Life and
for Retir

MW01115527

The Essential Handbook for Estate Planners

Seventh Edition, Revised
2011

Natalie B. Choate

Ataxplan Publications, Boston, Massachusetts

Updates for this book are published at our website:

> ## *www.ataxplan.com*

Life and Death Planning for Retirement Benefits

The Essential Handbook for Estate Planners
Seventh edition, completely revised

By Natalie B. Choate

Published by: Ataxplan Publications
               Post Office Box 51371
               Boston, Massachusetts 02205-1371

Publisher's Cataloging-in-Publication Data
Choate, Natalie B.
       Life and Death Planning for Retirement Benefits: The Essential Handbook for Estate Planners—7th ed. / Natalie B. Choate
       p.   cm.
Includes bibliographical references and index.

ISBN 978-0-9649440-4-6

       1. Estate planning - United States. 2. Tax planning - United States. 3. Retirement income - Taxation - United States. 4. Inheritance and transfer tax - United States. I. Choate, Natalie B. II. Title

KF 6585 .C43 2010

To Ian

Warning and Disclaimer

The rules applicable to qualified retirement plan benefits and IRAs are among the most complex in the tax code. I have read few works on this subject that were, in my view, completely accurate; in fact most that I have seen, including, unfortunately, earlier incarnations of this work, contain errors. Furthermore, even accurate information can become outdated quickly as IRS or Congressional policy shifts. Despite my best efforts, it is likely that this book, too, contains errors. Citations are provided so that practitioners can check any statements made in this book and reach their own conclusions regarding what the law is.

This book is intended to provide general information regarding the tax and other laws applicable to retirement benefits, and to provide suggestions regarding appropriate estate planning actions for different situations. It is not intended as a substitute for the practitioner's own research, or for the advice of a qualified estate planning or tax specialist. The author and publisher shall have neither liability nor responsibility to any person or entity with respect to any loss or damage caused, or alleged to be caused, directly or indirectly by the information contained in this book.

If you do not wish to be bound by the above, you may return this book to the publisher for a full refund.

About the author

Natalie B. Choate is an attorney with the Boston law firm of Nutter McClennen & Fish. Her practice is limited to consultations on estate planning for retirement benefits. She has chaired the Boston Bar Estate Planning Committee, the Boston Bar Employee Benefits Committee, and the American College of Trust and Estate Counsel Employee Benefits Committee. The National Association of Estate Planners and Councils awarded her the "Distinguished Accredited Estate Planner" designation. She has published widely and lectured in 49 states (sorry Montana!). Her comments on estate and retirement planning have been quoted in *The Wall Street Journal*, *Money*, *The New York Times, Newsweek, Forbes, Financial Planning* and *Financial World*. A Boston native, Miss Choate is a graduate of Radcliffe College and Harvard Law School.

SUMMARY CONTENTS

Introduction 23

Abbreviations used in this book 25

Chapter 1   The Minimum Distribution Rules 27

Chapter 2   Income Tax Issues 121

Chapter 3   Marital Matters 203

Chapter 4   Inherited   Benefits: Advising   Executors and
             Beneficiaries 243

Chapter 5   Roth Retirement Plans 316

Chapter 6   Leaving Retirement Benefits in Trust 394

Chapter 7   Charitable Giving 483

Chapter 8   Investment Issues; Plan Types 515

Chapter 9   Distributions Before Age 59½ 545

Appendix A: Tables 569

Appendix B: Forms 573

Appendix C: Resources 604

Bibliography 608

Index 615

TABLE OF CONTENTS: DETAILED

An even more detailed version of this Table of Contents is posted at
www.ataxplan.com

Introduction 23
    Terminology Used in this Book 24
    Abbreviations and Symbols 25

CHAPTER 1: THE MINIMUM DISTRIBUTION RULES 27

1.1 Introduction to the MRD Rules 27
1.1.01 Where to find the law 28
1.1.02 Which plans are subject to the MRD rules 28
1.1.03 MRD economics: The value of deferral 29
1.1.04 WRERA suspended MRDs for 2009 30
1.1.05 MRDs under defined plans, "annuitized" DC plans 32

1.2 MRD Fundamentals 33
1.2.01 The 12 Fundamental Laws of the MRD Universe 33
1.2.02 Which distributions count towards the MRD 36
1.2.03 Tables to determine Applicable Distribution Period (ADP) 38
1.2.04 What is a person's "age" for MRD purposes? 39
1.2.05 How to determine "account balance" for MRD purposes 40
1.2.06 How rollovers and MRDs interact 41
    A.   Adjustment required for outstanding rollovers 41
    B.   Other rollover effects on balance 42
    C.   Effect of rollover on RBD 42
    D.   Rollover can change applicable MRD rules. 42
1.2.07 Post-year-end recharacterization of Roth conversion 43
1.2.08 Valuation rules for determining account balance 44

1.3 MRDs During Participant's Life 44
1.3.01 *Road Map: How to compute lifetime MRDs* 45
1.3.02 The Uniform Lifetime Table: Good news for retirees 46
1.3.03 Lifetime MRDs: Much-younger-spouse method 47
1.3.04 Taking distributions from multiple plans 48
1.3.05 Separate accounts within a single plan 49

1.4 The RBD and First Distribution Year 50
1.4.01 Required Beginning Date (RBD); Distribution Year 50
1.4.02 RBD for IRAs and Roth IRAs 51
1.4.03 QRPs: RBD for 5-percent owner 51
1.4.04 QRPs, cont.: RBD for non-5-percent owner 52
1.4.05 RBD for 403(b) plans (including "grandfather rule") 53
1.4.06 What does "retires" mean? 54

1.4.07 RBD versus first Distribution Year: The limbo period 55
    A.   If the first year's MRD is postponed 55
    B.   No rollover or conversion until MRD taken 55
    C.   Death during the limbo period 55
1.4.08 Grandfather rule: TEFRA 242(b) elections 57
1.4.09 Effect of 2009 one-year suspension of MRDs 58

1.5 MRDs after the Participant's Death 59
1.5.01 Post-death MRD rules: Basics and overview 59
1.5.02 *Road Map for determining post-death MRDs* 60
    Step 1: Gather basic information 60
    Step 2: Gather specialized information 61
    Step 3: Determine whether the participant died before RBD . . . 61
    Step 4: Are you computing MRD for year of death or later year?62
    Step 5: Are there are multiple beneficiaries? 62
    Step 6: Do the benefits pass to a Designated Beneficiary? 62
    Step 7: Compute the MRDs 63
1.5.03 *Road Map, cont.: MRDs in case of death BEFORE the RBD* . . . 64
    A.   MRD for year of death regardless of who is beneficiary 64
    B.   Surviving spouse is sole beneficiary 64
    C.   Individual beneficiary who is not the surviving spouse . 65
    D.   See-through trust 65
    E.   Estate, non-see-through trust, other nonindividual 66
    F.   Multiple beneficiaries 66
1.5.04 *Road Map, cont.: MRDs in case of death AFTER the RBD* 66
    A.   MRD for year of death regardless of who is beneficiary 67
    B.   Surviving spouse is sole beneficiary 68
    C.   Individual beneficiary who is not the surviving spouse . 68
    D.   See-through trust 69
    E.   Estate, non-see-through trust, other nonindividual 69
    F.   Multiple beneficiaries 70
1.5.05 MRDs based on life expectancy of Designated Beneficiary 70
1.5.06 Death before the RBD: The 5-year (sometimes 6-year) rule 74
1.5.07 Life expectancy or 5-year rule: Which applies? 75
    Road Map: Three steps to tell whether the 5-year rule applies. . 75
1.5.08 Computing MRDs based on participant's life expectancy 78
1.5.09 Aggregation of inherited accounts for MRD purposes 80
1.5.10 Plan not required to offer stretch payout or lump sum 82
1.5.11 Switching between 5-year rule and life expectancy method 83
1.5.12 Who gets the benefits when the beneficiary dies 84
1.5.13 What is the ADP after the beneficiary's death? 85

1.6 Special Rules for the Surviving Spouse 87
1.6.01 *Road Map* of the special spousal rules 87
   A. Lifetime distributions: Much-younger-spouse method . 87
   B. Postponed Required Commencement Date 87
   C. Spouse's life expectancy recalculated 88
   D. Spouse can roll over inherited benefits 88
1.6.02 Definition of "sole beneficiary" 88
1.6.03 *Road Map: How to determine MRDs of surviving spouse* 89
1.6.04 Required Commencement Date: Distributions to spouse 93
1.6.05 Special "(B)(iv)(II) rule" if both spouses die young 94
1.6.06 When is a trust for the spouse the same as the spouse? 98

1.7 The Beneficiary and the"*Designated* Beneficiary 100
1.7.01 Significance of having a Designated Beneficiary 100
1.7.02 Who is the participant's beneficiary? 100
1.7.03 Definition of Designated Beneficiary 101
1.7.04 Estate cannot be a Designated Beneficiary 104
1.7.05 Multiple beneficiary rules and how to escape them 104
1.7.06 Multiple beneficiaries: Who must take the MRD? 105
1.7.07 Simultaneous and close-in-time deaths 107

1.8 Modifying MRD Results after the Participant's Death 108
1.8.01 The separate accounts rule 108
   A. IRS's statement of the separate accounts rule 109
   B. Separate accounts for ADP purposes 109
   C. Separate accounts for all other MRD purposes 110
1.8.02 How do you "establish" separate accounts? 112
1.8.03 Removing beneficiaries by Beneficiary Finalization Date 113
   A. 9/30 of year after death=Beneficiary Finalization Date. 113
   B. Removal by distributing beneficiary's share of benefits 114
   C. Effect of death prior to the BFD. 116

1.9 Enforcement of the MRD Rules 116
1.9.01 Who enforces the minimum distribution rules 116
1.9.02 Failure to take an MRD: 50% penalty and other effects 117
1.9.03 IRS waiver of the 50 percent penalty 118
1.9.04 Statute of limitations on the 50 percent penalty 119

CHAPTER 2: INCOME TAX ISSUES 121

2.1 Income Tax Treatment: General & Miscellaneous 121
2.1.01 Plan distributions taxable as ordinary income 121
2.1.02 Post-2010 tax increases; surtax on investment income 122
2.1.03 When does a "distribution" occur? 124

2.1.04 Actual distributions and deemed distributions 126
2.1.05 Whose income is it? Community property etc. 128
2.1.06 List of no-tax and low-tax distributions 128
     A.   Roth plans 128
     B.   Tax-free rollovers and transfers 128
     C.   Life insurance proceeds, contracts 129
     D.   Recovery of basis 129
     E.   Special averaging for lump sum distributions 129
     F.   Net unrealized appreciation of employer
          securities (NUA) 129
     G.   No tax on distribution of annuity contract 129
     H.   Return of IRA contribution 129
     I.   Income tax deduction for certain beneficiaries 129
     J.   Distribution to charitable entity 130
     K.   Qualified HSA Funding Distributions 130
     L.   QDROs and divorce-related IRA divisions 130
2.1.07 Income tax, MRD, and estate planning aspects of plan loans . . 131
2.1.08 Excess IRA contributions; corrective distributions 133

2.2 If the Participant Has After-tax Money in the Plan or IRA . . . 138
2.2.01 *Road Map: Tax-free distribution of participant's "basis"* 139
2.2.02 General rule: The "cream-in-the-coffee rule" of § 72 140
2.2.03 Participant's basis in a QRP or 403(b) plan 140
2.2.04 QRP distributions from account that contains after-tax money . 141
     A.   What is the "distribution" § 72 is applied to? 142
     B.   No aggregation of multiple plans 143
     C.   "Cream" rule exception for certain separate accounts . 143
     D.   "Cream" rule exception for pre-1987 balances 144
2.2.05 Partial rollovers and conversions: QRP distributions 145
     A.   Myron Example 145
     B.   Direct rollovers to traditional and Roth IRAs 147
     C.   Partial rollover of distribution containing basis 147
     D.   Successive 60-day rollovers 149
2.2.06 Participant's basis in a traditional IRA 150
2.2.07 Beneficiary's basis in an inherited IRA 151
2.2.08 How much of a traditional IRA distribution is basis? 152
     A.   The cream-in-the-coffee formula 152
     B.   Distribution Amount 153
     C.   Year-end Account Balance 154
     D.   Total Nondeductible Contributions 155
     E.   Outstanding Rollovers 155
     F.   The aggregation rule: Which IRAs must be aggregated 155
     G.   Cream-in-the-coffee formula: Examples 156
2.2.09 Partial rollovers and conversions: IRA distributions 158

2.2.10 Exceptions to the cream-in-the-coffee rule for IRAs 159
        A.   IRA-to-nonIRA-plan rollovers 159
        B.   Return of IRA contribution before tax return due date 159
        C.   QHSAFDs 159
        D.   Qualified Charitable Distributions 159

2.3 Income Tax Withholding 160
2.3.01 Withholding of federal income taxes: overview 160
2.3.02 Periodic, nonperiodic, and eligible rollover payments 160
2.3.03 Exceptions and special rules 163
2.3.04 Mutually voluntary withholding 164
2.3.05 How withheld income taxes are applied 164

2.4 Lump Sum Distributions 164
2.4.01 Introduction to lump sum distributions 165
2.4.02 First hurdle: Type of plan 165
2.4.03 Second hurdle: "Reason" for distribution 166
2.4.04 Third hurdle: Distribution all in one taxable year 168
2.4.05 Exceptions to the all-in-one-year rule 170
2.4.06 Special averaging: Participant born before 1936 171

2.5 Net Unrealized Appreciation of Employer Stock 172
2.5.01 NUA: Tax deferral and long-term capital gain 172
2.5.02 Reporting NUA distributions 173
2.5.03 Distributions after the employee's death 174
2.5.04 Basis of stock distributed in life, held until death 174
2.5.05 Election to include NUA in income 176
2.5.06 Should employee keep the LSD or roll it over? 176
2.5.07 NUA and partial rollovers 177

2.6 Rollovers and Plan-to-Plan Transfers 179
2.6.01 Definitions: rollovers, trustee-to-trustee transfers, etc. 180
        A.   Background: Rollover vs. trustee-to-trustee transfer . . 180
        B.   Definition of "rollover" and "rollover contribution." . 181
        C.   Direct rollovers. 181
        D.   Definition of "60-day" (indirect) rollover 182
        E.   Trustee-to-trustee transfer 182
2.6.02 Distributions that can (or can't) be rolled over 183
        A.   Inherited plans 183
        B.   MRD 183
        C.   Series payments 183
        D.   Corrective and deemed distributions 183
        E.   Hardship distributions 184
        F.   12-month limitation on IRA rollovers 184

G.   Plan loans 184
H.   After-tax money 184
2.6.03 Rollover in a year in which a distribution is required 184
A.   Everybody: First distribution of the year is the MRD . 185
B.   Everybody: Missed MRDs from prior years. 185
C.   Participant only: Plan can assume there is no DB 185
D.   Participant only: Rollovers in the age-70½ year 186
E.   Beneficiaries only: Rollover and the 5-year rule 187
F.   Exceptions to the no-rollover-of-MRDs rule 187
2.6.04 60-day rollover: Must roll over same property received 187
2.6.05 60-day rollovers: Only one IRA-to-IRA rollover in 12 months 188
2.6.06 60-day rollover deadline; exceptions and blanket waivers 191
2.6.07 Hardship waiver of 60-day rollover deadline 192
2.6.08 Avoid some rollover requirements with IRA-to-IRA transfer . . 197

2.7 *Retiree Road Map* 198
2.7.01 Plan-related issues to discuss with your client 199
2.7.02 Reasons to roll money from one plan or IRA to another 199
2.7.03 Best how-to rollover tips 201
2.7.04 How many IRAs should a person own? 201
2.7.05 How to take MRDs and other distributions 202

CHAPTER 3: MARITAL MATTERS 203

3.1 Considerations for Married Participants 203
3.1.01 *Road Map: Advising a Married Participant* 203
3.1.02 *Road Map: Advising the Surviving Spouse* 204
3.1.03 Simultaneous death clauses 207

3.2 Spousal Rollover; Election to Treat Decedent's IRA as Spouse's
3.2.01 Advantages and drawbacks of spousal rollover 208
3.2.02 Spousal rollover: QRPs and 403(b) plans 210
3.2.03 Rollover (or spousal election) for IRA or Roth IRA 211
A.   Spousal election: Code and regulations 211
B.   Spousal election for inherited Roth IRA 212
C.   Conditions that must be met 212
D.   How spouse makes the election 213
E.   When spousal election may be made 214
F.   Rollovers also permitted 214
3.2.04 Roth conversion by surviving spouse 215
3.2.05 Rollover or election by spouse's executor 215
3.2.06 Deadline for completing spousal rollover 216
3.2.07 Plans the spouse can roll benefits into 217

3.2.08   Rollover if spouse is under age 59½ 218
3.2.09   Spousal rollover through an estate or trust 220

3.3 Qualifying for the Marital Deduction 223
3.3.01   *Road Map: Leaving Benefits to Spouse or Marital Trust* 224
3.3.02   Leaving retirement benefits to a QTIP trust 225
3.3.03   IRS regards benefits, trust, as separate items of QTIP 227
3.3.04   Entitled to all income: State law vs. IRS 228
3.3.05   Ways to meet the "entitled" requirement; Income vs. MRD ... 229
3.3.06   Distribute all income to spouse annually 231
3.3.07   Do not require stub income to be paid to spouse's estate! 232
3.3.08   Combination marital deduction-conduit trust 233
3.3.09   General Power marital trust 234
3.3.10   Automatic QTIP election for "survivor annuities" 234
3.3.11   Marital deduction for benefits left outright to spouse 235

3.4 REA '84 and Spousal Consent 236
3.4.01   Introduction to the Retirement Equity Act of 1984 236
3.4.02   Plans subject to full-scale REA requirements 236
3.4.03   REA requirements for "exempt" profit-sharing plans 237
3.4.04   IRAs, Roth IRAs, and 403(b) plans 238
3.4.05   Various REA exceptions and miscellaneous points 239
3.4.06   Requirements for spousal consent or waiver 240
3.4.07   Spousal waiver or consent: Transfer tax aspects 241

CHAPTER 4: INHERITED BENEFITS: ADVISING EXECUTORS AND BENEFICIARIES 243

4.1 Executor's Responsibilities 243
4.1.01   *The Executor's Road Map* 243
4.1.02   Recharacterizing the decedent's Roth conversion 244
4.1.03   Who can make, withdraw decedent's IRA contribution? 247
4.1.04   Completing rollover of distribution made to the decedent 247
4.1.05   Executor's responsibilities regarding decedent's MRDs 251

4.2 Post-Death Transfers, Rollovers, & Roth Conversions 254
4.2.01   How to title an inherited IRA 254
4.2.02   Post-death distributions, IRA-to-IRA transfers 256
     A.   Nonspouse beneficiary cannot roll over a distribution received. 256
     B.   Post-death IRA-to-IRA transfers permitted 257
     C.   What can go wrong 259
4.2.03   Combining inherited IRAs 259

4.2.04 Nonspouse beneficiary rollovers from nonIRA plans 260
     A.   Legislative background 260
     B.   Types of nonIRA plans 261
     C.   Available only to a Designated Beneficiary 261
     D.   Direct rollovers only 262
     E.   Must roll to an "inherited IRA" 262
     F.   Applies to post-2006 post-death distributions 262
     G.   Cannot use rollover to "fix" the estate plan 263
     H.   Limits on the plan's obligations 263
     I.   Plan must distribute MRD before the transfer 264
     J.   Beneficiary's MRDs after the transfer 264
4.2.05 Nonspouse beneficiary Roth conversions 264

4.3 Federal Estate Tax Issues 267
4.3.01 Retirement benefits on the estate tax return 267
4.3.02 Problems paying the estate tax 267
4.3.03 Alternate valuation method (AVM) for retirement benefits ... 268
4.3.04 AVM, cont.: Distributions, other IRA events as "disposition" . 270
4.3.05 AVM, cont.: Sale of assets inside the IRA 273
4.3.06 Federal estate tax exclusion for retirement benefits 274
4.3.07 Valuation discount for unpaid income taxes 274
4.3.08 Deaths in 2010: One-year "repeal" of the federal estate tax ... 275

4.4 Qualified Disclaimers of Retirement Benefits 276
4.4.01 *Post-mortem disclaimer checklist* 277
4.4.02 Requirements for qualified disclaimer: § 2518 278
4.4.03 Income tax treatment of disclaimers 279
4.4.04 What constitutes "acceptance" of a retirement benefit 280
4.4.05 Effect of taking a distribution; partial disclaimers 282
4.4.06 Deadline for qualified disclaimer 284
4.4.07 To whom is the disclaimer delivered? 285
4.4.08 Who gets the disclaimed benefits and how do they get them? .. 286
     A.   Property must pass to "someone other than"
              disclaimant 286
     B.   Property must pass "without direction" by disclaimant 287
     C.   How to determine who gets the disclaimed benefits .. 288
4.4.09 Disclaimers, ERISA, and the plan administrator 288
     A.   Disclaimers and ERISA's anti-alienation rule 289
     B.   Disclaimers and the plan document 290
     C.   Effect of the plan's "state law" provision 291
4.4.10 Disclaimers and the minimum distribution rules 292
4.4.11 How a disclaimer can help after the participant's death 292

4.4.12 Double deaths: Disclaimer by beneficiary's estate 294
    A.   Who is the successor beneficiary? 294
    B.   If the fiduciary is also a beneficiary 295
4.4.13 *Building disclaimers into the estate plan:* **Checklist** 296

4.5 Other Cleanup Strategies 299
4.5.01 Check the plan's default beneficiary 299
4.5.02 Invalidate the beneficiary designation 299
4.5.03 Spousal election to take share of estate 300
4.5.04 Will (or beneficiary designation form) contest 301
4.5.05 Reformation of beneficiary designation form 301
4.5.06 Reformation of trust or will 303
4.5.07 Choose the right cleanup strategy 304
    A.   When to seek reformation and avoid disclaimer 305
    B.   When and how to use disclaimer 306

4.6 Income in Respect of a Decedent (IRD) 306
4.6.01 Definition of IRD; why it is taxable 307
4.6.02 When IRD is taxed (normally when received) 308
4.6.03 Tax on transfer of the right-to-receive IRD 308
    A.   Gift of right-to-receive IRD 308
    B.   Transfer from estate or trust to beneficiary 309
    C.   Transfer to a 100 percent grantor trust 309
4.6.04 Income tax deduction for estate tax paid on IRD 310
4.6.05 Who gets the § 691(c) (IRD) deduction 311
4.6.06 IRD deduction for deferred payouts 312
4.6.07 IRD deduction: Multiple beneficiaries or plans 313
4.6.08 IRD deduction on the income tax return 314

4.7 Road Map: Advising the Beneficiary 314

CHAPTER 5: ROTH RETIREMENT PLANS 316

5.1 Roth Plans: Introduction 316
5.1.01 Introduction to Roth retirement plans 316
5.1.02 Roth retirement plan abuses 317

5.2 Roth IRAs: Minimum Distribution and Income Tax Aspects . 318
5.2.01 Roth (and deemed Roth) IRAs vs. traditional IRAs 318
5.2.02 Roth IRAs and the minimum distribution rules 319
    A.   No lifetime required distributions. 319
    B.   Post-death MRD rules DO apply. 319

    C.   Roth *distributions* do not fulfill MRD for traditional
          IRA. 320
    D.   MRDs and recharacterizations 320
    E.   MRDs and Roth conversions 320
5.2.03 Tax treatment of Roth IRA distributions: Overview 321
5.2.04 Qualified distributions: Definition 323
5.2.05 Computing Five-Year Period for qualified distributions 324
    A.   Five-Year Period for participant. 325
    B.   Five-Year Period for beneficiaries. 325
5.2.06 Tax treatment of nonqualified distributions 327
5.2.07 The Ordering Rules 328

5.3 How to Fund a Roth IRA; Regular and Excess Contributions . 329
5.3.01 The eight ways to fund a Roth IRA 329
5.3.02 "Regular" contributions from compensation income 331
5.3.03 Applicable Dollar Limit for regular contributions 332
5.3.04 Who may make a "regular" Roth IRA contribution 333
    A.   No age limit. 333
    B.   Participation in an employer plan is irrelevant. 333
    C.   Income must be below certain levels. 333
    D.   Traditional IRA contribution followed by conversion . 335
5.3.05 Penalty for excess Roth IRA contributions 335

5.4 Conversion of Traditional Plan or IRA to a Roth IRA 336
5.4.01 What type of plan may be converted to a Roth IRA 337
    A.   Individual retirement accounts. 337
    B.   NonIRA plans. 338
5.4.02 Who may convert: age, plan participation, income, etc. 339
    A.   Age: Under 59½, over 70½, or in between. 339
    B.   Participation in other plan(s). 339
    C.   Prior conversion. 339
    D.   Filing status. 339
    E.   Income limit. 340
5.4.03 Tax treatment of converting traditional IRA to Roth IRA 340
5.4.04 Tax treatment of converting nonIRA plan to Roth IRA 342
5.4.05 Income spreading for conversions in 1998 or 2010 344
5.4.06 Failed conversions 345
5.4.07 Mechanics of traditional IRA-to-Roth IRA conversions 346
5.4.08 Mechanics of conversion from other traditional plans 347

5.5 Roth Plans and the 10% Penalty For Pre-Age 59½ Distributions
5.5.01 Penalty applies to certain Roth plan distributions 348
    A.   Qualified distribution 348
    B.   Nonqualified distribution from Roth IRA 349

C.   Nonqualified distribution from DRAC 349
D.   Conversion; distribution within 5 years 349
5.5.02 Roth conversion prior to reaching age 59½ 349
A.   Penalty does not apply to a Roth conversion. 349
B.   Penalty applies to certain distributions within five years after
        a conversion. 350
C.   Penalty applies to failed conversion 352
5.5.03 Conversion while receiving "series of equal payments" 352

5.6 Recharacterizing an IRA or Roth IRA Contribution 353
5.6.01 Which IRA contributions may be recharacterized 353
5.6.02 Income attributable to the contribution 354
5.6.03 How to recharacterize certain IRA/Roth IRA contributions ... 356
5.6.04 Partial recharacterizations 358
5.6.05 Deadline for Roth IRA contributions and conversions 358
5.6.06 Recharacterization deadline: Due date "including extensions" . 360
5.6.07 Same-year and immediate reconversions banned 363

5.7 Designated Roth Accounts 364
5.7.01 Meet the DRAC: Roth 401(k)s, 403(b)s, 457(b)s 364
5.7.02 DRAC contributions: Who, how much, how, etc. 365
A.   Who may contribute 365
B.   How much may be contributed 366
C.   Election is irrevocable 367
D.   What may be contributed to a DRAC 367
5.7.03 MRDs and other contrasts with Roth IRAs 368
5.7.04 DRACs: Definition of "qualified distribution" 368
A.   Qualified distribution triggering events 368
B.   How Five-Year Period is computed for DRAC 369
C.   List of never-qualified distributions 370
D.   QDROs and payments to beneficiaries 371
5.7.05 Nonqualified DRAC distributions 371
5.7.06 Rollovers of DRAC distributions: General rules 372
5.7.07 DRAC-to-DRAC rollovers 374
A.   May roll to any other DRAC 374
B.   Direct rollover 374
C.   Total direct rollover preserves basis in excess of value 374
D.   Direct rollover preserves holding period 374
E.   60-day ("indirect") rollover 375
5.7.08 DRAC-to-Roth-IRA rollovers: In general 376
A.   Who is eligible. 376
B.   Minimum distribution effects. 376
C.   Favorable effect on basis recovery. 376
D.   Rollover when basis is higher than market value 376

5.7.09 DRAC-to-Roth IRA rollovers: Effect on Five-Year Period 377
    A.   Rollover of a qualified distribution 378
    B.   Rollover if participant already has a Roth IRA 378
    C.   Danger: Rolling to participant's first Roth IRA 378
5.7.10 DRAC accounting may not shift value 379
5.7.11 In-plan conversions 379

5.8 Putting it All Together: Roth Planning Ideas and Principles .. 381
5.8.01 Roth plan or traditional? It's all about the price tag 381
5.8.02 Factors that incline towards doing a Roth conversion 384
5.8.03 Factors that incline against a Roth conversion 387
5.8.04 How participant's conversion helps beneficiaries 388
5.8.05 Annual contributions: Traditional vs. Roth plan 389
5.8.06 Roth plans and the estate plan 391

CHAPTER 6: LEAVING RETIREMENT BENEFITS IN TRUST 394

6.1 Trust as Beneficiary: Preliminaries 394
6.1.01 *Trust as beneficiary: **Drafting checklist*** 394
6.1.02 Trust accounting for retirement benefits 397
6.1.03 Trust accounting: Drafting solutions 399
6.1.04 "Total return" or "unitrust" method 401
6.1.05 Transferring a retirement plan out of a trust or estate 402
    A.   Transferability of retirement benefits. 402
    B.   Examples of fiduciary transfers of retirement plans .. 403
    C.   PLRs approving these transfers 405
    D.   IRA providers and plan administrators 406
6.1.06 Can a participant transfer an IRA to a living trust? 406
6.1.07 Individual retirement trusts (trusteed IRAs) 407

6.2 The Minimum Distribution Trust Rules 410
6.2.01 When and why see-through trust status matters 410
6.2.02 MRD trust rules: Ground rules 412
    A.   Should you discuss MRDs in the trust instrument? ... 412
    B.   Benefits and proceeds thereof 413
    C.   Benefits pass from one trust to another 413
    D.   Who tests compliance? 413
6.2.03 What a "see-through trust" is; the five "trust rules" 413
6.2.04 Dates for testing trust's compliance with rules 415
6.2.05 Rule 1: Trust must be valid under state law 415
6.2.06 Rule 2: Trust must be irrevocable 415
6.2.07 Rule 3: Beneficiaries must be identifiable 416
6.2.08 Rule 4: Documentation requirement 418
6.2.09 Rule 5: All beneficiaries must be individuals 421

6.2.10 Payments to estate for expenses, taxes 421
6.2.11 Effect of § 645 election on see-through status 423

6.3 MRD Rules: Which Trust Beneficiaries Count? 423
6.3.01 If benefits are allocated to a particular share of the trust 423
    A. Beneficiaries with respect to trust's interest in benefits. 424
    B. Subtrust named directly as beneficiary of the benefits 425
    C. Benefits allocated pursuant to trustee's discretion 425
    D. Instrument mandates allocation; no formula 425
    E. Mandated allocation pursuant to formula 426
    F. Mandatory allocation under state law 427
6.3.02 Separate accounts: benefits payable to a trust or estate 427
    A. No separate accounts for ADP purposes 427
    B. Separate accounts for purposes other than ADP 428
    C. Drafting to achieve separate accounts under one trust 429
6.3.03 Beneficiaries removed by Beneficiary Finalization Date 430
    A. Distribution on or before September 30 430
    B. Qualified disclaimer by September 30 431
    C. Other ways to "remove" a trust beneficiary. 432
6.3.04 Disregarding "mere potential successors" 432
6.3.05 Conduit trust for one beneficiary 433
    A. What a conduit trust is 433
    B. How a conduit trust is treated under the MRD rules . . 434
    C. Payments for beneficiary's benefit 435
    D. Payment of trust expenses 435
    E. Drawbacks of the conduit trust 436
    F. Conduit trust drafting pointers 437
    G. Conduit trusts for successive beneficiaries 437
6.3.06 Conduit trust for multiple beneficiaries 438
6.3.07 Accumulation trusts: Introduction 439
6.3.08 Accumulation trust: O/R-2-NLP 440
6.3.09 Accumulation trust: "Circle" trust 443
6.3.10 Accumulation trust: 100 percent grantor trust 443
6.3.11 Powers of appointment 445
6.3.12 Combining two types of qualifying trusts 447
    A. Conduit trust and 678 grantor trust 447
    B. Conduit distributions must begin at participant's death 447
    C. "Switch" trusts 448

6.4 Estate Planning with the MRD Trust Rules 449
6.4.01 Boilerplate provisions for trusts named as beneficiary 449
6.4.02 Advance rulings on see-through trust status 450
6.4.03 Should you use a separate trust for retirement benefits? 451
6.4.04 Planning choices: Trust for disabled beneficiary 451

6.4.05 Planning choices: Trusts for minors 454
6.4.06 Planning choices: Trust for spouse 459
6.4.07 Generation-skipping and "perpetual" trusts 461
6.4.08 "Younger heirs at law" as "wipeout" beneficiary 463

6.5 Trust Income Taxes: DNI Meets IRD 464
6.5.01 Income tax on retirement benefits paid to a trust 464
6.5.02 Trust passes out taxable income as part of "DNI" 465
6.5.03 Trust must authorize the distribution 468
6.5.04 Trusts and the IRD deduction 469
6.5.05 IRD and the separate share rule 470
6.5.06 IRD, separate shares, and discretionary funding 472
6.5.07 Income tax effect of transferring plan 473
6.5.08 Funding pecuniary bequest with right-to-receive IRD 475

6.6 *See-Through Trust Tester Quiz* 477

CHAPTER 7: CHARITABLE GIVING 483

7.1 Three "Whys": Reasons to Leave Benefits to Charity 483
A.   To benefit charity. 483
B.   Most tax-efficient use of retirement plan dollars. 484
C.   Accomplish other estate planning goals. 484

7.2 Seven Ways to Leave Benefits to Charity 484
7.2.01 Name charity as sole plan beneficiary 484
7.2.02 Leave benefits to charity, others, in fractional shares 484
7.2.03 Leave pecuniary gift to charity, residue to individuals 486
7.2.04 Formula bequest in beneficiary designation 487
7.2.05 Leave benefits to charity through a trust 487
7.2.06 Leave benefits to charity through an estate 488
7.2.07 Disclaimer-activated gift 488

7.3 MRDs and Charitable Gifts Under Trusts 489
7.3.01 Trust with charitable and human beneficiaries 490
7.3.02 If charitable gift occurs at the participant's death 491
7.3.03 If charitable gift occurs later 492

7.4 Income Tax Treatment of Charitable Gifts From a Trust or Estate
7.4.01 Background: trust income tax rules 494
7.4.02 DNI deduction, retirement benefits, and charity 495
7.4.03 Charitable deduction under § 642(c) 495
7.4.04 Timing of charitable deduction for trust or estate 499

7.4.05 Transferring benefits to charity avoids some rules 500
7.4.06 How to name a charity as beneficiary through a trust 502

7.5 Seven "Whiches": Types of Charitable Entities 503
7.5.01 Suitable: Public charity 503
7.5.02 Suitable: Private foundation 503
7.5.03 Suitable: Donor-advised fund 504
7.5.04 Suitable: Charitable remainder trust 504
7.5.05 Income tax rules for CRTs; IRD deduction 505
7.5.06 Solving planning problems with a CRT 507
7.5.07 Reasons NOT to leave benefits to a CRT 509
7.5.08 Suitable: Charitable gift annuity 510
7.5.09 Usually unsuitable: Charitable lead trust 510
7.5.10 Unsuitable: Pooled income fund 510

7.6 Lifetime Gifts of Retirement Benefits 511
7.6.01 Lifetime gifts from distributions 511
7.6.02 Give your MRD to charity 512
7.6.03 Gifts from a pre-age 59½ "SOSEPP" 513
7.6.04 Gift of NUA stock 513
7.6.05 Gift of other low-tax lump sum distribution 513
7.6.06 Give ESOP qualified replacement property to CRT 514
7.6.07 Qualified Charitable Distributions 514

CHAPTER 8: INVESTMENT ISSUES; PLAN TYPES 515

8.1 IRAs: Issues for Investors 515
8.1.01 Various investment issues for IRAs 515
        A.   IRA contributions, distributions, rollovers 515
        B.   Prohibited transaction: Standard account form 516
        C.   IRA, nonIRA transactions matched: Wash sale 516
8.1.02 Investment losses and IRAs 517
8.1.03 Restoring lawsuit winnings to IRA 519
8.1.04 Paying, deducting IRA investment expenses 520
8.1.05 IRAs owning "nontraditional" investments 522
        A.   Partnerships 523
        B.   Hedge funds and other "private" investments 523
        C.   S corporation stock 525
        D.   Real estate 525
        E.   Active business 526
8.1.06 IRAs and prohibited transactions 527

8.2 IRAs and the Tax on UBTI 530
8.2.01 UBTI: Rationale, exemptions, returns, double tax, etc. 530
8.2.02 Income from an IRA-operated trade or business 531
8.2.03 When investment income becomes UBTI 531
8.2.04 Income from debt-financed property 532

8.3 Types of Retirement Plans 534
8.3.01 Overview of types of plans 534
8.3.02 401(k) plan; elective deferral; CODA 535
8.3.03 403(b) plan 535
Deemed IRA, deemed Roth IRA. See ¶ 5.2.01. 535
8.3.04 Defined Benefit plan 535
8.3.05 Defined Contribution plan 538
8.3.06 ESOP (Employee Stock Ownership Plan) 539
8.3.07 Individual account plan. 539
8.3.08 Individual Retirement Account (IRA) 540
8.3.09 Keogh plan 540
Money purchase plan. See ¶ 8.3.10. 542
8.3.10 Pension plan 542
8.3.11 Profit-sharing plan 542
8.3.12 Qualified Retirement Plan 543
Roth IRA. See ¶ 5.2.01. 543
8.3.13 SEP-IRA, SIMPLE 544
Traditional IRA. See ¶ 8.3.08. 544
Trusteed IRA. See ¶ 8.3.08, ¶ 6.1.07. 544

CHAPTER 9: DISTRIBUTIONS BEFORE AGE 59½ 545

9.1 10% Penalty on Early Distributions 545
9.1.01 What practitioners must know 545
9.1.02 The § 72(t) penalty on early distributions 546
9.1.03 How the penalty applies to particular distributions 546
9.1.04 Enforcement of early distributions penalty 548

9.2 Exception: "Series of Equal Payments" 548
9.2.01 Series of substantially equal periodic payments (SOSEPP) 548
9.2.02 How this exception works 549
9.2.03 Notice 89-25 (A-12) and Rev. Rul. 2002-62 549
9.2.04 Steps required to initiate a SOSEPP 550
9.2.05 The three methods: RMD, amortization, annuitization 550
9.2.06 Variations on the three methods 552
9.2.07 Choose single or joint life expectancy 552
9.2.08 Notes on Joint and Survivor Life Table 553
9.2.09 Notes on Single, Uniform Lifetime Tables 553

9.2.10 What interest rate assumption is used 554
9.2.11 What account balance is used 554
9.2.12 Applying the SOSEPP exception to multiple IRAs 555
9.2.13 Starting a second series to run concurrently 556
9.2.14 Procedural and reporting requirements 556

9.3 Modifying the SOSEPP 556
9.3.01 Effects of a forbidden modification of series 556
9.3.02 When the no-modification period begins and ends 557
9.3.03 Exceptions for death or disability 557
9.3.04 Changing to RMD method after SOSEPP commences 557
9.3.05 When taking an extra payment is not a modification 558
9.3.06 What other changes do NOT constitute a modification? 558
9.3.07 What changes DO constitute a modification? 560
9.3.08 Effect of divorce on the SOSEPP 560
9.3.09 Transfers to, from, or among IRAs supporting a SOSEPP 561

9.4 Other Exceptions to the Penalty 563
9.4.01 Death benefits 563
9.4.02 Distributions attributable to total disability 563
9.4.03 Distributions for deductible medical expenses 564
9.4.04 QRPs, 403(b) plans: Early retirement 564
9.4.05 QRPs, 403(b) plans: QDRO distributions 565
9.4.06 ESOPs only: Dividends on employer stock 565
9.4.07 IRAs only: Unemployed's health insurance 566
9.4.08 IRAs only: Expenses of higher education 566
9.4.09 IRAs only: First-time home purchase 567
9.4.10 IRS levy on the account 568
9.4.11 Return of certain contributions 568
9.4.12 Qualified reservist distributions 568
9.4.13 Exceptions for tax-favored disasters 568

APPENDIX A: TABLES 569
APPENDIX B: FORMS: See detailed Table of Contents at page: ... 573
APPENDIX C: RESOURCES 604
        The Pension Answer Book 604
        Ataxplan Website 604
        Software 604
        Newsletters 605
        Quick Reference Guides 606
        Choate Special Reports 606

Bibliography 608

Introduction

This book is the professional advisor's guide to minimum required distributions, rollovers, Roth conversions, and dozens of other tax code creations that our clients must navigate if they own an IRA or participate in a qualified retirement plan. With this book, you can help your clients defer or reduce taxes, avoid penalties, and preserve their retirement benefits.

The tax rules governing retirement benefits grow ever more complex. Every day I hear of individuals who have stumbled on these rules and dropped their retirement benefits into the hands of the IRS. Yet with proper care and attention all the pitfalls can be avoided. The purpose of this book is to explain, for the benefit of my fellow estate planning lawyers, and all tax and financial services professionals involved in helping individuals plan for distribution and preservation of their retirement benefits, as many of the applicable rules and planning considerations as I can fit into 600 pages.

Don't let these rules trap you or your clients. Keep this book by your desk and get the facts. Find what you need quickly using the Index, Table of Contents, and Road Maps (see back cover). If you don't find the answer you're looking for, or you don't understand it, or you disagree with it, please email me at author@ataxplan.com.

Limitations of this Book

Many important aspects of planning for retirement distributions are *not* covered in this book, including investment alternatives and financial planning considerations generally. This book also does not cover: § 457 plans; qualified domestic relations orders (QDROs); stock options and other nonqualified forms of deferred compensation; ESOPs; creditors' rights; state tax issues; and community property.

This book is designed to explain estate planning and tax planning issues for the benefit of estate and financial planners who are counseling individuals (and their beneficiaries) who have assets in retirement plans. It does not cover issues which are of concern to plan administrators, but do not have a significant impact on planning decisions for the individual participant.

This book deals with the *federal* tax law applicable to retirement benefits. Planners will need to determine what impact, if any, state law has with respect to their clients.

Terminology Used in this Book

For meaning of "**retirement plan**," and the various types of plans, see ¶ 8.3.

The **participant** is the individual for whom the retirement plan account is established: the employee who has benefits in a qualified plan, or for whom a tax-sheltered annuity or mutual fund account was purchased; or the account owner in the case of an IRA. For ease of understanding, throughout this book, except in some examples, the "participant" is male and the feminine pronoun refers to the participant's spouse. Of course any statement would apply equally to a female participant and her male spouse. When discussing matters that apply only to qualified plans or 403(b) plans, sometimes **employee** is used instead of participant. When discussing an issue from the point of view of advising an individual client the participant is sometimes referred to as "the client" or occasionally "the decedent."

A **beneficiary** is a person or entity who inherits a retirement plan from a deceased participant (or from another beneficiary); someone who holds an "inherited" retirement benefit, as in "An individual's IRAs held as beneficiary cannot be aggregated with the individual's own IRAs for MRD purposes." During the participant's life, the "beneficiary" means the "beneficiary-apparent," i.e., the person or entity who is currently named as the participant's beneficiary and who is accordingly expected (unless something changes) to inherit the account at the participant's death; see, *e.g.*, ¶ 1.3.03(B). These definitions of beneficiary *always* apply in this book, and *usually* also apply in IRS pronouncements. A source of confusion is that the Code sometimes uses the word "beneficiary" to mean the person whom this book always (and the IRS usually) calls the participant, IRA-owner, or employee. For definitions of "**Successor Beneficiary**" and "**Contingent Beneficiary**," see ¶ 1.5.12.

For definitions of **rollover**, direct rollover, indirect rollover, 60-day rollover, trustee-to-trustee transfer, IRA-to-IRA transfer, custodian-to-custodian transfer, and plan-to-plan transfer, see ¶ 2.6.01.

Taxable account is the shorthand term for funds or assets that are outside any retirement plan, as in, for example, "The distribution was supposed to be transferred to an IRA but instead, by mistake, the funds were deposited in the participant's taxable account."

Traditional IRA or account refers to an IRA or retirement plan account that is not a "Roth" IRA or account; see ¶ 5.2.01.

Abbreviations and Symbols

¶   Refers to a section of this book.
§   Refers to a section of the Code unless otherwise indicated.

ADP	Applicable Distribution Period. ¶ 1.2.03.
AGI	Adjusted gross income.
CODA	Cash-or-deferred arrangement. ¶ 8.3.02.
COLA	Cost-of-living adjustment.
Code	Internal Revenue Code of 1986, as amended through September 27, 2010.
DB	Designated Beneficiary. ¶ 5.8.03.
DNI	Distributable net income. ¶ 6.4.02.
DOL	Department of Labor.
DQP	Disqualified person. ¶ 8.1.06.
DRAC	Designated Roth account. ¶ 5.7.01.
EGTRRA	The Economic Growth and Tax Relief Reconciliation Act of 2001 (Pub. L. 107-16).
ERISA	Employee Retirement Income Security Act of 1974.
FMV	Fair market value.
IRA	Individual retirement account or individual retirement trust under § 408 or § 408A.
IRD	Income in respect of a decedent. ¶ 4.6.01.
IRS	Internal Revenue Service.
IRT	Individual retirement trust (trusteed IRA). ¶ 6.1.07.
MAGI	Modified adjusted gross income.
MRD	Minimum Required Distribution. Chapter 1, first paragraph.
NUA	Net unrealized appreciation. ¶ 2.5.01.
O/R-2-NLP	Outright to now-living person. ¶ 6.3.06.
PLR	IRS private letter ruling.
PPA '06	The Pension Protection Act of 2006 (Pub. L. 109-280).
Prop. Reg.	Proposed Treasury Regulation.
PT	Prohibited transaction. ¶ 8.1.06.
QRP	Qualified Retirement Plan. ¶ 8.3.12.
RBD	Required Beginning Date. ¶ 1.4.01.
REA	Retirement Equity Act of 1984 (Pub. L. 98-397). ¶ 3.4.
Reg.	Treasury Regulation.
TRA '86	The Tax Reform Act of 1986 (Pub. L. 99-514).
UBTI	Unrelated business taxable income. ¶ 8.2.
WRERA	The Worker, Retiree, and Employer Recovery Act of 2008 (Pub. L. 110-458).

Acknowledgments

I am most grateful to those who took the time to read sections of the book and send me their thoughtful comments, almost all of which were incorporated into the book. Peer reviewers for this edition were Denise Appleby, Beverly Deveny, Robert M. Geurden, Christine Morgan, Beth Warach, and Denise Yurkofsky.

Numbers are tricky things; I thank Guerdon T. Ely, CFP, of Chico, California, for his patience and expertise (in both numbers and retirement benefits matters) in reviewing my numerical examples.

Appreciation for their hard work of cite checking goes to two newly minted lawyers, Yoav Sered and Aimee Fukuchi. As always, the book benefitted from comments of my private in-house former Harvard Law Review editor Ian M. Starr.

I send thanks also to the retirement benefits and estate planning experts who have always freely shared their expertise: Jonathan Blattmachr, Beverly Budin, Beverly DeVeny, Seymour Goldberg, Steve Gorin, Marcia Holt, Chris Hoyt, Mike Jones, Bob Keebler, Stephen J. Krass, Lou Mezzullo, Barry Picker, Ed Slott, Bruce Temkin, Kaye A. Thomas, Steve Trytten, and Dan Wentworth.

In gathering material for this book, I have talked with, listened to, or read the work of countless estate planners, actuaries, accountants, lawyers, financial planners, retirees, trust officers, mutual fund personnel, plan administrators, IRS and DOL staffers, plan participants, and writers who have studied the subject matter. I have learned from almost every encounter. While I did not manage to collect the name of every person whose comments, questions, and ideas helped me improve this book, that is no excuse not to thank: Heidi Adair, Sabrina Alvarez, Steve Brownlow, Barbara Camaglia, Keith Carpenter, Puneet Cham, Patrick Cunningham, Bob Daigle, David de Reyna, Joan B. Di Cola, Francine Duke, Jeff W. Eschman, Dave Foster, Jeffrey L. Gebauer, Wayne H. Gilbert, Kal Goren, Michael Haigh, Jane Hardin, Kristen L. Hartman, Emilee K. Lawson Hatch, Steve Holdsworth, David Hultstrom, Stephen Koster, Don Jansen, Terry Knox, Steven M. Laiderman, Alice Lonoff, Larry Malecky, Eric Manterfield, Charity A. McCarthy, Michael McGrath, David Metzger, Marcia L. Mueller, Shelly E. Nixon, Gregory T. Peacock, Scott Pohar, Mark Puttre, Jose Reynoso, Doyle Sanders, Stanley Schoenbaum, David Shayne, Heidi Rai Stewart, Michael L. Trop, Alan Wandalowski, Mark A. Watson, Tim Wyld, and Marily Zigarac!

1

The Minimum Distribution Rules

The minimum distribution rules dictate
when benefits must be distributed from
a retirement plan.

Minimum Distribution Road Maps
How to compute MRDs during the participant's life: ¶ 1.3.01, p. 45.
How to compute MRDs after the participant's death: ¶ 1.5.02, p. 60.

Congress wants tax-favored retirement plans to be *retirement* plans, not estate-building wealth transfer vehicles. To that end, Congress enacted § 401(a)(9), which compels certain annual distributions from plans beginning generally at age 70½ or, if earlier, death. § 401(a)(9) and its related regulations are called the "minimum distribution rules" or the "MRD rules." The **"minimum required distribution"** or **MRD** is the amount that must be distributed under these rules in a particular year.

This Chapter explains the minimum distribution rules applicable for 2003 and later years under the IRS's final minimum distribution regulations for defined contribution (DC) plans. See ¶ 1.1.01 regarding earlier years; see ¶ 1.1.05 regarding defined benefit plans and annuity payouts.

1.1 Introduction to the MRD Rules

The major attraction of the types of retirement plans discussed in this book (¶ 1.1.02) is the ability to accumulate funds inside the plan on a tax-deferred basis (or tax-free, in the case of a "Roth" plan). The minimum distribution rules dictate when this tax-sheltered accumulation must end. § 401(a)(9) tells us when benefits must start coming out of a retirement plan, and, once forced distributions start, how much must be distributed each year. Advisors need to know the MRD rules for planning purposes because these rules set the outer limits on plan accumulations, and because failure to comply with the rules involves substantial penalties (¶ 1.9.02).

The MRD rules come in two flavors: "life" (distributions required during the participant's life; see ¶ 1.3–¶ 1.4); and "death" (distributions required after the participant's death; see ¶ 1.5–¶ 1.8).

1.1.01 *Where to find the law*

Congress established the minimum required distribution (MRD) system in substantially its present form in the Tax Reform Act of 1986. The MRD rules are found in (the very brief) § 401(a)(9) of the Code and in the Treasury's (very lengthy) final MRD regulations: Reg. § 1.401(a)(9)-0 through § 1.401(a)(9)-9; § 1.403(b)-6(e)(2); § 1.408-8; and § 54.4974-2.

The final regulations described in this Chapter apply to all DC plan participants and beneficiaries for calendar years beginning after 2002. Reg. § 1.401(a)(9)-1, A-2(a); § 1.403(b)-6(e)(2); § 1.408-8, A-1(a). For the two versions of proposed minimum distribution regulations promulgated in earlier years, see the *Special Report: Ancient History* (Appendix C). For rules applicable to defined benefit plans (¶ 8.3.04), see ¶ 1.1.05.

1.1.02 *Which plans are subject to the MRD rules*

For definitions of plans referred to in this section, see ¶ 8.3.

The minimum distribution rules are contained in § 401(a)(9), which applies to **Qualified Retirement Plans (QRPs)**. The Code specifies that rules "similar to" the rules of § 401(a)(9) shall also apply to **IRAs** (§ 408(a)(6)) and **403(b) plans** (§ 403(b)(10)).

Because the minimum distribution *regulations* were first written for QRPs, they refer to the **participant** (the individual who earned the benefits; see p. 24) as the "employee." The Treasury has made the same regulations applicable (with certain variations) to IRAs. Reg. § 1.408-8, A-1(a). When applying the QRP regulations to an IRA, "the employee" is to be read as "the IRA owner." Reg. § 1.408-8, A-1(b). "Simplified employee pensions" (**SEP** or **SEP-IRA**; § 408(k)) and **SIMPLE** IRAs (§ 408(p)) are treated the same as other IRAs for purposes of § 401(a)(9), and accordingly are subject to the same MRD rules and regulations as "regular" traditional IRAs. Reg. § 1.408-8, A-2.

Roth IRAs are subject to the IRA minimum distribution rules *only* after the participant's death; the lifetime MRD rules do not apply to Roth IRAs. ¶ 5.2.02(A).

The Treasury has also made its QRP MRD regulations applicable (again with certain variations) to **403(b) plans**. Reg. § 1.403(b)-6(e).

1.1.03 *MRD economics: The value of deferral*

The most valuable feature of traditional tax-favored retirement plans is the ability to invest without current taxation of the investment profits. In most cases, investing through a retirement plan defers income tax not only on the investment profits but also on the participant's compensation income that was originally contributed to the plan. The longer this deferral continues, the better, because, generally, the deferral of income tax increases the ultimate value of the benefits.

As long as assets stay in the plan, the participant or beneficiary is investing not just "his own" money but also "Uncle Sam's share" of the participant's compensation and the plan's investment profits, i.e., the money that otherwise would have been paid to the IRS (and will eventually be paid to the IRS) in income taxes. Keeping the money in the retirement plan enables the participant or beneficiary to reap a profit from investing "the IRS's money" along with his own. Once funds are distributed from the plan, they are included in the gross income of the participant or beneficiary, who then pays the IRS its share (see Chapter 2). Thereafter the participant or beneficiary will no longer enjoy any investment profits from the government's share of the plan. Long-term deferral of distributions also tends to produce financial gain with a Roth retirement plan, even though income tax is not being deferred; see ¶ 5.1.01.

Despite the apparent goal of the MRD rules (assuring that tax-favored retirement plans are used primarily to provide retirement income), § 401(a)(9) permits the retirement account to stay in existence long past the death of the participant whose work created the benefit—*if* the participant leaves his retirement benefits to the right kind of beneficiary. If various requirements are met, the law allows the retirement benefits to be paid out gradually, after the worker's death, over the life expectancy of the worker's beneficiary. ¶ 1.5.05. The financial benefit of the long-term deferral of distributions permitted by the minimum distribution rules puts a premium on naming a beneficiary who will qualify for the life expectancy payout method.

Depending on investment returns, if the beneficiary is young, and takes no more than the MRD each year, the value of the inherited plan can soar, under the life expectancy payout method, by the time the *beneficiary* reaches retirement age. For example, a 38 year-old beneficiary who inherits a $500,000 traditional IRA and withdraws it using the life expectancy method will have $1,696,000 inside the IRA plus $1,432,000 *outside* the IRA in 30 years; if he cashes out the entire account when he inherits it, he will have (outside the IRA) only $1,470,000. This example assumes an 8% constant investment return for all assets and a 36% tax rate on all plan distributions and outside investment income; projections were prepared using Brentmark Retirement Plan Analyzer® and NumberCruncher® software (Appendix C).

Deferring income taxes is not always beneficial. See ¶ 5.8.02.

1.1.04 *WRERA suspended MRDs for 2009*

The "Worker, Retiree, and Employer Recovery Act of 2008" (WRERA) amended § 401(a)(9) by adding the following new subparagraph (H), entitled "Temporary waiver of minimum required distribution": "The requirements of…[§ 401(a)(9)] shall not apply for calendar year 2009 to" any defined contribution plan under § 401(a), § 403(a) or § 403(b); any governmental 457 plan; or "an individual retirement plan" (IRA). Notices 2009-9, 2009-5 IRB 419, and 2009-82, 2009-41 IRB 491, provide guidance on § 401(a)(9)(H).

Thus, anyone who otherwise would have been required to take a distribution from one of these types of plans in 2009—whether participant or beneficiary—could skip a year. Throughout this Chapter, though it may not be mentioned every single time, bear in mind that there was no MRD "for" the year 2009, and that:

✓   The one-year suspension generally did not change how *post-2009* MRDs are calculated. It did not *extend* lifetime or post-death life expectancy payouts, or somehow cause the year 2009 to "drop out" of the calculations when determining a person's "Applicable Distribution Period" (¶ 1.2.03). For example, a participant who is taking lifetime MRDs (¶ 1.3) will use his actual attained age in 2010 to compute the 2010 MRD, just as would have been the case if 2009 had been a "normal" year; he will not use his 2009 age for 2010, as if 2009 somehow did not exist. See IRS Publication 590, *IRAs* (2009), Examples 1 and 2 (p. 34); see also ¶ 1.5.05(D). For the one exception to this statement see the "5-year rule," ¶ 1.5.06.

✓   WRERA has the effect of extending *certain* deadlines by one year, namely the deadlines for: Distributions under the "5-year rule" for beneficiaries of decedents who died (before their Required Beginning Dates (RBDs)) in the years 2004–2009 (see ¶ 1.5.06); the Designated Beneficiary of a participant who died before his RBD to elect between a life expectancy payout and the 5-year rule (¶ 1.5.07(B), (C)); and the nonspouse Designated Beneficiary of a participant who died before his RBD to qualify for a life expectancy payout by completing a direct rollover of inherited benefits, to an "inherited IRA," from a plan under which the 5-year rule applied (¶ 4.2.04(J)).

✓   But WRERA did NOT change other MRD deadlines: The Beneficiary Finalization Date remains September 30 of the year after the year of the participant's death (¶ 1.8.03(A)). The date by which a see-through trust must deliver documentation to the plan administrator remains October 31 of the year after the year of the participant's death (¶ 6.2.08(A)). The date by which multiple beneficiaries must establish separate accounts for purposes of determining their Applicable Distribution Period (ADP; ¶ 1.2.03) remains December 31 of the year after the year of the participant's death (¶ 1.8.01(B)). The participant's RBD remains April 1 of the year after the year in which he reaches age 70½ (or retires, whichever is applicable) for purposes of determining whether he died before or after his RBD (¶ 1.5.02, Step 3), even if he reached age 70½ in 2008 or 2009.

✓   Although in theory there were "no MRDs in 2009," actually there were two types of MRDs that had to be paid, even in 2009. One was a 2008 MRD that was postponed until April 1, 2009 (2008 being the first distribution year); see ¶ 1.4.09(A). The other was a skipped MRD from any year earlier than 2009. See ¶ 1.9.02 and Notice 2009-82, Part V, A-8.

✓   For the effect on individuals who turned age 70½ in 2008 or 2009, see ¶ 1.4.09.

✓   Despite WRERA's suspension of MRDs, some plans
distributed 2009 "required" distributions anyway. The IRS
granted participants and surviving spouses (but not other
beneficiaries) who received these "nonrequired required
distributions" the right to roll them over within 60 days of
receipt (or by November 1, 2009, if later); see the *Special
Report: Ancient History* (Appendix C).

1.1.05 *MRDs under defined plans, "annuitized" DC plans*

Defined benefit plans are subject to an entirely different system
of MRDs than the defined contribution (DC) plan system explained in
this Chapter. For details on the defined benefit plan MRD system, see
Reg. § 1.401(a)(9)-6 and the *Special Report: When Insurance Products
Meet Retirement Plans* (Appendix C).

Advisors need to be aware of this alternative MRD system even
if they have nothing to do with MRD compliance for any defined
benefit plan because the defined benefit plan system *also* applies to any
portion of a DC plan that is "annuitized." Annuitize is a word that does
not appear in the dictionary; in the IRS lexicon, it means that all or part
of an individual's account in a DC plan is used to purchase an
immediate annuity. For example, suppose a participant wants to use
part of his IRA balance to purchase an immediate annuity from an
insurance company, i.e., he wants to convert that money into a stream
of periodic payments that the insurer guarantees will last for some
specified period of time or for specified lives. In exchange for that
promise the participant gives up his ownership of the money turned
over to the insurance company.

The IRA owner has two choices regarding how to use his IRA
money to buy an immediate annuity. He can cash out the IRA, pay the
resulting income tax, and then buy whatever kind of annuity contract
he wants (and can get an insurer to sell). Or he can buy the contract
"inside" the IRA. If he chooses the latter course, then the defined
benefit plan MRD rules step in. These rules limit what types of annuity
contract he can buy and how the contract (and the rest of the IRA) will
be treated for MRD purposes following the purchase. If your client is
considering such a purchase, you need to read the summary in the
following paragraph, and then read the regulation or *Special Report*
above cited.

The defined benefit plan MRD system is briefly summarized as
follows. First, the MRD rules limit the type of annuity contract that can

be purchased "inside" an IRA—basically, an immediate annuity contract purchased inside an IRA must provide for level periodic payments (or level plus certain permitted percentage annual increases or COLAs), beginning no later than the age-70½ year (or year of purchase, if later). The duration of the stream of payments may be for the life of the participant alone, or for the joint lives of the participant and his spouse-beneficiary, or for the joint lives of the participant and his nonspouse beneficiary (with, in this last case, limits on the size of the survivor annuity if the beneficiary is younger than the participant). The contract can have a minimum guaranteed term, provided it does not extend beyond, roughly, the participant's age 97.

Finally, following the purchase of this contract inside the IRA, the annuity contract and "the rest of the IRA" (i.e., the nonannuitized portion) are treated as *two separate plans* for all purposes of the minimum distribution rules. All distributions received under the annuity contract are considered MRDs from the "annuity" portion (so they cannot be rolled over; ¶ 2.6.03), and the non-annuitized portion must pay its own MRDs computed in the usual way (excluding the annuity contract when valuing the account).

1.2 MRD Fundamentals

This ¶ 1.2 explains the components of the minimum distribution system.

1.2.01 *The 12 Fundamental Laws of the MRD Universe*

Here are the basic principles underlying the minimum required distribution (MRD) scheme for defined contribution (DC; ¶ 8.3.05) plans. Note that many rules have at least one exception!

1. **MRDs start at a particular time.** The starting point for lifetime required distributions is approximately age 70½ (or upon later retirement in some cases); see ¶ 1.4 for explanation of the "first Distribution Year" and the "Required Beginning Date." The final Distribution Year for "lifetime" distributions is the year of the participant's death. ¶ 1.5.04(A). The starting point for post-death MRDs is measured from the participant's death. ¶ 1.5.05(B), ¶ 1.5.06, ¶ 1.5.08, ¶ 1.6.04.

2.   **The MRD must be taken by December 31 each year.** Once MRDs begin, the participant or beneficiary must take a distribution each and every calendar year, no later than December 31, as long as he lives (or until the plan runs out of money). Reg. § 1.401(a)(9)-5, A-1. There are several exceptions to this rule. First, the "5-year rule" does not require annual distributions; see ¶ 1.5.06. Second, in the case of lifetime MRDs, the distribution for the first Distribution Year can generally be postponed until the Required Beginning Date (RBD) (which occurs in the following year); see ¶ 1.4.01. Third, there were no MRDs for the year 2009; see ¶ 1.1.04. Fourth, see ¶ 1.2.06(D) for how to use rollovers to *stop* MRDs. Finally, MRDs can be delayed beyond the normal deadline in two situations: a review period for QDROs and (in the case of insured plans) delay caused by receivership of the insurance company; see Reg. § 1.401(a)(9)-8, A-7, A-8, regarding these exceptions.

3.   **Each year's MRD is determined by dividing the prior year-end account balance by a factor from an IRS table.** MRDs are computed by dividing an annually-revalued account balance by an annually-declining life expectancy factor. Reg. § 1.401(a)(9)-5, A-1(a). (Exception: This principle does not apply to post-death distributions under the 5-year rule. ¶ 1.5.06.) This life expectancy factor is obtained from an IRS table and is called the **Applicable Distribution Period (ADP)** or **divisor**; see ¶ 1.2.03 for more on the definition of these terms and where to find the IRS tables. The ADP is a divisor, not a percentage; see Kenny Example, ¶ 1.3.01. For how to determine the account balance, see ¶ 1.2.05.

4.   **There is no maximum distribution.** The formula tells you the *minimum required* distribution. The rules impose no maximum distribution; the participant or beneficiary is always free, as far as the IRS is concerned, to take more than the minimum (but see #6). See Reg. § 1.401(a)(9)-5, A-1(a), A-2.

5.   **Taking more than the required amount in one year does not give you a "credit" you can use to reduce distributions in a later year.** Each year stands on it own. Reg. § 1.401(a)(9)-5, A-

2. Taking larger distributions in one year *indirectly* reduces later MRDs by reducing the account balance.

6.   **The plan is not required to offer every option the law permits.** Generally participants and beneficiaries must accept whatever distribution options the plan happens to offer, provided the plan does not call for *slower* distributions than the minimum distribution rules would require. See ¶ 1.5.10. See ¶ 3.2.01 and ¶ 4.2.04 for use of post-death rollovers to solve this problem (in some cases).

7.   **The MRD cannot exceed 100 percent of the account balance.** "...[T]he required minimum distribution amount will never exceed the entire account balance on the date of the distribution." Reg. § 1.401(a)(9)-5, A-1(a). This rule can help if the account is "wiped out" before the MRD is taken; see ¶ 1.2.05.

8.   **Distributions before the first Distribution Year don't count.** The first year for which an MRD is required is called the "first Distribution Year." See ¶ 1.4.01. Distributions in years prior to that year have no effect on the computation of the MRD for the first (or any other) Distribution Year (other than indirectly, by reducing the account balance). Reg. § 1.401(a)(9)-2, A-6(a).

9.   **Distribution period does not involve an election.** Generally, determination of the ADP for benefits, either during the participant's life or after his death, does not involve an "election" on the part of the participant or beneficiary. The ADP is prescribed by law based on the identity of the participant and beneficiary. (This is in contrast to the now-obsolete 1987 proposed regulations (¶ 1.1.01), under which the participant had to make various irrevocable elections at his RBD.) For the exceptions to this rule, see ¶ 1.5.07 (if the participant dies before his RBD, leaving his benefits to a Designated Beneficiary, the beneficiary may have to elect between the life expectancy payout method and the 5-year rule) and ¶ 3.2.03 (surviving spouse may elect or be deemed to have elected to treat an inherited IRA as the spouse's own IRA).

10.   The regulations "overrule" the Code. You cannot compute MRDs simply by following the Internal Revenue Code. The IRS regulations have fundamentally altered the Code's approach in several ways. For example, the Code dictates that lifetime distributions must be made over the life expectancy of the participant or the joint life expectancy of the participant and his beneficiary. § 401(a)(9)(A)(ii). The regulations make the identity and life expectancy of the beneficiary almost irrelevant; see ¶ 1.3.02. For other examples, see ¶ 1.5.04 ("General Comments") and ¶ 1.5.07.

11.   MRDs are determined under the rules applicable to the plan that holds the benefits, not some prior plan where the benefits "used to live" prior to a rollover. Reg. § 1.401(a)(9)-7. See ¶ 1.2.06(D).

12.   Missing an MRD has consequences. A participant or beneficiary who misses an MRD becomes liable for a penalty; see ¶ 1.9.02.

1.2.02 Which distributions count towards the MRD

Regs. § 1.401(a)(9)-5, A-9(a), and § 1.408-8, A-11(a), state that, except as otherwise provided in A-9(b) or A-11(b) of such regulations, or as may later be otherwise provided by other IRS pronouncements, "all amounts distributed" from a plan or IRA during the applicable Distribution Year (or grace period; ¶ 1.4.01) "are taken into account in determining whether section 401(a)(9) is satisfied...." Distributions before the Distribution Year don't count; see ¶ 1.2.01, #8. Here is the MRD status of various other distributions:

A.   Distribution of an annuity contract does NOT count. When an employee's plan account or IRA balance is used to purchase an annuity contract, distributions under the contract must comply with MRD rules. Reg. § 1.401(a)(9)-5, A-1(e), § 1.401(a)(9)-8, A-2(a)(3); see ¶ 1.1.05. Distribution of a nonassignable annuity contract that complies with the MRD rules is a nontaxable event (¶ 2.1.06(G)) and does not count as a distribution for MRD purposes. Reg. § 1.401(a)(9)-8, A-10.

B.   **Corrective and deemed distributions do NOT count.** QRP contributions that are returned to the participant because they exceeded various contribution limits do not count towards the MRD requirement. Reg. § 1.401(a)(9)-5, A-9(b)(1)–(3). IRA contributions returned (together with the "earnings thereon") by the extended due date of the participant's tax return ("corrective distributions"; see ¶ 2.1.08) do not count. Reg. § 1.408-8, A-11(b)(1)–(3). Neither do plan loans that are treated as distributions due to failure to comply with the plan loan rules (¶ 2.1.07(A)), or the imputed income arising from life insurance held by a plan (see the *Special Report: When Insurance Products Meet Retirement Plans*, Appendix C). Reg. § 1.401(a)(9)-5, A-9(b)(4), (6).

C.   **ESOP dividends do NOT count.** Dividends on employer stock in an ESOP can be paid by the issuer directly to the participant or beneficiary. § 404(k). Such dividend payments do not count towards the MRD requirement. Reg. § 1.401(a)(9)-5, A-9(b)(5).

D.   **Nontaxable distributions DO count.** For two exceptions to this rule see "A" and "B" above. Reg. § 1.401(a)(9)-5, A-9(a) (second sentence), § 1.408-8, A-11(a). See PLR 9840041. The nontaxable portion of a QRP distribution is applied first to the MRD. Reg. § 1.402(c)-2, A-8. If the MRD amount exceeds the nontaxable portion of the distribution, then the rest of the MRD is "filled up" from the taxable portion. Any balance of the taxable portion remaining after the MRD is satisfied is eligible for rollover (¶ 2.6.03). See ¶ 2.2 for how to tell what portion of a particular distribution is nontaxable. See ¶ 1.3.05 if the employee has multiple accounts in a QRP.

E.   **Distributions in kind DO count.** (For an exception to this rule see "A.") A participant or beneficiary can take MRDs in kind as well as in cash. Plans are permitted to distribute property as well as cash. See Reg. § 1.401(a)(9)-5, A-9(a) (third sentence); § 1.402(a)-1(a)(1)(iii); Notice 89-25, 1989-1 C.B. 662, A-10; and instructions for IRS Forms 1099-R (2010), p. 7.

F.   **Trustee-to-trustee transfers generally do NOT count.** A direct transfer from one IRA to another IRA *of the same type* (traditional or Roth) is not treated as a distribution for purposes of fulfilling the MRD requirement. Reg. § 1.408-8, A-8(a). Thus, the MRD with respect to the transferring IRA for the year must still be satisfied. However, since that MRD can be satisfied by a distribution from another IRA (including the transferee IRA) (see ¶ 1.3.04), the IRA-to-IRA transfer can be done without distributing or holding back the MRD; see ¶ 2.6.08. For a transfer that is treated *as a rollover*, i.e., a direct rollover from a QRP or 403(b) plan to an IRA or Roth IRA (see ¶ 2.6.01(C), ¶ 4.2.04(D)), or a transfer (conversion) from a traditional IRA to a Roth IRA (¶ 5.4.07), the MRD must be distributed to the participant or beneficiary *before* the transfer or conversion occurs. See ¶ 2.6.03, ¶ 5.2.02(E).

G.   Payment of account expenses does not count. ¶ 8.1.04(A).

1.2.03 *Tables to determine Applicable Distribution Period (ADP)*

Annual MRDs are determined by dividing the prior year-end account balance by a life expectancy factor (from an IRS table) called the **Applicable Distribution Period (ADP)** or divisor. The term "ADP" is used to mean both, particularly, the numerical factor used as a divisor in computing the MRD for a particular year (¶ 1.2.01, #3) (as in "look up the ADP for age 78 in the Uniform Lifetime Table") and, more generally, the payout period that will apply to a particular participant or beneficiary (as in "the ADP is the oldest beneficiary's life expectancy"; ¶ 1.7.05(B)).

There are currently three tables in use for purposes of computing MRDs. All three tables are reproduced in full in IRS Publication 590, "Individual Retirement Arrangements." All three tables are "unisex" (life expectancy for men and women is the same).

Lifetime MRDs (¶ 1.3) are calculated using either the **Uniform Lifetime Table** (¶ 1.3.02) or (if the participant's sole beneficiary is his more-than-10-years-younger spouse) the **Joint and Last Survivor Table**. ¶ 1.3.03. The Uniform Lifetime Table is found at Reg. § 1.401(a)(9)-9, A-2, and in Appendix A of this book (p. 569). The Joint and Last Survivor Table is found at Reg. § 1.401(a)(9)-9, A-3 (not reproduced in this book).

Post-death MRDs based on the life expectancy of the surviving spouse (¶ 1.6.03(C), (D)); of a nonspouse Designated Beneficiary (¶ 1.5.05); or of the deceased participant (¶ 1.5.08); are calculated using the **Single Life Table**. The only post-death MRDs *not* governed by the Single Life Table are the MRD for the year of the participant's death (¶ 1.5.04(A)) and distributions under the 5-year rule (¶ 1.5.06). The Single Life Table is found at Reg. § 1.401(a)(9)-9, A-1, and in Appendix A of this book (pp. 571–572).

The IRS uses a different set of actuarial tables for estate and gift tax valuations; see § 7520. The *estate and gift tax* actuarial tables must be updated at least every 10 years. § 7520(c)(3). The 2009 updates to the transfer tax actuarial tables have *no effect* on the calculation of MRDs. The tables used to calculate MRDs were last updated in 2002. T.D. 8987, 67 FR 18987. They may be updated from time to time by the IRS. Reg. § 1.401(a)(9)-9, A-4.

1.2.04 *What is a person's "age" for MRD purposes?*

To obtain the ADP or divisor (¶ 1.2.03) from the IRS tables, you need to know the participant's or beneficiary's age. Age for MRD purposes means the age the person will attain on his birthday in the applicable Distribution Year; it is the age he will be at the end of the Distribution Year. Reg. § 1.401(a)(9)-5, A-4(a), (b); A-5(c).

The tricky part is that for some MRDs the age is determined only once, at the beginning of the payout period; this is called the "fixed-term" or "reduce-by-one" method. For other MRDs, the age is redetermined annually ("recalculation method"). The participant or beneficiary has no choice in this matter—the regulations dictate which method applies in which situation.

A.   **Recalculation method.** The recalculation method applies for purposes of computing all lifetime MRDs (¶ 1.3), including the MRD for the year of the participant's death if any (¶ 1.5.04(A)), and post-death MRDs when the surviving spouse is the sole beneficiary (¶ 1.6.03(D)). Under the recalculation method, <u>the individual's age is redetermined each year</u>, and the ADP used is the divisor applicable to the new age, instead of just deducting one from last year's divisor. Under the recalculation method, life expectancy never runs out as long as the distributee is alive: See "Kenny Example" (¶ 1.3.01); ¶ 1.3.02; and "Josephine Example" (¶ 1.6.03(D)).

B.   **Fixed-term method.** Under the "fixed-term method," you determine the person's age and the corresponding ADP in the *first* Distribution Year. In subsequent Distribution Years, the divisor is simply the prior year's divisor reduced by one; see Diane Example at ¶ 1.5.05(A). Some call this the "**reduce-by-one method**." Unlike with the recalculation method, you do not determine a new ADP each year based on the person's new age. With two exceptions, the fixed-term method is *always* used after the participant's death to determine MRDs to the beneficiary. The two exceptions are: the MRD for the year of the participant's death (¶ 1.5.04(A)); and MRDs during the surviving spouse's life, if she is the participant's sole beneficiary (¶ 1.6.03(D)). The fixed-term method is *never* used to calculate MRDs during the participant's lifetime.

1.2.05 *How to determine "account balance" for MRD purposes*

Each year, the MRD is determined by dividing the *prior year-end account balance* by the ADP. This section explains which account balance you use and what adjustments are required. See ¶ 1.2.08 for how to value the account balance.

The relevant account balance for an IRA is "the account balance of the IRA as of December 31 of the calendar year immediately preceding the calendar year for which distributions are required to be made." Reg. § 1.408-8, A-6. In the case of a qualified retirement plan (QRP), use "the account balance as of the last valuation date in the calendar year immediately preceding" the Distribution Year. Reg. § 1.401(a)(9)-5, A-3(a).

Here are the adjustments that are required (or not allowed) with respect to this account balance:

✓   The prior year-end balance must be increased by the amount of any "outstanding rollover" (rollover in transit as of the last day of the prior year). See ¶ 1.2.06(A).

✓   The prior year-end balance must be increased by the amount of any recharacterization, in the Distribution Year, of a Roth conversion that occurred in the prior year. See ¶ 1.2.07.

✓   If any portion of the account has been converted to an immediate annuity payout (e.g., for an IRA, via use of part of the account balance to purchase an immediate annuity), the annuity contract and the rest of the account are considered two separate plans for MRD purposes; see ¶ 1.1.05.

✓   If the participant chooses to postpone the MRD for the first Distribution Year into the second Distribution Year (see ¶ 1.4.01), the prior year-end account balance is NOT reduced by the amount of the postponed MRD when computing the MRD for the second Distribution Year. T.D. 8987, 2002-1 C.B. 852, 858, "Calculation Simplification." Regarding the possibility of a reduction of the prior year-end account balance by the amount of any other MRDs that were missed (not distributed) in prior years, see ¶ 1.9.02.

✓   Finally, with one exception, there is <u>no adjustment</u> allowed for post-year-end decreases in the value of the account, such as could occur through investment losses, a divorce in which part of the account is transferred to the participant's ex-spouse, or a creditor's seizing the account. The exception: The MRD is reduced as necessary so that it does not exceed the entire account balance on the date of the distribution. See ¶ 1.2.01, #7.

Biff Example: Biff's IRA is worth $1 million as of 12/31/05. He turns 74 in 2006, so his 2006 MRD is $42,017. In 2006, he gets divorced, and the divorce court awards Mrs. Biff half of Biff's IRA in a tax-free split under § 408(d)(6), so Biff's IRA is reduced to approximately $500,000. Biff still has to take out $42,017 in 2006. If the divorce court had awarded the *entire* account to Mrs. Biff, reducing Biff's account balance to zero before he had taken his 2006 MRD, the 2006 MRD would be reduced to zero (every cloud has a silver lining).

1.2.06 *How rollovers and MRDs interact*

This ¶ 1.2.06 explains how rollovers and plan-to-plan transfers affect application of the minimum distribution rules. See also ¶ 1.2.07 regarding recharacterization of Roth IRA conversions.

A.   **Adjustment required for outstanding rollovers.** You must increase the prior year-end balance (¶ 1.2.05) by any amount that was added to the account in the Distribution Year ("Year 2") and that represented a rollover from another plan or IRA, if the amount in question was distributed from such other plan or IRA in the *prior* calendar year ("Year 1"). The IRS calls such rollovers that are in transit from one account or plan to another on the last day of the year "**outstanding rollovers.**"

For purposes of computing MRDs for the *receiving* plan, the rollover amount is deemed to have been received in the prior calendar year (i.e., Year 1) and not the year it was actually received (Year 2). Reg. § 1.401(a)(9)-7, A-2, last sentence. If this rule did not exist, people could cheat by moving money around from account to account at the end of the year, so as to avoid having the funds count as part of the year-end account balance of *either* plan.

Reg. § 1.408-2(b)(6)(v), which states the opposite (outstanding rollovers added back to the distributing plan) was rendered obsolete by the final MRD regulations. See Reg. § 1.408-8, A-1.

B.   Other rollover effects on balance. Reg. § 1.401(a)(9)-7 contains other rules regarding the effect of rollovers and plan-to-plan transfers on the calculation of MRDs, but (except as noted in "A") a rollover or transfer *into* a plan or IRA has no effect on MRDs *from* that plan or IRA until the year after the rollover or transfer is received. Reg. § 1.401(a)(9)-7, A-2. The rollover or transfer has the effect of increasing the plan balance of the receiving plan, which increases the MRD for the year *following* the rollover.

C.   Effect of rollover on Required Beginning Date (RBD). Generally, if a rollover contribution (¶ 2.6.01(B)) or IRA-to-IRA transfer (¶ 2.6.08) is made into a new IRA (an account which contained nothing at the time it received the rollover contribution), there is no distribution required from such new IRA for the year in which the contribution comes into the account, because the prior year-end account balance was zero (for exceptions see "A," ¶ 1.2.07, and ¶ 1.6.03(B)). The RBD for the new account will be the later of (1) April 1 of the year after the year the participant reaches age 70½ or (2) December 31 of the year after the year of the rollover. See PLRs 1999-31049, 2001-23070.

D.   Rollover can change applicable MRD rules. MRDs are determined under the rules applicable to *the plan that holds the benefits*. It does not matter that the benefits may have previously been held in some other type of plan prior to a rollover. See Reg. § 1.401(a)(9)-7. This means that a rollover can change the MRD rules applicable to the rolled over assets. There are three situations in which an individual can use a rollover to stop (or head off) the flow of required distributions. Of course he must withdraw the MRD for the year of the rollover (if any) *before* doing the rollover; see ¶ 2.6.03.

✓   A participant who is over age 70½, and therefore is forced to take MRDs from his traditional IRAs (and from any QRPs maintained by any employer as to which the participant is a 5-percent owner), can staunch the flow of MRDs *if* he is still working for an employer as to which he is *not* a 5-percent owner and which maintains a QRP that accepts rollovers, by rolling over the benefits to this employer's QRP. See ¶ 1.4.04 and PLR 2004-53015.

✓   A participant can stop or prevent MRDs by rolling traditional plans and DRACs to a Roth IRA. See ¶ 5.2.02(A), ¶ 5.7.08(B).

✓   A surviving spouse beneficiary can use a rollover or Roth conversion to prevent, delay, or stop MRDs from a plan inherited from the deceased participant. See ¶ 3.2.01(A), (C), ¶ 3.2.04.

1.2.07 *Post-year-end recharacterization of Roth conversion*

A "Roth conversion" (see ¶ 5.4) can be "recharacterized" (reversed or undone) by transferring the "conversion contribution" (and its earnings) from the Roth IRA to a traditional IRA by a certain deadline. See ¶ 5.6.

If there is a Roth conversion in a particular year ("Year 1"), and that conversion is recharacterized in the following year ("Year 2"; see ¶ 5.6.06 for the deadline), the recharacterized conversion contribution, and the net income—or loss—allocable to it (which must be transferred to the traditional IRA along with the contribution itself in order to have a valid recharacterization; see ¶ 5.6.02) are added to the prior year-end account balance of the traditional IRA that received the recharacterized amount, for purposes of computing the MRD for *the year of the recharacterization* ("Year 2"). This rule applies to recharacterizations of both "failed" (¶ 5.4.06) and valid Roth conversions. Reg. § 1.408-8, A-8(b). Note that the amount added to the prior year-end balance is the amount that is actually transferred into the traditional IRA, NOT the prior year-end balance of the Roth IRA itself.

1.2.08 *Valuation rules for determining account balance*

¶ 1.2.05–¶ 1.2.07 explain which account balance is used and what adjustments to the balance are required. But the most important thing about that account balance is its value. The value of the account balance is what the ADP is divided into to determine the MRD.

IRA providers are required to provide the year-end fair market value (FMV) of the IRA to the IRS annually on Form 5498. Reg. § 1.408-8, A-10. There is one special valuation rule, governing how a variable annuity contract held inside a defined contribution (DC) plan is to be valued for MRD purposes. See Reg. § 1.401(a)(9)-6, A-12(a), or the *Special Report: When Insurance Products Meet Retirement Plans* (Appendix C). Surprisingly, except for that one rule, there is no guidance on how to determine FMV for MRD purposes. See Notices 2002-27, 2002-1 CB 814, and 2003-3, 2003-1 CB 257.

1.3 MRDs During Participant's Life

The minimum distribution rules come in two flavors, "life" and "death." This ¶ 1.3 and ¶ 1.4 explain the "life" rules, the rules that apply during the participant's life. For the post-death rules see ¶ 1.5–¶ 1.8.

An individual (the **participant**) who owns a retirement plan account must start taking annual "minimum required distributions" (MRDs) at a certain point in his life. This general statement does *not* apply to Roth IRAs, which are not subject to the lifetime distribution requirement; see ¶ 5.2.02(A). Accordingly, this ¶ 1.3 does not apply to Roth IRAs. Also, see ¶ 1.1.04 regarding the 2009 one-year suspension of MRDs.

For when lifetime MRDs must start, see ¶ 1.4. Once commenced, annual MRDs continue for the rest of the participant's life; for this rule and its exceptions, see ¶ 1.2.01, #2. Although the computation of *post-death* MRDs can be radically different depending who is the beneficiary of the plan (see ¶ 1.5), *lifetime* MRDs are computed the same way for most people. See ¶ 1.3.01 for the method most people use (and the list of people who do *not* use it).

1.3.01 *Road Map: How to compute lifetime MRDs*

Follow Steps 1–8 below to compute a participant's "lifetime" MRD for a particular year (the "Distribution Year") for a qualified retirement plan (QRP) or 403(b) plan account or traditional IRA. Reg. § 1.401(a)(9)-5, A-4(a). This calculation must be done separately for EACH IRA or plan account the participant owns; see ¶ 1.3.04. As a reminder, this method does *not* apply to defined benefit plans or to the "annuitized" portion of any DC plan; see ¶ 1.1.05.

Step 1: **Determine whether a distribution is required** for this year. If the participant has not yet reached his "first Distribution Year" (¶ 1.4.01), you're done—no MRD is required. For the first Distribution Year itself, see ¶ 1.4.07. If the participant has passed his RBD, a distribution is required. If a distribution *is* required for the year, proceed to Steps 2–8.

Step 2: **Determine the prior year-end account balance** for this plan or IRA. See ¶ 1.2.05–¶ 1.2.08.

Step 3: **Determine the participant's age.** See ¶ 1.2.04.

Step 4: **Obtain the ADP (divisor)** from the Uniform Lifetime Table (¶ 1.2.03) for the participant's age (Step 3), unless the sole beneficiary of the account is the participant's more-than-10-years-younger spouse (in which case see ¶ 1.3.03 for where to find the divisor).

Step 5: **Compute the current Distribution Year's MRD** by dividing the prior year-end account balance (Step 2) by the ADP (Step 4).

Step 6: **If the current Distribution Year is 2009**, reduce the amount obtained in Step 5 to zero. See ¶ 1.1.04.

Step 7: **Add any missed MRDs from prior years** to the amount obtained in Steps 1–6. See ¶ 1.9.02.

Step 8: **And the answer is…** The MRD for the current year is the amount determined under Step 7, or, if less, the total value of the account on the distribution date (see ¶ 1.2.05), unless the participant qualifies for one of two "grandfather rule" exceptions: For a QRP participant who has a pre-1984 "TEFRA 242(b) election" in effect (this is rare), see ¶ 1.4.08. For a 403(b) participant who has a pre-1987 account balance, see ¶ 1.4.05.

Here is an example of how to compute a lifetime MRD for a participant who does not qualify for any grandfather rule exceptions, has not failed to take the MRD in any prior year, and does not have a more-than-10-years-younger spouse as his sole beneficiary:

Kenny Example: Kenny turns 73 on his 2010 birthday. Under the Uniform Lifetime Table, the ADP (divisor) for age 73 is 24.7. On 12/31/09, the value of his IRA was $750,000; assume no adjustments (¶ 1.2.06(A), ¶ 1.2.07) are required. Divide $750,000 by 24.7; the result ($30,364) is Kenny's MRD for 2010. Kenny must withdraw $30,364 from his IRA sometime in 2010 (i.e., after December 31, 2009, and before January 1, 2011). In 2011, Kenny will reach age 74. To compute his 2011 MRD, he will use the age 74 factor from the Uniform Lifetime Table. This will be divided into the 2010 year-end account balance to produce the 2011 MRD. This is the "recalculation method" of determining life expectancy; ¶ 1.2.04(A).

1.3.02 *The Uniform Lifetime Table: Good news for retirees*

The divisors in the Uniform Lifetime Table represent the joint life expectancy of a participant age 70 (or older) and a hypothetical beneficiary who is 10 years younger than the participant. T.D. 8987, 2002-1 C.B. 852, 854, "Uniform Lifetime Table." Thus, the initial divisor under this table (for a participant age 70) is 27.4 years, which is the joint and survivor life expectancy of one person age 70 and another person age 60.

The expectancy factors in the Uniform Lifetime Table are redetermined annually: The table does not start with a 27.4-year distribution period and then reduce it by one each year. If the table used such a "fixed-term method," then all money would have to be distributed out of the plan by the time the participant reached age 97 (70 + 27). Instead, the divisor decreases by less than one most years. At age 75, the divisor is 22.9 (not 22.4), at age 89 it is 12.0 (not 8.4). The divisor never goes below 1.9, so if the participant takes only the MRD the account balance will never go to zero, regardless of how long the participant lives, unless it is wiped out by an external factor such as investment losses.

In fact, depending on the rate of investment return, there may well be more in the account when the participant dies than there was when MRDs began. For example, if the participant takes only the MRD starting at age 70½, and the account has a steady six percent annual investment return, the account will have more dollars in it at his death than it did when he started taking MRDs, if he dies prior to age 89.

Under this system, the life expectancy of the participant's actual beneficiary, or whether he even has a beneficiary, are almost irrelevant (for exception see ¶ 1.3.03). Nevertheless, the Uniform Lifetime Table is the IRS's way of implementing the Code's requirement that benefits be distributed either in full on the RBD, or, "beginning not later than the required beginning date...over the life of such employee or over the lives of such employee and a designated beneficiary (or over a period not extending beyond the life expectancy of such employee or the life expectancy of such employee and a designated beneficiary)." § 401(a)(9)(A)(ii).

1.3.03 *Lifetime MRDs: Much-younger-spouse method*

As generous as the Uniform Lifetime Table is, the participant enjoys even smaller MRDs if his sole beneficiary is his more-than-10-years-younger spouse.

"[I]f the sole designated beneficiary of an employee is the employee's surviving spouse, for required minimum distributions during the employee's lifetime, the applicable distribution period is *the longer of* the distribution period determined in accordance with...[the Uniform Lifetime Table] or the joint life expectancy of the employee and spouse using the employee's and spouse's attained ages as of the employee's and the spouse's birthdays in the distribution calendar year." Reg. § 1.401(a)(9)-5, A-4(b) (emphasis added). Note that this formulation mandates annual recalculation (¶ 1.2.04(A)) of the participant's and spouse's life expectancies.

The Joint and Last Survivor Table (¶ 1.2.03) will produce larger ADPs (divisors) and smaller MRDs than the Uniform Lifetime Table if the spouse-beneficiary was born in a year more than ten years later than the year of the participant's birth. For example, if the participant was born in 1941, the joint table will provide larger divisors than the Uniform Lifetime Table if the spouse was born in 1952 or later.

See ¶ 1.3.05 regarding separate accounts; and note the following additional points regarding this method:

A.   **No election required.** The participant does not have to elect to use the joint life expectancy of the participant and spouse as his ADP. If the participant's spouse is his sole beneficiary, then the participant's divisor is *automatically* the ADP determined under the Uniform Lifetime Table, or under the Joint and Last Survivor Table, whichever is larger.

B.   **Tests for whether spouse is sole beneficiary.** The spouse is the sole Designated Beneficiary for purposes of determining the participant's MRDs "if the spouse is the sole beneficiary of the employee's entire interest at all times during the distribution calendar year." Reg. § 1.401(a)(9)-5, A-4(b)(1). Marital status is determined on January 1 of each Distribution Year for purposes of computing that year's MRD; therefore the *death* of either spouse, or a *divorce*, during the Distribution Year does not cause the spouse to lose her status as "spouse" until the following calendar year. The spouse is deemed to be the "sole beneficiary" for the entire year if she is the sole beneficiary on January 1 of the year *and* the participant does not change his beneficiary designation prior to the end of the calendar year (or prior to the spouse's death, if earlier). Reg. § 1.401(a)(9)-5, A-4(b)(2). "Sole beneficiary" means sole *primary* beneficiary; see ¶ 1.6.02, ¶ 1.7.02.

C.   **Post-RBD changes permitted.** It is not required that the participant and spouse be married on the RBD or any other date prior to January 1 of the Distribution Year in question. If the participant has named some other beneficiary, he can change the beneficiary to his spouse (or marry after his RBD and name his new spouse as beneficiary); the determination of which table applies is made separately each Distribution Year.

1.3.04 *Taking distributions from multiple plans*

This section explains the rules for *participants* who are taking *lifetime* MRDs from more than one retirement plan. For rules applicable to *beneficiaries* taking distributions from *inherited* plans, see ¶ 1.5.09 instead.

If the participant has benefits in more than one <u>qualified retirement plan</u> (QRP), the MRD must be calculated separately for each such plan, and each such plan must distribute the MRD calculated for that plan. Reg. § 1.401(a)(9)-8, A-1. Thus if he participates in two pension plans and a 401(k) plan, he will receive three separate MRDs (even if all the plans are provided by the same employer).

A different rule applies for <u>IRAs</u>. The MRD must be calculated separately for each IRA, but (with exceptions noted below) the participant is not required to take each IRA's calculated amount from that IRA. He can total up the MRDs required from *all* of his IRAs and then take the total amount from one of the IRAs or from any combination of them. Reg. § 1.408-8, A-9. For purposes of this rule, all traditional IRAs—whether contributory, rollover, SIMPLE, or SEP—are treated the same; they may all be aggregated with each other. However, *Roth IRAs* may not be aggregated with any type of traditional IRA for this purpose; see ¶ 5.2.02(C).

This optional aggregation rule applies also to <u>403(b) accounts</u>. The MRD must be calculated separately for each 403(b) account, but (with exceptions noted below) the participant is not required to take each 403(b) account's calculated amount from that 403(b) account. He can total up the MRDs required from all of his 403(b) arrangements, and then take the total amount all from one of them or from any combination of them. Reg.§ 1.403(b)-6(e)(7).

Note that IRAs may be aggregated *only* with other IRAs, and 403(b)s may be aggregated *only* with other 403(b)s.

Now for the exceptions: An individual's IRAs held as *owner* may not be aggregated with IRAs he holds as *beneficiary*; an individual's 403(b) plans held as *employee* may not be aggregated with such individual's 403(b) plans held as *beneficiary*; and an individual's IRAs (or 403(b) plans) held as beneficiary of one decedent may not be aggregated with IRAs (or 403(b) plans) held as beneficiary of another decedent. Regs. § 1.408-8, A-9; § 1.403(b)-6(e)(7). Also, if any part of an IRA or 403(b) account has been "annuitized" (converted to an immediate annuity), the annuitized portion becomes subject to the defined benefit plan MRD rules and cannot be aggregated with amounts governed by the DC plan rules; see ¶ 1.1.05.

1.3.05 *Separate accounts within a single plan*

A QRP may maintain multiple accounts for a particular employee on the plan books, for example a rollover account, an employer contribution account, and an employee contribution account. These multiple accounts within a single QRP are treated as <u>one account</u> for MRD purposes during the employee's life. Reg. § 1.401(a)(9)-8, A-2(a). This rule is favorable to the employee, because he can withdraw his MRDs from his employee contribution account (which may contain after-tax dollars) first; see ¶ 1.2.02(D).

Though a single IRA payable to multiple beneficiaries can be divided into "separate accounts" (each payable to a different beneficiary) for MRD purposes after the owner's death (¶ 1.8.01), separate accounts treatment is *not* available for MRD purposes during the participant's life. Thus, it is not possible to use the much-younger-spouse method to calculate the MRD for the fractional portion of the account of which the spouse is the beneficiary if she is not sole beneficiary of the participant's entire account in the plan. Reg. § 1.401(a)(9)-8, A-2(a)(2).

1.4 The RBD and First Distribution Year

Computing lifetime MRDs (¶ 1.3) is much easier than figuring out when they start. This ¶ 1.4 explains what the "RBD" and "first Distribution Year" are for various types of retirement plans and looks at the anomalies created by the disconnect between the first Distribution Year and the RBD (¶ 1.4.07).

1.4.01 *Required Beginning Date (RBD); Distribution Year*

A year for which an MRD is required is called a "distribution calendar year" in the regulations (Reg. § 1.401(a)(9)-5, A-1(b)), a **Distribution Year** in this book. For plans subject to the lifetime MRD rules (¶ 1.1.02), the "first Distribution Year" is the year the participant reaches age 70½ (or, in some cases, retires, if later; see ¶ 1.4.04, ¶ 1.4.05). However, if the participant reached age 70½ (or retired, if later) in 2008 or 2009, see ¶ 1.4.09.

See ¶ 1.2.06(C) for the effect of rollovers and IRA-to-IRA transfers.

Normally, the deadline for taking the MRD for a particular Distribution Year is December 31 of such year (¶ 1.2.01, #2), but, for lifetime distributions only, in the case of the first Distribution Year, the deadline is April 1 of the *following* year. Reg. § 1.401(a)(9)-5, A-1(c). That postponed deadline for the first year's MRD is called the

Required Beginning Date or **RBD**. § 401(a)(9)(C). This postponement of the MRD for the first year does not apply to death benefits (¶ 1.5).

The RBD matters mainly for *compliance* purposes: The participant must start taking MRDs by that date to avoid penalty (¶ 1.9.02). Also, the calculation of post-death MRDs is different depending on whether death occurred before or after the RBD; see ¶ 1.5.02, Step 3. The RBD has little significance for *planning* purposes.

The starting point for determining the RBD is the attainment of age 70½, which is "the date six calendar months after the 70th anniversary of the employee's birth." Reg. § 1.401(a)(9)-2, A-3.

1.4.02 *RBD for IRAs and Roth IRAs*

The RBD for a <u>traditional IRA</u> is April 1 of the calendar year following the year in which the participant reaches age 70½, regardless of whether he is "retired." § 408(a)(6), § 401(a)(9)(C)(i)(I), (ii)(II). Exceptions: For participants who turned age 70½ in 2009, see ¶ 1.4.09(B); for certain rollover contributions, see ¶ 1.2.06(C).

<u>Roth IRAs</u> have no RBD. The participant is *never* compelled to take distributions from his Roth IRA. Minimum distribution requirements do not apply to a Roth IRA until after the participant's death. See ¶ 5.2.02.

1.4.03 *QRPs: RBD for 5-percent owner*

For a participant who is a "5-percent owner," the RBD for a QRP is the same as the RBD for a traditional IRA (¶ 1.4.02): April 1 of the calendar year following the year in which the participant reaches age 70½, regardless of whether he is "retired." § 401(a)(9)(C)(ii)(I); Reg. § 1.401(a)(9)-2, A-2(c). For participants who turned age 70½ in 2009, see ¶ 1.4.09(B).

More precisely, the "normal" RBD for QRPs (later of retirement or age 70½; see ¶ 1.4.04) is *not available* for "an employee who is a 5-percent owner (as defined in section 416) with respect to the plan year ending in the calendar year in which the employee attains age 70½...." "Once an employee is a 5-percent owner...distributions must continue to such employee even if such employee ceases to own more than 5 percent of the employer in a subsequent year." Notice 97-75, 1997-2 C.B. 337, "Background."

§ 416(i)(1)(B)(i) defines 5-percent owner as someone who owns "*more than* 5 percent of the outstanding stock of the corporation or stock possessing more than 5 percent of the total combined voting power of all stock of the corporation, or...if the employer is not a corporation, any person who owns more than 5 percent of the capital or profits interest in the employer" (emphasis added). Note that someone who owns exactly 5 percent is not a 5-percent owner—you must own more than 5 percent to be a 5-percent owner!

In determining ownership percentages under § 416, a modified version of the "constructive ownership" rules of § 318 applies. Under these complicated rules, a participant could be deemed, for purposes of the 5 percent test, to own stock held by various family members, trusts, estates, partnerships, or corporations; and stock options must be taken into account. Explanation of the constructive ownership rules is beyond the scope of this book.

1.4.04 QRPs, cont.: RBD for non-5-percent owner

The RBD for a QRP participant who is not a "5-percent owner" is generally "April 1 of the calendar year following the *later of* (I) the calendar year in which the employee attains age 70½, or (II) the calendar year in which the employee retires from employment" with the employer maintaining the plan. § 401(a)(9)(C); Reg. § 1.401(a)(9)-2, A-2(a). Emphasis added. See ¶ 1.4.03 for the meaning of "5-percent owner." See ¶ 1.4.06 for the meaning of "retires." Note the following:

✓   If the "later of" year was 2008 or 2009, see ¶ 1.4.09.

✓   A QRP participant who filed a "TEFRA 242(b) election" may have a *later* RBD than specified in § 401(a)(9)(C); see ¶ 1.4.08.

✓   A QRP is not required to recognize the "later of retirement or age 70½" RBD. A QRP may choose to require *all* employees to commence distributions by April 1 of the year following the year in which they reach age 70½, even non-5-percent owners who are not retired. Reg. § 1.401(a)(9)-2, A-2(e).

If the plan forces all employees to commence distributions by April 1 of the calendar year following the year they reach age 70½, things get complicated for the nonretired employee who is not a 5-percent owner: He has one RBD for certain purposes, but some of his "required" distributions from the plan are not considered "required" distributions for other purposes. Specifically, for purposes of *determining MRDs from that plan*, and *determining whether the employee died before or after his RBD for that plan*, the employee's RBD is the RBD set by the plan, *not* the RBD described in the statute. Reg. § 1.401(a)(9)-2, A-6(b).

However, any distributions the employee receives during the period that is after the employee has passed *the plan's* RBD but not his *statutory* RBD are eligible for rollover: Such distributions are not considered "required distributions" for purposes of the definition of eligible rollover distribution (see ¶ 2.6.03) until after the employee's *statutory* RBD. Somehow the distribution *is* an MRD when the check is cut, but it is *not* an MRD when the check arrives in the employee's mailbox! Notice 97-75, 1997-2 C.B. 337, A-10(c).

1.4.05 *RBD for 403(b) plans (including "grandfather rule")*

The RBD for all 403(b) plans is April 1 of the calendar year following the later of the year the participant reaches age 70½ or the year the participant retires. There is no possibility of a different rule for 5-percent owners (¶ 1.4.03) because all 403(b) plans are maintained by tax-exempt charitable organizations that have no "owners." Reg. § 1.403(b)-6(e)(7). In contrast to the rule for qualified plans, there is no apparent permission for the plan to establish an RBD earlier than that in the statute (compare ¶ 1.4.04).

A "grandfather rule" applies to pre-1987 balances in 403(b) plans if separately identified. See Reg. § 1.403(b)-6(e)(6). The Tax Reform Act of 1986 made the minimum distribution rules applicable, for the first time, to all 403(b) plans, but made this rule prospective only by exempting any pre-1987 403(b) plan balance from the new regime, provided such balance is accounted for separately. The pre-1987 account balance, while not subject to the full panoply of today's minimum distribution rules, is still subject to the more primitive predecessor of today's rules, the "incidental death benefits rule" (see below) of Reg. § 1.401-1(b)(1).

Here are the three advantages of qualifying for this grandfather rule:

✓   The age for starting lifetime required distributions from the pre-1987 balance is actual retirement or, if later, age 75 (not age 70½). See PLR 9345044.

✓   Required distributions from the grandfathered balance are computed under the **incidental death benefits rule** rather than in the manner explained at ¶ 1.3. Under this rule, any mode of distribution to the participant qualifies provided that it is projected *either* to distribute all the benefits over the lifetimes of the participant and his spouse-beneficiary *or* to distribute at least 50 percent of the benefits during the participant's life. Reg. § 1.403(b)-6(e)(vi); Rev. Rul. 72-240, 1972-1 C.B. 108; Rev. Rul. 72-241, 1972-1 C.B. 108, ninth paragraph.

✓   There are no requirements for how rapidly death benefits must be distributed if the participant dies before commencing distributions.

The pre-1987 grandfather amount is a frozen, fixed-dollar amount; investment earnings and gains do not increase the grandfathered balance. Reg. § 1.403(b)-6(e)(i). With the passage of time, new contributions to the plan and investment growth tend to make the pre-1987 balance an ever-smaller percentage of the overall plan balance, so in most cases it is not a significant planning factor. Also, any distributions taken from the plan that are in excess of the MRDs from the post-1986 balance are deemed to come first out of the pre-1987 balance. For more on the 403(b) grandfather rule, see the *Special Report: Ancient History* (Appendix C).

1.4.06 *What does "retires" mean?*

The meaning of "the calendar year in which the employee retires" (see ¶ 1.4.04, ¶ 1.4.05) is not always obvious. We do know that **"retirement"** means retirement "from employment *with the employer maintaining the plan.*" Reg. § 1.401(a)(9)-2, A-2(a); Reg. § 1.403(b)-6(e)(3). Emphasis added. It is not known whether retirement always means "separation from service" or whether some reduction of hours worked or responsibilities could be considered "retirement." Neither the regulations, nor any IRS Publication, nor Notice 97-75, 1997-2 C.B. 337 (which provides guidance to employers on the tax law changes made by the Small Business Jobs Protection Act of 1996) says anything on this point. Also, the statute reads as though there is only one "retirement" per employee; it is not known whether re-employment could "cancel" retirement, allowing MRDs to be discontinued until the employee retires *again*.

1.4.07 *RBD versus first Distribution Year: The limbo period*

The disconnect between the first Distribution Year and the RBD (¶ 1.4.01) creates a "limbo period," beginning January 1 of the first Distribution Year and ending on the RBD. Odd effects occur during this limbo period:

A.   **If the first year's MRD is postponed**, two MRDs are required in the second year (unless the second year was 2009; see ¶ 1.4.09(A)). The two MRDs in the second year will have different deadlines, be based on different account balances, and use different divisors.

Bernie Example: Bernie turns age 70½ in 2007, so 2007 is the first Distribution Year for his IRA. To calculate the 2007 MRD, he uses the 2006 year-end account balance and the Uniform Lifetime Table divisor for the age he attains on his 2007 birthday, which will be 70 if he was born before July 1, or 71 if he was born after June 30. He can take the 2007 MRD at any time from January 1, 2007, through April 1, 2008. There will then be *another* MRD for the year 2008, which must be taken between January 1, 2008, and December 31, 2008. The 2008 MRD will be based on the December 31, 2007 account balance and will use the Uniform Lifetime Table factor applicable for the age he attains on his 2008 birthday.

B.   **No rollover or conversion until MRD has been taken.** Even though the participant does not have to take the MRD for his first Distribution Year until April 1 of the second Distribution Year, he cannot, in the first Distribution Year (or any other Distribution Year) roll over (or convert to a Roth IRA) any funds from that plan or IRA to another plan or IRA until *after* he has taken the MRD for that Distribution Year; see ¶ 2.6.03(D) and ¶ 5.2.02(E). This rule does not apply to IRA-to-IRA transfers (¶ 1.2.08); see ¶ 1.2.02(F).

C.   **Death during the limbo period.** If the participant dies on or after January 1 of the year he turns age 70½ (or retires, whichever is applicable), but before April 1 of the following year, he has died *"before" his RBD* and therefore the rules of § 401(a)(9)(B)(ii),(iii), and (iv) (life expectancy of beneficiary or 5-year rule; ¶ 1.5.03) apply to distribution of his death benefits, not § 401(a)(9)(B)(i) (the at-least-as-rapidly rule; ¶ 1.5.04). Reg. § 1.401(a)(9)-2, A-6.

What becomes of the MRDs that have "accrued" for the age 70½ and age 71½ (if applicable) year(s) in such a case of death during the "limbo period?" Those MRDs are simply "erased." They need not be taken at all. If "Bernie" (see "A") had died on March 31, 2008, he would have died before his RBD. Because he died before he was required to start taking MRDs, *no one* has an obligation to take Bernie's 2007 and 2008 MRDs; they vanish. Even if he had taken part or all of his 2007 and 2008 MRDs before his death, his death would still be "before" his RBD for purposes of computing post-death MRDs. This conclusion is based on the following authorities:

- § 401(a)(9)(B)(i) provides that the "at-least-as-rapidly rule" applies "if distribution of the employee's interest has begun" in accordance with § 401(a)(9)(A)(ii) (the lifetime minimum distribution rules). Reg. § 1.401(a)(9)-2, A-6, provides that "distributions are not treated as having begun to the employee [for that purpose]...until the employee's [RBD].... Thus, section 401(a)(9)(B)(i) [the at-least-as-rapidly rule] *only* applies if an employee dies *on or after* the employee's" RBD. Emphasis added.

- "*If an employee dies on or after the required beginning date*, the distribution period applicable for calculating the amount that must be distributed during the distribution calendar year that includes the employee's death is determined as if the employee had lived throughout that year." Reg. § 1.401(a)(9)-5, A-4(a). Emphasis added. This is the only regulation that explicitly states a rule for the year of death. A-5 (which covers post-death MRDs in case of deaths both before and after the RBD) begins in each case with the year *after* the year of death.

- If the surviving spouse is the sole beneficiary of a deceased participant's IRA and elects to treat the IRA as her own (¶ 3.2.03), Reg. § 1.408-8, A-5(a) provides that, if the spousal election is made in the year of the participant's death, "the spouse is required to take a required minimum distribution for that year, determined with respect to the deceased IRA owner under the rules of A-4(a) of section 1.401(a)(9)-5, to the extent such a distribution was not made to the IRA owner before death." The referenced regulation is the one that says the balance of the year-of-death MRD must be taken by the beneficiary "if the employee dies *on or after*" the RBD. Emphasis added.

- Finally, Reg. § 1.401(a)(9)-3, A-1, provides that, if the employee dies before his RBD, "distribution of the employee's *entire interest* must be made in accordance with" the rules of § 401(a)(9)(B)(ii), (iii), and (iv). Those subsections refer only to the 5-year rule and payouts over the life expectancy of the designated beneficiary, with no reference to taking any distribution that the decedent would have been required to take had he not died.

These regulations lead to the conclusion that, since the decedent was not required to take an MRD for the age 70½ (or age 71½) year(s) if he died before his RBD, the beneficiary is not required to take the balance of the MRD for the year of death, because there is no MRD to take the balance of. There is no authority that contradicts this conclusion.

1.4.08 *Grandfather rule: TEFRA 242(b) elections*

TEFRA (1982) significantly expanded the coverage and stringency of the minimum distribution rules. TEFRA contained a grandfather rule, § 242(b)(2), which provided that, despite the new rules, a plan would not be disqualified "by reason of distributions under a designation (before January 1, 1984) by any employee of a method of distribution...(A) which does not meet the requirements of [§ 401(a)(9)], but (B) which would not have disqualified such [plan] under [§ 401(a)(9)] as in effect before the amendment" made by TEFRA. TRA '84 (which made more changes) continued the TEFRA grandfather rule: The TRA '84 changes would not apply to "distributions under a designation (before January 1, 1984) by any employee in accordance with a designation described in section

242(b)(2) of [TEFRA] (as in effect before the amendments made by this Act)." TRA '84, § 521(d)(2)-5.

To avoid the impact of TEFRA, there was a flurry of activity among sophisticated plan participants trying to make a "designation" by December 31, 1983 that would enable them to continue to use the older, more liberal rules. Participants with valid TEFRA 242(b) elections can postpone the start of MRDs past age 70½, until retirement (even if they own more than 5 percent of the employer), and their death benefits are not subject to the "5-year rule" (¶ 1.5.06) or the "at-least-as-rapidly" rule (¶ 1.5.04).

For the requirements of a valid TEFRA 242(b) election see Notice 83-23, 1983-2 C.B. 418, and Reg. § 1.401(a)(9)-8, A-13–A-16. For more detail regarding TEFRA 242(b) elections see the *Special Report: Ancient History* (Appendix C).

1.4.09 *Effect of 2009 one-year suspension of MRDs*

This section explains how the one-year suspension of MRDs in 2009 (¶ 1.1.04) affected participants whose first distribution year was 2008 or 2009 and whose RBD therefore fell in 2009 or 2010.

A. **First distribution year was 2008, RBD was in 2009.** A participant who attained age 70½ (or retired, whichever is applicable) in 2008, but postponed taking his 2008 MRD until 2009 (¶ 1.4.01), still had to take his 2008 MRD by April 1, 2009. Notice 2009-9, 2009-5 IRB 419.

B. **First distribution year was 2009, RBD was in 2010.** An individual who turned 70½ (or retired, whichever was applicable) in 2009 (so 2009 was his "first Distribution Year") did not have to take his 2009 MRD until April 1, 2010. Notice 2009-9 made it clear that this individual was excused from taking the 2009 distribution: "The 2009 RMD waiver under the Act *does apply* to individuals who may be eligible to postpone taking their 2009 RMD until April 1, 2010…." Emphasis added. But even though no distribution had to be taken by that date, April 1, 2010, is still considered to be such person's RBD for purposes of applying the post-death MRD rules (see ¶ 1.5.02, Step 3) and for purposes of the deadline for the *2010* MRD (i.e., it is 12/31/10, not 4/1/11). The RBD "with respect to any individual shall be determined without regard to" the one-year suspension of MRDs in 2009 for purposes of applying § 401(a)(9) for years after 2009. § 401(a)(9)(H)(ii)(I).

1.5 MRDs after the Participant's Death

After the participant's death, the minimum distribution rules apply to the beneficiary. The post-death MRD rules are more complicated than the lifetime MRD rules.

The good news is there are only four possible post-death payout methods: life expectancy of the surviving spouse, life expectancy of a nonspouse beneficiary, life expectancy of the participant, and the 5-year rule. What gets complicated is trying to figure out which one applies to your particular beneficiary and the particular plan he, she, or it inherited.

This ¶ 1.5 covers only the post-2002 MRD rules applicable to defined contribution (DC) or "individual account" plans. Regarding defined benefit plans or annuity payouts, see ¶ 1.1.05. Regarding earlier years, see ¶ 1.1.01.

Instead of this ¶ 1.5, see ¶ 1.4.08 for benefits subject to a "TEFRA 242(b) election," or ¶ 1.4.05 for pre-1987 403(b) plan balances.

1.5.01 *Post-death MRD rules: Basics and overview*

Post-death MRDs after 2002 are determined under the final regulations (¶ 1.1.01) *regardless of when the participant died*. When determining MRDs from the account of a participant who died prior to 2002, "the designated beneficiary must be redetermined....and the applicable distribution period...must be reconstructed" in accordance with the post-2002 rules described here. Reg. § 1.401(a)(9)-1, A-2(b)(1).

In the Code, "required beginning date" refers only to the starting date for lifetime distributions to the participant (¶ 1.4). The date by which post-death distributions to the *beneficiary* must begin does not have an official name; compare § 401(a)(9)(A) and (C) with § 401(a)(9)(B). In this book, **Required Commencement Date** means the deadline by which a beneficiary must start taking distributions.

The basic concept of the post-death MRD rules is simple: The participant's retirement benefits can be depleted gradually through annual distributions (beginning the year after the year of the participant's death) over the life expectancy of the participant's "Designated Beneficiary." ¶ 1.5.05. This is called the "**life expectancy**" (or "**stretch**") payout method and is generally considered a favorable way to distribute benefits, for reasons explained at ¶ 1.1.03. Alternatively, as is always true under the minimum distribution rules, the account can be depleted by any more rapid schedule of distributions; see ¶ 1.2.01, #4.

As we will see, this simple concept gets complicated in its application.

1.5.02 *Road Map for determining post-death MRDs*

To calculate minimum required distributions (MRDs) after the participant's death, START HERE and complete Steps 1 through 6. The chart at Step 7 will then tell you how to compute MRDs for your particular beneficiary, decedent, and plan. However, the plan is not required to allow all the payout options that the tax law permits; see ¶ 1.5.10.

For "double deaths" (the participant died; the beneficiary survived the participant; and then the beneficiary *also* died, before having withdrawn all of the money in the plan), FIRST determine MRDs applicable on the participant's death using this ¶ 1.5.02, plus either ¶ 1.5.03 or ¶ 1.5.04, whichever is applicable. THEN proceed to what happens on the beneficiary's later death, using ¶ 1.5.12 AND either:

- ▸ ¶ 1.6.03(E) or ¶ 1.6.05(C) (whichever is applicable), if the participant's sole beneficiary was his surviving spouse; or
- ▸ ¶ 1.5.13 if the participant's surviving spouse is not the sole beneficiary.

Step 1: Gather basic information you will need in every case to complete the rest of the steps:

- The participant's date of birth and date of death. You can skip the "birth date" part for a Roth IRA, or if you know the participant was younger than age 70½ at death.

- The identity of the participant's beneficiary(ies). For an individual beneficiary, you need to know the beneficiary's date of birth and whether the beneficiary is the surviving spouse of the participant. If the beneficiary is a trust, you need to know whether the trust qualifies as a see-through trust (see ¶ 6.2.03). See ¶ 1.7.02 for how to determine who is the participant's "beneficiary."

- The type of plan you are dealing with: traditional IRA, Roth IRA, QRP, or 403(b) plan (see ¶ 8.3).

Step 2: Gather specialized information you may need to compute the MRD in some cases:

- If the participant died on or after April 1 of the year after the year in which he reached age 70½, and the plan is a QRP or 403(b) plan, you need to know whether the participant had *retired* prior to his death and whether (in the case of a QRP) he was a "5-percent owner" with respect to that plan. See ¶ 1.4.03–¶ 1.4.06.

- If the plan is a 403(b) plan, is there a "pre-1987" account balance in the plan? If so, see ¶ 1.4.05; this Road Map will not work for the pre-1987 balance.

- If the plan is a QRP, did the participant have a TEFRA 242(b) election in effect since 1983? If so, see ¶ 1.4.08; this Road Map will not work for these benefits.

Step 3: Determine whether the participant died before, on, or after the RBD. See ¶ 1.4. If the decedent died BEFORE his RBD, use ¶ 1.5.03 to determine post-death MRDs. If the decedent died AFTER his RBD, use ¶ 1.5.04. Death *on* the RBD is treated as death *after* the RBD. Reg. § 1.401(a)(9)-2, A-6(a).

- ✓ If the plan is a *Roth IRA*, the death is always *before* the RBD, because Roth IRAs have no RBD. ¶ 5.2.02(A).

- ✓ If the participant died <u>before</u> April 1 of the year following the year in which he reached (or would have reached) age 70½ then he died BEFORE his RBD for all plans. See ¶ 1.4.07(C).

✓　　　If he died <u>on or after</u> that date, see ¶ 1.4 for how to determine the RBD for each of the decedent's plans; the RBD is not always easy to determine in this case, because different types of plans have different RBDs. The participant may have died before his RBD under some of his retirement plans but after the RBD for other plans. For the most confusing situations, see: ¶ 1.4.04, qualified plan's RBD is earlier than statutory RBD; and ¶ 1.2.06(C), new IRA created via rollover or transfer.

✓　　　Finally, even though a participant who turned age 70½ (or retired, whichever was applicable) in 2009 did not have to take an MRD for 2009, April 1, 2010, will still be considered his RBD when determining whether he died before or after his RBD for purposes of computing post-death MRDs. See ¶ 1.4.09(B).

Step 4: Are you computing the MRD for the year of death, or for a later year? If you are computing the MRD for the year of the participant's death, see ¶ 1.5.03(A) (if participant died before his RBD), ¶ 1.5.04(A) (if participant died on or after his RBD), and ¶ 1.7.06(A) (if there are multiple beneficiaries); and skip the rest of this ¶ 1.5.02. If you are computing MRDs for years AFTER the year of the participant's death, go on to Step 5.

Step 5: Are there are multiple beneficiaries? If there are multiple beneficiaries, you need to determine whether the "separate accounts rule" applies for purposes of determining the beneficiaries' ADPs. See ¶ 1.8.01(B). If the beneficiaries' interests constitute separate accounts for ADP purposes, then the beneficiary (and resulting ADP) are determined separately for each such separate account and the distribution options described in ¶ 1.5.03(B)–(F) or ¶ 1.5.04(B)–(F) (whichever is applicable) apply to *each separate account*. If there are multiple beneficiaries whose interests do *not* qualify as separate accounts for ADP purposes, then the distribution options are as described at ¶ 1.5.03(F) or ¶ 1.5.04(F), whichever is applicable.

Step 6: Do the benefits pass to a Designated Beneficiary, and if so who? See ¶ 1.7.03 for the definition of Designated Beneficiary. Note that the identity of the beneficiary is not finally fixed, for purposes of these rules, until September 30 of the year following the year of the participant's death; see ¶ 1.8.03. Accordingly, the "quiz answers" in ¶ 1.5.03(B)–(F) or ¶ 1.5.04(B)–(F) apply *once the identity of the beneficiary is finalized on September 30 of the year following the year of the participant's death.* Your choices for completing Step 6 are: the participant's surviving spouse (¶ 1.6.02); an individual who is not the participant's surviving spouse (¶ 1.7.03); a see-through trust (¶ 6.2.03); an estate, non-see-through trust, or other nonindividual beneficiary (¶ 1.7.04); and multiple beneficiaries (i.e., any combination of the foregoing) (¶ 1.7.05).

Step 7: Compute the MRDs:

If the beneficiary is...	...and the participant died before the RBD, see:	...and the participant died after the RBD, see:
Year of participant's death:		
Any beneficiary	N/A; no MRD. ¶ 1.5.03(A).	¶ 1.5.04(A).
Later years:		
The participant's surviving spouse	¶ 1.5.03(B)	¶ 1.5.04(B)
An individual (not the surviving spouse)	¶ 1.5.03(C)	¶ 1.5.04(C)
See-through trust	¶ 1.5.03(D)	¶ 1.5.04(D)
Participant's estate; a non-see-through trust; any nonindividual beneficiary.	¶ 1.5.03(E); 5-year rule applies (¶ 1.5.06)	¶ 1.5.04(E); life expectancy of participant (¶ 1.5.08)
Multiple beneficiaries	¶ 1.5.03(F)	¶ 1.5.04(F)

1.5.03 *Road Map, cont.: MRDs in case of death BEFORE the RBD*

To determine required distributions for retirement benefits of a participant who died *before his RBD,* first complete the steps at ¶ 1.5.02. Then read this ¶ 1.5.03. First read the general comments and caveats, and paragraph A. Then read the particular paragraph (B–F) that describes the beneficiary. See ¶ 1.5.02, Step 3, for explanation of the RBD.

General Comments and Caveats

Post-death MRDs from a *Roth IRA* are always determined using rules in this ¶ 1.5.03 (never ¶ 1.5.04). Reg. § 1.408A-6, A-14(b).

In *all* cases, see ¶ 1.5.10 for the ability of the plan to require faster distribution of the benefits than the MRD rules would require.

See ¶ 3.2 regarding the ability of the participant's surviving spouse to roll benefits over to her own IRA (or elect to treat an inherited IRA as her own); such a rollover or election would change the MRD rules applicable to the rolled over benefits; see ¶ 1.6.03(A), (B), for MRD effects.

A. **MRD for year of death (regardless of who is beneficiary).** Because the participant died before his RBD, there is no MRD for the year of his death. See ¶ 1.4.07(C). Required distributions will begin, at the earliest, the year *after* the year of the participant's death.

B. **Surviving spouse is sole beneficiary.** If the participant died before his RBD, leaving his benefits to his surviving spouse as sole beneficiary, the ADP is the surviving spouse's life expectancy, unless the 5-year rule applies. Reg. § 1.401(a)(9)-3, A-1(a). See ¶ 1.5.07 for how to determine whether the 5-year rule applies; see ¶ 1.5.06 for how to calculate distributions under the 5-year rule. See ¶ 1.6.02 for meaning of "spouse is sole beneficiary." See ¶ 1.6.03 for how to calculate MRDs based on the spouse's life expectancy. See ¶ 1.6.04 for when distributions to the spouse must commence (Required Commencement Date). See ¶ 1.5.12 and ¶ 1.6.05 for what happens if the spouse, having survived the participant, dies *before* that Required Commencement Date. See ¶ 1.5.12 and ¶ 1.6.03(E) for what happens if the spouse, having survived the participant and lived *beyond* her Required Commencement Date, dies before having withdrawn all of the benefits. See ¶ 3.2 for the surviving spouse's ability to roll over the inherited benefits to another retirement plan; see ¶ 1.6.03(A), (B), for MRD effects of such a rollover.

C.   **Individual beneficiary who is not the surviving spouse.** If the participant died before his RBD, leaving his benefits to one individual beneficiary who is not the participant's surviving spouse, the ADP is the beneficiary's life expectancy, unless the 5-year rule applies. Reg. § 1.401(a)(9)-3, A-1(a). See ¶ 1.5.07 for how to determine whether the 5-year rule applies, ¶ 1.5.06 for how to calculate distributions under the 5-year rule. See ¶ 1.5.05 for how to calculate annual distributions over the life expectancy of a nonspouse individual beneficiary and when such distributions must commence. See ¶ 1.5.12–¶ 1.5.13, for what happens if the beneficiary, having survived the participant, dies before having withdrawn all of the benefits.

D.   **See-through trust.** If the participant died before his RBD, leaving his benefits to a trust that qualifies as a "see-through trust" under the minimum distribution trust rules (see ¶ 6.2.03), then the individual beneficiary(ies) of the trust is (or are) treated (for most *but not all* purposes) as the participant's Designated Beneficiary(ies). If the sole beneficiary of the trust is the participant's surviving spouse, the ADP is the spouse's life expectancy (see ¶ 1.6.03(D) for how to calculate MRDs, ¶ 1.6.04 for when distributions to the trust must commence) unless the 5-year rule applies. See ¶ 1.6.06 for how to determine whether the spouse is considered the "sole beneficiary" of the trust. If the spouse is not the sole beneficiary of the trust, the ADP is the life expectancy of the oldest (or sole) trust beneficiary unless the 5-year rule applies. Reg. § 1.401(a)(9)-3, A-1(a), § 1.401(a)(9)-5, A-7(a)(1). See ¶ 1.5.05 for how to calculate annual distributions over the life expectancy of a nonspouse individual beneficiary (this method applies even if the spouse is the oldest of the multiple individual beneficiaries) and when such distributions must commence. See ¶ 1.5.07 for how to determine whether the 5-year rule applies and ¶ 1.5.06 for how to calculate distributions under the 5-year rule.

E.   **Estate, non-see-through trust, or other nonindividual beneficiary.** If the participant died before his RBD, leaving his benefits to his estate (¶ 1.7.04) or other "nonindividual" beneficiary, including a trust that does not qualify as a "see-through trust" (¶ 6.2.03), then the participant has "no Designated Beneficiary," and the "no-DB rule" applies. Reg. § 1.401(a)(9)-4, A-3. The no-DB rule in case of death before the RBD is the 5-year rule. Reg. § 1.401(a)(9)-3, A-4(a)(2). See ¶ 1.5.06 for how to calculate distributions under the 5-year rule.

F.   **Multiple beneficiaries.** If the participant died before his RBD, leaving his benefits to multiple beneficiaries, first determine whether the separate accounts rule applies for ADP purposes; see ¶ 1.8.01(B). If the separate accounts rule does apply for ADP purposes, determine the ADP for *each separate account* using the rules in these subparagraphs B–F based on the beneficiary(ies) of such separate account. If there are multiple beneficiaries whose interests do *not* constitute separate accounts for ADP purposes, then two special rules apply. First, unless all of the beneficiaries are individuals or see-through trusts (¶ 6.2.03), the participant is deemed to have "no Designated Beneficiary" and MRDs are determined under the 5-year rule; see ¶ 1.7.05(A) and see "E" above. Second, if all of the beneficiaries are individuals (or see-through trusts; ¶ 6.2.03), the ADP is either the life expectancy of the oldest Designated Beneficiary (Reg. § 1.401(a)(9)-5, A-7(a)(1)) or the 5-year rule; see ¶ 1.5.07 for how to determine which applies. See ¶ 1.5.05 for how to calculate annual distributions over the life expectancy of the oldest beneficiary, and when such distributions must commence. See ¶ 1.5.06 for how to calculate distributions under the 5-year rule.

1.5.04 *Road Map, cont.: MRDs in case of death AFTER the RBD*

To determine required distributions for the retirement benefits of a participant who died *on or after his RBD*, first complete the steps at ¶ 1.5.02. Then read this ¶ 1.5.04. First read the general comments and caveats. Then read paragraph A. Then read the particular paragraph (B–F) that describes the beneficiary in your case.

General Comments and Caveats

The rules in this ¶ 1.5.04 apply if the participant died on or after the RBD, regardless of whether the participant actually took any distributions before he died. Reg. § 1.401(a)(9)-2, A-6(a).

Post-death MRDs from a Roth IRA are *never* determined using rules in this ¶ 1.5.04; see ¶ 1.5.03 instead. Reg. § 1.408A-6, A-14(b).

Annual MRDs under paragraphs B–F must generally begin no later than the end of the year after the year of the participant's death. Reg. § 1.401(a)(9)-2, A-5. The exception: If the participant died in 2008, this Required Commencement Date is extended to December 31, 2010; see ¶ 1.5.05(B), ¶ 1.5.08. In addition, an MRD for the year of death itself may be required; see "A" below.

In *all* cases, see ¶ 1.5.10 for the ability of the plan to require faster distribution of the benefits than the MRD rules would require.

See ¶ 3.2 regarding the ability of the participant's surviving spouse to roll benefits over to her own IRA (or elect to treat an inherited IRA as her own); see ¶ 1.6.03(A), (B), for MRD effects of such a rollover or election.

Under the final regulations (¶ 1.1.01), the life expectancy of the beneficiary payout method is available to a Designated Beneficiary *regardless* of who (if anyone) was the participant's beneficiary as of the RBD. This is in contrast to the pre-2001 proposed MRD regulations, which would have severely limited post-death payout options once the participant lived past his RBD.

The Code provides that, if the participant dies after the RBD, the remaining portion of the participant's benefits "will be distributed at least as rapidly as under the method of distributions being used" to calculate the participant's MRDs during life. § 401(a)(9)(B)(i). This is called the **"at-least-as-rapidly rule".** The regulations pay lip service to the rule (see Reg. § 1.401(a)(9)-2, A-5), *but make no attempt to comply with it.* When a participant dies after the RBD the rate at which he was taking (or was required to take) his lifetime MRDs has *no bearing whatever* on the determination of MRDs after the year of his death. The "at-least-as-rapidly rule" has been administratively repealed by the IRS.

A.   **MRD for year of death (regardless of who is the beneficiary).** If the participant died on or after his RBD, and had not yet taken the entire MRD for the year of death, the balance must be taken by the end of that year by the *beneficiary* of the account. The amount of the MRD for the year of death is whatever the decedent was required to take (because the lifetime distribution rules apply through the year of death); minus what he actually did take in that year. "Thus, a minimum required distribution, determined as if the employee had lived throughout that year, is required for the year of the employee's death and that amount must be distributed to a beneficiary to the extent it has not already been distributed to the employee." Reg. § 1.401(a)(9)-5, A-4(a). The beneficiary owns the account once the participant dies, and the participant's estate has no right to take any distribution from it (unless the estate is the beneficiary). See PLR 1999-30052, paragraph [4]. For the effect of a qualified disclaimer on the year-of-death MRD, see ¶ 4.4.10. For who takes the year-of-death MRD if there are: multiple beneficiaries with respect to one plan or IRA, see ¶ 1.7.06(A); or with respect to multiple IRAs payable to one beneficiary or to different beneficiaries, see ¶ 1.5.09.

B.   **Surviving spouse is sole beneficiary.** If the participant died on or after his RBD, leaving his benefits to his surviving spouse as sole beneficiary, the ADP is the surviving spouse's life expectancy, or what would have been the life expectancy of the deceased participant, whichever is longer. Reg. § 1.401(a)(9)-5, A-5(a)(1). See ¶ 1.6.02 for meaning of "spouse is sole beneficiary." See ¶ 1.6.03(D) for how to calculate annual distributions over the spouse's life expectancy. See ¶ 1.6.04 for when distributions to the spouse must commence. See ¶ 1.5.08 for how to calculate MRDs based on what would have been the participant's life expectancy and when such distributions must commence. See ¶ 1.6.03(E) for what happens if the spouse, having survived the participant, dies before having withdrawn all of the benefits. The surviving spouse can also roll over the inherited benefits to another retirement plan; see ¶ 3.2. See ¶ 1.6.03(A), (B), for MRD effects of such a rollover.

C.   **Individual beneficiary who is not the surviving spouse.** If the participant died on or after his RBD, leaving his benefits to one individual beneficiary who is not the participant's surviving spouse, the ADP is the individual beneficiary's life expectancy, or (if greater) the life expectancy of the deceased participant.

Reg. § 1.401(a)(9)-5, A-5(a)(1). See ¶ 1.5.05 for how to calculate annual distributions over the life expectancy of a nonspouse individual beneficiary and when such distributions must commence. See ¶ 1.5.08 for how to calculate MRDs using what would have been the participant's life expectancy and when such distributions must commence. See ¶ 1.5.12–¶ 1.5.13 for what happens if the beneficiary, having survived the participant, dies before having withdrawn all of the benefits.

D.   **See-through trust.** If the participant died on or after his RBD, leaving his benefits to a trust that qualifies as a "see-through trust" under the IRS's minimum distribution trust rules (¶ 6.2.03), the ADP is the life expectancy of the oldest beneficiary of the trust, or (if greater) the life expectancy of the deceased participant. Reg. § 1.401(a)(9)-5, A-5(a)(1), A-7(a)(1), § 1.409(a)(9)-4, A-5. If the sole beneficiary of the trust is the participant's surviving spouse, see ¶ 1.6.03(D) for how to calculate annual distributions over the spouse's life expectancy and ¶ 1.6.04 for when distributions to the trust must commence. See ¶ 1.6.06 for how to determine whether the spouse is considered the "sole beneficiary" of the trust. If the spouse is not the sole beneficiary of the trust, see ¶ 1.5.05 for how to calculate annual distributions over life expectancy of a nonspouse individual beneficiary (this method applies even if the spouse is the oldest of the multiple individual beneficiaries) and when such distributions must commence. See ¶ 1.5.08 for how to compute MRDs based on what would have been the participant's life expectancy and when such distributions must commence.

E.   **Estate, non-see-through trust, or other nonindividual beneficiary.** If the participant died on or after his RBD, leaving his benefits to his estate (¶ 1.7.04) or other "nonindividual" beneficiary, including a trust that does not qualify as a "see-through trust" (¶ 6.2.03), then the participant has "no Designated Beneficiary," and the no-DB rule applies. Reg. § 1.401(a)(9)-4, A-3. The "no-DB rule" that applies in the case of death after the RBD is that the ADP is what would have been the participant's remaining life expectancy. Reg. § 1.401(a)(9)-5, A-5(a)(2). See ¶ 1.5.08 for how to compute MRDs based on what would have been the participant's life expectancy and when such distributions must commence.

F. **Multiple beneficiaries.** If the participant died on or after his RBD, leaving his benefits to multiple beneficiaries, see ¶ 1.7.06(A) regarding the MRD for the year of the participant's death. Then determine whether the separate accounts rule applies for ADP purposes for years after the year of the participant's death; see ¶ 1.8.01(B). If the separate accounts rule does apply for that purpose, then, for years after the year of the participant's death, determine MRDs for each separate account using the rules in these subparagraphs B–F based solely on the beneficiary(ies) of such separate account. If there are multiple beneficiaries whose interests do *not* constitute separate accounts for purposes of determining the ADP, then two rules apply. First, unless all the beneficiaries are individuals or see-through trusts, the participant is deemed to have "no Designated Beneficiary" and the "no-DB rule" applies, which is: The ADP is what would have been the participant's remaining single life expectancy. Reg. § 1.401(a)(9)-4, A-3 (third sentence), § 1.401(a)(9)-5, A-5(a)(2). See ¶ 1.5.08 for how to compute MRDs based on what would have been the participant's life expectancy and when such distributions must commence. Second, if all of the beneficiaries are individuals (or qualifying see-through trusts; see ¶ 6.2.03), the ADP is either the life expectancy of the oldest Designated Beneficiary (see ¶ 1.5.05 for how to compute) or (if greater) what would have been the remaining life expectancy of the participant (¶ 1.5.08). Reg. § 1.401(a)(9)-5, A-5(a)(1), A-7(a)(1).

1.5.05 *MRDs based on life expectancy of Designated Beneficiary*

Reg. § 1.401(a)(9)-5, A-5(c)(1), tells us how to compute MRDs when the ADP is the life expectancy of an individual Designated Beneficiary. This is the so-called "**life expectancy payout method**" (also called the "life expectancy of the beneficiary," "stretch payout," or "**stretch IRA**" method). This method applies when the participant died either *before* or *after* the RBD, and:

✓ Benefits are left to an individual nonspouse Designated Beneficiary and the ADP is the beneficiary's life expectancy. See ¶ 1.5.03(C), ¶ 1.5.04(C).

✓ Benefits are left to multiple Designated Beneficiaries whose interests are not treated as separate accounts for ADP purposes (¶ 1.8.01(B)) and the ADP is the life expectancy of the oldest beneficiary. ¶ 1.7.05(B), ¶ 1.6.03(C).

✓ Benefits are left to a "see-through trust" of which the surviving spouse is not sole beneficiary, and the ADP is the life expectancy of the oldest trust beneficiary. ¶ 1.5.03(D), ¶ 1.5.04(D).

The method of computing a beneficiary's life expectancy described in this ¶ 1.5.05 does NOT apply if the sole Designated Beneficiary is the surviving spouse (or a trust of which she is deemed to be the sole beneficiary); in that case see ¶ 1.6.03(D) instead.

A.   **How to compute the MRDs.** Annual MRDs over the life expectancy of a Designated Beneficiary are computed similarly to the MRDs to the participant during the participant's life (¶ 1.3.01): Each year's MRD is computed by dividing the prior year-end account balance by a life expectancy factor (called the "Applicable Distribution Period" (ADP) or divisor) obtained from an IRS table. Beyond that general similarity are differences in the details. Here is what you need to know to compute MRDs for a Designated Beneficiary:

✓ Determine the beneficiary's life expectancy based on his age on his birthday in the year after the year of the participant's death unless the surviving spouse is the sole beneficiary (in which case see ¶ 1.6.03(D) instead of this section). Reg. § 1.401(a)(9)-5, A-5(c)(1).

✓ The beneficiary's life expectancy is <u>always</u> computed using the *Single Life Table* (¶ 1.2.03). Reg. § 1.401(a)(9)-5, A-6.

✓ The beneficiary's MRDs for years after the year of the participant's death are computed using the <u>fixed-term</u>

method (¶ 1.2.04(B)), unless the surviving spouse is the sole beneficiary (in which case see ¶ 1.6.03(D) instead of this section). Reg. § 1.401(a)(9)-5, A-5(c)(1).

Diane Example: Bonnie died in 2004, leaving her IRA to her sister Diane as Designated Beneficiary. Assume that the ADP is Diane's life expectancy (see next paragraph). Diane's life expectancy is determined as of 2005 (the year after the year of Bonnie's death). Diane turns 46 on her birthday in 2005, so her life expectancy (ADP) from the Single Life Table is 37.9. For calculating her MRDs for 2006 (and later years), Diane deducts one from the prior year's ADP, so her 2006 divisor is 36.9, 2007 is 35.9, and so on. She never looks at the table again after the first Distribution Year.

For purposes of this particular computation, it does not matter whether Bonnie died before or after her RBD (¶ 1.5.02, Step 3), provided that (if Bonnie died before her RBD) Diane either elects or is defaulted into the life expectancy payout method (see ¶ 1.5.07), or (if Bonnie died after her RBD) Diane is younger than Bonnie (so Diane's life expectancy is the ADP; see ¶ 1.5.04(C)).

See ¶ 1.5.03(A) or ¶ 1.5.04(A) regarding the MRD for 2004 (the year of Bonnie's death). See "D" below regarding the 2009 one-year suspension of MRDs.

B.   Required Commencement Date. Distributions under the life expectancy payout to a nonspouse Designated Beneficiary begin the year <u>after</u> the year of the participant's death (Regs. § 1.401(a)(9)-2, A-5; § 1.401(a)(9)-3, A-3(a)), unless the participant died in 2008 in which case they begin in 2010 instead of 2009 (see "D"). Thus, the Required Commencement Date for a life-expectancy-of-the-beneficiary payout is December 31 of the year after the year of the participant's death (or December 31, 2010, if the participant died in 2008). In addition, a distribution for the year of death itself is sometimes required (computed under a different method); see ¶ 1.5.03(A) or ¶ 1.5.04(A). Once the life expectancy payout begins, a distribution must be taken every year (except 2009; see "D"), until the account has been entirely distributed. The "fundamental laws of MRDs" (¶ 1.2.01) continue to apply to the beneficiary just as they applied to the participant.

C.   Economic effects. Calculating MRDs by dividing an annually-revalued account balance by the beneficiary's life expectancy tends to produce gradually increasing payments over the years, so long as the plan has a positive investment return. As long as the beneficiary's remaining life expectancy is greater than [100/the plan's annual growth rate], the plan balance will be growing faster than the beneficiary is withdrawing it.

For example, if the plan is growing at eight percent per year, "100" divided by "growth rate" (100/8) equals 12.5; if the beneficiary's life expectancy is 20 years, the first year's MRD (1/20th, or 5%), is less than the plan's earnings for the year (1/12.5, or 8%), so the plan is growing at a faster rate than the MRDs are depleting it.

Eventually the beneficiary's life expectancy is reduced to the point that he is withdrawing more than the year's investment return. If the plan is growing at 8 percent per year, the crossover point would be reached 12.5 years before the end of the payout period. Even after this crossover point, the MRDs tend to keep getting larger; though the plan balance is now shrinking, the fraction applied to it grows larger.

Under the fixed-term method, the distribution period runs out eventually. The final MRD for "Diane" (see "A" above) will occur in the 38th year after Bonnie's death and will wipe out the remaining balance of the account. Thus, even though Diane may live more than 37.9 years after Bonnie's demise, her inherited IRA will run out of money no later than 2042.

D.   Effect of one-year suspension of MRDs. A beneficiary did not have to take the MRD that would normally have been required for the year 2009; see ¶ 1.1.04. The suspension of MRDs for 2009 does not affect the calculation of MRDs for 2010 or any other later year (other than indirectly, by possibly increasing the account balance). For example, a beneficiary's life expectancy is computed based on his age in the year after the year of the participant's death (see "A" above) even if that year was 2009. See IRS Publication 590, *IRAs* (2009), first example under "What Age(s) Do You Use With the Table(s)?", p. 37. If 2009 would have been the final year of the beneficiary's life expectancy payout, presumably the beneficiary had to withdraw 100 percent of the account no later than the end of 2010, rather than December 31, 2009, but there is no guidance on this point.

1.5.06 *Death before the RBD: The 5-year (sometimes 6-year) rule*

This ¶ 1.5.06 explains how to compute MRDs using the "**5-year rule**." The 5-year rule is the "no-DB rule" that applies in cases of death prior to the RBD: If the participant died prior to his RBD, and had no Designated Beneficiary, this is the rule under which MRDs are computed. See ¶ 1.5.03(E). But the 5-year rule can also sometimes apply even when there *is* a Designated Beneficiary; see ¶ 1.5.07.

Computing MRDs under the 5-year rule is very easy: All benefits must be distributed no later than December 31 of the year that contains the fifth anniversary of the participant's date of death. Reg. § 1.401(a)(9)-3, A-2.

Maude Example: Maude dies in 2010, before her RBD, leaving her IRA to her estate. Because an estate is not a Designated Beneficiary (¶ 1.7.04), the 5-year rule applies. ¶ 1.5.03(E). All amounts must be distributed out of the IRA no later than 12/31/2015.

The 2009 one-year suspension of MRDs (¶ 1.1.04) has a special effect on the 5-year rule: The 5-year period "shall be determined without regard to calendar year 2009." § 401(a)(9)(H)(ii)(II). Effectively, the "5-year rule" becomes the "6-year rule" for beneficiaries of decedents who died in the years 2004–2009. The deadline for such beneficiaries is the end of the year that contains the *sixth* anniversary of the participant's death.

Claude Example: Claude died in 2006, before his RBD, leaving his IRA to his estate. Because an estate is not a Designated Beneficiary (¶ 1.7.04), the 5-year rule applied, meaning that (but for WRERA) all amounts would have had to be distributed out of the IRA no later than 12/31/2011; WRERA extended that deadline to 12/31/2012.

The 5-year rule operates differently from the rest of the minimum distribution rules. Unlike all the other MRD payout methods (see ¶ 1.2.01, #2), the 5-year rule does not require annual distributions. The only requirement is that the entire plan balance must be distributed by December 31 of the year that contains the fifth anniversary of the participant's death (or sixth anniversary, in the case of deaths in 2004–2009). Reg. § 1.401(a)(9)-3, A-1(a), § 54.4974-2, A-3(c). Thus, a beneficiary taking distributions under this rule could spread them over all the years in the period (which could be up to six *taxable* years, in the case of deaths before 2004 or after 2009, or seven taxable years in the case of deaths in 2004–2009), or could wait until the last day of the period and take out all the money on that date, or anything in between.

Here are some other points to remember regarding the 5-year rule:

✓   Under the 5-year rule there is *no MRD at all* in years prior to the final year of the payout period. In the final year, the MRD is 100 percent of the account. Reg. § 54.4974-2, A-3(c); Notice 2007-7, 2007-5 IRB 395, A-17(b). This rule is significant in connection with computing the penalty for missed MRDs (¶ 1.9.02) and in determining whether a distribution is eligible for rollover (¶ 2.6.03).

✓   The 5-year rule ceases to have any application once the participant lives past his RBD. The 5-year rule is *never* available as a payout option in case of death on or after the RBD. § 401(a)(9)(B)(i). But since Roth IRAs have no RBD, the 5-year rule may apply to a Roth IRA even after the participant has passed his RBD on all his other retirement plans; ¶ 5.2.02(B).

1.5.07 *Life expectancy or 5-year rule: Which applies?*

When a participant dies before his RBD, it appears under the Code that the 5-year rule (¶ 1.5.06) applies *only* if there is no Designated Beneficiary, and that the life expectancy method *automatically* applies if the participant left his benefits to a Designated Beneficiary. § 401(a)(9)(B)(iii), (iv). The regulations use a different approach. Under the regulations, the plan can permit the Designated Beneficiary of a participant who died before his RBD to choose between the 5-year rule and the life expectancy payout method. Reg § 1.401(a)(9)-3, A-1.

A.   **Road Map: Three steps to tell whether the 5-year rule applies.** Here are the steps required to determine which method (5-year rule or life expectancy of the Designated Beneficiary) applies to benefits of a decedent who died before his RBD. First determine who the beneficiary is; see ¶ 1.7.02. Then:

1. If the participant died before his RBD with no Designated Beneficiary (¶ 1.7.03), you've finished the process: The 5-year rule (¶ 1.5.06) is the only distribution method available. § 401(a)(9)(B)(ii); Reg. § 1.401(a)(9)-3, A-4. Even in that situation, the plan may require a faster payout; see ¶ 1.5.10. If the participant's benefits are left to a Designated Beneficiary, proceed to Step 2.

2. The plan may provide that, even if the benefits are left to a Designated Beneficiary, the 5-year rule applies in some or all situations, with no option for the Designated Beneficiary to elect a life expectancy payout. If the plan has that rule and it applies to this beneficiary, the plan provision controls. Reg. § 1.401(a)(9)-3, A-4(b). See ¶ 4.2.04(J) for how to get out from under this rule.

3. A retirement plan may (but is not required to) allow a Designated Beneficiary to elect which method will apply. If the plan permits Designated Beneficiaries to elect between the 5-year rule and the life expectancy payout, then the following three *additional* rules apply:

    ✓   The election becomes irrevocable by the deadline for making the election (see "B" below).
    ✓   The plan can provide a default rule, under which the life expectancy method or the 5-year rule will automatically apply if the Designated Beneficiary fails to elect one method or the other by the applicable deadline.
    ✓   If the plan does not provide a default rule, the default rule is the life expectancy of the Designated Beneficiary. Reg. § 1.401(a)(9)-3, A-4(c).

If the beneficiary is defaulted into the life expectancy payout, but misses one or more MRDs (for example, because he was unaware of the existence of the account), the beneficiary can start taking annual MRDs as soon as he learns of the account; he will need to file Form 5329 to request a waiver of the penalty for missed years (see ¶ 1.9.03).

See PLR 2008-11028 for an example of this sequence. Another alternative is for the beneficiary to avoid the penalty by complying with the 5-year rule; see ¶ 1.5.11(C).

B.   **Deadline for Designated Beneficiary's election between life expectancy payout and 5-year rule: General rule.** Reg. § 1.401(a)(9)-3, A-4(c), provides that the deadline for making this election is "the *earlier of* the end of the calendar year in which distribution would be required to commence in order to satisfy the requirements for the life expectancy rule in section 401(a)(9)(B)(iii) and (iv)…or the end of the calendar year which contains the fifth anniversary of the date of death of the employee." This rule can produce different deadlines depending on whether the spouse *is* (see "C") or is *not* (see "D") the sole Designated Beneficiary. If the deadline computed under "C" or "D" would fall in 2009, it is extended to the end of 2010 as a result of the one-year suspension of MRDs (¶ 1.1.04). Notice 2009-82, 2009-41 IRB 491, Part V, A-2.

C.   **Deadline for election if the sole Designated Beneficiary is the surviving spouse (or a trust of which the spouse is deemed to be the sole beneficiary).** The deadline under § 401(a)(9)(B)(iv) that would appear to apply if the surviving spouse is the sole beneficiary of the account is the *earlier* of the end of the year in which the first distribution would be required to be made to her under the life expectancy payout method (¶ 1.6.04) or the end of the year containing the fifth anniversary of the participant's death. This creates a potential trap for surviving spouses of young decedents, with respect to a QRP or 403(b) plan that allows an election but provides the 5-year rule as the default election. For example, if the decedent dies after 2009 in the year he would have turned age 40, in Year 1, the election period expires in Year 6 (the year that contains the fifth anniversary of the date of death), when the decedent would have reached age 45. Under the life expectancy payout method, the surviving spouse would not have to take any MRDs until the year the decedent would have reached age 70½ (Year 30 or 31), but if she is defaulted into the 5-year rule in Year 6 then the entire remaining account balance becomes the "MRD" for Year 6, and here is what will happen to her in Year 6:

✓ If the inherited plan is a QRP or 403(b) plan, she will receive a distribution of the entire balance in Year 6. Being an MRD, this distribution will not be eligible for rollover; see ¶ 2.6.03(E).

✓ If the inherited plan is an *IRA* of which the spouse is the sole beneficiary, her failure to take the MRD in Year 6 would be deemed an election to treat the account as her own in that year; see ¶ 3.2.03(D), #3. The election would be effective for the year in which it is made, meaning that the entire account would NOT be treated as an MRD for such year after all! See ¶ 1.6.03(B).

D.   **Deadline for Designated Beneficiary's election if surviving spouse is not deemed to be the sole beneficiary** is generally the end of the year after the year of the participant's death.

1.5.08 *Computing MRDs based on participant's life expectancy*

This ¶ 1.5.08 explains *when* and *how* to compute MRDs using the "participant's life expectancy" as the ADP. The Required Commencement Date for MRDs computed using the participant's life expectancy as the ADP is the end of the year after the year of the participant's death. Reg. § 1.401(a)(9)-2, A-5. Exception: if the participant died in 2008 it is 12/31/2010 (see ¶ 1.1.04).

A.   **When to use the participant's life expectancy as the ADP.** There are two situations in which the participant's single life expectancy (i.e., what would have been his life expectancy if he had not died) is the ADP for distributions to a beneficiary. Both arise <u>only if the participant died on or after his RBD</u>:

✓ If the participant dies on or after his RBD with *no Designated Beneficiary*, the ADP is the *participant's* remaining single life expectancy. Reg. § 1.401(a)(9)-5, A-5(a)(2). This is the "no-DB" rule that applies in cases of death on or after the RBD. ¶ 1.5.04(E).

✓ If the participant dies on or after his RBD leaving the benefits *to a Designated Beneficiary*, then the ADP is the beneficiary's life expectancy or the participant's life expectancy, *whichever is longer*. Reg. § 1.401(a)(9)-5, A-5(a)(1). So if the Designated Beneficiary is older than the participant was, the beneficiary uses the participant's life expectancy as the ADP, not the beneficiary's own life expectancy. There is no election or choice involved in this situation; the MRDs are calculated based on the longer of the beneficiary's life expectancy or the participant's life expectancy.

Of course, as always, regardless of who is the beneficiary, the plan may require an even faster payout, see ¶ 1.5.10; or the beneficiary may choose to take a faster payout, or a lump sum, if permitted by the plan, ¶ 1.2.01, #4.

B.   **How to calculate the participant's life expectancy.** Use the IRS's Single Life Table (¶ 1.2.03) and find the divisor or "distribution period" (ADP) based on the age the participant had attained (or would have attained had he lived long enough) on his birthday in the year of his death. This number, reduced by one, is the divisor for the year *after* the year of the participant's death. The divisor is reduced by one each year thereafter (fixed-term method; ¶ 1.2.04(B)). Reg. § 1.401(a)(9)-5, A-5(a)(2), (c)(3).

Under § 401(a)(9)(H) (see ¶ 1.1.04), the beneficiary did not have to take the MRD that would otherwise normally have been required for the year 2009.

Cookie Example: Cookie died in July, 2006, at age 73, leaving her IRA to her estate. She had already taken her MRD for 2006. The estate's ADP is computed as follows. Cookie was born in November, 1932, so she would have turned age 74 on her 2006 birthday had she lived. The life expectancy factor for age 74 from the Single Life Table is 14.1. Therefore, the estate's divisor for 2007 is 13.1 (14.1 minus one). The first MRD to the estate (payable in 2007) is the account balance as of December 31, 2006, divided by 13.1. This MRD must be taken by 12/31/07. In 2008, the MRD will be the 12/31/07 account balance divided by 12.1. In 2009 (which would have been the "11.1" year) there is no MRD; see ¶ 1.1.04. In 2010, the MRD will be the 12/31/09 account balance divided by 10.1.

C.   **Other aspects.** The "participant's life expectancy" is never available as an optional ADP in cases of death before the RBD (and never applies to Roth IRAs, as to which death is always "before the RBD"; see ¶ 5.2.02(A)). Also, the Uniform Lifetime Table applies during the participant's life, and also applies for the year of his death (¶ 1.5.04(A)), but has *no possible application* after that point in computing distributions to a beneficiary. The Single Life Table is the ONLY table used to compute life expectancy payout-MRDs from inherited plans beginning with the year after the year of the participant's death, regardless of whether the ADP is the beneficiary's life expectancy (¶ 1.5.05(A)) or the participant's (this ¶ 1.5.08).

1.5.09 *Aggregation of inherited accounts for MRD purposes*

MRDs must be computed separately with respect to each inherited traditional QRP account, IRA, Roth IRA, and 403(b) account a beneficiary holds. Reg. § 1.408-8, A-9. Having computed the MRDs separately for each account, the beneficiary has some flexibility regarding which account he actually takes the MRDs from. The MRD from each inherited QRP must be taken from that QRP; multiple QRPs cannot be aggregated with each other for MRD purposes, even if maintained by the same employer. The flexibility pertains to IRAs and 403(b)s:

A.   **Accounts that may be aggregated if held by one beneficiary.** A beneficiary can take:

✓   The MRDs attributable to all traditional IRAs he inherited from one decedent from any one or more of the traditional IRAs inherited by that beneficiary from that decedent.

✓   The MRDs attributable to all Roth IRAs he inherited from one decedent from any one or more of the Roth IRAs inherited by that beneficiary from that decedent.

The regulation makes no distinction, for purposes of this rule, among different types of traditional IRAs the beneficiary may have inherited from the particular decedent; contributory IRAs, rollover IRAs, SEP-IRAs, and SIMPLE IRAs may all be aggregated. But the beneficiary can *not* aggregate inherited IRAs of any type with his own IRAs or with IRAs inherited from any other decedent, and can *not* aggregate traditional IRAs with Roth IRAs. See Reg. § 1.408-8, A-9, and Reg. § 1.408A-6, A-15.

Reg. § 1.403(b)-6(e)(7) provides similarly for multiple 403(b) plans inherited from the same decedent.

Mendel Example: Mendel dies, leaving two 403(b) plans, three traditional IRAs, and a Roth IRA to his daughter Chaya Sora as beneficiary. Assume the MRD rules require that all these retirement plans be distributed to Chaya Sora in annual installments over her life expectancy. After calculating her MRDs separately for each inherited 403(b) account and each inherited IRA, Chaya Sora can take the MRDs for both 403(b) plans from either one or both of the 403(b) plans. Similarly, she can take the MRDs for all three inherited traditional IRAs from any one or more of them. However, she cannot aggregate the inherited traditional IRAs with the inherited 403(b)s or inherited Roth IRA, or aggregate any of these inherited plans with her own 403(b) plans, IRAs, or Roth IRAs for purposes of fulfilling any MRD requirement.

B.   Different beneficiaries cannot aggregate accounts inherited from one decedent. The regulations do not allow multiple IRAs (or 403(b) plans) inherited by *different beneficiaries* from a single participant to be "pooled" so that MRDs paid to *one* beneficiary can fulfill the distribution requirement applicable to *another* beneficiary:

Jeffrey Example: Jeffrey dies, leaving two IRAs. One is payable to a QTIP marital trust (¶ 3.3.02), and one is payable to a credit shelter trust. The IRS's minimum distribution "trust rules" (¶ 6.2) are complied with, so the beneficiaries of the respective trusts are treated as Jeffrey's Designated Beneficiaries, and the life expectancy of the oldest beneficiary of each trust is used to measure the post-death MRDs to that trust from the two respective IRAs. Assume the credit shelter trust permits accumulation of income. To maximize income tax deferral and minimize estate taxes, the family would like to compute the MRD for both IRAs, then take that MRD for both IRAs entirely from the IRA payable to the marital trust. This way, the credit shelter trust would get the maximum available income tax deferral and what income taxes had to be paid would be paid by the marital trust, where at least they could reduce the surviving spouse's future taxable estate. The regulation does NOT allow this maneuver.

Does this conclusion (different beneficiaries cannot aggregate IRAs inherited from the same decedent) apply even for the year-of-death distribution? There is no IRS pronouncement supporting a different rule (different beneficiaries CAN aggregate) for the year-of-death distribution, so it seems wise to assume such aggregation is not permitted.

1.5.10 *Plan not required to offer stretch payout or lump sum*

A retirement plan is not required to offer all the payout options that the law allows. Reg. § 1.401(a)(9)-3, A-4(b). While most *IRAs* permit the life expectancy payout, the situation is just the opposite with QRPs. Most QRPs offer death benefits only in the form of lump sum distributions (or in some cases annuities), and do not offer the life expectancy payout method. A plan is not even required, when the 5-year rule applies, to allow the beneficiary to spread out distributions over the five years.

Nor is the plan required to offer a lump sum distribution. The plan can provide a restricted form of payout, such as instalment payments or an annuity; as long as the distribution method called for by the plan document is not *slower* than the minimum distribution rules would require, it's perfectly legal.

What can be done if the participant's retirement plan does not offer the payout options the participant or beneficiary wants?

✓ If the participant is living, and is entitled to take the money out of the plan, he can roll the benefits over to an IRA that will offer more suitable payout options for his beneficiaries.

✓ If the participant has already died, and the plan wants to distribute a lump sum but the beneficiaries want a life expectancy payout, see ¶ 4.2.04 regarding the ability of a Designated Beneficiary to transfer the distribution by direct rollover to an inherited IRA.

✓ Distribution by the plan of a nontransferable annuity contract is another way to salvage a deferred payout to the beneficiaries while satisfying the plan's desire to get rid of the money. The contract must call for distributions that comply with the minimum distribution rules. See ¶ 2.1.06(G), ¶ 1.2.02(A), and PLRs 2005-48027 and 2005-48028.

1.5.11 *Switching between 5-year rule and life expectancy method*

When a participant dies before his RBD (¶ 1.5.02, Step 3), and his Designated Beneficiary either elects or is defaulted into the 5-year rule or the life expectancy method (see ¶ 1.5.07), the Designated Beneficiary generally cannot switch to the other method. The exceptions to this rule are as follows:

A.   If permitted by the plan, a Designated Beneficiary can change his election prior to the deadline for making the election (¶ 1.5.07(B), (C)). Reg. § 1.401(a)(9)-3, A-4(c), third sentence.

B.   If a Designated Beneficiary is using the life expectancy payout method, then, unless the plan prohibits withdrawing more than the MRD (which would be rare), the beneficiary can take out the entire remaining balance at any time, including by the end of the 5-year period if all that is desired is a faster distribution. This has no effect on penalties (¶ 1.9.02) unless "C" applies.

C.   If there is *only one* Designated Beneficiary, and he withdraws all of the benefits by the end of the 5-year rule period (¶ 1.5.06), the penalty for any missed MRDs in earlier years is automatically waived, so to that limited extent a beneficiary can make a penalty-free switch from the life expectancy method to the 5-year rule even after the "election deadline" (¶ 1.5.07(B), (C)). Reg. § 54.4974-2, A-7(b). It is not clear why the IRS limits this reasonable provision to the situation in which there is only one Designated Beneficiary.

D.   If the nonspouse Designated Beneficiary of a QRP or 403(b) plan completes a direct rollover from the inherited plan to an inherited IRA by the end of the year after the year of the participant's death (or by the end of 2010, if the participant died in 2008), the Designated Beneficiary can elect to use the life expectancy payout method for the "inherited" IRA, even if under the original plan he would have been required to use the 5-year rule. See ¶ 4.2.04(J).

1.5.12 *Who gets the benefits when the beneficiary dies*

When the participant dies, the beneficiary becomes entitled to the benefits. ¶ 1.7.02, ¶ 4.2.01. This ¶ 1.5.12 explains who is entitled to receive the inherited benefits if the beneficiary, having survived the participant, and thus become entitled to the benefits, later dies before having withdrawn all the benefits from the plan.

The person or entity entitled to the benefits after the death of the original beneficiary is called the **successor beneficiary**. Reg. § 1.401(a)(9)-4, A-4(c), § 1.401(a)(9)-5, A-7(c). Who the successor beneficiary is depends on the terms of the plan or IRA agreement. The IRS doesn't really care who the account passes to at that point, since that has no effect on the ADP (see ¶ 1.5.13). Here are the alternatives:

A.   **Beneficiary names successor beneficiary.** Some plans and IRA providers allow the original beneficiary to name his own successor beneficiary. If the original beneficiary has named a successor beneficiary, the successor beneficiary steps into the shoes of the original beneficiary as owner of the account. See ¶ 4.4.04(C) regarding how designating a successor beneficiary affects the original beneficiary's ability to disclaim.

B.   **Beneficiary's estate**. Some plans and IRAs require the benefits to be paid to the original beneficiary's estate if the beneficiary dies before having withdrawn all the benefits he is entitled to. This is also likely to be where the benefits go if the original beneficiary dies without having named a successor beneficiary (but see "C"). In either case, the estate of the original beneficiary steps into the shoes of the original beneficiary as owner of the account. See ¶ 6.1.05 for ability to transfer the account out of the beneficiary's estate.

C.   **Successor beneficiary named by the plan.** At least one IRA provider spells out, in its IRA documents, individuals (for example, the deceased beneficiary's surviving spouse or children) who will succeed to the account if the original beneficiary (having survived the participant) dies before having withdrawn all of the benefits. Unlike with designating individuals to take if the *participant* dies without having named a beneficiary (see ¶ 1.7.03), there is no MRD advantage to having the plan specify individual *successor* beneficiaries, since the identity of the successor beneficiary has no effect on the ADP (see ¶ 1.5.13; see ¶ 1.6.05(C) for a rarely-applicable exception to this rule). See ¶ 4.4.12(A) for possible effect of such a provision on the ability of the original beneficiary's executor to disclaim the benefits.

D.   **Contingent beneficiary.** Some practitioners assume that, if the original beneficiary dies after the participant, the account passes to the *contingent beneficiary* named by the participant. This would typically NOT be true. A *contingent beneficiary* is not the same as a *successor beneficiary*. Usually, the participant's beneficiary designation form provides that the contingent beneficiary will receive the benefits only if the primary beneficiary *predeceases* the participant (or disclaims the benefits). Once the primary beneficiary *survives* the participant, the primary beneficiary (unless he disclaims the benefits; see ¶ 4.4) becomes the absolute owner of the account and the contingent beneficiary's interest is completely eliminated. The plan documents (including the participant's beneficiary designation; see "E") could provide otherwise, but typically they don't.

E.   **Participant names successor beneficiary.** Some participants would like to include provisions dictating what happens to the benefits remaining in the account if the original beneficiary dies after the participant but before withdrawing all the benefits. As noted at "D," this is something above and beyond naming a "contingent beneficiary" to take the benefits if the primary beneficiary does not survive the participant. There is nothing illegal about having the participant name a successor beneficiary, but it does raise property law and estate tax issues beyond the scope of this book. Most IRA providers do not allow this approach, unless the account is an individual retirement trust (IRT; ¶ 6.1.07). See ¶ 3.3.11 for marital deduction effects, ¶ 4.4.12(A) for possible disclaimer effects.

1.5.13 *What is the ADP after the beneficiary's death?*

¶ 1.5.12 explained how to determine who is the successor beneficiary. This ¶ 1.5.13 explains the Applicable Distribution Period (ADP; ¶ 1.2.03) that applies to the successor beneficiary.

Subject to two rarely-applicable exceptions, the death (in the case of an individual beneficiary) or termination of existence (in the case of a trust or estate named as beneficiary) of the original beneficiary has *no effect* on the ADP. The successor beneficiary simply steps into the shoes of the original beneficiary and continues to take out the benefits using the ADP that applied to the original beneficiary. Any such subsequent beneficiary is merely a "successor" to the original beneficiary's interest and is ignored in determining the ADP. Reg. § 1.401(a)(9)-5, A-7(c)(2).

For example, if the benefits were payable to a Designated Beneficiary who survived the participant but then died prior to having withdrawn all the benefits, the successor beneficiary continues to withdraw over what is left of the life expectancy of the original Designated Beneficiary (or of the deceased participant if applicable; see ¶ 1.5.04(B)–(D)), or at any faster rate required by the plan or desired by the successor beneficiary. This rule holds true even if the Designated Beneficiary, having survived the participant, dies before the Beneficiary Finalization Date; see ¶ 1.8.04.

Hugh Example: Hugh, as beneficiary of his mother's IRA, is taking MRDs in annual installments over his 34-year life expectancy. He dies 10 years into his 34-year ADP. At Hugh's death, ownership of the IRA passes to Regis, a successor beneficiary named by Hugh. MRDs to Regis continue to be calculated based on Hugh's life expectancy. Regis uses what's left of Hugh's 34-year ADP established at the time of Hugh's mother's death.

Similarly, if the benefits were payable to the participant's estate under the 5-year rule (¶ 1.5.03(E)) or over the participant's remaining life expectancy (¶ 1.5.04(E)), and the estate closes and transfers the inherited retirement plan out to the estate's beneficiaries (see ¶ 6.1.05), the estate beneficiaries can use up whatever is left of the 5-year rule or of the participant's life expectancy—but the transfer does *not* allow the beneficiaries to switch over to using a life expectancy payout.

Here are the two exceptions to the general rule:

✓ If the participant's sole Designated Beneficiary was the participant's surviving spouse, the ADP and/or method of computing life expectancy may change on the spouse's subsequent death; see ¶ 1.6.05(C) (if both the participant and his surviving spouse died before the end of the year in which the participant reached or would have reached age 70½) or ¶ 1.6.03(E) (otherwise) instead of this section.

✓   If the plan documents (or the participant's beneficiary designation form) required the original beneficiary to survive by a certain period of time in order to be entitled to the benefits, and the named beneficiary survived the participant but failed to meet that condition, see ¶ 1.7.02.

1.6 Special Rules for the Surviving Spouse

The Code provides special minimum distribution rules that apply when the beneficiary is the participant's spouse. These rules are intended to provide more favorable treatment when the spouse is the beneficiary, though the effect is not always favorable (see ¶ 1.6.05(C)). For most of the "special deals" the spouse must be the sole beneficiary. In *some* cases, a trust for the spouse's benefit can qualify for the same treatment available to the spouse individually; see ¶ 1.6.06.

"Spouse" vs. "Surviving Spouse"

The minimum distribution regulations often refer to the spouse as the participant's "surviving spouse" even while they are both alive. Of course, while the participant is alive his spouse is not yet (and may never become) the "surviving" spouse. In this book, as in the regulations, "spouse" and "surviving spouse" are used interchangeably.

1.6.01 *Road Map of the special spousal rules*

There are four special provisions that may apply when the participant's spouse is named as beneficiary:

A.   **Lifetime distributions: Much-younger-spouse method.** If the participant's sole beneficiary is his more-than-10-years-younger spouse, the participant's lifetime MRDs are computed using the Joint and Last Survivor Table rather than the Uniform Lifetime Table. See ¶ 1.3.03.

B.   **Postponed Required Commencement Date.** If the participant dies before his Required Beginning Date (RBD; ¶ 1.4) leaving benefits to his surviving spouse as sole beneficiary, see ¶ 1.6.04

regarding a possible later Required Commencement Date for MRDs to the spouse, and ¶ 1.6.05 for related rules if the spouse dies after the participant but prior to her Required Commencement Date.

C.   **Spouse's life expectancy recalculated.** When the surviving spouse is the sole beneficiary, and withdraws benefits using her life expectancy as the ADP, her life expectancy is recalculated annually; see ¶ 1.6.03(D). Other beneficiaries must use the fixed-term method (¶ 1.5.05).

D.   **Spouse can roll over inherited benefits.** The participant's surviving spouse can roll over benefits she inherits from the participant to another retirement plan. The spouse does NOT have to be the sole beneficiary to have this right (which, unlike A–C, is not a "minimum distribution rule"). See ¶ 3.2. A spouse who is the participant's sole beneficiary also has the right to treat an IRA inherited from the deceased spouse as her own IRA. See ¶ 3.2.03.

1.6.02 *Definition of "sole beneficiary"*

For purposes of the special minimum distribution rules applicable to a spouse-beneficiary (though not for purposes of the spousal rollover), the participant's surviving spouse must be the "sole" beneficiary. The spouse is the sole beneficiary if she, alone, will inherit all of the benefits if she survives the participant; in other words if she is the sole *primary* beneficiary. The fact that other beneficiaries are named as *contingent* beneficiaries (who will inherit if the spouse does not survive the participant) does not impair her status as "sole" beneficiary.

Bud Example: The beneficiary designation form for Bud's IRA provides: "I name my spouse, Louise, as my sole primary beneficiary, to receive 100 percent of all benefits payable under this Plan on account of my death if she survives me. If she does not survive me, the benefits shall instead be paid to my sister Gladys." The spouse, Louise, is Bud's sole beneficiary so long as both spouses are alive. She is Bud's sole beneficiary at his death if she survives him and does not disclaim the benefits. The fact that Gladys is named as a contingent beneficiary does not impair Louise's status as sole beneficiary.

Reminder: If the "separate accounts" rule applies for ADP purposes, the test of whether the spouse is the "sole beneficiary" is applied only to the separate account of which the spouse is beneficiary. Reg. § 1.401(a)(9)-8, A-2. See PLR 2001-21073 and ¶ 1.8.01(B).

The applicable *time* for determining whether the participant's spouse is the sole beneficiary differs depending on which tax provision is being considered:

✓   For purposes of computing *MRDs during the participant's life*, see ¶ 1.3.03.

✓   For purposes of the *post-death minimum distribution rules* (¶ 1.6.03–1.6.06), the spouse must be sole beneficiary as of September 30 of the year after the year of the participant's death (the Beneficiary Finalization Date; ¶ 1.8.03), and "a" beneficiary on the date of death (¶ 1.7.02). Reg. § 1.401(a)(9)-8, A-2(a)(2). In some cases, if the surviving spouse is just one of several beneficiaries on the date of death, it will be possible to "remove" the other beneficiaries (by means of disclaimer, distribution, or establishing separate accounts by 12/31 of the year after the year of the participant's death; ¶ 1.8.01(B)) so that the spouse can be deemed the sole beneficiary as of the Beneficiary Finalization Date.

✓   In the case of the spouse's right to elect to treat the deceased spouse's IRA as the spouse's own IRA (¶ 3.2.03), she can make this election at any time after the participant's death provided that she is the sole beneficiary as of the Beneficiary Finalization Date (¶ 1.8.03). See Reg. § 1.408-8, A-5(a).

1.6.03 Road Map: How to determine MRDs of surviving spouse

This is one of the more confusing aspects of the minimum distribution rules. There are several different ways to compute MRDs for benefits left to (or in trust for) a surviving spouse, though there is only one correct method for each particular situation.

Usually, the spousal rollover (see "A") or election ("B") provides better results (more deferral opportunities) for the surviving spouse and her beneficiaries than does holding the account as beneficiary (C–E). See ¶ 3.2.01(A)–(C) for why that is so. See

¶ 3.2.01(D) for when the spousal rollover or election should NOT be used. See ¶ 3.1.02(B) for whether to use a rollover or an election.

A.   **If spouse rolls over benefits to her own plan.** Unlike other beneficiaries, the surviving spouse has the ability to roll over, tax-free, to her own IRA or to her own account in any other eligible retirement plan, any QRP, IRA, or 403(b) benefits left to her by her deceased spouse. ¶ 3.2.02–¶ 3.2.04. Following such a rollover, the benefits are now in the spouse's own retirement plan, and are no longer in an "inherited plan." Accordingly, she takes MRDs as "participant" (¶ 1.3) rather than as "beneficiary" (¶ 1.5) beginning the year *after* the rollover (Reg. § 1.408-8, A-7); for requirements applicable to the distributing plan in the year *in which the rollover occurs*, see ¶ 2.6.03.

For the year following the rollover and later years, the spouse's RBD and MRDs will be determined in exactly the same manner as would be true for any other participant in that particular type of plan or IRA. For Roth IRAs, there will be no MRDs because Roth IRAs are not subject to the lifetime MRD requirement; see ¶ 5.2.02(A). For traditional plans and IRAs, see ¶ 1.4 for the RBD and ¶ 1.3 to determine the MRDs.

The surviving spouse *also* has the right to "roll over" inherited benefits to an IRA in the name of the deceased spouse; see ¶ 3.2.07. If benefits are held in or rolled over to such an "inherited" plan or IRA, see "D" for how to compute the spouse's MRDs.

B.   **If spouse elects to treat inherited IRA/Roth IRA as her own.** Unlike other IRA beneficiaries, the surviving spouse has the ability to elect to treat a traditional or Roth IRA that she (as sole beneficiary) inherits from the deceased spouse as *her own* traditional or Roth IRA. ¶ 3.2.03. Once she has made this election, the IRA is treated as the spouse's own IRA. If the account is a Roth IRA, see ¶ 3.2.03(B). If it is a traditional IRA, see ¶ 1.4 for the RBD and ¶ 1.3 for how to determine the MRDs.

The exception to this rule is that the MRD *for the year of the participant's death* is still based on the distribution rules applicable to the decedent. Reg. § 1.408-8, A-5(a); ¶ 1.5.03(A); ¶ 1.5.04(A). If the surviving spouse makes the election in the same year the participant died, MRDs will be calculated based on her being the participant beginning the *following* year.

If the spouse makes the election in any year *after* the year of the participant's death, her election is retroactive to the beginning of the year the election occurs, so MRDs will be calculated based on her being the participant beginning with the year of the election. Reg. § 1.408-8, A-5(a), fifth and sixth sentences. The "account balance" (¶ 1.2.05) used to compute the MRD for a traditional IRA for the year of the election in this case is (presumably; there is no IRS pronouncement on point) the prior year-end balance of the elected account, even though the account was not "hers" in such prior year.

C.   **If spouse is oldest of multiple Designated Beneficiaries.** If benefits are left to a see-through trust (¶ 6.2.03) of which the surviving spouse is the oldest beneficiary, but of which the spouse is not the *sole* beneficiary, then the trust's ADP is the life expectancy of the surviving spouse computed just as if the oldest Designated Beneficiary were someone other than the spouse. Reg. § 1.401(a)(9)-5, A-5(c)(1); see ¶ 1.5.03(D), ¶ 1.5.04(D), ¶ 1.5.05. When this rule applies, the spouse's later death will have no impact on the ADP; see "E" below.

D.   **During spouse's life, if spouse is sole Designated Beneficiary.** If the spouse is the sole beneficiary of the deceased participant; or if a trust is the sole beneficiary and the spouse is deemed to be the sole beneficiary of the trust (see ¶ 1.6.06(A), (B)); then the ADP for distributions to the spouse (or such trust) will generally be the surviving spouse's life expectancy. (The exceptions would be, if the participant died before his RBD and the spouse or trust elected or was defaulted into the 5-year rule, ¶ 1.5.07; or if the participant died after his RBD and the ADP is what would have been the participant's life expectancy because the participant was younger than the surviving spouse, ¶ 1.5.04(B).) The spouse's life expectancy will be determined using the Single Life Table (¶ 1.2.03) and the spouse's age on her birthday *in each year for which a distribution is required* (recalculation method; ¶ 1.2.04(A)). Reg. § 1.401(a)(9)-5, A-5(c)(2) (first sentence), A-6. See ¶ 1.6.02 for how to determine whether the spouse is the "sole beneficiary." For the effect of the 2009 one-year suspension of MRDs, see ¶ 1.5.05(D).

Josephine Example: Napoleon died, after his RBD, leaving his 401(k) plan to his younger surviving spouse, Josephine, as sole beneficiary. She is taking annual MRDs as Napoleon's beneficiary; she did not roll over the benefits to her own retirement plan. Each year, the plan sends an MRD to Josephine based on her life expectancy (from the Single Life Table) for her attained age on her birthday in the year of the distribution (i.e., her age as of the end of each Distribution Year). Josephine turned 46 in the year after Napoleon's death, so her "divisor" (ADP) for the first Distribution Year was 37.9. For the second Distribution Year, Josephine's divisor is not 36.9 (37.9 minus one—as it would be under the fixed-term method; see Diane Example, ¶ 1.5.05(A)); instead Josephine's second year divisor is 37.0 (the life expectancy of a person age 47). Josephine, as a surviving spouse-sole beneficiary, determines her divisor each year by going back to the Single Life Table and determining her new life expectancy based on her new age (recalculation method).

Note that the spouse does not have to "elect" to use the recalculation method; that's just how her MRDs are determined. If a surviving spouse made a mistake, for example, and computed her MRDs using the fixed-term method, that would not change the amount of her actual MRD; it would just mean that she was taking larger distributions than she was required to take. If she caught her error quickly enough, she could roll the excess back into a tax-deferred account to avoid paying tax on it.

E.   **MRDs to spouse's successor beneficiaries.** If "D" above applied during the spouse's life, and the spouse later dies before all the benefits have been distributed to her, here is how to compute MRDs for her successor beneficiary(ies): If the participant had died before his RBD, and the surviving spouse then died before her Required Commencement Date, see ¶ 1.6.05(C). Otherwise, the MRD for the year of her death must be paid out to the successor beneficiary to the extent the spouse had not already taken it by the time of her death, and any remaining benefits must be paid out (beginning the year after the year of the spouse's death) over the spouse's remaining life expectancy, using the fixed-term method (¶ 1.2.04(B)). This is computed based on the age she attained (or would have attained if she had lived long enough) on her birthday in the year of her death and reduced by one year for each year thereafter. Reg. § 1.401(a)(9)-5, A-5(c)(2). It is not clear whether this rule (successor beneficiaries take over what's left of the surviving spouse's life expectancy) applies even if the ADP that applied to the spouse herself was the participant's remaining life expectancy rather than her own (see ¶ 1.5.04(B)).

1.6.04 *Required Commencement Date: Distributions to spouse*

If the participant dies <u>on or after his RBD</u> (¶ 1.5.04), the Required Commencement Date for MRDs to the surviving spouse-beneficiary is the same as the Required Commencement Date for distributions to any other beneficiary: December 31 of the year after the year of the participant's death (or, if the participant died in 2008, December 31, 2010; ¶ 1.1.04). Reg. § 1.401(a)(9)-2, A-5. As is true for other beneficiaries, the spouse as beneficiary must also withdraw, by the end of the year of the participant's death, any part of the year-of-death MRD not distributed during the participant's life. ¶ 1.5.04(A).

If the participant dies <u>prior to his RBD</u>, and the spouse is the *sole* Designated Beneficiary (¶ 1.6.02), annual distributions to the spouse over her life expectancy do not have to begin until the *later of* the following years, "X" or "Y":

X: The year following the year in which the participant died (unless the decedent died in 2008, in which case the "X" year is 2010); or

Y: The year in which the participant would have reached age 70½ (unless the decedent would have reached age 70½ in 2009, in which case the "Y" year is 2010).

§ 401(a)(9)(B)(iv)(I); Reg. § 1.401(a)(9)-3, A-3(b); Notice 2009-82, Part V, A-2. Thus, the surviving spouse's "Required Commencement Date" is December 31 of whichever of the above two years (X or Y) is applicable. *However, the spouse may have to make an irrevocable election earlier than that deadline to preserve her rights; see ¶ 1.5.07(C).*

1.6.05 Special "(B)(iv)(II) rule" if both spouses die young

If the participant died before his RBD, and his spouse survives him, and the surviving spouse is the sole Designated Beneficiary (¶ 1.6.02), the spouse does not have to commence taking MRDs until the end of the year in which the participant would have reach age 70½, as explained at ¶ 1.6.04. § 401(a)(9)(B)(iv)(II) then provides a special rule that applies upon the surviving spouse's later death if she dies before this "Required Commencement Date."

Under the special **(B)(iv)(II) rule**, MRDs for years after the year of the spouse's death will *not* be based on the spouse's remaining life expectancy, as would normally be true for MRDs payable to successor beneficiaries (see ¶ 1.5.13, ¶ 1.6.03(E)). Rather, a new distribution period starts: The post-death rules of § 401(a)(9)(B)(ii) and (iii) will be applied "as if the surviving spouse were the employee" for purposes of determining MRDs to the successor beneficiary(ies) after her death…meaning that the benefits will have to be distributed over the life expectancy of *the surviving spouse's* Designated Beneficiary or under the 5-year rule (see ¶ 1.5.07).

The (B)(iv)(II) rule is quite confusing, so must be reviewed in detail:

A.   **Rule applies only if participant died before his RBD.** Under the structure of § 401(a)(9), the (B)(iv)(II) rule can apply *only* if the participant dies before his RBD. See Reg. § 1.401(a)(9)-3, A-1, confirming that § 401(a)(9)(B)(ii), (iii), and (iv) apply only if the employee (participant) "dies before the employee's required beginning date (and, thus, before distributions are treated as having begun in accordance with section 401(a)(9)(A)(ii))." Reg. § 1.401(a)(9)-5, A-5(b), reiterates that the special rules of "(B)(iv)" apply only if the employee dies before his RBD, as does IRS Publication 575 (2009), p. 33. (For the record, in PLR 2009-45011, the IRS erroneously applied the (B)(iv)(II) rule in a case where the participant died *after* his RBD.)

B.   **...*And* spouse dies before her Required Commencement Date.** The second condition that must exist for the (B)(iv)(II) rule to apply is that the surviving spouse-sole beneficiary of the account "dies before the distributions to such spouse begin." § 401(a)(9)(B)(iv)(II). Under the regulations, the date distributions "begin" means the date distributions are *required to begin*, not when they *actually begin*; and that Required Commencement Date is December 31 of the year in which the decedent would have reached age 70½ (or of the year after the year of the participant's death, if later; see ¶ 1.6.04). Reg. § 1.401(a)(9)-3, A-3(b), A-5, A-6.

Michelle Example: Michelle died after 2009 in Year 1 at age 68, leaving her IRA to her husband Bill as sole beneficiary. Had she lived, Michelle would have reached age 70 in Year 3, and would have reached age 70½ in Year 4, so her RBD would have been April 1, Year 5 (¶ 1.4.02). She died before her RBD, with her spouse as sole beneficiary, so Bill's Required Commencement Date is December 31 of Year 4 (the year Michelle would have reached age 70½). To comply with the minimum distribution rules, Bill takes what would be the Year 4 MRD (computed based on his life expectancy as beneficiary; see ¶ 1.6.03(D)) on November 1 of Year 4. He never elects to treat the IRA as his own (¶ 3.2.03). He dies on December 1, Year 4. Because he died before his Required Commencement Date, the (B)(iv)(II) rule applies; see "C" for how to determine MRDs after Bill's death. This is true even though he had actually started taking distributions, because he died before the date he was *required* to take distributions.

Grenville Example: Grenville dies after 2009 in Year 1 at age 68, leaving his IRA to his wife Rowena as sole beneficiary. Had he lived, Grenville would have reached age 70½ in Year 3, so his RBD would have been April 1, Year 4 (¶ 1.4.02). He died before his RBD, with his spouse as sole beneficiary, so Rowena's Required Commencement Date is December 31 of Year 3 (the year Grenville would have reached age 70½; ¶ 1.6.04). In order to comply with the minimum distribution rules, Rowena takes what would be the Year 3 MRD (computed based on her life expectancy as beneficiary; ¶ 1.6.03(D)) on November 1 of Year 3. She never elects to treat the IRA as her own (¶ 3.2.03). Rowena dies on January 1, Year 4. Because she died *after* her Required Commencement Date, the (B)(iv)(II) rule does not apply; see ¶ 1.6.03(E) for how to determine MRDs after Rowena's death. If Rowena had *not* taken the MRD for Year 3 by the deadline of December 31, Year 3, then such failure to take the MRD would have been deemed an election by Rowena to treat the IRA as her own, in which case a whole other set of rules would apply after her death; see

¶ 3.2.03(D)(3) regarding this deemed election and ¶ 1.6.03(B) for how to compute MRDs to the spouse's beneficiaries in that case.

C.   Post-death rules applied as if spouse is participant. If the (B)(iv)(II) rule applies (see "A" and "B"), then the benefits must be distributed, following the spouse's death, either by the end of the year that contains the fifth anniversary of *the spouse's* death (5-year rule; ¶ 1.5.06) or (if the benefits are payable to a Designated Beneficiary *of the surviving spouse*) in annual installments over the life expectancy of the *spouse's* Designated Beneficiary, commencing no later than December 31 of the year following the year of the *spouse's* death. ¶ 1.5.05; Reg. § 1.401(a)(9)-3, A-5, A-6, § 1.401(a)(9)-4, A-4(b). Essentially, the surviving spouse is treated as a "new" participant who died *before his RBD*.

The beneficiary to whom the benefits are paid at the spouse's death could be a successor beneficiary named by the surviving spouse (Reg. § 1.401(a)(9)-4, A-2) or by the plan; see ¶ 1.5.12, ¶ 1.7.02. The identity and status of the spouse's beneficiary will be determined as of the date of the spouse's death, and finalized on September 30 of the year after the year of the spouse's death (see ¶ 1.8.03). Note, however, that even if the surviving spouse has remarried, and named her new spouse as sole beneficiary, the special rule of § 401(a)(9)(B)(iv) does NOT apply a second time, to the new surviving spouse. Reg. § 1.401(a)(9)-3, A-5 (last sentence).

The effects of the "(B)(iv)(II) rule" are not harmful *if* the spouse has a Designated Beneficiary: The benefits can be distributed in annual installments over that Designated Beneficiary's life expectancy. Unfortunately, in most cases when the (B)(iv)(II) rule applies the spouse does not have a Designated Beneficiary:

✓   **If spouse holds as beneficiary:** Typically, the surviving spouse will have died without having had the time and/or the proper planning advice to name a successor beneficiary for her interest. If the surviving spouse dies before designating a successor beneficiary for her interest, the benefits (under most plans' and IRAs' default provisions; see ¶ 1.7.02) will pass to the spouse's *estate*—meaning that the benefits will not pass to a Designated Beneficiary and the 5-year rule will apply. ¶ 1.5.03(E).

Alphonse Example: Alphonse died at age 65, leaving his IRA to his wife, Heloise. Heloise died after Alphonse, but before the end of the year in which Alphonse would have reached age 70½, still holding the IRA as beneficiary. She had neither elected to treat the IRA as her own (¶ 3.2.03), nor named a successor beneficiary for her interest in Alphonse's IRA (¶ 1.5.12(A)). Under the terms of Alphonse's IRA, if a beneficiary has inherited the account, and dies without having named a successor beneficiary, any remaining balance in the account becomes payable to the beneficiary's estate. Under the special rule of § 401(a)(9)(B)(iv)(II), the minimum distribution rules now apply to this account "as if" Heloise were the participant and died before her RBD. Thus, the "new beneficiary" of the account is Heloise's estate and the 5-year rule applies because Heloise did not have a Designated Beneficiary. ¶ 1.5.07.

✓   **If benefits are left to a conduit trust for the spouse:** In PLR 2006-44022, a participant died before his RBD leaving an IRA to a trust. Litigation ensued among the participant's surviving spouse and other family members. The litigation was settled by an agreement reforming the trust, so that it became either a conduit trust (¶ 6.3.05) or a 100 percent grantor trust (¶ 6.3.10) (the ruling is not clear) for the surviving spouse's benefit, with remainder to her son. The surviving spouse then later died before she reached age 70½. (Actually, the wife's age at her death was not relevant; despite the wording of this ruling, the question under § 401(a)(9)(B)(iv)(II) is whether she died before the end of the year *the deceased participant* would have reached age 70½; see "B.") The IRS then applied the special (B)(iv)(II) rule. The IRS ruled that the son was not *the spouse's* Designated Beneficiary, because she "had not named a beneficiary of her interest in IRA X prior to her death." The result was that the 5-year rule applied to the IRA after the spouse's death. This result seems erroneous based on the IRS's own definition of Designated Beneficiary (see ¶ 1.7.02).

D.   Effect of suspension of MRDs in 2009. If under normal circumstances the surviving spouse's Required Commencement Date would have been December 31, 2009, a special rule applies. There were no MRDs for the year 2009 (¶ 1.1.04), so her Required Commencement Date is automatically extended to December 31, 2010. The special § 401(a)(9)(B)(iv)(II) rule will apply if she dies any time before the end of *2010*. Also, if the special rule applies in the case of a surviving spouse who died in 2008, leaving benefits to a Designated Beneficiary, normally her Designated Beneficiary would have to elect between a life expectancy payout and the 5-year rule by December 31, 2009; that deadline is extended to December 31, 2010. Notice 2009-82, Part V, A-2.

1.6.06 *When is a trust for the spouse the same as the spouse?*

A trust for the spouse's sole or primary benefit may be entitled to some of the special privileges that apply when the spouse individually is named as beneficiary:

A.   Spouse is sole beneficiary: conduit trust. The spouse is considered the sole beneficiary of the participant's account, for purposes of the special spousal rules explained at ¶ 1.6.03(D)–(E), ¶ 1.6.04, and ¶ 1.6.05, if she is the sole life beneficiary of a conduit trust that is named as sole beneficiary of the benefits. Reg. § 1.401(a)(9)-5, A-5(c)(2), A-7(c)(3), Example 2, paragraph (ii). See ¶ 6.3.05 for definition of "conduit trust."

However, for purposes of the spouse's right to elect to treat an inherited IRA as her own IRA (¶ 3.2.03), the spouse must be the sole beneficiary of the IRA and this requirement is not satisfied "[i]f a trust is named as beneficiary of the IRA...even if the spouse is the sole beneficiary of the trust." Reg. § 1.408-8, A-5(a). Thus a trust for the spouse's benefit (even a conduit trust) *cannot* exercise the spousal election or rollover rights that a spouse named individually as beneficiary can exercise. For the spouse's ability, in some cases, to use a rollover "through" the trust to achieve the same result, see ¶ 3.2.09.

B.   Spouse is sole beneficiary: grantor trust. If a trust is the sole beneficiary of the account, and the surviving spouse is treated as the owner of all of such trust's property under the "grantor trust rules" (¶ 6.3.10), she *should* be considered the sole beneficiary of that trust and accordingly should be considered the participant's "sole beneficiary" for purposes of the special spousal rules explained at ¶ 1.6.03(D)–(E), ¶ 1.6.04, and ¶ 1.6.05 (though *not* for purposes of the spousal rollover and the spousal election to treat an inherited IRA as the spouse's own IRA). However, the regulations do not discuss grantor trusts and there are no rulings confirming that the grantor trust rules apply in this context.

C.   **Typical QTIP-type trust: spouse is income beneficiary.** If the spouse does not have the right to demand distribution to herself of *either* (i) the entire amount of the participant's retirement benefits payable to the trust (as under a 100% grantor trust; see "B"), *or* (ii) whatever amounts are distributed from the retirement plan to the trust during her lifetime (as under a conduit trust; see "A"), the trust is not entitled to *any* of the privileges of the spouse. A typical example is a QTIP trust, under which the spouse is entitled only to "income" for life (with or without limited rights to principal). Many "credit shelter trusts" also fit this model.

Even if such a trust qualifies as a see-through trust (¶ 6.2.03), and the spouse's life expectancy is the ADP (because she is the oldest beneficiary of the trust; ¶ 1.5.03(D), ¶ 1.5.04(D)), "some amounts distributed from...[the retirement plan] to [the trust] may be accumulated in [the trust] during [the spouse's] lifetime for the benefit of [the] remaindermen beneficiaries." Therefore the remainder beneficiaries "count" as beneficiaries of the trust, and *the spouse is not the sole beneficiary of the trust.* Reg. § 1.401(a)(9)-5, A-7(c)(3), Example 1(iii). Thus, the delayed Required Commencement Date (and related rules) of § 401(a)(9)(B)(iv) (¶ 1.6.04–¶ 1.6.05) do *not* apply to benefits payable to such a trust. The special method of computing the spouse's life expectancy (¶ 1.6.03(D)) does *not* apply; the life expectancy of the oldest trust beneficiary is calculated on a fixed-term basis as described at ¶ 1.5.05. Rev. Rul. 2006-26, 2006-22 IRB 939.

1.7 The Beneficiary and the "*Designated* Beneficiary"

This ¶ 1.7 explains what a "beneficiary" is (¶ 1.7.02); the difference between a "beneficiary" and a "Designated Beneficiary" (¶ 1.7.03); the problems when an estate is a beneficiary (¶ 1.7.04); and special rules that apply when there are multiple beneficiaries (¶ 1.7.05–¶ 1.7.06). See ¶ 1.8 for the "separate accounts" rule and how to modify the MRD results after the participant's death.

1.7.01 *Significance of having a Designated Beneficiary*

The valuable income tax deferral permitted under the "life expectancy of the beneficiary" or "stretch" payout method (¶ 1.1.03, ¶ 1.5.05(C)) is available only for retirement plan death benefits that pass to a Designated Beneficiary. Not every beneficiary is a Designated Beneficiary. If there is deemed to be no Designated Beneficiary, the payout options (under the applicable "no-DB rule") will generally be less favorable than a payout over the life expectancy of an individual Designated Beneficiary.

Therefore, estate planners must understand the meaning of the term Designated Beneficiary and in most cases will want to take steps to assure that clients have a Designated Beneficiary so as to maximize the value of the client's retirement plans for the benefit of the client's chosen beneficiaries. However, there are situations in which it doesn't matter whether there is a Designated Beneficiary; see ¶ 6.2.01.

1.7.02 *Who is the participant's beneficiary?*

Like life insurance proceeds, retirement benefits generally pass, as nonprobate property, by contract, to the beneficiary named on the participant's beneficiary designation form for the plan in question. Unless otherwise provided in the beneficiary designation form or in the documents establishing the retirement plan, the provisions of the participant's *will* are *irrelevant* in determining who inherits his retirement benefits.

Most retirement plans and IRAs have a printed or on-line form the participant must use to name a beneficiary for his death benefits. Some plans and IRA providers will accept attachments to the printed form, or even a separate instrument in place of the plan's form.

For purposes of the post-death minimum distribution rules, the **beneficiary** means the person or persons who inherit the plan on the participant's death. For example, a beneficiary designation form typically names a primary beneficiary (such as the participant's spouse) and one or more contingent beneficiaries (such as the participant's issue) who will take the benefits if the primary beneficiary does not survive the participant. If the primary beneficiary survives the participant, the primary beneficiary is "the" beneficiary, unless the primary beneficiary "disclaims" the benefits (see ¶ 4.4.10).

If the primary beneficiary does not survive the participant, the contingent beneficiary becomes "the" beneficiary:

Regina Example: Regina designates her children A, B, and C as primary beneficiaries of her IRA, with the proviso that, if any child predeceases her, such child's issue (the contingent beneficiaries as to such child's share) take the share such child would have taken if living. B predeceases Regina, leaving two children and no other issue. Regina dies. There are no disclaimers or distributions prior to the Beneficiary Finalization Date. Regina's beneficiaries are A, C, and the two children of B. The children of A and of C (if any) are still merely "contingent" beneficiaries as of Regina's death and accordingly drop out of the picture; they are not entitled to anything. See ¶ 1.5.12(D), ¶ 1.6.02.

If the participant does not name a beneficiary; or if all of the beneficiaries named by the participant either fail to survive him or disclaim the benefits; then the benefits pass to the person(s) or entity(ies) named in the plan documents to take in that case, usually called the "**default beneficiary**." See ¶ 4.5.01. The default beneficiary is "the" beneficiary in this case.

Beneficiary designations can raise many issues: The form may contain ambiguous or unclear wording. The form may be missing or for some reason arguably ineffective. There may be a question as to which state's law governs the interpretation of the beneficiary designation form. Those subjects are beyond the scope of this book. This book assumes that the identity of the beneficiary is clear.

1.7.03 Definition of Designated Beneficiary

In order for benefits to be distributable over the life expectancy of the Designated Beneficiary, there must be a Designated Beneficiary. Not every beneficiary is a Designated Beneficiary. The Code defines

Designated Beneficiary as "any *individual* designated as a beneficiary by the employee." § 401(a)(9)(E); emphasis added. The regulations substantially expand this definition:

"A designated beneficiary is an individual who is designated as a beneficiary under the plan. An individual may be designated as a beneficiary under the plan either by the terms of the plan or, if the plan so provides, by an affirmative election by the employee...specifying the beneficiary. A beneficiary designated as such under the plan is an individual who is entitled to a portion of an employee's benefit, contingent on the employee's death or another specified event. ... A designated beneficiary need not be specified by name in the plan or by the employee to the plan in order to be a designated beneficiary so long as the individual who is to be the beneficiary is identifiable under the plan. The members of a class of beneficiaries capable of expansion or contraction will be treated as being identifiable if it is possible to identify the class member with the shortest life expectancy. The fact that an employee's interest under the plan passes to a certain individual under a will or otherwise under applicable state law does not make that individual a designated beneficiary unless the individual is designated as a beneficiary under the plan." Reg. § 1.401(a)(9)-4, A-1.

"Q-2. Must an employee...make an affirmative election specifying a beneficiary for a person to be a designated beneficiary under section 401(a)(9)(E)?"

"A-2. No, a designated beneficiary is an individual who is designated as a beneficiary under the plan whether or not the designation under the plan was made by the employee." Reg. § 1.401(a)(9)-4, A-2.

So, there are several key elements to achieving Designated Beneficiary status:

1.   Only individuals can be Designated Beneficiaries. An estate does not qualify; ¶ 1.7.04. A trust is not an individual, but, if various rules are complied with, you can "see through" the trust and treat the individual trust beneficiaries (for some *but not all* purposes) as if the participant had named them directly as beneficiaries. See ¶ 6.2.01, ¶ 6.2.03. It is not known whether a single-member LLC (or other single member entity) that is not treated for federal tax purposes as an entity separate from its owner would be regarded as an "individual" for this purpose. See Reg. § 301.7701-3.

2.   If there are multiple beneficiaries, all must be individuals and it must be possible to identify the oldest member of the group. See ¶ 1.7.05. You also must determine whether the separate accounts rule applies for ADP purposes. ¶ 1.8.01(B).

3.   Finally, the beneficiary must be designated either "by the terms of the plan" or (if the plan allows this; almost all plans do) by the participant.

If the participant fills out his beneficiary form naming "my spouse," or "my children," or "my friends Larry, Moe, and Curly," as his beneficiaries, and the specified individual(s) survive the participant and do not disclaim, there is no problem: We have individual beneficiaries designated by the participant, so there is a Designated Beneficiary whose life expectancy can be used as the ADP after the participant's death.

If the participant does not fill out a beneficiary designation form; or if all the beneficiaries he named fail to survive him or disclaim the benefits; we *still* have a Designated Beneficiary, *if* the plan fills the gap by specifying *individuals* who are then living to whom the benefits pass. QRPs, for example, generally provide that benefits will be paid to the participant's surviving spouse as default beneficiary; see ¶ 3.4.

In many cases, however, if the participant fails to fill out the beneficiary form (or if the beneficiaries he has specified fail to survive him), the plan or IRA will provide that the benefits are paid to the participant's estate. This will mean loss of the ability to use a beneficiary's life expectancy as the ADP; see ¶ 1.7.04.

In PLR 2006-50022, a beneficiary designation form stating that the beneficiary was to be determined "per my will" was apparently treated by all parties, including the IRS, as leaving the benefits to the participant's estate. In PLR 2008-46028, the IRS ruled that a beneficiary designation "as stated in wills" was not sufficient to establish a Designated Beneficiary.

A beneficiary named by the participant's executor is not considered a "beneficiary under the plan" and therefore cannot be a Designated Beneficiary; see ¶ 4.1.04(B). For the effect of post-death reformation of the beneficiary designation form, see ¶ 4.5.05.

1.7.04 *Estate cannot be a Designated Beneficiary*

If benefits are payable to the participant's "estate," the participant has no Designated Beneficiary, even if all beneficiaries of the estate are individuals. Reg. § 1.401(a)(9)-4, A-3, § 1.401(a)(9)-8, A-11; PLR 2001-26041.

The executor can transfer the inherited IRA to the estate beneficiaries (see ¶ 6.1.05); however, such a transfer will *not* have the effect of allowing the estate beneficiaries to use their own life expectancies for computing MRDs, even if the transfer is completed before the Beneficiary Finalization Date (¶ 1.8.03).

See ¶ 3.2.09 for whether a spousal rollover may still be available. See ¶ 4.4.11(C) regarding disclaimers in this situation.

By making a "§ 645 election," a decedent's revocable trust can be treated for income tax purposes as if it were (all or part of) the probate estate. See ¶ 6.2.11. If retirement benefits are payable to the participant's estate, there is no reason to believe that having the trust make a "645 election" would cause the trust, rather than the estate, to be treated as the beneficiary for MRD purposes.

1.7.05 *Multiple beneficiary rules and how to escape them*

This ¶ 1.7.05 and the following ¶ 1.7.06 explain the special minimum distribution rules that apply when a participant dies leaving his retirement benefits to *more than one beneficiary*. The post-death MRD Road Maps at ¶ 1.5.03(F) and ¶ 1.5.04(F) directed you here in that situation.

The IRS has two "multiple beneficiary rules," both of which have negative effects on post-death payout options, but allows two "escape hatches" to mitigate these negative results. The two multiple beneficiary rules are: If the participant has more than one beneficiary,

A.   The participant has no Designated Beneficiary unless all of the beneficiaries are individuals. Reg. § 1.401(a)(9)-4, A-3. See ¶ 1.5.06 and ¶ 1.5.08 for the "no-DB rules" applicable in this case; and

B.   If all of the beneficiaries are individuals, the ADP is the oldest beneficiary's life expectancy. Reg. § 1.401(a)(9)-5, A-7(a)(1). See ¶ 1.5.05 for how to compute this.

The two escape hatches from these rules are:

- ✓ The "separate accounts rule," discussed at ¶ 1.8.01–¶ 1.8.02; and

- ✓ The ability to "remove" a beneficiary prior to the "Beneficiary Finalization Date"; see ¶ 1.8.03.

1.7.06 Multiple beneficiaries: Who must take the MRD?

If there are multiple beneficiaries, and the separate accounts rule applies (see ¶ 1.8.01), then each beneficiary is responsible to take the MRD from such beneficiary's own separate account. What is not clear is, if there are multiple beneficiaries, and the separate accounts rule does NOT apply, to what extent do the minimum distribution regulations "care" about which beneficiary takes each year's MRD (provided the terms of the participant's beneficiary designation form are not violated)?

A.   Must year-of-death MRD be apportioned? If there are multiple beneficiaries, it appears that the MRD rules are satisfied as long as ANY beneficiary takes the balance of the year-of-death distribution; it is not required that each beneficiary take a pro rata share of the year-of-death MRD. See ¶ 1.5.04(A). Of course the parties need to keep track of which beneficiary's share any distribution comes out of.

Dorian Example: Dorian's IRA beneficiary designation form for his $1 million IRA specified that $50,000 was to be paid to his church and the balance equally to his two children. Assume the MRD for the year of his death is $40,000, of which Dorian had taken none. Prior to the end of the year of his death, $50,000 is distributed from the IRA to the church in full satisfaction of its share of the account. Since this distribution exceeded the MRD for the year, there is no need for the children to take any MRDs for that year from their shares.

Percy Example: Percy dies in Year 1, leaving his $1 million IRA equally to his two daughters Daisy and Lily. They immediately divide the inherited IRA into separate accounts (two $500,0000 inherited IRAs), one payable to each of them (see ¶ 1.8.01). Assume Percy's MRD for Year 1 is $40,000, which he had not yet taken at the time of his death. Daisy withdraws $40,000 from her share of the inherited IRA in Year 1. This distribution satisfies the distribution requirement for Year 1, and accordingly Lily does not have to take any MRD from *her* share of the IRA until Year 2.

The conclusion that the year-of-death MRD is not required to be distributed proportionately to all of the multiple beneficiaries is based on three IRS pronouncements: First, Reg. § 1.401(a)(9)-5, A-4(a), says that the year-of-death MRD must be distributed to "a" beneficiary, implying "any" beneficiary.

Second, the separate accounts rule (¶ 1.8.01) provides that the entire account is treated as a single account for MRD purposes unless and until separate accounts are "established"; and the establishment of separate accounts during the year the participant died is not recognized *for MRD purposes* until the year *after* the year of death. Reg. § 1.401(a)(9)-8, A-2(a)(2).

Third, in Rev. Rul. 2005-36 (¶ 4.4.05(A)) the distribution requirement for the year of death was satisfied where the distribution was made to only one beneficiary, even though (as a result of that beneficiary's later partial disclaimer) that beneficiary was *not* the sole beneficiary of the account.

However, there are plan administrators who take a different view, and require that each beneficiary to take a proportionate share of the year-of-death MRD.

B.   Must subsequent-year MRDs be apportioned? When the interests of multiple beneficiaries do not meet the requirements for "separate accounts," it is unclear whether the distribution requirement is imposed on the collective account (so that the requirement is satisfied as long as the total MRD amount for the account is distributed to any one or more of the account beneficiaries); or whether, alternatively, each beneficiary must take such beneficiary's pro rata share of the total MRD.

Under § 401(a)(9), the portion of the account payable to a Designated Beneficiary must be distributed over the life expectancy of that beneficiary; this suggests that each beneficiary has a personal obligation to take an annual distribution from his share. However, arguably the IRS has "overruled" this Code provision in its separate account regulations, by providing that: "Except as otherwise provided...[under Reg. § 1.401(a)(9)-8, A-2(a)(2), the separate accounts rule discussed at ¶ 1.8.01], if an employee's benefit under a defined contribution plan is divided into separate accounts under the plan, the separate accounts *will be aggregated* for purposes of satisfying the rules in section 401(a)(9). Thus, except as otherwise provided in this A-2, all separate accounts...*will be aggregated* for purposes of section 401(a)(9)." Reg. § 1.401(a)(9)-8, A-2(a)(1). Emphasis added.

If, as this regulation states, the plan is treated as a single account, then a distribution to *any* of the beneficiaries would satisfy the distribution requirement.

1.7.07 *Simultaneous and close-in-time deaths*

Different states have different laws regarding the effect of simultaneous or close-in-time deaths. State A may presume that the beneficiary predeceased the participant if they die simultaneously, in a common accident or catastrophe, or otherwise under such circumstances that it cannot be easily determined who survived whom. State B's law may provide that the beneficiary is deemed to have predeceased the participant if the beneficiary dies within 120 hours after his benefactor. Seymour Goldberg, CPA, author of the "E-Guide," *Inherited IRAs: What the Practitioner Needs to Know* (www.cpa2biz.com, Product #017270PDF), points out that some states have now adopted the "120-hour rule" as part of the "Uniform Simultaneous Deaths Act." Such a law could operate to change the "beneficiary" of an IRA in the case of simultaneous or close-in-time deaths unless the beneficiary designation form specifically overrides state law presumptions.

Some beneficiary designation forms provide that if the primary beneficiary fails to survive the participant by a particular period of time (such as 30 days) he loses the rights to the benefits, and the contingent beneficiary becomes "the" beneficiary. The IRS has approved a beneficiary designation that contained such a condition, and recognized the primary beneficiary as the Designated Beneficiary, where the primary beneficiary *did* survive for the required period of time. PLR 2006-10026.

There are no IRS pronouncements regarding who is considered the beneficiary for MRD purposes if the original beneficiary failed to survive for a period of survival required by the beneficiary designation form or by applicable state law, so that the formerly-contingent beneficiary becomes the only person entitled to the benefits.

Presumably, as long as the required period of survival did not extend beyond the Beneficiary Finalization Date (¶ 1.8.03), the IRS would recognize the formerly-contingent, now-primary beneficiary as "the" beneficiary, since he is entitled to the benefits "contingent on the employee's death or another specified event" (see ¶ 1.7.03, second paragraph). The IRS should not treat the formerly-contingent-now-primary beneficiary as a mere successor beneficiary (¶ 1.5.12), because the original primary beneficiary never became entitled to the benefits.

1.8 Modifying MRD Results after the Participant's Death

As noted, minimum required distributions (MRDs) after the participant's death are imposed on the participant's beneficiary. Who is required to take those distributions and over what period of time depends on the identity of the beneficiary. Generally, the identity of the beneficiary (and the resulting minimum distribution requirements) are determined as of the date of the participant's death. In this ¶ 1.8, we look at two ways you can modify the application of the minimum distribution rules *after* the participant's death: One is by dividing the participant's benefit into "separate accounts" for multiple beneficiaries (¶ 1.8.01–¶ 1.8.02); the other is by "removing" beneficiaries prior to the Beneficiary Finalization Date (¶ 1.8.03).

1.8.01 *The separate accounts rule*

In this ¶ 1.8.01, we look at how multiple beneficiaries can divide up an inherited IRA into separate inherited IRAs ("separate accounts"), one payable to each of the respective multiple beneficiaries. The rules discussed here apply to Roth IRAs as well as traditional IRAs.

Following the "establishment" of such separate accounts, the beneficiary of each such separate account will be responsible only for taking the MRDs from his account. Regarding apportionment of MRDs prior to such establishment, see ¶ 1.7.06. If the division into separate accounts occurs by a certain deadline, then the separate accounts get an additional benefit: The ADP for each separate account will be determined as if its share of the benefits had been left just to the beneficiary(ies) of that separate account; see "B."

If the benefits pass to multiple beneficiaries through a trust or estate that was named as beneficiary of the IRA, see "E."

Separate accounts treatment is also available for nonIRA plans. However, although employee contribution accounts in a QRP can be treated as separate accounts for income tax purposes (¶ 2.2.04(C)), they would not be treated as separate accounts for post-death MRD purposes unless they were payable to different beneficiaries. Reg. § 1.401(a)(9)-8, A-2(a).

Separate accounts treatment is NOT available for computing lifetime MRDs. ¶ 1.3.05.

A.   **IRS's statement of the separate accounts rule.** If the participant's benefit under a plan "is divided into separate accounts and the beneficiaries with respect to one separate account differ from the beneficiaries with respect to the other separate accounts of the employee under the plan, for years subsequent to the calendar year containing the date as of which the separate accounts were established, or date of death if later, such separate account under the plan is not aggregated with the other separate accounts under the plan in order to determine whether the distributions from such separate account under the plan satisfy section 401(a)(9). Instead, *the rules in section 401(a)(9) separately apply to such separate account....*" Reg. § 1.401(a)(9)-8, A-2(a)(2). Emphasis added.

In order for the beneficiaries' shares to be recognized as separate accounts, they must share pro rata in gains and losses after the participant's death; see "D."

B.   **Separate accounts for ADP purposes.** As explained at ¶ 1.7.05, the ADP for benefits payable to multiple beneficiaries is generally determined based on the life expectancy of the oldest member of the group (or on the applicable "no-DB rule" if not all the beneficiaries are individuals). These rules can be avoided if separate accounts (see "A") are established <u>by the end of the year after the year of the participant's death</u>. The regulation provides that "However, the applicable distribution period for each such separate account is determined disregarding the other beneficiaries of the employee's benefit only if the separate account is established on a date no later than the last day of the year following the calendar year of the employee's death." Reg. § 1.401(a)(9)-8, A-2(a)(2).

If separate accounts are established by that deadline, the beneficiary(ies) with respect to each such separate account will be considered the sole beneficiary(ies) of the account payable to such beneficiary(ies) for purposes of determining post-death MRDs; see the Road Map at ¶ 1.5.02, Step 5. For example, if the surviving spouse is the sole beneficiary of a separate account payable to her, her account will be subject to the special minimum distribution rules applicable when the surviving spouse is sole beneficiary (see ¶ 1.6.03–¶ 1.6.05), even though the IRA was originally left to multiple beneficiaries. See § 1.401(a)(9)-8, A-2(a)(2) (fourth sentence).

The suspension of minimum required distributions for the year 2009 (¶ 1.1.04) did NOT extend this deadline. Thus, beneficiaries of decedents who died in 2008 had to have completed the establishment of separate accounts by December 31, 2009, in order to have such accounts recognized for purposes of establishing the ADP, even though they did not have to take any MRD in 2009. Notice 2009-82, 2009-41 IRB 491, Part V, A-4.

C.   **Separate accounts for all other MRD purposes**. Multiple beneficiaries can establish separate accounts for their respective interests even after the deadline described at "B." Reg. § 1.401(a)(9)-8, A-2(a)(2). The advantage of establishing "late" separate accounts is that, even though the ADP will continue to be the same for all of the separate accounts, each beneficiary's MRD will be determined solely based on his separate account balance for Distribution Years following the establishment of the separate accounts. Each beneficiary will be responsible only for taking the MRD from his respective account; there is no need to worry about a penalty because some other beneficiary fails to take his MRD (see ¶ 1.9.02). Separate accounts allow each beneficiary to choose his own investments. The ADP for all the late-established separate accounts will continue to be the ADP that applied to the combined accounts on the Beneficiary Finalization Date (¶ 1.8.03). See also ¶ 6.3.02(B).

D.   **Pro rata sharing in gains and losses.** In order to establish separate accounts for any purpose, according to the regulations, the beneficiaries' interests must share pro rata in post-death gains and losses occurring prior to the division. This requirement comes from the definition of separate accounts: "[S]eparate accounts in an employee's account are separate portions of an employee's benefit reflecting the separate interests of the employee's beneficiaries under the plan as of the date of the employee's death for which separate accounting is maintained. The separate accounting must allocate all post-death investment gains and losses, contributions, and forfeitures, for the period prior to the establishment of the separate accounts on a pro rata basis in a reasonable and consistent manner among the separate accounts." Reg. § 1.401(a)(9)-8, A-3.

Chloe Example: Chloe dies in Year 1, leaving her IRA to her husband and daughter equally. They divide the inherited IRA into two separate inherited IRAs that qualify as separate accounts. Between the time Chloe died and the time the husband and daughter divide up the IRA into separate accounts some assets in the account decline in value and some increase, but no distributions are taken. The division must result in two accounts that are equal in value on the date of the division. They cannot (for example) give a larger share of the total account to daughter based on the theory that the assets that increased in value belonged to the daughter's share of the inherited IRA and the assets that declined belonged to the father's share.

Such pro rata sharing would be the norm for fractional or percentage interests in the benefits. A pecuniary gift will not meet this definition of "separate account" unless (under local law or under the terms of the plan documents) it will share in post-death pre-division gains and losses pro rata with the other beneficiaries' shares. If the beneficiary designation contains any pecuniary gifts that would not so share, the beneficiaries of the pecuniary gifts can be "eliminated" by distributing their gifts to them prior to the Beneficiary Finalization Date (see ¶ 1.8.03); if only fractional or percentage interest beneficiaries remain as beneficiaries on the Beneficiary Finalization Date, then this requirement is met.

E.   **If beneficiaries inherit through a trust or estate.** Multiple beneficiaries who inherit their shares of an IRA through a trust or estate can establish separate accounts for their respective

shares for all MRD purposes *except* determination of the ADP.
See ¶ 6.3.02.

F. **When the separate accounts become effective.** The division
of a single account into separate accounts is generally effective
for MRD purposes beginning with the year after the year in
which the division occurs, and for subsequent years. Reg.
§ 1.401(a)(9)-8, A-2(a)(2), first sentence. However, if the
separate accounts are established either in the year of the
participant's death or in the following year, the division will be
effective for purposes of calculating MRDs beginning with the
year after the year of the participant's death. T.D. 9130, 2004-
26 IRB 1082, "Explanation of Provisions," "Separate accounts
under defined contribution plans."

1.8.02 How do you "establish" separate accounts?

The way most often used to "establish" separate accounts in an
inherited IRA is to transfer the account assets directly, via IRA-to-IRA
transfer (¶ 2.6.08), from the single IRA that the deceased participant
owned at his death into separate "inherited IRAs" payable to the
respective beneficiaries.

In the case of a typical IRA payable to, for example, "my three
children A, B, and C, equally," immediately before the participant's
death the account is titled "John Doe, IRA." As a result of John Doe's
death, the account becomes an "inherited IRA," titled "John Doe,
deceased, IRA payable to A, B, and C, as beneficiaries" (or "A, B, and
C, as beneficiaries of John Doe"). See ¶ 4.2.01. Upon instruction from
the beneficiaries, the IRA provider creates three new empty inherited
IRAs, titled "John Doe, deceased, IRA payable to A [or B, or C] as
beneficiary" or "A [or B, or C] as beneficiary of John Doe," and
transfers equal amounts directly into the new accounts. Separate
accounts have been established.

If the decedent's account is not "physically" divided up, but the
IRA provider or plan administrator tracks each beneficiary's gains,
losses, and distributions separately, that should be sufficient to
constitute "establishment" of separate accounts.

Another way to accomplish the objective is for the participant
to divide his IRA into separate IRAs payable to the respective
beneficiaries *while he is still living*. For example, a participant leaving
his IRA partly to charity and partly to an individual beneficiary could

create two separate IRAs, one payable to each of the respective beneficiaries. Such separate IRAs have the nontax advantage of not requiring the beneficiaries to interact with each other after the participant's death. The disadvantages of having multiple IRAs while the participant is still alive include the additional paperwork, the difficulty of keeping the IRAs in the same relative proportion to each other when each contains different investments, and increased investment management fees applicable to multiple smaller accounts compared with one larger account.

1.8.03 *"Removing" beneficiaries by Beneficiary Finalization Date*

Establishing separate accounts for multiple beneficiaries (¶ 1.8.01–¶ 1.8.02) is one way to improve the MRD situation after the participant's death. Another is to prune the list of beneficiaries, eliminating "undesirable" beneficiaries by means of distributions and/or disclaimers prior to the "Beneficiary Finalization Date."

A.   **The Beneficiary Finalization Date.** The participant's beneficiaries for minimum distribution purposes are all the beneficiaries who, as of the date of the participant's death, are or might become entitled to inherit his benefits, *minus* any beneficiary who ceases to have an interest in the benefits by a certain deadline: "[T]he employee's designated beneficiary will be determined based on the beneficiaries designated as of the date of death who remain beneficiaries as of September 30 of the calendar year following the calendar year of the employee's death." Reg. § 1.401(a)(9)-4, A-4(a).

That deadline is called the **Beneficiary Finalization Date** in this book, though that term is not used in the regulations.

Although WRERA suspended the minimum distribution rules for the year 2009 (see ¶ 1.1.04), WRERA did NOT extend this deadline. Thus, beneficiaries of decedents who died in 2008 still had to be "removed" by September 30, 2009, if they were not to "count" for MRD purposes, even though no beneficiary had to take any MRD in 2009. Notice 2009-82, 2009-41 IRB 491, Part V, A-4.

Post-death planning cannot somehow designate a new crop of beneficiaries. Rather, "...any person who was a beneficiary as of the date of the employee's death, but is not a beneficiary as of that September 30 (*e.g.*, because the person receives the entire benefit to which the person is entitled before that September 30) is not taken into account in determining the employee's designated beneficiary for purposes of determining the distribution period for required minimum distributions after the employee's death." Reg. § 1.401(a)(9)-4, A-4(a).

So, *if* there are "good" beneficiaries (*e.g.*, individual beneficiaries with long life expectancies) who are *already named* by the deceased participant (*e.g.*, as contingent beneficiaries, or among a group of multiple beneficiaries), it is possible to eliminate other (*e.g.*, older or nonindividual) beneficiaries, so that by September 30 of the year after the year of death only the "good" beneficiaries are left.

There is a disconnect between the Beneficiary Finalization Date (September 30 of the year after the year of the participant's death) and the deadline for establishing separate accounts for ADP purposes (December 31 of the year after the year of the participant's death; see ¶ 1.8.01). Establishment of separate accounts during the year after the participant's death is effective retroactively to the beginning of the year; see ¶ 1.8.01(F). So an account that appears to have multiple beneficiaries as of the Beneficiary Finalization Date may actually be treated for MRD purposes as multiple separate accounts, with different beneficiaries, if separate accounts are established by 12/31 of the year after the year of death because (in that year) the establishment of separate accounts is retroactive to the beginning of the year.

For how the "removal" concept applies to beneficiaries of a trust that is beneficiary of an IRA, see ¶ 6.3.03. For use of disclaimers to "remove" beneficiaries, see ¶ 4.4.11(A).

B.   Removal by distributing beneficiary's share of benefits. One way to cure the multiple beneficiary problem is to distribute, to any nonindividual (or older) beneficiaries, the shares payable to them. If the amounts payable to the nonindividual (or older) beneficiaries are entirely distributed to them by the Beneficiary Finalization Date, then only the remaining (younger, individual) beneficiaries who still have an interest in the benefit will "count" for purposes of determining who is the Designated Beneficiary. Reg. § 1.401(a)(9)-4, A-4(a).

Distributing these shares of course means that any "undesirable" beneficiary who is being cashed out loses the benefit of continued deferral of distributions, the goal that the *other* beneficiaries are trying to achieve by cashing out the older or nonindividual beneficiary. This fact may or may not be a problem. It is not a problem if the "undesirable" beneficiary is a tax-exempt charity, which gets no tax advantage from deferring plan distributions, and which is "undesirable" only because it is a nonindividual. See "Frank Example" at ¶ 7.2.02(C).

It is also no problem if the "older individual" beneficiary being cashed out is the participant's surviving spouse who can roll over the benefits tax-free to her own retirement plan (¶ 3.2) and get continued deferral that way; see "Luther Example" below. Even with a nonspouse non-tax-exempt individual beneficiary, the cashout may be "no problem" if the beneficiary *wants* to be cashed out because he wants to spend the money immediately anyway. But if the older individual beneficiary does *not* want to take immediate distribution of his share this approach will not work; see "Shelly Example" below.

Luther Example: Luther dies in Year 1. His IRA beneficiary designation leaves the first $1 million of the account (a fixed dollar amount) to his wife, and the balance to their three children. The children would like to use "separate accounts" treatment for their shares, so each child's ADP would be based on his own life expectancy, but their mother is the oldest beneficiary of the IRA and her share does not qualify for separate account treatment because (as a fixed dollar amount) it does not share in gains and losses after Luther's death (¶ 1.8.01(D)). Before September 30 of Year 2, Luther's widow takes distribution of her $1 million share of the account in full, and rolls it over tax-free to her own IRA. Now she "doesn't count" as a beneficiary any more, and the children can establish separate accounts for their respective interests by 12/31 of Year 2.

Shelly Example: Shelly died in Year 1 at age 82, leaving her $1 million IRA to a see-through trust (¶ 6.2.03). The trust is to terminate at her death and be distributed in five equal shares to her sister (age 78), her nephew (age 52), and the three children (X, Y, and Z, ages 20, 24, and 25) of her deceased niece. The trustee transfers equal portions of the IRA to five separate inherited IRAs, one for each beneficiary (see ¶ 6.1.05). These are separate accounts for most minimum distribution purposes, but *not* for purposes of determining the ADP, because the IRA was left to a single funding trust and the division into separate shares/accounts occurred at the "trust level" not at the "beneficiary designation form level" (see ¶ 1.8.01(E), ¶ 6.3.02(A)). Accordingly, the ADP for *all* of the beneficiaries will be the life expectancy of the oldest trust beneficiary (¶ 1.5.04(D)) who remains as a beneficiary as of the Beneficiary Finalization Date (¶ 1.8.03). As of the date of death, the oldest beneficiary is Shelly's sister, but she cashes out her entire inherited IRA prior to September 30, Year 2; accordingly, she is no longer a beneficiary as of the Beneficiary Finalization Date. Shelly's nephew, who was the second oldest beneficiary as of the date of death, now becomes the oldest beneficiary. X, Y, and Z wish the nephew would cash out *his* share prior to the Beneficiary Finalization Date, so they could use the 50+-year life expectancy of the oldest one of them as their ADP. However, the nephew wants a payout over his 30-something year life expectancy, so he does *not* cash out his share. As of the Beneficiary Finalization Date, the oldest beneficiary is Shelly's nephew and his life expectancy becomes the ADP for all of the remaining beneficiaries.

C.   **Effect of death prior to the BFD.** A person who is a beneficiary as of the date of death, but then dies prior to the Beneficiary Finalization Date, does NOT thereby lose his status as a beneficiary for purposes of determining the ADP. Reg. § 1.401(a)(9)-4, A-4(c). He will still be considered a beneficiary—unless his benefits are entirely distributed (to him or to his estate) or disclaimed (by him or by his estate) prior to the Beneficiary Finalization Date. For what happens to the deceased beneficiary's interest at that point, see ¶ 1.5.12–¶ 1.5.13. The exception to this rule would be a beneficiary whose death erased his right to the benefits, due to his failure to survive long enough to meet a minimum survival period (see ¶ 1.7.07) or because his death caused him to "drop out" of the pool of beneficiaries (under a trust, for example).

1.9 Enforcement of the MRD Rules

1.9.01 Who enforces the minimum distribution rules

Compliance with the minimum distribution rules is one of the more than 30 requirements a qualified retirement plan (QRP) must meet to stay "qualified." § 401(a). The plan administrator is the enforcer of the QRP minimum distribution rules. Since disqualification of the plan would be a disaster for all concerned, the plan administrator is extremely concerned to make sure MRDs are distributed—even though the penalty for missing an MRD is imposed on the "payee" rather than on the plan. ¶ 1.9.02.

An IRA does not have to be "qualified" in the same way that QRPs must be qualified; the IRS does not issue individual determination letters for IRAs. Rev. Proc. 87-50, 1987-2 C.B. 647, § 4.03. The penalty tax for failure to take the MRD falls on the payee, not on the IRA provider.

However, IRA providers are required to report to the IRS annually, on Form 5498, the year-end account value of each IRA they hold and also whether an MRD is required from the account for the year in question. Reg. § 1.408-8, A-10. The IRA provider is also required to inform the IRA account holder that a distribution is required, and to either calculate or offer to calculate the amount of the MRD for the account holder. Notice 2002-27, 2002-1 CB 814.

1.9.02 *Failure to take an MRD: 50% penalty and other effects*

The Code imposes a penalty for failure to take an MRD. The penalty is 50 percent of the amount that was supposed to be, but was not, distributed. § 4974(a). For how to compute the penalty, see Reg. § 54.4974-1.

The penalty is imposed on the "payee" (nonpayee?). § 4974(a). Presumably, in the case of a single IRA left to multiple beneficiaries, each beneficiary is liable for a penalty only to the extent he fails to take *his particular share of the distribution*, though there is no authority or guidance on this point.

When it appears that a participant or beneficiary may owe the penalty for past years, remember that the MRD rules have changed over the years; it may be that based the rules in effect in the applicable year the individual did NOT violate the MRD rules. To determine MRDs for pre-2003 years see the *Special Report: Ancient History* (Appendix C).

An *individual participant or beneficiary* who has failed to take an MRD (or failed to take the full amount of the MRD) must file Form 5329 for each year for which an MRD was wholly or partly missed. If he hasn't yet filed his income tax return for the year the distribution was missed, and he is required to file a return for that year, the Form 5329 should be attached to the return (Form 1040; you cannot use Form 1040A or 1040EZ if you must file Form 5329; IRS Publication 590 (2009), p. 55). However, if he already has filed his tax return for the year the distribution was missed, or if he is not required to file a return for that year, he should file Form 5329 as a stand-alone form. See Reg. § 301.6501(e)-1(c)(4) and instructions for IRS Form 5329.

If the *fiduciary* of a trust or estate fails to take an MRD that should have been paid to the trust or estate (as beneficiary of an inherited IRA), the fiduciary should attach Form 5329 to the estate's or trust's Form 1041; see instructions for Form 1041 (2009), p. 29 (Schedule G, line 7).

When an MRD is not taken in the Distribution Year to which it is attributable, it is added to and considered part of the MRD for the next Distribution Year *for purposes of determining whether distributions in the subsequent year are eligible for rollover.* Reg. § 1.402(c)-2, A-7(a) (last sentence). (MRDs are not "eligible rollover distributions"; see ¶ 2.6.03.) However, it does not appear that the missed MRD is subject to the 50 percent extra tax in more than one year; see IRS Form 5329 (2009) and Instructions. Presumably, despite the "carryover" rule, if an MRD was missed in only one year, Form 5329 needs to be filed only for that year, not for all subsequent years until it is taken.

If an MRD has been missed, do you deduct the missed MRD from the "prior year-end account balance" when computing the MRDs for *subsequent* years? Nothing in the regulations authorizes such an adjustment for IRAs; see Reg. § 1.401(a)(9)-5, A-3.

If an individual postpones the MRD for his first Distribution Year beyond the end of the first Distribution Year (¶ 1.4.01), but then fails to take the MRD by the Required Beginning Date, Form 5329 should be filed for the year in which the RBD falls, not the first Distribution Year (to which the distribution was actually attributable). Instructions for IRS Form 5329 (2009), Line 50, p. 6.

1.9.03 *IRS waiver of the 50 percent penalty*

There are two paths to a waiver of the 50 percent penalty imposed by § 4974(a) for failure to take an MRD (¶ 1.9.02). One (rarely used) is the automatic penalty waiver for certain beneficiaries who comply with the 5-year rule; see ¶ 1.5.11(C).

The more often used way to negate the penalty is to request a penalty waiver from the IRS. The penalty can be waived by the IRS on a case-by-case basis (§ 4974(d)) "if the payee described in section 4974(a) establishes to the satisfaction of the Commissioner" that "(1) The shortfall...in the amount distributed in any taxable year was due to reasonable error; and (2) Reasonable steps are being taken to remedy the shortfall." Reg. § 54.4974-2, A-7(a). The request for a waiver is submitted with Form 5329; see IRS Publication 590 (*IRAs*).

The "payee" does *not* have to pay the penalty as a condition of requesting the waiver; that condition imposed by the IRS prior to 2005 no longer applies.

There are no published rulings or other IRS pronouncements regarding the standards used in determining whether there was "reasonable error."

Presumably the requirement that reasonable steps be taken to remedy the shortfall means that the taxpayer must take the distributions that were missed in prior years before requesting the waiver.

1.9.04 *Statute of limitations on the 50 percent penalty*

In general, the IRS must assess taxes within three years after a required return for those taxes was filed—and there is *no* statute of limitations if no return is filed. § 6501(a), (c)(3). The goal of participants and beneficiaries should be to assure themselves the protection of the three-year statute of limitations with respect to assessment of the 50 percent penalty tax for missed MRDs under § 4974.

A.   **What is the "return" you have to file?** A "return" for this purpose generally means "the return required to be filed by the taxpayer." In the case of the 50 percent penalty tax, the "return" is Form 5329 (see Reg. § 301.6501(e)-1(c)(4) and instructions for IRS Form 5329). This suggests that all participants over age 70½, and all beneficiaries (including trusts or estates named as beneficiaries) holding inherited retirement benefits, should file Form 5329 every year, even when they believe they owe no penalty.

The penalty for failure to take a required distribution is imposed by § 4974, which is part of Subtitle D ("Miscellaneous Excise Taxes") of the Code. In the case of an excise tax such as that under § 4974, "the filing of a return" for the applicable period "on which an entry has been made with respect to a tax imposed under a provision of subtitle D (including a return on which an entry has been made showing no liability for such tax for such period) shall constitute the filing of a return of all amounts of such tax which, if properly paid, would be required to be reported on such return for such period." § 6501(b)(4).

This suggests that just filing the annual income tax return, Form 1040, with a "zero" entry on the line for "Additional tax on IRAs, other qualified plans, etc.", could be sufficient to start the statute of limitations running even *without* filing Form 5329.

B.   **How to avoid the six-year statute.** § 6501(e)(3) provides that a *six-year* statute of limitations applies to Subtitle D taxes (which would include this penalty) "if the return omits an amount of such tax properly includible thereon which exceeds 25 percent of the amount of such tax reported thereon." If the taxpayer files a Form 5329 or 1040 showing zero as the amount of excise tax he owes, and the IRS later decides some tax was owed, it is obvious that the amount "omitted" will always be more than 25 percent of the amount shown on the return.

The Code provides a way out of this problem. "In determining the amount of tax omitted on a return, there shall not be taken into account any amount of tax…which is omitted from the return if the transaction giving rise to such tax is disclosed in the return, or in a statement attached to the return, in a manner adequate to apprise the Secretary of the existence and nature of such item." § 6501(e)(3). Therefore, to keep the statute of limitations at three years instead of six years, one would need to file (in addition to a return showing "zero" penalty owed) a description of the "item" in the "return (or in a schedule or statement attached thereto) in a manner sufficient to apprise the district director…of the existence and nature of such item." Reg. § 301.6501(e)-1(c)(4). A statement could be attached to the return listing the retirement plans owned by the taxpayer, his age, and other relevant facts, and explaining how the MRD was calculated (or why no MRD was required).

2

Income Tax Issues

How federal income taxes apply to retirement benefits, including special income tax deals such as NUA and LSD, rollovers, and tax withholding rules.

This Chapter examines all aspects of the federal income tax treatment of retirement benefits payable under defined contribution plans, except the following: "Income in Respect of a Decedent" (IRD; see ¶ 4.6); fiduciary income taxes (¶ 6.5, ¶ 7.4); the tax on "unrelated business taxable income" (¶ 8.2); and IRA losses (¶ 8.1.02). This book does not cover state income taxes or income tax treatment of qualified or nonqualified annuities.

2.1 Income Tax Treatment: General & Miscellaneous

Tax-sheltered investment accumulation is the main attraction of retirement plans. Chapter 1 explained how long that tax-sheltered accumulation can last. We now turn to how benefits are subjected to federal income tax once they are distributed (or deemed distributed) from a qualified retirement plan (QRP), IRA, or 403(b) plan (¶ 8.3).

2.1.01 *Plan distributions taxable as ordinary income*

The General Rule
A distribution from a retirement plan is taxable as ordinary income to the participant whose plan it is or (in the case of distributions after the participant's death) to the beneficiary who receives such distribution. § 402(a).

There are exceptions to the General Rule: For how a retirement benefit can be taxable even *without* a distribution's occurring, see ¶ 2.1.04. Regarding who is liable for the tax, see ¶ 2.1.05. For distributions that are nontaxable, or that are taxed more favorably than as "ordinary income," see ¶ 2.1.06.

Here is how we arrive at the General Rule. § 402(a) governs income taxation of distributions from qualified retirement plans (QRPs). § 402(a) provides that, except as otherwise provided in § 402, "any amount *actually distributed* to any distributee by any employees' trust described in section 401(a)…shall be taxable to the distributee, in the taxable year of the distributee in which distributed, under section 72 (relating to annuities)." Emphasis added.

§ 408(d)(1) provides similarly for distributions from IRAs, as § 403(b)(1) does for 403(b) plans.

If *cash* is distributed, the amount of cash distributed is the "amount actually distributed." If *property* is distributed, the "amount…distributed" is generally the fair market value of the property. Reg. § 1.402(a)-1(a)(1)(iii); Notice 89-25, 1989-1 C.B. 662, A-10. For exceptions, see ¶ 2.1.06(G) (annuity contract) and ¶ 2.5 (employer stock).

If the distribution occurs after the participant's death, it is *also* subject to the rules of § 691, governing "income in respect of a decedent" (IRD); see ¶ 4.6.

§ 72 is one of the most complicated sections of the Code. It has lengthy rules dealing with: taxation of distributions (and deemed distributions) from annuity contracts, employer plans, life insurance contracts, and modified endowment contracts; how the owner's "investment in the contract" (basis) is apportioned among distributions; and various penalties. This ¶ 2.1 covers only nonannuity distributions from QRPs, IRAs, and 403(b) plans, so there is no need to tackle most of the intricacies of § 72. The only parts of § 72 covered in depth in this book are: how to compute the participant's "investment in the contract" (basis) that may be distributed tax-free (¶ 2.2); and the penalty for certain distributions before age 59½ (see Chapter 9).

2.1.02 *Post-2010 tax increases; surtax on investment income*

As this book goes to press, several federal income tax increases are scheduled. One change is expiration of lower tax rates that were enacted in 2001; see "A." The others are part of the Patient Protection and Affordable Care Act of 2010, including the "reconciliation" provisions enacted with it, imposing new taxes on certain types of income; see "B" and "C."

A. **Expiration of EGTRRA tax cuts.** At the end of 2010, the so-called "Bush tax cuts" enacted as part of EGTRRA in 2001 and in 2003 are scheduled to expire. The effect will be to increase the highest marginal income tax bracket from 35 percent (as of 2010, effective for taxable income in excess of $373,650) to 39.6 percent (effective beginning at a lower level of taxable income). The maximum tax rate on long-term capital gain will increase from 15 percent to 20 percent; on qualified dividends, from 15 percent to 39.6 percent.

These tax increases only indirectly impact retirement benefits. EGTRRA's many changes in the *retirement plan rules* will not expire at the end of 2010, because they were made permanent by the Pension Protection Act of 2006. The indirect effect of these tax increases will be to increase the incentive for Roth conversions while today's lower rates still apply (see ¶ 5.8.02(B)), and to increase the relative attractiveness of investing inside a retirement plan (tax-deferred or tax-free) compared with investing outside a plan.

B. **"Medicare" surtax on compensation income.** The "Medicare" tax rate prior to 2013 is 2.9 percent (including both the "employer" and "employee" shares, with the "employer" share being tax-deductible for the employer), imposed on all wages and self-employment income. Beginning in 2013, an additional .9 percent surtax must be paid (by the employee or self-employed individual) on wages and self-employment income in excess of $200,000 ($250,000, in the case of married taxpayers filing a joint return).

C. **3.8% surtax on investment income.** Another tax increase is captioned the "Unearned Income Medicare Contribution." It is a 3.8 percent surtax applied to certain income of "high-income" taxpayers. See § 1411, effective for years after 2012.

The surtax applies to "net investment income" of individuals whose modified adjusted gross income (MAGI) exceeds a certain "threshold amount." Investment income includes "interest, dividends, annuities, royalties, and rents" and "net gain" attributable to the disposition of property. The "threshold amount" is $250,000 for "A taxpayer making a joint return...or a surviving spouse...." The threshold is half that amount for a married taxpayer filing separately; and $200,000 "in any other case."

Distributions from IRAs, Roth IRAs, qualified plans, 403(a) and 403(b) arrangements, and 457(b) plans are NOT subject to the surtax, but are included in computing the "threshold" amount, so the effect will be the same in many cases as if they were subject to the tax:

Chris Example: Chris and his wife have MAGI of $200,000 in 2013, including $50,000 of interest and dividends, before taking any IRA distributions. At this point they are not subject to the surtax, because their MAGI is below the $250,000 threshold. Then Chris takes $100,000 from his IRA (all pretax money). This increases their MAGI to $300,000, putting them above the threshold by $50,000. Their entire $50,000 of interest and dividends are now subject to the surtax.

D.   **Impact on trusts that are beneficiaries of retirement plans.** Trusts and estates have a much lower "threshold" than individuals. The dollar level at which the trust or estate enters the highest income tax bracket becomes the trust's or estate's "threshold" amount for purposes of the surtax. Under § 1(e), that level is $7,500 indexed for inflation. As of 2010, the $7,500 has increased to $11,200. With expiration of the "Bush tax cuts" (see "A"), the addition of this surtax means that trusts will pay a 43.4 percent tax on investment income beginning at about $11,500 of taxable income in 2013.

2.1.03 *When does a "distribution" occur?*

For purposes of the income tax Code, when are funds considered "distributed" from a retirement plan or IRA? When the plan administrator cuts the check, mails the check, or deducts the amount from the participant's account on its books? When the participant or beneficiary requests the distribution, receives the check, or negotiates the check? What if the check is payable to a retirement plan but is delivered to the participant? The date a distribution occurs matters for purposes of determining the deadline for completing a 60-day rollover (¶ 2.6.06) and when the distribution is includible in the recipient's gross income.

A.   **Check is received by the distributee.** If a check *payable to the participant* is received by the participant, there definitely has been a distribution. See, e.g., PLR 2004-42035, ruling there was a distribution because the employee had received the check from the plan, even though she had not cashed it. That's not surprising.

When an employee requests a direct rollover from a nonIRA plan to another plan or IRA (see ¶ 2.6.01(C)), IRS rules require the distributing plan to make the distribution check payable to the transferee plan or IRA, but permit the distributing plan to send or give the check *to the employee*. Reg. § 1.401(a)(31)-1, A-4. It sometimes occurs that the employee for whatever reason fails to deliver the check to the recipient plan or IRA within 60 days. The IRS has privately ruled that the 60-day deadline does not apply to direct rollovers, so the employee (or his executor, if the employee died holding the undeposited check) can complete the rollover (even more than 60 days after the check was sent out from the transferor plan) by simply depositing the check into the recipient plan or IRA account. See PLR 2010-05057 ("The distribution check was given to Taxpayer A, but made out to Company B, FBO Taxpayer A; thus the check was not payable to Taxpayer A and Taxpayer A lacked control over the check and could not have disposed of it....In short, Taxpayer A never received a distribution subject to the 60-day rollover requirement...") and PLR 2010-35044 (because this distribution was in the form of a direct rollover, "it was not subject to the 60-day rollover requirement," therefore no "hardship extension" was needed to enable the executor to deposit the plan's check).

These two 2010 PLRs reversed the IRS's earlier position, which was that a hardship extension (¶ 2.6.07) was required to allow completion of a direct rollover if the check had not been deposited within 60 days. See PLRs 2004-24009 and 2004-39049.

B. **If the check is never received.** What if the participant never receives the check the plan sends him? The IRS has issued inconsistent PLRs. In PLRs 2004-30031 and 2004-36017, the IRS ruled that, if the distribution check is never received, there has been no distribution (the 60-day rollover period, in PLR 2004-30031, being measured from the date of the replacement check that the plan issued to replace the lost check). But in PLR 2004-47042 the IRS ruled that the 60-day rollover deadline was measured from the date of the original (lost) check, *not* the date of the replacement check. § 408(d)(3)(A)(i)) says the deadline is "the 60th day after the day on which he [i.e., the participant or surviving spouse] receives the payment or distribution." Reg. § 1.408-4(b)(1) says the same. So, based on the Code and its own regulation, the IRS was right in PLRs 2004-30031 and 2004-36017 and wrong in 2004-47042.

2.1.04 *Actual distributions and deemed distributions*

Generally, a participant or beneficiary is taxable on QRP, IRA, or 403(b) benefits only if, as, and when such benefits are *actually distributed.* ¶ 2.1.01. The doctrine of "constructive receipt" (holding that income becomes taxable when it is "made available," not just when it is paid) does not apply to these benefits. Compare § 402(b)(2), dealing with tax treatment of distributions from "nonexempt" (nonqualified) employee benefit plans, providing that the employee is taxed on amounts "actually distributed *or made available.*" (If a QRP ceases to be qualified under § 401(a), income taxation would cease to be governed by § 402(a), with results beyond the scope of this book.)

Here are exceptions to the general rule—events that cause a participant or beneficiary to be currently taxable on retirement benefits *without* an actual distribution:

A.   **Pledging an IRA as security for a loan.** "If, during any taxable year of the individual for whose benefit an individual retirement account is established, that individual uses the account or any portion thereof as security for a loan, the *portion so used* is treated as distributed to that individual." § 408(e)(4) (emphasis added); see also Reg. § 1.408-4(d)(2). The IRS has allowed an exception to this rule for a pledge of IRA assets to secure a former employee's obligation to repay a pension plan distribution under certain circumstances; PLR 2006-06051.

B.   **Other assignments, pledges, or transfers.** Generally, assigning, pledging, or transferring an IRA or other retirement plan to another person causes a deemed distribution of the account. See ¶ 5.8.06(C); § 72(e)(4)(A)(ii); Reg. § 1.408-4(a)(2); and *Coppola v. Beeson*, 2005-2 USTC ¶50,503, 96 AFTR 2d 2005-5375 (5th Cir. 2005) (participant's pledge of his 403(b) account, as security for alimony he owed, treated as a distribution). However:

- QRP benefits are nonassignable, so this issue does not arise. § 401(a)(13).
- Regarding transfer of an IRA to a "grantor trust," see ¶ 4.6.03(C), ¶ 6.1.06.
- The transfer of the account from the participant to the beneficiary that occurs as a result of the participant's death is not a taxable event.
- See ¶ 2.1.06(L) regarding an exception for certain court-ordered transfers between spouses in connection with divorce.
- Regarding transfer of an inherited retirement benefit generally, see ¶ 4.6.03; regarding transfer from a trust or estate to the beneficiary(ies) of the trust or estate, see ¶ 6.5.07–¶ 6.5.08.

C.   **UBTI.** An otherwise tax-exempt retirement plan is subject to the income tax on unrelated business taxable income. ¶ 8.2.

D.   **Prohibited transaction with IRA.** See ¶ 8.1.06 for how a prohibited transaction involving an IRA can result in a deemed distribution of the entire IRA.

E.   **IRA acquires collectible.** The acquisition by any IRA (or by a self-directed account in a QRP) of a "collectible" (as defined in § 408(m)(2)) is treated as a distribution of the cost of the "collectible." § 408(m)(1).

F.   **QRPs: Certain loan events.** A loans made by a QRP to the participant may be treated as a distribution at the time the loan is made or if the loan is defaulted. See ¶ 2.1.07.

G.   **Roth IRA conversion.** Transferring or "rolling over" assets from a traditional plan or IRA to a Roth IRA is taxed as if it were a distribution. See ¶ 5.4.03, ¶ 5.4.04.

H.   **Plan-owned life insurance.** Ownership of a life insurance policy on the participant in his QRP account causes part of the cost of the insurance to be currently taxable income to the participant when premiums are paid from plan earnings or contributions. See the *Special Report: When Insurance Products Meet Retirement Plans* (Appendix C).

2.1.05 Whose income is it? Community property etc.

Generally any plan distribution that occurs during the participant's life is treated as gross income *of the participant*, regardless of who actually receives it.

In states that apply community property or similar "marital property" law, earnings of one spouse generally belong equally to both spouses. However, community property rules do not affect the income taxation of distributions from QRPs. The federal law giving the worker's spouse certain rights to the worker's QRP benefits (see ¶ 3.4) preempts state-law marital property rights such as community property.

An IRA, in contrast, is not subject to the federal spousal-rights rules, and thus may be community property under applicable state law. However, even if the spouses are co-owners of the IRA under their state's law, the Tax Court has ruled that distributions from the IRA are gross income *to the participant only*, under federal income tax law. *Morris*, 83 TCM 1104, T.C. Memo 2002-17; *Bunney*, 114 T.C. 259 (2000). See also PLR 2009-23027 (IRA paid to alimony trust for participant's spouse taxable to participant despite § 682).

A participant cannot reduce his income tax burden by, say, directing his IRA provider to distribute funds directly to his grandchildren, any more than you can avoid tax on your salary by endorsing your paycheck to your children.

2.1.06 List of no-tax and low-tax distributions

Though retirement plan distributions are generally taxable to the recipient, upon receipt, as ordinary income (¶ 2.1.01), there are exceptions. Here are the situations in which a distribution may be wholly or partly tax-free or may be taxed more favorably than as ordinary income:

A.   **Roth plans.** Qualified distributions from a Roth retirement plan are tax-free. ¶ 5.2.03, ¶ 5.7.04.

B.   **Tax-free rollovers and transfers.** Distributions can be "rolled over" tax-free to another retirement plan, if various requirements are met. See ¶ 2.6 for rollovers by the participant, ¶ 3.2 for rollovers by the surviving spouse, and ¶ 4.2.04 for rollovers by other beneficiaries. See ¶ 2.6.08 for why certain

IRA-to-IRA transfers are not taxable because they are not considered to be distributions at all.

C.   Life insurance proceeds, contracts. Distributions of life insurance *proceeds* from a QRP (after the participant's death) are partly tax-free; distribution of a life insurance *policy* on an employee's life to that employee may be partly tax-free as a return of basis. See the *Special Report: When Insurance Products Meet Retirement Plans* (Appendix C).

D.   Recovery of basis. If the participant has made or is deemed to have made nondeductible contributions to his plan account or IRA, these become his "basis" in the retirement benefits. This basis is nontaxable when distributed to the participant or beneficiary. See ¶ 2.2.

E.   Special averaging for lump sum distributions. Certain QRP lump sum distributions of the benefits of individuals born before January 2, 1936, are eligible for reduced tax. ¶ 2.4.06.

F.   Net unrealized appreciation of employer securities (NUA). Certain distributions of employer stock from a QRP are eligible for deferred taxation at long-term capital gain rates rather than immediate taxation at ordinary income rates. See ¶ 2.5.

G.   No tax on distribution of annuity contract. The distribution of an annuity contract (to either the participant or the beneficiary) is nontaxable, provided the annuity contract complies with the minimum distribution rules and is nonassignable by the recipient. Reg. § 1.402(a)-1(a)(2); see PLR 2006-35013. This includes a variable annuity contract; PLR 2005-48027. Instead, the recipient pays income tax on distributions received under the contract.

H.   Return of IRA contribution. See ¶ 2.1.08(D), (F), regarding special income tax treatment for IRA contributions that are returned to the contributor.

I.   Income tax deduction for certain beneficiaries. A beneficiary taking a distribution from an inherited retirement plan is entitled to an income tax deduction for federal estate taxes paid on the benefits, if any. ¶ 4.6.04–¶ 4.6.08.

J.   **Distribution to charitable entity.** If the beneficiary is income tax-exempt, it will not have to pay income tax on the distribution. See ¶ 7.5.01–¶ 7.5.04, ¶ 7.5.08.

K.   **Qualified Health Savings Account Funding Distributions** (QHSAFD). An IRA owner is permitted, once per lifetime, to transfer funds tax-free directly from an IRA to a Health Savings Account (HSA). § 223, § 408(d)(9). The individual can make such a transfer from his own IRA, or from an inherited IRA he holds as beneficiary. Notice 2008-51, 2008-25 IRB 1163. See ¶ 2.2.10(C) for the effect of a QHSAFD on basis. While HSAs are a tax-favored form of savings account (contributions are deductible from adjusted gross income; distributions are tax-free if used to pay medical expenses), the ability to transfer funds directly to the HSA from an IRA will be of use to few individuals. Most individuals will benefit more by contributing to the HSA from their taxable account, thereby getting an above-the-line income tax deduction (the HSA contribution reduces adjusted gross income; it is not an itemized deduction). The QHSAFD does not increase the amount that can be contributed to the HSA.

L.   **QDROs and divorce-related IRA divisions.** An individual can transfer all or part of his qualified retirement plan benefits to his spouse without being liable for income taxes on the transfer if the transfer is pursuant to a "qualified domestic relations order" (QDRO). § 402(e)(1), § 414(p). § 408(d)(6) allows similar tax-free division of an IRA between divorcing spouses. In both cases, the statutory requirements applicable to the state court order must be strictly followed. It is not clear whether the QDRO/408(d)(6) procedures for tax-free division of retirement benefits between spouses can be used for inherited benefits. This book does not cover divorce-related divisions of retirement plans; see, instead, Chapter 36 of *The Pension Answer Book* (Appendix C).

2.1.07 *Income tax, MRD, and estate planning aspects of plan loans*

A participant cannot borrow money from his IRA; such a loan would be a "prohibited transaction" (¶ 8.1.06), triggering a deemed distribution of the account. § 408(e)(2)(A).

Qualified retirement plans (QRPs) are permitted to make loans to employees from their plan accounts provided various requirements are met regarding the maximum <u>amount</u> of the loan and the <u>repayment terms</u>. § 72(p)(2). For explanation of these requirements, see Chapter 14 of *The Pension Answer Book* (Appendix C). Benefits in certain plans may not be used as security for a plan loan to the employee unless the spouse consents. § 417(a)(4); see ¶ 3.4.02.

A plan loan that meets the requirements of § 72(p)(2) is not treated as an income-taxable distribution at the time it is made. However, a plan loan can generate a "deemed distribution" or an "offset distribution." These two types of distributions have very different consequences; when the "distribution" results from a default under the loan it is not always clear which type it is (deemed or offset).

A.   **Deemed distribution caused by "flunking" § 72(p)**. If the loan does *not* meet the requirements of § 72(p) (either from the beginning, or because the employee later fails to meet the statutorily required repayment terms) the loan (or, if the problem is that the loan exceeded the permitted amount, the excess part of the loan) is treated as a <u>deemed distribution</u> to the employee. § 72(p)(1)(A). If, after the loan was treated as a deemed distribution, the employee does in fact repay the loan, then such repayments to the plan are treated as after-tax contributions to the plan for purposes of computing the employee's basis (investment in the contract). Reg. § 1.72(p)-1, A-4, A-10, A-11, A-21; ¶ 2.2.03(C). A deemed distribution under § 72(p):

- Is not an eligible rollover distribution (¶ 2.6.02); Reg. § 1.402(c)-2, A-4(d).

- Cannot be a tax-free "qualified distribution" if made from a DRAC (¶ 5.7.04(C)); Reg. § 1.402A-1, A-2(c), A-11; § 1.402(c)-2, A-4(d).

- Does not count towards fulfilling the minimum distribution requirement (¶ 1.2.02(B)); Reg. § 1.401(a)(9)-5, A-9(b)(4).

- Is subject to the 10 percent early distributions penalty if the participant is under age 59½ and no exception applies; see ¶ 9.1.03(D).

B.   **Plan loan offset distributions.** If the loan *complies* with § 72(p), we get away from the nonrollable deemed distribution that occurs when § 72(p) is violated. We then encounter another type of loan-related distribution, the "plan loan offset distribution" that occurs when the employee's termination of employment (or death) causes the loan to be accelerated. Typically, the plan requires the loan to be repaid immediately in that event, deducts the loan balance from the employee's account, and distributes to the employee (or beneficiary) the plan benefits minus the loan amount. The plan's repayment to itself is called a loan offset, and it is considered an <u>actual distribution</u>, includible in income (¶ 2.1.01) when the offset occurs (except to the extent it is rolled over). Reg. § 1.72(p)-1, A-13. As an "actual distribution," the plan loan offset:

✓   Does count towards the minimum required distribution (MRD) (if any) for the year. Reg. § 1.401(a)(9)-5, A-9(a); see ¶ 1.2.02.

✓   Is subject to the 10 percent early distributions penalty (§ 72(t)), unless an exception applies (¶ 9.4). For example, if the employee has retired at age 55 or later at the time the plan loan offset distribution to him occurs, there is no penalty; ¶ 9.4.04.

✓   Is an eligible rollover distribution (¶ 2.6.02), except to the extent it represents an MRD (¶ 2.6.03). The participant can "roll over" the non-MRD portion of the offset distribution using substituted funds. Reg. § 1.402(c)-2, A-9; PLR 2006-17037; IRS Instructions for Forms 1099-R and 5498 (2010), p. 3. See *Tilley v. Comm'r*, T.C. Summary 2008-86, in which the Tax Court ruled that, for purposes of computing the 60-day rollover deadline (¶ 2.6.06), the offset distribution was deemed to have occurred upon expiration of the loan's 90-day cure period. See PLR 2009-30051, in which an employee was granted a hardship waiver (¶ 2.6.07) of the 60-day rollover deadline for a plan loan offset distribution.

✓   Is treated as an "eligible rollover distribution" (or as part of such a distribution) for purposes of the mandatory 20 percent income tax withholding on eligible rollover distributions (¶ 2.3.02(C)). However, the plan is not obligated to withhold more than the cash (i.e., the non-offset) portion of the distribution. Reg. § 31.3405(c)-1, A-11. The plan does not have to offer the direct rollover option (see ¶ 2.6.01(C)) for this type of distribution as it does for other eligible rollover distributions. Reg. § 1.401(a)(31)-1, A-16.

C.   Who gets the "offset" when participant dies? If the decedent had borrowed money from his employer's QRP, the plan will typically "pay itself back" out of the employee's account before distributing the (net amount) to the beneficiary of the account, thereby creating a "plan offset distribution" (see "B" above) and its resulting phantom income.

The question is, *to whom* is the offset amount deemed distributed in this case? One possibility is that this is considered a distribution *to the participant's estate*, because it is discharging a debt of the decedent. Another view is that this is a distribution to the beneficiary(ies) of the account. Reg. § 1.402(c)-2, A-9(a), seems to support the "beneficiary" view, since it says that the plan offset distribution "can be rolled over by the employee *(or spousal distributee)*." Emphasis added. There is no other guidance.

2.1.08 *Excess IRA contributions; corrective distributions*

The Code allows IRA contributions to be returned to the contributor for a certain period of time. If three requirements are met (see A–C), the returned contribution gets special treatment for income tax purposes (see "D") and for purposes of the penalty on excess IRA contributions (see "E"). In this book, a returned IRA contribution that meets these requirements is called a **"corrective distribution,"** regardless of whether it was returned in order to correct a problem (such as an excess IRA contribution) or just because the participant changed his mind. The same rules apply to return of *Roth* IRA contributions. Reg. § 1.408A-6, A-1(d).

If an excess plan contribution is returned late, so it does not qualify as a corrective distribution, see F–H.

A. **Deadline for a corrective IRA distribution.** To qualify for the special income tax treatment (see "D"), the corrective distribution must be "received on or before the day prescribed by law (including extensions of time) for filing such individual's return for such taxable year." § 408(d)(4)(A). See ¶ 5.6.06 for what this deadline term means.

B. **Income attributable to returned IRA contribution.** The amount that must be distributed by the deadline is the contribution itself, "accompanied by the amount of net income attributable to such contribution." § 408(d)(4)(C). For how to compute the net income attributable to a returned IRA contribution, see ¶ 5.6.02.

C. **No deduction taken.** The participant must not take an income tax deduction for the contribution. § 408(d)(4)(B).

D. **Income tax and 10 percent penalty treatment.** As explained at ¶ 2.2.02 and ¶ 2.2.08, the general rule for tax treatment of IRA distributions (under § 408(d)(1) and § 72) is that any such distribution is included in gross income to the extent it exceeds the distributee's basis; and a proportionate allocation and aggregation rule (the "cream-in-the-coffee rule") applies for purposes of determining how much of such distribution is basis. Returned IRA contributions are an exception to these general rules: If the above three requirements A–C are met, the corrective distribution is not taxable under § 408(d)(1), and therefore is not taxable under § 72.

Rather, apparently, the distribution is taxable only under § 61, which is the general definition of gross income. Accordingly, it appears that the returned contribution itself is not taxable (because it is not "income"); only any net income "attributable" to the contribution that is distributed with it would be taxable. § 408(d)(4) provides that "for purposes of section 61, any net income [that is attributable to the contribution and accordingly is included in the distribution] shall be deemed to have been earned and receivable in the taxable year in which such contribution is made." Reg. § 1.408A-3, A-7, § 1.408A-6, A-1(d).

The net income so returned is also subject to the 10 percent penalty under § 72(t) if the participant is *under age 59½ at the time he withdraws the contribution*, unless an exception applies; see ¶ 9.1.03(B).

Wayne Example: Wayne, age 50, was eligible to, and did, contribute $3,000 to a new IRA (one that contained no other funds) in 2009. Wayne made no other contributions to, and took no distributions from, the IRA. By 2010, the investments in the IRA had earned $75 of interest. Wayne then cashes out the account in March 2010, prior to the due date of his 2009 tax return, receiving a distribution of $3,075. The $75 of earnings are included in his gross income for the year of the contribution (2009), *not* the year they are distributed (2010), and the 10 percent penalty ($7.50) is payable for the year 2009 unless an exception (¶ 9.2–¶ 9.4) applies.

E.   **Effect on six percent penalty.** A six percent penalty applies to excess IRA and Roth IRA contributions. § 4973(a), (f); Reg. § 1.408A-3, A-7. A corrective distribution that meets the requirements of § 408(d)(4) (see A–D above) is treated "as an amount not contributed" for purposes of this penalty. Thus, making a corrective distribution that meets the requirements of § 408(d)(4) gets the participant not only a special income tax dispensation, but also excuses him from the six percent penalty. § 4973(b) (second to last sentence), § 4973(f) (last sentence).

F.   **Late-returned excess contribution that did not exceed Applicable Dollar Limit.** See ¶ 5.3.03 regarding the maximum dollar amount that an eligible individual may contribute to an IRA in any particular year. If an individual makes contributions to his IRA for a particular year that are *within the Applicable Dollar Limit for that year*, but the individual is not eligible to contribute to the IRA in such year (because he did not have sufficient compensation income, or because he was too old; see ¶ 5.3.04), and this excess contribution (together with earnings thereon) is not returned to him in time to be a corrective distribution (see "A"), he will owe the penalty for the year the excess contribution occurred, but (as long as he did not take a deduction for the contribution) it can be returned to him tax-free even *after* the normal corrective-distribution deadline. § 408(d)(5); see Instructions for IRS Form 8606 (2009), pp. 4–5 ("Return of Excess Traditional IRA Contribution").

G.   **If correcting distribution is late: Income tax effect.** If an excess IRA contribution is not returned by the deadline (see "A"), the income tax treatment and the penalty treatment *both* change. Except as described in "F," there is no special income tax "deal" for an excess IRA contribution that has not been withdrawn by the applicable deadline. Unless the excess contribution can be "absorbed" into the following year's IRA contribution (see "H"), the participant should still withdraw the excess contribution (to avoid accruing *additional* annual excess-contribution penalties), but such withdrawal will be taxed under the usual cream-in-the-coffee rule (¶ 2.2.02, ¶ 2.2.08) unless the limited exception described at "F" applies. On the "bright" side, the excess contribution is added to the participant's basis in the IRA. See PLR 2009-04029.

H.   **If correcting distribution is late: Effect on 6% penalty.** If the excess contribution was not returned (with its net income) by the applicable deadline (see "A"), the participant owes the six percent penalty for the year the excess contribution occurred. This is true even if he qualifies for the special *income tax* treatment described at "F." The excess contribution is then "carried over" to the next year; and is treated, for purposes of computing the excess contributions penalty for such following year, as if it were a "regular contribution" for such following year, and for each succeeding year, until it is either "absorbed" or distributed. See Reg. § 1.408A-3, A-7.

An excess Roth IRA contribution can be "absorbed" as a regular contribution (¶ 5.3.02) for a succeeding year if the individual who made the excess contribution (1) is eligible to make a regular contribution to that account for such succeeding year and (2) does not use up his regular contribution limit by making a cash contribution for such succeeding year. Of course, the most that can be "absorbed" in any one year is the applicable contribution limit amount for that individual for that year (¶ 5.3.03). Note that:

- Once the year the original excess contribution was made has passed, the earnings on the contribution cease to be a factor with respect to the excess contributions penalty. The excess contribution is simply carried forward, dollar for dollar, with no growth factor, from year to year, until it is either "absorbed" or distributed (see § 4973(f)(2)). To the extent each additional year goes by without having the excess contribution either fully "absorbed" or distributed, there will be a six percent penalty each year.

- The fact that the participant can eliminate the excess-contributions penalty by merely withdrawing the *contribution* after the corrective-distribution deadline has passed, *without* withdrawing the earnings that were generated by the excess contribution, creates the potential for an abusive Roth IRA transaction. See ¶ 5.1.02.

I. **Excess contribution examples.** Here are some examples illustrating the discussion above; see also "Gideon Example" (¶ 5.2.02(E)) in connection with a Roth conversion.

Lola Example: Lola's father died in 2009, leaving his $300,000 401(k) plan (all pretax money) to Lola (age 48) as Designated Beneficiary. In 2010, Lola requested the plan administrator of the 401(k) plan to transfer the inherited 401(k) benefit to an "inherited IRA" (¶ 4.2.04). Due to an error by the financial institution, the funds were transferred into Lola's *own* IRA (one she owned as participant), not into an *inherited* IRA. Because the distribution was not properly rolled over pursuant to the requirements of § 402(c)(11), the $300,000 distribution from the 401(k) plan is included in Lola's gross income for 2010. Assume the maximum contribution Lola can legally make to her own IRA in 2010 is $5,000, so $295,000 of this improper rollover is an *excess contribution*. Lola must withdraw that excess contribution (and all net income attributable to it; assume the "income attributable" is $12,000) no later than October 15, 2011, to avoid being liable for a six percent penalty ($17,700) on the $295,000 excess contribution. Assume she withdraws the excess contribution and income thereon in early 2011. Here is how she will report these transactions on her tax return: $300,000 distribution from the inherited 401(k) plan in 2010 (this is includible in her income in 2010, but is not subject to the 10% penalty because the penalty does not apply to death benefits; see ¶ 9.4.01); additional income of $12,000 (the earnings on the contribution) reportable in 2010 and subject to the 10% penalty in 2010 (see "D" above); and $5,000 contribution to her own IRA for 2010.

Armande Example: Armande, age 45, is eligible to contribute $5,000 to a traditional IRA in 2010. By mistake he contributes $9,000. He has made an excess contribution of $4,000. By the time he discovers this error, in early 2011, the $4,000 excess contribution has already generated $3,000 of "net income attributable thereto" (¶ 5.6.02) due to Armande's spectacular investment success. To avoid a six percent excess contribution penalty for 2010 ($240), he would have to withdraw the $4,000 excess contribution and the $3,000 of "earnings" thereon...but the earnings would be subject to income tax *and* to the 10 percent penalty on "early distributions" (see "D" above) because Armande is under age 59½. So he would have to pay a $300 penalty to avoid a $240 penalty! He decides to pay the excess contributions penalty of $240 for 2010, leave the excess contribution in the IRA, and treat the 2010 excess contribution as part of his $5,000 "regular" IRA contribution for 2011. In 2011 he is eligible to contribute up to $5,000 to an IRA from his compensation income, so the $4,000 excess contribution carried over from 2010 will "absorb" most of his 2011 contribution.

2.2 If the Participant Has After-tax Money in the Plan or IRA

This ¶ 2.2 explains how to determine how much basis (after-tax money) a participant or beneficiary has in a traditional qualified retirement plan (QRP) or IRA, how much of such basis is deemed included in any particular distribution, and what happens if a distribution that includes some basis is rolled over *to more than one plan or IRA* or is *only partly rolled over*. See the "Road Map" in ¶ 2.2.01.

To answer the same questions with respect to a Roth IRA (or designated Roth account (DRAC)), see ¶ 5.2.06 (or ¶ 5.7.05). For treatment of return of basis under the minimum distribution rules, see ¶ 1.2.02(D). For the effect of UBTI on basis, see ¶ 8.2.01. For what happens if the total combined value of the participant's IRAs is less than the amount of his basis, see ¶ 8.1.02.

2.2.01 *Road Map: Tax-free distribution of participant's "basis"*

A retirement plan distribution is nontaxable to the extent it represents the recovery of the participant's "investment in the contract." § 72(b)(2). The **"investment in the contract"** is the money in the plan that the participant has already paid income tax on. For ease of reference, it is usually called the participant's **"basis"** or **"after-tax money"** in the plan or IRA. There is no double taxation; the participant is not taxed *again* when he takes that after-tax money out of the plan or IRA. The **pretax money** is the money inside the plan or IRA that has not yet been subjected to income tax.

Unfortunately, there is no quick easy way to explain the rules that govern after-tax money in a plan or IRA. There is a general rule with numerous exceptions, and there are different rules (and different exceptions) for plans than for IRAs. Here is your **Road Map for Tracking Basis:**

Step 1: How much basis does the participant have? To determine the participant's basis in a QRP, see ¶ 2.2.03. To determine the participant's basis in his traditional IRAs, see ¶ 2.2.06. To determine a beneficiary's basis in inherited IRAs, see ¶ 2.2.07.

Step 2: How much of a particular distribution is basis? See ¶ 2.2.04 to determine how much of any particular distribution from a QRP is deemed to be after-tax money. See ¶ 2.2.08 to determine what portion of any particular distribution from a traditional IRA is deemed to be after-tax money.

Step 3: How much of a partial rollover or Roth conversion is after-tax money? If a particular distribution is only partly rolled over, or only partly converted to a Roth IRA, how is after-tax money allocated between the rolled and nonrolled (or converted and nonconverted) portions? If a distribution is rolled over to multiple plans or IRAs, how is the after-tax money allocated among the various "destination" plans? See ¶ 2.2.05 to answer these questions with respect to QRP distributions, ¶ 2.2.08–¶ 2.2.10 for traditional IRA distributions.

2.2.02 General rule: The "cream-in-the-coffee rule" of § 72

Any distribution from a traditional retirement plan (or IRA) is deemed to carry out proportionate amounts of the pre- and after-tax money in all of the participant's account(s) in that plan (or all of the participant's traditional IRAs), unless an exception applies.

Here is how we arrive at that general rule: § 402(a) provides that QRP distributions are taxable under the rules provided in § 72. § 408(d)(1) provides similarly for distributions from IRAs, as § 403(b)(1) does for 403(b) plans.

§ 72 provides that any distribution from a retirement plan is deemed to carry out proportionate amounts of the pre- and after-tax money in the plan. See § 72(e)(8)(A), (B), (5)(D). Ed Slott, CPA, one of America's leading IRA experts, the author of several books on retirement distribution planning and publisher of *Ed Slott's IRA Advisor* newsletter (see Appendix C), calls § 72 the "**cream-in-the-coffee rule.**" Once after-tax money (cream) has been combined with the pretax money (coffee) in your retirement plan, every "sip" (distribution) taken from the plan will contain some cream and some coffee.

Of course, like everything else, the cream-in-the-coffee rule applies differently to IRAs and nonIRA plans, and has several exceptions (different exceptions for IRAs and nonIRA plans). So, the task of figuring how much of a particular distribution or rollover contribution consists of after-tax money will always start with the general "cream" rule, but then follow different tracks for IRAs and nonIRA plans. And remember, a totally different track applies for *Roth* IRAs—see ¶ 5.2.06.

Because § 72 was originally written to deal with distributions from annuity contracts, it often refers to the "contract," which can be confusing when dealing with a retirement plan.

2.2.03 Participant's basis in a QRP or 403(b) plan

This ¶ 2.2.03 explains how a participant can get "basis" in his QRP, and how to determine what the participant's basis is with respect to such a plan. Once you have determined what the participant's basis is, ¶ 2.2.04 explains how to tell how much of that basis is included in any particular distribution.

The participant's basis in a QRP consists of the sum of the following three components, A–C. In addition, some QRP participants may have basis in a life insurance contract held within the plan; see the *Special Report: When Insurance Products Meet Retirement Plans* (Appendix C).

A.   **Nondeductible employee contributions.** Some QRPs permit (or formerly permitted) employees to make after-tax contributions. The employee's nondeductible contributions become his basis or investment in the contract with respect to the plan benefits. Some 403(b) plans and government plans have mandatory employee contributions or permit participants to contribute their own after-tax money to the plan to purchase "past service credits"; these nondeductible contributions are added to the employee's investment in the contract. Regardless of the reason for the nondeductible contributions, the earnings on such contributions are *not* part of the employee's basis; the earnings are pretax money.

B.   **Employer plan contributions when plan was not qualified.** If the retirement plan was not a "qualified plan" at some time(s) during its history, employer contributions to the employee's account in the plan may have been treated as taxable income to the employee at the time of the contribution. Any such previously-taxed contribution becomes part of the participant's "investment in the contract." Reg. § 1.402(a)-1(a)(iv).

C.   **Plan loans that become deemed distributions.** See ¶ 2.1.07(A).

It is unusual for an employee to have any basis in a QRP, since most employees do not have defaulted or improper plan loans, previously-taxed employer contributions, or nondeductible employee contributions. When an employee does have significant basis in a QRP, consider converting the plan (or the employee contribution account in the plan, if that is the account that contains the after-tax money; see ¶ 2.2.04(C)) directly to a Roth IRA; see ¶ 5.4.04(B).

2.2.04 *QRP distributions from account that contains after-tax money*

Under the "cream-in-the-coffee" rule of § 72 (¶ 2.2.02), a distribution from a QRP generally carries out a pro rata share of the participant's pre- and after-tax money in the plan. § 72(e)(8)(A), (B),

(5)(D). This ¶ 2.2.04 looks at how this rule applies to particular distributions, and the exceptions to the general rule.

A.   **What is the "distribution" § 72 is applied to?** The threshold question is, what is the "distribution" to which the cream-in-the-coffee formula applies? While the participant is living, a QRP can send funds from the participant's account to the participant himself and/or to one or more "eligible retirement plans" on the participant's behalf (direct rollover; see ¶ 2.6.01(C)). Are transmittals to such different "destinations" treated as separate distributions?

This question is the subject of much controversy and disagreement (including contradictory IRS pronouncements). Not every plan administrator necessarily interprets the rules the same way.

One controversy concerns the proper classification of a distribution that is split between a direct rollover (¶ 2.6.01(C)) and an outright distribution to the participant. This commonly occurs when, for example, a participant retires and requests that part of his account be distributed directly to him and part be sent to an IRA via direct rollover. According to Notice 2009-68, 2009-39 I.R.B. 423 (p. 429), if a plan distributes funds to both the participant and an eligible retirement plan, that is considered *two separate distributions* for purposes of the cream-in-the-coffee rule. It is *not* considered a single distribution to the participant of which a portion is rolled over. See also Reg. § 1.402A-1, A-5(a), third sentence, which provides similarly for DRAC-to-DRAC direct rollovers (¶ 5.7.06), and the Instructions for Form 1099-R (2010), p. 4 ("If part of the distribution is a direct rollover and part of it is distributed to the participant, prepare two Forms 1099-R"); the same statement appeared on page 3 of the 2008 and 2009 Instructions for Form 1099-R.

Yes this treatment contradicts the IRS's own regulation dealing with income tax withholding, which treats the direct rollover and outright payment as *two portions of a single eligible rollover distribution*, when the "distributee elects to have a portion of an eligible rollover distribution paid to an eligible retirement plan in a direct rollover and to receive the remainder of the distribution...." Reg. § 31.3405(c)-1, Q-6. See also PLR 2009-26041, in which the IRS "blessed" a "direct rollover of the [participant's] entire account balance from Plan X into Plan Y, except the after-tax contributions...which were to be distributed directly to" the participant; such a split-up of the pre- and after-tax money is not possible if the direct rollover and outright distribution must be treated as two separate distributions as stated in Notice 2009-68.

This distinction is important, because if there are *two separate distributions*, each distribution carries out proportionate amounts of pre- and after-tax money. But if there is a *single distribution, part of which is rolled over to another plan*, an exception to the cream-in-the-coffee rule would apply and produce a different result; see ¶ 2.2.05(C).

> ### Is Notice 2009-68 the Last Word?
> The rest of the discussion in this book accepts the IRS's most recent pronouncement, Notice 2009-68, to the effect that an outright distribution and simultaneous direct rollover from the same account are treated as two separate distributions. However, as noted above, this IRS position is controversial and not consistent with some other IRS pronouncements. Furthermore, according to anecdotal evidence, many plan administrators seem to have their own rules about what constitutes a "distribution" and whether pre- and after-tax moneys can be separated and sent to different "destinations." When a participant or beneficiary requests a direct rollover of part of the participant's plan balance and an outright distribution of the rest, or multiple direct rollovers into different types of IRAs (traditional and Roth), the plan administrator who reports the distribution(s) to the IRS on Form 1099-R, and the tax preparer who reports the distribution(s) and any related rollovers or Roth conversions to the IRS on the participant's or beneficiary's tax return, will need to resolve the question of the proper tax treatment and determine which IRS pronouncement is applicable.

B.   **No aggregation of multiple plans.** *Unlike* with IRAs (see ¶ 2.2.08), there is no "aggregation rule" requiring multiple *nonIRA* plans to be considered as "one plan" for purposes of this determination. Thus, for example, a solo practitioner lawyer who has both a "solo 401(k) plan" and a defined benefit plan does not aggregate his two plans for purposes of determining the taxability of a distribution from one or the other. On the contrary, a single QRP might even be treated as multiple separate "accounts" for this purpose (see "C").

C.   **"Cream" rule exception for certain separate accounts.** In a defined contribution plan, usually, the employer maintains a separate accounting for the employee contribution account (i.e., the employee's after-tax contributions and the earnings thereon) and the employer contribution account (i.e., the employer's contributions and the earnings thereon). § 72 may be applied separately to these separate accounts. § 72(d)(2). In the lingo of § 72, the employee contribution account may be treated as a "separate contract" for purposes of § 72. This rule is favorable to the employee, because typically he has a higher basis in the employee-contribution account, so a distribution from that account (or direct Roth conversion of that account; see ¶ 5.4.08) might be largely tax-free if it is treated separately from the rest of his plan benefits.

Some employees are confused by this exception and think it means they can withdraw their after-tax contributions separately from any pretax money in the plan. That is not correct. The "employee contribution account" includes not only the employee's own contributions (which are indeed after-tax money) but *also* the earnings that have accrued on those contributions. The earnings are pretax money. A distribution from the employee contribution account is subject to the same rules of § 72 (though applied only to that separate account) as usual, meaning that a partial distribution from the employee contribution account would carry out proportionate amounts of the pre- and after-tax money *in that account* (unless some other exception applies).

Under some plans that allow the employee to make after-tax contributions to purchase "past service credits," the contributions are not kept in a separate account; the plan pays a single benefit based on both employer and employee contributions. A distribution from such a plan (even if the plan labels it as a return of the participant's after-tax contributions) is generally treated as a pro rata distribution of pretax and after-tax money, based on the value of the employee's entire account, rather than as a distribution from a separate employee contribution account. However, there are exceptions and grandfather rules, so § 72 must be carefully studied in these cases; see § 72(e)(8)(D) and PLRs 2001-15040, 2004-11051, and 2004-19036.

D.   "Cream" rule exception for pre-1987 balances. Pre-1987 balances are not subject to the current rules applicable to other balances. The Code provides that: "In the case of a plan which on May 5, 1986, permitted withdrawal of any employee contributions before separation from service, subparagraph (A) [of § 72(e)(8)] shall apply only to the extent that amounts received before the annuity starting date (when increased by amounts previously received under the contract after December 31, 1986) exceed the investment in the contract as of December 31, 1986." § 72(e)(8)(D).

In the form of notice the IRS provides to plan administrators (for them to give to a retiring employee receiving a distribution from his account), the IRS suggests telling the employee "If a payment is only part of your benefit, an allocable portion of your after-tax contributions is generally included in the payment. If you have pre-1987 after-tax contributions maintained in a separate account, a special rule may apply to determine whether the after-tax contributions are included in a payment"—but there's no statement of what that "special rule" is. Notice 2009-68, p. 428.

2.2.05 *Partial rollovers and conversions: QRP distributions*

This ¶ 2.2.05 explains what happens to the pre- and after-tax portions of a distribution made from a QRP to the participant if only *part* of the distribution is rolled over to an IRA (or the distribution is rolled into multiple recipient IRAs). Since Roth conversions are considered "rollovers" from the QRP to a Roth IRA (¶ 5.4.04), this ¶ 2.2.05 also applies to partial Roth conversions.

This section does not tell you *what constitutes a "distribution."* For that question, and for how to determine how much of any particular QRP distribution *is* after-tax money, see ¶ 2.2.04. Once you have identified a particular "distribution" made to the participant, *and* you have determined how much of that distribution is after-tax money, this ¶ 2.2.05 tells you what happens to the pre- and after-tax money included in that distribution if the participant (within 60 days; see ¶ 2.6.06) rolls over only part of the distribution (or rolls over all of it, partly to a traditional and partly to a Roth IRA).

A.   **Myron Example.** Myron is retiring. His $150,000 profit-sharing plan account at Acme Widget consists of $50,000 of after-tax money and $100,000 of pretax money. He does not have "separate accounts" for employer and employee contributions (¶ 2.2.04(C)); all this money is in one "account." None of the money is "pre-1986 contributions" (¶ 2.2.04(D)).

As discussed at ¶ 5.4.04(B), Myron can get a "bargain" Roth IRA by converting this QRP account to a Roth IRA. If he directs the plan to transfer his entire account to a Roth IRA by direct rollover (¶ 2.6.01(C)), he gets a $150,000 Roth IRA but has to pay income tax on only $100,000. We now turn to the more complicated question of what happens if he rolls over or converts only *part* of his profit-sharing plan account. Here are the possible scenarios:

Scenario 1:   Myron directs the plan to send $100,000 from the account to a traditional IRA via direct rollover and to distribute the other $50,000 to him. As explained, at ¶ 2.2.04(A), the IRS treats this as two separate distributions (according to Notice 2009-68), so each rollover carries with it proportionate amounts of the pre- and after-tax money. $33,333 of Myron's $50,000 distribution is taxable; the other $16,667 is considered a tax-free return of basis. The traditional IRA will have $33,333 of basis in it going forward.

Scenario 2:   Myron directs the plan to send $100,000 from the account to a *traditional* IRA via direct rollover and to send the other $50,000 to a *Roth* IRA via direct rollover. See "B" below for the results of this scenario.

Scenario 3:   Myron directs the plan to send $50,000 from the account to a Roth IRA via direct rollover and to leave the other $100,000 in the 401(k) plan. See "B" below.

Scenario 4:   Myron directs the plan to distribute the entire $150,000 to him. Within 60 days after that distribution, Myron "rolls" $100,000 to a traditional IRA. He keeps the rest of the distribution ($50,000) in his taxable account. See "C" below.

Scenario 4:   Myron directs the plan to distribute the entire $150,000 to him. Within 60 days after that distribution, Myron "rolls" $100,000 to a traditional IRA. After completing that rollover, but still within 60 days of the original distribution, he "rolls" the remaining $50,000 of the distribution into a Roth IRA. See "D" below.

B.   **Direct rollovers to traditional and Roth IRAs.** Suppose Myron directs the Acme plan to "transfer the $50,000 of after-tax money in my account to my Roth IRA via direct rollover," and to leave the $100,000 of pretax money in Myron's QRP account. Alternatively, assume Myron directs the plan to "send the $50,000 of after-tax money in my account to my Roth IRA and send the $100,000, of pretax money to my traditional IRA, in both cases via direct rollover."

Myron would *like* to think that what he has done is to "convert" the after-tax money to a Roth IRA, while either leaving the $100,000 of pretax money in the QRP account or rolling it directly to an IRA. But neither of these approaches would work to accomplish that result.

Instead, because of the "cream-in-the-coffee rule" (¶ 2.2.04), the $50,000 rollover to the Roth IRA would be deemed to consist of proportionate amounts of the pre- and after-tax money in the account, so two-thirds of the $50,000 conversion amount ($33,333) would be pretax money and accordingly would be includible in Myron's gross income. The $100,000 left in the profit-sharing plan account (or sent via direct rollover to a traditional IRA) would likewise be deemed to consist two-thirds of pretax money and one-third of after-tax money. § 72(e)(2)(B), (5)(A), (5)(D)(iii), and (8)(B); § 408A(d)(3).

To separate the "cream" (after-tax money) from the "coffee" (pretax money), Myron would have to find an exception to the cream-in-the-coffee rule. But the exceptions for separate accounts (¶ 2.2.04(C)) and "pre-1986 contributions" (¶ 2.2.04(D) do not apply to his case, and the exception for certain partial rollovers (see "C" below) does not apply to the scenarios described here in "B."

C.   **Partial rollover of distribution that contains after-tax money.** Suppose, instead, Myron directs the plan to distribute his entire $150,000 account to him. Within 60 days after that distribution, Myron "rolls" $100,000 (equivalent to the pretax money in the account) to a traditional IRA. He keeps the rest of the distribution ($50,000, equivalent to the after-tax money) in his taxable account.

The Code has a specific rule, in § 402(c)(2), dealing with the partial rollover of a QRP distribution that contains both pre- and after-tax money. The pretax money is deemed to be rolled over "first."

Here is how we reach that conclusion. § 402(a) tells us that distributions from QRPs are includible in gross income. ¶ 2.1.01. § 402(c)(1) then tells us that § 402(a)'s general rule of income-inclusion does *not* apply to the "portion" of any eligible rollover distribution that is transferred to another retirement plan. In other words, amounts properly "rolled over" to another plan are excluded from gross income despite § 402(a).

Then comes the mysterious § 402(c)(2). This section seems to say that, notwithstanding § 402(c)(1), the participant cannot roll over any after-tax money that was included in his plan distribution; except that (A) he *can* transfer after-tax money to a nonIRA plan *if* such transfer is accomplished via direct rollover, and (B) he *can* roll over after-tax money to an IRA. The last sentence of § 402(c)(2) then says that "in the case of a transfer described in subparagraph (A) or (B)" (i.e., *any* rollover to an IRA, or a *direct rollover* to another QRP), the amount transferred into the plan or IRA that receives the rollover "shall be treated as consisting first of the portion of the distribution that" would have been includible in gross income if it were not rolled over.

This last sentence of § 402(c)(2) clearly says that, if the employee receives a distribution from the plan, then rolls over only *part* of the distribution, the part rolled over is deemed to come first from the pretax money included in the distribution. This rule enables the employee to isolate the after-tax money *outside* the plan, while rolling over the pretax money to keep it tax-sheltered in an IRA. The IRS agrees with this conclusion; see Regs. § 1.402A-1, A-5(b), and § 1.402(c)-2, A-8; PLR 9840041; and IRS Publication 575, *Pension and Annuity Income* (2009), p. 26, which says: "If you roll over only part of a distribution that includes both taxable and nontaxable amounts, the amount you roll is treated as coming first from the taxable part of the distribution."

The last sentence of § 402(c)(2) *also* seems to say that, when a distribution is "split" between an outright distribution to the employee and a direct rollover to another eligible retirement plan, the direct rollover is treated as part of the "total distribution" and is deemed to come out of the pretax money first. However, as explained at ¶ 2.2.04(A), Notice 2009-68 contradicts this interpretation and regards the direct rollover and outright distribution as two separate distributions.

Therefore, if the employee wants to get his after-tax money out of the plan while continuing to defer distribution of the pretax money, the only way he can accomplish that (according to Notice 2009-68) is to take a total distribution of the entire plan balance, and then roll the pretax money over into another plan or IRA within 60 days. This approach unfortunately forces the employee to incur mandatory 20 percent income tax withholding on the taxable portion; see ¶ 2.3.02(C).

In Myron's case, he could take a total distribution of $150,000 from the plan, which would be subject to mandatory income tax withholding of 20 percent of the taxable portion. The taxable portion of the distribution is $100,000, so the withheld income tax would be $20,000, leaving Myron with $130,000 of cash. He then could roll $100,000 of this into a traditional IRA. If that is all he does, he would be deemed to have rolled the pretax money entirely into the traditional IRA. He will then be left with zero tax on the distribution, plus $30,000 of cash in his taxable account, and a $20,000 credit for the withheld tax on his income tax return for the year of the distribution.

D.   **Successive 60-day rollovers.** Suppose Myron, after receiving the $150,000 cash distribution of his entire account from the plan (minus $20,000 mandatory income tax withholding), and after rolling $100,000 over into a traditional IRA within 60 days (see "C" above), later (but still within 60 days after the original distribution) rolls the final $50,000 of the distribution into a Roth IRA. (Because $20,000 of his distribution was sent to the IRS as withheld income taxes he will have to make up that $20,000 using "substituted funds" in order to complete a rollover of the entire distribution; see Reg. § 1.402(c)-2, A-11.)

Now his entire $150,000 distribution has been rolled over. Did he succeed in rolling the pretax money to a traditional IRA and the after-tax money into a Roth IRA? Or has he simply rolled proportionate amounts of each into each IRA? Experts disagree on the answer to this question.

One expert says: The amount includible in income on account of a Roth conversion of a QRP distribution is, whatever would have been included if the amount contributed to the Roth had NOT been rolled over at all, citing § 408A(d)(3)(A)(i). If Myron had *not* rolled over the final $50,000 of the distribution he received, even the IRS agrees it would have been tax-free, because of the final sentence of § 402(c)(2) (see "C" above). Since that amount would not have been taxable if it had NOT been rolled over, § 408A(d)(3)(A)(i) says it is not taxable when it IS rolled over to a Roth IRA.

But another expert says: The concept of the "tax-free" second rollover (transferring the after-tax money into a Roth IRA) depends on the last sentence of § 402(c)(2). The last sentence of § 402(c)(2) tells us what happens when only PART of a particular distribution is rolled over. In this case, the ENTIRE distribution has been rolled over within 60 days. Therefore the "partial rollover" rule is irrelevant. There is one distribution, and if the entire distribution was rolled over within 60 days it doesn't matter how many IRAs that distribution was rolled into or in what sequence. § 402(c)(2) simply doesn't apply, so both rollovers will carry proportionate amounts of the pre- and after-tax money (and the Roth conversion is not "tax-free").

The IRS has not given its opinion. Advisors will need to make their own judgment with respect to this question.

2.2.06 *Participant's basis in a traditional IRA*

Here is a list of the ways that after-tax money can get IN to an IRA. A participant who acquires all (or part) of his ex-spouse's IRA in a divorce pursuant to § 408(d)(6) will thereby also acquire all (or part) of the ex-spouse's basis. For a beneficiary's basis in an inherited IRA, see ¶ 2.2.07. For how the after-tax money (basis) comes OUT of the IRA, see ¶ 2.2.08–¶ 2.2.10.

✓   **Nondeductible "regular" IRA contributions.** A participant may have after-tax money in his IRA as the result of nondeductible contributions made to the account in 1987 or later years. See § 408(o), added by § 1102 of TRA '86.

✓   **Excess IRA contributions not returned by due date of return.** See ¶ 2.1.08(G).

✓   **Contribution of a "qualified reservist distribution."** See ¶ 2.6.06(C).

✓   **Rollover of after-tax money from a QRP after 2001.** § 401(a)(31) and § 402(c)(2) permit nontaxable as well as taxable amounts to be rolled over from a QRP to a traditional IRA after 2001; see ¶ 2.6.02(H).

A participant is required to file Form 8606 for any year in which he either: makes a nondeductible contribution to an IRA (presumably including a rollover contribution that contains after-tax money); converts any part of an IRA to a Roth IRA (¶ 5.4); takes a distribution from a Roth IRA; or takes a distribution from a traditional IRA at a time when he had after-tax money in any of his traditional IRAs. Form 8606 is attached to the individual's Form 1040, but may be filed separately if the individual is not required to file Form 1040.

Part of the information reported on Form 8606 is the participant's basis in his traditional IRAs. To determine a client's basis in his traditional IRAs, therefore, theoretically, you need only look at his most recent Form 8606. Whether everyone who is supposed to file this form has actually done so, or has completed the form accurately, is another question.

2.2.07 *Beneficiary's basis in an inherited IRA*

An inherited IRA (¶ 4.2.01) is subject to various additional or different income tax considerations, though IRS publications, tax forms, and instructions do not always make that clear. See, in addition to this section, ¶ 2.1.07(C) (effect of plan loan at participant's death), ¶ 4.2 (rollovers and plan-to-plan transfers of inherited plans), and ¶ 4.6 (income in respect of a decedent).

For authority for the following statements, see Rev. Proc. 89-52, 1989-1 CB 632, § 3.01. See also IRS Publication 590 (2009), *Individual Retirement Arrangements (IRAs)*, "What if you inherit an IRA?," "IRAs with basis," p. 20. Neither Form 8606 nor the instructions to that Form (2009) give any indication of the separate treatment of inherited IRAs or of the proper method of reporting with respect to these accounts.

If the deceased participant had after-tax money in his IRA, the beneficiary takes over that basis after the participant's death. [This statement would appear to hold true even if the account is worth less than the participant's basis as of the date of death; § 1014(b) (applicable for deaths in years before and after 2010), providing for an adjustment bringing basis to date-of-death value, does not apply to "income in respect of a decedent" (IRD; see ¶ 4.6). § 1014(c). For deaths *in* 2010, see ¶ 4.3.08.]

Inherited IRAs are *not* aggregated with the beneficiary's own IRA(s) for purposes of determining how much of any distribution from either type constitutes tax-free return of basis. If a beneficiary inherits IRAs from more than one decedent, he must track basis separately for the IRAs he inherited from each decedent. The one exception to these statements applies to the surviving spouse—if she elects to treat an IRA she has inherited from the deceased spouse as her own IRA or rolls it over into her own IRA (see ¶ 3.2), the basis in the decedent's IRA is just added to hers. Inherited *traditional* IRAs are not aggregated with inherited *Roth* IRAs for any purpose. See ¶ 5.2.03(B).

2.2.08 *How much of a traditional IRA distribution is basis?*

Distributions from traditional IRAs are taxed under the cream-in-the-coffee rule of § 72 (¶ 2.2.02). § 408(d)(2); § 72(e)(2)(B), (5)(A), (5)(D)(iii), and (8)(B). For taxation of distributions from a *Roth IRA*, see ¶ 5.2.03.

A special aggregation rule applies to IRAs that does not apply to other plans: For purposes of determining how much of any particular distribution is a return of the participant's basis, all of the participant's (noninherited) IRAs are treated as a single giant IRA (aggregation of accounts; see "F" below) and all distributions during the year from the aggregated accounts are treated as one single distribution (see "B"). Since the conversion of funds from a traditional to a Roth IRA is treated as a distribution from the traditional IRA (¶ 5.4.03), these same aggregation rules are used to determine how much income a participant realizes when he converts funds from a traditional IRA to a Roth IRA. Reg. § 1.408A-4, A-7(a).

Here is the formula for determining how much of a particular year's distributions from (and Roth conversions of) traditional IRAs constitutes tax-free return of the participant's investment in the contract (basis), adapted from Notice 87-16, 1987-1 C.B. 446, Part III. The taxable portion of traditional IRA distributions and of Roth conversions of traditional IRAs are figured on different parts of IRS Form 8606 using this formula.

A.   **The cream-in-the-coffee formula.** The total amount of the participant's IRA distributions for the year is multiplied by a fraction. The numerator of the fraction is participant's total basis in the aggregated accounts ("Nondeductible Contributions"). The denominator is the [total balance of all his traditional IRAs as of the end of the year in which the distribution occurs] plus [the Distribution Amount].

Return of Basis = [Distribution Amount] X [The Fraction]

The Fraction is:

$$\frac{\text{Total Nondeductible Contributions}}{[\text{Year-End Account Balance} + \text{Distribution Amount} + \text{Outstanding Rollovers}]}$$

The following paragraphs explain the components of this formula and how it works.

B.   **Distribution Amount.** The Distribution Amount figures into the formula twice, once as part of the denominator of The Fraction and once as the multiplicand. Basically, the Distribution Amount is the sum of all "countable" distributions the participant took from any of his traditional IRAs during the calendar year, because all such distributions are treated as one single giant distribution. Each distribution is valued as of the date it is distributed. Any amount converted to a Roth IRA is treated as a distribution, and valued for this purpose on the date it is distributed out of the traditional IRA. § 408(d)(2). Use IRS Form 8606 and its instructions and related worksheets to compute the Distribution Amount; here are some points to consider (including which distributions "don't count"):

✓   Since all of the participant's traditional IRAs are treated as a single account, make sure you are looking at the right IRAs in figuring the Distribution Amount; see "F."

✓   IRA distributions that were rolled over to another traditional IRA or traditional QRP are NOT included in the Distribution Amount. IRA distributions that were rolled to another traditional IRA don't count because they will show up in the Year-end Account Balance. IRA distributions that were rolled into a QRP don't count because such rollovers were deemed to come out of the pretax money in the account first (see ¶ 2.2.10(A)); accordingly, they simply reduce the pretax money in the IRA without diminishing basis.

✓   There are other IRA distributions that are deemed to come "first" from the pretax money in the participant's aggregated IRAs; see ¶ 2.2.10(B)–(D). In order for the formula to work, these excepted distributions must be *excluded* from the Distribution Amount. Notice 87-16 does not mention this exclusion, because these exceptions did not exist in 1987, but the exclusion does appear on line 7 of IRS Form 8606 (2009).

✓   Exclude any distribution that was rolled into a *Roth IRA* (conversion) during the year, if that conversion amount is later recharacterized (¶ 5.6); see "C."

C.   **Year-end Account Balance.** This is the total combined account balance of all of the participant's countable traditional IRAs (for countable and excluded accounts see "F"), computed as of the end of the year in which the distribution occurs. § 408(d)(2)(C). Use IRS Form 8606 and its instructions and related worksheets to compute the Year-end Account Balance; here are some points to consider:

✓   There are special rules for returned contributions (both regular and excess), and for various disaster recovery assistance distributions. See Instructions for Form 8606.

✓   Recharacterizations of contributions made to any IRA for that year are taken into account, even if the recharacterization occurred after the end of the year. If the recharacterization occurred during the same year as the distribution/conversion, the recharacterized amount "automatically" is included in the Year-end Account Balance. If the recharacterization occurs after the end of the year, the amount that was transferred into the IRA after the end of the year to effect the recharacterization (i.e., the contribution plus or minus earnings or losses thereon) (NOT the actual year-end value of the amount that was recharacterized) is treated as part of the Year-end Account Balance of the IRA that receives the recharacterization contribution (even though the amount is not received until AFTER the end of the year).

Simon Example: On 11/30/09, Simon made a regular contribution of $3,000 to a Roth IRA for the year 2009. Without recharacterization, that contribution and its earnings would *not* affect his 12/31/09 *traditional* IRA account balance because that money is in a Roth IRA, not in a traditional IRA. After the end of 2009, but within the deadline for recharacterization (¶ 5.6.06), Simon recharacterizes that contribution as a contribution to a traditional IRA. That recharacterization is taken into account, meaning that the $3,000 Roth IRA contribution (plus or minus net income attributable thereto; see ¶ 5.6.02) IS included in the 12/31/09 Year-end Account Balance of Simon's traditional IRA for purposes of applying the cream-in-the-coffee rule (as well as for MRD purposes; see ¶ 5.2.02(D)).

D.   **Total Nondeductible Contributions.** This is the participant's basis in all of his traditional IRAs as of December 31 of the year preceding the distribution year, *plus* the amount of any nondeductible "regular" contribution (¶ 5.3.02) made to any of his traditional IRAs for the year of the distribution (even if made after the end of the year); see Instructions for IRS Form 8606 (2009), line 2. This number will be the numerator of The Fraction.

E.   **Outstanding Rollovers.** A rollover from one traditional IRA to another that is distributed from the first IRA within 60 days before the end of the distribution year, and is received by the recipient IRA AFTER year-end, must be included in the denominator of The Fraction. The IRS calls this an **outstanding rollover**. Notice 87-16, Part III. This is similar to the rule for minimum required distributions, where the Year-end Account Balance is increased by rollovers that are in "mid air" on December 31 (¶ 1.2.05).

F.   **The aggregation rule: Which IRAs must be aggregated.** § 408(d)(2) provides that: "For purposes of applying section 72 to any [IRA distribution]...(A) all individual retirement plans shall be treated as 1 contract, [and] (B) all distributions during any taxable year shall be treated as 1 distribution...." Here are the IRAs which must be (or must not be) aggregated with each other for purposes of determining the A–E amounts above.

"Individual retirement plans"to be aggregated include the participant's traditional IRAs, individual retirement annuities, and SEP and SIMPLE IRAs (¶ 8.3.13). See § 7701(a)(37); § 408(k)(1), (p)(1); Notice 87-16, Part III; and Instructions for IRS Form 8606 (2009), Line 6, p. 6. All such accounts the participant owns are considered one giant IRA; then, each distribution from any such account is counted as part of the Distribution Amount. § 72(e)(2)(B), (5)(A), (5)(D)(iii), and (8)(B). However:

✓ *Inherited* IRAs held as beneficiary are aggregated only with other inherited IRAs held as beneficiary of the same decedent; they are *not* aggregated with the individual's own IRAs; see ¶ 2.2.07.

✓ *Roth IRAs* are not aggregated with *traditional IRAs*. § 408A(d)(4)(A).

✓ IRAs of *husband and wife* are not aggregated. Each spouse's IRAs are aggregated only with other IRAs belonging to that spouse. See Notice 87-16, Part III, D7, and Instructions for IRS Form 8606 (2009), "Specific Instructions," first paragraph (page 5), stating that Form 8606 is completed separately for each spouse.

G.   Cream-in-the-coffee formula: Examples. The following "Gibbs" and "Ted" examples illustrate the formula:

Gibbs Example: Gibbs has $12,000 of nondeductible contributions in his traditional IRA at X Fund, which is now worth $30,000. He also has a traditional IRA worth $210,000 (as of the end of Year 1) at Y Fund. The larger IRA received no after-tax contributions; it contains only a rollover from a QRP maintained by Gibbs's former employer, plus some deductible IRA contributions Gibbs made prior to 1987. He has no other IRAs. In Year 1, he cashes out the $30,000 IRA. He thinks that, because that particular account contains his $12,000 of after-tax contributions, he will be taxable on only $30,000 - $12,000, or $18,000. However, because of § 408(d)(2), Gibbs's $30,000 distribution is *deemed* to come proportionately from *both* of his IRAs, even though it *actually* came from only one of them. Here is how the cream-in-the-coffee fraction applies to Gibbs's distribution:

Distribution Amount: $30,000
Total Nondeductible Contributions: $12,000
Year-end Account Balance: $210,000
Outstanding Rollovers: zero

Return of Basis = $30,000 X [$12,000 ÷ ($210,000 + $30,000)] = $1,500

The amount of gross income Gibbs must report is therefore $28,500 ($30,000 distribution minus $1,500 basis allocated to the distribution). His remaining basis in his traditional IRA is $10,500 ($12,000 total basis, less $1,500 used up in the Year 1 distribution).

Ted Example: As of August 1, 2010, when he converts the entire account to a Roth IRA, Ted has $50,000 in his traditional IRA, $40,000 of which is after-tax money. He never recharacterizes this conversion. On December 1, 2010, he retires from his job, and gets a distribution of $450,000 from his 401(k) plan, all of which is pretax money. He rolls the $450,000 into a traditional IRA on December 2, 2010. He makes no other contributions to (and receives no other distributions from) any traditional IRA in 2010. Ted *thinks* that he has made a Roth conversion that is only 20 percent ($10,000 ÷ $50,000) taxable, but his post-conversion rollover messes up the fraction. Here is how the cream-in-the-coffee fraction applies to Ted's Roth IRA conversion:

Distribution (conversion) Amount: $50,000
Total Nondeductible Contributions: $40,000
Year-end Account Balance: $450,000
Outstanding Rollovers: zero

Return of Basis = $50,000 X [$40,000 ÷ ($450,000 + $50,000)] = $4,000

The amount of gross income Ted must report is therefore $46,000 ($50,000 conversion minus $4,000 basis allocated to the conversion). His remaining basis in his traditional IRA is $36,000 ($40,000 total basis, less $4,000 used up in the conversion).

2.2.09 *Partial rollovers and conversions: IRA distributions*

This section explains how basis is apportioned in the case of a partial rollover or partial Roth conversion of an IRA distribution.

A.   **IRA-to-nonIRA plan rollovers.** When a distribution from a traditional IRA is rolled over to a QRP or 403(b) plan, the rolled-over money is deemed to come entirely out of the *taxable* portion of the traditional IRA distribution. § 408(d)(3)(H) (applicable to years after 2001). This rule is necessary because the *nontaxable* portion of an IRA cannot legally be rolled into a QRP or 403(b) plan. ¶ 2.6.02(H). See IRS Publication 590 (*IRAs*) (2009 edition, p. 23).

This exception creates the opportunity for a tax-free distribution from a traditional IRA. In the Gibbs Example (¶ 2.2.08(G)), if Gibbs participates in a QRP that accepts rollovers, Gibbs could take a total distribution of all his IRA balances, then roll over, to the QRP, every dollar above his $12,000 basis. Now he is left with just $12,000, outside any plan, all after-tax money. He can then keep this money outside the plan (thus effecting a distribution of his after-tax money while keeping all pretax money inside a plan), or he can roll the $12,000 into a Roth IRA, thus (apparently; the IRS has not commented on this technique) effecting a tax-free Roth conversion.

B.   **Partial IRA to Roth IRA conversion.** Generally, any IRA distribution consists proportionately of pre- and after-tax money, and the same is true for any transfer (conversion) from a traditional IRA to a Roth IRA. ¶ 2.2.08. If the participant takes a distribution from his IRA, and the distribution contains both pretax and after-tax money, and the participant rolls over (converts) only *part* of the distribution to a Roth IRA, the rollover would apparently consist of the same proportions of pre- and after-tax money as the distribution itself. See Reg. § 1.408A-4, A-1(b), (c), A-7(a); § 408(d)(1), (2); compare § 408(d)(3)(H); IRS Form 8606 (2009). Unlike with the special rules applicable to partial rollovers of QRP distributions (¶ 2.2.05(C)), and to IRA-to-nonIRA plan rollovers (see "A" above), there is no special exception to § 72 applicable to partial IRA-to-IRA (or IRA-to-Roth IRA) rollovers that would cause the pretax money to be deemed rolled first.

The only possible exception to this conclusion arises if the partial IRA distribution occurs in a year in which a minimum distribution is required. Reg. § 1.402(c)-2, A-8, provides that, in the case of a distribution from a *qualified plan*, where the distribution includes both pre- and after-tax money, the after-tax money is applied first to the MRD for the year. This has the effect of making more of the pretax money eligible for rollover. It is not clear whether this same rule also applies to IRA distributions.

2.2.10 *Exceptions to the cream-in-the-coffee rule for IRAs*

There are several exceptions to the proportionate allocation, cream-in-the-coffee, all-IRAs-aggregated, scheme described at ¶ 2.2.08:

A.   **IRA-to-nonIRA-plan rollovers.** See ¶ 2.2.09(A).

B.   **Return of IRA contribution before tax return due date.** Certain returned IRA contributions are taxed outside the § 72 "system." See ¶ 2.1.08(D), (F).

C.   **QHSAFDs.** A Qualified Health Savings Account Funding Distribution (see ¶ 2.1.06(K)) is deemed to come entirely from the pretax money in the individual's IRAs until the pretax money is exhausted. § 408(d)(9)(E).

D.   **Qualified Charitable Distributions.** Another exception is for "Qualified Charitable Contributions" (QCDs). A QCD is the distribution of up to $100,000 per year from the IRA(s) of an individual who is over age 70½ directly to an eligible charity; see ¶ 7.6.07. A QCD is deemed to come first out of the pretax portion of the individual's IRA. § 408(d)(8)(D). QCDs were available in tax years 2006–2009 *only*.

2.3 Income Tax Withholding

For the effect of income tax withholding on the recipient's right to roll over benefits, see ¶ 2.6.02 (first paragraph).

2.3.01 *Withholding of federal income taxes: overview*

Retirement plan distributions are subject to withholding of federal income taxes. This fact creates problems and planning opportunities. This book does not cover state or local withholding requirements.

Chapter 24, Subchapter A, of the Code (§ 3401–§ 3406) establishes the withholding of income tax at the source of payment. Though titled "Withholding from Wages," one section of the Chapter (§ 3405) also provides income tax withholding rules for QRPs, 403(b) plans, and IRAs.

¶ 2.3.02 explains the Code's general scheme for withholding from retirement plan distributions, including the different rules for different types of distributions. Exceptions and special rules are discussed at ¶ 2.3.03. ¶ 2.3.04 explains mutually voluntary withholding. Finally, ¶ 2.3.05 explains how withheld income taxes are applied to the recipient's tax liability for the year.

2.3.02 *Periodic, nonperiodic, and eligible rollover payments*

Here are the Code's opening bids on withholding from retirement distributions, including which ones the recipient can opt out of. (If the recipient wants the plan to withhold *more* income tax than is required, see ¶ 2.3.04.)

The withholding requirements distinguish between "periodic payments" (§ 3405(e)(2)), "nonperiodic distributions" (§ 3405(e)(3)), and "eligible rollover distributions" (§ 3405(c)(3)).

A.   **Periodic payments** from all types of retirement plans, including IRAs, are subject to withholding of taxes at the same rate as wages. § 3405(a)(1). The recipient can elect out of having anything withheld from a periodic payment, so the withholding is voluntary as far as the recipient is concerned. § 3405(a)(2). The Code defines "periodic payment" as a distribution that is "an annuity or similar periodic payment." § 3405(e)(2). See Reg. § 35.3405-1T, A-9.

B.   **Nonperiodic distributions other than "eligible rollover distributions"** (see "C") are subject to withholding at a flat rate of 10 percent. § 3405(b)(1). This rule applies to all types of plans, including IRAs. § 3405(b)(1), (e)(1)(A), (3), "Distributions from an IRA that are payable on demand are treated as nonperiodic payments." Instructions for IRS Form W-4P (2010), p. 3. The recipient can elect *out* of having anything withheld from a nonperiodic distribution, so again the withholding is voluntary from the participant's perspective. § 3405(b)(2). This exception does not apply to eligible rollover distributions; see "C."

In the case of a direct transfer from an IRA to another IRA, the paying plan *could* choose to treat the participant's request for a direct IRA-to-IRA transfer as an election not to have withholding apply. Reg. § 35.3405-1T, d-33. However, anecdotal evidence suggests that at least some IRA providers are not doing so; rather, they are requiring the IRA owner to elect out of withholding if the transfer is to a Roth IRA (i.e., it is a taxable transfer).

C.   **Eligible rollover distributions from QRPs** are subject to withholding at a 20 percent rate, and the recipient can *not* elect out of this withholding if the distribution is paid to him. The only way to make an eligible rollover distribution *not* subject to 20 percent withholding requirement is to have the distribution paid directly to an eligible retirement plan (direct rollover; ¶ 2.6.01(C)), such as an IRA or even a Roth IRA. § 3405(c); Notice 2008-30, 2008-12 IRB 638, A-6; PLR 2000-38055.

An "eligible rollover distribution" is a defined term meaning basically any distribution from a qualified plan (§ 402(c)(4)) or (after 2001) 403(b) plan that is eligible to be rolled over. § 3405(c)(3); § 402(f)(2)(A); see ¶ 2.6.02.

Because the surviving spouse as beneficiary has the same rollover options as the deceased participant would have had, the withholding rules apply to distributions to the surviving spouse in the same manner as to the participant. § 402(f)(2)(A). QRP distributions to a nonspouse Designated Beneficiary are eligible rollover distributions (and therefore subject to mandatory withholding) if the beneficiary does not choose a direct rollover; see ¶ 4.2.04. However, distributions to a beneficiary that is not a "Designated Beneficiary" cannot be rolled over and therefore are not subject to mandatory withholding.

IRA distributions are not subject to the mandatory 20 percent withholding rule; an IRA distribution cannot be an "eligible rollover distribution" *for withholding tax purposes* even if it is eligible to be rolled over.

The distinction between periodic payments and nonperiodic distributions is a little vague, but is not terribly important. Both types are subject to withholding by all types of plans, and with both types the recipient can elect out of having anything withheld (unless the distribution is an eligible rollover distribution). The only difference is the rate of withholding that applies if the recipient does not opt out of withholding. The significant distinction is between "eligible rollover distributions" and other payments, because withholding from an eligible rollover distribution is mandatory unless the distribution is sent by direct rollover to another retirement plan.

The mandatory withholding on eligible rollover distributions does not pose a problem if someone simply wants to get the money out of the QRP without simultaneously paying any income tax on the distribution. All such person has to do is have his distribution transferred directly (a "direct rollover") into an IRA, so the qualified plan does not have to withhold anything; and then take the money out of the IRA (electing out of withholding on the IRA distribution).

The person for whom "mandatory withholding" is *truly* mandatory is the person who wants to take a lump sum distribution from a QRP in order to qualify for special averaging treatment (¶ 2.4.06). This person cannot roll over any part of the distribution, and so will be forced to pay 20 percent income tax on it through withholding. He can get a refund when he files his tax return for the year of the distribution, if his total tax payments (including this withholding) exceed his actual tax liability.

D.   Roth conversion of eligible rollover distribution. Under § 3405(c)(2), as long as the recipient elects (under § 401(a)(31)) to have the eligible rollover distribution sent directly to an "eligible retirement plan," there is no required income tax withholding. "Eligible retirement plan" is not defined in § 3405(c), but is defined in regulations: "…[A]n eligible retirement plan is a trust qualified under section 401(a), an annuity plan described in section 403(a), or an individual retirement plan (as described in Sec. 1.402(c)-2, Q&A-2 of this chapter)." Reg. § 31.3405(c)-1, A-1(a).

The referenced section states that eligible retirement plan includes an individual retirement account under § 408(a). Notice 2008-30, 2008-12 IRB 638, A-1, A-6, makes clear that Roth IRAs are also eligible to receive direct rollovers, and that a direct rollover to a Roth IRA is *not* subject to the 20 percent mandatory income tax withholding: "...[A]n eligible rollover distribution that a distributee elects, under § 401(a)(31)(A), to have paid directly to an eligible retirement plan (including a Roth IRA) is not subject to mandatory withholding, even if the distribution is includible in gross income." Despite that clear statement, the IRS's instructions to employers in Publication 15-A (2010), at page 22, after stating that eligible rollover distributions are subject to mandatory 20 percent withholding, states that "However, you should not withhold federal income tax if the entire distribution is transferred...in a direct rollover to a *traditional IRA*, qualified pension plan [etc.]," making it sound as though mandatory withholding *does* apply to direct Roth rollovers.

2.3.03 *Exceptions and special rules*

A retirement plan is not required to withhold taxes from an eligible rollover distribution to the extent it is "reasonable to believe" that the distribution is not includible in the payee's income. § 3405(e)(1)(B)(ii); Temp. Reg. § 35.3405-1T, A-2. For example, a qualified distribution from a DRAC or Roth IRA, as a nontaxable distribution, would not be subject to withholding.

If the entire distribution consists of securities of the employer corporation (as defined in § 402(e)(4)(E)) (and up to $200 cash "in lieu of fractional shares"), there is no withholding. If the distribution consists of securities of the employer corporation plus cash and other property, the maximum amount the employer is required to withhold is the value of the cash and other property. § 3405(e)(8). In connection with determining the amount required to be withheld from that sort of mixed distribution, "it is reasonable to believe that all net unrealized appreciation [NUA] from employer securities is not includible in gross income." Temp. Reg. § 35.3405-1T, A-30; see ¶ 2.5 regarding NUA.

See ¶ 2.1.07(B) regarding withholding with respect to a plan loan offset distribution.

2.3.04 Mutually voluntary withholding

If the plan administrator does not want to withhold from a plan or IRA distribution any income taxes beyond the amount required by § 3405, the participant or beneficiary cannot force him to do so. Temp. Reg. § 35.3405-1T, A-6. However, if the plan administrator or IRA provider is agreeable, the parties can apparently agree to mutually voluntary withholding under § 3402(p)(3)(B) for such payments. See IRS Publication 575, "Pension and Annuity Income" (2009), p. 9, and Form W-4P (2010), line 3.

2.3.05 How withheld income taxes are applied

Withheld income taxes are applied as a credit against the taxpayer's income tax liability for the year of the distribution. § 31(a)(1). Although § 31 is titled "Tax Withheld on Wages," it applies to any amount "withheld as tax under chapter 24," which includes withholding from retirement plan distributions, since § 3402 and § 3405 are part of chapter 24.

§ 6654 (part of Subtitle F of the Code) imposes a penalty for underpayment of estimated income taxes, and also establishes how withheld income tax relates to the taxpayer's obligation to pay estimated taxes. For purposes of determining the penalty, the § 31 credit for withheld income taxes "shall be deemed a payment of estimated tax, and an equal part of such amount shall be deemed paid on each due date for such taxable year, unless the taxpayer establishes the dates on which all amounts were actually withheld...." § 6654(g)(1). This rule can help a participant or beneficiary who has underpaid his estimated taxes "catch up" (and possibly avoid the penalty for underpayment of estimated taxes) through a late-in-the-year distribution for which he elects income tax withholding.

2.4 Lump Sum Distributions

Through the years, the Code has provided a special gentle treatment for "lump sum distributions" (LSDs) from qualified retirement plans (QRPs). A person who wishes to obtain this special treatment is confronted with some of the most convoluted requirements known to post-ERISA man.

2.4.01 *Introduction to lump sum distributions*

Congress changed the rules on LSD treatment so often that the IRS was unable to keep pace with regulations. There are only assorted proposed and temporary regulations issued in 1975–1979 (under old Code § 402(c)), that became obsolete before they could be finalized. The instructions for IRS Forms 4972 and 1099-R are often the best indication of the IRS's interpretation of the LSD rules.

From 1992 through 1999, the definition of LSD was found in § 402(d); after 1999, it went back to its pre-1992 home, § 402(e). One special LSD deal, five-year forward averaging, ceased to be available for distributions after 1999.

To achieve the favorable tax treatments still available for LSDs, the taxpayer must clear various "hurdles," many of which are surrounded by hidden-issue "land mines." The requirements that must be met in order for a distribution to qualify as an LSD are summarized at ¶ 2.4.02–¶ 2.4.05. If a distribution clears those hurdles it is an LSD. That doesn't mean much, however, unless it meets further tests to qualify for particular favorable tax treatments:

❑   If the LSD meets *additional* tests, it can qualify for special averaging treatment. See ¶ 2.4.06.

❑   If the LSD includes employer stock, see ¶ 2.5.

The following aspects of LSDs are not treated here: LSDs in connection with a QDRO (§ 402(e)(4)(D)(v), (vii)); interplay with the § 691(c) deduction (¶ 4.6.04); an LSD paid to multiple recipients; and distribution of annuity contracts as part of an LSD.

2.4.02 *First hurdle: Type of plan*

Only distributions from § 401(a) "qualified plans" (pension, profit-sharing, or stock bonus) can qualify as LSDs. Both corporate plans and self-employed ("Keogh") plans can give rise to LSDs, but a distribution from an IRA, SEP-IRA, SIMPLE, or 403(b) plan can never qualify for LSD treatment. § 402(e)(4)(D)(i). Once money or stock has been "rolled" into an IRA, any special LSD or NUA deal is permanently lost. PLR 2004-42032.

2.4.03 *Second hurdle: "Reason" for distribution*

The distribution must be made following a triggering event. § 402(e)(4)(D)(i), I–IV. The triggering events are slightly different depending on whether the participant is a "common law employee" or is self-employed ("employee within the meaning of section 401(c)(1)").

If the participant is a common-law employee, the distribution must be made either:

▸   On account of the employee's death; or
▸   After the employee attains age 59½; or
▸   On account of the employee's "separation from service." § 402(e)(4)(D)(i), I–III.

If the participant is self-employed, the distribution must be made either:

◆   On account of the employee's death; or
◆   After the employee attains age 59½; or
◆   After the employee has become disabled within the meaning of § 72(m)(7). § 402(e)(4)(D)(i), I–II, IV.

A person is "disabled," according to § 72(m)(7), if he is "unable to engage in any substantial gainful activity by reason of any medically determinable physical or mental impairment which can be expected to result in death or to be of long-continued and indefinite duration."

These LSD "triggering events" are of significance primarily for determining whether there has been a distribution of 100 percent of the balance to the credit of the employee (¶ 2.4.04). Distributions before the triggering event are irrelevant for this purpose; see, *e.g.*, PLR 8541089 (distributions before age 59½ did not adversely affect LSD status of distribution occurring after reaching age 59½).

(a)   Landmine: separation from service

A treatise could be written on the subject of what constitutes "separation from service." "An employee will be considered separated from the service within the meaning of section 402(e)(4)(A) of the Code, only upon the employee's death, retirement, resignation or discharge, and not when the employee continues on the same job for a different employer as a result of the liquidation, merger or consolidation, etc., of the former employer." Rev. Rul. 79-336, 1979-2 C.B. 187. See, *e.g.*, PLRs 9844040, 1999-27048, 2001-48077. See PLR 2000-38050 holding that an executive employee who transitioned to being a consultant (independent contractor) had "separated from service" for LSD purposes. Defining "separation from service" is beyond the scope of this book. See instead *The Pension Answer Book* (Appendix C).

The frustrating technicalities of the term "separation from service" caused Congress to change to a different term—"severance from employment"—in defining when an elective deferral account may properly be distributed from a 401(k) plan (a subject not covered in this book); see § 401(k)(2)(B)(i)(I), effective for distributions after 2001. Unfortunately, Congress did not similarly amend § 402(e), so "separation from service" is still the term applicable in the definition of LSD. Most cases and rulings on the meaning of separation from service dealt with 401(k) plans; see, *e.g.*, PLR 2001-27053. Post-2001 401(k) pronouncements will no longer help on this question, since the two Code sections now use different terms.

(b)   Landmine: "on account of"

Occasionally taxpayers have had problems asserting that a particular LSD was made "on account of" a triggering event. For example, where the employee died leaving his QRP benefits to his surviving spouse, then she died after taking some distributions from the plan, the children who inherited the remaining QRP benefits at her death were not entitled to LSD treatment, because the payments to them were not "on account of" the employee's death (they were on account of the surviving spouse's death). *Gunnison*, 461 F.2d 496, 499 (7th Cir. 1972). But see PLR 2003-02048, in which a distribution received 10 years after taxpayer's separation from service was ruled to be "on account of" the separation from service.

If the triggering event is reaching age 59½, or becoming disabled, then the distribution does not have to be "on account of" the triggering event; it merely has to be "after" it. PLR 8541089. The treatment is available for someone who has attained age 59½ even if he has not terminated employment; see PLR 2004-10023.

2.4.04 *Third hurdle: Distribution all in one taxable year*

For the distribution to qualify as an LSD, the employee's entire balance must be distributed to him in one calendar year. As the Code puts it, there must be a "distribution or payment within one taxable year of the recipient of the balance to the credit of...[the] employee..." from the plan. § 402(e)(4)(D)(i). The "balance to the credit" includes *all* the participant's accounts in that plan—employ*ee* contribution, employ*er* contribution, rollover, *and* designated Roth! LSD treatment is NEVER available for a partial distribution. See PLRs 2006-34017 through 2006-34022.

For exceptions to the all-in-one-year rule, see ¶ 2.4.05.

This hurdle is surrounded by land mines. Clearly, if an employee takes out, say, one-third of his plan balance in Year 1 and leaves two-thirds in the plan, the distribution of the one-third portion in Year 1 does not qualify for LSD treatment because it is not a distribution of the entire balance. Now suppose the employee takes out the remaining two-thirds of his balance in Year 2. He has taken out 100 percent of his (remaining) plan balance in Year 2. Is the Year 2 distribution an LSD?

It *would* be, *if* the "balance to his credit" simply meant the balance as of the date of distribution—but that is not what it means. Rather, the rule means that the balance to the credit of the employee *as of the first distribution following the most recent triggering event* (¶ 2.4.03) must be distributed within one taxable year. See Notice 89-25, 1989-1 C.B. 662, A-6; Prop. Reg. § 1.402(e)-2(d)(1)(ii); Rev. Rul. 69-495, 1969-2 C.B. 100.

Elaine Example: After Elaine retired from Acme in Year 1 at age 64, she withdrew $60,000 from her $800,000 Acme Profit-sharing Plan account in order to fulfill her dream of traveling around the world in a submarine. Returning to the U.S. in Year 2, she withdraws the rest of her account. This final distribution would not qualify for LSD treatment because the entire balance that existed on the date of the most recent triggering event (separation from service) was not distributed all in one calendar year. In contrast, suppose Elaine, upon returning from her cruise, died on her way to the Acme benefits office. Now there is a new triggering event, the employee's death. Her beneficiary can elect LSD treatment for her remaining plan balance even though Elaine, had she lived, could not have done so. Or suppose Elaine had withdrawn the $60,000 for her cruise *before* she retired. Then her later separation from service would have been a new triggering event, and the final distribution would qualify for LSD treatment.

The IRS Instructions for Form 4972 (2009) make no reference to this requirement. Prior distributions from the same plan are referred to only in connection with the rule that if any prior distribution from the same plan was rolled over, subsequent distributions cannot receive special averaging treatment (see ¶ 2.4.06). These instructions give the impression that the IRS regards the triggering events as obsolete. However, unless the IRS has had an unpublicized change of heart, Notice 89-25 is still in effect. The Code's definition of LSD still includes the requirement that the distribution be of the "balance to the credit" of the employee which becomes payable "after the employee attains age 59½," or "on account of" the participant's death, separation from service, etc..

Failure to distribute the entire balance in one calendar year is a mistake you cannot fix. In PLR 2004-34022, a retiring employee intended to have all of the employer stock in his account in his employer's QRP distributed outright to him and to have all of the other assets in his account distributed directly to his IRA. Through a paperwork error, the distribution of employer stock occurred in 2002, but the transfer of the other assets did not occur until 2003. He did not have an LSD. The IRS ruled that it could not allow him an extension of the all-in-one-year deadline.

Here are more land mines surrounding this hurdle:

A.   Landmine: Post-distribution additions. Does a post-distribution addition to the employee's account retroactively destroy the LSD status of the distribution? That depends:

The "balance to the credit" of the employee (which must be distributed "in one taxable year") is determined as of the first distribution following the most recent triggering event. If there is an addition to the account *after* that date (for example, a new employer contribution), that new addition is *not* part of the balance that must be distributed within the same taxable year to qualify for LSD treatment. If it *is* distributed within the same year, it is treated as part of the LSD; if it is not distributed within the same year, its existence does not disqualify the LSD. Notice 89-25, A-6.

To avoid concerns about a late-appearing asset, when distributing all assets of an account (or when terminating the plan), have the plan trustee sign a blanket assignment of all remaining assets, claims, etc., known and unknown, to the recipient (participant or beneficiary, as the case may be). Thus, the recipient, not the plan trustee, becomes the owner of the stray interest, dividends, and class action claims that seem inevitably to turn up after the plan is liquidated, and the newly-discovered dollars do not cast doubt on the LSD status of the terminating distribution.

B.   **Landmine: aggregation of plans.** In determining whether the entire balance to the credit of an employee has been distributed, certain plans must be aggregated. Specifically all profit-sharing plans of the same employer are considered to be one plan for this purpose; all pension plans of the employer are treated as one plan; and all stock bonus plans are treated as one. § 402(e)(4)(D)(ii); PLR 2006-17039.

See PLR 2002-50036, in which the employer converted part of a pension plan to a stock bonus plan so employees could receive an LSD from the new stock plan without having to take anything from the pension plan.

Unfortunately it is not always easy to determine what type a particular retirement plan is. The employee is entitled to a summary plan description for each plan; that should tell what type it is.

But finding out what type of plan a particular retirement plan is does not necessarily end the problems with this requirement. For one thing plans may have to be aggregated, even if they are *not* both of the same type, if they have interrelated benefit formulas. Also, it may be impossible to obtain distribution of 100 percent of all similar plans. For example, the employer may have two pension plans (a defined benefit and a money purchase) that must be aggregated for purposes of this requirement, but the employer may permit lump sum distributions from only one of them.

If the employer maintains more than one plan, and it is proposed to take an LSD from only one of them, have the employer certify that this requirement is met.

2.4.05 *Exceptions to the all-in-one-year rule*

"[A]ccumulated deductible employee contributions" can be ignored in determining whether the employee has received a distribution of his entire plan balance. § 402(e)(4)(D)(i). This type of contribution, which was permitted under § 72(o) only for the years 1982–1986, is rarely encountered.

Another exception: "Dividends to ESOP participants pursuant to section 404(k)(2)(B) of the Code are not treated as part of the balance to the credit of an employee for purposes of the lump sum distribution rules...Thus, such distribution does not prevent a subsequent distribution of the balance to the credit of an employee from being a lump sum distribution." PLRs 9024083, 1999-47041.

Note that MRDs are *not* ignored in applying the all-in-one-year rule. If a retired participant or a beneficiary starts taking MRDs from the plan, he must take out the entire plan balance in the same calendar year he takes the first MRD, or he will lose out on LSD treatment.

2.4.06 *Special averaging: Participant born before 1936*

If an LSD meets certain *additional* requirements (no portion of the distribution may be rolled over, etc; see Form 4972), the LSD can be taxed separately, using the "10-year averaging" and/or "20 percent capital gain" methods. These two special tax deals are referred to collectively as the "**special averaging method**." An LSD for which a proper election is made to use these methods is excluded from the recipient's adjusted gross income (AGI), and is instead taxed using special rates. § 402(d)(3); § 62(a)(8). These Code sections have been repealed for years after 1999, but still apply under the "transition rule" that "grandfathers" participants born before 1936; see effective dates for amendments to § 62 and § 402.

The special averaging method is available only for individuals "who attained age 50 before 1 - 1 - 86." TRA '86 § 1122(h)(3), (5), (6), as amended by TAMRA '88, § 1011A(b), (13)–(15). The IRS variously interprets this as applying to anyone born before January *2*, 1936 (see IRS Form 4972 (2009), lines 3–4), or before January *1*, 1936 (see Notice 2009-68, 2009-39 IRB 423, p. 429). For more information regarding this grandfather rule, see Instructions for IRS Form 4972, and the *Special Report: Ancient History* (Appendix C).

2.5 Net Unrealized Appreciation of Employer Stock

This ¶ 2.5 describes the special favorable tax treatment available for "lump sum distributions" (and certain other distributions) of employer stock from a retirement plan. For definition of lump sum distribution, see ¶ 2.4.02–¶ 2.4.05. For Roth conversion of NUA stock, see ¶ 5.4.04(A). For charitable gifts of NUA stock, see ¶ 7.6.04.

2.5.01 *NUA: Tax deferral and long-term capital gain*

The Code gives special favorable treatment to distributions of employer securities (referred to here as "employer stock," though the "securities" could be stocks or bonds; § 402(e)(4)(E)) from a qualified plan. Some plans hold the employer securities inside some type of "single-stock fund" rather than directly; you may need an opinion of the plan's or other counsel regarding whether the particular securities held in your client's plan constitute "employer securities."

"Net unrealized appreciation" (NUA) is the excess of the stock's fair market value at the time of distribution over the plan's basis in the stock. Reg. § 1.402(a)-1(b)(2). If various requirements are met:

♦　　The NUA is excluded from the employee's gross income at the time the securities are distributed to the employee. § 402(e)(4)(A), (B). Accordingly, the employee is liable for income tax (and 10% early-distribution penalty, if applicable; ¶ 9.1.03(A)) only on the plan's basis in the stock.

♦　　When the stock is later sold, the NUA is taxed as long-term capital gain, regardless of how long the recipient (or the plan) held the stock. Reg. § 1.402(a)-1(b)(1)(i); Notice 98-24, 1998-1 C.B. 929; PLR 2004-10023. The sale proceeds attributable to the NUA and any post-distribution gain are not subject to the early-distribution penalty. ¶ 9.1.03(A).

Joe Example: Joe, age 53, retires from Baby Bell Corp. in 2009 and receives an LSD of his 401(k) plan, consisting entirely of 10,000 shares of Baby Bell stock. The plan's basis for that stock is $10 per share (total $100,000); the stock is worth $100 a share at the time of the distribution (total $1 million). The amount of the distribution includible in Joe's income is $100,000 ($10 plan basis per share times 10,000 shares). Joe must also pay the 10 percent early-distribution penalty on the $100,000 taxable portion of the distribution, unless an exception applies (¶ 9.4).

If Joe sells the stock immediately for $1 million, he will have long-term capital gain of $900,000. If he waits two months and sells the stock for $125 a share, he has a short-term capital gain of $250,000 ($25 appreciation between date of distribution and date of sale, times 10,000 shares) in addition to his long-term capital gain of $900,000. If he holds the stock for 12 months after receiving the distribution, all gain on any subsequent sale will be long-term capital gain.

The tax deferral/capital gain treatment is not available for all distributions of employer securities. It applies in only two situations:

✓   If the securities are distributed as part of a "lump sum distribution" (¶ 2.4.02–¶ 2.4.05), *all* the NUA is nontaxable at the time of the distribution. § 402(e)(4)(B).

✓   If the distribution is *not* an LSD, then only the NUA attributable to the *employee's* contributions is excludible. § 402(e)(4)(A).

2.5.02 *Reporting NUA distributions*

The employer or plan determines its "cost or other basis" in the plan-held employer securities using one of the methods in Reg. § 1.402(a)-1(b)(2), and thus determines how much of a distribution of employer securities is NUA. Notice 89-25, 1989-1 C.B. 662, A-1. The employer then reports the NUA amount in Form 1099-R (2009), Box 6. So Joe (see "Joe Example," ¶ 2.5.01) will receive a 1099-R from Baby Bell for 2009, indicating a "Gross distribution" of $1 million (in Box 1), a "Taxable amount" of $100,000 (in Box 2a), and "Net unrealized appreciation" of $900,000 (in Box 6). In Box 2b, "Total distribution" will be checked.

Different plans may use different methods of determining the plan's basis. For example, one plan might use, as its basis for stock allocated to "Joe's" account, the value of the stock at the time it was placed in Joe's particular account; another plan might use the historical value of the stock at the time it was originally acquired by the plan, even if it was not allocated to any employee's account until a much later time.

Joe does not have to file any special tax form to report his receipt of NUA stock. He does *not* have to file Form 4972, which is used only by those claiming the special tax treatments for those born before 1936 (¶ 2.4.06). He simply reports the "Gross distribution" amount (from Box 1 of Form 1099-R) on line 16a of his Form 1040, and the "Taxable amount" (from Box 2a of Form 1099-R) on line 16b, as a retirement plan distribution.

2.5.03 *Distributions after the employee's death*

The favorable tax treatment of NUA also applies when employer stock is distributed to the employee's beneficiary, provided the beneficiary takes an LSD of the employee's balance. If the beneficiary takes distribution of the benefits in some form other than an LSD, then the beneficiary can exclude only the NUA attributable to stock purchased with the employee's contributions. ¶ 2.5.01.

The IRS has ruled that the NUA, like other post-death retirement plan distributions, constitutes "income in respect of a decedent" (IRD; see ¶ 4.6) under § 691. Rev. Rul. 69-297, 1969-1 C.B. 131. Accordingly, when the participant's beneficiaries sell the employer stock that is distributed to them from the plan in a qualifying distribution, the NUA portion of the sale proceeds is long-term capital gain. They will get a § 691(c) deduction (¶ 4.6.04) for the estate taxes paid on the NUA.

2.5.04 *Basis of stock distributed in life, held until death*

When the employee receives a distribution of employer stock and the NUA is excluded from his income, his basis in the stock going forward is the value that *was* taxed upon distribution, *i.e.*, the plan's original cost basis in the stock. If the employee still holds the stock at death, the IRS has ruled that such stock does *not* receive a stepped-up basis (under § 1014(c)) to the extent the employee benefitted from exclusion of NUA. According to the IRS, the NUA retains its character as NUA even after the employee's death, and will constitute IRD to the employee's heirs when they eventually sell the stock. Only to the extent, if any, that the stock appreciated in value *after* it was distributed to the employee by the plan does it receive a stepped-up basis. Rev. Rul. 75-125, 1975-1 C.B. 254.

Note: § 1014(c) does not apply for deaths in 2010; see ¶ 4.3.08.

Though Rev. Rul. 75-125 has not been revoked, the IRS may have changed its mind on this issue. One indication of this is that the IRS has allowed NUA-stock recipients to assign their stock and its NUA to charitable remainder trusts (CRTs; ¶ 7.6.04); see PLRs 1999-19039, 2000-38050, and 2002-15032. If the NUA represented unrealized income, an assignment of it should trigger income tax, but the IRS in those PLRs did not rule that assignment of NUA stock to a CRT caused realization of the underlying income by the employee-assignor. Also, in PLR 2000-38050 (eighth ruling), the IRS ruled that NUA stock contributed by the employee to a charitable remainder trust *would* get a stepped-up basis to the extent the CRT was included in the employee's estate; this directly contradicts Rev. Rul. 75-125.

NUA: Expert Tips

When first advising an employee who holds NUA stock in his retirement plan, consider consulting with a more experienced practitioner. Advisors who counsel numerous NUA stock-holding retirees often know more about the subject than the plan's own counsel and/or an auditing IRS agent. Here are some tips and war stories from three advisors who have counseled numerous employees regarding the best disposition of their NUA stock:

Mark Cortazzo, CFP, Senior Partner of MACRO Consulting Group, Parsippany, NJ, reports that each employer has its own method of calculating the "basis" of the NUA stock; the employee may be able to take advantage of his particular employer's variation to increase his NUA benefit prior to retiring. He also points out that the plan's basis may be different for different shares of employer stock held in the employee's account, and that the employee is entitled (under IRS rules) to take advantage of this (for example, by specifying which particular shares will be rolled to an IRA and which will be distributed to the employee). However, the plan's reporting to the IRS (on Form 1099-R) will not differentiate; the plan may even insist on using average basis for all the stock. So the employee may need to negotiate with the company. Mark also has found shocking mistakes by employers, such as reporting multi-year distributions as being entitled to NUA treatment even though they clearly don't qualify.

Frank Duke, CPA, of Cincinnati, OH, recommends that the employee consider rolling over stock equal in value to the plan's "basis," and not rolling stock equal in value to the NUA. Using the basis allocation method blessed by the IRS in PLR 8538062 (see ¶ 2.5.07(B)), such a partial rollover potentially maximizes the tax benefits to the employee, who can realize long-term capital gain on the NUA portion whenever he decides to sell the nonrolled stock, while deferring income tax on the ordinary income portion that is rolled over until he later takes a distribution from the IRA.

Bob Keebler, CPA, of Green Bay, WI, and his colleagues at Keebler & Associates, do extensive work with NUA-holding employees and retirees. PLR 2002-15032, involving gifting NUA stock to a charitable remainder trust, is an example of their creative planning. Much of Bob's work involves computer modeling and hedging strategies to help clients maintain their employer stock (and favorable NUA treatment) while managing the risk of a one-stock portfolio.

2.5.05 *Election to include NUA in income*

The recipient can elect *out* of the favorable tax treatment, *i.e.*, can elect to have the NUA taxed as income when the distribution is received rather than deferring tax until the stock is sold. This option could be attractive if (i) the distribution qualifies for special averaging (see ¶ 2.4.06) and (ii) the total distribution is small enough that the tax under the special averaging method is less than the capital gain tax that will otherwise eventually have to be paid. Of course this decision is based on some guesswork, since it involves comparing today's special averaging rate with tomorrow's capital gain rate.

2.5.06 *Should employee keep the LSD or roll it over?*

For most retiring employees, rolling over, to an IRA, a lump sum distribution received from an employer plan is the best tax-saving and financial planning strategy. The opportunity for continued tax-sheltered growth of retirement assets inside an IRA offers the greatest financial value for *most* retirees.

An LSD that includes appreciated employer securities often provides an exception to this rule of thumb. Since the NUA is not taxed currently anyway, rolling it over is not necessary to defer tax on the NUA. Furthermore, rolling over NUA will convert this unrealized long-term capital gain into ordinary income, since IRA distributions cannot qualify for NUA treatment. Reg. § 1.402(c)-2, A-13(a), last two sentences. So which is better, taking an LSD of NUA stock and keeping the stock outside of any plan, to take advantage of the NUA deal? Or rolling over that stock to an IRA? The answer depends on multiple factors (as well as guesswork), and no one answer is right for everyone. Factors to consider include:

✓ **How old is the employee?** If he is under 59½, the currently-taxable part of the distribution will be subject to the 10 percent penalty (see Chapter 9) unless it qualifies for an exception or unless the tax can be eliminated by a partial rollover (¶ 2.5.07(B)). Also, the younger the employee is, the more attractive continued tax deferral through a total rollover becomes, because he has many more years to go before he must start taking minimum required distributions (MRDs; see Chapter 1). If he is near or past age 70½, on the other hand, MRDs are starting or have started already, so an immediate distribution at a low tax rate becomes more attractive relative to the limited possibilities for continued deferral.

✓ **What other plans does the participant have?** If the employee has substantial assets in other retirement plans, the chance to cash out some of his benefits at a relatively low tax rate can be appealing. But if this is the employee's only retirement plan, rolling it to an IRA could be more attractive.

✓ **How much of the distribution is NUA?** If the NUA is a substantial portion of the stock's value, taking the NUA deal becomes more attractive, even irresistible. If the NUA is a small portion, rolling over becomes more attractive. Thus, the advice to a 45-year-old executive who is switching jobs, whose employer stock is only 10 percent NUA, and who needs to save for retirement, may be to roll over the entire distribution (and forfeit the NUA deal), while the advice to a 71-year-old whose stock is 90 percent NUA and who has other retirement plans that are funded beyond his likely needs would be the opposite.

2.5.07 *NUA and partial rollovers*

Although it is a requirement, when claiming special averaging (see ¶ 2.4.06), that no portion of the LSD be rolled over, and indeed that no other qualifying distribution received in the same year be rolled over, no such requirement applies to obtaining the exclusion from income of the NUA portion of an LSD. For the effect of combining an NUA distribution and a partial rollover for a year in which a minimum distribution is required, see Elizabeth Example at ¶ 2.6.03(A).

A.   **Rolling over everything except the NUA stock.** If the employee receives a distribution that (1) meets the LSD requirements (¶ 2.4.02–¶ 2.4.05) and (2) includes employer securities, the employee can exclude from his income the NUA inherent in the securities, while rolling over to an IRA the assets other than the employer securities, which otherwise would be included in gross income. See PLRs 2004-10023, 2001-38030, 2001-38031, 2000-38052, 2000-38057, 9721036. In PLR 2000-03058, this split was accomplished by direct rollover of the nonstock assets to another plan and outright distribution of the stock to the employee.

If the LSD includes other assets besides the NUA stock it is usually desirable to roll over the nonstock assets, because there is no special tax advantage to not rolling them over. The only exception would be, if the LSD also qualifies for special averaging treatment (¶ 2.4.06), the employee should evaluate whether special-averaging gives him a low enough tax rate on the LSD to make it worthwhile *not* to roll over any part of the distribution, then pay tax on the taxable portion using the special averaging method.

B.   **Rolling over part of the NUA stock.** If the employee rolls over some but not all of the employer stock, the NUA and plan's "cost basis" must be allocated, somehow, between the rolled and the nonrolled stock.

Grace Example: Grace, age 52, receives an LSD of $1 million, consisting entirely of employer stock, of which $300,000 is the plan's cost basis and $700,000 is NUA. She rolls over 30 percent of the stock to an IRA within 60 days. How are the NUA and plan-basis allocated as between the rolled and nonrolled stock? Grace would *like* to allocate all of the $700,000 of NUA to the stock that is *not* rolled over, and allocate all of the $300,000 of plan-basis to the stock that *is* rolled over to the IRA. The advantages of that allocation are: She pays no current income tax and no 10 percent "premature distributions" penalty, because the "taxable income" part of the distribution ($300,000) was entirely rolled over; she pays no current income tax on the $700,000

NUA portion (because it's NUA); and when she eventually sells the NUA stock the first $700,000 of sales proceeds will be long-term capital gain.

Grace's preferred method of allocation would be correct according to § 402(c)(2), which provides that, in the case of a distribution which is partially rolled over to an IRA, the rolled portion "shall be treated as consisting first of the portion of such distribution that is includible in gross income...". See ¶ 2.2.05(C). This interpretation was endorsed by the IRS in the well-reasoned PLR 8538062, which is the only IRS pronouncement discussing this subject. This approach is consistent with other regulations on similar subjects. See Reg. § 1.402A-1, A-5(b), dealing with a partial rollover of a nonqualified distribution from a designated Roth account (taxable portion is deemed rolled over first); and Reg. § 1.402(c)-2, A-8 (if a partially taxable distribution is received in the same year as a distribution is required under § 401(a)(9), the nontaxable portion is allocated first to the MRD, which cannot be rolled over, and the taxable portion is therefore treated as an eligible rollover distribution to the maximum extent possible). See also PLR 9840041, in which an employee took a distribution of his entire balance from an employer plan, rolled over the taxable portion of the distribution, and did not roll over the nontaxable amounts.

Another approach would be to allocate NUA and ordinary income proportionately to the rolled and nonrolled stock; this approach appears possibly to have been used in PLR 2000-38050. Later PLRs dealing with partial rollovers of NUA stock do not discuss how basis and NUA are allocated between the rolled and nonrolled shares; see, e.g., PLRs 2002-43052, 2002-15032.

A third approach would be to allocate to each share of stock (whether rolled over or not) its actual cost basis from the plan's records; see ¶ 2.5.04 ("Expert Tips").

2.6 Rollovers and Plan-to-Plan Transfers

This ¶ 2.6 explains how a participant can transfer or "roll over" assets from one of his retirement accounts to another (or "roll" a distribution back into the same plan or IRA it came out of), without having the transferred or distributed amount included in his gross income. Unless otherwise indicated, the same rules described here for tax-free rollovers also apply to Roth IRA "conversions," which are in essence "taxable rollovers" (¶ 5.4.03(A)).

This ¶ 2.6 deals primarily with rollovers and transfers by the participant. For rollovers and transfers by a surviving spouse, see also ¶ 3.2; by nonspouse beneficiaries, see ¶ 4.2.

This book deals with rollovers from the perspective of planning and compliance for the individual participant or beneficiary, and thus deals only with transfers and rollovers *to or from IRAs*. Plan administration matters, and rollovers that do not involve IRAs, are not covered; see instead *The Pension Answer Book* (Appendix C).

2.6.01 *Definitions: rollovers, trustee-to-trustee transfers, etc.*

Rollovers and trustee-to-trustee transfers are both ways to move assets from one retirement plan to another. A rollover can also be a way to money assets out of a plan and then back in to the same plan. Beyond that, it is difficult to define these terms because they overlap.

A. **Background: Rollover vs. trustee-to-trustee transfer.** In dealing with "rollovers" and "transfers" from one plan to another, we are dealing with an evolving and confusing terminology.

A "rollover" originally meant the distribution of funds out of one retirement plan to the participant or surviving spouse, followed by the recipient's redepositing all or part of that distribution into the same or a different retirement plan—but now we also have "direct rollovers" (see "C") where the money passes directly from a nonIRA plan to an IRA, without spending any time in a "taxable account."

At one time, a "rollover" always meant a "tax-free rollover"—but now we also have taxable rollovers (called "Roth conversions"; ¶ 5.4.03, ¶ 5.4.04).

A "trustee-to-trustee transfer" once meant the transfer of funds directly from one IRA to another IRA of the same participant (or beneficiary), an approach that avoided many of the rules applicable to "rollovers" (see ¶ 2.6.08); but now we also have trustee-to-trustee transfers from a nonIRA plan to an IRA (direct rollover; see "C"), and these *are* subject to certain "rollover" rules, as well as IRA-to-IRA transfers that are both taxable and subject to (some of) the rollover rules (Roth conversions; see ¶ 5.4.03).

B.   **Definition of "rollover" and "rollover contribution."** Generally, a retirement plan distribution is not included in anyone's gross income if the distribution is "rolled over" to the same or a different "eligible" retirement plan or IRA, if various requirements are met. § 402(c)(1), § 408(d)(3). If the **rollover** meets all the requirements, but the recipient account is a *Roth IRA*, the rollover (Roth conversion) is a valid rollover but it is *taxable*; see ¶ 5.4.03, ¶ 5.4.04. For the requirements of a valid rollover, see ¶ 2.6.02–¶ 2.6.06. For ways to avoid these requirements, see ¶ 2.6.07–¶ 2.6.08. There are two ways to accomplish a rollover; see "C" and "D."

A "**rollover contribution**" is a contribution that comes into a retirement plan account by means of a direct rollover (see "C") or indirect or 60-day rollover (see "D"). A contribution that is not a rollover contribution is called a "regular contribution" (see ¶ 5.3.02).

C.   **Direct rollovers.** A direct rollover is one particular kind of trustee-to-trustee transfer. It is the transfer of assets directly from the participant's account in a qualified retirement plan (QRP), 403(b) plan, or governmental 457(b) plan ("nonIRA plan") to an account for the benefit of such person in a traditional or Roth IRA or in another eligible plan nonIRA plan. A direct rollover may be carried out for the benefit of the participant (upon retirement, for example) or for the benefit of the Designated Beneficiary (if the participant is deceased). A direct rollover of nonIRA plan benefits of a nonspouse Designated Beneficiary can be made only to an IRA or Roth IRA, not any other type of plan; see ¶ 4.2.04. The Code calls this a **direct trustee-to-trustee transfer**. § 401(a)(31)(A)(ii). The IRS (and this book) call it a **direct rollover**. See, *e.g.*, Reg. § 1.401(a)(31)-1.

Generally, when a plan is about to make an "eligible rollover distribution" to the participant, surviving spouse (¶ 3.2.02), or Designated Beneficiary (see ¶ 4.2.04(H)), the plan MUST offer the recipient the option of having the distribution sent, via direct rollover, to any eligible retirement plan (which includes a Roth IRA) and MUST comply with the employee's request for such a direct rollover. § 401(a)(31); Notice 2008-30, 2008-12 IRB 638, A-4. (There are exceptions for certain small distributions and multiple distributions.)

A direct rollover is considered to be a distribution followed by a rollover, which may mean spousal consent is required (see ¶ 3.4.02). Reg. § 1.401(a)(31)-1, A-15.

The plan *may* allow the recipient to have direct rollover of the distributions into multiple "destination" IRAs (*e.g.*, a traditional and a Roth); however, the plan is not *required* to offer that option. All that the plan is *required* to offer with respect to any one distribution is a menu of three choices: 1. Outright distribution of the entire amount; 2. Direct rollover of the entire amount to a single IRA; or 3. Partial outright distribution to the recipient with the balance directly rolled over to a single IRA. Reg. § 1.401(a)(31)-1, A-10. Since distribution of an eligible rollover distribution *to the recipient* will trigger mandatory withholding (¶ 2.3.02(C)), the plan could be "forced" to write up to three checks (one to an eligible plan as a direct rollover, one to the distributee, and one to the IRS).

D.   **Definition of "60-day" (indirect) rollover.** The IRS calls a distribution from a plan or IRA to the participant (or his surviving spouse), followed by the participant's (or spouse's) redepositing the distributed amount into the same or another plan or IRA a **60-day rollover** (because of the deadline normally applicable for completing the rollover; see ¶ 2.6.06); Reg. § 1.402A-1, A-5(a); or **indirect rollover** (see, *e.g.*, Reg. § 1.402A-1, A-4(b)).

E.   **Trustee-to-trustee transfer.** In a trustee-to-trustee transfer, assets are moved directly from one tax-favored retirement plan into another such plan, without the intervening step of being distributed "to" the participant or beneficiary. The distribution check is payable to the receiving plan, not to the participant or beneficiary; the funds spend no time in a taxable account. This book deals with only certain types of trustee-to-trustee transfers: Transfers from one IRA directly into another IRA in the name of the same participant or beneficiary (see ¶ 2.6.08, ¶ 4.2.02(B)) (usually called, in this book, **IRA-to-IRA transfers**); Roth conversions (¶ 5.4.07, #2); recharacterizations (¶ 5.6.03,#1); and **direct rollovers** (see "C" above). Transfers directly from one nonIRA plan to another nonIRA plan are beyond the scope of this book.

2.6.02 *Distributions that can (or can't) be rolled over*

Any distribution from a QRP, IRA, or 403(b) plan may be rolled over except those listed in A–G below. If income taxes have been withheld (¶ 2.3) from an **eligible rollover distribution** the participant or surviving spouse can nevertheless roll over the withheld amount by substituting other funds. Reg. § 1.402(c)-2, A-11; see PLR 2003-44024.

Before 2002, money could be rolled from a traditional IRA to a QRP or 403(b) plan only if the traditional IRA contained no contributions other than one or more distributions rolled from the same or another QRP or 403(b) plan, so-called "conduit IRAs." See § 408(d)(3)(A)(ii)–(iii), prior to repeal by EGTRRA, and Reg. § 1.408(b)(2), which is now obsolete. Now, pretax (but not after-tax; ¶ 2.2.09(A)) money can be rolled from *any* IRA "upstream" to a QRP.

Here is a list of the distributions that may NOT be rolled over:

A.   **Inherited plans.** A distribution from an inherited retirement plan may not be rolled over to the beneficiary's *own* plan by any beneficiary other than the participant's surviving spouse. For more on that rule, and the ability of a nonspouse Designated Beneficiary to transfer inherited nonIRA plan benefits via direct rollover to an "inherited" IRA, see ¶ 4.2.04. For the ability of the surviving spouse to roll over benefits paid to her, see ¶ 3.2.

B.   **MRD.** A minimum required distribution (MRD; Chapter 1) cannot be rolled over. See ¶ 2.6.03.

C.   **Series payments.** "[A]ny distribution which is one of a series of substantially equal periodic payments" made annually or more often (1) over the life or life expectancy of the participant, (2) over the joint life or life expectancy of the participant and a designated beneficiary, or (3) over a "specified period of 10 years or more" may not be rolled over. § 402(c)(4)(A). Reg. § 1.402(c)-2, A-5, explains how to determine whether a distribution is part of a series of substantially equal payments.

D.   **Corrective and deemed distributions.** Certain corrective or "deemed" distributions cannot be rolled over. See Reg. § 1.402(c)-2, A-4, for list.

E.   **Hardship distributions.** Hardship distributions cannot be rolled over. § 402(c)(4).

F.   **12-month limitation on IRA rollovers.** See ¶ 2.6.05 for a limit on the number of IRA distributions that may be rolled to another IRA within 12 months.

G.   **Plan loans.** A plan loan that is deemed distributed under § 72(p) (because the loan does not conform with the plan-loan rules) is not an eligible rollover distribution. A "plan loan offset" distribution (when the plan pays itself back out of the participant's account) *is* an eligible rollover distribution. See ¶ 2.1.07.

H.   **After-tax money.** Both pre- and after-tax money may be rolled over from a QRP to a traditional IRA; see ¶ 2.2.05(C). (Reg. § 1.402(c)-2, A-3, which provides to the contrary, has not been amended to reflect this 2001 law change.) However, after-tax money may *not* be rolled in the other direction (from an IRA to a QRP). § 408(d)(3)(A)(ii) generally allows rollovers from any traditional IRA to any other type of plan in years after 2001, but if the rollover is made from an IRA into a QRP, 403(a) or 403(b) plan, or 457 plan, only the *pretax* money in the traditional IRA may be rolled. § 402(c)(8)(B)(iii), (iv), (v), (vi).

2.6.03 *Rollover in a year in which a distribution is required*

A minimum required distribution (MRD) cannot be rolled over. § 402(c)(4)(B), § 403(b)(8)(A)(i), § 408(d)(3)(E). The following persons must navigate the traps described in A–E below:

✓   A participant who is seeking to roll over a distribution from his own plan or IRA.

✓   A surviving spouse seeking to do a rollover of benefits inherited from the deceased spouse. ¶ 3.2.

✓   A nonspouse Designated Beneficiary seeking to have benefits transferred from an inherited nonIRA plan to an inherited IRA (¶ 4.2.04).

✓   A participant, surviving spouse, or Designated Beneficiary seeking to do a Roth conversion of traditional benefits. See ¶ 5.2.02(E).

A.   **Everybody: First distribution of the year is the MRD.** The first "trap" is that *the first distribution received in any year* for which a distribution is required (Distribution Year) is considered part of the MRD for that year and thus cannot be rolled over. Reg. § 1.402(c)-2, A-7(a), § 1.408-8, A-4.

Elizabeth Example: Elizabeth, who retired several years ago, turned 70½ in Year 1, so her RBD is April 1, Year 2. Her 401(k) plan with her former employer contains $1 million of employer stock (with basis of $200,000 and NUA (¶ 2.5) of $800,000), plus $500,000 of cash. It is now February, Year 2, and Elizabeth, after consulting with several financial, tax, and estate planning advisors, has decided: to take an LSD in Year 2; keep the NUA stock in her own name (then later selling some of it or giving some to charity); and roll over the $500,000 of cash to her IRA. She wants the stock distribution in Year 2 to satisfy her combined MRD requirement for the 401(k) plan for both Year 1 and Year 2 (which is about $120,000). To make sure this happens, she takes a distribution of all of the NUA stock FIRST, in March, Year 2. Only AFTER that stock has been distributed to her does she request a direct rollover of the cash to her IRA (which of course must be completed by December 31, Year 2, in order to have an "LSD"; ¶ 2.4.04). If she had requested the rollover *first*, the plan would have had to distribute her MRDs to her from the cash fund before it could do a direct rollover of the rest; Elizabeth would then have received a nonrollable MRD in cash, and she would IN ADDITION have to pay tax on the basis portion of the NUA stock when that was distributed later in Year 2.

B.   **Everybody: Missed MRDs from prior years.** The last sentence of Reg. § 1.402(c)-2, A-7(a), indicates that any MRDs not taken in a prior year are not eligible to be rolled over in a later year.

C.   **Participant only: Plan can assume there is no DB.** The plan is not required to take into account whether a participant's Designated Beneficiary is his more-than-10-years-younger spouse (¶ 1.3.03). For purposes of computing the portion of any distribution that will be treated as "nonrollable" because it is an MRD (and as therefore not subject to mandatory 20 percent withholding applicable to "eligible rollover distributions"), the plan is entitled to assume that the participant has no Designated Beneficiary (and therefore to distribute to the participant an "MRD" computed using the Uniform Lifetime Table rather than the joint life expectancy of the participant and spouse). Reg. § 1.401(a)(31)-1, A-18(c); § 31.3405(c)-1, A-10. The participant can roll over the portion of such distribution that is in excess of the "true" MRD. Reg. § 1.401(c)-2, A-15.

D.   **Participant only: Rollovers in the age-70½ year.** Another "trap" is that the participant's first Distribution Year is not the year in which the required beginning date (RBD; ¶ 1.4) occurs; it is the year *before* the RBD. The first Distribution Year is the year the participant reaches age 70½ (or, in some cases, retires), even though the first MRD does not have to be taken until April 1 of the *following* year. Accordingly, any distribution received by the participant on or after January 1 of the first Distribution Year will be considered part of the MRD for that year, and thus cannot be rolled over. Reg. § 1.402(c)-2, A-7(a), (b). For similar problems facing Roth IRA converters, see ¶ 5.2.02(E), ¶ 5.4.02(A).

Leonard Example: Leonard turns 70½ on January 1, Year 1. On that date, he retires from his job at XYZ Corp. and asks the plan administrator of the XYZ retirement plan to send his benefits to his IRA in a direct rollover. The administrator replies that it will make a direct rollover of everything except the MRD for Year 1. Leonard is unhappy because he thought he could postpone all MRDs until his RBD in Year 2. Unfortunately for Leonard, if he insists on not taking any MRD in Year 1, then he also cannot do a rollover in Year 1. A direct rollover IS considered a "distribution" for purposes of the rule that MRDs cannot be rolled over, even though a direct rollover is NOT considered a distribution for income tax or withholding purposes! Note that if Leonard dies before April 1 of Year 2, and before removing his benefits from the retirement plan, his surviving spouse (¶ 3.2) or nonspouse Designated Beneficiary (¶ 4.2.04) could roll over Leonard's entire account balance, because death before the RBD simply "erases" the MRD for both the first and second distribution years. ¶ 1.4.07(C).

E.   **Beneficiaries only: Rollover and the 5-year rule.** If the 5-year rule (¶ 1.5.06–¶ 1.5.07) applies,100 percent of the remaining account balance becomes the "MRD" in the year that contains the fifth anniversary of the participant's death (or sixth anniversary, in the case of deaths in 2004–2009), and thus there can be no rollover in that year. However, no amount distributed prior to that year is considered an MRD, and thus there is no MRD-based restriction on rolling over distributions made prior to that year. Reg. § 54.4974-2, A-3(c); Notice 2007-7, 2007-5 I.R.B. 395, A-17(b).

F.   **Exceptions to the no-rollover-of-MRDs rule.** There are three quasi-exceptions to the no-rollover-of-MRD rule: One is when a plan has an earlier required beginning date than the statute requires; see ¶ 1.4.04. The second occurs when a surviving spouse who is named as sole beneficiary of an IRA is deemed to have elected to treat it as her own because of her failure to take an MRD as beneficiary; this rule in effect allows her to roll over that MRD in certain cases. See ¶ 3.2.03(D)(3), ¶ 3.2.06, ¶ 1.6.04. Finally, it was possible to roll over certain MRDs under transition rules when the final minimum distribution regulations were coming into effect.

2.6.04 60-day rollover: Must roll over same property received

A rollover cannot be used to "swap" property out of a retirement plan.

If property is distributed to a participant or surviving spouse from a QRP, and the recipient wants the distribution to be treated as a tax-free rollover to another plan or IRA (or as a valid conversion to a Roth IRA), the same property that was received from the first plan must be contributed to the recipient plan, IRA, or Roth IRA. § 402(c)(1)(C). The participant (or surviving spouse) cannot simply substitute some other asset of equal value; if he still owns the property that was distributed from the first plan, that is what must be contributed to the same or another plan to have a tax-free rollover (or valid Roth conversion as the case may be). Rev. Rul. 87-77, 1987-2 C.B. 115. The only exception is that if the participant (or surviving spouse) sells the property after receiving it from the first plan, the *sales proceeds* are rolled over rather than the property itself; no income is reportable as a result of the sale (because it is treated as if it had occurred inside a retirement plan). § 402(c)(6).

The Code does not authorize selling distributed property and rolling over the sale proceeds in connection with rollovers of IRA distributions; it blesses only rollovers of the "amount received (including money or other property)." § 408(d)(3)(A).

2.6.05 60-day rollovers: Only one IRA-to-IRA rollover in 12 months

A participant or surviving spouse may not roll over an IRA distribution to the same or another IRA "if at any time during the 1-year period ending on the day of...[the receipt of the distribution] such individual received any other amount...from an individual retirement account...which was not includible in his gross income because" it was a tax-free rollover to an IRA. § 408(d)(3)(B).

A.　　**How rule applies to multiple IRAs.** Under the statute, it appears that the tax-free rollover of a distribution from *any* IRA into the same or any other IRA prevents the tax-free rollover of any *other* IRA distribution that is received less than 12 months after the first distribution—regardless of which IRA the second distribution came from. However, the IRS applies the rule on an account-by-account basis. Once you have rolled over tax-free a distribution from one IRA (IRA #1) into another IRA (IRA #2), you cannot, within 12 months after the date of the distribution that was rolled over, do an IRA-to-IRA rollover of any *other* distribution from either of the two IRAs involved in the first rollover. IRS Publication 590 (2009), p. 24. However, you may (within that 12-month period) roll over a distribution from an IRA that was *not* involved in the first rollover.

For better or worse, this rule is easy to avoid with careful planning. It appears that if the participant divides his large IRA into many smaller IRAs he can then take a series of "60-day loans" from these respective IRAs, as long as he never takes a to-be-rolled distribution from any IRA that either distributed or received a rolled-over distribution within the preceding 12 months.

If the participant did not set up multiple IRAs in advance of doing his first distribution/rollover, some have asked whether the rule can be avoided by (1) doing an IRA-to-IRA transfer (¶ 2.6.01(E)) from an IRA that was "tainted" by being involved in the prior distribution and rollover to a brand new, "untainted" IRA, and then (2) doing the second distribution/rollover within 12 months from this new untainted IRA. There is no specific guidance on the point. It does not appear advisable to "push the envelope" like this. Since 1978, the IRS has been very generous in allowing the use of IRA-to-IRA transfers to finesse various rollover requirements including the once-per-year rule. At the same time, the IRS is understandably hostile to efforts to use the IRA as a source of short-term financing through a series of 60-day rollovers. The result of such an end run could be taxable income (and possibly penalties) for the client and possibly stricter rules for everybody else.

B. **Not a calendar year test.** The no-rollover period is twelve months from the date of receipt of the first distribution. Thus it is always necessary to look back into the prior calendar year, as well as to the current calendar year, in determining whether there has been a prior rolled-over distribution that would prevent the rollover of a second distribution.

C. **Distribution dates count, not rollover dates.** The rule prevents tax-free rollover of a *distribution* that occurs within 12 months of a prior *distribution* that was rolled over. Thus, if Distribution #2 is received less than 12 months after Distribution #1, waiting until 12 months have elapsed since the prior *rollover* does *not* cure the problem. Similarly, there is no prohibition against two tax-free rollovers within 12 months of each other, provided that the *distributions being rolled over* did not occur within 12 months of each other.

Barak Example: Barak received Distribution #1 from IRA "A" on January 2, Year 1, and rolled it into IRA "B" on February 28, Year 1. He received Distribution # 2 from IRA "A" on January 5, Year 2, and rolled it into IRA "B" on February 1, Year 2. Both distributions are tax-free: even though the second rollover occurred less than 12 months after the first rollover, the second *distribution* did not occur within one year of the first *distribution*.

D. **Exceptions to the one-per-12-months rule.** Neither a Roth conversion (¶ 5.4.07), nor the "recharacterization" of an IRA or Roth IRA contribution (¶ 5.6.03, #5), is treated as either a distribution or a rollover for purposes of this rule. For another exception to the one-per-year limit rule (for thwarted would-be first-time home buyers), see ¶ 2.6.06(A). There is an exception for distributions from a failed financial institution; see IRS Publication 590 (2009), p. 24.

The limit of one IRA-to-IRA rollover per year has no application to a direct transfer of funds or property from one IRA custodian to another IRA custodian (IRA-to-IRA transfer; see ¶ 2.6.08). In most cases, concerns about § 408(d)(3)(B) can be easily avoided by using an IRA-to-IRA transfer rather than a rollover.

§ 408(d)(3)(B) prevents the rollover into an IRA of a second distribution within 12 months from an IRA; it does not prevent a rollover of such a second IRA distribution into *some other kind of eligible retirement plan*, nor does it prevent multiple tax-free rollovers *into* an IRA from some other type of plan. Thus it would appear easy to avoid § 408(d)(3)(B) by rolling the second IRA distribution first into a QRP and then rolling it out again to another IRA shortly thereafter.

E.   Taxpayer cannot later choose which rollover is tax-free.

Yoav Example: In July, Yoav withdraws $60,000 from IRA #1, intending to roll it over tax-free to another IRA. Then he remembers that in April of the same year he received, and rolled over to IRA #2, a $1,000 distribution from IRA #1. He would rather pay tax on the $1,000 distribution he received in April than on the $60,000 distribution he received in July. He now wishes that he had said the $1,000 contribution to IRA #2 in April was part of his "regular" IRA contribution for the year, not a rollover of the distribution from IRA #1. Unfortunately, he can not now retroactively elect to treat the $1,000 he deposited in IRA #2 in April as a regular rather than a rollover contribution. In order for a contribution to qualify as a tax-free rollover the participant must elect, "*at the time the contribution is made*, to treat the contribution as a rollover contribution....This election is irrevocable." Reg. § 1.402(c)-2, A-13. Thus, when Yoav made his $1,000 contribution to IRA B in April he was required to irrevocably designate it either as a rollover or a regular contribution. If he said it was a rollover contribution when he made it, he cannot retroactively change that election.

2.6.06 60-day rollover deadline; exceptions and blanket waivers

A rollover *generally* must be completed no later than "the 60th day following the day on which the distributee received the property distributed." § 402(c)(3)(A); § 408(d)(3)(A). See also ¶ 2.1.03 regarding how this period is measured.

Unlike the due date for tax returns, the 60-day deadline is apparently not eligible for the automatic extension of time (under § 7503) to the next business day if the 60th day falls on a weekend or holiday. The IRS has granted hardship waivers of the deadline (¶ 2.6.07) in several cases where the deadline fell on a weekend or other "bank holiday." See PLRs 2006-06055, 2009-30052, 2009-51044, 2009-52066, and 2010-39041.

The deadline is 60 days, not two months. A distribution made on March 12th must be rolled over by May 11th; May 12th is too late. PLR 2005-23032.

There are several exceptions to the 60-day deadline. The most significant one is that an individual may seek a "hardship waiver" of the deadline; see ¶ 2.6.07. Here are other less commonly seen exceptions:

A. **First-time homebuyer.** There is a 120-day deadline rather than a 60-day deadline for the rollover of a "first-time homebuyer" distribution (¶ 9.4.09) if the distribution is not used to purchase the residence "solely by reason of a delay or cancellation of the purchase or construction of the residence." The recontribution of the thwarted homebuyer distribution is also not treated as a rollover for purposes of the once-per-12-months rule (¶ 2.6.05).§ 72(t)(8)(E); PLR 2004-23033.

B. **Disaster-based extensions.** The IRS tends to grant blanket extensions for this and other tax deadlines in the case of certain federally-recognized disasters. See the IRS pronouncement applicable to the disaster in question (*e.g.*, IRS News Release IR-2004-115 extending deadlines for taxpayers affect by Hurricane Frances).

C. **Qualified reservist distribution.** A qualified reservist distribution (QRD; ¶ 9.4.12) may be "rolled into" (i.e., contributed to) an IRA or Roth IRA at any time during the *two-year period* that begins on the day after the end of the active duty period. § 72(t)(2)(G). The rollover contribution of a QRD does not erase the taxable income that resulted from the original distribution. The only advantage of this type of rollover is that (if the reservist has enough cash to replace the money he withdrew during his active duty service) this provision enables him to replace the funds in his plan without regard to the normal limits on IRA contributions (¶ 5.3.03). Since there is no tax deduction allowed for the contribution, it is advisable to make the contribution to a Roth IRA, so future earnings on the contribution will be tax-free. The "rollover" is reported on Form 8606 as a nondeductible contribution to an IRA.

D.   **Automatic waiver for certain financial institution errors.** The deadline is *automatically* waived in the following circumstances: The participant received a distribution after 2001, and (within the 60-day limit) transmitted the funds to a financial institution and did everything else required (under the financial institution's procedures) to deposit the funds in an eligible retirement plan, but "solely due to an error on the part of the financial institution" the funds were not deposited into the eligible retirement plan within 60 days of the original distribution. Provided the funds are deposited in the eligible plan within one year of the original distribution, there is an automatic waiver of the rollover deadline, and no need to seek IRS approval. Rev. Proc. 2003-16 (see ¶ 2.6.07).

E.   **Frozen deposits.** What if the participant receives a distribution and deposits the money in a bank, and then the bank becomes insolvent so the participant can't get his money out in time to complete the rollover? The 60-day period does not include the time during which the money is "frozen," or end until at least 10 days after the money becomes "unfrozen." § 402(c)(7)(B), § 408(d)(3)(F).

2.6.07 *Hardship waiver of 60-day rollover deadline*

The IRS "may waive the 60-day requirement…where the failure to waive such requirement would be against equity or good conscience, including casualty, disaster, or other events beyond the reasonable control of the individual subject to such requirement." § 402(c)(3)(B); § 408(d)(3)(I) (effective for distributions after 2001). In Rev. Proc.

2003-16, 2003-1 C.B. 359, the IRS issued the following guidance for such hardship waivers; see also ¶ 2.6.06(D).

A.   **Procedure to request a waiver.** A participant or surviving spouse can request a hardship waiver of the rollover deadline by following the usual procedures for obtaining a private letter ruling.

Although the legislative history of EGTRRA indicates that Congress wanted the IRS to issue "objective standards" for granting hardship waivers of the 60-day deadline, the Rev. Proc. says only that the IRS will consider "all relevant facts and circumstances," such as "death, disability, hospitalization, incarceration, restrictions imposed by a foreign country or postal error;...the use of the amount distributed (for example...whether the check was cashed); and...the time elapsed since the distribution occurred."

Obtaining an IRS letter ruling requires payment of a "user fee" (filing fee). Under Rev. Proc. 2010-8, 2010-1 IRB 234, § 6.01(4), (14), requests for hardship waivers of the 60-day rollover deadline have their own user fee schedule, which is:

If the rollover is less than $50,000:	$ 500.
If the rollover is $50,000 or more, but less than $100,000:	$1,500.
If the rollover is $100,000 or more:	$3,000.

The next user fee schedule will be issued in Rev. Proc. 2011-8, in early 2011.

B.   **Earnings and MRDs during the out-of-plan gap period.** Getting a hardship waiver does not solve all the problems. For example, see the problem of designating a beneficiary for an IRA established by the participant's executor to receive a late rollover of a distribution made during the participant's life, ¶ 4.1.04(B).

Also, all that can be rolled over is the amount of the distribution, not any income earned on that distribution during the period of time the money was outside the IRA—regardless of how long that was, and regardless of what hardship prevented the participant from completing the rollover on a timely basis. Rev. Proc. 2003-16, § 3.04.

Another problem with long-delayed rollovers is what to do about minimum required distributions (MRDs; see Chapter 1) that would otherwise have accrued in the meantime. The waiver rulings typically specify that interim MRDs cannot be rolled over despite the extension (see ¶ 2.6.03) but do not specify how that nonrollable amount is to be determined.

Polly Example: Polly suffered from a mental disability in 2007, when she was age 69, and she cashed out her entire $500,000 IRA. She did not have the mental capacity to know what she was doing. In 2008, the year she reached age 70½, she was placed under guardianship and the guardian applied for a waiver of the 60-day deadline to allow the $500,000 distribution to be recontributed to the IRA. The waiver is granted by the IRS in 2009; the waiver specifies that any MRD cannot be rolled over. But there was no MRD for the year that the distribution came out of the IRA, in 2007, because Polly was only 69 years old. An MRD *would have accrued* in 2008 and 2009 if the money had still been in the IRA, but there was no "prior year-end balance" for either year because the account didn't exist. Accordingly it would appear that the guardian can roll over the entire $500,000 in 2009 and start taking MRDs in 2010. This does not "cheat" the IRS too much because Polly was taxable in 2008 and 2009 on the income earned by the $500,000 distribution outside the IRA (and she is not allowed to roll over that income "as if" it had been earned inside an IRA). There is no IRS guidance either confirming or denying the above conclusions.

C.   **Typical grounds for granting waiver: FI or FA error, illness, etc.** Following issuance of Rev. Proc. 2003-16, the IRS began issuing a flood of private letter rulings dealing with these deadline waiver requests. Most successful waiver requests involve one or more of the following situations:

Error by a financial advisor (FA) or financial institution (FI) is by far the most common reason for obtaining a deadline waiver, accounting for an estimated half of all requests. The "good" news is that the IRS *always* grants the waiver when the participant missed the deadline due to a processing error by an FI or FA. Generally the IRS seems to require the FI or FA to admit the mistake in writing. Typical are rulings in which the participant's new financial advisor or institution inadvertently established a regular taxable account instead of an IRA with funds transferred from prior advisor or institution, such as PLRs 2004-02028, 2004-04053, 2004-01023, 2004-20035, 2009-51040, 2010-14073. If the professional error involved erroneous tax advice rather than a straight processing error, the standards are a little tougher. If the advisor gave erroneous advice *about the rollover requirements* (such as telling the participant that the deadline is 90 days not 60 days), the IRS will generally grant the waiver; regarding other erroneous tax advice, see "E."

Distribution not requested. In many successful waiver requests, the original distribution was "involuntary," in that the participant hadn't requested it and often did not even realize it had occurred, or the participant was mentally incompetent to understand the consequences of withdrawing the funds. See PLRs 2004-21009, 2004-21008, 2004-27027, 2004-35017, 2004-36014, 2010-15040, 2010-16093.

Health problems, trauma: Many successful waiver requests involved participants who were hampered from initiating and/or completing the rollover by significant mental or physical health problems (of themselves or family members), a death in the immediate family, or other catastrophes. See PLRs 2004-30039, 2004-30040, 2004-36021, 2004-04051, 2004-12002, 2004-26020, 2004-30037, 2004-30038, 2004-36021, 2009-36048, 2010-15042, 2010-05059.

The waiver can be granted long after the original distribution. See PLRs 2003-27064 (rollover allowed more than a year after funds were stolen from IRA; loss had not been discovered immediately) and 2007-05031 (rollover allowed in 2005 of a "restorative payment" replacing losses incurred due to defalcations by the advisor in the years 2000–2004; see ¶ 8.1.03).

D.   **Typical grounds for denying waiver: Participant spent funds, etc.** The IRS is most likely to refuse a waiver when the taxpayer deliberately took the distribution (e.g., to qualify for Medicaid, PLR 2005-47024, or to pay medical expenses, PLR 2005-49023, or to complete a house closing, PLR 2005-44025); and/or showed no evidence of intent to roll it over until after the 60-day deadline (typically, when he discovers it is taxable; PLR 2005-46047, 2005-48030, 2005-49017, 2004-33029, 2004-22058); or he deliberately took it, intending to spend it and then replace the funds with other funds, but he did not receive the replacement funds in time to meet the 60-day deadline (PLRs

2004-17033, 2004-22053, 2004-23038, 2004-33022, 2004-36018, 2005-44025).

However, even if the participant did deliberately use his IRA as a "source of short-term financing," the IRS will grant the waiver if the participant had the replacement funds, and sent them in to the IRA provider, within the 60-day time limit, if the deadline was then missed due to financial institution error or other cause beyond the participant's control. See, *e.g.,* PLR 2010-16092.

E.   **Evolving and inconsistent IRS standards.** The IRS has grown more restrictive over the years when it comes to granting hardship waivers. In the early days some waiver requests were granted where the taxpayer really didn't have much of an excuse (e.g., taxpayer waited until the 58th day, then found the bank was closed for a long holiday weekend so she couldn't deposit the check; PLR 2004-11052).

More recently, the IRS has denied waivers for such "flimsy" excuses as: participant was busy getting ready to go on vacation (2007-30024); minor surgery (2007-51032); participant's father's cancer and death (2008-29030); participant's sibling's financial crisis (2010-02049); and participant's lack of a college education and lack of knowledge of legal, accounting, or tax matters (2010-03030).

The worst thing about the IRS's "evolving" standards is that the IRS is not consistent. The IRS has taken to reciting a mantra in the PLRs where it denies the waiver: A waiver will be granted *only* if the deadline was missed because of one of the factors listed in Rev. Proc. 2003-16. See, *e.g.*, PLRs 2007-27023, 2007-30023, 2010-15039. Yet this pious recital is absent in many PLRs which *do* grant a waiver, because the IRS regularly grants waivers when the ability to meet the rollover deadline was completely within the participant's control at all times and no factor listed in the Rev. Proc. existed; see, *e.g.*, PLRs 2006-06055, 2009-30052, 2009-51044, and 2009-52066 (waiver granted because the final day of the 60-day period fell on a bank holiday); PLRs 2007-15016 (participant received two distributions when he had requested one; he was granted a waiver despite no mention of any illness or other problem that prevented him from noticing the double distribution or rolling it over); and 2007-08085, 2007-26031.

Another inconsistency has to do with reliance on tax advice of a professional advisor. Sometimes erroneous tax advice is grounds for granting a waiver...and sometimes it isn't. In PLR 2006-17039, the IRS *refused* a waiver where a participant took a distribution of employer stock from his company plan, not intending to roll it over because his advisor told him the distribution qualified for NUA treatment (see ¶ 2.5). After the 60-day rollover deadline had passed, he found out the distribution did *not* qualify for NUA treatment. Says the IRS "We do not believe that Congress intended to permit the Service to retroactively correct tax treatment choices which do not produce the expected benefits even though...these choices were the result of erroneous advice" by the financial consultant. But in PLRs 2006-09019 and 2009-25047 the IRS *granted* waivers to widows who were told (incorrectly) by their advisors that distributions from their deceased husband's retirement plans were tax-free. What's the difference? The IRS mentions the widow's depression in PLR 2009-25047; is the IRS saying that it is reasonable to rely on professional tax advice only if you are mentally ill?

The most insidious trend in IRS waivers is that they will not grant the waiver if the *taxpayer himself* made a mistake that caused the rollover deadline to be missed (and the taxpayer was not incapacitated). For example, an individual who clearly requested a direct rollover to an IRA, but wrote the wrong account number on his form, so the money went into a taxable account by mistake, and nobody noticed the mistake until after the deadline had passed—the IRS did not grant a waiver, because they said the ability to complete the rollover was within his control at all times. See PLRs 2010-02049, 2010-03030, 2010-06035, 2010-07080, 2010-15039, and 2010-37038 for other examples of this trend.

The tragedy is that, in most of these hardship waiver-seeking cases, if the participant had just read his account statements when they came in, he would have discovered the mistake immediately and been able to fix it within 60 days.

2.6.08 *Avoid some rollover requirements with IRA-to-IRA transfer*

Some of the technical rules that apply to *rollovers* do not apply to *IRA-to-IRA* transfers (see ¶ 2.6.01(E) for definition).

✓   IRA-to-IRA transfers are not considered to be distributions from the transferor IRA, nor are they considered "contributions" or "rollovers" to the recipient IRA for IRS reporting purposes. PLR 2005-28031; Instructions for IRS Forms 1099-R and 5498 (2010), pp. 5, 14.

✓   The participant can do an IRA-to-IRA transfer in a year in which an MRD is required even before taking the MRD; the transferring IRA is not required to either pay out or hold back the MRD for the year, according to the Preamble to IRS final minimum distribution regulations, T.D. 8987, 67 FR 18987, 4/17/02 ("Other Rules for IRAs").

✓   An IRA-to-IRA transfer is not considered a rollover for purposes of the limit of one IRA-to-IRA rollover per 12 months (¶ 2.6.05). Rev. Rul. 78-406, 1978-2 C.B. 157.

✓   Since, in an IRA-to-IRA transfer, money is never distributed out of the IRA environment there is no 60-day deadline (¶ 2.6.06) to contend with, even if the check does not reach the recipient IRA within 60 days after being sent out from the transmitting IRA. See ¶ 2.1.03(A).

✓   Funds can be transferred via IRA-to-IRA transfer from one inherited IRA to another, even though distributions from an inherited IRA cannot be "rolled over." See ¶ 4.2.02(A), (B).

Note that a transfer from a traditional IRA to a *Roth* IRA must meet some requirements of a "rollover," even if it is carried out by means of an trustee-to-trustee transfer, according to Reg. § 1.408A-4, A-1—including the rules prohibiting the rollover of an MRD (see ¶ 5.2.02(E)) or of a distribution from an inherited IRA (¶ 4.2.05(A)).

2.7 Retiree Road Map

This road map is primarily for use when you are advising the individual who has money in a QRP, 403(b) plan, or IRA and who is planning to retire, or whose employment with the plan sponsor is ending for any reason. It also covers income tax issues continually faced by all IRA or plan participants, both during employment and after retirement, as well as tips for a successful rollover.

2.7.01 *Plan-related issues to discuss with your client*

Does your client have any of the following special situations involved in his/her employer's retirement plan?

Plan loan outstanding? See ¶ 2.1.07.

Appreciated employer stock owned in the plan, or that could be purchased in the employee's plan account? See ¶ 2.5. Anyone advising an employee (or the beneficiaries of a deceased employee) whose QRP account holds (or could purchase) employer stock MUST impress on the client the importance of considering the favorable NUA deal before the client does any of the following: sells the stock inside the plan; retires; takes a distribution from the plan; or rolls over anything from the plan to another plan or IRA.

Was your client born before January 2, 1936? See ¶ 2.4.06. Anyone advising a QRP participant (or the beneficiaries of a deceased QRP participant) who was born before January 2, 1936, should impress on the client the importance of considering the favorable special averaging deal before the client takes a distribution from the plan or (in the case of the participant or surviving spouse) rolls over anything from the plan to another plan or IRA.

Did your client make a TEFRA 242(b) election in 1984? See ¶ 1.4.10.

Does your client have after-tax money (basis or "investment in the contract") in any of his retirement plans or IRAs, and if so how much? Is the best use of the basis to convert the plan to a Roth IRA, or cash out the basis separately, or just leave it where it is? See ¶ 2.2.

Consider any special deals offered by the current plan, such as subsidized early retirement, subsidized joint and survivor annuity with spouse, annuity vs. lump-sum payout, or unique investment options.

2.7.02 *Reasons to roll money from one plan or IRA to another*

Roll from QRP to IRA to improve death benefit options: Many QRPs offer a lump sum as the only form of death benefit; see ¶ 1.5.10. A lump sum is fine if the beneficiary is the spouse (who can roll it over; ¶ 3.2) or a charity (which is income tax-exempt; ¶ 7.5). If the beneficiary is a nonspouse individual, or a see-through trust, and the beneficiary wants a life expectancy payout, the beneficiary can arrange to have the lump sum transferred to an inherited IRA after the participant's death (see ¶ 4.2.04), but query whether it is a good idea (during the estate *planning* phase) to count on the future occurrence of such post-death transfers. Also the post-death transfer option is not even available for an estate or non-see-through trust. By rolling benefits over to an IRA while still alive, the participant assures the availability of a deferred payout for all his beneficiaries (without the necessity and attendant risks of a "beneficiary rollover"), but takes away the option of a post-death Roth conversion by a nonspouse Designated Beneficiary (see ¶ 4.2.05).

...Or eliminate spousal rights: A person about to marry might roll QRP benefits to an IRA to avoid having federal spousal rights attach to the QRP benefits (see ¶ 3.4.); *unlike* the QRP benefits, the IRA could be protected from state-law spousal rights via a prenuptial agreement. A married person can withdraw from a "REA-exempt" profit sharing plan without spousal consent, and roll the distribution to an IRA that is not subject to federal spousal rights; see ¶ 3.4.03.

Participant under age 59½: Many of the exceptions to the 10 percent penalty on pre-age-59½ distributions (see Chapter 9) apply only to certain types of plans, or apply differently depending on the type of plan. Thus a participant under age 59½ might roll money from a QRP to an IRA to use the "SOSEPP exception" (¶ 9.2), which is easier to implement in an IRA, or the first-time-homebuyer (¶ 9.4.09) or higher-education-expenses (¶ 9.4.08) exceptions, which are only available for IRAs. However, an employee retiring at age 55 or older should not roll to an IRA if he wants to use the "early retirement" exception (¶ 9.4.04), which is available only for QRPs.

Participant approaching or past age 70½: For use of a rollover to prevent or stop MRDs, see ¶ 1.2.06(D).

Investment considerations. An IRA cannot own life insurance or make a loan to the participant, whereas a QRP can do these things.

Universal considerations: Some participants stay in (or leave) a QRP because the investment options and/or maintenance costs are better (or worse) than they would be in an IRA. Also, always consider state income tax effects; a few states offer income or estate/inheritance tax breaks for particular types of retirement plans, so rolling from one type of plan to another could destroy (or improve) the state income tax treatment. An individual concerned about possible creditors' claims should consider which type of plan is best protected; there is no universal answer to that question. While all tax-favored retirement plans receive a complete or nearly complete exemption in federal bankruptcy proceedings, protection varies wildly for inherited plans and also (for everyone) outside of bankruptcy, depending on state law (for IRA exemptions) and ERISA (which protects some but not all employer plans).

Using rollovers to "beat the system." See ¶ 2.6.05 regarding use of an IRA-to-QRP rollover (or a Roth conversion and recharacterization) to evade the once-in-12-months rule applicable to IRA-to-IRA rollovers.

2.7.03 *Best how-to rollover tips*

Use a 60-day rollover (¶ 2.6.01(D)) when it is needed—for example, to isolate after-tax money outside a QRP (see ¶ 2.2.05(C)) or when taking advantage of the NUA deal combined with a partial rollover (¶ 2.5.07). Otherwise, in order to: minimize the risk of mistakes and "lost" rollovers; avoid mandatory income tax withholding (¶ 2.3.02(C)); and avoid concerns with certain rollover rules; always use a direct rollover (¶ 2.6.01(C)) or IRA-to-IRA transfer (¶ 2.6.08) instead of a 60-day rollover.

Ed Slott tip: Do your rollover or transfer no later than November, so mistakes will be revealed in the December account statement and can be caught and fixed before year-end.

Roll or transfer securities, rather than selling the securities, transferring cash, and repurchasing the securities, to save commissions.

No matter how you accomplish your rollover or transfer, have the phone number of your account representative handy, then go on-line and watch the transactions like a hawk to catch, prevent, and/or fix mistakes.

Elect out of income tax withholding on rollovers and transfers if the IRA provider offers you the election. ¶ 2.3.

2.7.04 *How many IRAs should a person own?*

The more retirement plan accounts and/or IRAs a person owns, the greater the chance for making a mistake (accidental distribution, missed MRD, lost beneficiary designation form, etc.). Estate planning for multiple accounts is more expensive because the attorney must draft and coordinate multiple beneficiary designation forms. If the plans have different beneficiaries, the estate plan gets out of whack when the participant (or his legal guardian, or power of attorney-holder) takes distributions disproportionately. Therefore, ideally, all things being equal, the client should consolidate his retirement plans unless there is a good reason to keep separate plans, such as:

If one of the client's IRA investments involves a prohibited transaction risk, keep that asset in its own separate IRA, so if there is an IRA-disqualifying PT it will destroy only that one separate IRA, not all of the client's IRAs. See ¶ 8.1.06.

A client who is subject to taking MRDs, and who has a substantial IRA investment that becomes worthless after the end of the year but before the client has taken his MRD for the following year, will be grateful if the now-worthless investment was in a separate IRA as of the end of the prior year. See ¶ 1.2.05.

There can be some advantage to having separate IRAs payable to different beneficiaries, rather than having one big IRA payable to multiple beneficiaries, if the beneficiaries don't get along with each other or if not all of them are individuals, or if they are individuals of substantially different ages. See ¶ 7.2.02(D), ¶ 1.8.02.

At one time, keeping "rollover" IRAs separate from "contributory" IRAs enabled the participant to roll the "rollover IRA" into a QRP. This reason for keeping separate IRAs was eliminated years ago; see ¶ 2.6.02. But there is still a difference—a "pure" rollover IRA (one that contains only rollovers from QRPs and 403(b) plans, and no "regular" contributions) has greater protection in bankruptcy than a "contributory" IRA.

See ¶ 2.7.02 for reasons why a client might want to leave funds in (or transfer funds to) a particular *type* of retirement plan, even if that would mean having multiple plans and IRAs.

2.7.05 *How to take MRDs and other distributions*

Use extra voluntary income tax withholding from a retirement plan distribution to avoid a penalty on underpayment of estimated taxes. See ¶ 2.3.05.

Using the permissive aggregation of accounts for MRD purposes, take each year's IRA MRDs from the smallest account(s) first, to close them out and consolidate.

Save commissions! Take MRDs in kind rather than selling the asset inside the plan to take cash.

3

Marital Matters

Rules and estate planning concerns for the married participant and the surviving spouse.

This Chapter explains most of the rules and planning considerations that apply when advising married participants and their surviving spouses; matters covered in other Chapters are cross-referenced in the Road Maps (¶ 3.1.01, ¶ 3.1.02) and other appropriate sections. For convenience, the participant is referred to as male and the spouse as female. All statements apply equally to a female participant and her male spouse.

3.1 Considerations for Married Participants

3.1.01 *Road Map: Advising the Married Participant*

Here are matters to consider when advising a married participant whose marriage is recognized for federal tax purposes. For a participant who is about to *get* married, see item #6.

1.   The tax laws generally, though not always, favor naming the participant's surviving spouse, personally and outright, as Designated Beneficiary of retirement benefits. See ¶ 3.2.01. Name a trust for the spouse as beneficiary (rather than the spouse personally) only for a compelling estate planning reason, such as the surviving spouse's inability to handle money, creditor risks, conflict with other family members, estate tax savings, etc. See ¶ 6.4.06 regarding ways to leave benefits in trust for the surviving spouse.

2.   The client's spouse has certain rights, under federal law ("REA"; ¶ 3.4), to be named as beneficiary of certain types of retirement plans. Make sure the client is aware of these, if applicable, and the need to obtain spousal consent if any death benefits subject to REA are not to be left to the spouse. If there is any question about the spouse's willingness to consent to waive REA benefits in order to facilitate the estate plan (or to honor a consent once given), it becomes especially important to adhere strictly to the statutory requirements regarding the form of the consent (¶ 3.4.06). There is no guarantee that the plan's standard printed spousal consent form complies with REA. Consider supplying your own form, using the IRS-provided sample spousal consent forms.

3.   If naming a marital deduction trust as beneficiary, comply with the marital deduction requirements (including special provisions that must be included to assure compliance with the "entitled to all income" requirement). See ¶ 3.3.01.

4.   Be aware that *state laws* under which marriage or divorce revokes a beneficiary designation form will *not* apply to qualified retirement plan (QRP) benefits, but normally *would* apply to IRAs.

5.   Consider state community or marital property laws; see ¶ 2.1.05, ¶ 4.4.09, ¶ 4.5.03.

6.   When advising a client who is about to marry, point out that the client's new spouse will automatically be entitled to substantial inheritance rights under any QRP the client participates in, under "REA" (see ¶ 3.4), and that such rights cannot be waived in a prenuptial agreement. If the client does not want the soon-to-be-spouse to have such rights, the client should consider taking the benefits out of the QRP and rolling them to an IRA (if the client is entitled to withdraw the benefits); though IRAs are subject to state-law spousal inheritance rights, those can generally can be negated in a prenuptial agreement.

3.1.02 Road Map: Advising the Surviving Spouse

Here are the options available to a surviving spouse who is named as beneficiary of the participant's retirement benefits, either directly or through an estate or trust, and where to find the details on each alternative. For ease of reference, the participant is referred to as "he" and the surviving spouse as "she"; the same alternatives apply to the male surviving spouse of a female participant.

A. **Spousal rollover.** The spouse can "roll over," to another retirement plan, benefits left to her by the deceased participant. ¶ 3.2 explains the advantages and drawbacks of the "spousal rollover" (¶ 3.2.01), as well as its requirements (¶ 3.2.02, ¶ 3.2.03) and deadlines (¶ 3.2.06); the types of plans from which (¶ 3.2.02–¶ 3.2.03) and into which (¶ 3.2.04, ¶ 3.2.07) the spouse can roll over or transfer such inherited benefits; special considerations that apply if the surviving spouse is under age 59½ (¶ 3.2.08); when a spousal rollover is allowed for benefits that pass to the spouse through the participant's estate or a trust (¶ 3.2.09); and the extent, if any, to which the surviving spouse's executor can exercise a deceased surviving spouse's rights to initiate or complete a rollover (¶ 3.2.05).

B. **Election to treat decedent's IRA as spouse's own IRA.** See ¶ 3.2.03 regarding whether and how the surviving spouse can elect to treat an *IRA or Roth IRA* inherited from the deceased participant as the surviving spouse's own IRA or Roth IRA. An election to treat an inherited Roth IRA as the spouse's own enables the spouse to "carry over" the decedent's holding period for purposes of computing her "Five-Year Period" (see ¶ 5.2.05(B)), while a rollover to her own Roth IRA presumably would not give her that right. Except in that situation, there is no known planning reason to favor one approach over the other; rollover and spousal election have identical effects.

C. **Life expectancy payout to spouse as sole beneficiary.** By leaving the benefits in the inherited plan (or rolling them over to an "inherited" IRA in the name of the deceased participant, ¶ 3.2.07), the surviving spouse can hold benefits *as beneficiary* rather than rolling them over to her own IRA or plan to hold them *as "owner" (participant)*. For *why* a surviving spouse would choose to hold as beneficiary rather than as participant, see ¶ 3.2.01(D). As long as she holds the benefits as beneficiary (whether because she positively chose to continue holding as beneficiary or because she simply did not yet get around to rolling the benefits over to her own plan), she is subject to taking minimum required distributions (MRDs; see Chapter 1) as beneficiary. For when she must commence taking distributions as beneficiary, see ¶ 1.6.04. For how to calculate a payout based on the life expectancy of the surviving spouse as sole beneficiary, see ¶ 1.6.03(D). For how to calculate MRDs to the spouse's successor beneficiaries if she dies while holding the account as beneficiary, see ¶ 1.6.03(E) or ¶ 1.6.05(C).

D.   **If spouse is one of multiple beneficiaries.** Even if the surviving spouse is not the sole beneficiary of the account, she can still roll over distributions made to her as one of multiple beneficiaries (option A above). T.D. 8987, 2002-1 C.B. 852. Also, if the surviving spouse is not the sole beneficiary as of the date of death, but all the other beneficiaries are eliminated (via distribution or disclaimer, for example) by September 30 of the year after the year of the participant's death (the "Beneficiary Finalization Date"; see ¶ 1.8.03), the spouse *would* be considered the sole beneficiary for minimum distribution purposes and options B and C above would also be available.

Similarly, if the surviving spouse is not the sole beneficiary as of the date of death, but is one of multiple beneficiaries who have fractional or percentage shares, and the inherited account is divided into separate "inherited accounts" payable to the respective multiple beneficiaries no later than December 31 of the year after the year of the participant's death, the spouse would be considered the sole beneficiary of the separate account payable to her for minimum distribution purposes, and Options B and C would be available; see ¶ 1.8.01.

If the surviving spouse is just one of multiple beneficiaries as of the Beneficiary Finalization Date, and the separate accounts rule does not apply, see ¶ 1.5.03(F) or ¶ 1.5.04(F) for how to compute MRDs.

E.   **If benefits are payable to an estate or trust of which the spouse is a beneficiary.** See ¶ 3.2.09 regarding availability of the spousal rollover. If the benefits are not rolled over by the surviving spouse "through" the estate or trust as described at ¶ 3.2.09, use the Road Map at ¶ 1.5.02 to compute MRDs.

F.   **Spousal Roth conversion.** The surviving spouse has the option to convert inherited benefits to a Roth IRA. See ¶ 3.2.04.

G.   If the surviving spouse-beneficiary dies after the participant. If the participant dies leaving benefits to the surviving spouse, and then the surviving spouse also dies, see ¶ 3.1.03 for the effect of simultaneous deaths clauses; ¶ 4.4.12 for the ability of the surviving spouse's executor to disclaim benefits on her behalf; ¶ 3.2.05 and ¶ 4.1.02 for the extent (if any) to which the surviving spouse's executor can exercise the now-deceased surviving spouse's rollover and election rights; and ¶ 1.6.03(E) or ¶ 1.6.05(C) regarding MRDs in the year of the surviving spouse's death and thereafter.

H.   Other pitfalls and considerations. If the participant died before his Required Beginning Date (¶ 1.4), be aware of the deadline the spouse may face regarding electing between the life expectancy payout method and the 5-year rule; see ¶ 3.2.06, last paragraph. If the surviving spouse inherits, in 2010 or 2011, a Roth IRA that was created by a 2010 conversion, see ¶ 5.4.05.

3.1.03 Simultaneous death clauses

If the participant names his spouse as beneficiary, and they die simultaneously or within a short time of each other, it may be presumed under applicable state law or under the plan documents that the spouse predeceased the participant; see ¶ 1.7.07. A presumption that the spouse *survived* the participant, if contained in the participant's will or trust, will NOT govern retirement benefits payable directly to the spouse. To be effective, the presumption would have to be contained in the designation of beneficiary form; see ¶ 1.7.02. Such a presumption may be used, if the spouse's estate is smaller than the participant's, to equalize the estates for estate tax purposes.

Although it may be desirable for estate tax purposes, a presumption that the spouse survives the participant will often produce bad results under the minimum distribution rules. In most cases, the result of a presumption that the spouse survives in case of simultaneous deaths will be that benefits must be distributed over the remaining single life expectancy of the spouse, or by the end of the fifth year after the spouses' deaths. See ¶ 1.6.03(E), ¶ 1.6.05(C).

3.2 Spousal Rollover; Election to Treat Decedent's IRA as Spouse's IRA

This ¶ 3.2 deals with the surviving spouse's option to roll over, to another retirement plan, retirement benefits left to her by her deceased spouse (the "participant"). ¶ 2.6 explains what a rollover is and the rules governing rollovers generally; this ¶ 3.2 discusses additional rules and considerations that apply to the rollover or Roth conversion of inherited benefits by a surviving spouse.

When the surviving spouse inherits an IRA or Roth IRA as sole beneficiary, she has the additional option to elect to treat it as her own; see ¶ 3.2.03.

In this Chapter, spousal rollover generally means a rollover into the surviving spouse's *own* retirement plan; for rollover into another *inherited* plan, see ¶ 3.2.07.

3.2.01 *Advantages and drawbacks of spousal rollover*

The surviving spouse's ability to roll over inherited benefits to her own retirement plan gives her a powerful option, not available to other beneficiaries, to defer plan distributions. For one thing, she escapes a taxable lump sum payout from the plan, if that's the plan's only form of death benefit (see ¶ 1.2.01, #6, and ¶ 1.5.10). Also, by rolling over benefits to her own retirement plan, the spouse becomes the "participant" or "owner" with regard to those benefits under the minimum distribution rules. By taking distributions as owner, the surviving spouse gains the following deferral advantages (A–C) compared with taking the benefits as beneficiary. See "D" for the drawbacks and reasons NOT to rush into a spousal rollover.

The following discussion assumes the spouse rolls the inherited benefits over into an IRA in her own name; rollovers into a nonIRA plan are not discussed in this book. For rollovers into an "inherited" IRA, see ¶ 3.2.07.

A.   **Slower rate of MRDs (longer ADP).** The Applicable Distribution Period (ADP; ¶ 1.2.03) for anyone (even the surviving spouse) who holds inherited benefits as *beneficiary* is the beneficiary's *single* life expectancy. ¶ 1.5.03(B), (C), ¶ 1.5.04(B), (C). Distribution over the spouse's life expectancy guarantees that the benefits will be entirely distributed out of the plan by the time the spouse reaches (or would have reached) her late 80s. In contrast, the surviving spouse's MRDs from an IRA she holds as *owner* (participant) are determined using the Uniform Lifetime Table (¶ 1.3.01), under which her ADP is the *joint* life expectancy of the surviving spouse (as participant) and a hypothetical 10-years-younger beneficiary. If benefits are left to the spouse outright and rolled over to her own IRA, and she withdraws only the MRDs required under the Uniform Lifetime Table, the benefits are guaranteed to outlive the spouse; in fact they will probably be worth more, when she reaches her late 80s, than they were worth when she inherited the plan!

B. **Start new life expectancy payout after spouse's later death.** The surviving spouse can name her own Designated Beneficiary for the rollover IRA she holds as owner. After her death, MRDs will then be based on the life expectancy of her Designated Beneficiary (¶ 1.5.05). In contrast, when the surviving spouse holds the inherited benefits merely "as beneficiary," the ADP does not change after her death; it will continue to be what's left of her (single) life expectancy, just as would be true for any other beneficiary (see ¶ 1.5.13, ¶ 1.6.03(E)). The only exception is in the rare case when both spouses die young (¶ 1.6.05(C)).

C. **Later starting date for MRDs if participant was older than the surviving spouse.** If the surviving spouse is the sole beneficiary of an inherited plan, she must start taking MRDs over her life expectancy no later than the end of the year after the year of the decedent's death, or (if later) the end of the year in which the decedent would have reached age 70½; see ¶ 1.6.04. (Of course, she must also take the MRD for the year of death, if the participant died after his required beginning date (RBD) and had not taken it himself; see ¶ 1.5.04(A).) The required distribution of benefits *rolled into the surviving spouse's own IRA* does not begin until the surviving spouse reaches age 70½. Thus, the spousal rollover or election can provide a later commencement date for MRDs for a surviving spouse who was younger than the deceased participant. If the participant was younger than the spouse, see "D."

D.   When NOT to roll over to the spouse's own IRA. Though the rollover to the spouse's own IRA (or election to treat an inherited IRA as the spouse's own IRA; ¶ 3.2.03) is the best option in most cases, it is not always suitable. Consider the relative vulnerability of the benefits to claims of the participant's or spouse's <u>creditors</u> (a subject not covered in this book). If there is <u>after-tax money</u> in either the inherited plan or in the surviving spouse's own pre-existing IRA, consider converting the inherited plan or IRA directly to a Roth IRA (or converting the spouse's own IRAs to a Roth IRA) before carrying out a rollover of inherited benefits to the spouse's IRA, if a rollover would "dilute" the after-tax money that exists in either plan; see ¶ 2.2.08. If the surviving spouse is <u>under age 59½</u>, see ¶ 3.2.08.

If the surviving spouse is <u>older than the deceased spouse</u> was, the surviving spouse may want to leave the benefits in an inherited plan or IRA until the year the deceased spouse would have reached age 69½. If the participant died before his Required Beginning Date (RBD; ¶ 1.4), the surviving spouse does not have to take any distributions as beneficiary until the year the deceased spouse would have reached age 70½ (see ¶ 1.6.04), whereas (once she rolls the benefits over to her own IRA) she will become subject to taking MRDs as owner the year she herself reaches age 70½. By not rolling over the benefits until the year the deceased spouse would have reached age 69½, she avoids having to take any MRDs as beneficiary but delays having to take MRDs as owner as long as possible. See PLR 2009-36049 for an example of this type of planning. If using this approach, be sure to have the spouse name her own Designated Beneficiary for the "inherited" IRA; see ¶ 1.6.05(C).

3.2.02 *Spousal rollover: QRPs and 403(b) plans*

§ 402(c)(1) allows a participant in a qualified retirement plan (QRP) to roll over certain plan distributions to another QRP, or to any other eligible plan, if various requirements are met. ¶ 2.6.01(B). If death benefits are paid to the participant's surviving spouse, the rollover rules "apply to such distribution in the same manner as if the spouse were" the participant. § 402(c)(9). Whatever rollover options the deceased participant had, the surviving spouse has the same options. Reg. § 1.402(c)-2, A-12(a).

§ 403(b)(8) permits <u>rollovers</u> by a 403(b) plan participant, and (by "importing" § 402(c)(9)) also permits rollovers by the participant's surviving spouse. § 403(b)(8)(B); Reg. § 1.403(b)-2. See PLRs 9713018, 2001-01038, 2002-10066, 2002-49008, 2003-14029, 2003-17040, and 2009-36049 for examples of spousal rollovers of 403(b) benefits. The Code does not permit the surviving spouse to elect to treat a 403(b) plan as the spouse's own plan; § 403(b) has no provision comparable to § 408(d)(3)(C); Reg. § 1.403(b)-3, A-1(c)(2). Contrast IRAs (¶ 3.2.03).

There is no requirement that the surviving spouse be the sole beneficiary of the account to be entitled to the spousal rollover; she can roll over a distribution made to her even if she is one of multiple beneficiaries. See, *e.g.*, PLRs 2004-49041–2004-49042.

The tests for determining whether a distribution is an "eligible rollover distribution," and other rollover rules, are the same for the surviving spouse as they would have been for the deceased participant. The same rules apply regarding the direct rollover option (¶ 2.6.01(C)) and mandatory income tax withholding (¶ 2.3.02(C)). The distribution does not have to be the entire account balance; partial distributions are eligible for rollover, unless they are MRDs or part of a series of substantially equal payments (¶ 2.6.02).

3.2.03 *Rollover (or spousal election) for IRA or Roth IRA*

§ 408(d), in a backhanded way, permits a surviving spouse to treat the deceased spouse's IRA (including a Roth IRA) that is payable to her as beneficiary as if it were the spouse's *own* IRA (or Roth IRA).

A.   **Spousal election: Code and regulations.** The Code provides that distributions from an "inherited IRA" may not be treated as tax-free rollovers, but then says that for this purpose an "inherited IRA" does not include an IRA inherited by the surviving spouse. § 408(d)(3)(C). Thus by negative implication the surviving spouse may roll over distributions she receives from the deceased participant's IRA. (Note: In this book, "inherited IRA" means an IRA held by *any* beneficiary. See ¶ 4.2.01.)

Reg. § 1.408-8, A-5(a), provides that "The surviving spouse of an individual may elect...to treat the spouse's entire interest as a beneficiary in an individual's IRA (or the remaining part of such interest if distribution thereof has commenced to the spouse) as the spouse's own IRA." The effect of such an election with respect to a traditional IRA inherited by the surviving spouse is that subsequent MRDs are "determined under section 401(a)(9)(A) with the spouse as IRA owner and not section 401(a)(9)(B) with the surviving spouse as the...beneficiary." See ¶ 1.6.03(B) for how to calculate MRDs when the spouse elects to treat an inherited traditional IRA as her own.

B.   **Spousal election for inherited Roth IRA.** If the surviving spouse as sole beneficiary of the deceased participant's Roth IRA elects to treat the Roth IRA as her own, then "the Roth IRA is treated *from that date forward* as though it were established for the benefit of the surviving spouse and not the original Roth IRA owner." Reg. § 1.408A-2, A-4. Emphasis added. Accordingly, there will be no further MRDs required until the spouse's death, because she now holds the account as owner rather than as beneficiary and the lifetime MRD rules do not apply to Roth IRAs (see ¶ 5.2.02(A)). It is not clear whether the MRD for the year of the election is erased "retroactively" as is the case with a spousal election regarding a traditional IRA; compare Reg. § 1.408-8, A-5(a), discussed at ¶ 1.6.03(B).

Following the spousal election, the decedent's basis in the account (his contributions) would be combined with the surviving spouse's own basis/contributions to her own Roth IRAs for purposes of applying the Ordering Rules (¶ 5.2.07) to any nonqualified distribution (¶ 5.2.06). Finally, once the spouse elects to treat the inherited Roth IRA as her own, the account ceases to be a "death benefit" for purposes of exceptions to the early-distributions penalty; see ¶ 3.2.08.

There is one exception to the rule that the elected Roth IRA becomes "indistinguishable" from any Roth IRA established by the spouse herself: The exception is that she gets to "keep" the decedent's years of Roth IRA ownership, if longer than her own, for purposes of computing the Five-Year Period; see ¶ 5.2.05(B).

See also ¶ 3.2.04 regarding the surviving spouse's ability to convert an inherited *traditional* plan or IRA to a Roth IRA.

C.   **Conditions that must be met for spouse to make this election.** "In order to make this election, the spouse must be the sole beneficiary of the IRA and have an unlimited right to withdraw amounts from the IRA." See ¶ 1.6.02 for definition of "sole beneficiary."

The requirement that the spouse be the "sole" beneficiary to make this election is satisfied (as to a "separate account" within the IRA) if the spouse is the sole beneficiary of such separate account, even if she is not the sole beneficiary of the participant's entire interest in the IRA. ¶ 1.8.01.

If the spouse has limited her rights to withdraw from the IRA (for example, through a prenuptial agreement), or if the beneficiary designation form limits the spouse's rights to withdraw from the IRA (for example, by specifying that she may withdraw only the income or only the MRD), then the spouse can NOT elect to treat the IRA as her own because she does not have the unlimited right to withdraw from the account.

D.   How spouse makes the election. Reg. § 1.408-8, A-5(b) provides three ways the surviving spouse can elect to treat the deceased participant's IRA or Roth IRA as the spouse's own IRA or Roth IRA.

    1.   Affirmative election. Ideally, with proper advice and planning, the spouse makes the election by "redesignating the account as an account in the name of the surviving spouse as IRA owner rather than as beneficiary."

    2.   Spouse contributes to the account. Another way to make the election is for the spouse to make a contribution to the account (other than a rollover of another retirement plan or IRA inherited from the deceased spouse). Since contributions (other than rollovers of other inherited plans from the same decedent) to an inherited IRA are not allowed, the spouse is deemed to have elected to treat the account as her own if she makes that type of contribution to it. Reg. § 1.408-8, A-5(b)(2).

    3.   Failure to take an MRD. The third way to make the election is for the surviving spouse to fail to take, by the applicable deadline, "any amount" that is required to be distributed to her as a beneficiary under the minimum distribution rules. Reg. § 1.408-8, A-5(b)(1); PLR 2001-21073. Note that even a $1 shortfall in the MRD would trigger this deemed election (under the "any amount" standard).

If the participant died after his RBD, then the beneficiary (including a surviving spouse who is beneficiary) is required to take the MRD for the year of the participant's death to the extent he did not take it himself. See ¶ 1.5.04(A). As an MRD, this distribution cannot be rolled over by a surviving spouse-beneficiary; furthermore, she cannot roll over the inherited plan until after she has taken this MRD. ¶ 2.6.03. Even if the inherited plan is an IRA and the spouse elects to treat the account as her own in the same year as the participant died she still has to take out this distribution. Reg. § 1.408-8, A-5(a). Because this MRD must be taken *regardless* of whether the spouse elects to treat the inherited IRA as her own, it is not clear whether the surviving spouse's failure to take *this* MRD in full would be deemed an automatic election by her to treat the inherited IRA as her own; it seems that it should NOT trigger that rule, but there is no authority or guidance on point.

E.   **When spousal election may be made.** The spousal election may "be made at any time after the individual's date of death," including after the surviving spouse's own RBD or Required Commencement Date. See PLR 9311037.

F.   **Rollovers also permitted.** The Code and regulations never explicitly state that the surviving spouse (*without* electing to treat the deceased participant's IRA as the surviving spouse's own IRA) can simply roll over distributions that she receives from the decedent's IRA, as she can with distributions she receives from a QRP or 403(b) plan inherited from the deceased participant (¶ 3.2.02). The Preamble to the final minimum distribution regulations (¶ 1.1.01) corrects this oversight by stating that "If the spouse actually receives a distribution from the IRA, the spouse is permitted to roll that distribution over within 60 days into an IRA in the spouse's own name to the extent that the distribution is not a required distribution, regardless of whether or not the spouse is the sole beneficiary of the IRA owner." TD 9897, 67 FR 18987 (4/17/02). For examples of spousal rollovers of distributions from inherited IRAs, see PLRs 9842058 and 2009-34046.

3.2.04 *Roth conversion by surviving spouse*

See Chapter 5 regarding Roth IRAs (¶ 5.2) and "conversions" from traditional plans and IRAs into Roth IRAs (¶ 5.4).

Since the surviving spouse has, with respect to QRP and 403(b) benefits left outright to her, every option the deceased participant would have had for those benefits (see ¶ 3.2.02), the surviving spouse can roll over the benefits into a Roth IRA just as the deceased participant could have done (see ¶ 5.4.01(B)). She can also roll traditional IRA benefits inherited from the deceased participant into a Roth IRA (see ¶ 3.2.03(F)). The recipient Roth IRA could be either her own Roth IRA or a Roth IRA in the name of the deceased participant payable to the surviving spouse as beneficiary (see ¶ 3.2.07).

Having converted an inherited traditional plan or IRA to a Roth IRA, the surviving spouse would have the same options as other Roth-converters to (1) recharacterize the conversion (see ¶ 5.6) or (2) (in the case of a 2010 conversion), include the conversion income in 2011–2012 rather than in 2010 (¶ 5.4.05). Once the inherited benefits are moved into a Roth IRA in the name of the surviving spouse they cease to be subject to any requirement of paying MRDs for the rest of the spouse's life; while inherited IRAs (either Roth or traditional) are required to distribute MRDs, Roth IRAs are not subject to the "lifetime" MRD rules. See ¶ 5.2.02(A).

3.2.05 *Rollover or election by spouse's executor*

If the surviving spouse is named as beneficiary, and she survives the participant, but then she dies before taking a distribution from the inherited benefits, the surviving spouse's death completely terminates any possibility of a spousal rollover for funds that are still inside the first spouse's retirement plan when the surviving spouse dies.

In the case of an IRA inherited by the spouse as sole beneficiary, the IRS has not allowed the executor of a surviving spouse's estate to exercise the surviving spouse's "personal" right to treat the deceased participant's IRA as the now-deceased surviving spouse's own IRA. See PLRs 9237038 and 2001-26036. And, in the case of any type of plan or IRA, there is no law or regulation that would permit the surviving spouse's executor to roll over a distribution that such executor takes from the plan. As one lawyer put it, "She can't roll over in her grave" (Colin S. Marshall, 1997).

If a distribution was made from the decedent's plan to the surviving spouse *while she was still living*, and she then died before completing the rollover of such distribution to the same or another plan, see ¶ 4.1.05 regarding her executor's ability to complete the rollover on her behalf.

3.2.06 *Deadline for completing spousal rollover*

There is no deadline, as such, for completing a spousal rollover. Of course, once any benefits are actually *distributed* to the spouse, they must be rolled over within 60 days (unless a hardship extension is obtained). ¶ 2.6.06, ¶ 2.6.07. See PLR 2009-31061 for an example of a surviving spouse obtaining a hardship waiver of the 60-day deadline. But the Code provides no specific time limit based on the participant's death after which it becomes "too late" for the spouse to roll over distributions. See, *e.g.*, PLR 2002-22033, in which the participant died in 1985 and his surviving spouse was allowed to roll over the benefits to her IRA in 1997.

However, even though there is no deadline as such, other events can diminish or eliminate the spouse's ability to roll over the benefits. For one thing, if the spouse dies before initiating (or completing) the rollover, the spouse's death may make it impossible (or very difficult) for the rollover to occur (or be completed); see ¶ 3.2.05.

Also, the minimum distribution rules (Chapter 1) can reduce or eliminate the spouse's ability to roll over inherited benefits. As long as the account remains in the name of the deceased participant, the surviving spouse must take MRDs from the account as beneficiary once she reaches her Required Commencement Date (¶ 1.6.04). MRDs cannot be rolled over; see ¶ 2.6.03.

However, if the plan is an IRA, and the surviving spouse is the sole beneficiary, her failure to take any part of the MRD would be deemed an election to treat the account as her own; see ¶ 3.2.03(D), #3. This would *cancel out* the obligation to take an MRD *as beneficiary* for that year and subsequent years (except that making the election in the year of the participant's death does not cancel out the obligation to take the MRD for such year; see ¶ 3.2.03(D), #3).

If the participant died before his Required Beginning Date (RBD), and the 5-year rule applies (¶ 1.5.07), then there is no MRD until the year in which the fifth anniversary of the participant's death occurs, but in that year the entire account becomes the "MRD." See ¶ 1.5.06. If the inherited plan is an <u>IRA of which the spouse is the sole beneficiary</u> her failure to cash out the account by the end of that year would be deemed an election to treat the account as her own (¶ 3.2.03(D), #3); otherwise, the deadline for completing the spousal rollover would appear to be December 31 of the year that contains the *fourth* anniversary of the participant's death. See PLR 2002-42044, in which the spouse was allowed to roll over the balance of a decedent's plan in the fourth year after his death. Note that if the participant died in any of the years 2004–2009 the "5-year rule" becomes the "6-year rule"; see ¶ 1.5.06.

Some plans and IRAs provide that the beneficiary of a participant who died before his RBD must elect to use the life expectancy payout method by a certain date, or else be defaulted into the 5-year rule; see ¶ 1.5.07(A), #3. Thus, a surviving spouse of a young decedent could find herself defaulted into the 5-year rule years before she would have been required to take any distributions under the life expectancy payout method; see ¶ 1.6.04. Since (except, apparently, in the case of an inherited IRA of which she is the sole beneficiary) this could mean she is stuck in the fifth year with a nonrollable distribution of the entire account, this once again illustrates the importance of studying the plan documents and the rollover-or-not decision, and having the spouse take the necessary actions to carry out her decision, as soon as possible after the participant dies.

3.2.07 *Plans the spouse can roll benefits into*

The surviving spouse can roll benefits into any type of eligible retirement plan the deceased employee could have rolled into, including a QRP or IRA. § 402(c)(9); see ¶ 2.6.01. Prior to 2002, a surviving spouse could roll over benefits inherited from the deceased spouse into an IRA but *not* into a QRP; Reg. § 1.402(c)-2, A-12, has not been updated to reflect this change.

This book covers only spousal rollovers into IRAs. For rollover (conversion) into a Roth IRA, see ¶ 3.2.04.

The spouse can roll the inherited benefits into <u>her own IRA</u>—either a pre-existing IRA that she already owns, or to a new IRA established to receive this rollover. She can establish an IRA just to receive the rollover, even if she is not herself eligible to contribute to an IRA; see, *e.g.*, PLR 2009-36049 (rollover of deceased spouse's IRA into new IRA established to receive the rollover by a surviving spouse who was already over age 70½). There is no prohibition against her commingling any of her own pre-existing IRAs with any rollovers from the deceased participant's plan, or from combining inherited benefits from multiple plans or IRAs left to her by the deceased participant. Once a surviving spouse rolls benefits over to her own IRA, she becomes the owner of the benefits (participant) in every way.

Alternatively, the surviving spouse may roll the benefits into an IRA that is in the name of the deceased participant-spouse and payable to the surviving spouse as beneficiary ("inherited IRA"; see ¶ 4.2.01). See Notice 2009-68, 2009-39 IRB 423: "If you receive a payment from the Plan as the surviving spouse of a deceased participant, you have the same rollover options that the participant would have had...In addition, if you choose to do a rollover to an IRA, you may treat the IRA as your own or as an inherited IRA." See also Reg. § 1.408-8, A-7, which provides that "If the surviving spouse of an employee rolls over a distribution from a qualified plan, such surviving spouse may elect to treat the IRA as the spouse's own IRA...." The fact that the spouse's election to treat the IRA as her own occurs *after* she has rolled over the distribution into that IRA indicates that the IRA into which she rolled the distribution was an IRA in the decedent's name. See PLR 9608042 for an example.

As with rollovers into her own IRA, an inherited IRA into which the spouse rolls a distribution from the decedent's plan can be either a pre-existing IRA (PLRs 9418034, 9842058, 2006-08029), or a new inherited IRA created for this purpose (PLRs 2004-50057, 2009-36049).

3.2.08 *Rollover if spouse is under age 59½*

A surviving spouse who is under age 59½ faces a dilemma. If she leaves the inherited benefits in the deceased participant's plan, she can withdraw the benefits whenever she wishes penalty-free, because the 10 percent penalty on early distributions does not apply to death benefits. ¶ 9.4.01. However, she may be forced to take annual MRDs as beneficiary (see ¶ 1.6.04)), and if she dies while the benefits are still in the deceased participant's account the distribution options after her death will *usually* be less favorable than the options available if she had rolled over the benefits to her own IRA; see ¶ 1.6.03(E), ¶ 1.6.05(C).

Alternatively, the spouse could take the benefits out of the deceased participant's account and roll them over to her own retirement plan, an action that will usually produce better distribution options for her beneficiaries upon her later death (¶ 3.2.01(B)); but once the benefits are rolled to her own plan, they become "her" benefits, and the death benefit exception no longer applies. She will not be able to withdraw from the rollover account until she reaches age 59½, unless she pays the 10 percent penalty or qualifies for an exception (¶ 9.2–¶ 9.4). Here are strategies to deal with this dilemma.

Note that strategies A, C, and D involve the spouse's taking part of the benefits as beneficiary and rolling over the rest. Reg. § 1.408-8, A-5(a), (see ¶ 3.2.03(A)) allows the surviving spouse to treat her interest in an IRA inherited from the participant "or the remaining part of such interest if distribution thereof has commenced to the spouse" as the spouse's own IRA. So, the spousal election can be made even after the spouse has taken one or more distributions as beneficiary. See PLRs 2001-10033, 2002-42044.

A.   **Leave benefits in decedent's plan until spouse reaches age 59½, then roll them over.** While she is under age 59½, the spouse can withdraw funds as needed penalty-free under the death benefits exception. If her death prior to completing the rollover would produce undesirable tax results for her beneficiaries, she can buy life insurance to protect against that risk. If she will reach age 59½ before the end of the year in which the deceased participant would have reached age 70½, AND the decedent's plan allows her to name her own successor beneficiaries, AND she does so, this option does not produce bad results EVEN IF the surviving spouse herself dies before she reaches age 59½: Her designated beneficiaries' life expectancies would be the ADP. See ¶ 1.6.05(C).

B.   **Roll to spouse's IRA, use SOSEPP if money later needed.** The spouse could roll all of the inherited money over immediately to her own IRA, to stop or prevent having to take MRDs as beneficiary if applicable, and to assure that the best possible distribution options will be available to her beneficiaries regardless of when she dies. If she later needs funds from the rollover IRA while she is still under age 59½, she can use the "series of substantially equal periodic payments" exception (¶ 9.2) to avoid the 10 percent penalty.

C. **Roll some to spouse's plan, leave some in decedent's plan.**
Estimate the spouse's needs prior to age 59½, leave that amount in the deceased participant's account (so she can withdraw it penalty-free), and roll over the rest to the spouse's own IRA.

D. **Roll to an "inherited" IRA.** If the spouse wants to leave the benefits in the decedent's plan for a while, but the plan in question insists that the spouse must take a lump sum distribution of the benefits immediately (¶ 1.5.10), the spouse can roll over that distribution to an IRA in the name of the decedent, payable to her as beneficiary, in order to preserve its status as a penalty-free death benefit until such later time as she chooses to roll it over to her own plan. See ¶ 3.2.07.

3.2.09 *Spousal rollover through an estate or trust*

If the participant's benefits are left to his estate or a trust as beneficiary, the surviving spouse can roll over benefits that are paid to her as a beneficiary of the estate or trust, *provided* the spouse has, and exercises, the right to demand payment of the benefits to herself.

There is no statute, regulation, or case stating this principle. Nevertheless, it is the IRS's most longstanding, consistent, and logical position in the entire field of employee benefit distributions. Dozens of private rulings have affirmed this principle consistently since 1993. Yet in all that time the IRS has never stated the rule in any form that could be cited as precedent (such as a regulation or Revenue Ruling). In view of the longstanding consistent and clear IRS position as indicated by dozens of PLRs, IRA custodians may be willing to rely on an opinion of counsel in accepting spousal rollovers under these circumstances; this approach would save the surviving spouse substantial expense and delay (compared with having to obtain a PLR).

The IRS has approved spousal rollovers with respect to every type of retirement plan covered by this book, through either an estate or trust or both, wherever the spouse has the right to the benefits, either because she is sole beneficiary of the estate or trust, or because she has the right to and does demand the benefits in fulfilment of her share; see "A." However, if the spouse's receipt of the benefits depends on *the discretion of a third party*, or on *meeting a standard for distribution*, then the rollover is not allowed; see "B." If only some but not all of the benefits are subject to the spouse's unfettered right to withdraw them, then only that portion is eligible for rollover; see "C." For the legal basis for this IRS position, see "D."

If the participant has already died, leaving benefits to a trust that does not meet this standard, and the survivors want to have the benefits qualify for a spousal rollover, see ¶ 4.5 regarding ways to modify, invalidate, or otherwise sidestep the participant's documents.

There are a few rulings that deviate from these rules, always in favor of even more liberally allowing the spouse to do the rollover, but these should be regarded as anomalous; see PLRs 8920060, 1999-13048, and 2006-15032.

A.   **Spousal rollover of all types of plans through estate, trust, or both.** Here is a partial list of PLRs approving the spousal rollover under these circumstances for various types of retirement plan benefits through the participant's estate, a trust, or both (i.e., where benefits are paid first to the participant's estate, thence to a pourover trust, and from there to the spouse). PLRs involving IRAs as community property include 2009-35045 and 2009-50053.

Estates: IRA payable to estate: PLRs 2002-10066, 2002-36052, 2004-06048; IRA annuity payable to estate: 2004-05017; 403(b) plan or annuity payable to estate: 2002-10066, 2002-49008, 2003-14029, 2003-17040; defined benefit plan payable to estate: 2003-05030; QRP payable to estate: 2002-11054, 2002-12036.

Trusts: IRA payable to a trust: 2001-30056, 2002-42044, 2009-34046, 2009-35045, 2009-50053; portion of IRA payable to a trust (where the rest of the IRA was payable, through the same trust, to other beneficiaries): 2004-49040; QRP payable to a trust: 2002-08031. See also PLR 1999-18065.

Estate and trust: IRA payable to an estate which passed to a trust: 2001-36031.

Generally, the surviving spouse must roll the money over within 60 days after it is distributed from the decedent's plan, but (as with other rollovers; see ¶ 2.6.07) the spouse can obtain a waiver of the 60-day deadline in cases of hardship. See PLR 2004-05017. Alternatively, the spouse can effect the rollover using a direct trustee-to-trustee transfer (¶ 2.6.01(E)); see, *e.g.*, PLR 2009-50058.

If the distribution is from a QRP and the plan withholds income taxes from the distribution, the spouse can "roll over" the withheld tax money by substituting other funds. PLR 2003-44024, citing Reg. § 1.402(c)-2, A-11.

Of course, the spouse cannot roll over any portion of the distribution that constitutes an MRD; see ¶ 2.6.03 and PLR 2009-35045.

B.   No rollover if spouse's rights limited by standard or subject to third party discretion. In PLR 2006-18030, the surviving spouse was entitled under the trust terms only to income necessary for health, support, etc.; the rollover was denied because the spouse was not the sole "payee" of the IRA payable to the trust. See also PLR 2009-44059. However, if the surviving spouse *herself* is the trustee who exercises the discretion to allocate and/or pay the benefits to herself, the rollover is allowed. See PLRs 2009-34046, 2009-35045, 2009-50053.

C.   Partial rollover allowed if only some of the benefits meet the requirements. See PLR 2004-49040, in which the spousal rollover was allowed for the portion of the IRA payable to the surviving spouse through a trust, where the rest of the IRA was payable, through the same trust, to other beneficiaries.

In PLR 1999-18065, the decedent's IRA could apparently have been allocated either to the marital trust (which the surviving spouse had the right to withdraw) or to the credit shelter trust (of which the surviving spouse was only the life beneficiary), and the surviving spouse was not the sole trustee (she was co-trustee with a corporation). The IRS allowed the rollover only for the portion of the IRA that exceeded the amount ($620,000) that *could* have been allocated to the credit shelter trust, even though no portion of the IRA actually was allocated to the credit shelter trust. PLR 2003-14029 is similar.

If the participant's will or trust (or applicable state law) allows or requires debts, expenses, and/or taxes to be paid out of the estate or the trust, and therefore arguably out of the retirement benefits that are payable to that estate or trust, does that potential liability represent a possible limit on the spouse's ability to take the benefits out of the estate or trust? Most of the PLRs don't even mention this subject, but some do mention it and allow the rollover anyway; see PLRs 2001-

36030, 2001-30056. In PLR 2009-34046 (allowing the spousal rollover through a trust), the taxpayer "recited" that all debts, expenses, etc., were paid out of assets other than the IRA; the IRS does not comment on this aspect.

D.   **Legal basis for IRS's position allowing rollovers.** The IRS in some of the rulings (*e.g.*, PLR 2004-06048) recites that the Preamble to the Final Regulations provides "that a surviving spouse who actually receives a distribution from an IRA is permitted to roll that distribution over...even if the spouse is not the sole beneficiary.... A rollover may be accomplished even if IRA assets pass through either a trust or an estate." However, the cited Preamble does not contain the second sentence "quoted." T.D. 8987, 2002-1 C.B. 852.

In most of the rulings, the IRS recites that benefits may be rolled over by a surviving spouse only if the benefits pass to the spouse *from the decedent*, and that the general rule is that benefits that pass to the spouse through an estate or a trust are *not* deemed to pass to the spouse from the decedent. Then in each and every ruling the IRS goes on to say that, based on the facts of *this particular case*, the IRS will not apply the general rule!

One recent ruling suggested a possible shift towards a more appropriate approach of setting a standard that all taxpayers can rely on. PLR 2009-34046 stated that "the general rule will not apply in a case where the surviving spouse is the sole trustee of the decedent's trust and has the sole authority and discretion under trust language to pay the IRA proceeds to herself...." However, a more recent PLR (2009-35045) goes back to the "this set of facts" language.

3.3 Qualifying for the Marital Deduction

This ¶ 3.3 describes how retirement benefits left to the participant's surviving spouse, or to a trust for her life benefit, can qualify for the federal estate tax marital deduction if the surviving spouse is a U.S. citizen, and provides details on the most-used methods of so qualifying. This discussion assumes the reader is familiar with the uses and requirements of the federal estate tax marital deduction, and so explains only how the marital deduction rules apply uniquely to *retirement benefits*.

If the participant's spouse is not a U.S. citizen, additional rules apply that are not covered in this book; see § 2056A. For more on the marital deduction generally; and details on how to qualify retirement benefits for the marital deduction if the spouse is not a U.S. citizen, or if using the less common methods; see the author's *Special Report: Retirement Benefits and the Marital Deduction (Including Planning for the Noncitizen Spouse)* (Appendix C).

For deaths in 2010, see ¶ 4.3.08 regarding the one-year "repeal" of the federal estate tax.

3.3.01 *Road Map: Leaving Benefits to Spouse or Marital Trust*

§ 2056, which creates the federal estate tax marital deduction, provides a general rule (the deduction is allowed for the value of property "which passes or has passed from the decedent to his surviving spouse"; § 2056(a)), followed by an exception to the general rule (no deduction is allowed if the property that passes to the surviving spouse is a "life estate or other terminable interest"; § 2056(b)(1)), followed by several exceptions to the exception (certain terminable interests do qualify for the marital deduction after all!). The key to qualifying for the marital deduction, therefore, is to make sure that any property left to the surviving spouse either (1) is not a "terminable interest," or (2) if it is a terminable interest, it qualifies for one of the exceptions to the "terminable interest rule." Here are the steps to follow:

A. **Choose a method.** Benefits can qualify for the marital deduction if left to the spouse outright (¶ 3.3.11), to a "QTIP" marital trust (¶ 3.3.02), to a "General Power" marital trust (¶ 3.3.09), or in certain forms of annuity (¶ 3.3.10).

B. **If using a trust, take three extra steps.** If leaving benefits to a QTIP or General Power marital trust, you need to cover three additional points to make sure the benefits qualify for the marital deduction. First, you need to understand the IRS's concept of how the "terminable interest rule" applies to retirement benefits payable to a marital trust; see ¶ 3.3.03. Second, you need to assure that the "income of the retirement plan" is determined correctly for marital deduction purposes; see ¶ 3.3.04. Third, you must make sure the spouse is "entitled" to all that income; see ¶ 3.3.05–¶ 3.3.08.

C.   Don't forget MRDs. Work out how the minimum distribution rules (Chapter 1) will work with the method you have chosen. See comments under each method, and ¶ 3.3.07–¶ 3.3.09.

D.   Pay attention to funding formula. If the benefits are payable to a trust that is to be divided, at the participant's death, between a "marital trust" and a "credit shelter" (or bypass) trust, it is recommended that either the division be by means of a "fractional" (rather than a "pecuniary") formula, or, if a pecuniary formula is used, that the benefits be made payable directly to the marital trust so they don't become subject to the pecuniary formula; see ¶ 6.5.08.

E.   Spousal consent. Finally, under certain types of retirement plans, benefits cannot be left to a trust without the consent of the participant's spouse. See ¶ 3.4.

3.3.02 *Leaving retirement benefits to a QTIP trust*

The most popular method of leaving retirement benefits to benefit the surviving spouse is leaving the benefits to her outright (¶ 3.3.11). The second most popular is to leave benefits to a "qualified terminable interest property" (QTIP) trust.

The "classic" QTIP trust provides for all income of the trust to be paid to the surviving spouse for her life, with the principal being paid to the donor's issue on the spouse's death. The spouse may or may not be given access to the principal of the trust during her life (such as through a standard based on health and support, or in the trustee's discretion, or through a 5-and-5 power). The spouse may or may not be given a limited power to appoint the principal at her death. However, the ultimate choice of remainder beneficiaries remains with the participant-donor; compare the General Power marital trust (¶ 3.3.09).

Leaving retirement benefits to a QTIP trust is no tax bargain. Making benefits payable to a marital trust, as opposed to the spouse individually, often results in forced distribution of the benefits sooner (see "B") than would be the case if the spouse personally were named as beneficiary. In addition to the loss of deferral, income-taxable retirement plan distributions to the trust (to the extent not passed out to the spouse as "distributable net income"; ¶ 6.5.02) are taxed to the trust. Trust income tax rates reach the top federal bracket at a much lower level of taxable income than individual rates do; ¶ 6.5.01.

If the client is determined not to leave any assets outright to his spouse, but is unhappy about the adverse MRD and income tax effects of a QTIP trust, consider making the benefits payable to the credit shelter trust, and using other assets to fund the marital trust. Although using this approach with income-taxable benefits is contrary to the usual rule of thumb ("don't waste your credit shelter paying income taxes"), this move could substantially increase the potential deferral for the benefits *if* the spouse is not a beneficiary of the credit shelter trust and the beneficiaries of the credit shelter trust are much younger than the spouse, because MRDs will be spread out over a longer life expectancy period if the trust qualifies as a see-through (¶ 6.2.03).

A.   **How a QTIP trust qualifies for the marital deduction.** Property qualifies for the estate tax marital deduction as QTIP if (1) the spouse is entitled for life to all of the income from the property payable at least annually, (2) no person has the power to appoint any of the property to someone other than the spouse during her lifetime, and (3) the decedent's executor irrevocably elects, on the decedent's estate tax return, to treat the property as QTIP. § 2056(b)(7). See ¶ 3.3.04 for how to determine the "income" the spouse is entitled to. See ¶ 3.3.05–¶ 3.3.06 for how to meet the "entitled" requirement. See ¶ 3.3.03 for requirement of a separate QTIP election for the benefits.

Terminable interests are generally not eligible for the marital deduction, but § 2056(b)(7) allows the marital deduction for this type of trust, even though it definitely is a "terminable interest." To assure the estate tax is merely deferred not eliminated, § 2044 provides that the surviving spouse's estate includes any property for which the marital deduction was elected at the first spouse's death.

B.   **MRD effects.** If the trust qualifies as a see-through trust under the IRS's minimum distribution trust rules, then the Applicable Distribution Period (ADP) for benefits payable to the trust can be based on the life expectancy of the oldest trust beneficiary. See ¶ 6.2 for how to determine if the trust qualifies as a see-through, and ¶ 1.5.03(E) or ¶ 1.5.04(E) for the ADP. Note that, even if the trust qualifies as a see-through, distributing the benefits over the single life expectancy of the surviving spouse (as the oldest trust beneficiary) results in *substantially less deferral* than would be available if the spouse were named as outright beneficiary and rolled over the benefits to her own plan; see ¶ 3.2.01(A)–(C).

3.3.03 *IRS regards benefits, trust, as separate items of QTIP*

Every estate planning lawyer should know how to draft a trust that complies with the marital deduction requirements. Many practitioners assume that, once the standard marital trust is drafted, and the trust is named as beneficiary of the participant's retirement benefits, qualification of those benefits for the estate tax marital deduction is assured (assuming the spouse survives the participant and does not disclaim her interest in the marital trust).

The IRS has a different view. The IRS's position is that, when a retirement plan benefit is payable to a marital trust, both the retirement plan benefit *and* the trust must meet the marital deduction requirements. In the IRS's view, the retirement plan itself is an item of "terminable interest property" separate from the marital trust. Rev. Ruls. 2006-26, 2006-22 IRB 939, and 2000-2, 2000-1 C.B. 305. This IRS positions has two implications:

A. **What to do on the estate tax return.** Rev. Ruls. 2006-26 and 2000-2 require the executor, on the estate tax return (Form 706), to elect QTIP treatment for *both* the retirement benefit *and* the marital trust when retirement benefits are payable to a marital trust, confirming the approach seen in PLR 9442032 as well as Rev. Rul. 89-89, 1989-2 C.B. 231.

B. **How to draft the trust and beneficiary designation form.** The IRS does not require that all the marital deduction language must be recited in the beneficiary designation form as well as in the trust instrument. Although that would be one way to comply with the IRS's directive, Rev. Rul. 2000-2 says that the governing instrument requirements are satisfied with respect to a retirement benefit payable to a marital trust if (1) the marital trust document contains the required language (*e.g.*, giving the spouse the right to all the trust's *and the plan's* income annually) and (2) the retirement plan document does not contain any provisions which would prevent the trustee of the marital trust from complying with the trust's provisions with respect to the plan.

Accordingly it is advisable to specify in the trust instrument not only that the spouse is entitled to all income *of the trust* (which is the standard marital deduction trust language) but in addition to specify that the spouse is entitled to all income *of any retirement plan payable to the trust*. See Form 4.5, Appendix B. If dealing with a would-be marital deduction trust that does not contain this language, and the participant is already deceased, check to see whether the applicable state has enacted a statute automatically correcting this defect.

3.3.04 *Entitled to all income: State law vs. IRS*

One requirement a trust must meet if it is to qualify for the marital deduction is that the spouse must be "entitled for life to all of the income" of the trust. See ¶ 3.3.05 for how to meet the "entitled" part of this requirement. ¶ 6.1.02(D) explains how "income" must be determined, with respect to a retirement plan that is payable to the marital trust, in order to satisfy the marital deduction requirement that the spouse be entitled to the "income."

A marital trust does not have to specify how "income" will be determined with respect to a retirement plan payable to the trust. If the spouse is entitled to the income of the retirement plan, then the trustee must determine that income in a manner that satisfies the IRS requirements, but the trust instrument does not have to spell out how that is done.

In Rev. Rul. 2006-26, the IRS ruled that the "10 percent rule" method of determining "income" with respect to a retirement plan (included in the widely adopted Uniform Principal and Income Act of 1997, "UPIA 1997") does *not* satisfy the marital deduction requirement for income; see ¶ 6.1.02(C). Does this mean that every marital trust drafted prior to that ruling must be amended? No.

Any trust that contains the specific direction that the trustee must pay the surviving spouse *the income of any retirement plan payable to the trust* does not have to be amended to reflect Rev. Rul. 2006-26, for the following reason. Under the IRS's logic, the "income of the retirement plan" means, as noted in ¶ 6.1.02, either the internal investment income of the account or an acceptable unitrust alternative. In the IRS's view, the 10 percent rule dictates how the trustee is to allocate plan distributions in determining the income *of the trust*, but has nothing whatsoever to do with the income *of the plan*! Therefore if the instrument specifically requires the trustee to pay the spouse the income of the trust's share of the plan, the trustee is required to pay her the internal income of the trust's share of the plan (or unitrust amount, if applicable), *regardless* of whether the UPIA 1997 10 percent rule applies to the trust.

While this IRS interpretation probably makes a hash of the UPIA drafters' intent (it seems clear they thought the "income of the plan" was 10 percent of the MRD), it is a blessing for estate planners, because it means that most marital trusts drafted since 1989 with retirement benefits in mind will *not* have to be amended due to Rev. Rul. 2006-26, despite the widespread adoption of UPIA 1997 by state legislatures. The IRS view that the benefits and the trust itself constitute separate items of QTIP has been known since Rev. Rul. 1989-89, 1989-2 C.B. 231, and accordingly many estate planners have long included the extra language specifying that the spouse must receive income "of the plan" as well as "of the trust." For example, the requirement that the trustee pay the spouse the income of the plan, not merely of the trust, has been part of the sample forms in this book since its first edition (1996). See Form 4.5, Appendix B.

A marital trust that is named as beneficiary of a retirement plan, and which states that the surviving spouse is entitled to all income "of the trust," but does *not* specifically state that the spouse is entitled to all income of the trust's interest *in the retirement plan*, should be amended if applicable state law would not require income of the plan to be paid to the surviving spouse.

Trustees of existing marital trusts that hold inherited retirement benefits, where the participant has already died, do not have the option of amending the trust. If the trust does not contain its own IRS-acceptable definition of income with respect to retirement benefits, and does not contain the magic words that the spouse is entitled to the income of the plan, and is governed by the UPIA 1997 10 percent rule, the trustee faces a dilemma. Rev. Rul. 2006-26 indicates that such a trust may not qualify for the marital deduction. However, if the federal estate tax return has been filed and accepted, with the marital deduction allowed, it's not clear what the IRS can do about it at this stage. Fixing this problem is beyond the scope of this book.

3.3.05 *Ways to meet the "entitled" requirement; Income vs. MRD*

In determining whether the spouse is "entitled for life to all of the income" of a marital trust, the same rules apply to both QTIP (¶ 3.3.02) and General Power (¶ 3.3.09) marital trusts. Reg. § 20.2056(b)-7(d)(2). The simplest, most-used, and generally recommended method of meeting the "entitled" requirement is for the trust instrument to require the trustee to withdraw from the plan, each year, and distribute to the surviving spouse, all income of the retirement plan. This method is explained in ¶ 3.3.06.

The primary reason one might wish to investigate *other* methods would be to achieve greater deferral of the retirement plan distributions; if the trustee does not have to withdraw the "income," the theory is, that income can be allowed to accumulate tax-deferred or tax-free inside the retirement plan. Looking into these other alternatives is worthwhile only if there is likely to be any income in excess of the MRD amount; see "A." For more on these other alternatives, see "B."

A.   **Does the "income" actually exceed the MRD?** Regardless of whether the trustee is required to withdraw "income" from the retirement plan, the trustee must withdraw the minimum required distribution (MRD) annually. See Chapter 1. Thus, if the trust instrument requires the trustee to withdraw the "income" annually, what it is really requiring is that the trustee withdraw from the retirement plan each year the income or the MRD, whichever is the larger amount; see PLR 2005-22012 for an example of a marital trust that specified the trustee had to withdraw the greater of the two amounts. The trustee must calculate both amounts each year in any case.

The MRD may be more or less than the income. The spouse is entitled to the "income," but the marital deduction rules do not require that she receive the entire MRD (if that is larger than the income). f the income of the retirement plan benefit is greater than the MRD, it would be desirable not to have to distribute the excess amount out of the retirement plan if such distribution *could* have been deferred until later under the minimum distribution rules.

The maximum period of deferral for benefits left to a classic QTIP trust that qualifies as a "see-through" (¶ 6.2.03) is the life expectancy of the oldest trust beneficiary (¶ 1.5.03(D), ¶ 1.5.04(D)), who is (in most cases) the spouse. If the surviving spouse is age 51 or older at the participant's death, the MRD based on her life expectancy (¶ 1.5.05) will be more than three percent of the benefits: The "divisor" at age 51 under the Single Life Table is 33.3, which translates to an MRD of three percent of the value of the plan. Each year the divisor declines and the corresponding percentage increases (¶ 1.2.01, #3). Thus, unless the income rate of the retirement benefit is more than three percent, the MRD for a spouse over age 51 will be more than the income—meaning that the trustee will have to withdraw more than the income. Thus, in many cases, *there is no advantage to allowing the trustee to accumulate income inside the retirement plan because the minimum distribution rules will prevent him from doing so.*

B.   Other methods of complying with "entitled" requirement. If the current distribution of "all income" would result in significant acceleration of distributions, the planner will look for a way to avoid such current distribution. Other methods of meeting the "entitled" requirement are permitted in IRS regulations and by Rev. Rul. 2006-26.

One approach that some have considered is to treat the retirement plan as "unproductive" (i.e., non-income-producing) property, which can be held in a marital trust if the surviving spouse is given the right to demand that it be made income producing (see Reg. § 20.2056(b)-5(f)(4)) or if compensating payments are made to her from other assets of the trust (Reg. § 20.2056(b)-5(f)(5)). The problem with this approach is that it is clear (from Rev. Rul. 2006-26) that the IRS does not consider the IRA to be unproductive property if it is invested in income-producing property. Nor is it clear that distributions to the spouse from *other* (non-retirement plan) assets held by the marital trust could be used to replace the missing income payments with regard to the retirement plan, since the IRS regards them as separate items of QTIP.

A more viable approach is to give the surviving spouse the right to demand the income, rather than distributing it to the spouse automatically, as permitted by Reg. § 20.2056(b)-5(f)(8). Use of this method of complying with the entitled-to-all-income requirement involves substantial additional complications. For more on this alternative, see the author's *Special Report: Retirement Benefits and the Marital Deduction (Including Planning for the Noncitizen Spouse)* (Appendix C).

3.3.06 *Distribute all income to spouse annually*

The easiest way to comply with the all-income requirement is to require the trustee to withdraw from the retirement plan each year, and distribute to the spouse, the "income" of the retirement plan. Reg. § 20.2056(b)-5(f)(8). This method was "blessed" by the IRS in Rev.

Rul. 89-89, 1989-2 C.B. 231, and Rev. Rul. 2006-26, and is believed to be the most commonly used by estate planners. See, *e.g.*, PLRs 9321035, 9321059, 9418026, and 9348025. For an example of a form using this method, see Form 4.5, Appendix B. Unless the "income" substantially exceeds the MRD, this method does not have significant tax drawbacks (beyond the usual drawbacks of leaving retirement benefits to a marital trust in the first place; see ¶ 3.3.02).

Even if use of this method does require distribution to the spouse of an amount significantly greater than the MRD, that would not mean loss of deferral if the spouse rolls over the excess to her own retirement plan. The IRS has repeatedly ruled that a surviving spouse may roll over retirement plan distributions that are made to her through a trust if she was entitled to receive that amount; see ¶ 3.2.09. While these rulings generally involved the spouse's rolling over a one-time at-death distribution of the entire plan balance, PLRs 2005-43064 and 2009-44059 affirm that the same principle would allow the spouse to roll over any distributions she is entitled to receive (through the trust) from the inherited retirement plan to the extent such distributions exceed the MRD (which cannot be rolled over; ¶ 2.6.03).

Prior to 2000, the IRS's position was that the distribution from the plan of all income annually was the *only* method available for a retirement benefit payable to a trust to qualify for the marital deduction. Rev. Rul. 89-89, 1989-2 C.B. 231. In Rev. Rul. 2000-2, 2000-1 C.B. 305, the IRS reversed this position and acknowledged that a marital trust funded with retirement benefits can use other methods permitted in its regulations for meeting the "entitled for life to all income" requirement. Rev. Rul. 2000-2 announced that it "obsoleted" Rev. Rul.89-89, which led to some confusion among practitioners. The method "blessed" in Rev. Rul. 89-89 for complying with the entitled-to-all-income requirement (namely, requiring annual distribution of all plan income to the spouse) still works; Rev. Rul. 2000-2 obsoleted Rev. Rul. 89-89 only to the extent Rev. Rul. 89-89 said this was the *only* method that worked.

3.3.07 *Do not require stub income to be paid to spouse's estate!*

Suppose a marital deduction trust receives income throughout the year, collects it in a bank account, and then periodically distributes everything in the account to the surviving spouse—say, quarterly or annually. What happens if the surviving spouse dies after the trust has collected some income but before the trust has gotten around to distributing that income to her?

The trustee is NOT required to pay this "stub income" to the surviving spouse's estate as a condition of qualifying for the marital deduction. Reg. § 20.2056(b)-7(d)(4) specifically provides that "An income interest does not fail to constitute a qualifying income interest for life solely because income between the last distribution date and the date of the surviving spouse's death is not required to be distributed to the surviving spouse or to the estate of the surviving spouse." Yet some trust-drafters, apparently under the mistaken impression that such a provision is required as a condition of qualifying for the marital deduction, include in their marital trusts a provision that such stub income must be paid to the estate of the surviving spouse. The result of including this provision is that the surviving spouse's estate (a nonindividual; ¶ 1.7.04) will be considered a countable beneficiary of the trust for minimum distribution purposes, causing the trust to "flunk" the IRS's minimum distribution trust rules (unless the trust is a conduit trust; see ¶ 6.3.05). See ¶ 6.2.09.

3.3.08 *Combination marital deduction-conduit trust*

A marital trust can also be a conduit trust. Under a conduit trust, the trustee must distribute to the conduit beneficiary (the surviving spouse in this case) ALL distributions the trustee receives from the retirement plan that is payable to the trust; see ¶ 6.3.05. There are two ways to draft a combination marital trust-conduit trust.

One method is to require the trustee to withdraw from the plan each year, and distribute to the spouse, the income of the trust's share of the retirement plan for such year or the MRD for such year, whichever is greater (and to distribute to the spouse any additional amounts the trustee withdraws from the plan). This combination is used by some practitioners who want a relatively simple structure that clearly qualifies for the marital deduction and as a see-through trust for minimum distribution purposes. See Form 4.7, Appendix B.

Another method which might be of interest if the participant has many years to go before he will reach age 70½ is to require the trustee to pass all plan distributions out to the spouse (as always is required under a conduit trust), but give the spouse only the right to *demand* income (¶ 3.3.05(B)) rather than requiring the trustee to automatically *distribute* all income regardless of demand. Since such a trust could defer the commencement of distributions until the participant would have reached age 70½ (¶ 1.6.06(A)), this approach could substantially extend the deferral of distributions compared with a standard QTIP trust. *All* plan distributions could be deferred until the year the participant would have reached age 70½. This approach makes a difference only if the participant died at a relatively young age.

3.3.09 *General Power marital trust*

A General Power marital trust is similar to a QTIP marital trust (¶ 3.3.02), in that the surviving spouse must be entitled to all of the trust's income for life. What is different is that the spouse must *also* have the right to appoint the principal to herself *or her estate*, which gives the spouse much more control than a QTIP trust gives her. It is used less often than a QTIP, since a client willing to give the spouse this much control would usually be willing to name the spouse as outright beneficiary. For MRD purposes, if spouse is given the power to appoint the trust property at her death to her own estate, the trust will be deemed to have a nonindividual beneficiary (¶ 1.7.04), and accordingly will not qualify as a see-through trust (¶ 6.3.11) unless it is a conduit trust (¶ 6.3.05) or (possibly) a 100 percent grantor trust as to the spouse (see¶ 6.3.10).

3.3.10 *Automatic QTIP election for "survivor annuities"*

§ 2056(b)(7)(C) provides that "[i]n the case of an annuity included in the gross estate of the decedent under section 2039...where only the surviving spouse has the right to receive payments before the death of such surviving spouse—(i) the interest of such surviving spouse shall be treated as a qualifying income interest for life, and (ii) the executor shall be treated as having made" a QTIP election for such property unless the executor elects *not* to have QTIP treatment apply. Retirement plan benefits are considered annuities, includible in the participant's estate under § 2039, whether or not paid in the form of true annuities, and thus are subject to this rule. Reg. § 20.2039-1(b).

The automatic QTIP treatment for "annuities" is a nice backup when retirement benefits are left outright to the spouse (¶ 3.3.11). It can also be helpful when retirement benefits are paid in the form of a true annuity and payments could continue after the surviving spouse's death.

If the first spouse's estate is not large enough to be subject to estate taxes, so the estate "does not need" the automatic QTIP election to eliminate estate tax, see Rev. Proc. 2001-38, 2001-1 C.B. 1335, which makes certain "unnecessary" QTIP elections automatically void. If the automatic QTIP election applicable to an annuity in the first estate is voided, the value of the annuity remaining at the surviving spouse's subsequent death would not be includible in his estate *under § 2044*; see PLR 2003-18039. (The asset may still be included in the surviving spouse's estate under some *other* Code provision.)

3.3.11 *Marital deduction for benefits left outright to spouse*

Death benefits payable directly to the spouse outright in a lump sum should qualify for the marital deduction, if the spouse is a U.S. citizen and entitled to withdraw all the benefits. See, *e.g.*, PLR 8843033. Where the spouse is named as sole beneficiary, with the unrestricted right to withdraw all the benefits, no part of the participant's interest in the plan passes to someone other than the spouse or her estate, so the spouse has not received a "terminable interest" (¶ 3.3.01).

There is one possible quibble with this conclusion. If the participant or plan document has also named a successor beneficiary (¶ 1.5.12(C), (D)), to receive the remaining benefits if the spouse survives the participant but dies before having withdrawn all the benefits, some might argue that the spouse has a nondeductible terminable interest under § 2056(b)(1). The author does not believe that this scenario creates a nondeductible interest. The spouse's interest meets the description of a deductible interest in § 2056(b)(5), which provides that an interest is not a nondeductible terminable interest if the spouse is entitled to all the income for life and has the right (exercisable by her alone and in all events) to appoint the principal to herself with no person having the power to appoint it to someone other than her. Compare Reg. § 20.2056(b)-5(g)(2). But in any case, at worst, the spouse's outright interest as beneficiary would qualify for the "automatic QTIP election" under § 2056(b)(7)(C) (see ¶ 3.3.10).

To eliminate the concern, the beneficiary form could recite that the spouse has the right to withdraw all income and principal of the benefits, tracking the wording of § 2056(b)(5) and Reg. § 20.2056(b)-5(f)(8), when (1) the participant is naming his spouse outright as beneficiary and (2) the participant or plan document names a successor beneficiary (other than the spouse's estate) who will be entitled to receive the benefits that the spouse does not withdraw during her lifetime.

3.4 REA '84 and Spousal Consent

This ¶ 3.4 describes the federal rights granted to spouses of retirement plan participants by the "**Retirement Equity Act of 1984**" ("**REA**"), and discusses the estate planning implications of these rights. The applicable law is in IRC § 401(a)(11) and § 417, and the virtually identical ERISA § 205 (29 U.S.C. § 1055); and Regs. § 1.401(a)-20 and § 1.417(e)-1.

The purpose of this ¶ 3.4 is to provide a brief overview of REA's requirements and exemptions, for estate planners. For complete explanation of REA, see Chapter 10 of *The Pension Answer Book* (Appendix C). This book does not cover state law spousal rights such as community property.

3.4.01 *Introduction to the Retirement Equity Act of 1984*

Retirement plans fall into three categories with respect to REA's requirements: plans that are subject to the full panoply of REA requirements (all pension plans, some profit-sharing plans, some 403(b) plans; ¶ 3.4.02); plans that are subject to a modified version of the REA requirements (some profit-sharing plans and some 403(b) plans; ¶ 3.4.03); and plans that are totally exempt from REA's requirements (IRAs, Roth IRAs, and some 403(b) plans; ¶ 3.4.04). With respect to covered plans, the Supreme Court has held that REA preempts state spousal rights laws such as community property; *Boggs v. Boggs*, 570 U.S. 833 (1997).

3.4.02 *Plans subject to full-scale REA requirements*

If a plan is fully subject to REA, then, generally (for exceptions see ¶ 3.4.05), ANY benefits distributed by that plan to a married employee MUST be distributed in the form of a "qualified joint and survivor annuity" (QJSA), unless the employee has waived that form of benefit and the employee's spouse consents to the waiver. If a married employee covered by such a plan dies before retirement, then the plan MUST pay his surviving spouse a "qualified pre-retirement survivor annuity" (QPSA) unless she has waived the right to receive the QPSA. The spousal consent or waiver must meet certain requirements. ¶ 3.4.06. The plan must offer additional joint annuity options after 2007 as a result of PPA '06; see § 417(a). Plan loans may require a spousal consent; see ¶ 2.1.07.

A QJSA is an annuity (1) for the life of the participant with a survivor annuity for the life of his spouse which is not less than 50 percent of (and is not greater than 100 percent of) the amount of the annuity which is payable during the joint lives of the participant and spouse, and (2) which is the actuarial equivalent of a single annuity for the life of the participant.

The definition of a QPSA is even more elaborate. Basically, it is supposed to be the annuity the spouse would have received under the QJSA had the employee lived to retirement, retired with a QJSA, then died. In the case of a defined contribution plan (¶ 8.3.05), the value of the QPSA is defined as an annuity equal in value to 50 percent of the employee's account balance. § 417(c)(2).

All *pension plans* are subject to the QJSA/QPSA requirements described in this ¶ 3.4.02. Defined benefit plans (¶ 8.3.04) and Money Purchase plans (¶ 8.3.10) are in this category. § 401(a)(11)(B). Other types of qualified retirement plans (QRPs), namely, profit-sharing and stock bonus plans, may or may not be subject to these rules, depending on whether they fit into the "exemption" (which is not really an exemption, just a modified version of the requirements) described at ¶ 3.4.03.

3.4.03 *REA requirements for "exempt" profit-sharing plans*

Certain QRPs are exempt from the QJSA/QPSA requirements of REA described at ¶ 3.4.02. Although this type of plan could be any type of QRP other than a "pension" plan, i.e., it could be a profit-sharing or stock bonus plan, these plans are called here "exempt profit-sharing plans." However, these plans are not "exempt" from *REA*, because (as a condition of being exempt from the QJSA/QPSA requirements) they still have to provide a spousal death benefit.

A qualified retirement plan that is *not* a pension plan is generally not subject to the QJSA/QPSA requirements described at ¶ 3.4.02. The exceptions would be, if the plan offers retirement benefits in the form of annuities, or was merged with a pension plan, or if it has a benefit formula that is integrated with a pension plan, then the plan is subject to the pension plan rules. See Reg. § 1.401(a)-20, A-4, A-5.

Most significantly for estate planning, in order to be "exempt" from the QJSA/QPSA requirements, a profit-sharing plan must provide "that the participant's nonforfeitable accrued benefit is payable in full, upon the participant's death, to the participant's surviving spouse (unless the participant elects, with spousal consent that satisfies the requirements of section 417(a)(2), that such benefit be provided instead to a designated beneficiary)." Thus, the only way a profit-sharing plan can be "exempt" from the QJSA/QPSA requirements is by paying 100 percent of the participant's account to the participant's spouse at the participant's death unless the spouse consents to waive this right.

Even though it must offer certain spousal benefits under REA, an exempt profit-sharing plan is still critically different from a pension plan. Under an exempt profit-sharing plan, the employee can withdraw ALL his benefits from the plan whenever the plan permits him to do so (typically, upon separation from service, although some profit-sharing plans permit in-service distributions) WITHOUT the consent of his spouse. He can then roll the benefits over to an IRA and continue to enjoy tax deferral without any further obligations to his spouse under federal law (¶ 3.4.04).

The trade-off is that, if the employee dies BEFORE having withdrawn the benefits from the plan, 100 percent of his benefits (including proceeds of any life insurance policy held in the plan) must be paid to the surviving spouse, unless she has consented to waive this right. Reg. § 1.401(a)-20, A-12(b).

3.4.04 IRAs, Roth IRAs, and 403(b) plans

IRAs and Roth IRAs are not subject to REA; neither ERISA § 205 nor IRC § 401(a)(11) applies to IRAs or Roth IRAs (with the possible exception of SEP-IRAs and SIMPLEs, a subject beyond the scope of this book).

Finally, we come to the special case of 403(b) plans. Although 403(b) plans are subject to some of the same § 401(a) requirements as qualified plans (see § 403(b)(10), (12)), § 401(a)(11) is not one of the 401(a) provisions "imported" into § 403(b), which would make it at first appear that 403(b) plans are not subject to REA. However, even though the tax Code REA provisions don't apply, *some* 403(b) plans are subject to ERISA—which has its own set of QJSA/QPSA requirements. Therefore, "to the extent that section 205 [of ERISA] covers section 403(b) contracts and custodial accounts they are treated as section 401(a) plans" for purposes of the QJSA/QPSA requirements. Reg.§ 1.401(a)-20, A-3(d). Therefore, some 403(b) plans are subject to REA and some are not.

The 403(b) plans NOT covered by ERISA (and therefore not subject to REA) are those funded exclusively by means of elective employee deferrals (salary reduction agreements). 403(b) plans funded in whole or in part by employer contributions are subject to ERISA and therefore also to the REA requirements. DOL Reg. § 2510.3-2(f).

403(b) plans that are subject to ERISA and offer annuity benefits to the participant will be subject to REA's full QJSA/QPSA requirements, just like a pension plan (¶ 3.4.02). A 403(b) plan that is subject to ERISA but that does *not* offer annuity benefits (*i.e.*, a plan funded exclusively with mutual fund custodial accounts pursuant to § 403(b)(7)) can use the alternative compliance procedure available to "exempt" profit-sharing plans (¶ 3.4.03).

3.4.05 *Various REA exceptions and miscellaneous points*

There are exceptions to the REA requirements, even for covered plans. These exceptions, are usually not significant in estate planning, but may be significant in a particular client's situation.

For example, no spousal consent is required for distribution of benefits to the participant when the total value of his benefits is under $5,000. Reg. § 1.411(a)-11(c)(3). There are modified rules for ESOPs (§ 401(a)(11)(C)) and exceptions for certain benefits accrued before REA's effective date (1984). No spousal consent is required if "it is established to the satisfaction of a plan representative that the consent...may not be obtained because there is no spouse, because the spouse cannot be located...." § 417(a)(2)(B).

Even the "significant" exceptions can be insignificant if the plan negates the exception by giving the spouse more rights than REA requires, usually for reasons of administrative convenience. For example, REA does not require that a QPSA, or 100 percent-death-benefit-in-lieu-of-QPSA, be paid to a spouse who was married to the participant for less than a year prior to the date of death. § 417(d); § 401(a)(11)(D). However, many retirement plan designers decided it was easier to grant the same rights to *all* spouses, regardless of the length of the marriage.

Similarly, the value of the legally-required QPSA (which is supposed to be equivalent only to the survivor pension the spouse would have received under a QJSA) is less than the total value of the employee's accrued benefit in the plan. However, some plans simply award every nonconsenting spouse 100 percent of the value of the participant's benefit, presumably because that is administratively easier than figuring out for each individual employee and spouse what would have been the relative values of their shares under a QJSA.

The spouse loses her REA rights upon divorce or legal separation or her "abandonment" of the participant. Reg. § 1.401(a)-20, A-27. (Instead, she may receive a share of the benefits through a "qualified domestic relations order" issued in connection with the divorce; see § 414(p).)

3.4.06 *Requirements for spousal consent or waiver*

§ 417 and regulations contain elaborate rules that must be complied with in order to have a valid spousal consent to the participant's waiver of the QPSA or the QJSA. The IRS has published sample spousal consent forms. Notice 97-10, 1997-1 C.B. 370.

REA creates serious, and sad, difficulties when a mentally disabled spouse is unable to consent to the desired estate plan. In that case consent can be provided only by the spouse's legal guardian. Reg. § 1.401(a)-20, A-27.

✓   The participant's waiver of a QPSA, and the spouse's consent to such waiver, must be given after the beginning of the plan year in which the participant reaches age 35, and prior to the employee's death. § 417(a)(6)(B). The IRS, unlike the Code itself, permits waiver of the QPSA even *before* the participant reaches age 35, provided the participant goes through the waiver/consent process *again* after reaching age 35. Reg. § 1.401(a)-20, A-33.

✓   For exempt profit-sharing plans (¶ 3.4.03), the spousal consent for waiver of the 100 percent-death-benefit may be provided "at any time," including before the participant reaches age 35. Reg. § 1.401(a)-20, A-33(a).

✓   Waiver of the QJSA benefit must occur not more than 90 days prior to the annuity starting date, so it is impossible to lock in spousal consent far in advance.

✓   REA rights cannot be waived in a prenuptial agreement, because the employee's affianced is not at that point the "spouse," even if the agreement is executed within the applicable election period. Reg. § 1.401(a)-20, A-28. A prenuptial agreement can, however, settle the parties' rights with respect to division of retirement benefit in case of divorce, because REA does not provide any spousal rights in the benefits in case of divorce (that subject being left to the divorce court).

✓   "No consent is valid unless the participant has received a general description of the material features, and an explanation of the relative values of, the optional forms of benefit available under the plan in a manner which would satisfy the notice requirements of section 417(a)(3)." Reg. § 1.417(e)-1(b)(2)(i). Although this disclosure must be provided to the *participant* rather than to the spouse, the spouse's consent to the participant's waiver of the QJSA or QPSA must "acknowledge the effect" of the election. § 417(a)(2)A)(i). This probably means that the spouse should see the same disclosures provided to the participant, in order that the spouse may understand the effect of the waiver.

✓   An election in proper form "designates a beneficiary (or a form of benefits) which may not be changed without spousal consent (or the consent of the spouse expressly permits designations by the participant without any requirement of further consent by the spouse), and...the spouse's consent acknowledges the effect of such election and is witnessed by a plan representative or a notary public...." § 417(a)(2)(A). See Reg. § 1.401(a)-20, A-31, for more on the form of spousal consent.

✓   If the spouse consents to the participant's naming a trust as beneficiary, later amendments to the trust do not require a subsequent spousal consent. Reg. § 1.401(a)-20, A-31(a).

3.4.07 *Spousal waiver or consent: Transfer tax aspects*

Would a surviving spouse's waiver of REA benefits, after the participant's death, be considered a disclaimer? And, if it is a disclaimer, is it a "qualified" disclaimer if the spouse's rights "vested" in her before the participant's death, so that the disclaimer is "too late" if made more than nine months after such vesting? See ¶ 4.4.06 regarding the deadline for a qualified disclaimer.

There is no concern about possible gift tax implications of a spousal waiver *before* the participant's death, because § 2503(f) provides that, "If any individual waives, *before the death of a participant*, any survivor benefit, or right to such benefit, *under § 401(a)(11) or 417* ["REA" benefits, in other words], such waiver shall not be treated as a transfer of property by gift for purposes of this chapter" (emphasis added). This gift tax exemption for lifetime spousal waivers or REA benefits seems to suggest that:

♦ Spousal waivers of REA-guaranteed benefits *after* the participant's death *could be* treated as a gift-taxable transfers. However, GCM 39858 (which was issued in 1989, though it is inexplicably dated 9/9/81) negated this suggestion, stating that § 2503(f) creates "no inference" that Congress intended to impose gift tax on spousal waivers that occur *after* the participant's death. GCM 39858 involved a spousal disclaimer of REA-guaranteed benefits and does not mention any deadline for such a disclaimer earlier than nine months after the participant's death, holding that: "There is no evidence that Congress intended to preclude a spouse from disclaiming or renouncing benefits under a qualified plan payable after the participant's death."

♦ Since the statutory exemption is limited to REA-guaranteed benefits, and many plans actually grant the spouse *more* rights than REA guarantees (see ¶ 3.4.05), a spousal waiver of such excess benefits *could be* treated as a gift-taxable transfer. There have been no cases or rulings on this question.

4

Inherited Benefits: Advising Executors and Beneficiaries

Considerations that apply in administering and distributing retirement plan benefits after the participant's death.

This Chapter examines tax considerations that apply after the death of a retirement plan participant; it deals with *inherited* retirement benefits. It begins with the "Executor's Road Map" (¶ 4.1.01) and ends with the "Beneficiary's Road Map" (¶ 4.7). See also ¶ 2.1.07 (tax effects of plan loans outstanding on the date of death) and ¶ 9.1.04 (death benefits exempt from the 10% "early distributions" penalty).

In this Chapter, unless otherwise specified, the "executor" means the executor, administrator, or personal representative of the estate of a deceased retirement plan participant.

4.1 Executor's Responsibilities

This ¶ 4.1 discusses an executor's responsibilities that are uniquely related to the decedent's retirement benefits.

4.1.01 *The Executor's Road Map*

Here are matters an executor needs to consider with respect to the decedent's retirement benefits that do not arise with respect to other assets. If the estate is the beneficiary of any of the decedent's retirement plans, the executor should also review the "Beneficiary's Road Map," ¶ 4.7.

✓ Whether the executor can or should "recharacterize" any traditional or Roth IRA contributions made by the decedent. ¶ 4.1.02.

✓ Whether the executor may make contributions (or withdraw contributions made) on the decedent's behalf to an IRA. ¶ 4.1.03.

✓ Whether the executor should seek to "roll over" any retirement plan distributions made to the participant prior to his death. ¶ 4.1.04.

✓ Whether the decedent took all "minimum required distributions" he was supposed to take, and if not, what the executor must do about it if anything. ¶ 4.1.05.

✓ How to report retirement benefits on the participant's federal estate tax return and pay the estate tax. ¶ 4.3.

✓ Whether the executor can or should disclaim any retirement benefits on the decedent's behalf. See ¶ 4.4.11(C) and ¶ 4.4.12.

4.1.02 *Recharacterizing the decedent's Roth conversion*

Chapter 5 explains Roth IRAs, how they differ from "traditional" IRAs, and how an individual, after having made a contribution to one type of IRA, can change his mind and "recharacterize" the contribution so it is deemed to have been contributed to the other type (see ¶ 5.6). Although certain "regular contributions" to IRAs can be recharacterized, most recharacterizations will involve undoing Roth IRA "conversions" (¶ 5.4); the rest of this ¶ 4.1.02 deals with the post-mortem recharacterization of a Roth conversion done by the decedent.

This discussion assumes that the decedent died prior to the deadline for recharacterizing his Roth conversion; see ¶ 5.6.06. According to the regulations, the recharacterization election "may be made on behalf of a deceased IRA owner by his or her executor, administrator, or other person responsible for filing the final Federal income tax return of the decedent under section 6012(b)(1)." Reg. § 1.408A-5, A-6(c).

Although this sounds reasonable, there is a significant "mechanical" problem with the regulation's approach. A recharacterization is accomplished by transferring the conversion contribution, plus earnings thereon, out of the Roth IRA and into a traditional IRA by means of an IRA-to-IRA transfer. See ¶ 5.6.03.

Unless the estate is the beneficiary of the Roth IRA, it is not clear how the executor will persuade the IRA sponsor to transfer the money to a different IRA when the executor does not have title to the account; the *beneficiary* owns the account from the moment the participant dies. ¶ 4.2.01.

IRA sponsors could alleviate this "mechanical" problem (and gift tax concerns; see below) by including in their IRA documents a provision to the effect that, if the sponsor receives timely notice from the deceased participant's executor that any contribution to the account is being recharacterized, the sponsor will forthwith transfer the contribution in question (plus or minus earnings thereon) to an IRA of the other type, with the same IRA sponsor, and with terms identical (except as required to reflect that it is the other type of IRA) to the existing account; and that the beneficiary designation applicable to the original IRA will also apply to the account created by the recharacterization. The IRS could help by including such a provision in its Forms 5305 and 5305-A (sample IRA/Roth IRA documents). See PLR 2002-34074 in which an IRA sponsor proceeded in that manner (presumably without the benefit of having such language in its documents).

If such a provision is not included in the IRA sponsor's documents, the estate planner should consider including it in the beneficiary designation form. See ¶ 5.8.06 for other issues the estate planner should consider in connection with Roth conversions and recharacterizations.

However, this solution is neither simple nor foolproof:

♦   The documents would need to protect the IRA provider by providing a mechanism for it to determine with finality who is the "executor" entitled to make this election; the amount of the recharacterized contribution and the earnings thereon; and whether the recharacterization was done within the applicable deadline.

♦   If the beneficiary cashes out the Roth IRA before the executor recharacterizes the contribution to it, the executor loses the ability to recharacterize. Recharacterization requires an IRA-to-IRA transfer, which can't be done once the account has been distributed. See ¶ 5.6.03(A)(1). This seems to be a trump card held by the beneficiary, unless the plan documents provide that the beneficiary may not withdraw from the account prior to the recharacterization deadline without the executor's consent.

Because of this "mechanical" problem, the IRS might have to revise its regulation to specify that the beneficiary (rather than the executor) has the power to recharacterize the Roth conversion. Here are other issues and concerns with respect to a post-mortem recharacterization of a pre-mortem Roth conversion:

✓   **Fiduciary problems.** If the Roth IRA is payable to a beneficiary other than the estate itself, there is a conflict of interest, with respect to the recharacterization decision, between the probate estate (which would get to "keep" the income taxes the decedent would otherwise have owed on the Roth conversion, if the conversion is recharacterized) and the beneficiary of the Roth IRA (whose IRA distributions will be income-taxable instead of tax-free if recharacterization occurs). Unless the will provides to the contrary, the executor's fiduciary duty to the estate may require him to recharacterize any Roth conversion (assuming the executor can figure out *how* to do so), in order to recoup the income taxes and so maximize the estate value.

✓   **Estate tax consequences.** If recharacterization does *not* occur, any income tax owed by the estate on the Roth conversion would be deductible for federal estate tax purposes as a debt of the estate, despite the fact that the executor could have undone the conversion and thus "cancelled" the income tax debt. See Reg. § 20.2053-6(f).

✓   **Gift tax concern.** If recharacterization requires the consent of the Roth IRA beneficiary (which would appear generally to be the case, unless the account documents provide otherwise), and as a result of the Roth IRA beneficiary's consent the beneficiaries of the probate estate are "enriched" at the formerly-Roth-IRA beneficiary's expense, there may be a question whether the Roth IRA beneficiary has made a gift to the estate beneficiaries (unless the beneficiaries of the Roth IRA and of the estate are the same people in the same proportions).

✓   **"Acceptance" is not a concern.** One requirement of disclaiming retirement benefits (¶ 4.4) is that the beneficiary must not have taken any actions to "accept" the inherited account. *No such requirement applies to the recharacterization election.* Thus, the Roth IRA beneficiary could register the IRA in his name as an inherited IRA (see ¶ 4.2.01) and/or change the investments inside the account (compare ¶ 4.4.04), *without* adversely impacting the ability to recharacterize.

4.1.03 *Who can make or withdraw decedent's IRA contribution?*

See ¶ 2.1.08 regarding a participant's ability to "cancel" an IRA contribution by withdrawing the contribution (and earnings thereon) prior to the extended due date of his tax return. If the participant died prior to that deadline without having withdrawn the contribution, can the executor or account beneficiary exercise this right on the deceased participant's behalf? The beneficiary, not the executor, owns the IRA upon the participant's death (¶ 4.2.01). Absent contrary language in the IRA documents, it would appear that only the beneficiary has the right to withdraw an IRA contribution or any other moneys held in the IRA.

As to whether an executor can make a regular IRA contribution on behalf of the decedent, the only guidance is PLR 8439066, in which the IRS ruled that an executor could *not* make a regular IRA contribution on behalf of the decedent (or the decedent's surviving unemployed spouse).

4.1.04 *Completing rollover of distribution made to the decedent*

If the participant receives a distribution, but then dies before rolling it over to another plan, can the participant's executor complete the rollover?

Note: This ¶ 4.1.04 deals with rolling over, after the participant's death, a distribution that occurred prior to the participant's death. If the distribution did not occur prior to the participant's death, there is no rollover to "complete"—even if the participant had requested the distribution and direct rollover prior to his death and done everything necessary to effectuate such distribution/rollover. See PLR 2002-04038, denying beneficiaries the right to complete a deceased participant's rollover in those circumstances. See also ¶ 3.2.05.

Note also: If the pre-death distribution took the form of a "direct rollover," where the distributing plan sent out a check payable to the transferee IRA, and the participant died before the check got deposited into the transferee IRA, the executor can deposit the check in the transferee IRA; see ¶ 2.1.03(A).

The ability of survivors to roll over *post-death* distributions is covered in ¶ 3.2 (surviving spouse) and ¶ 4.2 (other beneficiaries).

A.   **Rollovers by surviving spouses and others.** Rev. Proc. 2003-16, 2003-1 C.B. 359, appears to concede that an executor can complete a rollover of a distribution made to the decedent prior to his death. The Rev. Proc. states that the IRS will consider requests for waiver of the 60-day deadline applicable to rollovers (¶ 2.6.06) if the failure to timely complete the rollover is due to (among other possible causes listed) "death." Thus, with an IRS hardship waiver (¶ 2.6.07), an executor definitely *can* roll over a distribution made to the participant, if the participant's death prevented the participant from completing the rollover within 60 days of the distribution.

If the decedent's rollover can be completed by the executor *more than* 60 days after the distribution date (under grant of an IRS hardship waiver), then must it not be true that the executor can complete the rollover (without an IRS waiver) *within* 60 days of the original distribution? Despite Rev. Proc. 2003-16, however, the IRS for a while permitted post-death rollovers of pre-death distributions only when the requestor was the participant's surviving spouse. In these PLRs, it usually appears that the surviving spouse had been the sole beneficiary of the plan from which the pre-death distribution was taken. See, *e.g.*, PLRs 2004-15012, 2004-20037, 2004-18045, and 2005-20038. But requests by nonspouse executors were denied, on the grounds that only the participant and the surviving spouse were permitted to roll over a distribution. See, *e.g.*, PLR 2004-15011.

Then, in 2005, the IRS started allowing post-death rollovers of pre-death distributions by nonspouse executors more liberally, under circumstances that clearly met the "hardship waiver" standard. Several such rulings involved a distribution that was "unintentional" (provider error in PLR 2005-02050 and 2007-40020; participant's lack of mental capacity when he received the distribution in PLRs 2005-16021 and 2007-40020; clerical error by attorney in fact in PLR 2005-16022). Two of the rulings also involved some financial institution error (erroneous income tax withholding in PLR 2005-02050; failure to issue 1099-R in PLR 2005-16022) as well as evidence that the participant had attempted to complete the rollover prior to his death. Three (PLRs 2007-17021, 2007-42027, and 2009-10069) involved individuals who died after requesting the distribution but before or shortly after receiving the check. In PLR 2009-24056, the participant's severe medical problems prevented him from completing the rollover prior to death. Meanwhile, the IRS also continued to allow post-death rollovers of pre-death distributions by surviving spouses. See PLRs 2005-23029, 2007-17021, and 2007-19018.

However, understandably, the post-death rollover was not allowed where the distribution had occurred more than three years prior to the participant's death, and the participant had spent the entire distribution prior to his death. PLR 2007-35029.

B.   **But no "Designated Beneficiary" allowed!** In order for inherited retirement benefits to be eligible for the favorable "stretch" (life expectancy of the beneficiary) payout method under the minimum distribution rules (¶ 1.5.05), the benefits must be payable to a "Designated Beneficiary." ¶ 1.7.01. Inherited benefits are always payable to some "beneficiary," but not just any old beneficiary qualifies as a *Designated* Beneficiary. ¶ 1.7.03. The IRS's position is that an IRA created by the participant's executor (to receive a rollover of a distribution made prior to the participant's death) cannot possibly have a "Designated Beneficiary" for minimum distribution purposes. See PLRs 2001-26036, 2005-16021, 2005-16022, 2005-20038, 2007-17021, 2007-19018, 2007-40020, 2009-10069 and 2009-24056.

This IRS position is unfortunate. It is not clear why, if (for example) a participant withdrew funds from his IRA when mentally incompetent (as was the case in PLR 2007-40020), and the IRS agrees that the funds should be restored to the IRA after the participant's death to avoid hardship, the IRS would object to having the funds restored to an IRA that has a "Designated Beneficiary," even if the beneficiary is designated by the executor (pursuant to a court order or other proper procedures). The IRS had no problem with allowing Designated Beneficiary status for an IRA established post-death (as a result of an executor's "recharacterization" of the decedent's Roth IRA contribution) in PLR 2002-34074 (see ¶ 4.1.02).

The IRS *might* recognize a Designated Beneficiary for MRD purposes if the rollover is made into a pre-existing account (created by the deceased participant) that already had a Designated Beneficiary (as opposed to a new account created by the executor). For example, in PLR 2005-23029, the distribution was to be rolled back into the same IRA it came out of, which had a Designated Beneficiary (the surviving spouse), and the IRS did not recite its mantra about not having a Designated Beneficiary. Similarly, in PLR 2005-20038, the IRS said the surviving spouse could roll his deceased wife's IRA distribution either back into the original IRA she had taken the money from (IRA X), or into a new IRA established in the name of the deceased wife; and went on to say that, unless the money was rolled back into IRA X, the recipient account "will not have a Designated Beneficiary." This implies that rolling the distribution back *into the account the participant took it out of* would allow the participant's beneficiary designation to apply to the rolled funds.

C.   **Executor must check pre-death distributions.** Executors must add a new item to their checklists: Determine whether the decedent received any eligible rollover distribution that was not rolled over, and (if so) whether it would be possible and advantageous (to the estate beneficiaries) to complete that rollover on the decedent's behalf.

Distributions even further back than 60 days prior to the date of death (i.e., the normal rollover deadline; see ¶ 2.6.06) could be eligible to be rolled over, under the hardship waiver provisions (see ¶ 2.6.07), if the decedent was hospitalized, disabled, incarcerated, unaware of thefts from his account, or for some other reason unable to complete the rollover within the allotted time. Thus, there is no maximum on the "look-back period" the executor should investigate for incomplete rollovers, other than this: There is no need to investigate distributions prior to 2002, since only post-2001 distributions are eligible for the hardship waiver of the 60-day rollover deadline.

The post-death rollover of a pre-death distribution could change the substantive estate plan if the beneficiary of the IRA (into which the rollover is contributed) is not the same as the beneficiary of the estate (where the distribution was sitting prior to the rollover). This would appear to be a problematic step for the executor to take, unless the same beneficiaries will inherit the funds in the same proportions either way.

The executor should obtain a court order blessing the proposed rollover if it is not specifically authorized in the will. If the rollover is going in to an account that the participant himself had established, and it is clear that the participant intended to roll the distribution into this account, then the court should approve the rollover as carrying out the decedent's intent. If there is no preexisting IRA to roll the money into, or if the distribution was unintentional (for example because the participant was mentally incompetent), or if for some other reason it is not clear to whom the participant intended to leave this particular asset, here are two routes to consider:

✓   One option is for the beneficiary of the rollover IRA to be the estate itself. Even if the estate is the beneficiary of the account (so there is "no Designated Beneficiary" for minimum distribution purposes, and thus no "life expectancy of the Designated Beneficiary" payout; ¶ 1.7.04) the rollover could make possible several years of continued deferral (compared with simply leaving the money outside a retirement plan) under the "no-DB" rules. See ¶ 1.5.06, ¶ 1.5.08.

✓   Another possibility is to get court permission to name the estate beneficiaries directly as beneficiaries of the proposed rollover IRA. Although current indications are that the IRS will not accept post-death beneficiary designations as sufficient to establish a Designated Beneficiary for minimum distribution purposes (see "B"), the estate might still be better off with this approach if the estate beneficiaries are charities (see ¶ 7.2.01), or if estate assets are vulnerable to creditors' claims or increased administration expenses; and possibly you or a judge or someone else will persuade the IRS to change its mind about allowing executor-named beneficiaries to be considered Designated Beneficiaries.

4.1.05 *Executor's responsibilities regarding decedent's MRDs*

The Code requires an individual to take annual distributions (called "minimum required distributions" or "MRDs" in this book) from such individual's retirement plans beginning at a certain point.

See Chapter 1. Failure to take an MRD results in a 50 percent excise tax under § 4974. See ¶ 1.9.02.

It may appear to an executor upon preliminary examination that the decedent did not take all of his MRDs. Before concluding that the participant owed a penalty, consider the possibility that for some or all of the years in question the decedent may have qualified for a "grandfather" rule, or for some other reason may actually *not* have been required to take distributions. See ¶ 1.3.01.

But if the decedent actually *did* fail to take MRDs during his life, to what extent does that failure become the executor's problem? The following discussion assumes the IRS had made no demand, prior to the participant's death, for payment of excise taxes under § 4974. If the IRS had made such a demand, then the estate and/or the beneficiaries could be subject to *transferee liability* for the decedent's excise taxes. Transferee liability is beyond the scope of this book.

A.   **MRD for the year of death.** If a participant died on or after his required beginning date (RBD), then a minimum distribution was required to be made during the year of his death. If he died before having taken the full required amount, the responsibility to take whatever portion of the year-of-death MRD the participant did *not* take prior to his death passes to the beneficiary of the account. See ¶ 1.5.04(A). Similarly, if a beneficiary dies in a year in which the beneficiary is required to take an MRD from an inherited plan or IRA, the responsibility to take the balance of the MRD for that year, and subsequent years, passes to the successor beneficiary of the account. See ¶ 1.5.13. Thus, the executor of the participant's (or beneficiary's) estate does *not* need to be concerned with the MRD for the year of the participant's (or beneficiary's) death unless the estate is the beneficiary (or successor beneficiary) of the account.

B.   **Missed MRDs for years prior to year of death.** Since it was the participant's personal responsibility to take his MRDs for any applicable years prior to his death, and the participant who owed the penalty under § 4974 for failure to take any such distributions, it would not appear that the *beneficiaries* of the retirement plan have any liability for *penalties* the deceased participant owed for MRDs that the decedent didn't take.

C.   Executor's responsibility for decedent's excise tax. An executor has personal liability (up to the value of the estate he is administering) for his decedent's federal *estate, income, and gift* taxes. § 2204(a), § 6905(a). The penalty for failure to take an MRD is an *excise* tax imposed by § 4974 which is part of Subtitle D. There does *not* seem to be an equivalent imposition of personal liability on the executor for the decedent's *excise taxes.*

The executor *does* have the responsibility to file the decedent's income tax return (§ 6012(b)), and the income tax return has a line (line 58 on the 2009 Form 1040) for the entry of "Additional tax on IRAs, other qualified plans, etc. (attach Form 5329 if necessary)." Form 5329 does not mention executors in its instructions. However, the IRS apparently thinks the executor is responsible for this return since the IRS includes "excise taxes" in Form 4810, the form the executor uses to request prompt assessment of "any tax" "for which return [sic] is required in the case of a decedent." § 6501(d).

All this suggests that the executor must try to determine whether the decedent took his MRDs *for any year for which the executor has to file Form 1040 on behalf of the decedent* (excluding the year of death itself, unless the estate is the beneficiary of the plan; see "A").

If the participant died after having filed his own returns for all years prior to the year of death, then the executor is "off the hook." The only year for which the executor has to file a Form 1040 for the participant would be the year of death, and the MRD penalty is not involved on that return (see "A").

D.   Executor seeking waiver of decedent's penalty. If the executor determines that the return he files on the decedent's behalf should report the failure to take the MRD, the executor should seek a waiver of the penalty if appropriate. See ¶ 1.9.03. Unless the retirement plan is actually payable to the estate, the executor is not in a position to take the missed distributions out of the plan as a way of remedying the shortfall, which is a condition of getting an IRS waiver of the penalty, because the beneficiaries control the account, even though the executor (i.e., the probate estate) owes the penalty.

4.2 Post-Death Transfers, Rollovers, & Roth Conversions

This ¶ 4.2 explains how and to what extent a *nonspouse beneficiary* can do benefit transfers, rollovers, and Roth conversions after the participant's death. For a spouse beneficiary see ¶ 3.2.

4.2.01 *How to title an inherited IRA*

During the participant's life, the IRA will be titled "John Doe IRA," "IRA of John Doe," or similarly. On the participant's death, the ownership of the account automatically passes to the participant's beneficiary, by operation of the contract (the IRA agreement and beneficiary designation form). At that point, the IRA becomes an "**inherited IRA**." Some IRA providers use the term "**beneficiary IRA**" or "**decedent IRA**" for such accounts. Even though the account "automatically" becomes an inherited/beneficiary/decedent IRA at the moment of the participant's death, some IRA providers reserve one or more of these titles exclusively for an account that the *beneficiary* has opened to receive and/or hold death benefits payable to such beneficiary from a decedent's plan or IRA.

The step of correctly titling the inherited account is extremely important. Errors can easily occur at this stage. It sometimes happens that, instead of simply updating the paperwork to show that the account is now an inherited IRA, the parties succeed in distributing the entire account balance, thereby causing immediate taxation of the entire amount and permanent loss of further deferral (see ¶ 4.2.02(A)), or depositing the funds in the nonspouse beneficiary's own IRA (see ¶ 4.2.04(E)). The request to the IRA provider should be in writing and emphasize that you are NOT requesting a distribution or rollover of the account at this time, merely informing them that the account is now an inherited IRA.

In this book, "**inherited IRA**" means an IRA inherited by any beneficiary (*including* the surviving spouse, and including a nonindividual such as an estate, trust, or charity). The IRS also generally uses the term "inherited IRA" to mean an IRA held as beneficiary by *anyone* (even the spouse); see Reg. § 54.4981A-T, A-d(10)(b), and Notice 2009-28, 2009-39 IRB 423; the IRS also uses the term "beneficiary IRA" (see Notice 2008-30, 2008-12 IRB 638, A-7). (Of course, once a surviving spouse rolls over the inherited IRA to her own IRA (or elects to treat the IRA she inherited as her own IRA) (see ¶ 3.2), the account becomes "her" IRA and ceases to be an "inherited" IRA in any sense.)

Inherited IRA: No Code Definition

The Internal Revenue Code does not define "inherited IRA." The Code provides that "in the case of an inherited" IRA, distributions from the account may not be rolled over (and rollover contributions may not be accepted). § 408(d)(3)(C). But instead of defining inherited IRA, § 408(d)(3) says only that an IRA *"shall be treated as* inherited if-- (I) the individual for whose benefit the account or annuity is maintained acquired such account by reason of the death of another individual, and (II) such individual was not the surviving spouse of such other individual." Emphasis added. All this sentence tells us is that, *for purposes of the rule that rollovers are not allowed for inherited IRAs,* an IRA held by the surviving spouse as beneficiary is NOT treated as an inherited IRA. The rule does not mention IRAs held by *non*individual beneficiaries, because the rule allowing rollovers of IRA distributions (§ 408(d)(3)(A)) only applies to distributions to the *individual* for whom the account is maintained.

Someone notifies the IRA provider of the participant's death. The IRA provider then typically has the beneficiary sign a new account agreement, appropriate to an "inherited IRA," and retitles the account accordingly. See Rev. Proc. 89-52, 1989-2 CB 632, and Notice 2007-7, 2007-5 IRB 395, A-13. An inherited IRA (or plan account) should be titled so as to make clear that it is an inherited account, and to indicate the names of the both the beneficiary (who now owns it) and the deceased participant (whose account it originally was). For example:

Individual: If the beneficiary is an individual, the inherited IRA or plan account could be titled "John Doe, deceased, f/b/o Junior Doe," or "Brian Young as beneficiary of Joan Smith" (see Rev. Proc. 89-52, § 3.01) or similarly.

Estate: For an IRA or plan account that is payable to the deceased participant's estate, the titling could be "John Doe, f/b/o Estate of John Doe," or "XYZ Bank, Executor of the estate of John Doe, as beneficiary of John Doe," or something similar.

Trust: An IRA or plan account held by a trust as beneficiary could be titled "John Doe, f/b/o John Doe Testamentary Trust," or "XYZ Bank, Trustee of the John Doe Revocable Trust, as beneficiary of John Doe," or similarly.

The IRS requires the IRA provider to show the name of the decedent, as well as the name and taxpayer identification number of the beneficiary, when reporting value of and distributions from an inherited IRA. Rev. Proc. 89-52, § 3.01; see Instructions for IRS Forms 1099-R and 5498 (2010), p. 15.

See ¶ 4.4.04(B) regarding preserving the option of disclaimer by the beneficiary when retitling the account.

4.2.02 *Post-death distributions, IRA-to-IRA transfers*

For definitions of (and differences among) "direct rollovers," "60-day rollovers," and "IRA-to-IRA transfers, "see ¶ 2.6.01.

A.   **Nonspouse beneficiary cannot roll over a distribution received.** If, after the participant's death, the retirement plan or IRA makes a distribution to a beneficiary who is not the participant's surviving spouse, that distribution cannot be rolled over. It cannot be rolled back into the plan or IRA it came out of, or into any other plan or IRA. Not within 60 days, not within 60 seconds. Not to the beneficiary's own IRA and not to an inherited IRA. This rule applies to every beneficiary who is not the participant's surviving spouse, whether or not such beneficiary is a "Designated Beneficiary" (¶ 1.7.03).

A nonspouse beneficiary's taking a distribution from an inherited plan, even if accidental or unintentional, is a mistake that cannot be fixed; the IRS simply does not have the power to authorize the recontribution of the distributed amount to the same or another plan. See PLR 2005-13032.

The rule permitting nonspouse beneficiary rollovers (¶ 4.2.04) applies only to *direct* rollovers (¶ 2.6.01(C)); it is not applicable when money is distributed to the beneficiary rather than being transferred directly to an inherited IRA. § 402(c)(9), § 408(d)(3)(C), Rev. Proc. 89-52, 1989-1 CB 692, § 3.01.

Here are the limitations on and quasi-exceptions to the above rule:

✓　　The above rule applies to distributions that occur after the death of the participant. For the executor's possible ability to roll over distributions made *prior* to the participant's death, see ¶ 4.1.04.

✓　　For the ability of a surviving spouse, as beneficiary of the plan or IRA, to roll over distributions made to her, see ¶ 3.2. If the beneficiary is a trust or estate, but the surviving spouse is the beneficiary of the trust or estate, see ¶ 3.2.09 for the possible ability of the surviving spouse to roll over a distribution made to her "through" the trust or estate.

✓　　For the ability of nonspouse Designated Beneficiaries to effect a direct rollover of benefits from an inherited nonIRA plan to an inherited IRA, see ¶ 4.2.04.

✓　　*All* IRA beneficiaries are permitted to do certain "IRA-to-IRA transfers"; see "B" below.

✓　　Finally, there is a "grandfather rule": A nonspouse beneficiary who inherited an IRA from someone who died <u>before 1985</u> could elect to treat the inherited IRA as the beneficiary's own IRA. See 1987 version of Prop. Reg. § 1.408-8, A-4; this grandfather rule is not mentioned in the final regulations. The nonspouse beneficiary of a participant who died after 1984 cannot do this. § 408(d)(3)(C).

B.　　**Post-death IRA-to-IRA transfers permitted.** Any IRA beneficiary (including an estate, a see-through trust, a non-see-through trust, a surviving spouse, and a nonspouse individual) can authorize a direct transfer from one IRA inherited from a particular participant to another "inherited IRA" of the same type (traditional or Roth) in the name of the same participant and payable to that same beneficiary. The IRS calls such transfers **"trustee to trustee transfers."** This book calls them **"IRA-to-IRA transfers."** See ¶ 2.6.08. This rule applies to inherited IRAs only; a nonspouse beneficiary can NOT do a "trustee to trustee transfer" of benefits either to or from a *nonIRA* plan except as explained at ¶ 4.2.04–¶ 4.2.05.

IRA-to-IRA transfers are permitted because, under Rev. Rul. 78-406, 1978-2 C.B. 157, an IRA-to-IRA transfer is not considered a "distribution" or a "rollover." An IRA-to-IRA transfer is not even a reportable event (unless combined with a Roth conversion); see IRS Instructions for Forms 1099-R and 5498 (2010), p. 5. Thus, an IRA-to-IRA transfer avoids several of the rules and prohibitions that apply to "60-day rollovers." See ¶ 2.6.08.

Although Rev. Rul. 78-406 involved an IRA-to-IRA transfer by a living participant, it is cited by the IRS in letter rulings as being equally applicable "if the trustee to trustee transfer is directed by the beneficiary of an IRA after the death of the IRA owner as long as the transferee IRA is set up and maintained in the name of the deceased IRA owner for the benefit of the beneficiary." PLR 2007-07158; see also, *e.g.*, PLRs 2002-23065, 2003-49009, 2006-16040, and 2006-47030. Because an IRA-to-IRA transfer is not a "rollover," it is not subject to the prohibition against rollovers by a nonspouse beneficiary (see "A").

For an IRA-to-IRA transfer in connection with:

♦ A post-death recharacterization of a pre-death Roth conversion, see ¶ 4.1.02.
♦ The transfer of an inherited IRA out of a trust or estate to the beneficiaries of the trust or estate, see ¶ 6.1.05.

Here are examples of other common types of IRA-to-IRA transfers that are carried out after a participant dies:

Transfer to another IRA provider: Father dies, leaving his IRA at ABC Bank to Daughter. Daughter opens an "inherited IRA" at XYZ Brokerage Firm in the name "Daughter as beneficiary of Father," and directs ABC Bank to transfer all the funds from Father's IRA at ABC Bank directly into the new "inherited" IRA at XYZ Brokerage Firm. ABC issues a check for Father's entire IRA balance payable to "XYZ Brokerage Firm, as Custodian of Father IRA, f/b/o Daughter as beneficiary." (Before issuing the check, ABC may require Daughter to sign paperwork establishing an "inherited IRA" at ABC Bank; see ¶ 4.2.01.) Daughter brings the check to XYZ Brokerage Firm which deposits the check into her newly created "inherited IRA."

Dividing among multiple beneficiaries: Mother dies leaving her IRA at DEF Mutual Fund Co. to her three children, A, B, and C. Upon learning of her death, DEF Co. retitles the account "Mother, deceased, IRA, payable to A, B, and C, beneficiaries." That is not an IRA-to-IRA transfer; that is simply retitling the account to reflect Mother's death. ¶ 4.2.01. The children then request that the account be divided into separate accounts (see ¶ 1.8.01). DEF Co. creates three separate inherited IRAs, each one titled "Mother, deceased, IRA, payable to [one of the children] as beneficiary." An equal-value amount of Mother's IRA assets is moved via IRA-to-IRA transfer to each child's separate inherited IRA. Each IRA provider may have its own procedures for these transfers dealing with such issues as whether it will: require the account to be converted to cash before being divided; allow the children to agree how assets will be divvied up among the three separate inherited IRAs instead of requiring equal allocation of each asset; and/or allow one child to peel off his share into a separate inherited IRA even if the other children don't participate.

C.   **What can go wrong.** If, in the process of attempting to carry out an IRA-to-IRA transfer of an inherited IRA, the funds are distributed to the beneficiary (i.e., money is deposited in the beneficiary's <u>taxable account</u>) by mistake, there is no remedy, because a nonspouse beneficiary cannot roll over a distribution—even if the distribution was made in error. See "A" above.

If funds from an inherited IRA that are supposed to be transferred directly into another inherited IRA (in the names of the same deceased participant and beneficiary) are instead moved into the beneficiary's *own* IRA, the transfer would not conform with the requirement recited in the PLRs "decided" under Rev. Rul. 78-406 (see "B" above). Such an erroneous transfer would presumably be treated as a taxable distribution to the beneficiary from the inherited IRA followed by a regular (probably excess; see ¶ 2.1.08) contribution to the beneficiary's own IRA. See ¶ 4.2.04(E).

4.2.03 *Combining inherited IRAs*

For <u>income tax purposes</u>, IRAs inherited from one decedent are aggregated with (and only with) other IRAs of the same type (traditional or Roth) inherited from that same decedent; see ¶ 2.2.07.

For <u>minimum distribution purposes</u>, the minimum distribution is computed separately for each IRA, inherited or otherwise. Having computed the MRD separately for each account, however, an individual is entitled to take the MRD for all of certain "aggregate-able" IRAs from any one or more of the IRAs in that group. As with income taxes, the individual's own IRAs may be aggregated only with each other for this purpose, and IRAs inherited from a particular decedent may be aggregated only with other IRAs inherited from that same decedent. Reg. § 1.408-8, A-9.

Based on these income tax and minimum distribution rules, it would appear that a beneficiary *should* be able to merge any traditional (or Roth) IRA inherited from a particular decedent with any other traditional (or Roth) IRA inherited from that same decedent, for convenience of management. However, there is no authority or guidance on this. See ¶ 4.2.04(E).

4.2.04 *Nonspouse beneficiary rollovers from nonIRA plans*

A nonspouse "Designated Beneficiary" (see "C") can have funds transferred, by direct rollover (see "D"), from certain types of inherited nonIRA plans (see "B") into an "inherited IRA" (see "E") or inherited Roth IRA (see ¶ 4.2.05). A surviving spouse as beneficiary has more expansive options; see ¶ 3.2.07.

This ¶ 4.2.04 deals only with money that was *still in the plan* at the time of the participant's death. For money that was distributed *prior to the participant's death*, see ¶ 4.1.04 instead. If not certain when the distribution occurred, see ¶ 2.1.03.

A.   **Legislative background.** Prior to the Pension Protection Act of 2006 (PPA '06), the Code permitted no one other than the participant and his surviving spouse to "roll over" money from one retirement plan to another. PPA '06 for the first time allowed a limited type of rollover by a Designated Beneficiary other than the surviving spouse. After 2006, a Designated Beneficiary is permitted to transfer certain inherited nonIRA plan benefits, *by direct rollover only*, into an "inherited" IRA. § 402(c)(11).

The main benefit of this type of transfer is that it allows a Designated Beneficiary to take advantage of a deferred "stretch" payout of the benefits over his life expectancy, even if the plan he actually inherited permitted only a lump sum distribution form of benefit. See ¶ 1.5.10. In Notice 2007-7, Section V, the IRS addressed the MRD effects and other details of nonspouse beneficiary rollovers. Notice 2007-7 was further clarified in a special edition of the IRS's *Employee Plan News* (http://www.irs.gov/pub/irs-tege/se_021307.pdf).

Beginning in 2010, plans are required to offer the direct rollover to a Designated Beneficiary. See § 402(f)(2)(A) as amended by WRERA; ¶ 2.6.01(C); and "E" below.

B.   **Types of nonIRA plans.** § 402(c)(11) applies to 403(b) plans and governmental 457(b) plans (¶ 5.4.01(B), #3) as well as to qualified retirement plans (QRPs). § 403(b)(8), § 457(e)(16)(B). For ease of reference this section will speak mostly of QRPs, but all statements apply equally to 403(b) and governmental 457(b) plans.

C.   **Available only to a Designated Beneficiary.** The direct rollover to an inherited IRA is available *only* for an "individual who is a designated beneficiary." § 402(c)(11)(A). A Designated Beneficiary means an *individual* (or group of individuals) who are named as beneficiary(ies) of the plan by the participant or under the terms of the plan. See ¶ 1.7.03.

Though a trust is not an individual, "a trust maintained for the benefit of one or more designated beneficiaries shall be treated in the same manner as a designated beneficiary" for purposes of the nonspouse beneficiary rollover provision, to the extent provided in rules prescribed by the Treasury. § 402(c)(11)(B). The IRS has confirmed that Reg. § 1.401(a)(9)-4, A-5 (see ¶ 6.2.03) will apply for purposes of determining whether a trust named as beneficiary is eligible to use the nonspouse beneficiary rollover under § 402(c)(11). Notice 2007-7, A-16.

Since the option to transfer inherited plan benefits to an inherited IRA is limited to Designated Beneficiaries, an estate or non-see-through trust will *not* be able to use the nonspouse beneficiary rollover to achieve *any* type of gradual payout from a plan that permits only a lump sum distribution; the estate or such a trust will be stuck with whatever payout options the plan allows. The estate or trust can *not* compel the plan to pay distributions out to the estate or trust over five years (¶ 1.5.06) or over what would have been the decedent's life expectancy (¶ 1.5.08), even though the minimum distribution rules would have permitted such a payout; see ¶ 1.5.10.

D.   **Direct rollovers only.** Only *direct rollovers* (¶ 2.6.01(C)) to an inherited IRA are permitted. § 402(c)(11)(A). If the plan distributes funds to the nonspouse *beneficiary* instead of to the *inherited IRA*, then the distribution is taxable and rollover of the distributed amount becomes impossible. See ¶ 4.2.02(A). However, if the beneficiary takes a partial distribution, he can still have a direct rollover of the *rest* of the benefits—the part he did NOT take out of the plan—to an inherited IRA.

E.   **Must roll to an "inherited IRA."** The nonspouse beneficiary direct rollover may be made *only* to an "inherited IRA" (i.e., one titled as described at ¶ 4.2.01) which is "established for the purpose" of receiving this distribution. § 402(c)(11)(A); Notice 2007-7, A-13. Regarding whether such accounts can later be combined with other IRAs inherited from the same decedent, see ¶ 4.2.03.

A nonspouse beneficiary can never "roll" an inherited plan to the *beneficiary's own* IRA or Roth IRA, only to an *inherited* IRA or Roth IRA. If a nonspouse beneficiary rolls a distribution from an *inherited* plan into the beneficiary's *own* traditional or Roth IRA, the rollover would be treated as, first, a taxable distribution from the inherited plan (because it is a plan distribution that does not meet the requirements of a qualified rollover under § 402(c)(11)); followed by a regular contribution (almost always an excess contribution) to the beneficiary's own IRA (or Roth IRA). See ¶ 5.3.02, ¶ 5.4.06, ¶ 2.1.08. This mistake cannot be fixed by "recharacterization"; see ¶ 5.6.01.

F.   **Applies to post-2006 post-death distributions.** The nonspouse beneficiary rollover is available for any otherwise-qualifying post-2006 distribution even if the date of death was before 2007. See PLRs 2007-17022 and 2007-17023, permitting beneficiaries to use § 402(c)(11) in 2007 to cause a direct rollover of plan benefits of a participant who had died in 2005. A distribution made *prior to 2007* cannot be rolled over by the nonspouse beneficiary. Also, the beneficiary rollover provision applies only to *post-death* distributions; for post-death rollovers of *pre-death* distributions, see ¶ 4.1.04. If not certain whether the distribution occurred before or after the participant's death, see ¶ 2.1.03.

G.   **Cannot use rollover to "fix" the estate plan.** The nonspouse beneficiary rollover can NOT be used to "create" a Designated Beneficiary when there is no Designated Beneficiary.

For example, suppose widowed Father dies without having named any beneficiary for his 401(k) plan. Under the plan terms, the benefits are payable to Father's estate (see ¶ 1.7.02). Father's three children are the sole beneficiaries of his estate. An estate cannot be a Designated Beneficiary. ¶ 1.7.04. Even if § 402(c)(11) permitted the estate to transfer the inherited 401(k) plan to an "inherited" IRA (which it does not do; see "C"), that would not permit the family to change the beneficiary of the plan from "the estate" to "the children."

Similarly, if the benefits are payable outright to a minor beneficiary, the beneficiary's guardian cannot use § 402(c)(11) to change the beneficiary to a trust for the minor; all the guardian can do is direct the benefits to be sent via direct rollover to an inherited IRA that is payable outright to the minor. (Once that direct rollover is completed, see ¶ 4.6.03(C) regarding the possibility of transferring the inherited IRA to a trust on the minor's behalf.)

H.   **Limits on the plan's obligations.** See ¶ 2.6.01(C) regarding choices the plan must offer to a recipient of retirement benefits regarding where the plan will "send" a distribution. It is not clear, when there are multiple Designated Beneficiaries, whether the plan is required to give each beneficiary the entire menu of choices or whether the plan can require all beneficiaries to agree on one of the distribution methods on the permitted "menu."

If the plan is restrictive on this, and there are multiple Designated Beneficiaries who want different outcomes (for example, some want immediate outright distribution of their shares, others want to establish separate inherited IRAs for their shares), the beneficiaries would have to proceed by having the plan transfer the entire benefit to a single inherited IRA payable to all of them collectively, then divide up the inherited IRA using IRA-to-IRA transfers (see ¶ 4.2.02), thus allowing each beneficiary to preserve or cash out his newly-created separate "inherited IRA."

I.　**Plan must distribute MRD before the transfer.** Since a minimum required distribution (MRD) is not an eligible rollover distribution (see ¶ 2.6.03), the plan must distribute the MRD for the year in which the rollover occurs *before* the plan transfers the (rest of the) inherited plan account to the "inherited" IRA.

J.　**Beneficiary's MRDs after the transfer.** In Notice 2007-7, A-19, the IRS decreed that the minimum distribution rules applicable to the "inherited IRA" which received the direct rollover would generally be the same as the rule that applied to the benefit while it was still in the original plan. So if the original plan decreed that the 5-year rule would apply to all death benefits of participants who died before the RBD (see ¶ 1.5.07(A), #2), the same 5-year rule would automatically apply to the inherited IRA into which the benefits were transferred via nonspouse beneficiary rollover.

Since this rule in Notice 2007-7 would basically defeat the entire Congressional purpose in allowing nonspouse beneficiary rollovers, the IRS does allow one escape hatch: IF the rollover is completed by a certain deadline, then the benefits can be distributed from the inherited IRA using the life-expectancy-of-the-beneficiary as the Applicable Distribution Period (¶ 1.2.03). If the participant died in 2008, the deadline is December 31, 2010. See ¶ 1.1.04 and Notice 2009-82, 2009-41 IRB 491, Part V, A-3. If the participant died in any other year, the deadline is December 31 of the year after the year in which the participant died. Notice 2007-7, A-17(c)(2) ("Special Rule").

4.2.05 *Nonspouse beneficiary Roth conversions*

This ¶ 4.2.05 explains how *certain* beneficiaries can convert *certain* inherited traditional retirement plans to inherited Roth IRAs by means of the "nonspouse beneficiary rollover" described at ¶ 4.2.04.

For how to advise a beneficiary who has inherited a Roth IRA (i.e., an IRA that is ALREADY a Roth at the time of the participant's death), see the following instead of this section: ¶ 5.2.05(B), "Computing Five-Year Period for beneficiaries"; ¶ 5.2.06, "Jules and Jim Example"; and ¶ 4.1.02.

A.   **Nonspouse beneficiary cannot convert an inherited IRA.**
The participant's surviving spouse can convert a traditional
IRA she has inherited from the participant to an inherited (or to
her own) Roth IRA; see ¶ 3.2.04. No other beneficiary
(regardless of whether such beneficiary is an individual, a trust,
or an estate) can convert an *inherited IRA* to a Roth IRA.

§ 408A(c)(6)(A) provides that "No rollover contribution may
be made to a Roth IRA unless it is a qualified rollover contribution."
"Qualified rollover contribution" is defined in § 408A(e). It includes
a rollover from an individual account plan (i.e., an IRA), but *only* if
such rollover meets the requirements of § 408(d)(3). One requirement
of § 408(d)(3) is that no rollover may be made from an inherited IRA.
An "inherited IRA" for this purpose means an IRA acquired by an
individual by reason of the death of another individual who was not the
acquirer's spouse (see ¶ 4.2.01). § 408(d)(3)(C). Thus, nonspouse
beneficiaries have never been, and are not now, able to "roll" money
from an inherited IRA to a Roth IRA. PLR 2000-13041.

If the funds are transferred from an inherited *traditional* IRA to
an inherited *Roth* IRA, that would be a "failed" Roth conversion
(¶ 5.4.06) and would be treated as a taxable distribution to the
beneficiary from the inherited IRA followed by a regular (excess)
contribution to the inherited Roth IRA. Reg. § 1.408A-8(b)(4),
§ 1.408A-4, A-1(a), A-3(b).

IRA-to-IRA transfers can be used to avoid a number of the
restrictions that apply to *rollovers*; see ¶ 2.6.08. However, an IRA-to-
IRA transfer can not be used to avoid *this* restriction because the IRS's
regulation on Roth IRA conversions says that any transfer from a
traditional IRA to a Roth IRA will be treated as (and must meet the
requirements for) a rollover, even if the "conversion" is accomplished
by an IRA-to-IRA transfer or even just by "redesignating" the account
as a Roth. Reg. § 1.408A-4, A-1(a), (c).

B.   **Code allows Roth conversions from other inherited plans.**
The definition of qualified rollover contribution (to a Roth
IRA) in § 408A(e) includes a rollover from a qualified
retirement plan (QRP) if the rollover meets the requirements of
§ 402(c). *Unlike* the provision defining qualified rollovers from
an IRA (§ 408(d)(2); see "A" above), § 402(c) does *not* prohibit
rollovers of inherited plans. Accordingly, a Designated
Beneficiary who is entitled to a direct rollover of inherited QRP

benefits (see ¶ 4.2.04) can require the QRP to transfer the benefits into either an inherited traditional IRA or an inherited Roth IRA. Notice 2008-30, 2008-12 IRB 638, A-7.

Qualified rollover contribution as defined in § 408A(e) also includes a rollover from a 403(a) or (b) plan if it meets the requirements of § 403(b)(8), and a rollover from a governmental 457(b) plan if it meets the requirements of § 457(e)(16). Since § 403(b)(8) and § 457(e)(16)(B) incorporate § 402(c)(9) and § 402(c)(11), nonspouse beneficiary Roth conversions *are* permitted for inherited 403 plans and governmental 457 plans in the same manner as for inherited QRPs.

C.   **Nonspouse beneficiary Roth conversions: Various matters.**
A Designated Beneficiary who converts an inherited nonIRA plan to an inherited Roth IRA has the same option other Roth converters have to defer income on a 2010 conversion into 2011–2012 (see ¶ 5.4.05); § 408A(d)(3)(A)(iii) does not except beneficiary conversions. He also has the same ability as other Roth converters to "recharacterize" (undo; see ¶ 5.6) that conversion by transferring the contribution and earnings thereon to a traditional inherited IRA. Notice 2008-30, A-7. However, once he recharacterizes he can never "reconvert" (¶ 5.6.07) because he can't convert an inherited IRA (see "A").

The minimum distribution rules apply to a beneficiary Roth conversion in the same manner as for other nonspouse beneficiary rollovers; see ¶ 4.2.04(I).
Computation of the Five-Year Period (¶ 5.2.05(B)) for a beneficiary Roth conversion is unclear. For a Roth IRA that the beneficiary inherits from the deceased participant, we know the participant's holding period "carries over" to the beneficiary; see ¶ 5.2.05(B). Does this same "carryover" rule also apply to an "inherited" Roth IRA created by the beneficiary in connection with a nonspouse beneficiary Roth conversion, i.e., if the decedent had already completed his Five-Year Period with respect to his own Roth IRAs, do the beneficiaries get the benefit of that for an "inherited" Roth IRA they created? There is no IRS guidance on this.
Even if the beneficiary wants, and can afford, a Roth conversion, he will get much more value by converting his own plans or IRAs to a Roth IRA than by converting an inherited plan to an inherited Roth IRA, if the cost is the same. "His own" Roth IRA would

have no MRDs during his lifetime (¶ 5.2.02(A)), and could be left to his surviving spouse for a spousal rollover (¶ 3.2), or to another Designated Beneficiary for a stretch payout (¶ 1.5.05), after his death. In contrast, an inherited Roth IRA would have to be distributed, starting the year after the year of the participant's death, over the beneficiary's single life expectancy (with no possibility of flipping to a more extended payout after his death). ¶ 1.5.03(C), ¶ 1.5.13.

4.3 Federal Estate Tax Issues

This ¶ 4.3 discusses how retirement benefits are treated for federal estate tax purposes. This section applies only if the participant dies at a time when the federal estate tax is in effect, meaning (as of this writing) either before or after 2010; see ¶ 4.3.08 for 2010 deaths.

4.3.01 *Retirement benefits on the estate tax return*

All retirement plan death benefits, including IRAs, 403(b) plans, and nonqualified deferred compensation plans, as well as qualified retirement plans (QRPs) and annuity contracts (except for proceeds of life insurance) that are includible in the estate are included as "annuities" under § 2039, to be reported on Schedule I of the estate tax return, regardless of whether the benefits are payable in the form of an annuity. § 2039; Reg. § 20.2039-1(b); Instructions for IRS Form 706 (Sept. 2009), Schedule I.

To complete a 706, it is necessary to determine the value of the decedent's retirement benefits as of the date of death. If a plan administrator refuses to provide information to the executor of the estate of a deceased employee, on the grounds that the estate was not the named beneficiary of the plan benefits, the executor might remind the plan administrator of the administrator's obligation under federal law to file an estate tax return for assets it holds if the executor is unable to file such a return due to the plan administrator's refusal to supply information. § 6018(b); see Form 5.5, Appendix B.

4.3.02 *Problems paying the estate tax*

How to pay the estate tax is always a problem when a major portion of the estate consists of nonprobate assets, because such assets pass directly to the beneficiaries. The executor (who controls only the probate estate) may not have enough assets under his control to enable him to pay the estate taxes, or the assets he controls may not be the assets that are supposed to be burdened with the tax. He is left chasing the recipients of the nonprobate assets to recover their shares of the tax.

Retirement benefits that pass directly to a beneficiary other than the estate are nonprobate assets and thus can put the executor into this difficult position. Compounding the problem, retirement benefits are often nonattachable, making the executor's job of recovering taxes owed to the estate by the beneficiaries of the plans even more difficult or impossible. In the planning stage, consider who will pay the estate taxes on the retirement benefits and with what funds. The key is to make sure that the fiduciary who will be responsible for paying the tax will have control of the money.

Here are examples of how executors have dealt with this problem:

✓   A decedent left his IRA to beneficiaries who were not U.S. citizens or residents. The will required these beneficiaries to pay their proportionate share of the estate taxes, but the executor had no way to even find let alone demand payment from these beneficiaries. The executor obtained a court order barring the IRA provider (a U.S. bank) from distributing anything from the IRA to the foreign beneficiaries until they had settled with the executor regarding the estate taxes.

✓   In PLR 2004-40031, section 8.7(v) of the trust that was named as beneficiary of the participant's plans gave the trustee discretion to pay the participant's expenses of last illness, estate taxes, and probate costs. The estate was insolvent, so the trustee and an estate creditor sought a court order to pay some of the estate's expenses from the trust. Though applicable state law exempted the retirement benefits from claims of the participant's and beneficiary's creditors, the court nevertheless ordered the trust to use the benefits to pay the estate's liabilities "because no other assets existed" to defray these expenses.

4.3.03 *Alternate valuation method (AVM) for retirement benefits*

Though normally assets are valued for federal estate tax purposes as of the date of death, § 2032(a) provides that, generally, if the estate so elects, "In the case of property *distributed, sold, exchanged, or otherwise disposed of,* within 6 months after the decedent's death such property shall be valued as of the date of distribution, sale, exchange, or other disposition. In the case of property not distributed, sold, exchanged, or otherwise disposed of, within 6 months after the decedent's death such property shall be valued as of the date 6 months after the decedent's death." Emphasis added. The executor must elect this "alternate valuation method" (AVM) for all assets of the estate or none, and can elect it only if the effect of the election is to decrease both the gross estate and the estate tax. § 2032(a), (c).

There is no authority regarding how the AVM applies to IRAs. The question is, what events occurring within six months after the date of death would constitute a *distribution, sale, exchange, or other disposition* with respect to the IRA, that would "freeze" the alternate estate tax valuation as of the date of the event? See ¶ 4.3.05 regarding sales of assets inside the IRA; see ¶ 4.3.04 regarding distributions and other events.

Only self-directed individual-account plans (such as the typical custodial IRA) raise the question posed here regarding the application of § 2032. Defined benefit plan (¶ 8.3.04) death benefits are typically payable in the form of a survivor annuity, which must be valued for estate tax purposes using the IRS's tables for valuing life estates, annuities and terms-for-years (if it is not a commercial annuity) (Reg. § 20.2031-7(a)) or based on the cost of comparable annuity contracts (if it is a commercial annuity contract) (Reg. § 20.2031-7(b), § 20.2031-8(a)(1)). The AVM rule for annuity contracts is in Reg. § 20.2032-1(f)(1).

Some retirement plans are neither self-directed individual account plans nor true annuities. For example, the decedent may have participated in a profit-sharing plan under which the investment decisions are made by the plan trustees rather than by the participant. This type of plan typically provides to participants and beneficiaries only annual or quarterly statements, showing the total account value, but not listing particular securities. Unless the decedent happened to die on a plan valuation date, the decedent's interest in the plan must be valued by obtaining an interim valuation from the plan trustees (which they may or may not be willing or able to provide) or by interpolating the values as of the last plan valuation date before and the first plan valuation date after the date of death (adjusting these valuations as necessary to reflect plan contributions and distributions during the period). In the case of such "other plans" the executor will presumably use, for the alternate valuation, the same interpolation method used to value the benefit on the date of death.

4.3.04 AVM, cont.: Distributions, other IRA events as "disposition"

Executors need to know whether various common IRA events would cause the asset to be deemed "disposed of" for purposes of the AVM. A disposition is an event "by which property ceases to form a part of the gross estate." A *mere change in form* is not a disposition.

The regulation's phrase "ceases to form a part of the gross estate" is unfortunate. It does not convey a clear meaning. The only way it makes sense is if it means that the asset ceases to be owned by the person or entity who received it from the decedent (whether that person or entity is the probate estate, a trust, a retirement plan beneficiary, or a surviving joint owner).

A.   **Mere change in form is not a disposition.** To illustrate the difference between a "disposition" and a "mere change in form," the IRS cites certain corporate transactions, and appears to make the difference hinge on whether the transaction triggers realization of income for income tax purposes, although the regulation does not explicitly say that is the criterion. See Reg. § 20.2032-1(c)(1).

Prop. Treas. Reg. § 20.2032–1(f), providing that "changes in value due to post-death events other than market conditions" will not be taken into account for AVM purposes, has no bearing on the IRA questions discussed here. The types of post-death IRA events we are considering have no effect on the *value* of the asset; the only issue is whether such events have the effect of *closing the alternate valuation period*, a subject not addressed in the proposed regulation.

Let us now look at particular post-death IRA "events" and see how they fit in to the AVM picture. Regarding a sale of securities "inside" the IRA, see ¶ 4.3.05.

B.   **Retitling the account.** For how to retitle an inherited plan on the death of the participant, see ¶ 4.2.01. This bit of paperwork does not constitute a sale, distribution, or other disposition of the asset for alternate valuation purposes. The retitling step merely formalizes the change of ownership of the account that has *already occurred* (at the moment of the participant's death).

The sole purpose of this step is for the IRA provider to get the beneficiary's address and Social Security number so it knows who owns the account. This "event" does not even rise to the level of a "mere change of form," let alone a "disposition" of the asset.

C.   **Transfer of account to a different custodian.** An IRA beneficiary can cause his inherited IRA to be transferred to a different IRA custodian. See ¶ 4.2.02. Following the transfer, the account remains as an inherited IRA titled in the name of the decedent payable to the beneficiary. Such changes are common where, for example, the beneficiary prefers to have the asset placed with his own financial advisor. If the change involves no sale of securities, and no taxable distribution, just an intact transfer of the inherited investments to a different IRA provider, there would not appear to be any basis for an argument that the transfer was a "disposition." The same beneficiary owns the same securities in the same format (an inherited IRA) both before and after the transfer. If any IRA activity should be treated as a "mere change of form," this would be it.

D.   **Dividing the account.** It can be to the advantage of multiple beneficiaries of a single inherited IRA to divide it into separate inherited IRAs, one payable to each of them. See ¶ 1.8.01. An argument could be made that this is a "mere change in form," and not a disposition. For one thing, such a division is nontaxable, and thus is analogous to the nontaxable corporate reorganizations the IRS described as mere changes of form in Reg. § 20.2032-1(c)(1). For another, the same individuals own the same securities in the same proportions and in the same format (inherited IRA) both before and after the division. If the taxable/nontaxable dichotomy is the bright line test, then this would be a "mere change in form."

However, when an inherited IRA is divided among multiple owners, the beneficiaries are not required to take proportionate shares of each asset in the account; they may elect to take different securities as part of their respective shares. For example, Beneficiary A might take the stocks, B might take the bonds, and C might take the cash. This "swap" would not be an income-taxable event, provided each beneficiary received the correct total value he was entitled to, because all the assets are still inside the tax-deferred IRA account. However, if the beneficiaries did not take proportionate shares of each and every security in the account, query whether they have engaged in an "exchange" of inherited assets, triggering closing of the AVM period.

E.   **Spouse's election to treat account as spouse's own account.** When the surviving spouse is the sole beneficiary of the decedent's IRA, the surviving spouse can elect to treat the inherited IRA as her own IRA. ¶ 3.2.04. Following such election (which can occur by default in some cases, without any overt act by the surviving spouse) the minimum required distributions for the account are determined based on the surviving spouse as "owner" rather than as "beneficiary." The fact that this transformation is not a taxable event suggests that the spousal election is a mere change of form that does not close the AVM period. On the other hand, since the assets are no longer in the "decedent's IRA," they are now in the "surviving spouse's IRA," they have arguably ceased to be "part of the gross estate," which would suggest the AVM period has closed.

F.   **Distribution from the account.** IRA distributions that are reportable as such to the IRS and recipient by the IRA provider on Form 1099-R are generally taxable (though a particular distribution might not be taxable, for example, to the extent it represents return of the participant's "basis" in the IRA, or if it is "rolled over" within 60 days by the surviving spouse as beneficiary, or if it is a qualified distribution from a Roth IRA).

Although any withdrawal from the IRA would be considered a "distribution" for income tax purposes (¶ 2.1.01), it would not necessarily be so considered for AVM purposes. Under the regulations, only an executor or trustee can "distribute" property for AVM purposes. Reg. § 20.2032-1(c)(2). Accordingly, distributing assets out of an IRA within six months after the date of death would not "freeze" the value of such assets for alternate valuation purposes *unless* either the IRA is in the form of a trust under § 408(a)(8) (¶ 6.1.07) or such distribution is considered an "other disposition."

Though property can be "distributed" for AVM purposes only by an executor or trustee, "Property may be 'sold, exchanged, or otherwise disposed of' by" a much broader group of recipients, including the executor, trustee, donee, heir, devisee, surviving joint tenant or "any other person," presumably including an IRA beneficiary. See Reg. § 20.2032-1(c)(3).

When a security is distributed out of an IRA to the beneficiary, it is a mere change of the form of ownership: The same individual beneficiary owns the same asset (the security inherited from the decedent) both before and after the distribution. The asset now has changed income tax characteristics, but the beneficiary has not parted with the risk of ownership of the asset. This analysis suggests that a distribution should be treated as a mere change of form.

On the other hand, this particular change of form is a potentially income-taxable event, which the IRA provider must report to the IRS on Form 1099-R (even if the distribution is nontaxable; see Instructions for IRS Form 1099-R (2010), p. 3). By analogy to the regulations' position on corporate reorganizations, an income tax-triggering distribution would be an "other disposition."

4.3.05 *AVM, cont.: Sale of assets inside the IRA*

The next question is whether the IRA is treated for AVM purposes as an asset itself (so all the executor needs to do is use the value of the IRA six months after the date of death as the AVM method value), or whether the IRA is treated as a collection of individual securities, so that the beneficiary's sale of a security *inside the IRA* within six months after the date of death would cause the AVM period to end for that security (with the results of reinvestment of the proceeds of the sale being irrelevant for estate tax valuation purposes). There is no authority or guidance on this point. Sometimes the collection-of-securities approach would favor the taxpayer; in other cases it would favor the IRS.

Since IRAs are usually reported and valued on the estate tax return as a collection of individually-valued securities, and the beneficiary who owns the IRA controls whether and when such securities are sold, this author believes the "security by security" approach is most appropriate. The gist of the alternate valuation rules is that the person who inherits the estate-taxable asset gets tax relief if the inherited asset declines in value within a limited period of time after the decedent's death. The maximum relief period is six months, and the period is shortened if the person voluntarily removes from himself the risk of further decline in value by (for example) selling the asset. If the IRA beneficiary sells a security inside the IRA, he has ended the risk of decline in value of the asset he inherited. If he then chooses to reinvest the proceeds, the U.S. Treasury should not have to bear the risk of decline in value of the new investment chosen by the beneficiary.

4.3.06 *Federal estate tax exclusion for retirement benefits*

At one time, retirement benefits were not subject to the federal estate tax. Though the estate tax exclusion for benefits was diminished and then repealed in the early 1980s, there are some "grandfathered" individuals: If the decedent died holding benefits in a qualified retirement plan and had separated from the service of the employer that sponsored the plan prior to 1985; or at his death held benefits in an IRA as to which he had irrevocably elected a form of benefit prior to 1984; then the estate may be entitled to a partial or full exclusion of the benefits from the federal estate. For details, see Instructions to IRS Form 706 (Estate Tax Return; Sept. 2009), Schedule I, p. 18, and the *Special Report: Ancient History* (Appendix C).

4.3.07 *Valuation discount for unpaid income taxes*

It has been suggested that the value of a retirement benefit should be discounted because the asset is subject to unpaid income taxes. The proponents of this theory assert that a "willing buyer" would pay less for a retirement plan benefit because subsequent distributions from the retirement plan or IRA to the willing buyer would be taxable.

This theory is wrong. If the beneficiary assigns the benefit to a buyer, the seller's recognition of income upon sale is mandated by § 691(a)(2). See CCM 2006-44020 (¶ 6.5.08). The "willing buyer" then has a basis equal to what he paid for the benefit, so the willing buyer can liquidate the entire benefit immediately with no income tax whatsoever (except to the extent he receives more from the plan than he paid for it). Cases recognizing a discount for future income taxes in the *valuation of corporate stock* have no relevance to the *valuation of a retirement plan benefit*, because the buyer of corporate stock does not get a "basis step-up" for appreciated assets held b the corporation (so the company he is buying has an ongoing "built in" liability for income tax on such appreciation). See, *e.g.*, *Estate of Jameson v. Comm'r*, 267 F. 3rd 366 (5th Cir., 2001). But taking a valuation discount on retirement benefits for built-in income taxes is not a defensible position. *Estate of*

Smith v. U.S., 93 AFTR 2d 2004-556 (1/16/2004); *Est. Of Kahn v. Comm'r*, 125 T.C. No. 11 (2005); and PLR 2002-47001 concur.

4.3.08 Deaths in 2010: One-year "repeal" of the federal estate tax

Effective January 1, 2010, and until January 1, 2011 (unless the law is changed before the end of 2010), there is no federal estate tax or generation-skipping transfer (GST) tax. The federal estate tax and GST tax ceased to exist for deaths after 2009. The gift tax still is in place, with a lifetime exemption of only $1 million and a tax rate equal to the top income tax rate (35%, as of 2010). The estate and GST taxes are scheduled to re-appear for deaths in 2011 and later, with an exemption of only $1 million.

The new-basis-at-death rule died with the estate tax—almost. Generally, for deaths before (and after) 2010, a beneficiary who inherited (or who inherits) property got (or will get) a new income tax basis for that property, equal to its date of death value (even if the decedent's taxable estate was or is not large enough to be subject to estate tax). See § 1014(a), as in effect for years before and after 2010.

In contrast, the beneficiary of a decedent who dies *in the year 2010* will generally inherit the decedent's income tax basis, instead of getting a new "stepped up basis" equal to the date of death value of the inherited property. § 1022(a). This is called "carryover" basis, because the decedent's basis in the property "carries over" to the beneficiary. However, the law effective for deaths in 2010 is not "pure" carryover basis; it is carryover basis with several exceptions:

✓ The carryover basis rule applies generally only to appreciated assets. If an asset had *declined* in value, so the value on the date of death was less than the decedent's basis, the beneficiary's basis is the date-of-death value, *not* the decedent's original basis.

✓ The survivors are allowed to apply *some* basis step up, under two separate provisions. First, the decedent's executor can allocate up to a total of $1.3 million (plus the amount of certain pre-death depreciation and losses) of basis step-up among the decedent's appreciated assets. § 1022(b). The executor gets to choose which appreciated assets get this step-up.

✓   Second, an additional $3 million of pre-death appreciation can
       be sheltered with respect to property passing to the surviving
       spouse. § 1022(c).

However, "property which constitutes a right to receive an item
of income in respect of a decedent" (IRD; ¶ 4.6) has never been entitled
to a new basis at death. § 1014(c). Instead, an individual who inherits
IRD takes over the decedent's basis (carryover basis). This was true
under the "old law" (pre- and post-2010) and is also true for deaths in
2010; NONE of that $1.3, $3 million, or other step-up can be allocated
to *retirement benefits*. Retirement benefits (and other IRD items)
continue to be frozen out of any basis step-up at death, just as was true
prior to the estate tax "repeal." § 1022(f).

Will Congress put the estate tax back into force before 2011?
If so, will the revived estate tax apply to deaths that occurred prior to
the legislation? If so, is that constitutional? And what exemption will
Congress allow? Will they raise the $1 million exemption slated to
arrive in 2011? Will they revive stepped-up basis along with the estate
tax, or give us an estate tax PLUS carryover basis? These matters are
unknown as this book goes to press.

4.4 Qualified Disclaimers of Retirement Benefits

A disclaimer is the refusal to accept a gift or inheritance.
Federal tax law recognizes that a person cannot be forced to accept a
gift or inheritance. Therefore, a disclaimer (provided it meets the
requirements of § 2518; ¶ 4.4.02) is not treated as, itself, a gift.
§ 2518(a). Since the person making the disclaimer never accepted the
property in the first place, the theory goes, he never owned it and
therefore he could not have given it away.

Disclaimers of inherited retirement benefits can be useful in
post mortem planning. However, not every refusal to accept an
inheritance is a *qualified* disclaimer, entitled to the blessings of § 2518.
If a beneficiary renounces an inheritance in a manner that does not
meet the requirements of § 2518, the renunciation would be considered
(for purposes of the federal gift tax) as a transfer to the person who
received the property as a result of the renunciation, potentially
resulting in imposition of gift taxes (and income tax; see ¶ 4.4.03).

4.4.01 *Post-mortem disclaimer checklist*

Use the checklist at ¶ 4.4.13 for building retirement-benefit disclaimers into the estate plan. After the participant has died, use *this* checklist to prepare for and/or carry out disclaimers of his retirement benefits:

A. **Delay "acceptance" until disclaimer decision is made.** Upon the death of a client, all plan and IRA beneficiary designations should be reviewed as soon as possible. Either (1) no benefits should be distributed to any beneficiary until this review is completed or (2) if a beneficiary wants to take a distribution (other than the MRD for the year of death; see ¶ 4.4.05(A)) the request for the distribution should be accompanied by a statement that the beneficiary is not thereby accepting the entire account (just the amount distributed) (see ¶ 4.4.05(B)). No beneficiary should exercise investment (or other) control over inherited plan benefits until this review is completed; see ¶ 4.4.04. If any beneficiary designation appears undesirable, consider the use of a qualified disclaimer, if that will cause the benefits to pass to the "right" beneficiary (see ¶ 4.4.08).

B. **How to do partial disclaimers.** If making a partial disclaimer, review Reg. § 25.2518-3, which discusses and gives examples of disclaimers of part of an inheritance. Follow the "successful" examples, and the rules stated in Rev. Rul. 2005-36 (¶ 4.4.05(A)) as closely as possible.

C. **Comply with state law requirements.** See ¶ 4.4.03. Should a beneficiary's disclaimer comply with the law of the participant's domicile? The beneficiary's domicile? Or the state where the plan or IRA is administered? If there is any doubt, comply with all of the above!

D. **Comply with requirements of the plan or IRA.** Check whether the plan or IRA has its own requirements for disclaimers and comply with those (see ¶ 4.4.09(B)).

E. **Keep the disclaimer short**. It's tempting to recite, in the disclaimer, who will receive the property as a result of the disclaimer, but it's a bad idea. If you mention who the property will pass to, it looks as if the disclaimant is trying to direct who will receive the property, or to make the disclaimer conditional on the property's passing to those recipients, either of which actions would make the disclaimer not qualified under § 2518. ¶ 4.4.02(A), ¶ 4.4.08(B).

F.   **Know where the property will go before disclaiming it.** Investigate THOROUGHLY who will receive the property as a result of the disclaimer. A child (*e.g.*) may assume that if he disclaims an inheritance from his father this will cause the inheritance to pass to his mother, only to find out later that the disclaimer caused the property to pass to some distant relatives of the father. See ¶ 4.4.08(C).

4.4.02 *Requirements for qualified disclaimer: § 2518*

Here are the requirements for a qualified disclaimer under § 2518; see ¶ 4.4.03 for why it is important for the disclaimer to be "qualified."

A.   The disclaimer must be irrevocable, unqualified (unconditional), and in writing. § 2518(b). Yes, that's right: In order to be qualified, the disclaimer must be unqualified! Verbal, revocable, and conditional disclaimers are not qualified disclaimers.

B.   The person who is disclaiming (the "disclaimant") must not have "accepted the interest disclaimed or any of its benefits." § 2518(b)(3). See ¶ 4.4.05, ¶ 4.4.05.

C.   The disclaimer must be delivered by a certain deadline. For retirement plan death benefits, the deadline is normally nine months after the participant's death. See ¶ 4.4.06.

D.   The disclaimer must be delivered to the correct party(ies). See ¶ 4.4.07.

E.   The property must pass, as a result of the disclaimer, *to someone other than the disclaimant.* See ¶ 4.4.08(A).

Exception: Property can pass to the decedent's spouse as a result of the disclaimer, even if she is also the disclaimant. § 2518(b)(4).

F.   The property must pass, as a result of the disclaimer, to whoever it passes to *without any direction on the part of the disclaimant*. Disclaimers by the surviving spouse are NOT excepted from this rule. § 2518(b)(4). See ¶ 4.4.08(B).

G.   A disclaimer can be qualified under § 2518 even if it is not valid under state law. § 2518(c)(3). The income tax effects of a qualified disclaimer that is not valid under state law are uncertain; see ¶ 4.4.03.

4.4.03 *Income tax treatment of disclaimers*

Disclaimers are primarily a gift tax concept; the point of having a "qualified disclaimer" is to avoid having a gift tax imposed on the disclaimant's act of refusing to accept an inheritance. However, when the inherited property is a *retirement plan*, the income tax consequences of this act may be even more important than the gift tax effects.

§ 2518 recognizes qualified disclaimers "for purposes of this subtitle." § 2518 is part of Subtitle B of the Code, "Estate and Gift Taxes." Income taxes are governed by Subtitle A. Except for a minor provision dealing with disclaimers of powers by a trust beneficiary (§ 678(d)), there is no Code provision dealing with the effect of disclaimers *for purposes of Subtitle A.*

The IRS Chief Counsel's office has filled the statutory gap, at least with respect to certain disclaimers. GCM 39858 ruled that a disclaimer of retirement benefits, if it meets the requirements of § 2518 and applicable state law, shifts the income tax burden of the benefits from the disclaimant to the person who receives the benefits as a result of the disclaimer.

GCM 39858 did not purport to decide the income tax effects of a disclaimer that was either *not qualified* under § 2518 or *not valid under state law*. The IRS has at least once treated a nonqualified disclaimer of QRP benefits as effective to transfer the income tax burden of the benefits to the person who took the benefits as a result of the disclaimer. See PLR 9450041. Nevertheless, a nonqualified disclaimer is clearly outside the safe harbor of GCM 39858.

There are cases in which "you don't care," for *gift tax purposes*, whether a disclaimer is qualified. See, *e.g.*, PLR 2005-32024. However, when the disclaimed property is a retirement plan, it is normally vital to have the disclaimer not be treated as an assignment, since assignment of a retirement plan generally results in loss of the income tax-sheltered status of the benefits. ¶ 4.6.03.

The rest of this ¶ 4.4 discusses how the qualified disclaimer requirements apply to disclaimers of retirement benefits. ¶ 4.5 discusses the planning uses (and pitfalls) of qualified disclaimers of retirement benefits.

4.4.04 What constitutes "acceptance" of a retirement benefit

One requirement of a qualified disclaimer is that the disclaimant must not "have accepted the interest disclaimed or any of its benefits." § 2518(b)(3). Under Reg. § 25.2518-2(d)(1), acceptance must involve some action on the part of the beneficiary. Mere passive title-holding is not acceptance. Rather, "Acceptance is manifested by an affirmative act which is consistent with ownership...," such as accepting "dividends, interest or rent from the property" (Reg. § 25.2518-2(d)(4), Examples (6), (11)) or "[D]irecting others to act with respect to the property" (Reg. § 25.2518-2(d)(4), Example (4)).

If a beneficiary causes inherited benefits to be transferred to a different account after the participant's death (¶ 4.2.02), that probably constitutes "directing others to act" with respect to the benefits and therefore constitutes acceptance. However, a direction as to only part of the benefits would not necessarily be considered acceptance of the whole; see PLR 2005-03024, in which a surviving spouse exercised control by selling some securities in a joint account that had passed to her by right of survivorship but was not thereby deemed to have accepted the *entire* account (just the securities she had traded), and was accordingly allowed to disclaim the rest of the account.

"[A]cceptance of any consideration in return for making the disclaimer" is treated as acceptance of the property. Reg. § 25.2518-2(d)(1), last sentence; (d)(4), Example (2).

A.　　**Exception for certain fiduciary actions.** This ¶ 4.4.04(A) discusses whether a person who is both a beneficiary and a fiduciary of the inherited property can disclaim an interest *as beneficiary* despite having taken actions with respect to the property in his capacity *as fiduciary*. For disclaimers by a fiduciary *in his capacity as fiduciary* see ¶ 4.4.08(B) (last paragraph), ¶ 4.4.11(B), (C), and ¶ 4.4.12(B).

Actions taken by a person who is both a beneficiary and a fiduciary "in the exercise of fiduciary powers to preserve or maintain the disclaimed property" do not constitute acceptance *as beneficiary.* Reg. § 25.2518-2(d)(2).

Shirley Example: Shirley dies. Her will leaves her house to her three children A, B, and C, and names C as executor. To fulfill his duties as executor under applicable state law, C arranges for insurance, security, and maintenance for the house. These actions taken as executor would not preclude his disclaiming his interest as beneficiary.

This exception can lead practitioners astray. This is a very limited exception for which the IRS provides no examples in the regulations. The only fiduciary powers blessed are "to preserve or maintain the disclaimed property." Any exercise of discretionary powers *to direct the enjoyment of the property*, even if exercised in a fiduciary capacity, would preclude a qualified disclaimer of the property by the individual in his personal capacity, unless the exercise of discretion is limited by an ascertainable standard. ¶ 4.4.08(B).

B.   Titling of account not determinative. The fact that a retirement plan account is retitled in the name of the beneficiary after the death of the participant does not in and of itself mean the beneficiary has accepted the account. See Reg. § 25.2518-2(d)(4), Example (6); PLR 8817061 (a surviving spouse's filing an election to take a statutory share of the decedent's estate did not constitute acceptance of the statutory share; the spouse could disclaim part of the statutory share); and PLR 9214022 (¶ 4.4.05(B)).

Rachel Example: Rachel dies, leaving her IRA (at Brokerage Firm X) to her husband Isaac. Isaac informs Brokerage Firm X of Rachel's death. Firm X retitles the account "Rachel, deceased, IRA, for the benefit of Isaac, beneficiary." Firm X sends Isaac paperwork explaining the account agreement, its fees, and his rights regarding rollover and investments. If this is all that happens, Isaac has not accepted the IRA. But: If Isaac gives Firm X any instructions regarding the account, such as buying or selling investments, he has accepted the account (or at least those investments; see above). If he takes a withdrawal from the account, see ¶ 4.4.05. If he names a successor beneficiary for his interest, see "C."

C.   **Naming a successor beneficiary.** A beneficiary's designating a successor beneficiary for his interest in the account is probably not "acceptance," *unless* the beneficiary dies while that designation is in effect (i.e., before he disclaims), in which case see ¶ 4.4.12(A). This conclusion is reached by analogy from the way the regulations deal with a disclaimer by the holder of a power of appointment: "The exercise of a power of appointment to any extent by the donee of the power is an acceptance of its benefits," says Reg. § 25.2518-2(d)(1), but this apparently does not include an *executory* exercise: See Reg. § 25.2518-2(d)(4), Example (7), in which B has a testamentary power of appointment under A's trust, and signs a will which would exercise the power, but then makes a qualified disclaimer of the power before he dies (so the "exercise" is never activated).

4.4.05 *Effect of taking a distribution; partial disclaimers*

Taking a distribution from an inherited retirement plan does not necessarily constitute acceptance of the entire plan.

A.   **Taking MRD for year of death not acceptance of entire plan.** The IRS has issued a safe-harbor ruling that a beneficiary can receive and keep the minimum required distribution (MRD) from the decedent's IRA for the year of the participant's death (¶ 1.5.04(A)) and still disclaim all or part of *the rest* of such beneficiary's interest in the decedent's IRA. Rev. Rul. 2005-36, 2005-26 IRB 1368. There is one minor limitation: By taking the MRD, the beneficiary is deemed to have accepted not only the MRD itself but also the "income" that the plan earned on that "pecuniary amount" (as the IRS calls it) between the date of death and the date the MRD is distributed to the beneficiary. See the Ruling for how to compute this income.

B.   **Taking other distributions from the plan.** If the beneficiary takes out more than just the year-of-death MRD (and income thereon), such excess distribution is not within the safe harbor of Rev. Rul. 2005-36. However, he has still not necessarily accepted the entire plan; the Code permits a beneficiary to disclaim part of an inheritance while accepting other parts of it. A person may disclaim "any interest" in property. § 2518(a). Reg. § 25.2518-3 is entirely devoted to disclaimers of "less than an entire interest." Several types of partial disclaimers are recognized, including a disclaimer relating to "severable property."

Severable property is "property which can be divided into separate parts each of which, after severance, maintains a complete and independent existence. For example, a legatee of shares of corporate stock may accept some shares of the stock and make a qualified disclaimer of the remaining shares." Reg. § 25.2518-3(a)(1)(ii). When a beneficiary inherits an estate, or a joint securities account, the beneficiary has inherited in effect a collection of severable property. The beneficiary can take some assets from the inherited collection and disclaim others. See Reg. § 25.2518-3(d), Example (17).

The IRS has in rulings allowed beneficiaries to accept some assets from an estate, trust, or joint investment account and later disclaim other assets. Although they did not involve retirement plan accounts, PLRs 8113061, 8619002, 9036028, 9214022, and 2005-03024 support the conclusion that a beneficiary may take a distribution from a typical self-directed IRA (which is, like an estate or a joint investment account, a collection of severable property) without being deemed to have accepted the entire account and therefore without being precluded from disclaiming all or part of the rest of the account. (The only exception would be if the distributions taken could somehow be construed as representing the "income" of the entire account; see ¶ 4.4.04.) Rev. Rul. 2005-36 also supports this conclusion, in that it created a safe harbor for one type of partial acceptance (taking the MRD for the year of death), and did not rule out the possibility of a qualified disclaimer even if other distributions had been taken.

If the beneficiary thinks of this issue before he takes a distribution, he can eliminate the concerns by either executing a partial disclaimer *before* he takes the distribution, or sending in to the IRA provider, along with the request for a distribution, a statement that the beneficiary is not accepting the entire account, just the amount of this distribution.

If the beneficiary does disclaim part of the account, see Rev. Rul. 2005-36 for elaborate rules regarding how the "income" of the retirement plan must be apportioned between the portions disclaimed and not disclaimed.

Taking a distribution *would* preclude a later disclaimer if the retirement benefit is not a collection of "severable" property. For example, if the plan in question is a defined benefit plan (¶ 8.3.04), and the death benefit is a life annuity of $100 per month, as soon as the beneficiary accepts the first $100 check, he has accepted the entire benefit, because there is no way to "sever" the annuity.

C.   **Automatic deposit of benefits not acceptance.** It is common for a participant to arrange his retirement plan so that periodic distributions are automatically deposited in his bank account. If the bank account is a joint account co-owned with the retirement plan beneficiary, the mere continuation of the automatic deposits after the participant's death would not, *in itself,* constitute acceptance of the retirement plan. Since there has been no action by the beneficiary, it would not even constitute acceptance of the amounts deposited, unless the beneficiary actually withdraws from the automatically-deposited amounts. See PLR 2000-03023.

4.4.06 *Deadline for qualified disclaimer*

At first it appears the deadline for disclaimers of retirement benefits is simply stated: nine months after the participant's death. When stated with all its exceptions and wrinkles, however, the deadline is more complicated.

A.   **Nine months after participant's death (or beneficiary's 21st birthday).** § 2518(b)(2) states that a person's qualified disclaimer must be delivered "not later than the date which is 9 months after the later of--(A) the day on which the transfer creating the interest in such person is made, or (B) the day on which such person attains age 21."

Normally, in the case of retirement plan death benefits, the date of transfer is the date of the participant's death, so the deadline for a disclaimer is nine months after that date (or, if later, the beneficiary's 21st birthday). Reg. § 25.2518-2(c)(3)(i). The fact that the deadline for finalizing the identity of the Designated Beneficiary for minimum distribution purposes is September 30 of the year after the participant's death (¶ 1.8.03) does NOT mean that the deadline for making a qualified disclaimer is extended to that date; the MRD rules have *no effect* on the deadline for a qualified disclaimer.

If the deadline for delivering the disclaimer falls on a Saturday, Sunday, or legal holiday (see Reg. § 301.7503-1(b) for definition), the deadline is extended to the next day which is not a Saturday, Sunday, or legal holiday. Reg. § 25.2518-2(c)(2).

In rules borrowed from the deadline for filing tax returns, the IRS provides that "a timely mailing of a disclaimer" to the correct person (¶ 4.4.07) "is treated as a timely delivery." Reg. § 25.2518-2(c)(2). See Reg. § 301.7502-1(c)(1), (2), and (d), for requirements of "timely mailing."

B.   **Is the starting point ever earlier than the date of death?** A qualified disclaimer must be made within a certain time period "after the...date of the transfer creating the interest" being disclaimed. If a beneficiary acquires rights in the participant's benefits earlier than the date of death we need to consider whether the time starts earlier. An irrevocable designation of beneficiary prior to the participant's death could raise this problem if the beneficiary then attempted to disclaim the benefits. However, irrevocable beneficiary designations are rare (nonexistent?) with qualified plans and IRAs.

A more realistic concern is whether the Federal law that gives married persons certain rights in each other's retirement benefits causes the surviving spouse to have acquired rights in the participant's benefits more than nine months before the date of death; see ¶ 3.4.07.

4.4.07 *To whom is the disclaimer delivered?*

§ 2518(b)(2) requires that the disclaimer be "received by the transferor of the interest, his legal representative, or the holder of the legal title to the property to which the interest relates." Reg. § 25.2518-2(b)(2) adds one more candidate, "the person in possession of such property," but provides no further elucidation and no examples.

In the case of retirement benefits, the disclaimer cannot be delivered to "the transferor" (the participant) because he is dead, so that leaves "his legal representative" (i.e., the executor or administrator of the participant's estate), "the holder of the legal title to the property," and "the person in possession." The legal title to retirement benefits is generally held by the trustee (of a QRP or individual retirement trust) or custodian (of an individual retirement account or 403(b) mutual fund account), who also has "possession" of the retirement plan's assets.

The "or" in the Code and Regulation makes it appear that § 2518(b)(2) would be satisfied if the disclaimer is delivered *either* to the executor of the participant's estate *or* to the trustee or custodian of the retirement plan, i.e., that you have a choice regarding where to send the disclaimer. However, see Reg. § 25.2518-2(a)(3) and § 25.2518-2(c)(2), both of which speak of delivery to "*the person*" described in Reg. § 25.2518-2(b)(2), as though in the case of any particular asset there is only one correct recipient of the disclaimer.

Regardless of which destination would satisfy § 2518(b)(2), it is normally *also* necessary to comply with applicable state law, which may have different requirements about where the disclaimer must be delivered. When in doubt, send to "all of the above."

For what it's worth, in PLR 9016026 a qualified disclaimer of QRP benefits was filed with the employer and the plan trustee; in PLR 9226058, a qualified disclaimer of an IRA was filed with the Probate Court. Other letter rulings discussing qualified disclaimers of retirement benefits don't say where the disclaimers were filed.

4.4.08 *Who gets the disclaimed benefits and how do they get them?*

When a beneficiary disclaims inherited benefits, the benefits will generally pass to the person or entity who would have been entitled to the benefits if the disclaimant had predeceased the participant. *To whom* those benefits pass as a result of the disclaimer, and *how they pass to such person*, are very important questions. If the benefits do not pass to the right type of person (see "A" below) in the right way (see "B"), the disclaimer is not qualified. Even aside from the tax consequences, the disclaimant also normally cares about who gets the benefits as a result of the disclaimer; see "C."

A.   Property must pass to "someone other than" disclaimant. § 2518(b)(4) requires that the property must pass, as a result of the disclaimer, either to the transferor's (i.e., the participant's) *surviving spouse* or to *someone other than the disclaimant*. Passing the benefits by means of a disclaimer from an individual primary beneficiary to a trust named as contingent beneficiary works as a *qualified* disclaimer only if the disclaiming primary beneficiary is (1) the surviving spouse or (2) not a beneficiary of the trust.

PLR 2008-46003 involves a disclaimer disaster caused by violation of this rule. The participant's prenuptial agreement required her to leave her IRA to a QTIP trust for the life of her spouse. The participant's children were the remainder beneficiaries of the QTIP trust. Instead of doing what she had agreed to do, the participant named her children directly as beneficiaries of her IRA.

Perhaps what the family should have done when this was discovered at the participant's death was to go to state court seeking an order enforcing the prenuptial agreement and reforming the beneficiary designation to say what the prenuptial agreement said it should say (see ¶ 4.5.05). Instead, the children disclaimed their rights as named beneficiaries of the IRA. The disclaimer caused the IRA to pass to the participant's estate as default beneficiary, whence it passed to the QTIP trust. However, the children did NOT disclaim their remainder interests under the QTIP trust. Thus, despite the disclaimer, this IRA was going to pass right back to the disclaiming children (on the surviving husband's later death), as remainder beneficiaries of the QTIP trust, so the disclaimer violated § 2518(b)(4) and was not a qualified disclaimer.

As a nonqualified disclaimer, the children's well-intentioned action was treated as a *taxable gift of the entire IRA value* by the children to the QTIP trust. There was no marital deduction for the transfer to the QTIP trust because, as far as the IRS was concerned, the IRA went from the *participant to the children* to the QTIP, not directly from the participant to the QTIP. There is no mention of the income tax effects (see ¶ 4.4.03).

B.   **Property must pass "without direction" by disclaimant.**
§ 2518(b)(4) also requires that the property pass, as a result of the disclaimer, to whomever it passes to *without any direction on the part of the disclaimant*. Disclaimers by the surviving spouse are NOT excepted from this rule.

If a surviving spouse named as outright beneficiary is to disclaim, she cannot thereafter retain any discretionary distribution powers over the disclaimed benefits (unless limited by an ascertainable standard; Reg. § 25.2518-2(e)(1)). For example, if the spouse is disclaiming benefits that will pass, as a result of her disclaimer, to a credit shelter trust for the benefit of the deceased participant's issue, she cannot be a trustee of that trust if the trustee has, say, discretionary power to "spray" trust income among the issue; nor can she have a power of appointment enabling her to, *e.g.*, decide which issue will receive the trust after her death. See PLR 2005-22012, in which the surviving spouse (because of this rule) disclaimed her testamentary power of appointment under a trust with respect to an IRA that flowed to such trust by virtue of her disclaiming the IRA as beneficiary.

The requirement that property must pass "without any direction" on the part of the disclaimant would presumably preclude a disclaimer by one discretionary trust that causes the disclaimed property to pass to a second discretionary trust with the same trustees.

C.   How to determine who gets the disclaimed benefits. Generally, unless the plan documents provide otherwise, the disclaimed benefits pass as if the disclaimant had died before the participant. For example, normally a disclaimer by the primary beneficiary will cause the property to pass to the contingent beneficiary, and a disclaimer by all named beneficiaries will cause the benefits to pass to the default beneficiary under the plan document. Sometimes the beneficiary designation form specifies one contingent beneficiary in case of the primary beneficiary's disclaimer, and a different contingent beneficiary if the primary beneficiary actually predeceases the participant. See ¶ 4.4.13(C).

4.4.09 *Disclaimers, ERISA, and the plan administrator*

One concern is whether a plan administrator of a qualified retirement plan (QRP) might cite ERISA requirements in refusing to recognize a disclaimer. A plan administrator might take the position that the plan requires the benefits to be paid to the beneficiary named by the participant, and the plan has no authority to pay the benefits to someone else if the named beneficiary is in fact living; that ERISA requires the plan to be administered in accordance with its terms; and that ERISA preempts state laws including disclaimer statutes.

"ERISA," which stands for the Employee Retirement Income Security Act of 1974, refers to the constellation of requirements that apply under the United States Code to "employee pension benefit plans" (usually called "retirement plans") as defined in 29 U.S.C. § 1002 (§ 3(2)(A) of ERISA). There are two concerns regarding enforceability of a disclaimer with respect to a qualified retirement plan: Does a disclaimer violate ERISA's "anti-alienation" requirement? See "A." And, does the disclaimer contravene the terms of the plan document? See "B."

These issues are of no concern to IRA administrators, since IRAs are not subject to ERISA and its preemption rule.

A.   **Disclaimers and ERISA's anti-alienation rule.** One of the requirements a retirement plan must meet in order to be "qualified" under § 401(a) is that the plan document must provide that benefits under the plan "may not be assigned or alienated," except through the medium of a "qualified domestic relations order" (QDRO; § 414(p)), which is a court-ordered transfer of benefits between spouses in connection with a divorce. § 401(a)(13). This "anti-alienation rule" is also a requirement applicable to retirement plans under ERISA. 29 U.S.C. § 1056(d)(1).

In GCM 39858 (¶ 4.4.03), the IRS stated that disclaimers do not violate ERISA, and that a disclaimer is not an "assignment or alienation" of plan benefits of the type forbidden by § 401(a)(13). The IRS has blessed disclaimers of QRP benefits in several letter rulings; see PLRs 9016026, 9247026, and 2001-05058.

In *Kennedy, Executrix, v. Plan Administrator for DuPont Savings and Investment Plan et al.*, 129 S.Ct. 865 (2009), the Supreme Court (confirming GCM 39858) held that a beneficiary's giving up the right to an inherited benefit under a QRP does not constitute an assignment or alienation, provided the beneficiary does not attempt to direct where the inherited benefit will go. Although *Kennedy* dealt with a divorcing spouse's waiver of her rights to benefits under her ex-husband's plan, the same principle would apply to a disclaimer which, under federal tax law, must not involve any direction by the disclaimant regarding who shall inherit the asset as a result of the disclaimer. ¶ 4.4.08(B). In fact the Court compared the spousal waiver to a disclaimer, pointing out that the law of trusts serves as a backdrop to ERISA, and "*the general principle that a designated spendthrift beneficiary can disclaim his trust interest* magnifies the improbability that a statute written with an eye on the old law would effectively force a beneficiary to take an interest...." Emphasis added. The plan involved in *Kennedy* had a specific provision permitting disclaimer, which the court quoted favorably. *Kennedy* should put an end to any notion that a disclaimer violates ERISA's anti-alienation requirement.

B.   **Disclaimers and the plan document.** Another ERISA requirement applicable to QRPs is that the plan administrator must administer the plan in accordance with "the terms of the plan." 29 U.S.C. § 1132(a)(1)(B). The Supreme Court has twice held that this ERISA rule preempts any state law that would require the plan administrator to deviate from the terms of the plan document:

1.   In *Egelhoff v. Egelhoff*, 532 U.S. 141 (2001), the named beneficiary under the plan was (as in *Kennedy*) the participant's ex-spouse. Under Washington state law, which otherwise applied to these individuals, the designation of the participant's spouse as beneficiary would have been automatically revoked by their divorce. Had Washington state law been applied to the QRP benefits in question, the former spouse would have been treated as having predeceased the participant. The Court ruled that the Washington state law was preempted by ERISA; the ex-wife, as the named beneficiary under the plan, was still entitled to the benefits because *nothing in the plan documents* said that divorce revoked her rights as named beneficiary.

2.   In *Boggs vs. Boggs,* 520 U.S. 833 (1997), the Court held that a state's community property law purporting to grant the participant's spouse the right to transfer part of the participant's plan benefits was preempted by ERISA because the right, as in *Egelhoff*, would require the plan administrator to look beyond the plan documents to determine who was entitled to the benefits.

These holdings would appear to "overrule" PLR 8908063, in which the IRS ruled that a plan must conform to a state's "slayer" statute, and not pay benefits to the person who murdered the participant, even if that person is named as beneficiary under the plan.

In *Kennedy* (see "A" above), there was a conflict between the participant's divorce agreement (under which the participant's ex-wife Liv had waived her rights to the benefits) and the written beneficiary designation form on file with the plan (under which Liv was the named beneficiary). The Court viewed the divorce agreement as a valid "federal common law waiver" of the benefits by Liv, but held that a federal common law waiver, like a state law revoking a beneficiary designation in case of divorce, would have to give way to the *superior rule* that the plan administrator must carry out the terms of the plan document.

The point of this rule, the Court explains in *Kennedy*, is to avoid forcing "plan administrators to examine numerous external documents purporting to be waivers and draw them into litigation like this over those waivers' meaning and enforceability." The *Kennedy* Court reiterates the importance of "holding the line" "in holding that ERISA preempted state laws that could blur the bright-line requirement to follow plan documents in distributing benefits." ERISA and the Court favor "a uniform administrative scheme, [with] a set of standard procedures to guide processing of claims...."

The *Kennedy* case leads to the following conclusion: A plan may choose to recognize disclaimers—or not. If the plan document specifies that disclaimers are not recognized, then the plan administrator cannot honor a disclaimer, regardless of state law.

C.   **Effect of the plan's "state law" provision.** Some plan documents, as in *Kennedy*, explicitly recognize disclaimers. Such a plan is obviously required to honor a disclaimer that satisfies the plan's requirements regarding disclaimers.

Other plans do not specifically mention disclaimers, but do recite that they are governed by a particular state's laws to the extent not preempted by ERISA. Under *Egelhoff* and *Boggs*, state law is pre-empted only to the extent it would require the plan administrator to do something that is not in accordance with the plan documents. With respect to disclaimers, however, the Supreme Court has stated in *Kennedy* that there is a federal common law right of waiver and/or disclaimer and that these rights do not, per se, violate ERISA. Since ERISA does not preempt disclaimers, and in fact federal law favors the right of disclaimer, according to *Kennedy*, it would appear that a plan that is to be administered in accordance with the law of a particular state (except to the extent preempted) is required by the terms of the plan document to honor a disclaimer that complies with such state's law.

4.4.10 *Disclaimers and the minimum distribution rules*

Who is liable for the § 4974 penalty for a missed MRD
(¶ 1.9.02) for the year of the participant's death if a qualified disclaimer
causes the identity of the beneficiary to change after the end of the
year?

Howard Example: Howard died in November, Year 1, after his RBD,
leaving his IRA to his daughter Stephanie. Howard's MRD for Year 1
was $30,000; he had not yet taken that distribution at the time of his
death. In January, Year 2, Stephanie disclaimed the entire IRA by
means of a qualified disclaimer. As a result of Stephanie's disclaimer,
the contingent beneficiary, Howard's son Milton, became "the"
beneficiary. Accordingly, it appears that Milton is liable for the 50
percent penalty for failure to take the Year 1 MRD—even though at no
time in Year 1 could he have legally accessed the account!

4.4.11 *How a disclaimer can help after the participant's death*

Disclaimers have proven to be of great value in cleaning up
beneficiary designations where the deceased participant named the
"wrong" beneficiary. See, *e.g.*, PLR 9442032 where a disclaimer was
used to allow retirement benefits to flow to the decedent's "credit
shelter trust" that otherwise would have been unfunded.

A.   **Changing the Designated Beneficiary.** A qualified disclaimer
made by September 30 of the year after the year of the
participant's death (the "Beneficiary Finalization Date"; see
¶ 1.8.03) is effective to "remove" the disclaimant as a
beneficiary of the disclaimed portion for purposes of
determining who is the participant's Designated Beneficiary
under the minimum distribution rules. Reg. § 1.401(a)(9)-4, A-
4(a). The fact that the Beneficiary Finalization Date is not until
September 30 of the year after the year of death does *not* extend
the deadline for making a qualified disclaimer. ¶ 4.4.06.

By means of a qualified disclaimer, an older beneficiary (such
as a surviving spouse or child) can disclaim the benefits and allow
them to pass to a younger contingent beneficiary (such as a child or
grandchild) and the younger beneficiary will then be "the Designated
Beneficiary" with respect to the disclaimed portion. MRDs with respect

to the disclaimed portion will be determined based on the identity of the beneficiary who takes as a result of the disclaimer rather than on the identity of the original beneficiary who disclaimed.

Trust beneficiaries can disclaim interests or powers they have under the trust, to help the trust qualify as a "see-through trust" under the IRS's minimum distribution trust rules. See ¶ 6.3.03(B).

B.   Salvaging spousal rollover. If the participant dies having named the "wrong" beneficiary, it may be possible to get the benefits to the spouse (so she can roll them over) by having the named beneficiary disclaim the benefits. This strategy works if, as a result of the disclaimer, the benefits pass outright to the spouse either as contingent beneficiary, or as the default beneficiary under the plan (¶ 1.7.02).

If the default beneficiary under the plan is the participant's estate, this strategy still works *if* (as a result of the disclaimer) the benefits will pass (through the estate) outright to the spouse as residuary beneficiary under the participant's will or by intestacy. See ¶ 3.2.09.

In PLR 9045050, the participant named a trust as his beneficiary. The spouse was a trustee of the trust. Upon the participant's death, the spouse, as trustee, made a qualified disclaimer of the benefits. As a result of the disclaimer, the benefits passed to the spouse outright rather than to the trust, and she rolled them over. PLR 1999-13048 (see ¶ 3.2.09) was similar.

In PLR 9450041, benefits were redirected from a marital trust to the spouse via a chain of qualified and nonqualified disclaimers; the rollover was allowed.

In PLR 2005-05030, a participant died without having named a beneficiary for his retirement plans. The benefits therefore became payable to his estate, which in turn was left to "Trust #2." The beneficiaries of Trust #2 were the participant's spouse, issue, sister, sister's issue, sister-in-law, and sister-in-law's issue. Qualified disclaimers were filed by the spouse, and all the then-living issue (two daughters and two grandchildren), and by the sister and sister-in-law and *their* then-living issue (seven nieces and nephews). As a result of these disclaimers, the trust passed to the surviving spouse under applicable state law, and the IRS approved the spousal rollover.

C.   **Disclaimer by participant's estate.** When retirement benefits are payable to the *participant's own estate*, the IRS has ruled that the participant's executor may not disclaim the benefits because the participant had "accepted" his own retirement benefits (¶ 4.4.04). PLR 9437042.

4.4.12 *Double deaths: Disclaimer by beneficiary's estate*

If the beneficiary of a retirement plan dies after becoming entitled to the benefits, the beneficiary's executor generally can disclaim the benefits on the beneficiary's behalf if permitted by state law. This approach is often useful when a husband and wife die within a short time of each other, and the first spouse to die named the surviving spouse as primary beneficiary and their children (or a see-through trust for their children) as contingent beneficiary. The executor of the now-deceased surviving spouse disclaims the benefits (and any interests granted to the now-deceased surviving spouse under any trust named as contingent beneficiary) on behalf of the now-deceased surviving spouse, allowing the benefits to flow directly to the next generation (or to the trust for the next generation). As a result of the disclaimer, the participant's original "contingent beneficiary" becomes the "primary beneficiary," which often produces better results under the minimum distribution rules. See PLR 2000-13041 for an example.

The deadline for this type of disclaimer is nine months after the death of the *participant* (not nine months after the subsequent death of the primary beneficiary).

Here are issues to consider with respect to such disclaimers:

A.   **Who is the successor beneficiary?** When a beneficiary dies after becoming entitled to the benefits, the person who succeeds to the deceased beneficiary's interest is called the successor beneficiary. ¶ 1.5.12. If the successor beneficiary is not the deceased beneficiary's own estate there are two potential obstacles to a disclaimer by the beneficiary's executor:

First, if the <u>beneficiary himself</u> had designated a successor beneficiary (¶ 1.5.12(A)), then a qualified disclaimer by the beneficiary's executor is probably not possible. The beneficiary's death would cause his "executory" designation of a successor beneficiary (¶ 4.4.04(C)) to be considered "executed," and this would be deemed acceptance by the beneficiary, precluding disclaimer. *Estate of Engelman*, 121 T.C. 54 (2003).

Second, if there is a successor beneficiary (other than the participant's own estate) who has been designated <u>by the participant</u> (¶ 1.5.12(D)), one case held that the successor beneficiary is automatically entitled to ownership of the benefits upon the death of the original beneficiary, so the estate of the original beneficiary had no standing to disclaim. *Nickel v. Estate of Estes*, 122 F. 3d 294 (5th Cir. 1997). Though this case has been criticized (and might not be followed by other courts), if there is a designated successor beneficiary, that successor beneficiary is likely to claim the benefits, citing this case.

B.   **If the fiduciary is also a beneficiary.** When the beneficiary's executor disclaims benefits that are payable (as a result of the beneficiary's death) to the now-deceased beneficiary's estate, the interest he is disclaiming is the *deceased beneficiary's* interest in those benefits. Thus, the executor of the now-deceased original beneficiary can make such a disclaimer on behalf of the deceased beneficiary even if the executor in his *individual* capacity (1) is a beneficiary of the original beneficiary's estate and (2) will receive the benefits personally as a result of the estate's disclaimer.

Such a disclaimer *appears* to violate the rule that the disclaimed assets must pass to someone other than the disclaimant (¶ 4.4.08(A)), since the asset is beneficially owned by the same individual both before and as a result of the disclaimer. However, it does not violate that rule, because when he disclaims in his capacity as *executor of someone's estate* he is not deemed to be disclaiming on behalf of *himself individually as beneficiary* of that estate.

See *Dancy*, 872 F. 2d 84 (4th Cir. 1989), in which a son, as executor of his mother's estate (of which he was also the sole beneficiary), was allowed, on her behalf, to make a qualified disclaimer of her interest as surviving joint owner of certain property she held with her husband. This disclaimer was allowed even though the son was also the beneficiary of the husband's estate which would receive the property as a result of the disclaimer; and PLRs 9015017 and 8749041 (involving similar situations).

4.4.13 Building disclaimers into the estate plan: Checklist

It is wise, at the planning stage, to anticipate the possibility of disclaimers. For example, the participant may be trying to choose between naming his spouse as beneficiary, to achieve deferral of income taxes via a spousal rollover, on the one hand, and naming a credit shelter trust as beneficiary, on the other hand, to take advantage of his unified credit. Each choice has its merits and a clear "winner" may not be apparent during the planning phase.

The participant may decide to make the benefits payable to the spouse as primary beneficiary, because his main goal is to provide for the spouse's financial security, but provide that, if the spouse disclaims the benefits, the benefits will pass to the credit shelter trust. If funding the credit shelter trust appears to be the more attractive alternative at the time of the participant's death, the spouse can activate the credit shelter plan by disclaiming the benefits, which will then pass to the credit shelter trust as contingent beneficiary. PLR 9320015 illustrates this type of planning. See also PLR 2005-22012 (benefits payable to spouse as primary beneficiary, with marital trust as contingent beneficiary if spouse disclaimed, and family trust as second contingent beneficiary if spouse also disclaimed all her interests in the marital trust, and participant's children as third contingent beneficiaries if spouse also disclaimed all her interests in the family trust); PLR 2005-21033 is identical.

While it is wise to consider the possibility of disclaimers, the apparent flexibility of disclaimers can tempt planners to rely excessively on future disclaimers as a way of carrying out the estate plan. One justification offered for this approach is that it avoids the need to spend time analyzing the choices at the planning stage. Thus, professional fees are lower—at the planning stage. The estate plan relies on the fiduciaries and beneficiaries to make the decisions later, after the participant's death, when a more informed choice can be made. Before making important estate planning goals dependent on prospective disclaimers by beneficiaries or fiduciaries, or whenever considering the impact of disclaimers on an estate plan being drafted, use this checklist for issues to be reviewed.

A. **Consider risks and drawbacks of disclaimers.** Disclaimers are not a simple solution:

    1.   One requirement of a qualified disclaimer is that the disclaimant must not have "accepted" the disclaimed property. See ¶ 4.4.04. If the surviving spouse is the sole beneficiary, and is considering a disclaimer, no one can exercise investment authority over the account pending her decision, unless the benefits are in a trusteed plan under which the trustee can exercise such authority. Assets in a custodial or self-directed plan would essentially be frozen, since the participant's powers of attorney or grants of investment authority would expire at his death and the spouse could not grant new authority without accepting the account.

    2.   Disclaimers generally have an inexorable deadline of nine months after the date of death. ¶ 4.4.06. Thus, an estate plan that depends on disclaimers requires rapid action *post mortem.*

    3.   No matter how apparently cooperative and disclaimer-friendly the proposed disclaimant may have been in the planning stage, he could have a change of heart and not sign a disclaimer when the time comes.

    4.   If estate taxes will be due on the disclaimed property, who will pay them? The decedent's will may contain a tax payment clause that does not operate correctly if there is a disclaimer.

B. **Consider having disclaimer occur at trust level.** If it is anticipated that a beneficiary might want to make a "formula" disclaimer (*e.g.,* a surviving spouse as primary beneficiary disclaiming an amount sufficient to fully fund the participant's credit shelter trust), consider the practicalities of drafting such a formula, getting the plan administrator to accept it, and carrying out its terms all within a brief nine-month window after the participant's death.

If that looks like it might be difficult to accomplish, or if there is any other reason to anticipate that the plan administrator may pose obstacles to the disclaimer (see ¶ 4.4.09), consider naming, as primary beneficiary, a trust which gives the surviving spouse the right to (1) all income for life, plus (2) principal if needed for health or support, plus (3) an unrestricted power to withdraw all principal during her life, plus (4) a general power of appointment at death. If she wants to keep the retirement benefits, she can withdraw them from this trust and roll them over; see ¶ 3.2.09. If she wants to convert the trust to a "credit shelter trust" for her life benefit, she can disclaim rights (3) and (4). If she wants to disclaim all interests, she can do that. She can disclaim any of these rights as to all or a fractional portion of the trust, if the trust contains the proper language. In doing all this, she will need to deal only (or primarily) with the (friendly, expert, understanding) trustee. This sidesteps the problems of dealing with the (cold, bureaucratic, nonexpert) plan administrator.

C.	**Consider naming different contingent beneficiaries for death vs. disclaimer.** The most common use of this dual designation of contingent beneficiary is where: (1) the primary beneficiary is the spouse and (2) the contingent beneficiary in case of the spouse's disclaimer is a trust of which the spouse is a life beneficiary, and (3) the contingent beneficiary in case of the spouse's death is the same person (or group of people) who is the remainder beneficiary of the trust at the spouse's death. See Form 3.4, Appendix B.

D.	**Facilitate disclaimers.** When a disclaimer is anticipated at the estate planning stage, take steps beforehand to facilitate that process, including: spousal waiver of REA rights (¶ 3.4), if needed; instructions to the beneficiaries regarding the choices that will be available to them and what considerations should be applied in making the choices; granting disclaimer authority to fiduciaries, along with guidelines for exercise of the power to disclaim; and review the plan documents, § 2518 requirements, and state law to make sure these pose no obstacles to the proposed disclaimers.

4.5 Other Cleanup Strategies

When a retirement plan participant dies leaving benefits to a beneficiary who is not the ideal choice, there are other "cleanup strategies" besides disclaimers. Some cleanup strategies are described in other parts of this book:

✓   See ¶ 1.8.03 and ¶ 7.2.02(C) for how a post-death distribution can eliminate an "undesirable" beneficiary for minimum distribution purposes. See ¶ 6.3.03 for the same strategy with respect to a trust.

✓   See ¶ 1.8.01(A) for how dividing an inherited plan into separate accounts can improve minimum distribution results.

✓   See ¶ 3.2.09 for achieving a spousal rollover of benefits that are payable to a trust or estate.

4.5.01 *Check the plan's default beneficiary*

If the participant failed to name a beneficiary (or no named beneficiary survived the participant), the plan document or IRA agreement will indicate who is the **default beneficiary**. See ¶ 1.7.02. Don't assume the estate is the default beneficiary. In the case of a qualified retirement plan (QRP), the Retirement Equity Act of 1984 (REA) requires that all or part of the death benefits pass to the surviving spouse if the participant was married for more than a year at the time of his death. See ¶ 3.4. Whether or not REA requires the benefits to be paid to the surviving spouse, the QRP or IRA may provide for a human default beneficiary such as surviving spouse, children, issue, or next of kin.

4.5.02 *Invalidate the beneficiary designation*

If the participant actually named the "undesirable" beneficiary, investigate whether the beneficiary designation could be invalidated. Perhaps the participant was incompetent, or did not comply with the formalities required by the plan to have a valid designation. This approach could be fruitful *if* invalidating the designation would reinstate a more favorable prior beneficiary designation or default beneficiary.

In *Liberty Life Assurance Co. of Boston v. Kennedy*, 358 F.3rd 1295 (11th Cir. 2004), a court found that the decedent's will was effective as a beneficiary designation under the terms of an employee life insurance plan governed by ERISA, where (1) the will specifically disposed of the insurance proceeds, (2) the plan permitted any writing to constitute a beneficiary designation (i.e., the employer's forms did not have to be used), and (3) the plan permitted posthumously-delivered beneficiary designations to be effective. The will terms superceded the beneficiary designation form that was on file with the employer (which named a former spouse as beneficiary).

In PLR 2003-17033, the deceased husband's IRA beneficiary designation was complex, possibly unclear, and evidently considered to produce an undesirable result. Three years before his death, the participant and his spouse had signed an agreement providing that, on the death of either spouse "title to all property" would immediately vest outright in the survivor. "It has been represented that this agreement applies to...[the IRA]. It has been further represented that this agreement is being treated as the beneficiary designation with respect to" the IRA. The IRS allowed the spouse to roll over the IRA.

4.5.03 *Spousal election to take share of estate*

Most practitioners concur that spousal rights in IRAs and other "nonERISA" plans are governed by state rather than federal law. Perhaps applicable state law gives the surviving spouse the right to claim a statutory share of a nonERISA plan. Some states give the spouse the right to claim a share of all marital assets (including IRAs) *and* the right to choose which assets will be used to fulfill her statutory share. A surviving spouse could exercise these rights by taking the retirement plan in fulfilment of her share and rolling it over to her own retirement plan. This strategy may not be helpful if the spouse is required to waive other benefits, or otherwise give up too much to exercise the right, or for a QRP (spousal rights under which cannot be governed by state law due to REA's preemption; see ¶ 3.4.01). See PLR 2001-50036, permitting rollover of the portion of an IRA payable to the surviving spouse as part of her statutory share of the estate.

4.5.04 *Will (or beneficiary designation form) contest*

In PLR 2001-27027, the decedent owned several IRAs and a QRP. In a compromise settlement, "after strenuous negotiations" among family members, the decedent's estate plan was set aside, and "Of Decedent's property, other than joint property but including the amounts from the IRAs and Plan, Y percent will pass to Spouse and Z percent will pass to Son. Daughter will receive $X." Spouse's share was less, in value, than she would have received under the will and trust. The IRS found that the dispute was bona fide and the settlement was within the range of reasonable settlements, and permitted spousal rollover of the portion of the IRAs payable to the spouse under the settlement agreement. PLR 2007-07158 (¶ 4.5.05) also involved revising a beneficiary designation form as part of the settlement of litigation over an inheritance.

4.5.05 *Reformation of beneficiary designation form*

Consider state court proceedings to reform a defective beneficiary designation. See ¶ 4.5.06 for discussion of which state court actions are binding on the IRS.

There have now been five PLRs involving beneficiary designation forms that were reformed by state court action after the death of the participant, PLRs 2006-16039 and 2006-16040 (both dealing with the same beneficiary designation form), 2006-52028, 2007-07158, and 2007-42026. Only three of these (2006-16039, 2006-16040, and 2007-42026) dealt with the *minimum distribution* effects of the reformation, and the newest of these three may cancel out the result in the first two.

The first two were PLRs 2006-16039 and 2006-16040, in which the participant had an IRA that named his wife as primary beneficiary and his two daughters as contingent beneficiaries. He moved the IRA to a different firm and instructed the new firm to prepare a beneficiary designation form identical to that of the old IRA. The new firm mistakenly did not insert the name of any contingent beneficiary and apparently the participant didn't notice this mistake when he signed the form, with the result that his estate was the default contingent beneficiary of the account at the time he died. His wife survived him for only a short time, and her executor disclaimed the benefits on her behalf (see ¶ 4.4.12). A court reformed the beneficiary designation form to name the daughters as contingent beneficiaries, so that the disclaimed benefits would pass to them rather than to the decedent's estate, and the IRS ruled that the daughters would be treated as the decedent's "Designated Beneficiaries" for minimum distribution purposes. This is a classic case of reformation to correct a "scrivener's error."

In PLR 2007-42026, however, the IRS refused to honor a post-death reformation for MRD purposes. The participant had named his spouse as primary beneficiary. Though he had named his daughter as contingent beneficiary on a prior beneficiary designation form, there was no contingent beneficiary named on the form that was in effect at the participant's death. Unlike in PLRs 2006-16039 and 16040, where the financial institution testified that its own error had caused the contingent beneficiary line to be left blank, in PLR 2007-42026 the IRA provider had actually mailed the participant a new form, after his wife died, to name his daughter as beneficiary of the IRA, but the participant never signed it. Because there was no named beneficiary, the IRA would pass to the participant's estate as beneficiary. Two years after the participant's death a court order was obtained reforming the beneficiary designation to name the daughter as beneficiary. The IRS refused to grant a ruling that the daughter should be treated as the participant's "Designated Beneficiary" for minimum distribution purposes.

One could say that this negative ruling simply reflects the factual differences between the 2006 and 2007 PLRs, but that's not what the ruling says. The language of the later ruling suggests rather that the IRS is closing the door on post-death reformations as a way to improve the Designated Beneficiary situation for MRD purposes, reversing the prior longstanding trend of the IRS's apparent strong approval of post-death "cleanup" actions; see ¶ 4.5.06 for more on the longstanding trend and the new IRS position.

Though the outlook is cloudy for reformation of a beneficiary designation form as a way to improve the minimum distribution results, it still can be useful for other "cleanup" jobs, such as undoing a designation signed under "undue influence" (PLR 2007-07158) or (as a way to reduce probate costs) redirecting benefits from an estate (as named beneficiary) to a trust (that was the residuary beneficiary of the estate) (see PLR 2006-52028).

4.5.06 *Reformation of trust or will*

"[A]bsent specific authority in the Code or Regulations, the [post-death] modification of...[a trust] will not be recognized for federal tax purposes." —Frances V. Sloan, IRS, in PLR 2010-21038.

The post-death "reformation" of the decedent's trust or will should be granted by a court and recognized by the IRS if it appears that (for example) the attorney who drafted the document made a mistake and did not write what the now-deceased client told him to write. But many PLR requests involving post-death reformations do not involve such "scrivener's errors." Rather, it often appears that the income tax effects of the estate plan were simply ignored until after the client's death, at which point "reformation" was used (by collusion among the beneficiaries, with the consent of a compliant judge) to redraft the documents in a way that (they hoped) would produce better income tax results. The IRS is not going to accept this type of "reformation." See, e.g., PLR 2009-44059, in which the participant died leaving his IRA to a trust for the benefit of his surviving spouse and issue. The surviving spouse and the remainder beneficiaries, with state court blessing, agreed to terminate the trust (so the surviving spouse could roll over the IRA held in the trust). The IRS denied the rollover.

How can the IRS ignore a state court order reforming a will or trust? It's easy. With regard to questions of state law, state probate court judgments and rulings are NOT binding on the IRS. The only state court whose judgment the IRS must defer to on such questions is the highest court in the state. *Estate of Bosch*, 387 U.S. 456 (1967). Thus, generally, the IRS is not impressed with lower state court orders, and will make its own independent judgment regarding state law matters, even if you have a court order supporting your position.

A.   **Reformation of trust to achieve see-through status.** See ¶ 6.2–¶ 6.3 for the rules a trust must comply with in order to qualify as a "see-through trust" for minimum distribution purposes (so that benefits can be paid out to the trust over the life expectancy of the oldest trust beneficiary rather than under the "no-DB" rules). The IRS has in the past "blessed" post-mortem court actions that caused noncomplying trusts to be reformed, settled, divided into separate trusts, or otherwise re-engineered to comply with the trust rules. See, *e.g.*, PLRs 2002-

18039, 2005-22012, 2005-37044, 2006-08032, 2006-20026, 2007-03047, and 2007-04033.

Despite this string of favorable rulings, however, PLR 2007-42026 (¶ 4.5.05) signaled a changing IRS attitude towards post-death state court actions reforming or interpreting trusts for minimum distribution purposes. PLR 2010-21038 (see quote at the beginning of this section) states the new IRS position on trust reformations loud and clear. In this PLR, "B" died leaving his IRA to a trust for "C" and "D." C and D had both lifetime and testamentary powers of appointment over the trusts, including the power to appoint to charity (i.e., a nonindividual beneficiary). After B's death, the trustee obtained a court order reforming the trust—eliminating the charitable beneficiaries, prohibiting use of retirement benefits to pay taxes, requiring pass-through of IRA distributions to the individual beneficiaries, etc.—then sought an IRS ruling that the trust qualified as a see-through. The IRS refused to grant the ruling, citing, in support of its position, numerous cases as well as the possibility of collusive reformations solely for the purpose of reducing federal tax. The IRS ruled that "B" had "no DB."

B.   **Reforming will or trust for other reasons.** There are reasons other than attempting to achieve see-through status why a post-death reformation could improve results with respect to retirement benefits. In PLR 2008-50004, the decedent's IRAs became payable to his estate as beneficiary, as a result of a disclaimer by the named beneficiary of the IRA. The will provided for certain charitable bequests without specifying the funding source for payment of these bequests. A court reformed the will to provide that the IRAs would be the source of funding the charities' shares of the estate, and the IRS allowed the transfer of the IRAs to the charities (see ¶ 6.1.05, ¶ 7.4.05) in fulfilment of these shares. The combination of disclaimer and reformation diverted the IRAs to the charities without payment of income tax.

4.5.07 *Choose the right cleanup strategy*

Consider carefully what cleanup strategy to use. A "cleanup" does not always work as expected.
      For example, PLR 2008-46028 (also issued as PLR 2008-49020) involved a state court's *interpretation* of a beneficiary

designation form rather than a reformation. The decedent's IRA beneficiary designation form said only, in the space provided for the name of the beneficiary, "as stated in wills." The participant's will left all of his estate (aside from some specific bequests of tangible personal property) to "Trust T." Trust T provided for disposition of the entire trust (other than specific gifts of certain real estate) to eight individuals in specified percentages.

Rather than obtaining a state court order simply confirming that the meaning of the beneficiary designation form was that the beneficiary of the IRA was "Trust T," the executor obtained a state court order ruling that: The eight individuals should be treated as having been named *directly* as beneficiaries by the participant; the individuals were "Designated Beneficiaries" of the participant's IRA within the meaning of the Code and regulations; and the "separate accounts" rule (¶ 1.8.01) was applicable in determining the applicable distribution periods for each beneficiary's share of the benefits!

Not only did this court ruling contradict the clear sense of the beneficiary designation form (which pointed to the beneficiary of the WILL, not the beneficiaries of the TRUST), it put the state court in a position of interpreting the federal minimum distribution regulations. Furthermore, it attempted an end-run around the IRS's rule that (even if a trust IS named as beneficiary), all trust beneficiaries must use the life expectancy of the OLDEST trust beneficiary as the ADP (¶ 6.3.02). The IRS refused to accept the state court order in any respect, ruling that the beneficiary designation form failed to indicate ANY beneficiary, therefore the benefits were payable by default to the participant's estate. One can only speculate whether, if the court order had been limiting to just interpreting the beneficiary designation form as naming the trust as beneficiary, the IRS might have accepted it.

A.   **When to seek reformation and avoid disclaimer.** If the decedent *tried* to do something, or *thought he had done* something, or *had agreed to do* something, but that "something" did not end up getting done in the actual documents in effect on his death, the correct strategy is to reform the documents so they reflect what the decedent tried to do, thought he had done, or was supposed to do. A disclaimer is usually not the right strategy in this situation. See PLR 2008-46003, discussed at ¶ 4.4.08(A).

B.   **When and how to use disclaimer.** If there is no evidence that the decedent had tried or agreed to do something that did not in fact get done, but the beneficiaries just don't like whatever it is the decedent did, then reformation is *not* the right remedy. Disclaimer *may* be an appropriate way for the beneficiaries to try to get things to be the way they want them to be.

Elmer Example: Elmer has three children, X, Y, and Z. He dies. He leaves his probate estate to all three children equally, but names only X as beneficiary of his IRA. He named no contingent beneficiary; the IRA documents provide that Elmer's estate is the default beneficiary. X wants to share the IRA equally with his siblings, for the sake of fairness. Seeking reformation of the beneficiary designation form is not advisable, because there is no evidence that Elmer *tried* to name all three children as IRA beneficiaries but was thwarted by the IRA provider's mistake, or that Elmer *believed* he had named all three children; no one knows why X ended up as sole beneficiary of the IRA. Even if a court and the IRA provider went along with the reformation, the IRS probably would not accept it (see ¶ 4.5.05–¶ 4.5.06), with the result that X might be treated as having made an income taxable assignment and taxable gift of the IRA to his siblings, and also causing loss of Designated Beneficiary treatment. Instead, X should disclaim an undivided two-thirds interest in the IRA and *also* disclaim any right he has (as a beneficiary of Elmer's estate) to share in this particular asset. The disclaimer will allow X to keep his one-third of the IRA as Designated Beneficiary, and allow the other two siblings to receive one-third each through the estate. Inheriting their shares through the estate will have less favorable income tax consequences (no life expectancy payout), but under these facts it is just not possible to achieve the goal of shifting part of the IRA to them and also get them Designated Beneficiary treatment.

4.6 Income in Respect of a Decedent (IRD)

When the participant dies, the plan benefits become payable to his beneficiaries. The beneficiaries must pay income tax on the inherited benefits because such benefits are "income in respect of a decedent" (IRD) under § 691. § 61(a)(14).

This ¶ 4.6 provides the basics of the IRD rules, with emphasis on how the rules apply to retirement benefits. For any questions not answered here, see the highly-recommended book *The Estate Planner's Guide to Income in Respect of a Decedent*, by Alan S. Acker (Bibliography).

Generally, the same income tax rules apply to beneficiaries as applied during the participant's life: Benefits are taxable only when they are actually distributed (¶ 2.1.01), distributions are taxable as ordinary income unless one of the exceptions listed at ¶ 2.1.06 applies, etc. However, additional considerations arise:

❏   **Rollovers:** The ability to use a rollover (¶ 2.6) to avoid income tax on a distribution is curtailed or in some cases eliminated, unless the beneficiary is the participant's surviving spouse; see ¶ 4.2 and ¶ 3.2 regarding beneficiary rollovers.

❏   **IRD deduction:** The beneficiary is entitled to an income tax deduction for federal estate taxes paid on the inherited benefits. See ¶ 4.6.04–¶ 4.6.08.

❏   **Kiddy tax:** The "kiddy tax" may apply: Under § 1(g), a child who is under age 24 may be taxable on his "unearned income" at his *parents'* income tax rate. Income resulting from a distribution from an inherited retirement plan is considered "unearned income" for this purpose. Reg. § 1.1(i)-T, A-6, A-9.

❏   **No more $5,000 death benefit exclusion.** For beneficiaries of participants who died prior to August 21, 1996, up to $5,000 of employee death benefits could be excluded from the beneficiary's income. This "$5,000 death benefit exclusion" no longer exists. See former § 101(b), repealed by the Small Business Job Protection Act of 1996.

4.6.01 *Definition of IRD; why it is taxable*

Income in respect of a decedent (IRD) is not defined in the Code. The IRS defines it as "amounts to which a decedent was entitled as gross income but which were not properly includible in computing his taxable income for the taxable year ending with the date of his death or for a previous taxable year...." Reg. § 1.691(a)-1(b).

Death benefits under qualified plans, 403(b) plans, and IRAs are IRD. Rev. Rul. 92-47, 1992-1 C.B. 198; Reg. § 1.663(c)-5,

Example 9; PLR 9341008. IRD does not qualify for any "basis step-up" at the decedent's death; see ¶ 4.3.08.

4.6.02 When IRD is taxed (normally when received)

Normally, IRD is includible (when received) in the gross income of the person or entity who acquired, from the decedent, the right to receive such income. § 691(a)(1).

Colin Example: Colin's estate is named as beneficiary of Colin's IRA, which is entirely pretax money. The estate withdraws money from the IRA. The withdrawal is includible in the estate's gross income as IRD. § 691(a)(1)(A).

Barbara Example: The beneficiary designation for Barbara's 403(b) account (which is entirely pretax money) provides that the first $20,000 of the account shall be distributed to Lucy, and the balance shall be paid to Tom. Upon Barbara's demise, Lucy withdraws her $20,000; that distribution is includible in her gross income as IRD. Whenever Tom withdraws from the account, such withdrawals will be includible in his gross income as IRD. § 691(a)(1)(B).

4.6.03 Tax on transfer of the right-to-receive IRD

Although much less common than distributions, there is another event that can cause IRD to be taxable. If the person or entity who inherited the right-to-receive the IRD from the decedent transfers that right-to-receive-IRD to someone else, § 691(a)(2) provides that the IRD is immediately taxable, *to the transferor*. A distribution from a retirement plan is IRD; the retirement plan account *itself* is a right-to-receive IRD. (Even without § 691(a)(2), the transfer of a *retirement plan* by gift or pledge would normally be a taxable event anyway; see ¶ 2.1.04(C).)

Here are examples of how a transfer of the right-to-receive IRD could occur:

A.   Gift of right-to-receive IRD.

Stokely Example: Stokely is named as beneficiary of his father's IRA. After taking distributions for several years after his father's death (and including such distributions in his income as IRD), Stokely decides he does not need this money and wants his sister to have it. He gives the inherited IRA to his sister. His gift is a transfer of the right-to-receive IRD, and the full value of the IRA becomes immediately taxable *to Stokely* under § 691(a)(2).

B. **Transfer from estate or trust to beneficiary.** Although the Stokely Example is unrealistic, there is one type of transfer of the right-to-receive IRD that is very common, and that is the transfer of an inherited retirement plan by an estate or trust to the individual beneficiary(ies) of the estate or trust. See ¶ 6.1.05. This type of transfer may or may not be taxable; see ¶ 6.5.07–¶ 6.5.08.

C. **Transfer to a 100 percent grantor trust.** Rev. Rul. 85-13, 1985-1 C.B. 184, established the principle that transactions between an individual and trust all of whose assets are deemed owned by such individual under the "grantor trust rules" (¶ 6.3.10) are not considered taxable transactions under the income tax Code, because "A transaction cannot be recognized as a sale for federal income tax purposes if the same person is treated as owning the purported consideration both before and after the transaction."

If a beneficiary transfers an inherited IRA to a trust of which he is considered the sole owner under § 678 (one of the "grantor trust rules"), the transfer, being a nonevent for income tax purposes, should not trigger deemed income under § 691(a)(2), *provided* that (under the terms of the transferee trust) the benefits cannot be distributed to anyone other than that beneficiary during his lifetime. Two PLRs confirm this conclusion. In PLR 2006-20025, an IRA that had been left to the participant's disabled child outright as beneficiary was transferred to a "special needs trust" ("(d)(4)(A)" type, since the child was establishing it for his own benefit) established by the child's guardian on his behalf, with probate court approval. In PLR 2008-26008, an IRA left outright to the participant's minor child as beneficiary was transferred to a trust for the minor's benefit established by the child's guardian on his behalf, with probate court approval. In both cases the trusts were irrevocable. The IRS ruled the transfers were nontaxable.

4.6.04 *Income tax deduction for estate tax paid on IRD*

The federal estate tax paid on IRD is deductible for federal income tax purposes by the recipient of the IRD. § 691(c). State estate taxes are *not* deductible.

To determine the amount of the deduction, first determine the estate tax due on the entire estate. Next, determine the net value of all items of IRD that were includible in the estate (for definition see § 691(c)(2)(B)). The estate tax attributable to the IRD is the difference between the actual federal estate tax due on the estate and the federal estate tax that would have been due had the net value of the IRD had been excluded from the estate.

Harvey and Emma Example: Harvey dies in 2009, leaving his $5 million taxable estate (including a $1 million pension plan) to his daughter Emma. The federal estate tax in 2009 on a $5 million taxable estate was $675,000. If the $1 million IRA were excluded from the taxable estate, the taxable estate would be only $4 million, and the federal estate tax would be $225,000. Thus the amount of federal estate tax attributable to the IRA is $675,000 – $225,000, or $450,000. Emma will be entitled to an income tax deduction of $450,000 which she can claim when she receives the $1 million pension distribution.

Note that:

1.   The deductible portion of the estate tax is computed at the marginal rate, not the average rate; this is favorable to the beneficiary. In the Harvey and Emma Example, even though the IRA constituted only 20 percent of the taxable estate, it accounted for 67 percent of the estate tax, so the IRD deduction equals 67 percent of the total estate tax.

2.   The federal estate tax is repealed for deaths in 2010, then reinstated (under EGTRRA's sunset provision, § 901) for deaths in 2011 and later. See ¶ 4.3.08. EGTRRA did not repeal or amend § 691, so if federal estate taxes are paid (because the participant died in a year in which the estate tax was in effect), they can be deducted when the beneficiary receives a distribution from the plan, even if the distribution occurs in 2010.

3.   The estate tax does not have to be paid before the deduction can be taken, as long as it is owed and attributable to the IRD. PLR 2000-11023.

4.   There is a limited deduction for generation-skipping transfer (GST) taxes; see § 691(c)(3). Computation of the § 691(c) deduction becomes more complex if a marital, charitable, or state death tax deduction is involved; see Reg. § 1.691(c)-1(a)(2). These topics are beyond the scope of this book. See instead, the highly-recommended *Estate Planner's Guide to Income in Respect of a Decedent* by Alan S. Acker (Bibliography).

The IRD deduction can create an incentive to cash out retirement benefits soon after the participant's death if the IRD is a relatively small part of a large estate. If the estate is large, the marginal estate tax bracket will be high, and that will make a relatively larger share of the IRD tax-free upon distribution. The beneficiary who receives the retirement plan distribution will therefore not lose too much of the distribution to income taxes, and can reinvest the after-tax distribution in property that will produce long-term capital gains and/or dividends, both of which (currently) enjoy relatively low income tax rates. In contrast, if the estate is not so large (so the estate tax and the resulting § 691(c) deduction are low), and/or if the retirement plan is a large portion of the estate (if it is large enough, the "tax attributable" to the IRD tends to be closer to the average rate of tax on the estate than to the highest marginal bracket applicable to the estate), there is less incentive for beneficiaries to take early distributions.

4.6.05 *Who gets the § 691(c) (IRD) deduction*

The § 691(c) deduction goes to the person who receives the IRD, regardless of who paid the estate tax.

Jack Example: Jack dies in 2002 with an estate of $3 million. He leaves his $1 million IRA (which is entirely IRD) to his daughter Jill. He leaves his $2 million probate estate (which is not IRD) to his son Alex. Alex pays the federal estate tax of $897,500. The § 691(c) deduction goes to Jill because she received the IRD, even though Alex paid the estate tax.

4.6.06 *IRD deduction for deferred payouts*

Calculating the § 691(c) deduction is easy when the beneficiary receives a distribution of the entire benefit all at once, but what if the retirement benefit is distributed in installments over the life expectancy of the beneficiary? Clearly the deduction will also be spread out; but how much of the deduction is allocated to each payment? How much of each distribution represents "IRD" that was included in the gross estate, and how much represents income earned by the retirement plan after the date of death?

When IRD is in the form of a joint and survivor *annuity*, the Code requires that the deduction be amortized over the surviving annuitant's life expectancy and apportioned equally to the annuity payments received by the survivor. § 691(d). No official source discusses the allocation of the deduction to nonannuity payouts, such as instalment payments. For discussion of possible alternative methods, see Christopher Hoyt articles cited in the Bibliography. For possible future developments in this area, keep an eye on regulations and rulings under § 2056A, where the question of which retirement plan distributions constitute IRD and which constitute post-death earnings is critical to application of the deferred estate tax on a "qualified domestic trust" (QDOT).

Meanwhile, the method used by many practitioners could be called the "IRD comes out first" method: All distributions from the retirement plan are assumed to be coming out of the IRD (rather than out of the post-death earnings of the plan) until the § 691(c) deduction has been entirely used up.

Jack Example, continued: In the Jack Example, assume that the total § 691(c) deduction was $427,600, which is 42.76 percent of the total $1 million IRA. Suppose the IRA has grown to be worth $1.2 million by the time Jill takes her first withdrawal of $30,000. She assumes the distribution comes entirely from the $1 million original principal of the IRA (from the IRD, in other words) and none of it from the $200,000 of post-death earnings, so Jill takes a deduction equal to 42.76 percent of her $30,000 distribution, or $12,801. She keeps doing this until she has received a total of $1 million of distributions from the IRA, at which point she has used up all of her $427,600 § 691(c) deduction.

A beneficiary can "lose" his IRD deduction if the value of the inherited IRD declines. Suppose that, instead of increasing in value after his death, Jack's IRA had declined in value from the $1 million used for estate tax purposes to just $400,000 a year after his death. Jill cashes out the IRA, receiving $400,000. It *seems* as if this distribution should be tax-free, because Jill was entitled to a $427,600 IRD deduction and she received only $400,000 total from the IRA...but the IRD deduction doesn't work that way. Jill is entitled to a deduction of only 42.76 percent of each distribution she receives. Her IRD deduction on the $400,000 IRA distribution is only $171,040.

What happened to the rest of Jill's IRD deduction? It just disappeared. After all, the purpose of the IRD deduction is to ease the pain of including the IRD in income. If the IRD ceases to exist due to a decline in value, the beneficiary does not suffer the pain of including it in income and so does not need the deduction. See IRS Publication 559, "Survivors, Executors and Administrators" (2009), page 12.

Suppose that, instead of cashing out the IRA, "Jill" keeps it alive until eventually its investments appreciate back to their original value. Presumably the unused IRD deduction can be fully applied to distributions from the re-appreciated account despite the fact that the value on which estate tax was paid was "lost" for some period of time (there is no authority on this point).

4.6.07 *IRD deduction: Multiple beneficiaries or plans*

If multiple beneficiaries inherit IRD items from the same decedent, the IRD deduction is apportioned among them in proportion to the amount of IRD each receives. § 691(c)(1)(A).

It is not clear whether the deduction must be apportioned among multiple plans inherited by a single beneficiary. Suppose a beneficiary inherits an IRA and a 403(b) plan, each worth $100,000, and she is entitled to a § 691(c) deduction of $80,000 for this $200,000 of IRD. The IRA experiences investment losses and becomes worthless, while the 403(b) plan doubles in value to $200,000. She cashes out the 403(b) plan. Can she use the entire § 691(c) deduction against the $200,000 403(b) distribution? Or is she required to apportion half the deduction to the now-vanished IRA, so she can never use it?

4.6.08 *IRD deduction on the income tax return*

On the bright side: Certain miscellaneous itemized deductions are deductible only to the extent the total of such deductions exceeds two percent of the individual's adjusted gross income (AGI). § 67(a).

The § 691(c) deduction is *not* one of those, so it may be deducted without regard to the two percent floor. § 67(b)(7). Because it is not subject to the two percent floor, this deduction *is* allowed in computing the alternative minimum tax (AMT). § 56(b)(1)(A)(i).

On the negative side, the § 691(c) deduction is subject to § 68, under which an individual's itemized deductions are reduced (in years before and after 2010) by an amount equal to as much as three percent of the individual's AGI in excess of an annually-adjusted threshold amount, or (if less) 80 percent of total itemized deductions. § 68(a), (b). EGTRRA repealed § 68 effective in 2010, but EGTRRA's sunset provision reinstates it in 2011 at 2001 levels. The § 68 reduction of itemized deductions does not apply to trusts or estates; see ¶ 6.5.04.

4.7 Road Map: Advising the Beneficiary

Here are matters the advisor needs to review with a client who has inherited a retirement plan. If the client is the deceased participant's surviving spouse, see also ¶ 3.1.02, "Road Map: Advising the Surviving Spouse."

✓   Go through the post-mortem disclaimer checklist at ¶ 4.4.01. If the benefits are not to be disclaimed, consider:

✓   Other ways to "clean up" the estate plan after the participant's death, if he named the "wrong" (or no) beneficiary for his retirement plan. ¶ 4.5. If benefits are payable to the "right" beneficiary, move on to:

✓   How to correctly title an inherited IRA. ¶ 4.2.01.

✓   Advise the beneficiary regarding the option for Roth conversion of the inherited plan if that option is available; see ¶ 4.2.05.

✓   Assist the beneficiary with transferring the account to the beneficiary's own preferred financial institution if that option is available and desired. ¶ 4.2.02–¶ 4.2.04.

✓   Compute the beneficiary's minimum required distributions (MRDs) using the Road Map for determining post-death MRDs at ¶ 1.5.02. Make sure the beneficiary understands the obligation to take MRDs and help him comply with it by offering to compute the MRDs and sending annual reminders.

✓   Determine whether there is after-tax money in the inherited plan and if so how it will be distributed; see ¶ 2.2.07.

✓   If the participant's estate is subject to federal estate tax, advise the beneficiary regarding the IRD deduction, how much it is and how to take it; see ¶ 4.6.04–¶ 4.6.08.

✓   Make sure the inherited benefits are integrated into the beneficiary's own estate plan, for example, by advising the beneficiary to name a successor beneficiary for his interest. See ¶ 1.5.12(A).

5

Roth Retirement Plans

Roth retirement plans offer the possibility of tax-free distributions to those who are eligible (and can afford) to adopt them.

This Chapter covers everything the advisor needs to know about "Roth" retirement plans except the following matters that are covered in other Chapters: Roth conversions by the participant's surviving spouse (see ¶ 3.2.04) or nonspouse beneficiary (¶ 4.2.05); the executor's responsibilities with respect to a deceased participant's Roth conversion (¶ 4.1.02); the tax on "unrelated business taxable income" (UBTI) (¶ 8.2); and tax treatment of investment losses (¶ 8.1.02) and management fees (¶ 8.1.04).

5.1 Roth Plans: Introduction

"Tax-free compounding is the best thing in the world." –Jonathan G. Blattmachr, Esq.

5.1.01 Introduction to Roth retirement plans

Prior to the debut of the Roth IRA in 1998, all retirement plans had the same basic tax structure: Contributions to the plan might or might not be tax deductible; and all distributions from the plan in excess of the participant's after-tax contributions would be includible in the recipient's gross income.

§ 408A established a new kind of IRA, called a Roth IRA, effective in 1998. Roth IRA contributions are never deductible, but distributions are normally tax-free. Thus, income tax on the plan's investment returns is not merely deferred, it is eliminated—at the cost of payment of income tax up front on the plan contributions. In addition to tax-free distributions, the Roth IRA offers other advantages over traditional IRAs: no minimum required distributions during the participant's life (¶ 5.2.02(A)); no maximum age for making contributions (¶ 5.3.04(A)); and the ability to withdraw the participant's own contributions, separately from any earnings thereon, income tax-free at any time (¶ 5.2.06).

Congress later added another type of Roth plan (the "designated Roth account" or "DRAC"; ¶ 5.7) and more ways to acquire a Roth plan (¶ 5.3.01).

Because the investment accumulations inside a Roth plan are tax-free (not merely tax-deferred, as with traditional plans), long-term deferral of Roth distributions becomes even more important than deferral of the taxable distributions under conventional plans. The longer the money stays inside the Roth account, the more tax-free income is generated for the participant and beneficiaries. See ¶ 1.1.03.

5.1.02 *Roth retirement plan abuses*

The potential for tax-free investment returns tempts some to misuse the Roth IRA. In a blatant abuse of the Roth IRA retirement savings vehicle, some individuals have attempted to shift income into their Roth IRAs by such means as having the Roth IRA form a wholly-owned entity (such as an LLC), then shifting value into that entity by (for example) selling property to it at bargain prices. The goal of these schemes is to shelter income in the tax-free Roth.

In Notice 2004-8, 2004-4 IRB 333, the IRS attacked these devices as being: disguised IRA contributions in violation of the limits on annual IRA contributions and the requirement that only cash may be contributed to an IRA (¶ 5.3.02); listed transactions for purposes of the anti-tax-shelter regulations (see Reg. § 54.6011-4); and possibly prohibited transactions (see ¶ 8.1.06). The IRS will dismantle the transactions through denial of deductions (for, *e.g.*, excessive payments from a business to the Roth IRA-owned entity) or re-allocation of income, deductions, etc., among the persons and entities involved pursuant to § 482; see CCA 2009-17030 for example.

Since 2004, the number of questionable Roth IRA schemes has only grown. Articles and seminars tout ideas for "investment vehicles" that will reduce the value of your IRA (for tax purposes only of course) thus facilitating a cheaper Roth conversion. In September 2010 the Justice Department obtained an injunction prohibiting a Missouri lawyer from promoting Roth IRA "ideas" of this type. See also the IRS website page regarding abusive retirement plan transactions, http://www.irs.gov/retirement/article/0,,id=118821,00.html. Advisors should stay far away from "planning ideas" like these.

5.2 Roth IRAs: Minimum Distribution and Income Tax Aspects

Roth IRAs are just like traditional IRAs except where the tax Code says they are different. The differences arise in the treatment of distributions (normally tax-free from Roth IRAs), deductibility of contributions, and application of the minimum distribution rules.

5.2.01 *Roth (and deemed Roth) IRAs vs. traditional IRAs*

For federal income tax purposes, Roth IRAs are treated just like traditional IRAs except where the Code specifies different treatment. § 408A(a); Reg. § 1.408A-1, A-1(b). Thus, if any question about Roth IRAs is not specifically answered in § 408A or the regulations, the answer should be the same as for a traditional IRA. Here are the ways in which a Roth IRA is NOT the same as a traditional IRA:

✓   The minimum distribution rules apply differently to the two types of IRAs. See ¶ 5.2.02(A).

✓   "Qualified" distributions from a Roth IRA are income tax-free, whereas traditional IRA distributions are generally taxable. See ¶ 5.2.03–¶ 5.2.05.

✓   As with a traditional IRA, the participant's after-tax contributions to a Roth IRA are not taxed again when they are withdrawn from the account; but there is a big difference between Roth and traditional IRAs in how you determine whether a particular distribution consists of the participant's own contributions. See ¶ 5.2.06–¶ 5.2.07.

✓   There are different eligibility requirements for making contributions to a Roth versus a traditional IRA. See ¶ 5.3.04, ¶ 5.4.02.

Deemed IRAs: An employer who maintains a qualified retirement plan may permit employees to make voluntary contributions to "a separate account or annuity established under the plan." § 408(q)(1)(A); Reg. § 1.408(q)-1. The separate account must meet the requirements of § 408 (traditional IRA) or § 408A (Roth IRA). The separate account (called a **deemed traditional IRA** or **deemed Roth IRA**) is then treated in all respects the same as a "regular" traditional or Roth IRA and is generally not subject to the qualified plan requirements.

Since a deemed Roth IRA is treated in all respects the same as a "real" Roth IRA, all discussion in this book about Roth IRAs applies equally to deemed Roth IRAs. Deemed IRAs seem to be rare (nonexistent?); at least, this author has never encountered one.

5.2.02 *Roth IRAs and the minimum distribution rules*

The minimum distribution rules (see Chapter 1) do not apply to a Roth IRA until after the participant dies. Thus, withdrawals beginning at age 70½ that are mandated for traditional IRAs simply do not apply to Roth IRAs. After the participant's death, the minimum distribution rules *do* apply to the Roth IRA beneficiary.

A.   **No lifetime required distributions.** The lifetime minimum required distribution (MRD) rules generally require that a participant must take annual distributions from an IRA beginning at approximately age 70½, using a distribution schedule designed to assure that the projected death benefits to the participant's beneficiary will be no more than "incidental benefits" compared with the value of the projected distributions to the participant. See ¶ 1.3. These "lifetime MRD rules" do not apply to Roth IRAs. § 408A(c)(5) provides that § 401(a)(9)(A) (which contains the lifetime minimum distribution rules) and the "incidental death benefits" rule do not apply to Roth IRAs. There is no "Required Beginning Date" (RBD; ¶ 1.4) for a Roth IRA.

B.   **Post-death MRD rules DO apply.** Once death occurs, the minimum distribution rules *do* apply to Roth IRAs. The Roth IRA is not exempted from any minimum distribution rules other than § 401(a)(9)(A) and the incidental death benefits rule, both of which apply only during the participant's life, so distributions must begin coming out of the Roth IRA after his death. Since there is no RBD for a Roth IRA, the post-death minimum distribution rules will *always* be applied "as though the Roth IRA owner died before his" RBD. Reg. § 1.408A-6, A-14(b).

For how to compute MRDs from a Roth IRA after the participant's death, see ¶ 1.5.02–¶ 1.5.03. If the participant's surviving spouse inherits the Roth IRA, see ¶ 1.5.03(B) for how to compute MRDs to her so long as she holds the account as beneficiary. If she rolls the account over to her own Roth IRA (¶ 3.2.03(B), (F)), it then becomes "her" Roth IRA, and there are no further distributions required until after her death.

C.   **Roth *distributions* do not fulfill MRD for traditional IRA.** *Distributions from* a Roth IRA cannot be used to fulfill a distribution requirement with respect to any other kind of IRA. Traditional and Roth IRAs are NOT aggregated for MRD purposes. Reg. § 1.408A-6, A-15.

D.   **MRDs and recharacterizations.** See ¶ 1.2.07 regarding effect of a recharacterization (¶ 5.6) occurring after the end of the conversion year on calculation of the MRD for the year of the recharacterization.

E.   **MRDs and Roth conversions.** Beginning in the first year that a minimum distribution is required from the traditional plan or IRA (the year the participant reaches age 70½ in the case of lifetime MRDs from a traditional IRA; ¶ 1.4.07), such plan or IRA may not be converted to a Roth IRA until *after* the MRD for the year of the conversion has been distributed out of the traditional plan or IRA. Reg. § 1.408A-4, A-6(a), (b); see ¶ 1.4.07(B), ¶ 2.6.03.

If funds are rolled or transferred from a traditional plan or IRA to a Roth IRA *before* the MRD for the year of the conversion has been distributed out of the traditional plan or IRA, the conversion cannot be a valid Roth conversion to the extent of the MRD. The IRS created a special rule to deal with this situation: The IRS treats the MRD that was improperly "rolled" to the Roth IRA "as if" (1) the MRD had been distributed out of the traditional plan and (2) the recipient then contributed the same amount to the Roth IRA as a "regular contribution" (¶ 5.3.02). Reg. § 1.408A-4, A-6(c).

Because of this special IRS rule there will be no penalty for failure to take the MRD (¶ 1.9.02); the MRD is deemed to have been distributed, and the Roth conversion (to the extent the converted amount exceeded the MRD) is valid. However, the "deemed" regular contribution to the Roth IRA will usually result in an "excess contribution" to the Roth IRA, either because the deemed contribution is larger than the permitted maximum regular contribution (¶ 5.3.03) or because the person is not eligible to make a regular contribution to a Roth IRA at all. A person who is eligible to *convert* to a Roth (¶ 5.4.02) may be ineligible to make a *regular* contribution to a Roth IRA (¶ 5.3.04). An excess contribution to the Roth IRA will generate an excess-contribution penalty (¶ 5.3.05) unless the excess contribution (along with the net income attributable to it) is withdrawn from the Roth IRA prior to the deadline for corrective distributions; see ¶ 2.1.08.

Gideon Example: Gideon, age 78 and retired, converted his $1 million traditional IRA to a Roth IRA in 2010. Unfortunately he failed to take the 2010 MRD from the traditional IRA before doing the conversion. Assume his 2010 MRD was $50,000. The good news is that the $50,000 is treated as if it were distributed to him from the traditional IRA, so he does *not* have to pay the penalty for failure to take an MRD. The bad news is he has made an excess contribution of $50,000 to the Roth IRA. To avoid a six percent penalty on that excess contribution, he must withdraw the $50,000 (plus net income attributable to it) by October 15, 2011. There is no possibility of treating any part of this improper rollover contribution as a proper "regular" contribution to the Roth IRA; because Gideon is retired, he has no compensation income, and thus is not eligible to make regular contributions to any IRA (¶ 5.3.02). Compare "Armande Example," ¶ 2.1.08(I).

5.2.03 *Tax treatment of Roth IRA distributions: Overview*

"Qualified distributions" from a Roth IRA are income tax-free. It is relatively easy to qualify for "qualified" distributions; see ¶ 5.2.04–¶ 5.2.05. The requirements for a qualified distribution from a designated Roth account (DRAC) are slightly different; see ¶ 5.7.04. *Non*qualified distributions from Roth IRAs may or may not be tax-free; see ¶ 5.2.06 (¶ 5.7.05 for nonqualified DRAC distributions).

Regarding the tax basis of property distributed from a Roth IRA, see ¶ 8.1.01.

A.   Qualified vs. nonqualified distributions. Qualified distributions from a Roth IRA are not included in the recipient's gross income for federal income tax purposes, regardless of whether the recipient is the participant or a beneficiary. § 408A(d)(1); Reg. § 1.408A-6, A-1(b)(2).

Shane Example: Shane has a Roth IRA. He receives qualified distributions from it. These are excluded from his gross income. Shane dies, leaving his Roth IRA half to his son and half to the Shane Family Trust. The son and the trust both take MRDs and other distributions from the Roth IRA, all of which are qualified distributions. These qualified distributions are income tax-free (regardless, in the case of the trust, of whether they are treated as "income" or "principal" for trust accounting purposes).

B.   **Aggregation of Roth IRAs for income tax purposes.** See ¶ 2.2.08 for the rule (in § 408(d)(2)) that all of an individual's IRAs are generally aggregated (treated as one account) for purposes of determining how much of any particular distribution constitutes a return of the participant's after-tax contributions. § 408A(d)(4)(A) provides that "§ 408(d)(2) shall be applied separately with respect to Roth IRAs and other individual retirement plans." This means that the taxation of distributions from *traditional* IRAs is computed without regard to the existence of, or distributions from, *Roth* IRAs in the same year; and that all of the participant's Roth IRAs are treated as one single account for purposes of applying the Ordering Rules (¶ 5.2.07). Note, however, that:

✓   *Beneficiaries:* A Roth IRA that an individual holds *as beneficiary of a deceased person* is NOT aggregated with the individual's own Roth IRA(s); it is aggregated only with other inherited Roth IRAs the individual holds as beneficiary of the same decedent. Reg. § 1.408A-6, A-11.

✓   *Spouses:* The Roth IRAs of a husband and wife are not aggregated with each other; each spouse's Roth IRAs are aggregated only with other Roth IRAs of that spouse. Aggregation applies to Roth IRAs of the "individual." Reg. § 1.408A-6, A-9.

✓   *Returned, recharacterized, contributions:* The aggregation rule does *not* apply for purposes of computing net income attributable to a returned or recharacterized IRA contribution. See ¶ 5.6.02. That computation is done with respect only to the particular account that received the contribution that is being returned or recharacterized. Reg. § 1.408-11(c)(3), § 1.408A-5, A-2(c)(4).

C. **Actual vs. deemed distributions.** Generally, funds in a Roth IRA are treated as distributions only when actually distributed from the account. See ¶ 2.1.01. For events that may cause a "deemed" distribution from an IRA (including a Roth IRA) without an actual distribution, see ¶ 2.1.04.

5.2.04 *Qualified distributions: Definition*

"Qualified distributions" are distributions that occur after a five-year waiting period has elapsed *and* a "triggering event" has occurred. For how to compute the five-year waiting period, see ¶ 5.2.05. The most common "triggering events" are attaining age 59½ and death. For most people, therefore, getting tax-free qualified distributions from their Roth IRA will be a matter of waiting five years and being over age 59½.

More precisely, a qualified distribution is one that is made after the Five-Year Period (¶ 5.2.05) has elapsed; and which *in addition* (§ 408A(d)(2)(A)):

1.   Is made on or after the date the participant attains age 59½; or

2.   Is made after the participant's death; or

3.   Is "attributable to" the participant's being totally disabled (as defined in § 72(m)(7); see ¶ 9.4.02); or

4.   Is a "qualified special purpose distribution," i.e., a distribution of up to $10,000 for certain purchases of a "first home." § 408A(d)(2)(A)(iv), (5); § 72(t)(2)(F), (8); see ¶ 9.4.09.

These conditions for a qualified distribution from a Roth IRA resemble the requirements for avoiding the 10 percent "early distributions" penalty of § 72(t) (¶ 5.5), but are not identical. For example, withdrawals from a Roth IRA to pay higher education expenses are not qualified distributions, even though such withdrawals from an IRA are exempt from the 10 percent penalty (¶ 9.4.08).

Note that certain distributions probably or definitely can NOT be qualified distributions, *even if* the Five-Year Period and triggering event requirements are met:

♦　**Corrective distributions.** If various requirements are met, an IRA (or Roth IRA) contribution that is returned (together with any earnings thereon) to the contributor by a certain deadline is deemed never to have been contributed; see ¶ 2.1.08 regarding such "corrective distributions." The "earnings" distributed along with a returned IRA contribution cannot be a qualified distribution, and therefore will be taxable (and will be subject to the 10% penalty if the individual is under age 59½ and no exception applies). Reg. § 1.408A-6, A-1(d). The IRS might apply this principle to the earnings on *any* excess Roth IRA contribution, regardless of whether the excess contribution was returned to the contributor as part of a corrective distribution, although the IRS has made no pronouncement on this subject to date; see ¶ 5.1.02.

♦　**Prohibited transactions.** Engaging in a prohibited transaction with a Roth IRA causes the account to lose its exempt status, and to be deemed to be entirely distributed as of the first day of the year in which the prohibited transaction occurs. § 408(e); § 408A(a); Reg. § 1.408A-1, A-1(b). Since the deemed distribution is coming from an account that no longer qualifies as a Roth IRA, it is presumably not a qualified distribution, though the regulations do not explicitly say that. Compare Reg. § 1.402A-1, A-11 (¶ 5.7.04(C)) which does explicitly say that the income resulting from engaging in a prohibited transaction with a DRAC cannot be a qualified distribution.

5.2.05 *Computing Five-Year Period for qualified distributions*

Satisfying a five-year waiting period (called in this book "the **Five-Year Period**") is one of two tests a Roth IRA owner must pass in order to have tax-free "qualified distributions" (¶ 5.2.04) from his Roth IRA.

A.   **Five-Year Period for participant.** The Five-Year Period (called in the statute the "**nonexclusion period**") for *all* of a participant's Roth IRAs begins on January 1 of the first year for which a contribution was made to *any* Roth IRA maintained for that participant. § 408A(d)(2)(B); Reg. § 1.408A-6, A-2.

Fred Example: On May 3, 1999, Fred put $1,000 into his Roth IRA. Fred's Five-Year Period starts January 1, 1999, and is completed on December 31, 2003. The first year in which he can possibly have a qualified distribution is 2004. If he makes further contributions (either regular or rollover) to the same (or any other) Roth IRA, those contributions do NOT start a new Five-Year Period running. In 2006, Fred converts his $100,000 traditional IRA to a Roth IRA. This new Roth IRA instantly meets the Five-Year Period requirement, because Fred has already completed the Five-Year Period for every Roth IRA he will ever own. If Fred is already over age 59½, he can immediately take qualified distributions from his newly-created Roth IRA in 2006.

If a Roth IRA contribution is entirely recharacterized (¶ 5.6.03), it is treated as if it had never been made. If Fred had recharacterized his 1999 Roth IRA contribution, that contribution would not start the Five-Year Period running.

The Five-Year Period is computed differently for a DRAC. ¶ 5.7.04(B). The method of computing the Five-Year Period for a Roth IRA does not change just because the Roth IRA receives a rollover from a DRAC, *regardless of how long the DRAC had been in existence.* See ¶ 5.7.09.

B.   **Five-Year Period for beneficiaries.** The five-year holding period requirement is not eliminated by the participant's death; the inheriting beneficiaries still must fulfill this requirement to have qualified distributions (see "Jules and Jim Example," ¶ 5.2.06). The deceased participant's holding period for the inherited Roth IRA carries over to the beneficiary. Reg. § 1.408A-6, A-7(a). The Five-Year Period is determined separately with respect to the beneficiary's OWN Roth IRAs and for the Roth IRAs he has inherited from each decedent. Reg. § 1.408A-6, A-7(b). It is not clear whether or how this "carryover" concept applies to an "inherited" Roth IRA that is created by means of a Roth conversion by a Designated Beneficiary (¶ 4.2.05(C)).

As usual, there are special rules for the surviving spouse: If the beneficiary of the Roth IRA is the surviving spouse, she gets to carry over the deceased participant's holding period *even if* she elects to treat the Roth IRA as her own Roth IRA (¶ 3.2.03), so in effect she gets to use her own holding period or the deceased spouse's holding period, whichever is longer. Reg. § 1.408A-6, A-7(b).

Scott Example: Scott contributes to his first Roth IRA in 2008. His Five-Year Period will therefore be completed December 31, 2012. He dies in 2010, leaving the Roth IRA in equal shares to his wife (age 45) and daughter (age 22). The wife and daughter divide the account into two separate equal inherited Roth IRAs, one payable to each of them (¶ 4.2.02(B)). The wife elects to treat the separate Roth IRA payable to her as her own Roth IRA.

For Scott's daughter, the Five-Year Period for her inherited Roth IRA will be completed December 31, 2012, because she "carries over" Scott's holding period. Accordingly, for the daughter, all distributions from the inherited Roth IRA after 2012 will be "qualified distributions," because she will have met both the Five-Year Period requirement and the triggering event requirement. Scott's death was the triggering event for her inherited Roth IRA. She started her own first Roth IRA in 2010. She will complete the Five-Year Period with respect to any (noninherited) Roth IRA she may ever own at the end of 2014, but will not meet the triggering event test with respect to *her own* Roth IRAs until she reaches age 59½, or is disabled, etc.

For the Roth IRA payable to Scott's wife that she has elected to treat as her own, her election erases Scott's death as a triggering event, because the Roth IRA is now considered her own Roth IRA (not an inherited Roth IRA), and she owns it as participant (not beneficiary). Reg. § 1.408A-6, A-3. For distributions after 2012 she will have met her Five-Year Period requirement, based on *Scott's* holding period, which she gets to carry over. If she had started a Roth IRA of her own prior to 2008 (the year Scott started his), her Five-Year Period would be based on her *own* Roth IRA. But regardless of which holding period start date applies, she will still not have qualified distributions from this or any of her other (noninherited) Roth IRAs until she attains age 59½ or becomes disabled, etc.

5.2.06 *Tax treatment of nonqualified distributions*

A **nonqualified distribution** is one made before the Five-Year Period (¶ 5.2.05) is up; or which is made (either before or after expiration of the Five-Year Period) before any triggering event (age 59½, disability, death, etc.; ¶ 5.2.04) has occurred. A nonqualified distribution is not *per se* excludible from gross income. However, even if a distribution is not "qualified" it receives favorable tax treatment compared with distributions from a traditional IRA.

A Roth IRA contains two types of money. First, it contains the participant's contributions; since these amounts were already included in the participant's gross income, these originally-contributed funds will not be included in his income *again* when they are later distributed. Thus, the amount of the participant's contribution(s) to the Roth IRA constitutes the participant's basis (or "investment in the contract") in the Roth IRA. § 72(b)(2); see ¶ 2.2.01. If the account has grown to be worth more than this basis, the rest of the account value (which represents the earnings and growth that have occurred since the contribution; the IRS calls this portion the "**earnings**") has not yet been taxed (and may *never* be taxed if it is distributed in the form of a qualified distribution).

The general rule is that all distributions from a Roth IRA are deemed to come *first* out of the participant's contributions. See ¶ 5.2.07. Thus, if the participant or beneficiary wants to get money out of the Roth IRA, but does not meet the requirements for a qualified distribution, he can still withdraw money income tax-free, up to the amount the participant contributed:

Jules and Jim Example: In 2007, Jules converted his $400,000 traditional IRA to a Roth IRA. This was Jules's first Roth IRA. He died in 2009, leaving the account (now worth $500,000) to his son Jim. Jim, as the Designated Beneficiary of the account, must start taking MRDs in 2010 (see ¶ 1.5.05). Jules's death is a "triggering event," but the Five-Year Period will not be up until December 31, 2011, so the distributions Jim is required to take in 2010 and 2011 are not qualified distributions. Nevertheless, these distributions are tax-free to Jim, because they are deemed to come out of the $400,000 of contributions Jules already paid tax on.

In contrast to this favorable treatment afforded to Roth IRAs, all distributions from a *traditional* IRA are deemed to come *proportionately* from the "basis" (nontaxable) portion and the post-contribution earnings (taxable) of all of the participant's aggregated IRAs. See ¶ 2.2.08.

You Can Never Stop Tracking "Basis" Vs. "Earnings!"

It might appear that once the client has met the requirements for a qualified distribution (*e.g.*, he is over age 59½ and has completed the Five-Year Period), he could breathe a sigh of relief and stop keeping track of how many dollars in the Roth account constituted "basis" versus "earnings." Not so! There is always the possibility that a nonqualified distribution may occur even after that point—for example, if there is a prohibited transaction (¶ 5.2.04). The example in the regulations is a disabled individual who receives a qualified distribution from a DRAC, then later ceases to be disabled and takes another distribution from the DRAC before reaching age 59½. Reg. § 1.402A-1, A-7. See the last sentence of ¶ 5.7.06 for how to eliminate the need for such tracking with respect to a DRAC.

5.2.07 *The Ordering Rules*

Any distribution from a Roth IRA is deemed to come from the following sources, in the order indicated. § 408A(d)(4)(B); Reg. § 1.408A-6, A-9. These rules are referred to in this book as the **Ordering Rules**. These rules apply to all Roth IRA distributions *except* corrective distributions (¶ 2.1.08) (Reg. § 1.408A-6, A-9(e)) and recharacterizations (¶ 5.6).

1.   Any distribution is deemed to come, first, from the participant's contributions to his Roth IRA(s), to the extent that all previous distributions from his Roth IRA(s) have not yet exceeded the contributions; and

2.   If the participant has made both "regular" (¶ 5.3.02) and "rollover" (conversion) (¶ 5.4) contributions, the distributions are deemed to come, first, from the regular contributions, then from rollover contributions on a first-in, first-out, basis; and

3.   Once it is determined that the distribution is deemed to come from a particular rollover contribution (conversion), the dollars that were includible in gross income by virtue of that

conversion (¶ 5.4.03) are deemed distributed first. (All of the rollover would have been included in income except the participant's own after-tax money that was part of the conversion; see ¶ 2.2.) This particular ordering rule matters *only* to someone who is under age 59½ at the time of the Roth IRA distribution (see ¶ 5.5.02); and

4.   Finally, once all contributions have been distributed, the balance of the distribution comes out of earnings. Whew!

Fortunately, practitioners will rarely if ever need to consult the Ordering Rules:

♦   For most people, the Ordering Rules matter only for purposes of determining whether a nonqualified distribution is subject to income tax; the Ordering Rules essentially mean that the participant's already-taxed contributions to the Roth IRA come out *first* and accordingly distributions from the Roth IRA are NOT taxable until the total distributed exceeds those contributions.

♦   The Ordering Rules matter also for someone who converts a traditional plan to a Roth IRA before reaching age 59½, and then takes a distribution within five years after the conversion and while still under age 59½. The Ordering Rules will apply in determining whether the 10 percent penalty applies to the distribution. See ¶ 5.5.02.

5.3 How to Fund a Roth IRA;
Regular and Excess Contributions

This section lists every known way to fund a Roth IRA; explains the rules for "regular" Roth IRA contributions; and tells how you can incur an "excess" Roth IRA contribution.

5.3.01 *The eight ways to fund a Roth IRA*

The law provides at least eight ways to fund a Roth IRA. Each method has its own rules and eligibility requirements.

- An individual who has compensation income (and whose adjusted gross income is under certain levels) can make a "**regular contribution**" to a Roth IRA. See ¶ 5.3.02–¶ 5.3.04.

- A participant who owns a traditional retirement plan or IRA can transfer funds (or "roll over" distributions) from the traditional plan or IRA to a Roth IRA. This is called a "Roth **conversion**." See ¶ 5.4.

- A participant can roll money from a **DRAC** into a Roth IRA. See ¶ 5.7.08.

- See ¶ 3.2.04 for the ability of a **surviving spouse** (or ¶ 4.2.05 for other **Designated Beneficiary**) to transfer funds from an inherited traditional plan to a Roth IRA.

- Certain **U.S. military death gratuities** can be contributed to a Roth IRA. For details, see § 408A(e)(2) and IRS Publication 590 ("IRAs"; 2009 ed., p. 63). This type of contribution is not covered in this book.

- A **qualified reservist distribution** (¶ 9.4.12) may be contributed to a Roth IRA; see ¶ 2.6.06(C).

- Certain individuals who received compensation in connection with the **Exxon Valdez** oil spill can contribute up to $100,000 of their settlement to a Roth IRA or other eligible retirement plan. For details, see § 504 of the Emergency Economic Stabilization Act of 2008 and IRS Publication 590 ("IRAs"; 2009 ed., p. 27–28, 64). This type of contribution is not covered in the Code or in this book.

- Certain **qualified airline employees** can contribute to a Roth IRA (only), within 180 days of receipt, certain payments they receive in connection with the bankruptcy of a "commercial passenger airline carrier." See § 125 of the Worker, Retiree, and Employer Recovery Act of 2008 and IRS Publication 590 ("IRAs"; 2009 ed., p. 64). This type of contribution is treated as a qualified rollover contribution to the Roth IRA (see ¶ 5.4), and is not covered in the Code or in this book.

5.3.02 *"Regular" contributions from compensation income*

One way to fund a Roth IRA is by making what the IRS calls "regular" (as opposed to "rollover"; ¶ 5.4) contributions to it. This section discusses the requirements for making a regular contribution to a Roth IRA, as contrasted with the rules governing regular contributions to a traditional IRA. See ¶ 2.1.08 and ¶ 5.6.01 for how to change your mind about your IRA or Roth IRA contribution after you've already contributed.

As with traditional IRAs, **only cash** may be contributed. § 408A(a), § 408(a)(1). See ¶ 5.6.05(A) regarding the **deadline** for making a regular Roth IRA contribution.

"Regular" Roth IRA Contributions: An Elastic Term

The term "regular" Roth IRA contribution normally means a permissible annual-type contribution to the Roth IRA from compensation income, as described in this ¶ 5.3.02. However, the regulations say that *any* contribution to a Roth IRA that is not a qualified rollover contribution is a "regular contribution." Reg. § 1.408A-3, A-1. So certain contributions that are intended to be rollovers or Roth conversions, but don't meet the rollover requirements, such as a "failed conversion" (¶ 5.4.06) or the attempted rollover of an MRD (¶ 5.2.02(E)), would be categorized as "regular" Roth IRA contributions. A so-called regular contribution arising out of a failed conversion will typically be an excess contribution (¶ 5.3.05). Adding to the confusion, a proper and legal tax-free rollover from a DRAC to a Roth IRA is treated as a "regular contribution" to the Roth IRA for purposes of applying the Ordering Rules (¶ 5.7.08(C)).

An individual must have compensation income in order to be eligible to make a regular contribution to either a traditional or a Roth IRA. Reg. § 1.408A-3, A-3. The individual's contributions to either type of IRA for a particular year may not exceed the amount of such individual's compensation income for such year (or, if less, the dollar limit described in ¶ 5.3.03). An individual who does not have compensation income, or whose compensation income is not high enough to support the full maximum contribution to an IRA, but whose spouse does have sufficient compensation income, can (if otherwise eligible) make a regular contribution to an IRA or Roth IRA based on the "working" spouse's income. § 219(c)(1)(B)(ii).

"**Compensation**" is partly defined in § 219(f)(1). It includes self-employment income (§ 401(c)(2)), and does *not* include pension, annuity, or deferred compensation payments. It includes taxable alimony and separate maintenance payments (§ 71). It includes (since 2004) nontaxable combat pay; see IRS Publication 590 ("IRAs"; 2009 ed., p. 8). It includes "wages, commissions, professional fees, tips, and other amounts received for personal services...." Reg. § 1.408A-3, A-4. See Rev. Proc. 91-18, 1991-1 C.B. 522, for further detail.

5.3.03 *Applicable Dollar Limit for regular contributions*

This brief summary of the amount that may be contributed as a "regular" contribution to an IRA or Roth IRA is included for convenience. For more detail (and annual updates) on the maximum IRA contribution, see IRS Publication 590, § 219 and related regulations, or Denise Appleby Quick Reference charts (Appendix C).

The maximum annual regular *Roth* IRA contribution amount derives from the maximum annual regular *traditional* IRA contribution amount. The maximum amount that may be contributed to all of a person's *traditional* IRAs for a particular year is the lesser of a particular dollar amount (called in this book the "Applicable Dollar Limit") or the individual's compensation income (¶ 5.3.02) for the year. The maximum regular contribution for a particular year to all of a person's *Roth* IRAs is the exact same amount—minus the amount of regular contributions made to any traditional IRA(s) for that person for that year. § 408A(c)(2).

The Applicable Dollar Limit is the *general dollar limit,* plus (if the individual is age 50 or older as of the end of the year) the "*catch-up contribution.*"

The general dollar limit is $5,000 for the years 2008–2011, to be increased by cost-of-living adjustments (COLA) if there is sufficient inflation in future years. § 219(b)(5)(A), (D); see Notice 2009-94, 2009-50 IRB 848, and www.irs.gov. The catch-up contribution (permitted only for the 50-and-older set) is $1,000 for 2006 and later years (with no COLA). § 219(b)(5)(B).

An individual who has compensation income (¶ 5.3.02), and who meets the other eligibility requirements (see ¶ 5.3.04 for Roth IRAs, § 219 for traditional IRAs) may contribute to either a traditional IRA or a Roth IRA (whichever he is eligible to contribute to), or both if he is eligible to contribute to both, provided that the total contributed to both types of accounts for the year may not exceed the lesser of

(1) the Applicable Dollar Limit or (2) the individual's compensation income for the year.

Contributions made on the individual's behalf to a SEP-IRA or a SIMPLE (¶ 8.3.13) are ignored for this purpose; these are considered *employer* contributions, and as such have no effect on the maximum the *individual* may contribute to his own traditional or Roth IRA. § 408A(f).

5.3.04 *Who may make a "regular" Roth IRA contribution*

Any individual who has compensation income (¶ 5.3.02) may make a "regular" contribution to a Roth IRA—*provided* that his income is below certain levels.

A.   **No age limit.** There is no maximum age for contributing to a Roth IRA, as there is for contributions to a traditional IRA; a taxpayer can contribute to a Roth IRA even after age 70½. § 408A(c)(4); compare § 219(d)(1); § 408(o)(2)(B)(i).

B.   **Participation in an employer plan is irrelevant.** An otherwise-eligible person who meets the income test may contribute to a Roth IRA regardless of whether he also participates in a retirement plan at his place of employment. Active participation in an employer plan is relevant only for determining whether a contribution to a *traditional* IRA is deductible. See § 219(g)(3).

C.   **Income must be below certain levels.** Only an individual whose "modified adjusted gross income" (MAGI) is below certain limits can legally make a regular contribution to a Roth IRA. The income test for making a regular contribution to a Roth IRA is not the same as the income test that applied (through 2009) to determine eligibility to convert a traditional plan to a Roth IRA (¶ 5.4.02(E)). Also unlike the income limit formerly applicable to Roth conversions, the income limit applicable to making "regular" Roth IRA contributions did *not* disappear at the end of 2009.

The definition of MAGI for purposes of the Roth IRA income limits starts with the MAGI definition used under § 219(g)(3) (income limits for making a deductible contribution to a traditional IRA when the individual is also a participant in an employer plan). However, MAGI for purposes of Roth contribution eligibility does NOT include the deemed distribution amount (¶ 5.4.03–¶ 5.4.04) that results from converting a traditional retirement plan or IRA to a Roth IRA. § 408A(c)(3)(B)(i). The gross income resulting from a Roth conversion is disregarded *solely for purpose of determining whether the taxpayer's MAGI is low enough to make him eligible to contribute to a Roth IRA.*

For example, the gross income resulting from a 2010 Roth conversion is excluded from MAGI for purposes of determining whether the individual is eligible to make a regular contribution to a Roth IRA in the years 2010–2012, regardless of whether that conversion income is included in his gross income in 2010 or in 2011–2012 (¶ 5.4.05). The conversion income is includible in the individual's "real" gross income, and he has to pay tax on it—it is just excluded from the "MAGI" figure for purposes of determining eligibility.

In order for an individual to be eligible to contribute the full Applicable Dollar Limit (ADL) (¶ 5.3.03) to a Roth IRA, his MAGI may not exceed a certain "**applicable dollar amount**." The applicable dollar amount depends on filing status, and is adjusted upwards, after 2006, for post-2005 inflation. The applicable dollar amount was originally $95,000 for a single taxpayer, $150,000 for a married taxpayer filing a joint return, or $zero for a married taxpayer filing a separate return. § 408A(c)(3)(A). The 2010 applicable dollar amounts are $105,000 (single), $167,000 (married filing jointly), and $zero (married filing separately). Notice 2009-94, 2009-50 IRB 848.

If MAGI exceeds these levels, the Applicable Dollar Limit amount the individual can contribute to a Roth IRA phases downward. It is reduced to zero once his income exceeds the applicable dollar amount by $15,000 (or by $10,000 in the case of a married taxpayer filing separately or married taxpayers filing jointly). § 408A(c)(3)(A), (B)(ii). Note that the phase-out applies to the *entire* ADL (including the over-50 catch-up amount), not just to the general dollar limit.

So, for 2010, a single taxpayer can contribute a reduced amount of the ADL if his income is between $105,000 and $120,000 (zero if income exceeds $120,000). A married taxpayer filing jointly can contribute a reduced amount of the ADL if the couple's income is between $167,000 and $177,000 (zero if income exceeds $177,000). A married taxpayer filing separately can contribute a reduced amount of the ADL if his income is between zero and $10,000 (zero if income exceeded $10,000).

An individual who is prevented from contributing the full ADL to a Roth IRA because of the income limit can contribute his reduced ADL to the Roth and the balance of the ADL to a traditional IRA (if he is under age 70½). Reg. § 1.408A-3, A-3(d), Example 4.

D.   Regular traditional IRA contribution followed by conversion. An individual who has compensation income, is under age 70½, and is prevented from making a regular contribution to a Roth IRA due to the income limit can make a regular contribution to a traditional IRA, then convert that to a Roth IRA. This anomalous situation arises because there is an income ceiling applicable to *regular* Roth IRA contributions but no income ceiling applicable to either traditional IRA contributions or Roth *conversions*.

There is no waiting period or minimum holding period following the making of a contribution to a traditional IRA before the individual can convert it to a Roth IRA, just as (before direct plan-to-Roth IRA conversions were permitted; see ¶ 5.4.01(B)) there was no waiting period that prevented an eligible individual who rolled money from a traditional nonIRA retirement plan to a traditional IRA from immediately converting the traditional IRA to a Roth IRA.

Sandy Example: In 2010, Sandy, age 28, has compensation income of $300,000 and participates in a 401(k) plan at her job. Because of her high income, she is not eligible to make a regular contribution to a Roth IRA. So instead she makes a nondeductible regular contribution of $5,000 to a traditional IRA on June 1, 2010. Soon thereafter she converts the account to a Roth IRA. If she has no other IRAs at any time during 2010, her conversion will be "tax-free," because the converted account contains nothing other than her own after-tax contribution. If she does have other IRAs in 2010, the conversion will be taxed under the "cream-in-the-coffee" rule; see ¶ 5.4.03(B).

5.3.05 *Penalty for excess Roth IRA contributions*

There is an excise tax of six percent imposed on "regular" contributions to Roth IRAs in excess of the applicable limits (¶ 5.3.03), just as there is for excess contributions to traditional IRAs. § 4973; Reg. § 1.408A-3, A-7. See ¶ 2.1.08 regarding the penalty on (and how to correct) excess IRA contributions.

5.4 Conversion of Traditional Plan or IRA to a Roth IRA

The other main way to create a Roth IRA, besides making annual-type "regular" contributions from compensation income (¶ 5.3), is to transfer funds to a Roth IRA from a traditional IRA or nonIRA plan. The amount so transferred is generally included in the participant's gross income as if it had been distributed to him. § 408A(d)(3)(A)–(C). This type of contribution is called a **"qualified rollover contribution"** in the Code (§ 408A(c)(3)(B)), a "**Roth conversion**" in this book.

Since there is no limit on the amount that can be converted from a traditional plan or IRA to a Roth IRA, a conversion contribution can be a much more substantial amount than the few thousand dollars per year maximum regular Roth IRA contribution (¶ 5.3.03).

This Chapter describes the Federal income tax treatment of Roth conversions. State income tax treatment is not covered in this book.

See ¶ 5.5 for how a Roth conversion interacts with the 10 percent penalty on early distributions. See ¶ 5.6.05(B) regarding the deadline for completing a Roth conversion.

> This ¶ 5.4 deals with Roth IRA conversions by the participant. Regarding the ability or inability of a beneficiary to convert an *inherited* plan or IRA to a Roth IRA, see ¶ 3.2.04 (for the surviving spouse) or ¶ 4.2.05 (for other beneficiaries).

Prior to September 27, 2010, a Roth IRA was the only possible destination for "conversions." See Reg. § 1.401(k)-1(f)(3), third sentence. Effective after that date, distributions from traditional cash-or-deferred (CODA) plan accounts (¶ 5.7.01) can be "converted" into a DRAC (see ¶ 5.7.11), but (other than such "in-plan conversions") funds from a traditional plan or IRA can be rolled only into a Roth IRA and can NOT be rolled or converted to a DRAC.

5.4.01 *What type of plan may be converted to a Roth IRA*

Here are the types of traditional retirement plans a participant may "convert" to a Roth IRA.

A. **Individual retirement accounts.** An "individual retirement plan" may be converted to a Roth IRA. § 408A(d)(3)(B), (C); Reg. § 1.408A-4, A-5. "**Individual retirement plans**" include individual retirement accounts (IRAs) and individual retirement trusts (IRTs; ¶ 6.1.07) under § 408(a), (h). Traditional IRA-to-Roth IRA conversions have been permitted since 1998. See ¶ 5.4.03 for the *tax treatment* of converting an IRA. See ¶ 5.4.07 for *how to convert* an IRA.

The Code provides that a SEP-IRA (§ 408(k)) or SIMPLE IRA (§ 408(p)) cannot be "redesignated" as a Roth IRA. § 408A(f). That prohibition is almost meaningless because, in the real world, a traditional IRA is not normally converted to a Roth IRA by being "redesignated" as a Roth IRA; it is converted by having assets transferred from the traditional IRA to an entirely different account (with a different account number and form of agreement) that is a Roth IRA. The IRS clarifies (in Reg. § 1.408A-4, A-4) that "An amount in an individual's SEP IRA can be converted to a Roth IRA on the same terms as an amount in any other traditional IRA," subject to two limitations:

✓ A SIMPLE IRA distribution "is not eligible to be rolled over into" a Roth IRA "during the 2-year period...which begins on the date that the individual first participated in any SIMPLE IRA Plan maintained by the individual's employer....". Reg. § 1.408A-4, A-4(b); and,

✓ Contributions under the SEP or SIMPLE plan may not be made to a Roth IRA. Reg. § 1.408A-4, A-4(c).

Accordingly, an employee whose only retirement plan is a SEP-IRA, and who wants a Roth and nothing but a Roth, must go through this two-step dance: Employer contribution goes into the (traditional) SEP-IRA, and the employee pulls it out and transfers it to a Roth IRA.

If the employee's plan is a SIMPLE, he must satisfy the two-year waiting period before performing the second step of the "dance."

B. **NonIRA plans.** Prior to 2008, the Code permitted rollovers into Roth IRAs only from IRAs and DRACs (¶ 5.7). Thus, someone who desired to "convert" money in a traditional nonIRA retirement plan had to first roll the money to an IRA, then convert the IRA. The expanded rollover provision effective in 2008 and later years permits rollovers into Roth IRAs directly from several *additional* types of eligible retirement plans, eliminating the necessity of the two-step process in the conversion of nonIRA plans (though the two-step process continues to exist hypothetically in the tax treatment of these conversions; see ¶ 5.4.04(A)). See ¶ 5.4.04 for the *tax treatment* of nonIRA plan-to-Roth conversions. See ¶ 5.4.08 for *how to convert* a nonIRA plan. Here are the types of nonIRA plans that may be converted directly to Roth IRAs:

1.   Qualified retirement plans under § 401(a) ("QRPs"). § 408A(e) (first sentence), § 402(c)(8)(B)(iii).

2.   403(a) and (b) contracts and plans. § 408A(e) (first sentence), § 402(c)(8)(B)(iv), (vi).

3.   457(b) plans maintained by a State, political subdivision of a State, and any agency or instrumentality of a State or political subdivision of a State. § 408A(e) (first sentence), § 402(c)(8)(B)(v), § 457(e)(1)(A). This type of plan is called in this book a "**governmental 457(b) plan**." Rollovers from a nongovernmental 457 plan (§ 457(e)(1)(B)) to a Roth IRA are not permitted.

See § 408A(e), as amended by PPA '06, § 824. This change rendered Reg. § 1.408A-4, A-5, obsolete.

5.4.02 *Who may convert: age, plan participation, income, etc.*

This ¶ 5.4.02 explains who is eligible to convert a plan or IRA to a Roth IRA, including the effects (or noneffects) of age (A), participation in other plans (B), prior conversions (C), filing status (D), and income (E).

If a person converts a traditional IRA or plan to a Roth IRA but is not eligible to do so (for example, if he reconverts a traditional IRA to a Roth too soon after recharacterizing; see "C"), the result is a "failed conversion." See ¶ 5.4.06. Prior to 2010, a person could be ineligible to convert to a Roth based on his filing status ("D") or income ("E").

A. **Age: Under 59½, over 70½, or in between.** Any IRA owner or plan participant can convert his traditional plan or IRA to a Roth IRA regardless of his age; you are never too young or too old to convert to a Roth IRA. However, if the participant is under <u>age 59½</u>, see ¶ 5.5 regarding how the 10 percent penalty on early distributions applies to certain post-conversion distributions. Also, an individual who is turning (or is past) age 70½ in the conversion year must take the MRD for that year *before* he can convert any money from the account to a Roth IRA; see ¶ 5.2.02(E).

B. **Participation in other plan(s).** An individual can convert his traditional plan or IRA to a Roth regardless of what other plan(s) he may be participating in that year.

C. **Prior conversion.** There is generally no limit on the number of times a participant can convert all or part of any traditional plan or IRA to a Roth IRA. A person who converts part of his traditional IRA to a Roth IRA is free at any later time (in the same or a later year) to convert more of the same or another plan or IRA to a Roth IRA. The only exception is a waiting period that applies to someone who has *un*converted (recharacterized) and then wants to *re*convert the same amount; see ¶ 5.6.07.

D. **Filing status.** For conversion of plan distributions made in 2010 and later years, there is no filing status test; anyone can convert regardless of his income tax filing status. For years prior to 2010, a person who used the filing status "married filing separately" could not do a Roth conversion. See the *Special Report: Ancient History* (Appendix C).

E. **Income limit.** For conversion of plan distributions made in 2010 and later years, there is no income test; anyone can convert regardless of his income level. For distributions occurring in years prior to 2010, an individual was not eligible to convert if his modified adjusted gross income exceeded $100,000. For details, including how MAGI was computed for purposes of this now-obsolete test, see the *Special Report: Ancient History* (Appendix C).

5.4.03 *Tax treatment of converting traditional IRA to Roth IRA*

A rollover from a traditional IRA to a Roth IRA is generally treated, for income tax purposes, as a *distribution* from the traditional IRA. The term "conversion" is often used (including in § 408A) for the rollover of funds from a traditional IRA to a Roth IRA, which is a taxable event, just as a handy way to distinguish that type of rollover from a "normal" rollover, which is nontaxable (¶ 2.6.01).

A. **A Roth conversion is a "taxable rollover."** Under § 408(d)(3), rollovers generally are nontaxable. However, § 408A(d)(3)(A) provides that "Notwithstanding" § 408(d)(3), "there shall be included in gross income any amount which would be includible were it not part of a qualified rollover contribution." Thus, Roth conversions *are* taxable despite § 408(d)(3). Whatever amount of a traditional IRA is converted or rolled over to a Roth IRA is taxed exactly as if it had been distributed from the traditional IRA and not rolled over, with the following exceptions:

- For conversions in 1998 or 2010, special "income spreading" treatment is allowed; see ¶ 5.4.05.

- If the converted property includes an annuity contract, the contract must be valued at fair market value for purposes of determining the amount of income includible by reason of the conversion, even if some different valuation method might have applied for determining the contract's value for minimum distribution purposes (¶ 1.2.08) or for purposes of computing the distributee's income if the contract had been distributed and not converted to a Roth IRA. Reg. § 1.408A-4, A-14. For more on this rule, see the *Special Report: When Insurance Products Meet Retirement Plans* (Appendix C).

So how are IRA distributions (and accordingly Roth conversions) taxed? Generally, all IRA distributions are taxable, but there are exceptions. For a catalogue of no- and low-tax distributions that are mostly *not* relevant to Roth conversions, see ¶ 2.1.06. The one significant exception that DOES apply to Roth conversions is the rule that the participant's own after-tax IRA contributions are not taxable when distributed to him (or converted to a Roth IRA); see "B."

B.   **Treatment of after-tax money in participant's IRA(s).** The amount converted from a traditional IRA to a Roth IRA is includible in the participant's gross income except to the extent it is excluded from income as a return of the participant's basis (investment in the contract); to that extent it is nontaxable. Reg. § 1.408A-4, A-7(a). For how to determine how much basis the participant has in his IRAs, see ¶ 2.2.06. To determine much of any particular IRA-to-Roth IRA conversion is treated as a tax-free conversion of the participant's basis, see ¶ 2.2.08–¶ 2.2.10. Someone with after-tax money in an IRA who also participates in a QRP that accepts rollovers, and who is therefore able to roll money from his IRA to his QRP account, can apparently follow the sequence described at ¶ 2.2.09(A) to achieve a tax-free Roth IRA conversion of only the after-tax money in the IRA. Except for that sequence, there is no known way to convert only the after-tax money.

C.   **Realizing a loss on a Roth conversion.** Suppose the individual's traditional IRA consists entirely of after-tax money, and the value of the IRA (at the time of conversion to a Roth) is less than his basis:

Tucker Example: Tucker made nondeductible contributions totaling $20,000 to a traditional IRA in the years leading up to 2010. This was and is his only IRA, and he made no contributions to it in 2010. As of the date in 2010 when he does his conversion to a Roth the account is worth only $17,000. What becomes of his "missing" $3,000 of basis?

A transfer from a traditional to a Roth IRA is to be taxed as if it were a distribution that was not rolled over. § 408A(d)(3)(A)(i). If Tucker's IRA had been totally distributed to him, rather than being rolled to an IRA, he would have been entitled to deduct the $3,000 loss as a miscellaneous itemized deduction. See ¶ 8.1.02. Accordingly, it would appear that Tucker would report a miscellaneous itemized deduction of $3,000 on his Form 1040 for 2010 as a result of the Roth conversion.

5.4.04 *Tax treatment of converting nonIRA plan to Roth IRA*

In adding plan-to-Roth-IRA rollovers, Congress applied the same rule it had used to make IRA conversions taxable (see ¶ 5.4.03(A)), just throwing a few more Code sections into the "notwithstanding" clause: "Notwithstanding sections *402(c)*, *403(b)(8)*, 408(d)(3), and *457(e)(16)*, there shall be included in gross income any amount which would be includible were it not part of a qualified rollover contribution." § 408A(d)(3)(A)(i), (B), and (C), as in effect after 2007. Emphasis added.

Notice 2008-30, 2008-12 IRB 638, Section II, questions 1–7, and Notice 2009-75, 2009-39 IRB 436, provide guidance on plan-to-Roth-IRA conversions.

For conversions in 2010, special "income spreading" treatment is allowed; see ¶ 5.4.05. If the assets converted include an annuity contract, see ¶ 5.4.03(A).

A.　　**The fictional two-step process.** The income tax treatment of a Roth conversion directly from a nonIRA plan employs a fiction: "For this purpose, the amount included in gross income is equal to the amount rolled over, reduced by the amount of any after-tax contributions that are included in the amount rolled over, *in the same manner as if the distribution had been rolled over to a non-Roth IRA that was the participant's only non-Roth IRA and that non-Roth IRA had then been immediately converted to a Roth IRA.*" Notice 2009-75, A-1(a). Emphasis added.

Thus, the one-step process of transferring funds directly from the nonIRA plan to a Roth IRA is treated as if it were a two-step process, with the distribution passing through a hypothetical traditional IRA on its way to the Roth IRA. The two-step fiction means that special tax treatments that might otherwise be available for (*e.g.*) a lump sum distribution (LSD; ¶ 2.4) from the nonIRA plan are NOT available for a Roth conversion, even if the amount converted otherwise qualifies as a "lump sum distribution."

For example, if an employee takes an LSD of appreciated employer stock from the employer's QRP, the "net unrealized appreciation" (NUA) inherent in the stock receives special income tax treatment if it is not rolled over to an IRA; see ¶ 2.5. If the employee rolls (converts) the NUA stock directly to a Roth IRA, the conversion will be fully taxable as ordinary income (except to the extent of any after-tax money included in the distribution; see "B"), just as if the stock had been rolled to a traditional IRA that was then converted to a Roth IRA. The special tax deal that applies to NUA stock can NOT be combined with a Roth conversion of the stock.

B.   **If the plan contains after-tax money.** The conversion of funds from a QRP to a Roth IRA presents a planning opportunity if the participant's account contains after-tax money; see ¶ 2.2.01, ¶ 2.2.03.

Myron Example: Myron is retiring. His $150,000 profit-sharing plan account at Acme Widget includes $50,000 of after-tax money. He instructs the plan to transfer the entire account to a Roth IRA via direct rollover. § 401(a)(31); see ¶ 2.6.01(C). Myron's Roth conversion of his $150,000 account is "cheap" because only the $100,000 of pretax money in the account is included in his gross income. He gets a $150,000 Roth IRA but has to pay income tax on only $100,000.

What if Myron converts only part of his profit-sharing plan account to a Roth? Is it possible for Myron to convert just the after-tax money to a Roth, thereby achieving a "tax-free" Roth conversion? See ¶ 2.2.04–¶ 2.2.05 for the rules governing the income tax treatment of partial and "split" distributions from QRPs and partial or "split" rollovers and conversions of QRP distributions and continuation of the "Myron Example."

C.   **Income tax withholding.** A direct rollover from a QRP to a Roth IRA (or any IRA) is not subject to the mandatory 20 percent income tax withholding that normally applies to the distribution of an eligible rollover distribution from a qualified plan (¶ 2.3.02(C)). However, any distributee and plan administrator can arrange for voluntary withholding even for a direct rollover. Notice 2008-30, A-6. It would presumably not be advisable to arrange for such withholding on a Roth conversion, since it would reduce the amount going into the Roth IRA. It is generally considered more favorable to pay the income tax resulting from a Roth conversion from funds held outside any retirement plan (see ¶ 5.8.01(A)).

5.4.05 *Income spreading for conversions in 1998 or 2010*

For rollovers in **1998** ONLY, the gross income resulting from a Roth conversion could be spread equally over the four taxable years 1998–2001. For details on this election, and on the acceleration of taxation in case of distributions from the converted account prior to 2001, see the *Special Report: Ancient History* (Appendix C).

The income resulting from a Roth conversion in **2010** can be reported in two equal instalments in 2011 and 2012 instead of being reported in 2010. § 408A(d)(3)(A)(iii). Note the following points (in which the "individual" is a participant who converted his traditional IRA or nonIRA plan, or a Designated Beneficiary who converted an inherited nonIRA plan (¶ 4.2.05), to a Roth account in 2010):

• The individual's only choices are to have all of his 2010 Roth conversions taxed in 2010, or to have all of them taxed half in 2011 and half in 2012. The individual cannot make partial elections, or make different elections for different conversions occurring in 2010.

• It appears that a husband and wife can make different elections if both do conversions in 2010, even if they file a joint return; however, there is no official confirmation of this conclusion at this writing.

• It is the income from the 2010 conversion(s) that is pushed forward into 2011 and 2012. The individual does not simply calculate the tax at 2010 rates, then pay the tax half in 2011 and half in 2012. If the individual accepts the election to push the income forward, the income resulting from the 2010 conversion(s) will be taxed at whatever rates apply to the individual in 2011 and 2012.

- The election is irrevocable and must be made on the tax return for 2010. § 408A(d)(3)(A), last sentence. If no election is made the default result is that the income is deferred into 2011 and 2012. § 408A(d)(3)(A)(iii).

- An individual who elects to have 2010 conversion income spread into 2011 and 2012, but then withdraws funds from the Roth account in 2010 or 2011, will have the inclusion of those withdrawn amounts accelerated (added to the amount that would *otherwise* be includible in his income for the withdrawal year on account of the conversion; i.e., zero in 2010 or half the conversion amount in 2011). § 408A(d)(3)(E)(i).

- If an individual who has elected to spread 2010 conversion income forward into 2011–2012 dies before all the income has been included on his return, all remaining conversion income is accelerated into the taxable year ending with his death. § 408A(d)(3)(E)(ii)(I). The one exception to this rule is that if a converting participant's surviving spouse acquires the Roth account that was the subject of this election, she can continue the deferral. § 408A(d)(3)(E)(ii)(II).

5.4.06 *Failed conversions*

"The term **failed conversion** means a transaction in which an individual contributes to a Roth IRA an amount transferred or distributed *from a traditional IRA*...in a transaction that does not constitute a conversion under Sec. 1.408A-4 A-1." Reg. § 1.408A-8, A-1(b)(4) (emphasis added). Although this definition has not been explicitly extended to include defective conversions *from nonIRA plans*, such conversions are probably deemed included in this definition by virtue of the fact that a Roth conversion from a nonIRA plan is treated for tax purposes "as if" it passed through a traditional IRA on its way to the Roth; see ¶ 5.4.04(A).

A failed conversion is generally treated for tax purposes as if the amount transferred to the Roth IRA had been (1) distributed from the original plan or IRA and then (2) contributed to the Roth IRA as a "regular contribution" (¶ 5.3.02). See Regs. § 1.408A-4, A-3(b) and § 1.408A-4, A-6(c) and ¶ 5.2.02(E). A failed conversion should be corrected by recharacterization (¶ 5.6). Reg. § 1.408A-4, A-3. If not so corrected, a failed conversion has the following effects:

✓   The deemed distribution will normally result in the distribution's being included in the recipient's gross income, with no option to spread the income over future years (¶ 5.4.05). The income-spreading option is available only for Roth conversions, not for other distributions.

✓   The deemed distribution will be subject to the 10 percent early-distribution penalty if the individual is under age 59½ and no exception applies. ¶ 5.5.02(A).

✓   Typically the deemed regular contribution to the Roth IRA resulting from a failed conversion will be an "excess contribution." See ¶ 5.3.05, CCA 2001-48051.

5.4.07 *Mechanics of traditional IRA-to-Roth IRA conversions*

There are three methods a participant can use to convert assets from a traditional IRA to a Roth IRA:

1.   A distribution from a traditional IRA may be contributed (rolled over) to a Roth IRA within 60 days after the distribution is made. See ¶ 2.6.06 and ¶ 5.6.05(B) regarding this deadline.

2.   An amount may be transferred directly from the traditional IRA to the Roth IRA, with the same or a different trustee (or custodian). See ¶ 2.6.01(E).

3.   The traditional IRA can simply be "redesignated" as a Roth IRA maintained by the same trustee or custodian; this is treated as a transfer of the entire account balance. Reg. § 1.408A-4, A-1(b)(3).

All three of these transactions are considered rollovers ("a distribution from the traditional IRA and a qualified rollover contribution to the Roth IRA"). Although a Roth conversion generally must meet the requirements applicable to other types of rollovers (see, *e.g.*, ¶ 5.2.02(E)), a Roth conversion is *not* considered a rollover for purposes of the one-rollover-per-year limitation in § 408(d)(3)(B) (see ¶ 2.6.05), so a Roth conversion may occur even if it is within 12 months of a tax-free traditional IRA-to-IRA rollover. Reg. § 1.408A-4, A-1(a), (c).

Prior to the arrival of Roth IRAs, "rollovers" were always tax-free, and most people still associate that word with tax-free transfers from one retirement plan to another. In contrast, the rollover of funds from a traditional IRA to a Roth IRA is taxable. ¶ 5.4.03(A).

Both partial and total conversions are allowed. An eligible individual (¶ 5.4.02) may choose to convert all, part, or none of his traditional IRA to a Roth IRA. There is no minimum or maximum dollar or percentage amount that must or may be converted.

5.4.08 *Mechanics of conversion from other traditional plans*

A participant can transfer a distribution from a traditional 401(a), 403, or governmental 457(b) plan to a Roth IRA either by direct rollover or by 60-day (indirect) rollover. ¶ 5.4.01(B). See ¶ 2.6.01 for definitions of direct, indirect, and 60-day rollover. The direct rollover is preferable because it avoids the mandatory 20 percent withholding of federal income taxes otherwise applicable to the taxable portion of the distribution. ¶ 2.3.02(C).

Generally, when a plan is about to make a distribution to an employee, the plan MUST offer the employee the option of having the distribution sent, via direct rollover, to any eligible retirement plan (which includes a Roth IRA) and MUST comply with the employee's request for such a direct rollover. See ¶ 2.6.01(C).

Plan-to-Roth IRA rollovers, like traditional IRA-to-Roth IRA rollovers, are called "qualified rollover contributions." Only traditional IRA-to-Roth IRA transfers are also called "conversions," according to the IRS in Notice 2008-30, Section II, Introductory paragraph. This book uses "conversion" for both types of rollover.

A major difference between converting a traditional IRA to a Roth, and converting money from a nonIRA plan, has to do with the participant's ability to obtain a distribution that he can convert. An IRA owner, regardless of age or employment status, is generally free (at least under the tax Code) at any time to withdraw money from his account. He will be taxable on the distribution, and will owe a penalty on the distribution if he is under age 59½ and doesn't qualify for an exception, but nobody can stop him from taking the distribution if he wants to do so and is willing to pay the taxes.

Not so with a qualified plan. Most qualified plans prohibit *any* distributions prior to attaining retirement age or severance of employment. 401(k) plans are generally forbidden to distribute the employee's elective deferral account prior to age 59½ or termination of service. § 401(k)(2)(B)(i). There is a hardship exception to that rule, but hardship distributions cannot be rolled over. § 402(c)(4)(C). Plans that do permit "in-service distributions" often restrict such distributions to employees over age 62. § 401(a)(36). So, realistically, the advisor is likely to encounter the opportunity for plan-to-Roth conversions mainly when the participant is leaving the service of the employer that sponsors the plan (but see ¶ 5.7.11 regarding "in-plan conversions").

5.5 Roth Plans and the 10% Penalty For Pre-Age 59½ Distributions

Generally, there is a 10 percent "additional tax" (penalty) on distributions from a retirement plan that occur while the participant is younger than age 59½. § 72(t). For details on this "early distributions" penalty, and the more than one dozen exceptions to the penalty, see Chapter 9. This ¶ 5.5 discusses the 10 percent penalty as it applies to Roth IRAs and DRACs (¶ 5.7).

5.5.01 *Penalty applies to certain Roth plan distributions*

The 10 percent penalty under § 72(t) applies to pre-age 59½ distributions from Roth IRAs the same as it applies to such distributions from traditional IRAs, under the rule that Roth IRAs are treated the same as traditional IRAs unless § 408A provides otherwise. Reg. § 1.408A-6, A-5. Similarly, there is nothing in the Code that exempts distributions from DRACs (¶ 5.7) from the 10 percent penalty. If the distribution qualifies for any exception from the penalty, there is no penalty. See ¶ 9.2–¶ 9.4 for the exceptions to the 10 percent penalty. If no exception applies, then:

A.   **Qualified distribution.** A qualified distribution (from either a DRAC or Roth IRA) is excluded from gross income. See ¶ 5.2.03(A), ¶ 5.7.04. Since the 10 percent penalty applies only to amounts includible in gross income (*with one exception; see*

¶ *5.5.02*), the penalty does not apply to any qualified distribution. See § 72(t)(1); Notice 87-16, 1987-1 C.B. 446, Question D9.

B.   **Nonqualified distribution from Roth IRA.** In the case of a nonqualified distribution from a Roth IRA (¶ 5.2.06), the portion of the distribution allocable, under the Ordering Rules (¶ 5.2.07), to the *earnings* of the Roth IRA would be includible in the participant's gross income and would accordingly be subject to the penalty. Reg. § 1.408A-6, A-5(a).

C.   **Nonqualified distribution from DRAC.** In the case of a nonqualified distribution from a DRAC (¶ 5.7.05), the portion of the distribution allocable to the earnings of the account would be includible in the participant's gross income and would therefore be subject to the penalty. See Reg. § 1.402A-1, A-3.

D.   **Conversion followed by distribution within five years.** See ¶ 5.5.02 for a special rule that may result in a penalty being applied to the return of the participant's own contribution.

5.5.02 *Roth conversion prior to reaching age 59½*

Roth conversions before age 59½ are very confusing, because there are TWO of everything:
- There are TWO separate parts of the Roth IRA, the contribution(s) and the earnings.
- There are TWO different taxes to worry about, the income tax and the 10 percent penalty.
- There are TWO completely different five-year holding periods!

A.   **Penalty does not apply to a Roth conversion.** The 10 percent penalty does not apply to the deemed distribution that results from converting a traditional retirement plan or IRA to Roth status. § 408A(d)(3)(A)(ii); § 402A(c)(4)(D); Reg. § 1.408A-4, A-7(b); Notice 2008-30, A-3. Thus a young person may convert his traditional plan or IRA to a Roth IRA without penalty.

However, this does not mean he can forget about the 10 percent penalty. The 10 percent penalty can still come into the picture in several ways. For one thing, the penalty would apply to any income taxes withheld from the conversion amount (¶ 2.3); such a tax payment would not qualify for the "conversion exception" since it is sent to the IRS and *not* converted to a Roth IRA. Also, the penalty applies to nonqualified distributions of *earnings* from the Roth account; see ¶ 5.5.01(B), (C). And:

B.   **Penalty applies to certain distributions within five years after a conversion.** Though a person who is under age 59½ can convert to a Roth IRA without penalty, he has to come up with the money to pay the income tax on the conversion from some source *other* than the newly-converted Roth IRA money, because he will owe the penalty to the extent he taps that money, under the following special rule:

If a participant who is under the age of 59½ receives a distribution from a Roth IRA or DRAC; and "any portion" of that distribution is allocable (see ¶ 5.2.07 for Roth IRAs, ¶ 5.7.05 for DRACs) to funds that were rolled over to the Roth account from a traditional plan account or IRA; and "the distribution is made within the 5-taxable-year period beginning with the first day of the individual's taxable year in which the conversion contribution was made"; then the § 72(t) penalty will apply to "such portion" of the distribution to the extent such portion was includible in the employee's gross income (unless an exception applies). § 408A(d)(3)(F); Reg. § 1.408A-6, A-5(b); Notice 2008-30, A-3. See ¶ 9.2–¶ 9.4 for the exceptions to the 10 percent penalty.

The § 72(t) penalty generally does not apply to distributions from a governmental 457(b) plan. Accordingly, if the distribution comes from a DRAC in a 457(b) plan it will generally not be subject to the penalty even if it represents a Roth conversion within five years; see ¶ 5.7.11. The exception: 457 distributions that represent money rolled into the 457 plan from another type of plan are subject to the penalty. § 72(t)(1), (9); § 4974(c).

Note that this five-year period is *not the same* as the Five-Year Period for determining "qualified distributions" (¶ 5.2.05). The latter begins in the first year *any* contribution is made to *any* Roth IRA; the former begins, as to any conversion of a traditional plan to Roth status, with the year of that *particular* conversion. Reg. § 1.408A-6, A-5(c).

Note also that this penalty applies *even though* the distribution is not included in gross income in the year it occurs.

Rand Example: Rand, age 32, converted his $100,000 traditional IRA to a Roth IRA in 1999. He had no basis in the traditional IRA, so the entire $100,000 was includible in his gross income in 1999. He has no other Roth IRAs, and makes no other contributions to this one. In 2002, at age 35 (i.e., within five years after the conversion, and while he is still under age 59½) he withdraws $20,000 from the Roth IRA. Under the Ordering Rules, this distribution is deemed to come out of the portion of the 1999 conversion-contribution that was includible in his gross income in 1999, and therefore it is subject to the 10 percent penalty *in 2002*.

This special penalty rule that makes a conversion-contribution "off limits" for five years after the conversion does not prevent the participant from withdrawing (tax- and penalty-free) *other* contributions he has made (to the same or another Roth account) that are not subject to the rule:

Leslie Example: In 2004, Leslie (age 40) converted a $100,000 traditional IRA to a Roth IRA. In 2009, when that Roth IRA had grown to $140,000, Leslie made a regular contribution (¶ 5.3.02) of $5,000 to the same account. In 2010, he does another conversion, transferring $50,000 more from his traditional IRA to the same Roth IRA that holds all his prior contributions and earnings. In 2011, the Roth IRA has grown to $210,000, and Leslie, now age 47, withdraws $15,000 from the account to pay the income tax on his 2010 conversion. Assume he does not qualify for any of the exceptions to the 10 percent penalty. Under the Ordering Rules (¶ 5.2.07), this distribution is deemed to come first from his 2009 regular contribution ($5,000), and the balance ($10,000) is deemed to come from his 2004 conversion contribution of $100,000. There is *no income tax* on this distribution, since it is deemed (under the Ordering Rules) to be coming entirely from his own already-taxed contributions; see ¶ 5.2.07. There is also *no penalty* applicable to withdrawal of his 2009 $5,000 "regular" contribution, because the special penalty rule applies only to *conversion* contributions. Since the rest of his 2010 distribution is deemed to come from his 2004 conversion, which happened more than five years earlier, there also is no 10 percent penalty on the distribution of this "old and cold" conversion money.

C.   Penalty applies to failed conversion. A person who recharacterizes a Roth conversion (¶ 5.6), then attempts to "reconvert" the same amount to a Roth IRA prior to expiration of the waiting period (¶ 5.6.07), has a "failed conversion" (¶ 5.4.06). His attempted *re*conversion does not qualify for the penalty exception applicable to successful Roth conversions. Reg. § 1.408A-4, A-3(b) (last sentence).

5.5.03 *Conversion while receiving "series of equal payments"*

The 10 percent penalty does not apply to IRA distributions that are part of a "series of substantially equal periodic payments" (SOSEPP; see ¶ 9.2). Generally, qualification for the "SOSEPP" exception is lost (and a recapture tax imposed) if the series is "modified" prior to the date the participant attains age 59½, or, if later, the fifth anniversary of the first payment (yet *another* five-year rule!); see ¶ 9.3.

If a participant who is receiving a SOSEPP from a traditional IRA converts the traditional IRA to a Roth IRA, the conversion is "not treated as a distribution for purposes of determining whether a modification" of the series has occurred, so the conversion itself does not trigger the loss of the penalty-exempt status of the series. Reg. § 1.408A-4, A-12.

However, the conversion does not mean that the participant can stop taking his periodic payments. "[I]f the original series...does not continue to be distributed in substantially equal periodic payments *from the Roth IRA* after the conversion, the series of payments will have been modified and, if this modification occurs within 5 years of the first payment or prior to the individual becoming disabled or attaining age 59½, the taxpayer will be subject to the recapture tax of section 72(t)(4)(A)." Reg. § 1.408A-4, A-12; emphasis added.

This statement in Reg. § 1.408A-4 seems to assume that the participant converted the entire traditional IRA to a Roth IRA. If he converted only part of the traditional IRA to a Roth IRA, it is not clear whether the rest of his "series" payments would have to come all from the Roth IRA, or proportionately from the new Roth IRA and the (now-diminished) traditional IRA; or whether the participant could take the payments from whichever of the two accounts he chooses.

5.6 Recharacterizing an IRA
or Roth IRA Contribution

The law provides broad relief to a taxpayer who wishes to "adjust" an IRA contribution by switching the contribution from a Roth IRA to a traditional IRA or vice versa. § 408A(d)(6). The IRS calls this relief "recharacterizing" an IRA contribution. It is available to anyone who changes his mind about which type of IRA he wants his "regular" contribution to go to, or about a Roth conversion he has done, as well as to someone who need to correct a Roth conversion or contribution for which he was ineligible (¶ 5.3.04, ¶ 5.4.02). Reg. § 1.408A-5, A-10, Example 2. Since recharacterization applies only to *IRA contributions*, it is not available for in-plan conversions; see ¶ 5.7.11.

A taxpayer who is unhappy with any IRA contribution he made for a particular year, or who discovers that he was not eligible to contribute to the type of IRA he contributed to, or who contributed more than he was entitled to contribute, may have other remedies besides recharacterization: See ¶ 2.1.08(A)–(E) regarding the ability to return an IRA or Roth IRA contribution ("corrective distribution"). See ¶ 2.1.08(H) regarding the "absorption" of excess IRA contributions.

5.6.01 *Which IRA contributions may be recharacterized*

Not all IRA contributions can be recharacterized. Here are IRA contributions that can be recharacterized:

✓   The only type of rollover contribution that can be recharacterized is a Roth conversion, i.e. a rollover from a traditional plan or IRA into a Roth IRA. The contribution (conversion) to a Roth IRA of a distribution from a traditional plan or IRA may be recharacterized as a contribution to a traditional IRA. Both valid Roth conversions and "failed" conversions (¶ 5.4.06) may be recharacterized. Reg. § 1.408-8, A-8(b).

✓   A regular contribution to an IRA or Roth IRA (¶ 5.3.02) can be reversed by means of a corrective distribution (¶ 2.1.08(A)-(E)), or (if the contributor was eligible to contribute the amount to the *other* type of IRA) by recharacterization (see the rest of this ¶ 5.6), or (if it is an excess contribution, but the contributor will be eligible to contribute to a Roth IRA in future years) by absorption (¶ 2.1.08(H)).

Here are IRA contributions that can NOT be recharacterized:

❑   If money has been rolled over from a *traditional* retirement plan into a *traditional* IRA via a tax-free rollover (whether by direct rollover or 60-day rollover), the taxpayer cannot later change his mind and "recharacterize" that as a Roth conversion by moving the rolled amount to a Roth IRA. "[A]n amount contributed to an IRA in a tax-free transfer cannot be recharacterized." Reg. § 1.408A-5, A-10, Example 4. The individual *can* convert to a Roth IRA the traditional IRA he has created via this rollover; he just cannot make such conversion "retroactive" to the original rollover.

❑   Similarly, employer contributions to a SEP or SIMPLE IRA may not be recharacterized as contributions to a Roth IRA, because the employer could not have made direct contributions to a Roth IRA in the first place. Reg. § 1.408A-5, A-5. But the employee may be able to convert the SEP or SIMPLE account to a Roth IRA; see ¶ 5.4.01(A).

❑   If a nonspouse Designated Beneficiary mistakenly rolls inherited nonIRA plan benefits into the beneficiary's *own* Roth IRA (rather than via directed rollover into an inherited Roth IRA; see ¶ 4.2.04(E), ¶ 4.2.05), recharacterization cannot cure the problem. The rollover is treated as a distribution followed by a *regular contribution* to the beneficiary's own Roth IRA; it can be recharacterized as a regular contribution to the beneficiary's own traditional IRA, but it cannot be recharacterized as a contribution to an inherited Roth IRA.

5.6.02 *Income attributable to the contribution*

One requirement that must be met in order for a returned IRA or Roth IRA contribution to qualify for the special income tax and penalty-avoidance treatment applicable to "corrective distributions" is that the "net income attributable" to the contribution must also be distributed (along with the returned contribution) by the applicable deadline. § 408(d)(4)(C); ¶ 2.1.08(B). Similarly, to recharacterize an

IRA contribution (¶ 5.6.03), not only the original contribution but also *any net income attributable to such contribution* must be transferred to the other type of IRA. § 408A(d)(6)(B); Reg. § 1.408A-5, A-2(a).

This ¶ 5.6.02 explains how to compute the net income attributable to an IRA or Roth IRA contribution for purposes of a corrective distribution or recharacterization.

Note that the "net income" may be a negative amount—a loss, in other words. See Reg. § 1.408A-5, A-2(b); A-2(c)(6), Example 1, and "Fouad Example" below.

There are two ways to compute the net income attributable to an IRA contribution:

Method 1: If the contribution in question was made to a separate IRA (traditional or Roth) that contained no other funds, *and* there have been no other contributions to or distributions from that separate IRA, then:

✓　　For a <u>corrective distribution</u>, distributing the entire account balance to the participant will satisfy the requirement of returning the contribution and net income attributable thereto. § 1.408-11(a)(2).

✓　　If the entire contribution is being <u>recharacterized</u>, transferring the entire account balance to the other type of IRA satisfies the requirement. Reg. § 1.408A-5, A-2(b); see Fouad Example below.

Because Method 1 is much simpler to apply than Method 2 (below), there is an advantage to keeping each year's Roth IRA conversion contributions in a separate Roth IRA account (not commingled with any pre-existing Roth IRA), until the deadline for recharacterizing such contributions (¶ 5.6.06) has passed.

Method 2: If Method 1 is not available, then the net income attributable to the contribution must be calculated using the following formula (Reg. § 1.408-11(a)(1)):

Net Income equals:

$$\text{Contribution} \times \frac{(\text{Adjusted Closing Balance} - \text{Adjusted Opening Balance})}{\text{Adjusted Opening Balance}}$$

See the regulation for details on this formula, and see Reg. § 1.408A-5, A-2, for examples of applying the formula to Roth recharacterizations.

For purposes of applying this formula, IRAs are *not* aggregated; earnings are computed only with respect to the actual account to which the contribution was made, even if the individual owns multiple IRAs. Reg. § 1.408-11(a)(2), § 1.408A-5, A-2(c)(4). Compare ¶ 5.2.03(B).

Fouad Example: Fouad converted $200,000 from his 401(k) plan to a new separate Roth IRA account in January 2010. This Roth IRA contained no other contributions, received no other contributions, and made no distributions. By November 2010, the account had declined in value to $160,000, and he decided to recharacterize. He closed the Roth IRA and transferred its entire value ($160,000) to a traditional IRA. He has successfully recharacterized his entire conversion, because he transferred to the traditional IRA the $200,000 contribution plus the "earnings thereon"; the "earnings" were a loss of $40,000. He can then "reconvert" this IRA to a Roth in 2011 (see ¶ 5.6.07).

5.6.03 *How to recharacterize certain IRA/Roth IRA contributions*

A recharacterization is effected by transferring the contribution that is to be recharacterized (plus earnings attributable thereto) to the other type of IRA by a certain deadline. § 408A(d)(7). A recharacterized contribution will be treated for income tax purposes as having been contributed to the transferee IRA (rather than the transferor IRA) "on the same date and (in the case of a regular contribution) for the same taxable year that the contribution was made to the" transferor IRA. Reg. § 1.408A-5, A-3. Although the Code makes it appear that *any* transfer of the IRA contribution amount to the other type of IRA before the applicable deadline is automatically treated as a recharacterization, the Regulation is clear that the treatment is elective. Reg. § 1.408A-5, A-1(a), (b), A-6.

For which contributions may NOT be recharacterized, see ¶ 5.6.01. For partial recharacterizations, see ¶ 5.6.04. For the deadline applicable to recharacterizations, see ¶ 5.6.06. See ¶ 1.2.07 regarding the effect of a recharacterization on calculation of the minimum required distribution.

Here are the requirements for effecting a recharacterization:

1.   Recharacterization is accomplished by moving the recharacterized traditional or Roth IRA contribution to the other type of IRA (Roth or traditional) by direct trustee-to-trustee transfer following the required notifications (see #3). A "60-day rollover" may *not* be used. Reg. § 1.408A-5, A-1(a). See ¶ 2.6.01 for the difference.

2.   Not only the original contribution but "any net income attributable to such contribution" must be transferred. Reg. § 1.408A-5, A-2(a). See ¶ 5.6.02.

3.   The election to recharacterize is made by providing notice and directions to the IRA sponsors involved, *on or before the date of the transfer*, to carry out the transfer of funds or property directly from the transferring IRA into the transferee IRA. Reg. § 1.408A-5, A-6(a).

4.   The election to recharacterize "cannot be revoked" after the transfer to the other type of IRA has occurred. Reg. § 1.408A-5, A-6(b).

5.   A recharacterization is "never treated as a rollover for purposes of the one-rollover-per-year limitation..., even if the contribution would have been treated as a rollover contribution by the...[transferee] IRA if it had been made directly to the" transferee IRA in the first place. Reg. § 1.408A-5, A-8. See ¶ 2.6.05 regarding the one rollover per year limitation.

6.   A Roth conversion that comes from a *nonIRA* plan (¶ 5.4.01(B)) is recharacterized by moving the converted amount (and earnings) out of the Roth IRA and *into a traditional IRA*, NOT back into the traditional nonIRA plan it was in prior to the Roth conversion. See Notice 2008-30, 2008-12 IRB 638, A-5, A-7.

7.   A "regular" contribution (¶ 5.3.02) made to *either type of IRA* for a particular year may be recharacterized as a contribution to the other type, by transferring the contribution (together with the "net income attributable" to the contribution) to the other type of IRA. § 408A(d)(6), (7).

5.6.04 *Partial recharacterizations*

Partial recharacterizations are permitted. Reg. § 1.408A-5, A-1(a).

However, you cannot "cherry pick" the assets you recharacterize so as to recharacterize only the "losers." If a participant converted his IRA to a Roth IRA at a time when the account contained 100 shares of Acme and 100 shares of Omega, and then a few months later the Acme had appreciated but the Omega had declined in value, the participant might like to recharacterize just the Omega stock. But the regulation's definition of the "income" on the account (the income that must be transferred to a traditional IRA along with the contribution being recharacterized; see ¶ 5.6.02) is based on the appreciation and depreciation *of the entire account*, not of the particular assets you might choose to recharacterize. Reg. § 1.408A-5, A-2(c)(5), (c)(6), Example 2.

If an individual converts his IRA to *multiple* Roth IRAs, the regulations permit him to "unconvert" one or more of the multiple Roths without undoing all of them. See Reg. § 1.408A-5, A-2(b), (c)(5), and (6), Example 2. Thus, a client might consider converting his IRA into several Roth IRAs, with portfolio assets whose values are less likely to move in tandem placed into separate Roth IRAs. That way, if one asset class declines in value prior to the deadline for recharacterizing the account, he can recharacterize just the Roth IRA that holds that asset class, and leave the other Roth IRAs alone. If using this strategy, the assets can be moved from a single traditional IRA directly into the multiple destination Roth IRAs; it is not necessary to first divide the assets into multiple traditional IRAs then convert those.

5.6.05 *Deadline for Roth IRA contributions and conversions*

The various deadlines for contributions, conversions, corrective distributions, and recharacterizations are extremely confusing. Some deadlines are based on the calendar year end, some on the extended due date of the return, and some on the *unextended* due date; and some of the deadlines qualify for an automatic extension—but you do not get the "automatic" extension unless you ask for it!

A.   **Deadline for "regular" contribution.** Starting with the easiest one: The deadline for making a regular contribution to a Roth IRA (¶ 5.3.02) for a particular year is the same as the deadline for contributing to a traditional IRA, i.e., the *unextended* due date of the tax return for that year, in other words, for most people, April 15 following the year in question. Reg. § 1.408A-3, A-2(b), § 219(f)(3).

For example, a contribution "for" the year 2009 may be made at any time after December 31, 2008, and before April 16, 2010. When a participant makes a regular IRA contribution between January 1 and April 15, the IRA provider must ask which year it is for, since between those dates it could be for either the year in which the contribution occurs or the prior year.

Meaning of "April 15"

The deadline for filing an individual's income tax return is the 15th day of the fourth month following the end of the individual's taxable year. § 6072(a). That means April 15th for most people. However, the actual deadline will be a bit later if April 15th falls on a weekend or holiday. § 7503. Also, the deadline may be extended for individuals in an area affected by a disaster; and of course the deadline is different for an individual whose taxable year is not the calendar year. In this book, "April 15" is used as shorthand for "the unextended due date of the individual's income tax return for the year in question, whatever that may be."

B.   **Deadline for "conversion" contribution.** Conversions are slightly more complicated. Because the conversion is technically a "rollover" (see ¶ 5.4.03(A), ¶ 5.4.04(A)), a conversion contribution is tied to the traditional plan distribution that is being "rolled over." Therefore a Roth IRA conversion that is supposed to be "for" the year 2010 must be tied to a *distribution that occurs in the calendar year 2010*. The due date of the 2010 return is *irrelevant*. A distribution made from a traditional plan in the calendar year 2010, if it is to be contributed to a Roth IRA, must be so contributed within 60 days after the date of the distribution. Reg. § 1.408A-4, A-1(b)(1). See § 402(c)(3)(A), § 408(d)(3), and ¶ 2.6.06.

The ability to recharacterize a "Year 1" IRA contribution until October 15 of "Year 2" (see ¶ 5.6.06) does *not* create an extended right to do Roth conversions between January 1 and October 15 of Year 2 that will count as Year 1 conversions.

January 1, 2010, would be the first date in 2010 on which an amount could be distributed out of a traditional IRA; therefore the earliest possible date for a "2010 Roth conversion" would be January 1, 2010 (same-day conversion of a January 1 distribution). The last possible date in calendar 2010 on which an amount could be distributed out of a traditional plan would be December 31, 2010. Therefore the last possible date for a "2010 conversion" would be 60 days after December 31, 2010 (the deadline for rolling over a distribution made on December 31, 2010). § 408(d)(3)(A)(i). Note that:

♦ Roth conversions are usually accomplished by transferring sums directly from a traditional plan or IRA into a Roth IRA. If both accounts are with the same administrator or IRA provider, the traditional plan distribution and the Roth IRA contribution would normally occur simultaneously. The 60-day deadline is irrelevant for direct transfers (see ¶ 2.1.03(A)).

♦ The IRS can extend the 60-day rollover deadline in cases of hardship. See ¶ 2.6.07. To date there is no published ruling in which this provision has been used to allow a longer period to complete a Roth IRA conversion.

♦ If a 2009 distribution is contributed to a Roth IRA in 2010 (within the applicable deadline for completing an indirect rollover) that is still considered a *2009* conversion for purposes of the eligibility tests (¶ 5.4.02(D), (E)). Reg. § 1.408A-4, A-2(a).

5.6.06 *Recharacterization deadline: Due date "including extensions"*

Generally, the deadline for recharacterizing an IRA contribution is the due date of the tax return for the applicable year *including extensions of time.* § 408A(d)(6), (7). So:

1. A regular contribution (¶ 5.3.02) to either a Roth IRA or a traditional IRA for a particular year, that was made by the *unextended* due date of the return for that year, can be

recharacterized by the *extended* due date of the return for that year.

2.   A <u>conversion contribution</u> to a Roth IRA may be recharacterized by the extended due date of the return for the taxable year in which the *distribution* that was converted to a Roth was distributed (which may not be the year the distribution was contributed to a Roth IRA; see ¶ 5.6.05(B)), and not the year the *recharacterization* occurred.

"Due date including extensions" or "extended due date" has a special meaning under IRS regulations. The taxpayer does not actually have to get an extension of his income tax return in order to go beyond April 15 for his recharacterization decision. Reg. § 301.9100-2(b) provides an automatic six-months extension (from the *unextended* due date of the return) for all "regulatory or statutory elections whose due dates are the...due date of the return including extensions *provided* the taxpayer timely filed its return for the year the election should have been made and the taxpayer takes" necessary corrective actions (such as filing an amended return if necessary). Emphasis added.

What's confusing is that there are two different "automatic" six-month extensions, neither of which is totally automatic. Any taxpayer can obtain a "automatic" six months' extension of time to file his income tax return (i.e., to October 15 instead of April 15)—but it's not truly automatic because to get this extension the taxpayer has to request it by April 15th, usually by filing Form 4868. Reg. § 1.6081-4.

Then there's the "automatic" six months extension of time to recharacterize an IRA contribution. This extension *is* automatic in the sense that the taxpayer doesn't have to request it; but to qualify for this automatic extension he has to "timely" file his income tax return. "Timely" filing the income tax return means filing the return by April 15 (*or* getting an extension of time to file from the IRS, and then filing the return by the extended due date).

Putting all these rules together, we find that if a taxpayer wants to recharacterize a regular Roth IRA contribution made for Year 1, or the Roth conversion of a Year 1 distribution, he must complete the necessary actions (¶ 5.6.03) by whichever one of the following deadlines applies:

A.   **October 15 if return is timely filed.** If he files his income tax return for Year 1 on or before its due date, he has until October

15 of Year 2 to complete the recharacterization. The "due date" of the Year 1 income tax return is April 15, Year 2, *unless* he obtains an extension of time to file the return, in which case the due date is whatever date the return was extended to. For example, if, on or before April 15, Year 2, he filed Form 4868 with the IRS requesting the "automatic" six months extension, the due date of his Year 1 return is October 15, Year 2. However, *regardless* of whether he got an extension of time to file his income tax return, as long as he filed the income tax return by whatever date it was due, the deadline for recharacterizing his IRA contribution is October 15, Year 2, under the automatic extension rule of Reg. § 301.9100-2(b).

B.   **April 15 if return is filed late.** If the individual does not file his income tax return for Year 1 on or before the date it is due (whether that due date is April 15 or some later date he qualified for under an extension), he must complete the recharacterization by April 15 of Year 2.

C.   **Disaster relief; "9100" relief.** For the taxpayer who misses the deadline for recharacterizing, there is still hope. First, Congress and the IRS sometimes grant blanket extensions of time and other relief to the victims of particular disasters. If the taxpayer is affected by such a disaster he may be entitled to complete a Roth recharacterization later than other taxpayers.

Second, there are procedures for applying to the IRS for relief in cases of good faith errors. See Reg. § 301.9100-1 *et seq.* Applying for relief on a Roth recharacterization gets it own special reduced "user fee" of $4,000. Rev. Proc. 2010-8, 2010-1 IRB 234, § 6.01(9). In dozens of private letter rulings, the IRS has been generous in using these relief provisions to grant extensions for recharacterizations of erroneous Roth conversions in deserving situations. See, *e.g.*, PLRs 2001-16053 (taxpayer erroneously believed that due date of her return was October 15 and that capital gain did not count toward the then-applicable $100,000 Roth conversion income limit); 2001-16057 (recharacterization of improper Roth conversion was late due to financial institution error); 2001-16058, 2001-19059, 2001-20040, 2001-22050, 2001-28058, and 2001-30058 (taxpayers unaware they didn't qualify for Roth conversion and unaware of recharacterization deadline); 2001-26040 (taxpayers had been erroneously advised that the Roth IRA conversion income limit then applicable was $150,000, that the deadline for a 1998 conversion was 4/15/99, etc.); and 2001-29040 (taxpayer ineligible to convert, and thought she had timely recharacterized all her Roth IRAs, but missed the deadline on one of them because she forgot about that account). For additional examples, see PLRs 2008-50052, 2008-26040, 2009-09073, 2009-21036, 2009-28044, 2009-48065, 2010-04037, and 2010-16095.

However, if the individual carried out a "legal" Roth conversion (i.e., he was eligible to and did properly convert), and seeks permission to recharacterize late due to a decline in value in the account following the conversion, the IRS is not likely to grant the extension absent evidence of some good reason why the individual missed the deadline, such as error by a professional advisor. See PLR 2010-24071.

5.6.07 *Same-year and immediate reconversions banned*

Once a recharacterization of an amount converted from a traditional IRA to a Roth IRA occurs, the individual "may not reconvert that amount" to a Roth IRA until the taxable year following the taxable year of the original conversion, or until at least 30 days have elapsed since the recharacterization, *whichever is later*. Thus, recharacterization cannot be used to flip back and forth quickly between traditional and Roth IRA status. Reg. § 1.408A-5, A-9. If the individual attempts to reconvert before the prescribed time period ends, the result is a *failed conversion*. See ¶ 5.4.06.

Essentially, this rule bars immediate "reconversions" only for an individual who converted *all* of his traditional IRAs to a Roth IRA. Someone who converted only part of his traditional IRAs can avoid the effect of the rule by simply converting *some other amount* immediately before or after he recharacterizes the first Roth conversion.

Brittany Example: Brittany's IRA (traditional IRA #1) in 2010 holds 30,000 shares of Acme stock worth $10 a share ($300,000). In January 2010 she moves 10,000 shares from her traditional IRA #1 to Roth IRA #1, thus effecting a $100,000 Roth conversion. A month later the Acme stock has declined to $7 per share, so her Roth IRA is worth only $70,000 and her traditional IRA only $140,000. Brittany wants to undo her Roth conversion that occurred at a higher price, but she wants to stick with her goal of converting about $100,000 worth of Acme stock in 2010. She recharacterizes the first conversion by moving the Acme stock out of Roth IRA #1 back to a new traditional IRA (IRA #2). She then immediately transfers another $100,002 worth of Acme stock (14,286 shares at $7) from traditional IRA #1 to Roth IRA #2. This new conversion is not banned because it is not a conversion of the same "amount."

A Roth conversion that was effected by transfer to a Roth IRA from a nonIRA plan can be recharacterized under § 408A(d)(6). Notice 2008-30, 2008-12 IRB 638, A-5. The rule banning same-year reconversions, by its explicit terms, applies only with respect to recharacterized conversions from *an IRA* to a Roth IRA, not to conversions from a nonIRA plan. The ban presumably also applies to plan-to-Roth-IRA conversions, under the rule that plan-to-Roth-IRA conversions are taxed "as if" the money went through a traditional IRA first on its way to the Roth IRA; see ¶ 5.4.04(A).

5.7 Designated Roth Accounts

In 2006, a new type of "Roth" plan joined the roster, the "designated Roth account" (DRAC) inside a "cash-or-deferred arrangement" (CODA) plan.

5.7.01 *Meet the DRAC: Roth 401(k)s, 403(b)s, 457(b)s*

Employees have long been permitted to make "elective deferral" (also called "salary reduction") contributions to workplace retirement plans. Under such a **cash-or-deferred arrangement** (**CODA**), the participant can choose either to receive a certain amount of his compensation in cash or to have such amount contributed to a vested account for his benefit in a retirement plan.

Needless to say, elective deferrals are subject to many complicated tax rules. Through 2005, the reward for successfully complying with these rules was that the amount of the elective deferral would be excluded from the participant's income. The deferred salary (and earnings thereon) would not be taxed until they were later distributed to the participant or his beneficiaries (typically after retirement or death).

Elective deferral contributions are treated as "wages" for purposes of the Federal Insurance Contributions Act (FICA). § 3121(a)(5)(C), (D), (H), (v)(1)(A). Since these contributions are subject to FICA taxes in any event, the employee's decision to have his elective deferral paid into a CODA plan account (whether traditional or Roth), or to himself in cash, will have *no effect* on either the employee's or the employer's FICA tax obligations.

Since 2006, the participant may have an additional option for his elective deferrals: Instead of deferring income tax on the deferred compensation, he can pay income tax on it currently and have it contributed to a **designated Roth account (DRAC)** within the plan; later qualified distributions from the DRAC will be tax-free. § 402A(d)(1). The portion of the elective deferral that the participant elects to have contributed to a DRAC is called a "designated Roth contribution." § 402A(a)(1).

Only "applicable retirement plans" are permitted to have DRACs. § 402A(a). Through 2010, "applicable retirement plans" included qualified (§ 401(a)) plans that have elective deferral (401(k)) provisions, and 403(b) plans, so DRACs are sometimes called "Roth 401(k)" or "Roth 403(b)" accounts. § 402A(e)(1). Governmental 457(b) plans are permitted to have DRACs effective in 2011 and later years. § 402A(e)(1). This book will refer only to 401(k) plans; unless specifically otherwise indicated the same rules apply to 403(b) and (after 2010) governmental 457(b) plans. Reg. § 1.403(b)-3(c)(1).

5.7.02 *DRAC contributions: Who, how much, how, etc.*

The rules discussed here apply, after 2005, to 401(k) and 403(b) plans and (after 2010) also to governmental 457(b) plans, all of which are collectively referred to here as "**CODA plans.**"

A.   **Who may contribute.** Any participant in a CODA plan can elect to have all or part of his elective deferral go into a DRAC, *if* his employer's plan permits designated Roth contributions (plans are not required to offer this option). A self-employed individual who has a self-employed (Keogh; ¶ 8.3.09) 401(k) plan can have all or part of his elective deferral contributed to a DRAC.

In contrast to Roth IRAs (¶ 5.3.04(C)), there is <u>no income ceiling</u> above which the participant is not allowed to make designated Roth contributions. § 402A. The DRAC was the first Roth retirement plan not to limit contributions to individuals with income below certain levels.

There is <u>no age limit</u> above which the participant cannot contribute to a Roth 401(k). Traditional IRAs are the only plans that do not allow contributions after the participant has reached age 70½.

An individual can contribute to a Roth 401(k) <u>even if he is also a participant in other retirement plans</u> offered by the same or another employer; however, participation in another plan may limit the *amount* that may be contributed (see "B").

B. **How much may be contributed.** The maximum amount that may be contributed to a DRAC is whatever maximum amount of elective deferral contribution the participant may make to his 401(k) plan for the year in question. § 402(g)(1)(B).

The dollar limit for elective deferrals in 2006 and later years is $15,000, plus an additional $5,000 "catch-up" contribution if the participant is 50 or older by the end of the year. § 402(g)(1)(B), (C). Cost-of-living adjustments (COLAs) increase both the base amount (§ 402(g)(4)) and the catch-up contribution (§ 414(v)(2)(C)) after 2006. For 2009–2011, the base and catch-up amounts are $16,500 and $5,500 respectively. Notice 2009-94, 2009-50 IRB 848; IR-2010-108. Note the contrast with IRAs, where the "catchup contribution" for individuals over age 49 is *not* subject to a COLA. ¶ 5.3.03.

To find each year's maximum permitted contribution amount, see Ed Slott's *IRA Advisor* newsletter or Denise Appleby's Quick Reference charts (Appendix C).

The DRAC option does not increase the amount the participant may contribute to a plan through elective deferrals. Rather, the participant may choose to put his total permitted elective deferral contribution amount into a DRAC, or into a traditional 401(k) account, or partly into each. For example, in 2010 an over-age-49 participant with sufficient compensation can (if permitted by his plan) contribute $22,000 to his regular 401(k) account, or $22,000 to a DRAC; or he can send part of his elective deferrals to a DRAC and part to a regular account, as long as the combined total so contributed does not exceed $22,000.

The elective deferral limits apply to an individual based on *all* elective deferral plans he participates in (with this or any other employer; § 402(g)); and § 415 also limits the amount that may be contributed. These limits are beyond the scope of this book; see instead Chapter 27 of *The Pension Answer Book* (Appendix C).

C.   Election is irrevocable. The election to have part of one's compensation contributed to a DRAC is irrevocable once the money has been contributed to the plan. Thus, a participant cannot retroactively designate a DRAC contribution as a regular contribution or vice versa. Reg. § 1.401(k)-1(f)(1)(i). This is *unlike* a Roth IRA, contributions to which can be withdrawn or recharacterized for a certain period of time, if the contributor changes his mind; see ¶ 5.6. The irrevocability of the DRAC decision will make planning more difficult; a participant might prefer to wait until the end of the year (when he has a better idea of his income and tax situation) to decide whether he wants a tax deduction now or tax-free income later.

D.   What may be contributed to a DRAC. The ONLY contributions that can go into a DRAC are: (1) certain rollovers from other DRACs (see ¶ 5.7.07); (2) a participant's post-2005 elective deferral contributions (Reg. § 1.401(k)-1(f)(3), third sentence); and (beginning 9/28/10), rollovers of distributions from the employee's "traditional" account in the same retirement plan (see ¶ 5.7.11). This means that:

✓   The employ*er* cannot make matching (or any other) contributions to a DRAC. The employer's matching contribution (if any), and any other employer contributions to the plan on behalf of the participant, must be made to the participant's "traditional" CODA account, regardless of whether the participant's contribution that is being "matched" was made to a traditional account or to a DRAC.

✓   Money cannot be rolled from a Roth IRA into a DRAC, even if that Roth IRA contains nothing but money rolled into it from the same or another DRAC. Reg. § 1.408A-10, A-5.

Elective deferrals may be contributed *prospectively only* to a DRAC. Once the participant has elected to have his deferral contribution sent to a traditional 401(k) account, he cannot later move the funds from the traditional account into a DRAC. Reg. § 1.401(k)-1(f)(1)(i). The only exception to that statement is, once he becomes entitled to a distribution from the traditional elective deferral account, he can roll such distribution from that account to a DRAC if permitted by the plan (see ¶ 5.7.11).

5.7.03 *MRDs and other contrasts with Roth IRAs*

A DRAC (unlike a Roth IRA) is part of a 401(k), 403(b), or governmental 457(b) plan. As such it is subject to all the same rules that apply to traditional accounts in such plans, except to the extent § 402A provides otherwise.

For example, DRACs are subject to the same lifetime and post-death minimum distribution rules as other plan benefits. Reg. § 1.401(k)-1(f)(3). A DRAC owner approaching age 70½ should consider rolling over his DRAC to a Roth IRA to avoid "lifetime" required distributions; see ¶ 5.2.02(A), ¶ 5.7.08, ¶ 5.7.09.

DRAC distributions are subject to the income tax withholding rules applicable to other distributions from qualified plans; see ¶ 2.3. DRACs are also subject to federally granted spousal rights (see ¶ 3.4), and the rules restricting distributions from elective deferral accounts (not covered in this book; see, instead, Chapter 27 of *The Pension Answer Book* (Appendix C)). Roth IRAs are subject to none of these. Other differences include the irrevocability of contributions (¶ 5.7.02(C)), the definition of qualified distributions (¶ 5.7.04), the treatment of nonqualified distributions (¶ 5.7.05), and the rollover rules (¶ 5.7.06–¶ 5.7.09).

5.7.04 *DRACs: Definition of "qualified distribution"*

As with a Roth IRA, there are two types of distributions from a DRAC, qualified distributions and other (nonqualified) distributions. Qualified distributions from a DRAC, like qualified distributions from a Roth IRA, are income tax-free. § 402A(d)(1); Reg. § 1.402A-1, A-2(a). However, the definition of qualified distribution is different for the two types of Roth plan. Each involves a five-year waiting period and a triggering event, but the computation of the Five-Year Period, and the triggering events, are not the same.

A.   Qualified distribution triggering events. A DRAC distribution is a qualified distribution only if it is either (1) made on or after the date the participant reaches age 59½, (2) made after his death, or (3) attributable to the participant's being disabled "within the meaning of section 72(m)(7)." An additional category of qualified distribution from a Roth IRA, the first-time homebuyer distribution, does NOT apply to DRACs; compare ¶ 5.2.04, #4. § 402A(d)(2)(A).

B. **How the Five-Year Period is computed for a DRAC.** As with Roth IRAs, DRACs have a five-year waiting period (called the "nonexclusion period" in the statute, the "Five-Year Period" in this book) before a qualified distribution can occur. § 402A(d)(2)(B). However, there is a difference in the way the Five-Year Period is calculated. With a Roth IRA, the Five-Year Period begins with the first year there is a contribution to *any* Roth IRA; see ¶ 5.2.05.

For a DRAC, in contrast, the Five-Year Period is five consecutive years beginning with the first year the employee made a contribution to a DRAC *in that particular plan* (i.e., the year the elective deferral was included in his income). § 402A(d)(2)(B)(i). If the employee takes distribution of the entire account during the Five-Year Period then later makes more contributions, the start of the Five-Year Period is not "redetermined"; it still begins with the *first* contribution. Reg. § 1.402A-1, A-4(c).

The Five-Year Period is computed plan-by-plan even for two plans maintained by the same employer. Reg. § 1.402A-1, A-4(a), (b). For the only exception to this rule (applicable to certain rollover amounts), see ¶ 5.7.07(D).

However, certain DRAC contributions do NOT start the Five-Year Period tolling. "A contribution that is returned as an excess deferral or excess contribution does not begin the 5 taxable-year period of participation. Similarly, a contribution returned as a permissible withdrawal under section 414(w) does not begin the 5 taxable-year period of participation." Reg. § 1.402A-1, A-4(a). (§ 414(w) came into effect in 2008, allowing for "eligible automatic contribution arrangements.") This rule avoids game-playing: The participant cannot start the five-year clock running with a contribution that is returned to him.

Once the Five-Year Period has elapsed, and the triggering event requirement is met, subsequent distributions are generally qualified; for exceptions, see "C."

Qualified status is determined based on *the year in which the distribution actually occurs*, not on some prior year to which it may relate. For example, a distribution received after completion of the Five-Year Period (and after a triggering event) is a qualified distribution, even if it is part of a series of substantially equal periodic payments that started prior to the completion of the Five-Year Period. T.D. 9324, "Preamble," "Determination of 5-Taxable-Year Period for Qualified Distributions."

For how to compute the Five-Year Period with respect to a reemployed **veteran**, see Reg. § 1.402A-1, A-4(e).

C.   **List of never-qualified distributions.** Certain DRAC distributions can not be qualified distributions, *even if* the Five-Year Period and triggering event requirements are met. Reg. § 1.402A-1, A-2(c), A-11. These never-qualified distributions are listed by cross-reference to Reg. § 1.402(c)-2, A-4:

  • Corrective distributions of excess plan contributions (including income thereon) made by the plan in order to comply with the § 415 limits. A-4(a).

  • Corrective distributions of excess deferral amounts (including income thereon) made to comply with the elective deferral limits of Reg. § 1.402(g)-1(e)(3) and the cash-or-deferred plan rules. A-4(b), (c).

  • Plan loans that are treated as deemed distributions under § 72(p). A-4(d). See ¶ 2.1.07(A).

  • Dividends paid on employer securities as described in § 404(k). A-4(e). See also Reg. § 1.402A-1, A-11.

  • The deemed income resulting from plan-owned life insurance. A-4(f). See ¶ 2.1.04(H).

  • The deemed income resulting from a prohibited transaction. A-4(g).

  • "Similar items designated by the Commissioner in revenue rulings, notices, and other guidance published in the Internal Revenue Bulletin." A-4(h).

The never-qualified category is needed to prevent game-playing. For example, if excess contributions (and earnings thereon) could be distributed tax-free as long as the participant had met the five-year and triggering event tests, then everyone over 59½ with five years of DRAC participation would have an incentive to transfer all his wealth into his DRAC. That would be an excess contribution, but any penalties could be avoided by distributing the excess contribution (and earnings thereon) back to himself by a certain deadline (see ¶ 2.1.08(D)); and if there were no income tax on the distributed earnings the participant would have done an end run around the Code's contribution limits.

Though the above list of never-qualified distributions generally tracks the list of distributions that are not "eligible rollover distributions," the regulations clarify that some distributions that are not *eligible rollover distributions* nevertheless CAN be *qualified distributions*. Hardship distributions, minimum required distributions, and distributions that are part of a series of substantially equal periodic payments fall into this category. Reg. § 1.402A-1, A-11.

D.   QDROs and payments to beneficiaries. In the case of a distribution to an alternate payee under a QDRO, or to a beneficiary, it is the death, age, or disability of the participant that determines whether the distribution is qualified. See Reg. § 1.402A-1, A-4(d), regarding QDRO payments from DRACs.

5.7.05 *Nonqualified DRAC distributions*

Though not automatically entitled to 100 percent tax-free treatment the way a qualified distribution is, a nonqualified distribution may be partly or wholly tax-free. However, the treatment of nonqualified distributions is one of the big differences between Roth IRAs and DRACs.

As is true with a Roth IRA, if the DRAC has appreciated since the original contribution(s), then the DRAC contains two kinds of money: the participant's contributions (which comprise the participant's basis in the account—the money he has already paid tax on—also called the "after-tax money" or "investment in the contract"; see ¶ 2.2.01), plus the appreciation (which is pretax money; the IRS calls this the "earnings"). Hopefully, the "earnings" will NEVER be taxed, because they will come out eventually in the form of a tax-free qualified distribution (¶ 5.7.04).

But if there is a nonqualified distribution, the earnings cannot come out tax-free. Accordingly, we need to determine how much of any nonqualified distribution represents a return of the participant's basis (tax-free) and how much is considered earnings (taxable), and here's where we find the difference between Roth IRAs and DRACs. With a Roth IRA, the participant's own contributions (i.e., the after-tax money) come out first. ¶ 5.2.06, ¶ 5.2.07. Accordingly, even nonqualified Roth IRA distributions are income tax-free until the entire basis has been distributed.

With DRACs, in contrast, there is no special rule allowing the participant's basis to come out first. So, the regular rule of § 72(e)(8) will apply—the "cream-in-the-coffee rule," under which any distribution carries out proportionate amounts of the participant's basis (after-tax money) and earnings (pretax money). Reg. § 1.402A-1, A-3; see ¶ 2.2.02. Thus, every nonqualified distribution from a DRAC will be partly taxable unless either (1) there has been no appreciation in the account since the original contributions or (2) the earnings portion is rolled over (¶ 5.7.06).

The participant's DRAC is treated as a separate account from the participant's *traditional* accounts in the plan for purposes of applying § 72. § 402A(d)(4). Thus, distributions can be taken from each category (traditional or Roth) separately, without their being aggregated for purposes of the "cream-in-the-coffee rule."

However, if the participant has more than one DRAC inside a single 401(k) plan (for example, an elective deferral account and a rollover account), these are treated as a single account for purposes of § 72. Reg. § 1.402A-1, A-9(a). The only exceptions to this are: If an account is divided between the participant and his spouse pursuant to a QDRO, each spouse's share of the employee's DRAC is treated as a separate account (or "separate contract," in the lingo of § 72; see ¶ 2.2.04(C)); and, the plan can split the DRAC into multiple separate accounts for the participant's multiple beneficiaries after the participant's death, and each such account will be treated as a separate "contract" under § 72. Reg. § 1.402A-1, A-9(b).

5.7.06 Rollovers of DRAC distributions: General rules

A distribution from a DRAC may be rolled over *only* to another DRAC or to a Roth IRA. § 402A(c)(3); Reg. § 1.402A-1, A-5(a). See

¶ 5.7.07 for the rules for DRAC-to-DRAC rollovers, ¶ 5.7.08 for DRAC-to-Roth IRA rollovers.

Though both direct rollovers and indirect (60-day) rollovers are permitted (see ¶ 2.6.01 for the difference), different rules apply to these two types of rollovers:

♦ If a DRAC pays a distribution from the participant's account directly to another DRAC (trustee-to-trustee transfer or direct rollover), that is treated as a separate distribution from "any amount paid directly to the employee," for purposes of determining how much of each of these "separate distributions" is after-tax money and how much is pretax money. Reg. § 1.402A-1, A-5(a), third sentence; A-6(a). Although this regulation addresses only direct rollovers from one DRAC to another, Notice 2009-68, 2009-39 IRB 423, at p. 429, provides the same rule for rollovers from *any* QRP to any other eligible retirement plan; see ¶ 2.2.04(A).

♦ If a distribution is paid to the participant (rather than being rolled directly to another plan or IRA), and the participant rolls over only *part* of the distribution (using a 60-day rollover), the part rolled over is deemed to come first out of the "earnings" portion of the distribution. § 402(c)(2), last sentence; Reg. § 1.402A-1, A-5(b). See ¶ 2.2.05(C) for more on this rule.

These rules for tracking the participant's "income" and "investment in the contract" in the distributing DRAC must be observed, in the case of a partial distribution from a DRAC, even if the distribution is a qualified distribution (so it is tax-free; ¶ 5.7.04), because of the possibility that the participant might later receive a *non*qualified distribution from that DRAC; see ¶ 5.7.05.

However, a DRAC or Roth IRA that *receives* a rollover of a qualified distribution from a DRAC is apparently *not* required to keep track of the basis and income "inside" that distribution, because a qualified DRAC distribution that is rolled into a DRAC or a Roth IRA comes in as "investment in the contract" for purposes of taxation of later distributions from that receiving account. Reg. § 1.402A-1, A-6(a), last sentence; § 1.408A-10, A-3(a), third sentence.

5.7.07 *DRAC-to-DRAC rollovers*

For general rules applicable to all rollovers of DRAC distributions, see ¶ 5.7.06. DRAC-to-DRAC rollovers are subject to several additional *very complicated* rules:

A.   **May roll to any other DRAC.** An eligible rollover distribution from a DRAC can be rolled to any other DRAC (including a DRAC in a different type of plan; for example, a 403(b) plan DRAC can be rolled into a 401(k) plan DRAC), *provided* the recipient plan offers DRACs as part of its own elective deferral program, and *provided* the rest of the rules in this ¶ 5.7.07 are complied with. Reg. § 1.402A-1, A-5(a); T.D. 9324 (Preamble).

B.   **Direct rollover.** The participant can do a DRAC-to-DRAC rollover by means of a direct rollover (¶ 2.6.01(C)) of any DRAC distribution. If the distribution from the first DRAC is a qualified distribution, then the entire amount rolled into the transferee DRAC is allocated to the participant's "investment in the contract" (basis) in the transferee DRAC. Reg. § 1.402A-1, A-6(a). See "C" for the advantage of rolling the *entire* DRAC distribution into the new DRAC by means of a *direct rollover.* See "D" for the advantage of rolling at least *some* of the DRAC distribution into the new DRAC by means of a *direct rollover.*

C.   **Total direct rollover preserves basis in excess of value.** If the ENTIRE account in the distributing DRAC is transferred by direct rollover to the recipient DRAC, and the employee's basis in the distributing DRAC exceeds the fair market value of the distribution, the employee's basis in the distributing DRAC becomes part of his basis in the recipient DRAC, despite the fact that his basis exceeds the account's value. This rule helps an employee whose DRAC is "under water" preserve his high basis when he changes jobs, and is a good reason to do a 100 percent DRAC-to-DRAC direct rollover in those circumstances. Reg. § 1.402A-1, A-6(b).

D.   **Direct rollover preserves holding period.** One advantage of doing a direct DRAC-to-DRAC rollover is that the participant's holding period from the transferor plan is tacked on to the holding period in the transferee plan for purposes of computing the Five-Year Period (¶ 5.7.04(B)). With an "indirect" (60-day) rollover, the years in the prior plan *will not count* in computing the Five-Year Period for the transferee plan. § 402A(d)(2)(B); Reg. § 1.402A-1, A-4(b).

E.   **60-day ("indirect") rollover.** If the participant actually receives the distribution (i.e., he did not arrange for a direct rollover), he generally has 60 days to roll all or part of that distribution into another DRAC; see ¶ 2.6.01(D), ¶ 2.6.06, for details on this deadline. Here are additional rules regarding such indirect DRAC-to-DRAC rollovers:

1.   The participant can roll the earnings (pretax) portion of the distribution to another DRAC, but the nontaxable portion of a DRAC distribution (the basis) may NOT be rolled to another DRAC by means of a 60-day rollover. This treatment is consistent with the rules that, in case of a partial indirect rollover, the portion rolled is deemed to come first out of the part of the distribution that would be taxable if not rolled over and that after-tax money cannot be rolled into a QRP except by direct rollover. § 402(c)(2); Reg. § 1.402A-1, A-5(a), second sentence. See ¶ 2.2.05(C).

2.   With a 60-day rollover, the transferee DRAC does NOT tack on the participant's holding period from the prior DRAC. Compare "D" above. The participant's Five-Year Period for the DRAC that receives the rollover is based on the first year he made a contribution to *that particular DRAC* (whether that first contribution was the rollover contribution or some other contribution). Reg. § 1.402A-1, A-5(c).

3.   Finally, since a 60-day rollover involves the distribution of an eligible rollover distribution to the participant, it is subject to mandatory 20 percent withholding of federal income tax from the taxable portion of the distribution. § 3405(c). To roll over the withheld amount, the participant must use substituted funds. ¶ 2.6.02.

5.7.08 *DRAC-to-Roth-IRA rollovers: In general*

For the *general* rules applicable to all rollovers of DRAC distributions, see ¶ 5.7.06.

A DRAC-to-Roth-IRA rollover may be accomplished by either direct rollover (¶ 2.6.01(C)) or 60-day (indirect) rollover (¶ 2.6.01(D)). Reg. § 1.402A-1, A-5(a). For the effect of such a rollover on computation of the Five-Year Period, see ¶ 5.7.09. For effect of a partial indirect rollover on basis, see ¶ 2.2.05(C). Here are *additional* rules and considerations that apply to DRAC-to-Roth-IRA rollovers:

A.   **Who is eligible.** A rollover from a DRAC to a Roth IRA is permitted *even if* the participant is not otherwise eligible to contribute to a Roth IRA (¶ 5.3.04). Reg. § 1.408A-10, A-2. He can establish a Roth IRA purely for the purpose of receiving a rollover from his DRAC. Both a qualified and a nonqualified DRAC distribution can be rolled to a Roth IRA—provided, of course, that it's an eligible rollover distribution; see ¶ 2.6.02.

B.   **Minimum distribution effects.** Rolling over from a DRAC to a Roth IRA will end the requirement of lifetime MRDs with respect to the rolled funds. ¶ 5.2.02(A). For a rollover in a year when a distribution is required, see ¶ 2.6.03. Also, if the rollover occurs after the participant's Required Beginning Date (RBD; ¶ 1.4), the rollover changes the method of computing the Applicable Distribution Period (ADP; ¶ 1.2.03) that will apply to the participant's beneficiaries from the "death post-RBD rules" to the "death pre-RBD rules"; see ¶ 1.5.02.

C.   **Favorable effect on basis recovery.** Rolling from a DRAC to a Roth IRA enables the participant (once the rollover is completed) to withdraw his own contributions tax-free from the Roth IRA while leaving any "earnings" inside the account, something he could NOT do with the DRAC, because the Roth IRA has more favorable rules for recovery of basis than a DRAC. Compare ¶ 5.2.06 with ¶ 5.7.05.

D.   **Rollover when basis is higher than market value.** There is a special rule for determining basis in the Roth IRA when there is a rollover into the Roth IRA from a DRAC, *if* the employee's basis in the DRAC exceeded the DRAC's value on the date of distribution: If the employee takes a distribution of the *entire balance* of his DRAC, and rolls PART of that distribution to a Roth IRA by means of a 60-day rollover, and at the time of the distribution his basis in the DRAC exceeded the market value of the DRAC, the excess basis is treated as a regular contribution to the Roth IRA (i.e., it is added to the employee's basis in the Roth IRA). Reg. § 1.408A-10, A-3(b).

Does this ability to preserve "excess basis" also apply to *direct* DRAC-to-Roth-IRA rollovers (not just 60-day rollovers), and to a rollover of the *entire* distribution (not just to partial rollovers)? The regulation specifically mentions only partial 60-day rollovers. The IRS *may* have intended that carryover of "excess" basis would also apply for direct rollovers of the entire account balance, by its cross reference to Reg. § 1.402A-1, A-6 (see ¶ 5.7.07(C)); it's not clear.

Preserving the "excess basis" could be important in two situations. One is if the participant or beneficiary later takes a *nonqualified* distribution from the Roth IRA. Such a distribution would be includible in income only to the extent the distribution exceeded the participant's basis. ¶ 5.2.06. The other advantage of preserving basis would occur if the individual cashed out all of his Roth IRAs, and the total sum received was less than the individual's basis in the account, so the individual would be entitled to a loss deduction. See ¶ 8.1.02.

5.7.09 *DRAC-to-Roth IRA rollovers: Effect on Five-Year Period*

The Five-Year Period for a Roth IRA begins January 1 of the first year the participant has any Roth IRA (¶ 5.2.05), *regardless* of whether the Roth IRA holds money rolled over from a DRAC; whatever holding period the DRAC owner had established in the plan that originally held the DRAC does NOT carry over to the Roth IRA, regardless of whether the DRAC-to-Roth-IRA rollover is a "direct rollover" or a "60-day rollover." Reg. § 1.408A-10, A-4.

With direct DRAC-to-*DRAC* rollovers, Congress specified that the employee's holding period carries over from one DRAC to the other. § 402A(d)(2)(B); see ¶ 5.7.07(D). However, Congress said nothing about a carryover of holding period in the case of a DRAC-to-*Roth-IRA* rollover, so the Regulations allow no such carryover.

This rule will adversely affect some (see "C"), but is not the disaster it at first appears (see "A" and "B").

A.   **Rollover of a qualified distribution.** If the DRAC distribution that is rolled over to the Roth IRA is *itself* a qualified distribution (¶ 5.7.04), then the entire rollover amount is treated as a "regular contribution" to the Roth IRA. Reg. § 1.408A-10, A-3(a). A regular contribution can be withdrawn from a Roth IRA at any time, income tax-free. ¶ 5.2.06. Thus, only the post-rollover earnings on the rollover amount may be subject to a "fresh start" Five-Year Period in order to become tax-free qualified distributions. Reg. § 1.408A-10, A-4(b), Example 3.

B.   **Rollover if participant already has a Roth IRA.** If the participant had already established a Roth IRA prior to the rollover, the money rolled from the DRAC gets the benefit of the years the participant's pre-existing Roth IRA has already completed towards the Roth IRA Five-Year Period (regardless of whether the DRAC distribution is rolled into the pre-existing Roth IRA or into a brand new Roth IRA). If the participant has already completed the Five-Year Period with respect to the existing Roth IRA(s) he owned prior to the rollover, then the rollover from the DRAC gets the benefit of that—even if the money was in the *DRAC* for less than five years. See Reg. § 1.408A-10, A-4(b), Example 1.

C.   **Danger: Rolling to participant's first Roth IRA.** The person who may be hurt by this rule is someone who had no prior Roth IRA, and had completed one or more years in his DRAC at the time he rolls a *non*qualified distribution from the DRAC to a Roth IRA. He loses the years he had completed, and starts the 5-year clock over again. Because his rollover was NOT of a qualified distribution, only his basis in the DRAC (i.e., the amount of his already-taxed contribution(s) to the DRAC) is treated as a "regular contribution" to the Roth IRA. The rest of the rollover is treated as "earnings," meaning that it cannot be distributed tax-free except in a qualified distribution. Reg. § 1.408A-10, A-4(b), Example 2.

This will make little difference to a person who is rolling from the DRAC to a Roth IRA when he is under age 54½ because, absent disability, he will have to wait five or more years ANYWAY before he can have a qualified distribution from the Roth IRA. However, it could be tough for a person who has accumulated many years in the DRAC and then rolls to a Roth IRA *shortly before reaching age 59½*. If the first year for which he has ever owned a Roth IRA is the year he establishes a Roth IRA with his DRAC rollover, he will have to wait five *more* years to have a qualified distribution from that Roth IRA:

Bryon Example: Bryon, age 38, establishes a $15,000 DRAC in 2006 in his employer's 401(k) plan. He makes no further contributions to the DRAC. In 2026, he retires at age 58 and rolls over the DRAC (now worth $45,000) to a Roth IRA. This is his first Roth IRA; accordingly, computation of his Five-Year Period for the Roth IRA starts with the year of the rollover (2026), so he cannot have a qualified distribution from the Roth IRA until 2031. His basis in the DRAC ($15,000) will be treated as his only "investment in the contract" in the Roth IRA. Though he can withdraw that basis tax-free at any time, he cannot withdraw the post-2006 earnings ($30,000 at the time of the rollover) tax-free until 2031. If he had just waited until he had reached age 59½ before rolling the DRAC to a Roth IRA, the rolled distribution would have been a qualified distribution and the fresh-start rule would have applied only to post-rollover earnings (see "A"), not to ALL earnings.

5.7.10 *DRAC accounting may not shift value*

The plan must maintain separate records for the participant's traditional and Roth accounts in the 401(k) plan until the DRAC has been completely distributed. § 402A(b)(2), Reg. § 1.401(k)-1(f)(2). The IRS fears that employers will try to arrange the plan accounting so that profits are shifted into the DRAC; the regulation provides that any transaction or methodology that has the effect of transferring value into a DRAC from another account violates the requirements of § 402A. However, swapping assets between accounts at fair market value is permitted. Reg. § 1.402A-1, A-13(a). A plan that holds a DRAC must keep track of each participant's investment in the contract and also the Five-Year Period for such participant. Reg. § 1.402A-2, A-1.

5.7.11 *In-plan conversions*

A new "in-plan conversion" option was added effective September 27, 2010, by the Small Business Jobs Act of 2010, for any 401(k), 403(b), or (after 2010) governmental 457(b) plan that offers both traditional and designated Roth elective deferral accounts: When an employee who has a traditional account in the plan becomes entitled to a distribution from that account, he can elect to have the distribution rolled directly into a DRAC in the same plan. In other words he can elect to "convert" the distribution to Roth status *while keeping it in the employer's plan.* § 402A(c)(4). Prior to this change in the law the only way an employee could convert an existing traditional nonIRA plan balance to Roth status was by rolling the distribution to a Roth IRA. See IRS Notice 2010-84, 2010-51 (11/29/10), for rules applicable to this new "in-plan conversion" option.

2010 in-plan conversions are subject to the same option to elect forward income-averaging (into 2011 and 2012) as other 2010 Roth conversions (¶ 5.4.05), except that the individual may make a different election for his 2010 in-plan conversions than he makes for all his 2010 Roth IRA conversions. Notice 2010-84, A-10. In-plan conversions are also subject to the same waiver and recapture provisions regarding the 10 percent early-distributions penalty as other Roth conversions (¶ 5.5.02). Notice 2010-84, A-8.

The plan may is not required to offer in-plan conversions, even if it offers DRACs. Notice 2010-84, A-4. Since an in-plan conversion is technically a rollover of a plan distribution, a plan can allow the in-plan conversion only if the plan account holder is entitled to a distribution under the plan. However, the plan can allow distributions for purposes of in-plan conversions (1) under any circumstances where the plan could legally allow distributions from the employee's account and (2) without being required to permit any *other* options for such distribution. Notice 2010-84, A-4. For example, the plan could permit in-service distributions solely for purposes of in-plan Roth conversions, without having to permit employees to take the money out of the plan. In-plan conversions are available to the surviving spouse as beneficiary but not to other Designated Beneficiaries. Notice 2010-84, A-14.

The recharacterization option (¶ 5.6) does not apply to in-plan conversions, making the conversion decision in effect irrevocable. Notice 2010-84, A-6. Because of the added flexibility offered by the recharacterization option, a Roth IRA conversion would be preferable to an in-plan conversion if both choices are available to the distributee. It appears that the in-plan conversion will be of interest only to the participant who is entitled to funds out of his plan account, wants to do a Roth conversion, and has a strong preference for keeping the money inside a qualified plan for reasons such as creditor protection or investment options; or who wants to do a Roth conversion but is not permitted by the plan to roll the money to an outside Roth IRA.

5.8 Putting it All Together:
Roth Planning Ideas and Principles

This ¶ 5.8 looks at planning decisions and ideas connected with Roth retirement plans. It covers the decision of whether to go into a Roth plan in the first place (¶ 5.8.01–¶ 5.8.05); and the estate planner's concerns in connection with Roth plans and conversions (¶ 5.8.06).

5.8.01 *Roth plan or traditional? It's all about the price tag*

A Roth IRA is a nice asset to own. It offers the ability to generate income tax-free investment accumulations that can be spent in retirement or left to heirs, and the additional advantage of no required distributions during the participant's life. And *unlike* with a traditional IRA, the participant can withdraw his own contributions income tax-free anytime he wants to.

There theoretically could be some drawbacks that would make a Roth IRA "worse" to own than a traditional IRA: For example, it's possible that some states' laws haven't caught up with the Roth idea yet, so that a Roth in such a state would be more vulnerable to state taxes and/or creditors' claims. Also, some planners speculate that a Roth is an "inferior" inheritance vehicle because beneficiaries are more likely to cash it out quickly because it's tax free, whereas they might go along with deferring distribution of a traditional plan that they would have to pay income tax on if they cashed it out. And (even aside from the income tax cost) the bump in taxable income generated by a Roth IRA conversion could "look bad" on an application for college financial aid or other means-tested benefit. But these drawbacks are speculative or applicable to few people.

The only *significant widely-applicable* drawback of a Roth plan is the cost. Generally, the price is payment of income taxes on the amount going *in* to the Roth retirement plan—taxes that could have been deferred (via a traditional retirement plan) until the money was taken *out* of the retirement plan. The debate is not whether a Roth IRA is a good type of retirement plan to own. The debate is about the price tag: Is it worth it, and can you afford it?

Which is better: to pay the taxes up front and get tax-free distributions later or to defer the taxes?

A. **Analyzing the cost and benefits of a Roth conversion.**
Professionals who have crunched the numbers for many clients
generally conclude that the following factors will result in a
Roth conversion's being profitable for the converting
participant and/or his beneficiaries:

   1. The income tax payable on the conversion will be less
       than would otherwise apply to withdrawals from the
       account if it stayed in traditional form.

   2. The funds stay in the Roth account for some number of
       years, the longer the better. This factor could mean
       (depending on the planner) that the money stays in the
       Roth IRA for some absolute certain number of years to
       achieve a "break even point," or simply that it stays in
       the Roth account longer than it would have been
       allowed (under the minimum distribution rules) to stay
       in a traditional plan.

   3. The income tax resulting from the conversion is paid
       with assets that are not inside any retirement account.

   4. The Roth investments do not decline in value.

Not all professionals agree on the relative weight of these
factors, and or even that all these factors are relevant to the decision.
Also, if one factor is positive enough, that factor alone may make the
Roth approach profitable even if the other factors are not present. For
example, work done by IRA expert Bob Keebler, CPA, and his firm
has shown that prepaying a 35 percent tax (via a 2010 Roth conversion)
on retirement assets that would otherwise be taxed at 43.6 percent (see
¶ 2.1.02) can produce a profit for the client in just 10 years (compared
with leaving all the money in a traditional IRA) even if the account
itself must be depleted to pay the conversion income tax—i.e.,
factor #1 trumps factor #3 if the rate increase is substantial enough.

B. **What goes into the spreadsheet.** Should *your client* convert to
a Roth IRA? A spreadsheet cannot give "the answer." A
spreadsheet just regurgitates the inputs you give it. Computer
projections of the benefits of a Roth conversion are based on
assumptions as to future tax rates, investment returns (inside

and outside the IRA), and withdrawal amounts. Different professionals running different computer programs may reach different conclusions regarding the profitability of converting to a Roth IRA. Creating inputs *truly applicable to the client's personal situation* is a daunting task.

✓ What income tax rates do you assume will apply to the client's traditional IRA withdrawals, Roth conversion, and outside investment income? Make sure the projections you are using are based on the actual taxes that would be payable on a specific amount of taxable income (not simply on a "marginal" tax bracket). With federal income tax law being extremely complex, and subject to rapid and substantial change, and with the client's personal circumstances being subject to changes that can affect his personal income tax picture regardless of what is happening to the Code in general, how much weight or certainty can you accord to a projected income tax rate? How does any applicable state income tax affect this?

✓ When do you assume the money will be distributed? Some projections assume that all plans and Roth IRAs are liquidated at the participant's death. This approach fails to evaluate the potential advantage of paying the benefits out gradually to a younger generation beneficiary after the participant's death. Also consider the possibility that the money may unexpectedly need to be withdrawn sooner due to illness or other setbacks.

✓ Do you assume the same investment returns for assets inside a Roth IRA, inside a traditional plan, and outside a plan?

You can not know for sure what the client's future tax rates, spending needs, or investment results will be. If the client's tax rate and investments go up, and his spending needs stay level or decline, the Roth conversion could be very profitable. If the client's tax rate and investments decline and/or spending needs accelerate, a Roth conversion could be a costly mistake. The future is unknowable. Unless the conversion is free (see ¶ 5.8.02(A)), the client might be best advised to convert some but not all of his plans to a Roth, and to consider converting more in a later year.

C.   **Beyond the spreadsheet.** There can be factors that incline a client towards or away from a Roth plan without regard to what the spreadsheet says; see ¶ 5.8.02, ¶ 5.8.03. Also, for some (many?) clients, personality outweighs computer projections: Some individuals are constitutionally attracted to Roth conversions, others are instinctively repelled by them. There can be a tendency (among advisors as well as clients) to use the computer projections and other factors not to help decide what to do, but to justify what has already been decided.

One regrettable tendency is to regard the Roth conversion decision as an all-or-nothing proposition. There are advisors who push all their clients towards Roth conversions and advisors who practically forbid their clients to convert. Clients want to convert everything or they want to convert nothing. Perhaps Roth lovers and Roth haters should both consider partial Roth conversions.

5.8.02 Factors that incline towards doing a Roth conversion

Here are factors that can tilt the balance in favor of a Roth conversion.

A.   **If conversion is "cheap" or "free."** Whether a Roth conversion will "make a profit" involves a cost-benefit analysis. If the cost is zero the decision is easy—there are only benefits. Similarly, if the cost is very low, the benefits do not have to clear a very high hurdle for the Roth conversion to win the contest. This factor makes the Roth conversion decision easy for an individual who is in a zero tax bracket temporarily (due, for example, to a net operating loss from a business). This factor also tends to make the Roth conversion favorable if the plan to be converted consists substantially of "after-tax money."

B.   **Future tax rate expected to be higher.** This factor favors a Roth conversion for a person whose personal tax rate is likely to go higher in the foreseeable future, either because of changes in his personal circumstances or because a general future tax increase is likely to apply to him.

For example, a retiree whose annual gross income (including investment income and retirement plan distributions) is likely to exceed $250,000 (in the case of a married individual; $200,000 for a single person) in future years will be subject to the 3.8 percent surtax on investment income after 2012 (see ¶ 2.1.02), resulting in a marginal tax rate of 43.6 percent on such income. A Roth conversion at the 2010 top marginal rate of 35 percent could benefit this client. Since qualified Roth IRA distributions do not increase gross income, converting to a Roth could help keep the client's future gross income below the threshold that would trigger the expected top future tax rate.

Another example: When a married person dies, the surviving spouse often will continue to receive almost as much income as the couple received while both were living, but the tax rates applicable to that income will sharply increase when the surviving spouse is filing as a single individual compared with the "married filing jointly" rates that previously applied. This prospect could encourage a married couple to start doing Roth conversions while both are living, especially if one of them is not healthy.

This factor is also at work in setting up Roth IRAs for young family members (¶ 5.8.06(C)) and when a low-income parent converts to a Roth for the benefit of high-income heirs (¶ 5.8.04(B)).

C.   **Participant does not want or need MRDs.** Money can stay in a Roth IRA much longer than in a traditional IRA, because of the different minimum distribution rules that apply (¶ 5.2.02(A)). This factor makes Roth IRAs attractive to individuals who would prefer to preserve their IRAs intact for heirs, or who do not want to deal with the annual hassle and penalty risk of MRDs.

D.   **Spend down "outside" assets.** An individual concerned about potential creditors' claims should consider the relative vulnerability of his assets outside vs. inside an IRA. If (based on the configuration of his assets, the nature of the potential claims, and applicable state or bankruptcy exemption laws) he concludes that assets inside an IRA are better protected than "outside" assets, he can convert his IRA to a Roth IRA, thereby spending down the outside assets, and using them to beef up the relative value of the "inside" assets, by prepaying the income taxes on the IRA. A person who is concerned about his own tendency to (wastefully?) spend "outside" assets could use a Roth conversion to decrease those outside assets in a productive way.

E.   **Diversification of tax risk.** The Code changes constantly. Recent decades have seen changes that discriminated against retirement plan assets (such as the 15% excise tax on "excess" plan accumulations and distributions that applied, under § 4980A, from 1987–1996, and the low 15 percent tax rate applicable through 2010 to certain dividends and capital gains earned outside a plan); as well as changes that favor retirement benefits (for example, the 3.8% investment income surtax (¶ 2.1.02) will not apply to retirement plan distributions). A client can diversify his tax risk by placing some bets on every "box": traditional plan, Roth IRA, and outside investments.

F.   **Control of taxable income levels.** To control levels of taxable income, ideally, a retiree would have a combination of traditional and Roth retirement plans and outside investments. That way, taxable income can be increased (to use up deductions or take advantage of lower tax brackets) by taking more from the traditional plans, or spending can be financed without increasing taxes by withdrawing from a Roth IRA or outside investments. A large slug of income in the conversion year could result in many later years of lower income for purposes of graduated income tax brackets, Medicare premiums, and the taxability of Social Security benefits (§ 86).

G.   **Longevity insurance.** Roth IRAs have appeal for retirees who expect to live beyond the average life expectancy due to their genetic heritage and/or health. A traditional IRA participant approaching age 70½ faces forced distributions that may substantially diminish the account over a long life span. With a traditional IRA, the way to maximize tax deferral is to die prematurely, leaving benefits to a young beneficiary. By converting the traditional IRA to a Roth IRA, this person can eliminate the forced lifetime distributions and reverse the usual rule of thumb: The way to minimize taxes with a *Roth* IRA is to live as long as humanly possible, deferring the commencement of ANY distributions until that way-later-than-normal death (and then leave the benefits to a young beneficiary to get the long life expectancy payout).

5.8.03 *Factors that incline against a Roth conversion*

Here are factors that tilt in favor of not spending money to convert existing traditional plans to a Roth IRA.

A.   **Investment risk.** If the client's investments decline in value, that is a "bad thing" regardless of whether the investments were held in a traditional or a Roth plan. Nevertheless, it is financially worse when the decline occurs inside a Roth plan, because the client has also lost the income tax money he paid for the conversion. At least when investments tank inside a traditional plan, Uncle Sam is sharing the loss. (This factor would be of less concern to someone whose IRA investments are in cash or some type of guaranteed-return annuity product.)

Ruby Example: Ruby has a $1 million IRA and $350,000 of cash outside her IRA. She converts the IRA to a Roth and spends the $350,000 of cash paying the income tax on that conversion. Then the IRA's value declines to $700,000. Ruby ends up with $700,000 of after-tax money (inside the Roth IRA). If she had *not* converted, the IRA would have shrunk to $700,000 and she would still have the outside cash; she could then have cashed out the $700,000 IRA, paid tax of only $245,000 on that distribution, and been left with $755,000 of after-tax money instead of $700,000.

B.   **Future tax rate lower.** The Roth deal is unfavorable if the benefits would be subject to income taxes at a lower rate when they come out than the rate the participant paid to convert the plan to a Roth. For Americans (the majority?) who will be in a lower bracket after retirement than they are during their working years, the Roth conversion seems unlikely to be profitable.

C.   **Legislative risk.** Prepaying the income tax would also presumably turn out to be a bad deal if the income tax is replaced by a value-added tax (VAT), or if income tax rates are substantially reduced when Congress adds a VAT. One skeptic won't "Roth" because he expects that retired baby boomers will use their electoral clout to cause Congress to make *all* pensions wholly or largely tax-free.

A perhaps more realistic worry is that Congress, in a desperate search for revenue, will seek ways to diminish the benefits of the Roth account, especially if there are massive conversions by "the rich" trying to keep their taxes in check. Presumably Congress would not simply declare that Roth distributions are taxable after all, but they could: make Roth IRAs subject to lifetime minimum distribution rules, or faster post-death minimum distribution rules; mandate that all of a Roth's earnings accrued after a certain date would be taxable; subject Roth distributions to income tax, with a credit being given for taxes previously paid; and/or count Roth IRA distributions as income for purposes of Medicare premiums, the taxability of Social Security benefits, the alternative minimum tax, or the "threshold" for the post-2012 surtax on investment income (¶ 2.1.02).

The question is, how much weight should be given to these prospective scenarios? Should a client bet everything on these possible outcomes and convert nothing to a Roth IRA, despite a projection that (if these negative rule changes do NOT occur) the Roth conversion would be favorable for him?

5.8.04 *How participant's conversion helps beneficiaries*

Beneficiaries of a traditional IRA can NOT convert that inherited IRA to a Roth. ¶ 4.2.05(A). If the participant converts his IRA to a Roth IRA prior to death, that conversion can benefit his beneficiaries:

A.   **Reduce estate taxes.** Converting to a Roth IRA can reduce the participant's *estate taxes* by removing the income taxes due on the Roth conversion from the gross estate. Unlike gift taxes payable on gifts made within three years of death, income tax paid (or due) on a Roth conversion is NOT brought back into the estate for purposes of computing estate taxes. If the participant dies owning a traditional retirement plan, and the estate is subject to estate taxes, the plan beneficiaries do get an income tax deduction for the federal estate taxes paid (the "IRD deduction"; see ¶ 4.6.04). However the IRD deduction often does not fully eliminate the "double tax" effect, because (1) the beneficiaries get no income tax deduction for *state* estate taxes and (2) as an itemized deduction, the IRD deduction may be reduced if the beneficiary has a high income (see § 68). For deaths in 2010, see ¶ 4.3.08.

B. **Low bracket parent, high bracket children.** A participant may do a Roth conversion to save *income taxes* for his beneficiaries:

Rhonda Example: Rhonda is a widow, age 65, living happily on her Social Security payments plus $50,000 a year withdrawn from a substantial traditional IRA. Her children are all in the highest income tax bracket, and some day those high brackets will apply to distributions the children take from the traditional IRA they inherit at her death. She can convert some of the traditional IRA to a Roth IRA each year to use up her lower income tax brackets. The high-bracket children will pay no income tax on distributions from the inherited Roth IRA.

C. **Simplify beneficiaries' lives.** Even if the pure mathematics indicate no advantage to having the participant pay the income tax on the retirement benefits now by converting to a Roth (rather than having the beneficiaries pay it later when they inherit a traditional plan), it would be a convenience to the beneficiaries to inherit a Roth IRA (distributions from which are tax-free) rather than a traditional IRA, so they do not to have to wrestle with the valuable but complicated IRD deduction every year (see "A").

5.8.05 *Annual contributions: Traditional vs. Roth plan*

This section discusses the choice between contributing to a Roth IRA vs. contributing to a traditional IRA, and contributing to a DRAC vs. a traditional 401(k), 403(b), or governmental 457(b) account.

A. **Traditional vs. Roth IRA.** An individual who has compensation income, and whose AGI is under the limits described at ¶ 5.3.04(C), has the option to contribute to a Roth IRA. If he is under age 70½ (as of the end of the tax year) he *also* has the option to contribute to a traditional IRA instead of to a Roth IRA, or to contribute part of his maximum permitted regular contribution amount (¶ 5.3.03) to each type of IRA. Assuming he wants to contribute to an IRA, and is eligible to contribute to either type, which type should he contribute to?

The decision is easy if the choice is between a Roth contribution and a *nondeductible* contribution to a traditional IRA. If there is no tax deduction for the IRA contribution, then the Roth option is "free." A Roth IRA is always better than a traditional IRA if it's free. See ¶ 5.8.02(A). A traditional IRA contribution is either totally or partially nondeductible if the individual and/or his or her spouse participates in a workplace retirement plan and had modified adjusted gross income (AGI) in excess of certain amounts. § 219(g)(3)(B).

Similarly, the decision is easy if the individual's taxable income is so low he is not subject to income tax, since, again, he gives up nothing by opting to contribute to the Roth IRA.

If neither the individual (nor his spouse) is an active participant in an employer plan; or, if he (or his spouse) is an active participant in an employer plan, but his (or their) AGI is low enough that he can get a tax deduction for a contribution to a traditional IRA; *and* his (or their) tax bracket is higher than zero; then his choice is between a *deductible* traditional IRA contribution (which could save him some current income taxes) and the nondeductible Roth IRA contribution. He should consider the factors discussed at ¶ 5.8.01–¶ 5.8.04 in making this choice.

B.   Traditional CODA account vs. DRAC. Which participants in a cash-or-deferred arrangement (CODA) plan should choose the DRAC (¶ 5.7)? By choosing the DRAC, the individual gives up the immediate tax savings of having the contribution excluded from his income in exchange for the hope of tax-free distributions later. The choice could be made considering whichever of the factors listed in ¶ 5.8.01–¶ 5.8.04 are applicable.

Eric Example: Eric has a choice of building his savings either inside or outside retirement plans. He prefers to maximize his savings inside tax-favored retirement plans, because he believes such savings are safer from potential creditors and from his own tendency to overspend. He also finds investing easier inside a retirement plan, because there is no need to track the cost basis and holding period of each investment. He figures that by contributing $15,000 to a traditional 401(k) he's really stashing away only about $10,000, because (based on his income tax bracket) the plan "owes" the government roughly 33 percent income tax on the contribution. He will have to pay that "debt" when he withdraws money from the traditional plan. With a Roth account, he is in effect increasing his plan contribution. Contributing $15,000 to a Roth plan is equivalent to contributing $22,500 to a traditional plan.

5.8.06 *Roth plans and the estate plan*

Here are matters the estate planner needs to consider in connection with a client's Roth plans or conversions.

Note: Though qualified distributions from Roth IRAs and DRACs are exempt from *income tax*, these accounts are not exempt from *estate tax*; they are includible in the participant's gross estate just as traditional plans and IRAs are (see ¶ 4.3).

A.   **Choice of death beneficiary.** Roth benefits generally should not be left to <u>charity</u>; there is no point in prepaying the income taxes on money being left to a tax-exempt entity. This principle may require an individual who participates in a CODA plan to designate different beneficiaries for his DRAC and traditional accounts in the plan. See Form 3.7, Appendix B.

A Roth plan could ease the problems of leaving retirement benefits to a "qualified domestic trust" (QDOT; § 2056A) for the benefit of a <u>noncitizen spouse</u>, as compared with leaving traditional (taxable) benefits to such a trust. Many of the problems of leaving traditional retirement benefits to a trust for a noncitizen spouse arise from the fact that such benefits are taxable as income in respect of a decedent; see the *Special Report: Retirement Benefits and the Marital Deduction (Including Planning for the Noncitizen Spouse)* (Appendix C). The Roth plan eliminates this problem.

By leaving Roth plan death benefits (rather than traditional plan death benefits) to his grandchildren (or to a "see-through trust" for their benefit), the participant gives his beneficiaries the advantage of long-term tax-free investment accumulations and does not "waste" any of the <u>GST exemption</u> (see ¶ 6.4.07) paying income taxes. For economic advantages of a "stretch" payout of a retirement plan to young beneficiaries, see ¶ 1.1.03; for how to achieve a stretch payout for a trust named as beneficiary, see ¶ 6.2–¶ 6.3.

Whenever a client is leaving retirement benefits to a trust that is likely to accumulate some of the plan distributions, be aware that a trust goes into the highest income tax bracket (and will become subject to the 3.8% investment income "surtax"; ¶ 2.1.02) at a very low level of taxable income (see ¶ 6.5.01). If the client can prepay the income tax at a lower rate by converting the plan to a Roth IRA that option should be considered.

Using a Roth IRA to fund a credit shelter trust for the life benefit of the participant's surviving spouse, or a QTIP trust, does not make best use of the Roth IRA, for the following reason. The way to maximize the tax-free accumulation in a Roth IRA is to leave it outright to the participant's surviving spouse, who then rolls it over to her own Roth IRA and takes no distributions from it during her lifetime. At her death she leaves it to a younger beneficiary for a stretched-out tax-free life expectancy payout. This approach allows total accumulation of all earnings inside the tax-free Roth as long as either spouse is living, with a life expectancy payout to a younger beneficiary after both spouses' deaths.

In contrast, the longest distribution period possible for a Roth IRA left to a *trust* for the benefit of the spouse is the spouse's life expectancy; the account will be distributed over her life expectancy (not accumulated during her lifetime), and be reduced to zero at the end of her life expectancy. See ¶ 3.3.02(B).

B.   Document changes needed to anticipate Roth conversion. The client's durable power of attorney should give the power-holder the power to convert any traditional plan or IRA to a Roth IRA and to recharacterize any IRA contribution made by the client. See Form 5.1, Appendix B.

Since the client's executor may have the power to recharacterize a Roth conversion made by the client (see ¶ 4.1.02), the client's estate planning documents may need to be amended to guide the executor or facilitate (or inhibit) a post-mortem recharacterization. Consider:

✓   Including in the will an equalizing bequest to the Roth IRA beneficiary to compensate him for loss of the account's tax-free status if the executor recharacterizes.

✓   Including in the beneficiary designation form language that will prevent the Roth IRA beneficiary from blocking the executor's recharacterization of a Roth conversion.

✓   Giving the executor instructions, guidance, and/or protection regarding the recharacterization decision. Approaches that various practitioners have suggested include requiring recharacterization if the account value drops by more than certain percentage (and forbidding it otherwise), or requiring recharacterization if requested by certain beneficiaries. See Form 5.3, Appendix B.

C.   **Gifts with Roth IRAs.** Depositing money in a Roth IRA for teenage children, grandchildren, etc., has appeal as a gifting technique if the young family members have summer or after-school jobs that generate compensation income on which an IRA contribution can be based. The projections of what a $5,000 contribution will grow to by the time the 15-year-old child reaches age 65 can be staggering. What gives pause is that there is no way to prevent the donee from taking the money out of the account once he reaches the age of majority.

For this idea to work, the child must have compensation income. ¶ 5.3.02. If a parent pays his toddler a salary for performing household chores, the IRS might maintain that the child has received a gift, not compensation, and that Roth IRA contributions based on this "compensation" are excess contributions subject to a penalty (¶ 5.3.05).

Donating cash to another individual's Roth IRA is a cash gift and does not create any particular problems. However, if the participant assigns *his own* Roth IRA by lifetime gift "to another individual," the gift causes the Roth IRA to be deemed distributed to the owner-donor, and accordingly it ceases to be a Roth IRA. Reg. § 1.408A-6, A-19.

6

Leaving Retirement Benefits in Trust

Minimum distribution, income tax, and
trust accounting considerations when
retirement benefits are left in trust

6.1 Trust as Beneficiary: Preliminaries

This ¶ 6.1 provides, first, a checklist for drafting a trust to be named as beneficiary of a retirement plan. The rest of ¶ 6.1 covers how trust accounting rules apply to retirement benefits payable to a trust as beneficiary; the transfer of retirement benefit accounts into and out of trusts; and the "individual retirement trust" (or "trusteed IRA" or "IRT").

6.1.01 Trust as beneficiary: Drafting checklist

When the estate plan calls for naming a trust as beneficiary of retirement benefits, use this checklist to review planning and drafting considerations uniquely applicable to such assets:

1. Is there a strong estate planning reason to name a trust as beneficiary, or is there a way to achieve the planning goals without incurring the risks and complications of naming a trust?

In view of the complications and other disadvantages involved in making retirement benefits payable to a trust, the bias is in favor of leaving the benefits outright to the intended beneficiaries unless there is a compelling reason to leave them in trust. The rest of this checklist deals with drafting the trust, once it has been decided to name a trust as beneficiary.

2.   If the trust contains special provisions dealing with retirement
        benefits, be sure you define "retirement benefits."

3.   Draft the dispositive terms so they will operate on the
        retirement benefits in accordance with the donor's intent. For
        example: If the trust's dispositive terms will distinguish
        between "income" and "principal" consider how these terms
        will apply to the retirement plan and to distributions from it.
        See ¶ 6.1.02. If a beneficiary is given the annual right to
        withdraw "five percent of the trust principal," will the
        withdrawal power apply to the gross value of any retirement
        benefit that is payable to the trust (with or without a reduction
        for the built-in income tax "debt")? Or will it apply only to
        amounts the trustee has actually withdrawn from the retirement
        plan?

4.   If the trust is intended to qualify for the federal estate tax
        marital deduction, comply with the requirements described in
        ¶ 3.3.02–¶ 3.3.09 and ¶ 6.1.02(D).

5.   Determine whether see-through trust status is important
        (¶ 6.2.01), and, if it is important, make sure the trust complies
        with IRS's MRD trust rules. ¶ 6.2–¶ 6.3. "Precatory" language
        urging the trustee to take steps to achieve the stretch payout is
        not enough; see ¶ 4.5.06(A). The trust should be drafted so that
        it qualifies as a see-through trust *without* the necessity of any
        trust amendments or reformations after the client's death.

6.   If the trust is to be divided into multiple shares or subtrusts for
        the benefit of different beneficiaries upon the client's death, see
        ¶ 6.3.01 regarding whether, if retirement benefits are allocated
        only to one particular share, beneficiaries of the other shares are
        disregarded for MRD purposes, and ¶ 6.3.02 regarding how the
        "separate accounts" rule applies to trusts. If the benefits are to
        pass to multiple beneficiaries, and separate accounts treatment
        is important, leave the benefits to the various beneficiaries
        directly (i.e., do not leave the benefits to a trust to be divided
        among the multiple beneficiaries) in the beneficiary designation
        form. See Form 3.5, Appendix B. For the same reason, if
        leaving benefits to a trust for the participant's surviving spouse,
        and the trust is to pass outright to the participant's issue on the

death of the surviving spouse, name the trust as beneficiary only if the participant's spouse survives the participant; name the issue directly as contingent beneficiaries if the spouse does not survive. See ¶ 6.3.02 and Form 3.4, Appendix B.

7.   To avoid the issue of whether funding a pecuniary bequest with the "right to receive IRD" is a taxable transfer (¶ 6.5.08), avoid having retirement benefits pass through a pecuniary funding formula. If benefits must pass to a trust, make them payable to a trust that will not be divided up. If benefits are going to a trust that will be divided, either specify clearly (in both the beneficiary designation form and the trust instrument) which trust share these retirement benefits go to (so that the benefits pass to the chosen share directly, rather than through the funding formula), or use a fractional formula (fulfillment of which does not trigger immediate realization of IRD) rather than a pecuniary formula (which may).

8.   Including a spendthrift clause poses no MRD issues, even in a conduit trust. Since the Code itself imposes spendthrift restrictions on retirement plans (see § 401(a)(13)), such clauses are favored by government policy.

9.   Consider whether certain classes of income should be directed to certain beneficiaries. For example, in a trust that authorizes the trustee to accumulate retirement plan distributions (¶ 6.3.07), the trust could direct the trustee to distribute all "investment income" to the life beneficiary, to avoid having the post-2012 "surtax" on investment income (¶ 2.1.02) imposed on the trust; this could make sense if it is expected that the trust beneficiary will probably not have a high enough income to incur the surtax. Such an allocation of a specific class of income is respected for income tax purposes if it has independent economic effect; see ¶ 7.4.03(E).

10.   If the trust has charitable and noncharitable beneficiaries, either direct the retirement benefits to be used to fund the charitable gifts (if the goal is to have the benefits pass income tax-free to the charities) or forbid such use (if the goal is to achieve a stretch payout for the trust's individual beneficiaries).

6.1.02 *Trust accounting for retirement benefits*

Suppose a trust is the beneficiary of a deceased client's $1 million IRA. The trust provides that the trustee is to pay all income of the trust to the client's surviving spouse for life, and at the spouse's death the trustee is to distribute the principal of the trust to the client's children. The trust receives a $50,000 minimum required distribution (MRD; see Chapter 1) from the IRA. Is that distribution "income" that the trustee is required to pay to the spouse? Or is it "principal" that the trustee must hold for future distribution to the client's children? Or some of each?

A.   **Trust accounting income vs. federal gross income.** A retirement plan distribution generally will constitute gross income to the trust for federal income tax purposes (¶ 6.5.01), but that same distribution may be "principal" (or "corpus," to use the IRS's preferred term) for trust accounting purposes:

Jorge Example: Jorge dies leaving his $1 million 401(k) plan to a trust for his son. The trustee is to pay the trust "income" to the son annually, and distribute the "principal" to the son when he reaches age 35. The 401(k) plan distributes a $1 million lump sum to the trustee a few days after Jorge's death. This is not a "required" distribution; the trustee simply requested the distribution from the plan. Barring an unusual provision in the trust instrument or applicable state law, the entire $1 million plan distribution is considered the trust "corpus." On the federal income tax return for the trust's first year, the trust must report the $1 million distribution as gross income, because it is "income" for income tax purposes even though it is "principal" for trust accounting purposes. The trustee invests the money that's left after paying the income tax on the distribution, and pays the income (interest and dividends) from the investments each year to Jorge's son.

B.   **Trust accounting income vs. MRD.** See Chapter 1 and ¶ 6.2–¶ 6.3 regarding the "minimum distribution rules." MRDs and trust accounting income are totally different and unrelated concepts.

C.   **State law; the 10 percent rule of UPIA 1997.** If the "trust accounting income" attributable to a retirement plan held by the trust is not the same as federal gross income, and is not the same as the MRD, what is it? Unless the trust has its own definition (which is the preferred solution; see ¶ 6.1.03(B)), the answer is determined by state law.

For example, the 1997 Uniform Principal and Income Act ("UPIA"), which was adopted by a majority of states, provides trust accounting rules for retirement plan distributions. UPIA § 409 governs the trust accounting treatment of (among other things) any "payment" from an IRA or pension plan.

UPIA § 409(c), which governs IRA and most other retirement plan distributions, provides: If "all or part of the payment is required to be made, a trustee shall allocate to income 10 percent of the part that is required to be made during the accounting period and the balance to principal." This is known as "the **10 percent rule**." A nonrequired payment is allocated entirely to principal.

Unfortunately, the 10 percent rule will provide too little income in most cases, especially if the benefits are being paid out over a long life expectancy. For example, if the trust's Applicable Distribution Period (ADP; ¶ 1.2.03) is the 40-year life expectancy of the oldest trust beneficiary (¶ 6.2.01), the first year's MRD will be [account balance] ÷ [40], i.e., only 2.5 percent of the value of the retirement benefits. That is already a low percentage, and the "income" portion of the distribution under UPIA § 409(c) would be only 10 percent of that. It seems unlikely that a trust donor would choose this method of determining the amount of "income" distributed to the life beneficiary.

D.   **Income for a marital deduction trust.** Trust accounting sometimes matters for tax purposes; most importantly for estate planners, the definition of "income" matters for purposes of the federal estate tax marital deduction. Generally, the surviving spouse must be entitled for life to all income of a trust in order for such trust to qualify for the federal estate tax marital deduction. § 2056(b)(7). This subsection "D" discusses what the "income" is that the spouse must be "entitled to" with respect to *retirement benefits* left to a trust, in order for such trust to qualify for the federal estate tax marital deduction. See ¶ 3.3.01–¶ 3.3.07 for how to meet the "entitled" (and other) requirements to obtain the marital deduction for retirement benefits left to a trust.

A definition of "income" provided by the governing instrument or by applicable state law will be accepted for tax purposes if it "provides for a reasonable apportionment between the income and remainder beneficiaries of the total return of the trust for the year...." See § 643(b) and Regs. § 1.643(b)-1, § 20.2056(b)-5(f)(1). The IRS found that the UPIA 1997's 10 percent rule (see "C" above) of determining income *does not satisfy the marital deduction income requirements* of § 20.2056(b)-5(f)(1) and § 1.643(b)-1, because the amount of the...[MRD] is not based on the total return of the IRA (and therefore the amount allocated to income does not reflect a reasonable apportionment of the total return between the income and remainder beneficiaries)." Rev. Rul. 2006-26, 2006-22 I.R.B. 939; emphasis added.

The IRS then explained what it views as the "income" of a retirement plan that the surviving spouse must be entitled to when such plan is payable to a marital deduction trust: either the plan's internal investment income ("trust-within-a-trust" concept; see ¶ 6.1.03(C)) or an acceptable (i.e., 3%–5%) annual "unitrust" percentage amount (see ¶ 6.1.04).

Because of problems with the 10 percent rule, the American College of Trust & Estate Counsel (ACTEC), through its Employee Benefits Committee, and other interested groups are seeking to have the UPIA amended to eliminate it. A number of states have modified § 409 so that retirement plan distributions received by the trust are accounted for using a unitrust or trust-within-a-trust approach rather than the 10 percent rule. Unfortunately, most states' approaches still do not satisfy the IRS's definition, because their rules account only for *distributions* the trustee receives from the retirement plan, not for the investment results "inside" the retirement plan. Some other states have not adopted the 1997 UPIA at all. The bottom line is that every drafter and trustee must check the applicable state law regarding its definition of "income" with respect to retirement benefits payable to the trust.

6.1.03 *Trust accounting: Drafting solutions*

There are three ways to avoid the problems discussed in ¶ 6.1.02: draft a totally discretionary trust (see "A" below); define income as it applies to retirement plan benefits (see "B" and "C"); or use the "unitrust" approach (see ¶ 6.1.04). For a marital deduction trust, use "C" or the "unitrust" approach; do not use "A."

This ¶ 6.1.03 gives an overview of this subject; it does not provide sufficient detail to enable the drafter to prepare a trust instrument without studying the applicable state law and IRS standards set forth in regulations under § 643 and in Rev. Rul. 2006-26. Also, this discussion deals with planning approaches; the trustee of a trust that is *already operative* needs to comply with the terms of the instrument and applicable state law to determine the trust's income, and does not have the option to simply adopt whatever method is appealing.

A.   **Draft so the definition of "income" doesn't matter.** The trust accounting question may be unimportant in a totally discretionary trust. For example, if the trust provides that the trustee shall pay to the life beneficiary "such amounts of the income and/or principal of the trust as the trustee deems advisable in its discretion from time to time," it will make no difference whether the internal income of (or a distribution from) a particular retirement plan is treated as income or principal for trust accounting purposes. The beneficiaries' substantive rights do not depend on whether a particular asset or receipt is classified as income or principal.

However, if the trustee's compensation is based on differing percentages of trust income and principal, even a totally discretionary trust will have to resolve the income/principal question regarding the retirement benefits. Also, this approach generally cannot be used for a marital deduction trust (¶ 6.1.02(D)).

B.   **Draft your own definition of income.** Another way to deal with the trust accounting problem is to provide, in the trust instrument, how retirement benefits are to be accounted for. This solution is recommended because even if the applicable state law definition at the time the trust is drafted suits the client's needs, the state law could change.

What should such a trust accounting provision say? First determine what the client is trying to accomplish. If the client wants his beneficiary to receive the "income" of the trust, find out what the client thinks that means with respect to the retirement benefits. Second, see ¶ 6.1.02(D) if the trust must comply with the IRS's definition of income.

C.   **"Trust within a trust" approach.** One approach, which works for IRAs and other "transparent" defined contribution plans where the trustee controls the plan's investments, and can readily determine exactly how much income those investments earn and when, is to treat the retirement plan as a "trust-within-a-trust": Investment income earned inside the plan is treated as trust income just as if it had been earned in the trust's taxable account. The IRS has approved this approach for marital deduction trusts. ¶ 6.1.02(D).

Debra Example: Debra's trust provides that after her death the trustee shall pay all "income" of the trust (including income of any retirement plan payable to the trust as beneficiary) to Debra's son Winston annually. The trust is the beneficiary of Debra's IRA, and also holds stocks and bonds in a taxable account. In Year X, the trust earns $4,000 of interest and dividends in the taxable account, and the IRA receives $3,000 of interest and dividends from its investments. The trustee withdraws from the IRA $3,000 (or the MRD for Year X, whichever is greater; see ¶ 6.2), and distributes $7,000 to Winston.

The trust-within-a-trust approach will not work for a defined benefit plan (¶ 8.3.04), or any other plan where the trustee cannot readily get the information needed to compute the plan's internal income. Thus, there must be some type of default rule to cover these plans. A unitrust approach is recommended for the default rule, if permitted by applicable state law; see ¶ 6.1.04.

6.1.04 *"Total return" or "unitrust" method*

A trend in trust drafting is to eschew "income" and "principal" concepts in favor of a "total return" (also called "unitrust") approach: The life beneficiary receives a fixed percentage (unitrust percentage) of the value of the trust's assets each year, rather than receiving the traditional trust accounting income of rents, interest, and dividends. The UPIA 1997 (¶ 6.1.02(C)) permits the unitrust method of trust accounting.

The IRS will accept a definition of income based on the unitrust method if that method is permitted by state law *and* the annual fixed percentage to which the income beneficiary is entitled is not less than three nor more than five percent of the trust's value (with "value" either being determined annually or being averaged on a multiple year basis). Reg. § 1.643(b)-1.

Retirement benefits pose a valuation problem for the unitrust approach: Should the built-in income tax liability be deducted from the nominal value of the benefits? That issue can be avoided by distributing, each year, the required percentage of the retirement plan assets and the required percentage of the nonretirement assets. This method of implementing the unitrust approach was blessed, for a marital deduction trust, in Rev. Rul. 2006-26 (¶ 6.1.02(D)).

6.1.05 *Transferring a retirement plan out of a trust or estate*

When a trust terminates, the trustee can transfer, intact, to the residuary beneficiaries of the trust, any IRA or other retirement plan then held by the trust. The same applies to the participant's estate (if the benefits pass to the estate as either named or default beneficiary), and to the estate of a beneficiary who dies prior to withdrawing all the benefits from an inherited retirement plan: The estate can transfer the IRA or plan to the estate's beneficiaries. This ¶ 6.1.05 explains the legal basis under which such transfers are permitted. See ¶ 6.5.07–¶ 6.5.08 for the federal income tax effects of such a transfer.

A.   **Transferability of retirement benefits.** An IRA is transferable. The owner of an IRA (whether such owner is the participant or the beneficiary of the account) can transfer the ownership of the account to another person or entity. Nothing in § 408 (the statute the creates IRAs) prohibits transferring an IRA; on the contrary, the Code recognizes that IRAs can be assigned, since it discusses transfer of an IRA in connection with divorce (§ 408(d)(6)) and pledging the account as security for a loan (§ 408(e)(4)). The Treasury confirmed in CCA 2006-44020 that an IRA is transferable. The question is not whether the account can be transferred; the question is whether such transfer will terminate the account's status as an IRA, causing an immediate deemed distribution. See ¶ 2.1.06.

With respect to nonIRA plans, such as QRPs, the plan account generally "may not be assigned or alienated" (§ 401(a)(13)(A)); this is ERISA's "anti-alienation rule" (see ¶ 4.4.09(A)). The anti-alienation rule is intended to prevent assignment (voluntary or involuntary) of the benefits to creditors of the participant or beneficiary, or any attempt to borrow against or sell the benefits. The rule has no bearing on the disposition of the benefits at the death of the participant (when the benefits are "assigned" to the beneficiary), or at the subsequent death of the beneficiary (which, again, causes the benefits to be "transferred" to someone else) or upon the termination of the existence of the beneficiary (in the case of an estate or trust which is closing). Transfers of benefits out of a trust or estate to the trust or estate beneficiary(ies) are transfers *to* the participant's beneficiary, not transfers *away* from the beneficiary.

Numerous PLRs have recognized these principles; the PLRs take it for granted that the benefits can be transferred out of an estate or trust, and address only the income tax consequences of such transfers. See "C" below. For an opposing viewpoint, see "D" below.

A trust can make such a transfer to its beneficiaries regardless of whether the trust qualifies as a "see-through trust" under the minimum distribution rules (¶ 6.2); an estate can make such a transfer even though an estate can NEVER qualify as a "Designated Beneficiary" (¶ 1.7.04).

The transfer of an inherited retirement plan or IRA from a trust or estate to the beneficiary(ies) of the trust or estate has *no effect* on the Applicable Distribution Period for the benefits. Such a transfer is *solely* for the purpose of allowing the trust or estate to terminate or otherwise cease to have control of the benefits. Furthermore, there is not much point in doing this type of transfer (and the plan probably won't allow it anyway) if the plan is a qualified plan and is payable to the estate, because the plan will normally pay benefits only in the form of a lump sum. The transfer procedure is most useful for IRAs, not other types of plans. Do NOT confuse these transfers with the nonspouse beneficiary rollover to an inherited IRA (¶ 4.2.04).

See Form 5.4, Appendix B, for how to request such a transfer.

B.   Examples of fiduciary transfers of inherited retirement plans. Here are some common examples of situations in which such transfers are called for:

Foster Example: Division into marital and family trusts. Foster dies, leaving his IRA to the Foster Revocable Trust as beneficiary. The Foster Revocable Trust provides that, upon Foster's death, the trustee is to divide all assets of the trust into two separate trusts, the Marital Trust and the Family Trust, pursuant to a fractional formula. All retirement benefits are to be allocated to the Marital Trust. The trustee instructs the IRA provider to change the name of the owner of the inherited IRA (see ¶ 4.2.01) from "Foster Revocable Trust, as beneficiary of Foster, deceased," to "Marital Trust, as beneficiary of Foster, deceased." The trustee has transferred the IRA from the Foster Revocable Trust to the Marital Trust.

Stanley Example: Trust termination upon spouse's death. Stanley names his testamentary trust as beneficiary of his IRA. The trust provides that, after Stanley's death, the trustee is to pay income of the trust to Mrs. Stanley for life. On her death, the trust is to terminate, with the principal of the trust passing to Stanley's son Yishai. The trustee takes annual MRDs from Stanley's IRA computed using the life expectancy of Mrs. Stanley, which is 18 years, as the ADP (¶ 6.2.01). Mrs. Stanley dies 12 years later. It is now time for the trust to terminate. There are still six years left in the ADP. The trustee instructs the IRA provider to change the titling of the inherited IRA from "Stanley Testamentary Trust, as beneficiary of Stanley, deceased," to "Yishai, as successor beneficiary of Stanley, deceased." The trustee has transferred the IRA from the testamentary trust to the trust's remainder beneficiary.

Noah Example: Division among multiple children. Noah dies, leaving his IRA to the Noah Family Trust as named beneficiary. The trust provides that, upon Noah's death, the trust is to be divided into three equal shares, one for each of Noah's sons Shem, Ham, and Japheth. Shem and Ham are to receive their shares outright; Japheth's share is to be held in trust for him for life, with remainder outright at Japheth's death to Japheth's issue, if any, otherwise to Shem and Ham outright. Upon learning of Noah's death, the IRA provider titled the IRA "Noah Family Trust, as beneficiary of Noah," and the trust's taxpayer identification number was attached to the account. See ¶ 4.2.01. The trustee now instructs the IRA provider to divide the IRA into three equal accounts, and to change the titling of two of those accounts. One account is to be retitled "Shem, as beneficiary of Noah," and the other "Ham, as beneficiary of Noah." The trustee has transferred two thirds of the IRA from the trust to these two sons. The Social Security numbers of Shem and Ham will be associated with those two inherited IRAs. The third inherited IRA created out of Noah's IRA stays in the trust (to be held for the life benefit of Japheth), so its titling (and associated taxpayer identification number) do not change for now.

C.   **PLRs approving these transfers.** Many private letter rulings have approved the transfer of inherited IRAs and other plans from the trust named as beneficiary of the plan to the individual trust beneficiaries. PLR 2001-31033 (Rulings 5, 6, and 7) is typical. This ruling allowed the transfer of "IRA Y" from a terminating trust to the participant's children, C and D. From the ruling: "The provision of Trust X which provides for its termination does not change either the identity of the individuals who will receive the IRA Y proceeds or the identity of the designated beneficiary of IRA Y.... Furthermore, the Trust X termination language which results in distributions from IRA Y being made directly to Taxpayers C and D instead of initially to Trust X and then to Taxpayers C and D was language in Trust X approved by [the participant] during his lifetime which reflects [the participant's] intent to pay his children directly instead of through Trust X."

Other rulings approving the transfer of a retirement plan from a trust to the trust beneficiaries (without requiring termination of the plan account or otherwise triggering immediate income tax) are: regarding IRAs, PLRs 2000-13041, 2001-09051; 2003-29048 (IRA payable to a trust divided into four "sub-IRAs," each to be held by one of the individual trust beneficiaries); 2004-33019; 2004-49040–2004-49042; 2005-26010; 2006-15032; 2006-18023 (involving a nonqualified annuity); 2007-40018; 2007-50019; 2008-03002 (annuity contract); 2008-26028; and 2009-35045. Regarding transfer of an inherited IRA to *charitable* residuary beneficiaries, see 2006-52028 (discussed at ¶ 7.4.05)

For rulings permitting Beneficiary IRAs to be opened directly in the name of the individual trust beneficiaries (rather than first in the name of the trust), where the IRA was payable to a trust that was to terminate immediately upon the participant's death and be distributed outright to the individual beneficiaries, see PLRs 2005-38030, -38031, -38033, and -38034.

PLRs 2002-34019 and 2008-50058 permitted retirement benefits to be transferred, intact, out of an estate to the estate beneficiaries. In PLR 2010-13033, an IRA was payable to an estate; the IRS permitted transfer of the IRA from the estate to the "pourover" trust that was beneficiary of the estate, and thence to the trust's beneficiaries. For more PLRs, see ¶ 6.5.07(B).

Unfortunately, PLRs cannot be cited as authority. ¶ 6.4.02. The PLRs discussed above cite Rev. Rul. 78-406, 1978-2 C.B. 157, which established the rule that an IRA-to-IRA transfer is not a "distribution" and accordingly does not have to meet the requirements of a "rollover" (see ¶ 2.6.08). However, Rev. Rul. 78-406 did not deal with transferring an *inherited* IRA, let alone transferring it from a terminating trust (or estate) to the trust (or estate) beneficiaries. It referred to the transfer from one IRA to another IRA in the same name (the name of the participant), which is not quite the same as a transfer from an IRA in the name of a trust as beneficiary to an IRA in the name of an individual or charity as successor beneficiary.

D.   **IRA providers and plan administrators.** Some *IRA providers* (see   www.ataxplan.com/bulletin_board/ira_providers.htm) readily permit these transfers, upon receipt of proper instructions from the fiduciary of the trust or estate, plus (in some cases) an opinion of counsel. However, some IRA providers do not allow these transfers, either because the IRA provider has concluded they are not legally permissible or because the IRA provider's computer systems cannot accommodate them.

A fiduciary faced with an IRA provider's refusal to allow transfer of an inherited IRA to the trust or estate beneficiaries has four choices: #1. Cash out the plan and give up further deferral. #2. Keep the trust or estate open until the end of the ADP, to preserve continued deferral of distributions, but at the cost of ongoing administration expenses. #3. Get a ruling from the IRS, if that will convince the IRA provider to allow the transfer. #4. Move the account (still in the name of the estate or trust), by means of an IRA-to-IRA transfer (¶ 2.6.01(E), ¶ 2.6.08) to a more cooperative financial institution, and *then* transfer it to the beneficiaries. Since options #1–#3 involve substantially increased taxes or costs, #4 is encouraged.

6.1.06 *Can a participant transfer an IRA to a living trust?*

A participant's transfer of an IRA (or other retirement plan account) to a trust that is entirely a grantor trust as to him (¶ 6.3.10) should not be treated as an "assignment" of the account, since an individual and his grantor trust are deemed to be in effect "the same person" under Rev. Rul. 85-13, 1985-1 C.B. 184, *provided* that no person other than the participant can receive any distributions from the trust during the participant's life. The trust into which the IRA is transferred would be named as both owner and beneficiary of the IRA.

If the trust permits distributions to anyone other than the participant during the participant's life, the transfer might (despite Rev. Rul. 85-13) be considered a transfer of the benefits to another person, which would terminate the account's status as an IRA. See ¶ 2.1.04(B). Thus, the typical living trust provision that allows distributions to be made during the grantor's lifetime for the benefit of the grantor's dependents may not be suitable for a trust that is to hold the grantor's retirement benefits prior to his death.

Before permitting an IRA owner to transfer his IRA into a grantor trust, the IRA provider might require that the trust be irrevocable and nonamendable. If the grantor transfers his IRA to an amendable or revocable trust, the IRA administrator would have no way to know whether the trust had later been revoked or amended in some way that would disqualify the IRA.

To date there is no ruling or authority confirming or contradicting these conclusions with respect to a *participant's* transfer of his benefits to a grantor trust. See ¶ 4.6.03(C) regarding the ability of a *beneficiary* to assign an inherited plan to a grantor trust.

6.1.07 *Individual retirement trusts (trusteed IRAs)*

Individual retirement arrangements can be established in either of two legal forms, a custodial account (§ 408(h)) or a trust (§ 408(a)); both are treated identically for all tax purposes. Most IRAs are established as custodial accounts rather than as trusts. This Chapter deals with naming a trust as beneficiary of an IRA or other retirement plan; however, it should be noted that in some cases an IRA owner can use a "**trusteed IRA**" (also called an "**individual retirement trust**," or "**IRT**") in place of a standard custodial IRA payable to a separate trust as beneficiary. A Roth IRA can also be in the form of a trusteed IRA.

An IRT can combine the *substantive terms* of a trust and the *tax characteristics* of an IRA or Roth IRA. The client (IRA owner) puts the trust terms and conditions into the IRT document. The document must comply with the minimum distribution rules and all other requirements of § 408, but otherwise there's no limit on what it may provide, other than what the IRT provider is willing to accept.

Troy Example: Troy has a $1 million trusteed IRA with XYZ Trust Company. XYZ manages the investments and pays the annual MRD to Troy, along with such additional distributions as Troy may request from time to time. Upon Troy's death, XYZ, as Trustee and IRA provider, continues to hold the account for the benefit of Troy's beneficiary, his wife Joy. As provided in the IRA-trust document, XYZ pays to Joy, annually, the greater of the MRD or the income earned by the IRA, and such additional amounts as XYZ, as trustee, deems advisable for her health and support. After Joy's death, XYZ pays annually to Troy's children, in equal shares, the MRD. As each child reaches age 40, he gains the right to withdraw additional amounts from his share of the trusteed IRA.

Here are some reasons why a client might consider using an IRT instead of the more common custodial IRA:

✓   **Participant's disability**. The IRT agreement can authorize the trustee to use the IRT assets for the participant's benefit during disability. An IRA custodian will not perform those duties; custodial IRA assets can be used for the benefit of the disabled participant only through the mechanism of a durable power of attorney or guardianship.

✓   **Limit beneficiary's access**. An IRA beneficiary can generally withdraw the entire account at will. An IRT can limit the beneficiary's withdrawal rights so that the beneficiary can withdraw only the MRDs; or MRDs plus additional payments (such as for health or support). Thus, it may be used in place of a conduit trust in some cases. See ¶ 6.3.05, ¶ 6.4.05(A).

✓   **Limit beneficiary's control at beneficiary's death**. Under an IRT, but not under most custodial IRAs, the *participant* can specify the "successor beneficiary," i.e., the person or entity who will become the owner of the account after the original beneficiary's death. See ¶ 1.5.12(E).

✓   **Avoid complications of MRD trust rules.** A trust named as beneficiary of a custodial IRA must meet complicated IRS requirements to qualify as a "see-through trust" (¶ 6.2–¶ 6.3). An IRT does not have to jump through these hoops, because the trust is not the beneficiary of an IRA—it *is* the IRA.

There are two types of trusteed IRAs, custom-drafted and (for lack of a better word) "pre-approved prototype." The "prototype" form of IRT is a complete trust agreement for which the IRA provider has obtained IRS approval. It comes as a pre-printed booklet (similar to the documents establishing "custodial" IRAs, but longer), which functions as an adoption agreement. The IRA participant is given "check the box" choices for various popular trust provisions, such as: the beneficiary can withdraw only the MRD (or, for a spouse-beneficiary, the greater of the account's income or the MRD); or MRDs plus more if needed for health or support, or in the trustee's discretion; with or without the right to greater control upon reaching a certain age. If the participant's estate planning goal is met by one of these "canned" options, the participant can avoid paying a legal fee to draft a trust agreement by using a trusteed IRA.

More customizable trusteed IRAs also exist. *Any* bank can serve as trustee of a trusteed IRA; no special IRS approval is required. The bank needs to be familiar with the requirements applicable to IRA providers. Then, all that is required is for the participant and IRA provider to enter into a trust agreement that complies with § 408. The parties can use IRS Form 5305, "Traditional Individual Retirement Trust Account" (or 5305-R for a trusteed Roth IRA), adding any extra provisions appropriate for the client's estate plan as an attachment (part of "Article VIII" of Form 5305, "additional provisions"). The estate planning lawyer should have a leading role in preparing this document. IRS approval is not required and in fact cannot be obtained for an individual's IRA or IRT.

An IRT has some drawbacks: The provider's fee (or minimum account size) is typically higher than for a custodial IRA because more services are provided, but that may be appropriate if the client needs the services. Also, since the IRT must pass all MRDs out to the IRT beneficiary directly, the IRT is not suitable for a client who wants MRDs accumulated and held in the trust for future distribution to the same or another beneficiary.

6.2 The Minimum Distribution Trust Rules

As explained in Chapter 1, once a retirement plan or IRA owner (the "participant") dies, the retirement plan or IRA must make certain annual minimum required distributions (MRDs) to the beneficiary(ies) of the account. The most desirable form of post-death payout, generally, is annual instalments over the life expectancy of the beneficiary, because this allows the longest tax deferral (or tax-free accumulation, in the case of a Roth plan). See ¶ 1.1.03, ¶ 1.5.05. This sought-after "stretch" or "life expectancy" payout is available only for benefits payable to a "Designated Beneficiary" (¶ 1.7.03), which generally means an individual. However, IRS regulations allow a trust to qualify for this favorable form of payout if various requirements, explained in this ¶ 6.2 and in ¶ 6.3, are met.

6.2.01 When and why see-through trust status matters

If retirement benefits are left to a "see-through trust" (¶ 6.2.03), the benefits can be distributed in annual instalments over the life expectancy of the oldest trust beneficiary, just as if the benefits had been left to an individual human Designated Beneficiary (¶ 1.5.05). In contrast, if the trust does not qualify as a see-through trust under the rules explained here, the retirement benefits must be distributed under the "no-DB rules." The no-DB (no Designated Beneficiary) rules require that all sums be distributed out of the plan within five or six years after the participant's death, if the participant died before his required beginning date (RBD) (¶ 1.5.06); or (if the participant died *after* his RBD) over the remainder of what would have been the participant's life expectancy (¶ 1.5.08). Distribution over the life expectancy of a beneficiary usually provides substantially longer deferral than distribution under the no-DB rules.

The fact that a trust qualifies as a see-through trust does not mean that the trust is the best choice as beneficiary of the retirement benefits. Making benefits payable to a trust of which the participant's surviving spouse is the life beneficiary results in substantially less deferral than would be available (via the spousal rollover) for benefits left to the spouse outright *even if* the trust qualifies as a see-through; see ¶ 3.3.02(B). Also, benefits left to a trust may be subjected to high trust income tax rates (¶ 6.5.01), even if the trust qualifies as a see-through.

Another reminder: Complying with the IRS's minimum distribution trust rules is not a prerequisite of making retirement benefits payable to a trust. If a trust named as beneficiary of a retirement plan flunks the rules, the trust will still receive the benefits; the trust just will not have the option of using the life expectancy of the oldest trust beneficiary as the Applicable Distribution Period (ADP; ¶ 1.2.03) for those benefits.

There are some situations in which it may make little or no difference whether the trust complies with the trust rules:

✓ **Client's goals; beneficiaries' needs.** It may be appropriate to sacrifice the deferral possibilities of the life expectancy payout method in order to realize the client's other goals. See ¶ 6.4.05(D) for an example. Similarly, if it is expected that the retirement plan will have to be cashed out shortly after the participant's death to pay estate taxes or for other reasons, there is no point in making the trust qualify as a see-through.

✓ **Trust beneficiary older than participant (plans that permit stretch payouts).** If the participant dies after his RBD, leaving benefits to a see-through trust, the ADP is the life expectancy of the participant or of the oldest trust beneficiary, whichever is longer. If the trust is not a see-through, the ADP is the participant's life expectancy. If the participant is past his RBD, and the oldest trust beneficiary is the same age as (or older than) the participant, the ADP will be the same *whether or not the trust qualifies as a see-through*. Thus, qualifying as a see-through trust is IRRELEVANT if (1) the participant was past his RBD when he died and (2) the oldest trust beneficiary is either close in age to or older than the participant. *However*, if the plan in question pays death benefits only in the form of a lump sum (see ¶ 1.5.10), a trust-named-as-beneficiary will have to qualify as a see-through trust *even if* the participant died after his RBD and was younger than (or the same age as) the oldest trust beneficiary, IF the trust wants to stretch distributions over the participant's remaining life expectancy. The trust will be able to use that "short stretch" payout only if it can have the lump sum transferred out of the lump-sum-only plan by direct rollover to an inherited IRA (see ¶ 4.2.04); and the nonspouse beneficiary rollover option is available only to individual beneficiaries and *see-through* trusts. See ¶ 4.2.04(C).

✓　　**Charitable trust.** Passing the trust rules is irrelevant for an income tax-exempt charitable remainder trust; see ¶ 7.5.04.

✓　　**Lump sum is best form of distribution.** There is no need to comply with the MRD trust rules if the trust qualifies for and plans to take advantage of a lump sum distribution income tax deal such as that available for "net unrealized appreciation" (NUA) of employer stock or for a participant born before 1936. See ¶ 2.4–¶ 2.5.

6.2.02 MRD trust rules: Ground rules

Here are introductory points regarding how to deal with the "minimum distribution trust rules."

A.　　**Should you discuss MRDs in the trust instrument?** The MRD trust rules do NOT require the trust instrument to specify that the trustee must withdraw the annual MRD from the retirement plan. § 401(a)(9)(B) requires the MRD to be distributed from the plan or IRA to the trust-named-as-beneficiary whether or not the trust instrument mentions the subject.

Nevertheless, practitioners frequently do mention the requirement of withdrawing the MRD in the trust instrument, because it doesn't hurt to remind the trustee that he is supposed to comply with the minimum distribution rules. Also, including language dealing with the minimum distribution rules makes it clear that the drafter was aware of these rules and that the dispositive terms of the trust are not meant to conflict with them. In a marital deduction trust (¶ 3.3) it is common to specify that the trustee must withdraw from the retirement plan "the greater of" the income (that the spouse is entitled to under the marital deduction rules) and the MRD.

Finally, if it ever becomes necessary to interpret the trust instrument in some unforeseen fashion, the court will look to the grantor's intent, so specifying that the grantor intends the trust to qualify as a see-through should help in that situation.

Avoid tying trust distributions too tightly to the minimum distribution rules, which could result in the beneficiary's receiving more or less than the trust-grantor envisioned if the minimum distribution rules are changed. This happened when § 401(a)(9)(H) suspended minimum required distributions for the year 2009 (¶ 1.1.04). Under a trust that permitted the trustee to distribute to the beneficiary ONLY the "required" distribution and nothing else, the beneficiary received no distributions at all in 2009.

B.   **Benefits and proceeds thereof.** For purposes of minimum distribution rule testing, a trust's interest in a retirement plan includes not just the retirement plan itself and the distributions from the retirement plan, but also the proceeds resulting from the trust's reinvestment of the retirement plan distributions. Reg. § 1.401(a)(9)-5, A-7(c)(1), third sentence.

C.   **Benefits pass from one trust to another.** If the beneficiary of the trust is *another* trust, then *both* trusts must qualify under the trust rules. Reg. § 1.401(a)(9)-4, A-5(d). (Note: the IRS seems to ignore this requirement in some letter rulings.) However, if the second trust can be disregarded under the rules discussed at ¶ 6.3, the second trust does *not* need to comply with the trust rules. Under a conduit trust, for example, the trust's remainder beneficiaries are disregarded. ¶ 6.3.05(B). Thus, the remainder beneficiary of a conduit trust can be a trust that does *not* comply with the trust rules.

D.   **Who tests compliance?** The person primarily responsible for verifying that the trust qualifies as a see-through trust is the trustee. The trustee is the one who must comply with the minimum distribution rules by correctly calculating (and taking) the annual required distribution, because the trust will have to pay the penalty for failure to take the MRD (¶ 1.9.02). The trustee should obtain a legal opinion regarding the trust's qualification as a see-through trust. The plan administrator of a QRP also cares about compliance, because failure to comply could lead to plan disqualification.

6.2.03 *What a "see-through trust" is; the five "trust rules"*

The Code allows retirement plan death benefits to be distributed in annual instalments over the life expectancy of the participant's Designated Beneficiary. ¶ 1.5.01. Although the general rule is that a Designated Beneficiary must be an *individual* (¶ 1.7.03), the regulations allow you to name a *trust* as beneficiary and still have a

Designated Beneficiary for purposes of the minimum distribution rules. Reg. § 1.401(a)(9)-4, A-5(b), contains the IRS's four "minimum distribution trust rules" (also called the MRD trust rules):

1.   The trust must be valid under state law. ¶ 6.2.05.

2.   "The trust is irrevocable or will, by its terms, become irrevocable upon the death of the" participant. ¶ 6.2.06.

3.   "The beneficiaries of the trust who are beneficiaries with respect to the trust's interest in the employee's benefit" must be "identifiable...from the trust instrument." ¶ 6.2.07.

4.   Certain documentation must be provided to "the plan administrator." ¶ 6.2.08.

If the participant dies leaving his retirement benefits to a trust that satisfies the above four requirements, then, for most (not all!) purposes of § 401(a)(9), the beneficiaries of the trust (and not the trust itself) "will be treated as having been designated as beneficiaries of the employee under the plan...." Reg. § 1.401(a)(9)-4, A-5(a). However, treating the trust beneficiaries as if they had been named as beneficiaries directly does not get you very far if the trust beneficiaries themselves do not qualify as Designated Beneficiaries. Accordingly, Rule 5 is that:

5.   All trust beneficiaries must be individuals. ¶ 6.2.09–¶ 6.2.11.

The IRS calls a trust that passes these rules a **see-through trust**, because the effect of passing the rules is that the IRS will look through, or see through, the trust, and treat the trust beneficiaries as the participant's Designated Beneficiaries, just as if they had been named directly as beneficiaries of the retirement plan, *with two significant exceptions*: First, "separate accounts" treatment is never available for purposes of determining the ADP for benefits paid to multiple beneficiaries through a single trust that is named as beneficiary; see ¶ 6.3.02(A). Second, a trust cannot exercise the spousal rollover option, even if it is a see-through. Reg. § 1.408-8, A-5(a). See ¶ 1.6.06.

6.2.04 *Dates for testing trust's compliance with rules*

The regulations give no specific testing date for the requirement that the trust must be <u>valid under state law</u>. The examples in the regulation refer to a trust that is valid under state law *as of the date of death.* ¶ 6.2.05. The <u>irrevocability requirement</u> must be met as of the date of death. ¶ 6.2.06.

For the <u>documentation requirement</u> deadline, see ¶ 6.2.08.

The requirement that the <u>beneficiaries be identifiable</u> must be met as of the date of death. However, if the trust flunks this requirement as of the date of death, it *may* be possible to cure the problem by actions prior to the Beneficiary Finalization Date. See ¶ 6.3.03.

The requirement that <u>all beneficiaries must be individuals</u> must be met as of the Beneficiary Finalization Date. See ¶ 6.2.10, ¶ 6.3.03.

6.2.05 *Rule 1: Trust must be valid under state law*

The first rule is that "The trust is a valid trust under state law, or would be but for the fact that there is no corpus." Reg. §1.401(a)(9)-4, A-5(b)(1). There is no PLR, regulation, or other IRS pronouncement giving an example of a trust that would flunk this requirement.

A testamentary trust can pass this test, despite the fact that, at the moment of the participant's death, the trust is not yet in existence; see Reg. §1.401(a)(9)-5, A-7(c)(3), Examples 1 and 2. There is no requirement that the trust be "in existence" or be funded at the time it is named as beneficiary or at the participant's death. The requirement is that the trust, once it is funded with the retirement benefits *after* the participant's death, must be valid under state law.

6.2.06 *Rule 2: Trust must be irrevocable*

The second rule is: "The trust is irrevocable or will, by its terms, become irrevocable upon the death of the" participant. Reg. § 1.401(a)(9)-4, A-5(b)(2); § 1.408-8, A-1(b).

Including in the trust the statement "This trust shall be irrevocable upon my death" is not necessary, since any testamentary trust or "living trust" automatically becomes irrevocable upon the testator's or donor's death, and therefore passes this test. On the other hand it does no harm to include this sentence, and inclusion may avoid the necessity of argument with possible future plan administrators and auditing IRS agents who may not be familiar with estate planning. See Form 4.1, Appendix B.

(Prior to revision of the minimum distribution regulations in 2001–2002, the IRS trust rules required the trust to be irrevocable as of the participant's RBD. That rule has been abolished.)

A trustee's power, after the participant's death, to amend administrative provisions of the trust should not be considered a power to "revoke." However, there is no authority or IRS guidance on this point.

Unfortunately, it is not clear what the IRS is driving at with Rule 2. The IRS has never given an example of a trust that does not become irrevocable at the participant's death. Perhaps the regulation-writers are thinking of a situation where someone *other than* the participant has a power to "revoke" the trust after the participant's death, as in some community property trusts.

6.2.07 *Rule 3: Beneficiaries must be identifiable*

"The beneficiaries of the trust who are beneficiaries with respect to the trust's interest in the employee's benefit" must be "identifiable within the meaning of A-1 of this section from the trust instrument." Reg. §1.401(a)(9)-4, A-5(b)(3). The entirety of what "A-1 of this section" provides on the meaning of the word "identifiable" is the following: "A designated beneficiary need not be specified by name in the plan or by the employee to the plan...so long as the individual who is to be the beneficiary is identifiable under the plan. The members of a class of beneficiaries capable of expansion or contraction will be treated as being identifiable if it is possible to identify the class member with the shortest life expectancy." Reg. § 1.401(a)(9)-4, A-1.

For the effect of a power of appointment on the question of whether there are unidentifiable beneficiaries, see ¶ 6.3.11.

A.   **Must be possible to identify the oldest trust beneficiary.** One meaning of this rule is that it must be possible to determine who is the *oldest person* (see "B," below) who could ever possibly be a beneficiary of the trust, because that is the person whose life expectancy is used as the ADP after the participant's death. Reg. § 1.401(a)(9)-4, A-5(c), § 1.401(a)(9)-5, A-7(a)(1).

Thus, if the trust beneficiaries are "all my issue living from time to time," and at least one such issue is living at the participant's death, the members of that class of potential beneficiaries are considered "identifiable," even though the class is not closed as of the applicable date, because no person with a shorter life expectancy can be added later. The oldest member of the class can be determined with certainty, because the participant's issue who are born after his death must be younger than the oldest issue of the participant who is living at his death. Reg. § 1.401(a)(9)-4, A-1.

Actually, there *is* theoretically a problem even with this common provision. If people who are issue by virtue of adoption are to be included, there is a potential for violating the rule. After the participant's death, one of his issue could adopt someone who was born earlier than the person who was the oldest beneficiary of the trust when the participant died. It is not known whether the IRS would ever raise this "issue," but to avoid the problem the trust could provide that older individuals cannot later be added to the class of beneficiaries by adoption. See Form 4.3, Appendix B.

The rule that it must be possible to identify the oldest member of a class of beneficiaries is similar to the rule against perpetuities, in that the mere *possibility* that an older beneficiary could be added to the trust after the applicable date is enough to make the trust flunk this rule, regardless of whether any such older beneficiary ever is *actually* added (unless the potential older beneficiary can be disregarded under the rules explained at ¶ 6.3.04).

Kit and Julia Example: Kit leaves his IRA to a trust that is to pay income to his daughter Julia for life, and after her death is to pay income to her widower (if any) for his life, with remainder to Kit's grandchildren. Kit dies, survived by Julia and several grandchildren, none of whom disclaims his interest in the trust. Kit's trust flunks Rule 3, because Julia, after Kit's death, *could* marry a new husband who is older than she. Thus an older beneficiary *could* be added to this trust after the applicable date, and accordingly as of the applicable date we cannot "identify" the oldest beneficiary of the trust.

The "identifiable" test is applied, first, as of the date of death. If the trust flunks the requirement as of the date of death, but the "unidentifiable" beneficiaries are "removed" by some means prior to the Beneficiary Finalization Date (¶ 6.3.03), the trust would "pass." Unfortunately, if a trust flunks this test as of the date of death it often is not the type of mistake that can be fixed by the usual remedies of disclaimer or distribution. In the Kit and Julia Example, Julia's future husband(s) can't disclaim (and the trustee can't distribute their share of the trust by the Beneficiary Finalization Date) because we don't know who they are yet—that's the whole problem!

B.   **What does "oldest beneficiary" mean?** For MRD purposes, "older" does not necessarily mean "born first"; it means having a shorter life expectancy. For MRD purposes, everyone born in the same year has the same life expectancy. See PLR 2002-35038.

C.   **Anyone in the world younger than a certain individual.** Sometimes the IRS expresses the "identifiable" requirement thus: "…the identity of the beneficiaries…can be determined by perusing…[the trust's] terms." PLRs 2005-21033, 2005-22012, and 2005-28031 use that exact phrase, and PLR 2002-09057 uses similar wording. What this phrase means, if anything, has yet to be established. If the IRS is suggesting that the "identifiable" test requires only that the identity of the beneficiaries can be determined from the trust instrument then the rule is redundant: A trust under which the identities of the beneficiaries could NOT be determined by "perusing" the trust instrument would presumably not be valid under state law and therefore would violate Rule #1 (¶ 6.2.05).

To date, the IRS has not used Rule 3 in any published ruling to disqualify trusts that are payable to broad or amorphous classes of unknown future beneficiaries or where access to the benefits is dependent on the trustee's discretion. In PLR 2002-35038, the IRS approved a trust where the remainder interest could be appointed to any individual in the world who was not born in a year prior to the birth-year of the donor's oldest issue living at the donor's death. (This ruling is flawed, because the IRS fails to consider what becomes of the benefits if the power of appointment is not exercised; see ¶ 6.3.11.)

6.2.08 *Rule 4: Documentation requirement*

The trustee of the trust that is named as beneficiary must supply certain documentation to the plan administrator. Reg. § 1.401(a)(9)-4, A-5(b)(4). In the case of a qualified plan, **"plan administrator"** is the statutory title of the person responsible for carrying out the plan provisions and complying with the minimum distribution rules; the employer must provide the name, address, and phone number of the plan administrator to all employees in the Summary Plan Description. In the case of an IRA, the IRA trustee, custodian, or issuer is the party to whom the documentation must be delivered. Reg. § 1.408-8, A-1(b).

A.   **Post-death distributions.** The <u>deadline</u> for supplying the required documentation with respect to post-death distributions is October 31 of the year after the year of the participant's death. Reg. § 1.401(a)(9)-4, A-6(b).

Although § 401(a)(9)(H) suspended minimum required distributions for the year 2009 (see ¶ 1.1.04), the suspension did NOT extend this deadline. Thus, the trustee of a trust named as beneficiary of a decedent who died in 2008 (or 2009) still had to supply the required documentation no later than October 31, 2009 (or 2010), even though the trust was not required to take any MRD in 2009. Notice 2009-82, 2009-41 I.R.B. 491, Part V, A-4.
Here is the <u>documentation required</u> to be supplied to the plan administrator by that deadline. The trustee of the trust must *either*:

1.   "Provide the plan administrator with a final list of all beneficiaries of the trust (including contingent and remaindermen beneficiaries with a description of the conditions on their entitlement) as of September 30 of the calendar year following the calendar year of the employee's death; certify that, to the best of the trustee's knowledge, this list is correct and complete and that the [other "trust rules"] are satisfied; and agree to provide a copy of the trust instrument to the plan administrator upon demand…"; or

2.   "Provide the plan administrator with a copy of the actual trust document for the trust that is named as a beneficiary of the employee under the plan as of the employee's date of death."

Supplying a copy of the trust (#2) is an easier way to comply than providing a summary of the trust (#1). However, some retirement plans may require the summary-certification method of compliance (#1), since it relieves the plan administrator of the burden of reading the trust and determining whether it complies with the trust rules.

B.   **Lifetime distributions.** The identity of the beneficiaries is irrelevant to the calculation of lifetime MRDs if the participant is using the Uniform Lifetime Table (¶ 1.3.01). Therefore, the participant has no need to comply with the documentation requirement or other trust rules for his lifetime distributions *unless*: (1) the participant has named a trust as his sole beneficiary; (2) the participant's more-than-10-years-younger spouse is the sole beneficiary of the trust (see ¶ 1.6.06); and (3) the participant wants to use the spouses' joint life expectancy (rather than the Uniform Lifetime Table) to measure his MRDs. In such cases, see Reg. § 1.401(a)(9)-4, A-6(a), regarding the documentation to be supplied.

No deadline is specified for supplying documentation in the case of lifetime MRDs. The conservative assumption would be that the deadline is the beginning of the distribution year in which the spouses' joint life expectancy is to be used as the ADP. The person who must fulfill this requirement is *the participant* (not the trustee, as is the case when the participant dies).

C.   **If incorrect trust documentation is supplied.** If the participant (in the case of lifetime MRDs) or the trustee (in the case of post-death MRDs) completes the certifications incorrectly, or sends a copy of the wrong trust instrument to the plan administrator, the regulations let the *plan* off the hook.

The plan will not be disqualified "merely" because of these errors, provided "the plan administrator reasonably relied on the information provided and the required minimum distributions for calendar years after the calendar year in which the discrepancy is discovered are determined based on the actual terms of the trust instrument." Reg. § 1.401(a)(9)-4, A-6(c)(1). This wording suggests that the trust can still qualify as a see-through, even though incorrect information was provided to the administrator initially. The 50 percent penalty (which is payable by the person required to *take* the MRD; see ¶ 1.9.02) will be still be based on what should have been distributed "based on the actual terms of the trust in effect." Reg. § 1.401(a)(9)-4, A-6(c)(2).

6.2.09 *Rule 5: All beneficiaries must be individuals*

The result of compliance with the first four rules is that the trust beneficiaries will be treated, for *most* purposes, as if the participant had named them directly as beneficiaries (for exceptions see ¶ 6.3.02(A) and ¶ 1.6.06). The next step, therefore, is to make sure that these trust beneficiaries qualify as Designated Beneficiaries, *i.e.*, that they are individuals. ¶ 1.7.03.

The first pitfall under this rule is that an estate is not an individual and therefore an estate cannot be a Designated Beneficiary. See ¶ 1.7.04. Therefore, if any part of the trust's interest in the benefits will pass to the participant's estate, there is a risk that the participant has no Designated Beneficiary; see ¶ 6.2.10. Once that hurdle is cleared we consider which trust beneficiaries, if any, can be disregarded in applying this rule. See ¶ 6.3.

6.2.10 *Payments to estate for expenses, taxes*

Typically, a trust provides that the trust must or may contribute funds to the decedent-trustor's estate for payment of the decedent's debts, expenses, and taxes. Such a provision raises a concern: If the estate (a nonindividual) is deemed to be a beneficiary of the trust, the trust will "flunk" Rule #5 (¶ 6.2.09).

However, despite suggestions in some PLRs (see, *e.g.*, PLR 9809059) that such a provision might disqualify a trust, there is no evidence that the IRS really does (or ever did) take this position. There is no published instance of any trust's ever having lost see-through status on account of such a clause. Many PLRs blessing see-through trusts do not even mention the subject; see PLRs 2002-08031, 2002-11047, 2002-18039, 2003-17041, 2003-17043, and 2003-17044.

If this type of clause *is* a problem, the risks of disqualification can easily be avoided either at the planning stage or (with a bit more care) in the post-mortem stage. Every letter ruling that *does* mention such a clause in a trust finds some reason why the trust nevertheless qualifies as a see-through. The IRS has recognized trusts as see-throughs, despite a trust clause calling for payments to the estate for debts, expenses, and/or taxes, where:

✓ The trust forbade the distribution of *retirement benefits* to the participant's estate (PLRs 2002-35038–2002-35041) or to any nonindividual beneficiary (PLRs 2004-10019–2004-10020).

PLR 2004-53023 refers favorably to trust language that would "wall off" the benefits from being used to pay the decedent's debts and expenses (though the trust in question did not contain such language).

✓   The trustees asserted either that applicable state law prohibited use of the retirement benefits for this purpose (either directly, or indirectly through the application of some fiduciary standard), or that state law exempted such benefits from creditors' claims. See PLRs 2002-23065, 2002-28025, and 2006-08032 for examples of this language; other PLRs with similar language and holdings are 2001-31033; 2002-21056, 2002-21059, 2002-21061; 2002-35038; 2002-44023; 2004-10019–2004-10020; 2005-38030; and 2006-20028.

✓   The participant's estate was a beneficiary of the trust as of the date of death (by virtue of the estate's right to receive funds from the trust for payment of debts, expenses, and/or taxes), but the estate was "removed" as a beneficiary by complete distribution of its share of the trust prior to (or "as of") the Beneficiary Finalization Date (¶ 6.3.03). In PLRs 2004-32027–2004-32029, "as of" September 30 of the year after the year of the participant's death, the trustee had withdrawn, from the IRA that was payable to the trust, sufficient funds to pay all anticipated debts, expenses, and taxes of the participant's estate, including a reserve for income taxes that would be due on the IRA distributions themselves. The IRS ruled that on the applicable September 30 the only remaining beneficiaries of the trust were the participant's three children. See ¶ 6.3.03(A).

✓   The benefits were subject to the trust's contingent liability to pay additional estate taxes even *after* the Beneficiary Finalization Date (for example, if the tax bill were later increased as a result of audit) because there were no other assets available. PLRs 2004-32027–2004-32029, 2004-40031.

In short, there is no PLR or other IRS pronouncement in which the IRS has disqualified a trust either on the basis of a clause permitting the trustee to make payments to the participant's estate, or on the basis of the trust's actually making such payments. The IRS seems to agree it would be absurd to disqualify a trust merely because the retirement benefits payable to it may be liable for the participant's debts, administration expenses, and estate taxes. *All* retirement benefits are potentially subject to those liabilities regardless of whether a trust is the named beneficiary. While the threatening IRS hints on the subject make it worthwhile to draft to avoid the issue (see Form 4.2, Appendix B), there is little to fear even if a trust does contain this clause.

6.2.11 *Effect of § 645 election on see-through status*

A deceased participant's revocable trust can make an election to be treated as if it were the decedent's probate estate, or part of the probate estate, for income tax purposes during the administration period. § 645. A trust's "645 election" does not adversely affect the trust's see-through status. Even though the effect of such an election is that the estate and trust are treated as one entity "for all purposes of Subtitle A" of the Code (Reg. § 1.645-1(e)(2)(i), (3)(i)), "...the IRS and Treasury intend that a revocable trust will not fail to be a trust for purposes of section 401(a)(9) merely because the trust elects to be treated as an estate under section 645, as long as the trust continues to be a trust under state law." TD 8987, 67 FR 35731, 2002-1 C.B. 852, 857 ("Trust as Beneficiary").

6.3 MRD Rules:
Which Trust Beneficiaries Count?

There is no special difficulty in determining whether the trust is valid under state law (Rule 1; ¶ 6.2.05), and irrevocable at the participant's death (Rule 2; ¶ 6.2.06), or that proper documentation has been supplied to the plan administrator (Rule 4; ¶ 6.2.08(A)). The hard part of testing a trust under the MRD trust rules is determining whether all trust beneficiaries are individuals (Rule 5; ¶ 6.2.09), and which trust beneficiary is the oldest (Rule 3; ¶ 6.2.07). The difficulty is determining which trust beneficiaries "count" for purposes of these two rules, and which beneficiaries may be disregarded.

6.3.01 *If benefits are allocated to a particular share of the trust*

This ¶ 6.3.01 deals with the following situation: Retirement benefits are payable to a trust. Upon the participant's death, that trust is divided or split into two or more separate shares or "subtrusts," and the retirement benefits are allocated to fewer than all of such shares or subtrusts. A typical example would be a trust that divides, upon the participant's death, into a marital trust and a credit shelter trust and under which the benefits are allocated entirely to the marital trust; see Foster Example, ¶ 6.1.05(B). Another common case is a trust under which the benefits are entirely allocated to the share of one of multiple beneficiaries, or may *not* be used to fund a particular beneficiary's share.

The question discussed here is whether the "identifiable" and "all-beneficiaries-must-be-individuals" tests (MRD trust rules 3 and 5; ¶ 6.2.03) are applied to the entire trust (i.e., all possible beneficiaries of all shares and subtrusts created by the trust instrument), or rather are applied only to the beneficiary, share, or subtrust that ends up with the retirement benefits. Can we disregard beneficiaries of shares/subtrusts that do not receive any portion of the retirement benefits? As the following discussion shows, the answer to this question is surprisingly unclear.

A.   **Beneficiaries with respect to the trust's interest in the benefits.** Reg. § 1.401(a)(9)-4, A-5(a), tells us that, if the trust rules are complied with, "the beneficiaries of the trust (and not the trust itself)" will be treated as having been designated as beneficiaries by the employee. Although A-5(a) uses the phrase "beneficiaries of the trust," all other references to the see-through trust concept specify that it is not *all* beneficiaries of the trust who are so treated, but rather only the beneficiaries of the trust *with respect to the trust's interest in the employee's benefit.* See Reg. § 1.401(a)(9)-4, Q-5; A-5(b)(3), (c); § 1.401(a)(9)-8, A-11 (last sentence).

Thus, the regulations seem to state that, even if the benefits are payable to a funding trust (such as the participant's revocable living trust), we are not required to test all potential beneficiaries of the *funding trust,* if the benefits are allocated only to certain beneficiaries or to particular subtrusts created under the funding trust. Instead, this wording suggests, we look only at the beneficiaries of the subtrust(s) that actually receive(s) (or possibly only at beneficiaries that *could* receive) the retirement benefits, because they are the only beneficiaries "with respect to the trust's interest in the benefits." Unfortunately the IRS pronouncements (all of which are in private letter rulings) are not consistently supportive of this view; see (C)–(F) below. Sometimes the IRS seems to confuse this question with the entirely different issue of "separate accounts" treatment (¶ 6.3.02).

B.   **Subtrust named directly as beneficiary of the benefits.** One thing is clear: If the participant's beneficiary designation form names the subtrust directly as beneficiary of the plan, rather than naming the funding trust, then the only beneficiaries who "count" for purposes of the trust rules are the beneficiaries of the subtrust named as beneficiary. PLR 2006-07031. See Form 3.5, Appendix B, for a sample beneficiary designation form leaving benefits in separate shares directly to separate trusts established under a single trust instrument.

C.   **Benefits allocated pursuant to trustee's discretion.** If the trustee has discretion to decide which assets to use to fund which subtrust, and exercises its discretion by allocating the benefits to one particular beneficiary (or share), can other beneficiaries (or beneficiaries of other shares) be disregarded in applying the MRD trust rules?

This seems like the worst case for convincing the IRS that other beneficiaries of the trust should be ignored, yet ironically it is one situation in which there is a favorable PLR squarely on point! See PLR 2002-21061 (issued under the 2001 proposed regulations; see ¶ 1.1.01), in which all pre-residuary beneficiaries of a trust (including charities) were ignored in determining the Applicable Distribution Period (ADP; ¶ 1.2.03) for retirement benefits payable to the trust, because the trustees (although they *could* have used the benefits to fund the pre-residuary bequests) were legally and financially able to, and did, satisfy the pre-residuary bequests out of other assets of the trust, and the pre-residuary beneficiaries did not have the right under state law to demand that they be paid out of the retirement benefits.

D.   **Instrument mandates allocation; no formula.** If the trust instrument requires that the benefits *must* be allocated to a certain subtrust or to certain beneficiaries, or mandates that the benefits *cannot* be paid to certain beneficiaries or shares, regardless of the amount of the benefits or any other factors, beneficiaries of the shares to which the benefits absolutely cannot under any circumstances be allocated *should* be disregarded.

Trevor Example: Trevor's IRA is payable to the Trevor Trust. At his death the assets of the Trevor Trust are to be divided between a marital trust and a credit shelter trust. The trust requires that all retirement benefits are to be allocated to the marital trust, even if that means the credit shelter trust is underfunded. Can the beneficiaries of the credit shelter trust be disregarded in applying the MRD trust rules?

It appears the answer to this should be yes, in view of PLR 2006-20026 (see "E") and the language of the regulation (see "A"). However, in view of the IRS vagueness on these issues, if it is important to Trevor that the credit shelter trust beneficiaries be disregarded, he should name the marital trust *directly* as beneficiary of his IRA (see "B").

Some PLRs mention, as part of a favorable ruling on see-through trust status, the fact that the trust in question forbade the distribution of retirement benefits to the participant's estate. These PLRs *imply* that the IRS will disregard trust beneficiaries who are forbidden, by the terms of the trust, to share in the retirement benefits. However, these rulings are not conclusive, because the IRS has never on the record ruled that a trust was not a see-through trust merely because the benefits were subject to an obligation to contribute to payment of the deceased participant's debts, expenses, or estate taxes. See ¶ 6.2.10.

E.   **Mandated allocation pursuant to formula.** Many trusts that create a marital and credit shelter trust (or other subtrusts) by means of a formula specify that retirement benefits are to be allocated to a particular subtrust to the extent possible, and used to fund other subtrusts only if there are no other assets that can be used for such purpose. If the formula and the "to the extent possible" language compel the trustee to allocate the benefits entirely to (say) the marital trust, can the credit shelter trust beneficiaries be disregarded in applying the trust rules?

The PLRs on point are contradictory. In PLR 1999-03050, decided under the proposed regulations (¶ 1.1.01), the IRS ruled that beneficiaries of other shares could *not* be disregarded; the ruling dealt with this as a "separate accounts" issue (see ¶ 6.3.02). However, in

PLR 2006-20026, involving an IRA and QRP payable to "Trust T," the IRS ruled exactly the opposite way. Trust T was to be divided into Subtrusts A and B upon the participant's death by means of a formula. As a result of applying the formula, the benefits "had to be allocated to Subtrust B." The ruling then proceeded to analyze only Subtrust B, with no mention of the terms or beneficiaries of Subtrust A. This suggests that the IRS has changed its mind since PLR 1999-03050, and is willing to ignore the beneficiaries of other trust shares, where the funding formula forces the trustee to allocate the benefits to one particular share.

F.   **Mandatory allocation under state law.** If applicable state law mandates that the benefits be allocated to one particular beneficiary, subtrust, or share, do we disregard beneficiaries of all other shares in applying the MRD trust rules? The IRS has ruled both ways on this question. In PLRs 2005-28031–2005-28035, the IRS said "no"; these rulings offer no argument or basis for the conclusion. In contrast, PLR 2007-08084 seems to suggest that beneficiaries whose shares cannot (because of applicable state law standards) be funded with the retirement benefits CAN be disregarded.

6.3.02 *Separate accounts: benefits payable to a trust or estate*

For ease of reference, this discussion will deal with inherited IRAs. Though the same rules apply to all types of benefits subject to the minimum distribution rules, "separate accounts" treatment almost always involves inherited IRAs (including Roth IRAs).

When a participant leaves his IRA in fractional or percentage shares to multiple beneficiaries, the inherited account may, if this is permitted by the IRA agreement, be divided into separate "inherited IRAs," one payable to each of the multiple beneficiaries. Once this division occurs, the separated accounts are treated as separate inherited IRAs for most purposes of the minimum distribution rules (generally, beginning the year *after* the division). See ¶ 1.8.01–¶ 1.8.02. However, there is a significant exception to the separate accounts rule for retirement benefits payable to a trust:

A.   **No separate accounts for ADP purposes.** Separate inherited IRAs established after the participant's death are NOT treated as separate accounts *for purposes of determining the Applicable*

Distribution Period (even if the division into separate accounts occurs on or before December 31 of the year after the year of the participant's death), if the division into separate accounts occurs by operation of a single trust that is named as beneficiary. See Reg. § 1.401(a)(9)-4, A-5(c), as applied in PLRs 2003-17041, 2003-17043, 2003-17044, and 2004-32027–2004-32029; compare ¶ 1.8.01(B).

Accordingly, if a participant wants a life expectancy payout to be available for each of multiple beneficiaries based on each such beneficiary's *own* life expectancy (or for each of multiple separate trusts based on the life expectancy of the oldest beneficiary of *each* such trust), the participant should name the individuals (or trusts) directly as beneficiaries *in the beneficiary designation form*, rather than naming a single funding trust as beneficiary of the retirement plan. See PLR 2005-37044; ¶ 6.3.01(B); and Form 3.5, Appendix B.

Prior to issuance of the final minimum distribution regulations in 2002, separate accounts treatment *was* available for multiple beneficiaries taking under a single trust. See PLR 2002-34074 (issued in May 2002, after the final regulations were issued, though this PLR was decided under the proposed regulations; ¶ 1.1.01).

B.   **Separate accounts for purposes other than ADP.** Although Reg. § 1.401(a)(9)-4, A-5(c), states that separate accounts cannot be established *for any purpose of the minimum distribution rules* for benefits that are left to multiple beneficiaries through a single funding trust, PLRs make clear that in fact the IRS means such separate accounts CAN be established for all MRD purposes *other than* determining the ADP. See ¶ 1.8.01(C). Thus, for example, if an IRA is payable to a trust that is to terminate immediately upon the participant's death and be distributed outright to the decedent's three children, the trust can divide the IRA into separate inherited IRAs and transfer one such separate inherited IRA to each of the children (see ¶ 6.1.05). Thereafter, the children's respective separate inherited IRAs (or "sub-IRAs" as the IRS calls them in some PLRs) will be treated as "separate accounts" for all minimum distribution purposes *except* determination of the ADP. The ADP for all three children's shares will continue to be based on the life expectancy of the oldest child. See PLRs 2000-13041 and 2002-35038–2002-35041.

Similarly, the IRS has allowed separate accounts treatment for all purposes other than determining the ADP for retirement benefits that pass through an <u>estate</u>. See PLRs 2006-46025; 2006-47029 and 2006-47030, in which two children inherited an IRA through their parent's estate and were allowed to split it into two separate inherited IRAs, one payable to each child. Even though the IRS ruled that "separate account treatment" was not available, the IRS *also* said the accounts *would be treated as separate accounts,* i.e., each child's MRDs would be determined solely with respect to his "sub-IRA." What the IRS apparently meant was, separate accounts would not be available *for ADP purposes.* PLRs 2006-46025, 2006-46027, and 2006-46028 (involving three children who inherited through a parent's estate) are similar.

C.   **Drafting to achieve separate accounts under one trust instrument.** If a participant wants to leave his IRA in separate shares, with each share to be held in trust for a different beneficiary, AND wants each such IRA-share to be payable over the life expectancy of the primary beneficiary for whom it is held, the participant should take the following two steps:

Step 1: He must cause a separate trust to be established for each such beneficiary. These separate trusts can be established (i.e. set up and funded) after his death, and can all be established under a single trust instrument, as long as each such trust is (at the time it receives the inherited benefits) a separate trust under applicable state law, with its own taxpayer identification number (TIN) and filing its own annual tax return. It is not possible to have separate account treatment for any MRD purpose for shares of a single IRA that are payable to a single trust that has multiple beneficiaries, even if the multiple beneficiaries have "separate shares" under the single trust for other income tax purposes (¶ 6.5.05).

Step 2: He must name each such to-be-established separate trust directly as a beneficiary of his retirement plan. He can do this either by establishing a separate IRA during his lifetime that is payable only to that particular trust, or by having a single IRA that is payable in specified shares to the respective trusts. See Form 3.5, Appendix B.

6.3.03 *Beneficiaries "removed" by Beneficiary Finalization Date*

A person or entity who is a beneficiary of the participant's retirement plan as of the date of the participant's death ceases to "count" as a beneficiary if he, she, or it does not "remain" as a beneficiary as of September 30 of the calendar year following the calendar year of the employee's death (the "Beneficiary Finalization Date"). See ¶ 1.8.03.

A beneficiary does not "remain" such if such beneficiary's interest in the benefits has been eliminated by either distribution (see "A"), disclaimer (see "B"), or other means (see "C"). The death of a beneficiary prior to the Beneficiary Finalization Date would eliminate him as a beneficiary only if his rights did not pass to his estate; see ¶ 1.8.03(C).

Although § 401(a)(9)(H) suspended the minimum distribution rules for the year 2009 (see ¶ 1.1.04), the suspension did NOT extend this deadline. Thus, the beneficiary of a participant who died in 2008 (or 2009) will be "countable" unless (through distribution, disclaimer, or otherwise) he, she, or it ceased to be a beneficiary no later than September 30, 2009 (or 2010), even though the beneficiary was not required to take any MRD in 2009. Notice 2009-82, Part V, A-4.

Here is how the Beneficiary Finalization Date concept applies to retirement benefits that are payable to a trust as beneficiary. The determination of who are the trust beneficiaries for purposes of determining the trust's "see-through" status is made as of the date of death, but may be modified by one of the following methods:

A.   **Distribution on or before September 30.** Suppose retirement benefits are payable to a trust that has multiple beneficiaries. For purposes of qualifying for a payout of these benefits based on the life expectancy of one or more young individual beneficiaries of the trust, the trustee may wish to "eliminate" one or more nonindividual beneficiaries of the trust (to satisfy the "all beneficiaries must be individuals" rule; ¶ 6.2.09) or one or more older beneficiaries (so the trust's ADP will be based on the life expectancy of a younger "oldest trust beneficiary"; ¶ 6.2.01). There are three ways that distribution can be used to "eliminate" an older and/or nonindividual beneficiary; note in each case that such option is available only if permitted by the trust instrument.

One is by distributing, to the beneficiary you are seeking to remove, his, her, or its share of the benefits, so that, as of the Beneficiary Finalization Date, the remaining beneficiaries of the trust and of the retirement benefits are all individuals (or all younger individuals). For example, see PLRs 2004-49041–2004-49042, in which the participant left his IRA to a trust that was to be distributed, in specified percentages, to his wife and daughters. The wife took distribution of her percentage in full by the Beneficiary Finalization Date (and rolled it over to her own IRA; see ¶ 3.2.03(F), ¶ 3.2.09). Therefore she was disregarded in determining who was the oldest beneficiary of the trust, and the older daughter's life expectancy was the ADP for both daughters' shares of the IRA (¶ 6.3.02(A)).

Another way is to distribute other assets (not the retirement benefits) to the "undesirable" beneficiary in full payment of his, her, or its share of the trust, so that, as of the Beneficiary Finalization Date, the only remaining beneficiaries of the trust and of the benefits are the "desirable" individual beneficiaries. See PLRs 2006-08032, 2006-10026, 2006-10027, and 2006-20026 for examples of this technique.

Finally, the trustee could transfer the retirement benefits out of the trust, intact, to an individual trust beneficiary (¶ 6.1.05), before the Beneficiary Finalization Date, so that, as of the Beneficiary Finalization Date, the (young, individual) transferee is the only beneficiary of the benefits. The other (older and/or nonindividual) beneficiaries of the trust are disregarded because they have ceased to have any interest in the retirement benefits (do not "remain" as beneficiaries).

Merely allocating the benefits to one particular share of a trust would *not* be sufficient to allow beneficiaries of other shares of the trust to be disregarded, according to PLRs 2005-28031–2005-28035.

B. **Qualified disclaimer by September 30.** If a beneficiary disclaims his entire interest by the Beneficiary Finalization Date, he no longer "counts" as a beneficiary. See ¶ 4.4.11(A). If the disclaimant was the oldest beneficiary, the next oldest beneficiary's life expectancy will become the ADP. Reg. § 1.401(a)(9)-4, A-4(a). See PLRs 2004-44033 and 2004-44034, in which "A" died leaving her IRA to a trust for the life benefit of her sister, with remainder to A's two nieces. The sister (who was older than the nieces) disclaimed her interest in the trust, so that the two nieces became the sole beneficiaries, and the older niece's life expectancy became the ADP.

Similarly, disclaiming a power of appointment can eliminate potential appointees who would otherwise be "unidentifiable" and cause the trust to flunk Rule 3 (¶ 6.2.07). See PLR 2004-38044, discussed at ¶ 6.3.11(B).

C. **Other ways to "remove" a trust beneficiary.** The regulation cites distribution and disclaimer simply as *examples* of ways in which a person who was a beneficiary as of the date of death could cease to be a beneficiary as of the Beneficiary Finalization Date. Reg. § 1.401(a)(9)-4, A-4(a). Certain post-death amendments of the trust, made before the Beneficiary Finalization Date pursuant to express provisions included in the trust instrument, have been recognized by the IRS for MRD purposes; see PLR 2005-37044 (discussed at ¶ 6.3.12(C)), and PLR 2005-22012. Also, any beneficiary whose rights are terminated prior to the Beneficiary Finalization Date by operation of the trust terms would not be a countable beneficiary:

Axel Example: Axel dies leaving his IRA to a trust which provides that, until his daughter Rose reaches age 35, the trustee will use income and principal for Rose's benefit. When Rose reaches age 35, the trust will terminate and all trust property will pass outright to Rose. If Rose dies before reaching age 35, the trust will terminate and all property will pass to a charity. On the date of Axel's death, Rose is age 34½. Based on the terms of the trust as they exist at Axel's death, the trust has two beneficiaries, Rose and the charity, and "flunks" the MRD trust rules because one beneficiary is not an individual. Six months after Axel's death, Rose turns age 35 and becomes the sole beneficiary of the trust. Since this is before the Beneficiary Finalization Date, the trust qualifies as a see-through trust; the nonindividual beneficiary does not "remain" as a beneficiary as of September 30 of the year after the year of Axel's death.

6.3.04 *Disregarding "mere potential successors"*

We now come to the last stand: trust beneficiaries who either definitely will, or someday may, receive a share of the retirement benefits that are payable to the trust, and who have not been "removed" as of the Beneficiary Finalization Date. Which members of this group can we disregard, if any?

Reg. § 1.401(a)(9)-5, A-7(c), the "**mere potential successor rule**," tells us which beneficiaries in this group are disregarded in applying the trust rules. Reg. § 1.401(a)(9)-4, A-5(c). The mere potential successor rule has been stated differently in each version of the regulations (1987 and 2001 proposed, 2002 final). The final regulation's version is as follows:

"(c). Successor beneficiary–(1) A person will not be considered a beneficiary for purposes of determining who is the beneficiary with the shortest life expectancy...or whether a person who is not an individual is a beneficiary, *merely because the person could become the successor* to the interest of one of the employee's beneficiaries after that beneficiary's death. However, the preceding sentence does not apply to a person who has any right (including a contingent right) to an employee's benefit beyond being a *mere potential successor* to the interest of one of the employee's beneficiaries upon that beneficiary's death." Emphasis added.

How does the "mere potential successor" rule apply to a trust? For purposes of testing trust beneficiaries for "mere potential successor" status, the world can be divided into two types of trusts: "conduit trusts" (¶ 6.3.05–¶ 6.3.06) and "accumulation trusts" (¶ 6.3.07–¶ 6.3.11).

6.3.05 *Conduit trust for one beneficiary*

"Conduit trust" is not an official term. It is a nickname used by practitioners (and occasionally by the IRS) for one type of see-through trust, namely, a trust under which the trustee has no power to accumulate plan distributions in the trust. The IRS regards the conduit beneficiary as the sole beneficiary of the trust; all other beneficiaries are considered mere potential successors and are disregarded.

See ¶ 6.4.04(A) with regard to using a conduit trust for a disabled beneficiary, ¶ 6.4.05(A) for a minors' trust, ¶ 6.4.06(A) for a trust for the benefit of the participant's spouse. See ¶ 6.3.06 regarding a conduit trust for multiple beneficiaries. See Forms 4.6–4.8, Appendix B, for sample conduit trust forms.

A.   **What a conduit trust is**. Under a **conduit trust**, the trustee is required, by the terms of the governing instrument, to distribute to the individual trust beneficiary any distribution the trustee receives from the retirement plan (1) after the participant's death and (2) during the lifetime of such beneficiary. The trustee has no power to retain inside the trust ("accumulate," in IRS terminology) *any* plan distribution that is made after the donor's death during the lifetime of the individual conduit trust beneficiary. Note that:

✓   The "conduit" provision must come into effect immediately upon the participant's death. If the conduit requirement does not begin to apply until some later point in time (such as after the later death of the participant's surviving spouse) the trust is *not* a conduit trust; see ¶ 6.3.12(B). A trust cannot start out as an accumulation trust (say, during the life of the spouse), then flip to being a conduit trust for the remainder beneficiary (say the children) after the life beneficiary's death and still qualify as a see-through. The reason is that the trust may have *already* accumulated plan distributions (during the spouse's lifetime), so the trust does not meet the definition of a conduit trust at the participant's death.

✓   The trustee must pay out *all* distributions the trust receives from the retirement plan, not just "minimum required distributions."

As the IRS describes it in Reg. § 1.401(a)(9)-5, A-7(c)(3), Example 2, "*all amounts* distributed from A's account in Plan X to the trustee while B is alive will be paid *directly* to B upon receipt by the trustee of Trust P... *No amounts* distributed from A's account in Plan X to Trust P are accumulated in Trust P during B's lifetime for the benefit of any other beneficiary." Emphasis added.

B.   How a conduit trust is treated under the MRD rules. With a conduit trust for one individual beneficiary, the retirement benefits are deemed paid "to" that individual beneficiary for purposes of the minimum distribution rules, and accordingly the "all beneficiaries must be individuals" test is met. As the IRS explains in Reg. § 1.401(a)(9)-5, A-7(c)(3), Example 2, under a trust with these terms, "...B [the conduit beneficiary] is the *sole designated beneficiary* of A's account in Plan X for purposes of determining the designated beneficiary under section 401(a)(9)(B)(iii) and (iv)....the residuary beneficiaries of Trust P are *mere potential successors* to B's interest in Plan X." Emphasis added.

All potential remainder beneficiaries (the persons who would take the remaining benefits if the conduit beneficiary died before the benefits had been entirely distributed) are disregarded because the IRS regards them as mere potential successors to the conduit beneficiary's interest.

The conduit trust for one individual beneficiary is a safe harbor. It is guaranteed to qualify as a see-through trust, and it is guaranteed that all remainder beneficiaries (even if they are charities, an estate, or older individuals) are disregarded under the MRD trust rules.

C.   **Payments for beneficiary's benefit.** Payment to the legal guardian of a minor or disabled beneficiary should be considered payment "to" the beneficiary for this purpose. See ¶ 6.3.12(A) regarding making the conduit payments to a trust that is a 100 percent grantor trust as to the beneficiary. See ¶ 6.4.04(A) regarding making the payments to a special needs trust in the case of a disabled beneficiary.

D.   **Payment of trust expenses.** In PLRs 2004-32027–2004-32029, the IRS ruled that "The use of Trust T assets to pay expenses associated with the administration of Trust T (in effect, expenses associated with the administration of the Trust T assets for the benefit of [the participant's three children])...does not change" the conclusion that the trust had only individual beneficiaries. The IRS refers to "Trust T" in PLRs 2004-32027–2004-32029 as "a valid, conduit, see-through trust," even though the trust terminated immediately upon the death of the participant and was distributed outright to the participant's three children. In other words, Trust T was not the "classic" conduit trust that remains in existence after the participant's death, passing out all plan distributions to the conduit beneficiary. Nevertheless, since the IRS calls it a "conduit trust," the conclusion that payment of trust expenses out of the retirement plan assets does not adversely affect conduit status should remain valid. In PLR 2006-20026, the IRS blessed a conduit trust under which "asset management fees" would be paid directly to the trustee of the conduit trust out of the retirement plan assets, and would "not flow through" the trust.

E.   **Drawbacks of the conduit trust.** The conduit trust is not suitable for every situation, because it lessens the trustee's control considerably. Also, to work as intended, the conduit trust depends upon the minimum distribution rules' staying exactly as they are under present law; if changes in the law require or encourage faster distributions, the trust beneficiary will receive the money much sooner than the participant intended.

Practical problems include the apparent requirement of "tracing" retirement plan distributions. The trustee must show that each distribution received from the plan is paid "directly" to the conduit beneficiary "upon receipt" by the trustee. Thus, the plan distributions need to bounce into and out of the trustee's bank account in short order. Possibly the trustee could arrange to have distributions sent directly from the IRA or plan to the conduit beneficiary (bypassing the trust's bank account).

There is no indication that the trust can take "credit" for distributing to the conduit beneficiary something other than the actual distribution received from the retirement plan. For example, suppose the minimum distribution from the IRA to a particular conduit trust for a particular year is $10. Early in the year (before taking any distribution from the IRA) the trustee pays $15 to the conduit trust beneficiary (from other assets of the trust). Now the trustee receives the $10 MRD from the IRA. The trustee apparently must pass the $10 IRA distribution out to the conduit beneficiary upon receipt by the trust, even though the trustee has already paid the beneficiary more than that amount during the year in question.

There is also the risk that the trust will receive a larger-than-intended distribution by mistake. There are cases where a trustee has requested a small distribution, or even just sent in the paperwork to have the IRA titled as an inherited IRA payable to the trust, and the IRA provider has erroneously cashed out the entire IRA and placed the funds in a taxable account in the name of the trust. One negative effect of such an erroneous distribution is loss of deferral (because a nonspouse beneficiary cannot "roll over" a distribution from an inherited plan, even if the distribution was made in error; ¶ 4.2.02(A)).

The negative effects are compounded if the erroneous distribution is paid to a conduit trust, under which the trustee is compelled to immediately pass out the entire plan distribution to the conduit beneficiary (even if that has the effect of terminating the entire trust).

Finally, the conduit trust does not work for a client whose goal is to keep the retirement plan proceeds in the trust for the benefit of later beneficiaries. If the conduit beneficiary lives to a normal life expectancy he will have received all or almost all of the benefits and the remainder beneficiary will receive little or nothing.

F.   **Conduit trust drafting pointers.** There are two ways to create a conduit trust. One is by including "conduit" provisions (that apply only to the participant's retirement benefits) in a trust document for a trust that will also hold other assets. The other approach is to have a separate "stand-alone" trust that holds no assets other than retirement benefits that are eligible for a life expectancy payout. See ¶ 6.4.03. A participant considering leaving benefits to a stand-alone conduit trust might consider using an "individual retirement trust" (IRT) instead. ¶ 6.1.07.

G.   **Conduit trusts for successive beneficiaries.** Here is a question that comes up repeatedly regarding conduit trusts:

Question: If there is a conduit trust for one beneficiary (call him Child), and after that beneficiary's death the trust converts to being a conduit trust for another beneficiary (call her Grandchild), does the ADP switch to the life expectancy of the beneficiary of the second trust (Grandchild in this example) when the first conduit beneficiary dies? Or if there is a conduit trust for the benefit of the participant's spouse ("Spouse"), which passes to the children at her death, does the trust switch to using the children's life expectancy as the ADP after Spouse dies?

Answer: No. The ADP is always and irrevocably established at the participant's death based on the life expectancy of the participant's Designated Beneficiary (or applicable "no-DB rule"). See ¶ 1.5.13. For a rarely-applicable exception to this rule, see ¶ 1.6.05(C). By leaving benefits to a conduit trust of which Child (or Spouse) is the conduit beneficiary, the result you get is that the ADP for benefits payable to the trust is the single life expectancy of Child (or Spouse). But that's ALL you get: Just because you use a conduit trust does NOT mean that the ADP somehow switches or flips upon the Child's (or Spouse's) later death and allows the trust to stretch subsequent distributions over the *next* beneficiary's life expectancy.

6.3.06 *Conduit trust for multiple beneficiaries*

Though the IRS's only example on point deals with a conduit trust for just one beneficiary, the principle should also work with multiple beneficiaries. However, even more is required to draft a conduit trust for multiple beneficiaries. To have a conduit trust for multiple beneficiaries, the requirements would be (based on the language in the IRS regulation):

1.   All distributions the trust receives from the retirement plan must be immediately paid out to one or more of the conduit beneficiaries; and

2.   As long as *any member* of the conduit group is living, no plan distributions can be accumulated in the trust for possible distribution to *other* beneficiaries.

Warren Example: Warren dies leaving his IRA to a trust for his children. The trust provides that, as long as any child of Warren is living, the trustee must pay out, to one or more of such children, in such proportions as the trustee deems advisable for their education, support, and welfare, any and all amounts the trustee receives from the IRA, upon receipt. The trust terminates when there is no child of Warren living who is under the age of 40, and the IRA is to be transferred in equal shares at that time to such of Warren's children as are then living. Warren's trust "works" as a conduit trust, since only the children can receive benefits from the IRA as long as any child is living. However, this approach does not provide any benefits for the issue of a deceased child of Warren.

Davis Example: Davis's trust is the same as Warren's, except that Davis's trust provides that, upon the death of any child of Davis during the term of the trust, such child's share would be held in trust for later distribution to the deceased child's issue. Davis's trust would *not* qualify as conduit trust, because plan distributions may be accumulated in the trust while some members of the conduit group are still living. In a conduit trust for one beneficiary (¶ 6.3.05), we "don't care" what the trust terms provide after the death of the conduit beneficiary, because those subsequent beneficiaries are disregarded as mere potential successors to the conduit beneficiary. In a conduit trust for multiple beneficiaries, the "we don't care" point is not reached until ALL of the permissible conduit beneficiaries have died.

6.3.07 *Accumulation trusts: Introduction*

Any trust that is not a conduit trust is called in this book an **accumulation trust** (the IRS does not use this term), meaning that the trustee has the power to accumulate plan distributions in the trust. Under an accumulation trust (except, probably, in the case of a 100% grantor trust; ¶ 6.3.10) some or all of the potential remainder beneficiaries *do* "count" (i.e., they are not disregarded) for purposes of the MRD trust rules.

From Reg. § 1.401(a)(9)-5, A-7(c): "Thus, for example, if the first beneficiary has a right to all income with respect to an employee's individual account during that beneficiary's life and a second beneficiary has a right to the principal but only after the death of the first income beneficiary (any portion of the principal distributed during the life of the first income beneficiary to be held in trust until that first beneficiary's death), *both beneficiaries must be taken into account* in determining the beneficiary with the shortest life expectancy and whether only individuals are beneficiaries." Emphasis added.

While a conduit trust is guaranteed to pass the IRS trust rules, an accumulation trust may or may not pass the trust rules. Under an accumulation trust, it may or may not be easy to figure out which beneficiaries are disregarded as mere potential successors, because the meaning of this term is clear in some situations but unclear in others. The regulations offer no other guiding principles and contain only one example of an accumulation trust that passes the rules, the ambiguous Example 1 of Reg. § 1.401(a)(9)-5, A-7(c)(3): "Under the terms of Trust P, all trust income is payable annually to B [spouse of the deceased participant, A], and no one has the power to appoint Trust P principal to any person other than B. A's children, who are all younger than B, are the sole remainder beneficiaries of Trust P. *No other person has a beneficial interest in Trust P*." Emphasis added.

In this example, the IRS is making the point that B and the children of A are all considered "beneficiaries" of Trust P, so the surviving spouse is not the sole beneficiary, but her life expectancy is used as the ADP because she is the oldest beneficiary. This example is defective, however, because it does not explain what happens under "Trust P" if all of A's children predecease B. Either the trust document or state law must have something to say on that point, but the IRS's example is silent. Yet the only way we would be entitled to disregard the contingent beneficiaries who take in that case is if they are considered "mere potential successors" (¶ 6.3.04) to the interests of A's children. The ambiguity is repeated in the IRS's use of the same example in Rev. Rul. 2006-26, 2006-22 I.R.B. 939.

The IRS has resolved this ambiguity in several private letter rulings (which of course are not authoritative); see ¶ 6.3.08(A). Based on these PLRs, the meaning of Example 1 is that we need not consider who would take the benefits if the children of A predecease the participant's surviving spouse B, because the children of A are outright (unlimited) beneficiaries, and accordingly any beneficiary who takes only if the children of A die before B is a "mere potential successor."

6.3.08 *Accumulation trust: O/R-2-NLP*

Under the approach exemplified in the PLRs discussed at "A" below, you test an accumulation trust by "counting" all successive beneficiaries down the "chain" of potential beneficiaries who could take under the trust, until you come to the beneficiary(ies) who or which will be entitled to receive the trust property *immediately* and *outright* upon the death of the prior beneficiary(ies). That "immediate outright" person, entity, or group is (or are) the last beneficiaries in the "chain" that you need to consider. If the immediate outright beneficiary(ies), and all prior beneficiaries in the "chain," are individuals, then the trust qualifies as a see-through trust, with the life expectancy of the oldest member of that group serving as the ADP. Any beneficiary who might receive the benefits as a result of the death(s) of the immediate outright beneficiary(ies) is ignored as a "mere potential successor."

These tests are applied at the time of the participant's death, "as if" the first trust beneficiary died immediately after the participant, and the next beneficiary in the chain died immediately after the first beneficiary, and so on until you reach the first "immediate outright" beneficiary, where you stop.

The tests are *not* re-applied at the later actual death of any beneficiary. It makes no difference who *in fact* inherits the benefits when the first beneficiary later dies. Rather, the "snapshot" of beneficiaries is taken once and only once, at the time of the participant's death, based on the identities of beneficiaries *who actually survived the participant* and on the *hypothetical death of each of these beneficiaries* immediately after the participant's death or immediately after the death of the prior beneficiary in the "chain."

This type of trust is called an **"outright-to-now-living-persons" (O/R-2-NLP) trust** in this book. It is recommended that practitioners use conduit trusts (¶ 6.3.05) and O/R-2-NLP trusts as often as possible when drafting trusts that are to be named as beneficiary of retirement benefits, since these are the only types of trusts as to which we have clear guidance that they "work." For how to have an O/R-2-NLP trust for a disabled beneficiary, see ¶ 6.4.04(B); for minors, see ¶ 6.4.05(B); for the participant's surviving spouse, see ¶ 6.4.06(B).

A.   **Authority for the O/R-2-NLP approach.** As explained at ¶ 6.3.07, the only example of a nonconduit see-through trust in the regulations is ambiguous. In PLR 2004-38044, the IRS resolved that ambiguity. In this PLR, "A" died, leaving his IRA payable to a trust. The trust benefitted the participant's spouse, B, for her life. Upon B's death the principal would be divided among the participant's "lineal descendants then living," with each descendant's share to be distributed to him outright (unless he was under age 30, in which case distribution was to be delayed until he had attained age 30).

At the time of the participant's death, his spouse survived him, and he had three living children, C, D, and E, and apparently no deceased children. The three children had *already attained age 30* at the time of the participant's death. Thus, if the spouse had died immediately after the trust's establishment, the three children would have taken the trust principal (including the remaining retirement benefits) *outright and immediately.*

Since the spouse's interest in the trust was "not unlimited" (she was entitled only to a life income interest, plus principal in the trustee's discretion), it was "necessary to determine which other beneficiaries of Trust Y must be considered in determining who, if anyone, may be treated as Taxpayer A's designated beneficiary...." In other words, if the first trust beneficiary is *not* entitled to outright distribution of the entire trust, or even of all distributions the trustee receives from the retirement plan, we must keep looking; we must also count as beneficiaries (for purposes of applying the tests in the IRS's MRD trust rules #3 and #5) the beneficiary(ies) who will take the trust when the first beneficiary dies.

However, the ruling goes on to say that we can stop our search once we reach the children who are the apparent remainder beneficiaries under this trust. *Because they will take their shares outright and immediately when the prior beneficiary dies*, we do not need to go further and find out who would take the benefits if any of these three children predecease the surviving spouse. From the ruling: "Since the right of each child to his/her remainder interest in the...[trust] was unrestricted at the death of Taxpayer A, it is necessary to consider only Taxpayers B through E [i.e., the spouse and the three children] to determine which of them shall be treated as the designated beneficiary of Taxpayer A's interest in" the IRA. (Note: The ruling should say "to determine which of them shall be treated as the *oldest* designated beneficiary"; all of them are Designated Beneficiaries, and the oldest Designated Beneficiary's life expectancy will be the ADP.) This is consistent with, and clarifies, Example 1 of Reg. § 1.401(a)(9)-5, A-7(c)(3).

Later PLRs 2005-22012, 2006-08032, and 2006-10026 confirm this interpretation of the regulation.

B.   Finding an "O/R" beneficiary (future issue don't count).
The O/R-2-NLP trust requires the existence of at least one now-living person who would be entitled to outright distribution of the benefits upon the prior beneficiary's death. It is not always easy to find a *younger individual* to name as outright immediate beneficiary after the first beneficiary's death.

Future unborn issue can NOT be counted for this purpose because you cannot assume they will ever exist. See, *e.g.*, PLR 2008-43042, in which father died leaving his IRA to a trust for his son "C." C was to receive all of the trust funds no later than age 40. If he died before reaching age 40, the trust would pass to C's descendants, if any, otherwise to C's "heirs at law." At the time of father's death, C had no descendants living. His "heir-at-law-apparent" was his mother. The IRS ruled that the countable beneficiaries of the trust were C and his mother. PLRs 2006-10026 and -10027 are similar.

6.3.09 *Accumulation trust: "Circle" trust*

One way to deal with the mystery of which beneficiaries are disregarded is to draft the trust so that there are no beneficiaries you *need* to disregard. If the trust property cannot be distributed to a nonindividual beneficiary, then it passes Rule 5 (¶ 6.2.09).

For example, if the trust provides "income to spouse for life, remainder outright to our issue living at spouse's death; provided, if at any time during spouse's life there is no issue of ours living, the trust shall terminate and be distributed to spouse," it is impossible for the trust assets to pass to anyone other than spouse or issue, all of whom are individuals. If spouse dies before issue, issue get the benefits. If issue die before spouse, spouse gets the benefits. This is nicknamed a "circle trust" because the group of beneficiaries is a closed circle. This approach could be appropriate for a client who is leaving benefits to a credit shelter trust for the spouse only to save estate taxes for his issue, and who would just as soon leave it outright to the spouse if it should happen that all the issue predecease the spouse.

This is also called the "last man standing" approach, because it provides for an accelerated termination if it should ever occur that only one member of the beneficiary-group is still living, with immediate outright distribution of the entire trust to that individual; see ¶ 6.4.05(B).

Note: Of course there is the possibility that simultaneous deaths may occur with the result that the benefits wind up passing to one or more beneficiaries' estates (i.e., nonindividual beneficiaries). Based on Reg. § 1.401(a)(9)-5, A-7(c)(3), Example 1, and the successful O/R-2-NLP PLRs (¶ 6.3.08(A)), this possibility is ignored when testing a trust for see-through status.

6.3.10 *Accumulation trust: 100 percent grantor trust*

Under the so-called "grantor trust rules," a trust beneficiary who is a U.S. citizen or resident is treated for purposes of the federal income tax as the "owner" of trust assets if such beneficiary has the sole unrestricted right to withdraw those assets from the trust. See § 678(a)(1), § 672(f), Reg. § 1.671-3. If an individual is deemed the owner of all of the trust's assets under § 678(a)(1), then retirement benefits payable to such trust *should be* deemed paid "to" such individual beneficiary for purposes of the minimum distribution rules, and the "all beneficiaries must be individuals" test would be met; however, there is no ruling on point.

In PLR 2000-23030, the decedent's IRAs were payable to a trust that was a grantor trust as to the surviving spouse. The IRS ruled that a transfer of the decedent's IRAs to or from this trust was deemed a transfer to or from the surviving spouse. See also PLR 2003-23012, in which the surviving spouse was recognized as the participant's Designated Beneficiary under the annuity rules of § 72 when benefits were payable to a trust deemed owned by the spouse under the grantor trust rules. However, neither of these rulings discussed whether the trust in question *qualified as a see-through trust*. The IRS has always been more lenient in allowing a spousal rollover through a trust (see ¶ 3.2.09) than in recognizing a trust as a see-through.

In PLRs 2006-20025 and 2008-26008 (discussed at ¶4.6.03(C)), the IRS allowed beneficiaries who inherited IRAs outright to transfer their inherited IRAs to "grantor trusts" for their own benefit, again lending support to the conclusion that a grantor trust will be deemed "the same as" the individual who is treated as the 100 percent owner of the trust property for income tax purposes. But there is no specific ruling to the effect that a trust that is named as beneficiary of a retirement plan and that is a grantor trust as to a particular individual qualifies as a see-through trust.

Treating the trust beneficiary as the "owner" of the benefits for income tax purposes would have two significant results: Income taxes on the trust's income would be imposed at the beneficiary's rate; and (presumably) the remainder beneficiary would not be considered a beneficiary of the trust for purposes of the minimum distribution rules. Thus an estate, older individuals, or charities could be named as remainder beneficiaries (to succeed to whatever part of the trust was not distributed to or withdrawn by the owner-beneficiary during his life) without loss of the use of the owner-beneficiary's life expectancy as the ADP. Similarly, a power of appointment that affected the trust property only after the death of the owner-beneficiary could be disregarded; see ¶ 6.3.11.

Under this model, the trust beneficiary would be given the unlimited right to withdraw the benefits (and any proceeds thereof) from the trust at any time. Until the beneficiary chose to exercise this right, the trustee would exercise ownership rights and responsibilities on the beneficiary's behalf, for example, by investing the trust funds, choosing distribution options, and distributing income and/or principal to or for the benefit of the beneficiary.

This type of trust would be uncommon, since anyone wanting to give such broad rights to the beneficiary would presumably leave the benefits outright to the beneficiary rather than in trust. However, this model could be useful for certain disabled beneficiaries (see ¶ 6.4.04(C)) or for a "qualified domestic trust" (QDOT) for the benefit of a noncitizen spouse (§ 2056(d)); see the *Special Report: Retirement Benefits and the Marital Deduction, Including Planning for the Noncitizen Spouse* (Appendix C).

6.3.11 *Powers of appointment*

If a remainder interest is subject to a power of appointment upon the death of the life beneficiary of the trust, all potential appointees, as well as those who would take in default of exercise of the power, are considered "beneficiaries," unless they can be disregarded under the rules discussed in this ¶ 6.3.

Under a <u>conduit trust</u> for a single beneficiary, the trust's remainder beneficiaries are disregarded. ¶ 6.3.05(B). Thus, the conduit beneficiary (or the trustee or anyone) can be given the power to appoint the trust assets remaining at the conduit beneficiary's death to anyone, even a charity, a non-see-through trust, an estate, or an older individual, and the trust will still qualify as a see-through with the ADP based on the conduit beneficiary's life expectancy. See, *e.g.*, PLR 2006-20026. For a trust with multiple conduit beneficiaries, it is more difficult to apply this rule; see ¶ 6.3.06.

With an <u>accumulation trust</u>, remainder beneficiaries generally must be counted. (The presumed exception is the 100 percent grantor trust; see ¶ 6.3.10.) Thus, if an accumulation trust (other than, presumably, a 100 percent grantor trust) is to qualify as a see-through, all such potential appointees, as well as those who will take in default of exercise of the power, should be: (1) identifiable (¶ 6.2.07), (2) individuals (¶ 6.2.09), who are (3) younger than the beneficiary whose life expectancy is the one the participant wants used as the ADP. The following examples illustrate the possibilities:

A.   **Power to appoint to "issue"** of the participant and/or spouse apparently is acceptable, because the power is limited to a small, clearly-defined group of "identifiable" younger individuals. See PLR 1999-03050 ("Trust B") approving a trust that granted the surviving spouse a testamentary power to appoint the principal "to and among the issue" of the participant and his spouse. If the power were not exercised, the property would pass at the surviving spouse's death to "the children or their issue, under the terms set forth in Trust M"; thus the potential appointees and the takers in default were the same group. A defect of this ruling is that the "terms" of "Trust M" under which the issue would take are not specified; see "E" below. Presumably the participant had some issue living at the time of his death, though curiously the PLR does not so state.

B.   **Power to appoint to spouses of issue.** A power to appoint property to someone's "spouse" is a classic example of creating a nonidentifiable beneficiary (unless it is limited to a particular identified spouse, or to spouses who are younger than the oldest trust beneficiary determined without reference to the power). See Kit and Julia Example, ¶ 6.2.07(A). In PLR 2004-38044, the participant's surviving spouse had the power to appoint the trust at her death to the participant's issue *and their spouses*; to enable the trust to qualify as a see-through, she disclaimed this power. See ¶ 6.3.03(B). As a result of the disclaimer of the power, the property would pass outright to the takers in default of exercise of the power, who were the decedent's issue.

C.   **Power to appoint to charity.** A trust that says "The trustee shall pay income to my spouse for life, and upon my spouse's death the principal shall be paid to such members of *the class consisting of our issue and any charity* as my spouse shall appoint by her will," would flunk this rule, because the benefits could pass under the power to a nonindividual beneficiary, the charity.

D.   **Power limited to younger individuals.** See ¶ 6.2.07(C).

E.   **Power to appoint to another trust.** Under many states' laws, a power to appoint to individuals includes the power to appoint *in trust for* such individuals. The IRS has never commented on the effect of such a state law (or of an explicit power in an instrument to appoint to another trust). Since the regulations require that, if benefits are distributable under one trust to another trust, *both* trusts must comply with the rules (¶ 6.2.02(C)), it would appear that any power of appointment that could be exercised by appointing the benefits to another trust would cause the first trust to flunk the trust rules *unless* the power is limited to appointing only to other trusts that comply with the rules. One requirement of a see-through trust is that a copy of the trust be given to the plan administrator by October 31 of the year after *the participant's* death (¶ 6.2.08(A)). Thus, the power could effectively not be exercised to appoint to a new trust; the power holder would be limited to appointing to other see-through trusts created by the participant at or prior to his death (if there are any such trusts).

6.3.12 *Combining two types of qualifying trusts*

As we have seen, there are several ways to qualify a trust as a see-through. What happens if you combine two methods in the same trust? Drafters sometimes look into that idea in an attempt to satisfy the client's desire to prevent the putative beneficiary from ever actually gaining access to the retirement benefits.

A.   **Conduit trust and 678 grantor trust.** If the trust beneficiary has the right to demand distribution of the entire trust to himself, it appears the trust qualifies as a see-through because it is a 100 percent grantor trust; see ¶ 6.3.10. A trust also qualifies as a see-through if the trustee is required to pass all plan distributions out to the beneficiary immediately (conduit trust; ¶ 6.3.05). What if the trustee is not required to automatically *distribute* all plan distributions to the beneficiary, but the beneficiary has the right to demand immediate payment to himself of *all distributions the trustee receives from the plan*? The IRS position regarding such a <u>hybrid grantor-conduit trust</u> is not known. Such a trust does *not* conform with the regulation's description of a conduit trust.

B.   **Conduit distributions must begin at participant's death.** Suppose a trust provides income to the participant's spouse for life, with remainder passing to the participant's issue, but with each issue's share to be held in trust until the beneficiary reaches age 30. To make the trust "pass" the trust rules, can the trust become a conduit trust for the issue on the surviving spouse's death? No. See ¶ 6.3.05(A).

Reminder: If the spouse *predeceases* the participant she does not "count" as a beneficiary, and terms that would have applied had she survived are *irrelevant*. If the spouse predeceases, you test the trust by looking ONLY at the terms that apply to the children's interests, so having a conduit trust for the children on the participant's death *if the spouse does not survive him* could be appropriate.

C.   **"Switch" trusts.** Under a "switch" or "toggle" trust, the trust is set up as a conduit trust for one beneficiary, but a "trust protector" is given the power to convert the trust, by amendment, to an accumulation trust. The amendment power may require the trustee to also change the remainder beneficiaries of the trust, if some of the remainder beneficiaries under the conduit trust would not be suitable under an accumulation trust.

The benefit gained by this elaboration is the flexibility to cut down on the beneficiary's access to the retirement plan. This flexibility would be desirable if the beneficiary is in financial trouble. But by definition this approach is helpful in this way *only* if the beneficiary gets into trouble during a very narrow window of time—either just before the participant's death (too late for the participant to amend his estate plan) or just after it (before the Beneficiary Finalization Date, which is the deadline by which the trust protector must exercise the amendment power).

The approach is based on PLR 2005-37044, which involved a trust under which a trust protector had and exercised such an amendment power. Following court proceedings to reform the trust to the IRS's liking, the IRS ruled that the exercise of the amendment power did not cause the trust to lose its see-through status, because the trust protector's actions: carried out specific provisions adopted by the participant (i.e., the trust protector did not simply substitute some provisions of its own devising); were effective retroactively to the date of death and so could "be treated as a part of" the original trust instrument; and were "treated as a disclaimer under the laws of" the applicable state. The finding that state law treated this trust amendment as a "disclaimer" is mysterious because the trust protector's action was not a disclaimer and was nothing like a disclaimer.

Some advisors advocate the "switch" trust as a planning technique, seemingly regarding this single rather messy PLR as if it established an IRS-approved prototype trust. Yet the IRS's subsequent turn against post-death trust modifications (see ¶ 4.5.06) makes it unclear whether this PLR could be duplicated today. An alternative view is that the "toggle" approach involves substantial complications, relying on a shaky "precedent," to obtain a modest benefit.

6.4 Estate Planning with the MRD Trust Rules

Now that we understand the minimum distribution trust rules (see ¶ 6.2–¶ 6.3), the next step is to see how these the rules affect estate planning choices.

6.4.01 *Boilerplate provisions for trusts named as beneficiary*

Many practitioners would like to have a blanket trust form that will work for all clients' situations without further fine tuning. This approach can be hazardous when dealing with retirement benefits.

It makes sense, if qualification for see-through trust status is important, to include a "boilerplate" provision either prohibiting the use of the retirement benefits for payments to the estate for debts, expenses, or taxes, or requiring that no such payments may be made from the retirement benefits either "at all" or "on or after the Beneficiary Finalization Date." See ¶ 6.2.10 and Form 4.2, Appendix B. If there are no assets available to pay debts, expenses, and taxes other than the retirement benefits, consider specifying that only certain plans may be used for this purpose, so that only the plans authorized to be so used will be "tainted" and the other(s) can be exempted from this problem; or have the participant take withdrawals during life so his estate will have sufficient nonretirement assets to pay these items.

Similarly, include provisions that: the trust will be irrevocable at the participant's death (¶ 6.2.06); certain adult adoptions occurring after the participant's death will be ignored (¶ 6.2.07(A)); and property may not be appointed to a non-see-through trust. See Forms 4.1, 4.3, and 4.4, Appendix B. However, do not be misled into thinking that any trust that includes these "boilerplate" provisions automatically qualifies as a see-through trust, eligible to take minimum distributions based on the life expectancy of the oldest of the primary trust beneficiaries. This is absolutely NOT the case!

Qualification as a see-through trust depends on the substantive terms of the trust. A trust that provides "income to my spouse for life, remainder to the Salvation Army," can NOT qualify as a see-through trust because of the "countable" nonindividual remainder beneficiary (namely the charity). Including a paragraph in such a trust to the effect that "retirement benefits cannot be paid to any nonindividual beneficiary" does not fix the problem; it just makes the trust even more defective because now (in this example) the remainder interest in the trust is not disposed of (and may therefore revert to the donor's estate, another nonindividual beneficiary). A "boilerplate" provision prohibiting distributions of retirement benefits to nonindividual beneficiaries can cause problems; see "Heather Example" at ¶ 7.3.03. *Qualification depends on the substantive terms of the trust*; see ¶ 6.2–6.3.

6.4.02 *Advance rulings on see-through trust status*

One expensive and time-consuming way to achieve certainty regarding the see-through status of a trust would be to seek a private letter ruling on this point while the client is still living. The IRS will not rule on "hypothetical" questions, but once the trust is named as the participant's beneficiary, the IRS should be willing to rule on whether the trust complies with the trust rules, as it did for a living taxpayer in PLR 2003-24018. However, the IRS stated in this PLR that it was "unable" to rule on the Applicable Distribution Period that would apply after the taxpayer's death until after the taxpayer had actually died.

The IRS certainly does not limit rulings to completed transactions; see, *e.g.*, PLR 2002-42044, in which a surviving spouse proposed (as co-trustee of the trust named as beneficiary of participant's IRA) to demand that the IRA be distributed to the trust, and then (as beneficiary of the trust) to withdraw the distribution from the trust and roll it over to her own plan. The IRS granted her requested rulings on these proposed transactions, even though these were just as "hypothetical" as the future death of the taxpayer in PLR 2003-24018.

In this chapter, PLRs are cited as "authority" for various propositions because of the lack of authoritative guidance. Of course, a PLR cannot be relied upon as authority by anyone other than the taxpayer who obtained it. Furthermore, the fact that the IRS approved a particular trust instrument in a PLR is not equivalent to an IRS endorsement of that form of trust. The firm that obtained the ruling should not attempt to sell the trust form to other taxpayers as, in effect, an IRS-approved prototype document.

However, a PLR can serve as "substantial authority" for a position taken on a tax return for purposes of avoiding a penalty. Reg.

§ 1.6662-4(d)(3)(iii). Also, a court might hold the IRS bound by a position that the IRS has taken consistently in numerous PLRs.

6.4.03 *Should you use a separate trust for retirement benefits?*

Should a client's retirement benefits be left to a separate trust that will hold no other assets? Or should the client's benefits be left to the same trust as the client's other assets, with that trust being modified to include special provisions that apply only to the retirement benefits?

Separate-trusters point to the many practical difficulties of having numerous special provisions that deal only with certain assets. For example, if there is a regular "family pot" trust for the decedent's minor children, with a conduit provision grafted onto it requiring the trustee to immediately pass out retirement plan distributions (see Form 4.8, Appendix B, for an example), will the trustee have to trace dollars in and out of the trust bank account? How quickly must the distribution be passed on before it merges into the rest of the trust's cash? Will the trustee, the client, or a later attorney amending the trust recognize and so preserve the intricate web of provisions governing the retirement benefits? But single-trusters pooh-pooh these difficulties as exaggerated or inapplicable, and remind us that separate trust treatment is impracticable for smaller retirement plans.

See also ¶ 6.4.05 (opening paragraph plus subsection (F)) and ¶ 6.1.07 for more discussion of when to have separate trusts versus one pooled trust (and related questions). See ¶ 7.3.03(B) ("Heather Example") for an example of when separate trusts should be used.

6.4.04 *Planning choices: Trust for disabled beneficiary*

Here are the options (A–D) available for a trust that is to be named as beneficiary of a retirement plan and that is intended to provide for a disabled beneficiary, when qualifying for see-through trust status is an important goal (¶ 6.2.01). Which option is best depends on whether the beneficiary must qualify for need-based government benefit programs, and on the identity of the remainder beneficiary. If qualification for benefit programs is a goal, the donor should consult with an attorney who specializes in drafting this type of trust. If the participant has *already died* and left benefits *outright* to a disabled beneficiary, see "E."

A.   **Conduit trust.** Under a conduit trust (¶ 6.3.05), all of the MRDs, as well as any other distributions the trustee receives from the retirement plan, would have to be promptly distributed to (or applied for the benefit of) the beneficiary. If such distributions are passed out to the disabled beneficiary, they would be considered available income or assets to the beneficiary, thus (unless the distributions are very small) forfeiting eligibility for welfare benefits. Thus, a conduit trust is normally not suitable to be named as beneficiary for a disabled individual if the goal is to avoid forfeiting eligibility for welfare-type disability benefits. If qualification for welfare benefits is not an issue (for example, because the family intends to provide for all of the beneficiary's care), a conduit trust could be suitable, especially if the donor wants the remainder interest to pass to charity.

To date there is no IRS ruling that would allow payments from a conduit trust to be made to a special needs trust for the benefit of a disabled beneficiary rather than directly to the beneficiary or his guardian or custodian; compare "D" below.

B.   **Accumulation O/R-2-NLP Trust.** Under most forms of "supplemental needs" trusts (designed to benefit a disabled beneficiary without causing loss of the beneficiary's eligibility for need-based government programs), the trustee has discretion regarding whether to distribute trust funds to or for the benefit of the disabled individual, but is prohibited from distributing funds for expenses that are paid for by the government programs such as support and medical care. Such a trust would be considered an accumulation trust for MRD purposes, but would still qualify as a see-through *if* the trust passes outright at the disabled beneficiary's death to other now-living individuals, such as the disabled beneficiary's siblings. See ¶ 6.3.08.

If an O/R-2-NLP trust is used, a charity cannot be named as remainder beneficiary. The chosen remainder beneficiaries should be (as siblings typically are) individuals who are close in age to (or younger than) the disabled beneficiary. The countable trust beneficiaries will be the disabled person and the remainder beneficiary(ies); the life expectancy of the oldest member of this group will be the ADP. Thus, drafting this type of trust is "easy" if there are siblings (or other suitable individual remainder beneficiaries) who are (1) living at the participant's death and (2) younger than or close in age to the disabled beneficiary—but impossible if there are no such suitable younger or close-in-age individual remainder beneficiaries.

C.   **Accumulation 100 percent grantor trust.** A trust that gives the beneficiary the unlimited right to withdraw all the trust property at any time would be treated as a 100 percent grantor trust (¶ 6.3.10). It could be a suitable way to provide for a mentally handicapped beneficiary who (1) does not need to qualify for need-based government benefits (because this type of trust would disqualify him) and (2) can exercise the right of withdrawal only through a legal guardian, especially if the guardian is also the trustee. For this type of beneficiary, this type of trust provides the benefits of a discretionary trust while (presumably; see ¶ 6.3.10) allowing the life expectancy of the handicapped beneficiary to be the ADP. It also allows distributions to be taxed at the beneficiary's tax rate. This approach can be particularly helpful if the beneficiary has no siblings or issue, where the only likely remainder beneficiaries are either much older individuals, the beneficiary's own estate, or charities.

D.   **Charitable remainder trust with payments to special needs trust.** If the donor is charitably inclined, consider making the retirement benefits payable to a charitable remainder trust (CRT; see ¶ 7.5.04) for the life benefit of the disabled beneficiary. The retirement benefits can be paid to the CRT free of income taxes, and the annuity or unitrust payments can be paid to a special needs trust for the disabled beneficiary rather than outright to him (as is normally required for CRTs) if various requirements are met, according to Rev. Rul. 2002-20, 2002-1 I.R.B. 794.

E.   **If the participant has already died.** Options A–D above apply during the planning stage, while the participant is alive and is trying to choose the best type of trust to name as beneficiary. If the participant has *already died*, and left the benefits *outright* to a disabled beneficiary, and qualification for government benefits is a concern, the disabled beneficiary's guardian could seek to have the benefits transferred to a "(d)(4)(A)" trust for the disabled beneficiary, as was done in PLR 2006-20025 (see ¶ 4.6.03(C)). In drafting such a trust, qualification as a see-through trust is NOT a concern. Because the benefits were left *outright* to an individual, the benefits have already qualified for the life expectancy payout; see-through trust status is a concern only when the *participant leaves benefits to a trust*, not when a beneficiary who has inherited benefits outright subsequently *transfers* such benefits to a trust.

6.4.05 *Planning choices: Trusts for minors*

Here are the options available for a trust intended to provide for minor beneficiaries, when qualifying for see-through trust status is an important goal (¶ 6.2.01). In deciding which to use, consider the donor's objectives: Is the donor's main goal to be sure that the "stretch" payout method is available? Or is the money most likely to be spent during the beneficiaries' childhood, for their education and care, rather than conserved for the beneficiaries' own retirement years? Also consider the value of the benefits and other assets: Are the benefits and nonbenefit assets each substantial enough to justify establishing separate trusts, one for the benefits and one for the other assets? Are the benefits substantial enough to justify establishing a separate trust for each minor beneficiary, or is the "family pot trust" approach better?

Naming a minor directly as beneficiary of a retirement plan is not recommended. This approach may cause the plan administrator not to release the benefits to anyone other than a legal guardian of the minor. In some states, subjecting property to legal guardianship is not only time consuming and expensive, it restricts how the money can be spent for the minor's benefit.

Here are ideas regarding different ways to leave retirement benefits for the benefit of minor beneficiaries:

A.   **Conduit trust (or IRT).** A conduit trust may make sense for benefits that are not intended to be the primary support source for the minor beneficiaries, such as a grandparent's IRA left to grandchildren who are supported by their parents. Also consider a trusteed IRA in this situation (¶ 6.1.07).

Even though a conduit trust partly defeats the purpose of leaving money in trust for a young beneficiary, some practitioners opt for this because it is a safe harbor and because they expect that the MRDs that would have to be passed out to the minor beneficiary (or his guardian or custodian) would be very small because of his young age. A conduit provision "inside" another trust may also be a good way to leave benefits to minors if the retirement benefits are not substantial enough to justify establishing a separate trust. The benefits are left to the same trust as all the other assets, but that trust contains "conduit" provisions requiring the trustee to pass through all retirement plan distributions. See Form 4.8, Appendix B.

On the other hand, if the benefits are a significant part of a trust fund that will be providing the primary source of support and education for an orphaned family, a conduit trust may not be a good match. The trustee would be required to distribute to one or more of the children, each year, all distributions the trustee receives from the retirement plan. Even assuming the trustee can pick and choose, each year, which member of the group will receive that year's distributions, the trustee has no discretion to accumulate distributions for possible later needs. If later changes in the minimum distribution rules, or in the income tax laws, make accelerated distributions either mandatory or desirable (*e.g.*, because tax rates are about to go up substantially), the trustee cannot comply with (or take advantage of) the changed tax rules without losing control of the funds.

B. **Circle Trust: Last man standing.** If a conduit trust is not suitable, so an accumulation trust for the minors must be named as beneficiary, the problem becomes, who will receive the benefits if the minor dies while the trust is still in effect? That contingent remainder beneficiary "counts" as a beneficiary for purposes of the minimum distribution trust rules, and it can be difficult to figure who that remainder beneficiary should be. (The minor's future unborn issue don't count; see ¶ 6.3.08(B).)

If the trust is for the benefit of several minors, one solution is to provide that if, at any time, there is only one beneficiary of the trust who is still living, the trust terminates at that time and all assets are distributed outright to that one. Thus, the living person who will receive the benefits outright on the death of all other beneficiaries is one of the children who are intended to be the sole or primary beneficiaries of the trust. This is the "Circle Trust" approach (see ¶ 6.3.09). This approach makes it unnecessary to name some remainder beneficiary the donor doesn't really want to name (see "C"). The drawback is that if the provision is triggered the benefits could pass outright to a very young individual (through his legal guardian or a custodian for his benefit). See Form 4.9, Appendix B.

C.   **O/R-2-NLP: Who will be the "NLP" remainder beneficiary?** To avoid using a conduit trust, and still qualify as a see-through, practitioners look for ways to make the minors' trust an O/R-2-NLP trust (¶ 6.3.08).

The typical minors' trust calls for the trust to terminate and be distributed outright to the minors as each reaches a certain age (for example, age 35), or when all of the siblings have either reached that age or died. To be a see-through under the O/R-2-NLP approach it is necessary to have a younger individual remainder beneficiary who will inherit the benefits outright if all of the minor children die *before* reaching the stated age.

With a trust for an *adult* beneficiary, the outright remainder beneficiary can usually be the then-living issue of the primary beneficiary, but that approach will not work with minor children who have no issue at the time of the participant's death. See ¶ 6.3.08(B).

Typically, the donor of a minors' trust would name a "wipeout" beneficiary, to take the trust property if all of the minor children die without issue while there is still money in the trust. The problem is, if the wipeout beneficiary is a charity or other nonindividual, the trust will flunk Rule 5 (¶ 6.2.09); and if the wipeout beneficiary is an individual who is older than the oldest minor child, the wipeout beneficiary's shorter life expectancy will be the ADP (¶ 6.2.07).

See PLR 2002-28025, which involved a trust for the benefit of two minors. The trust was to terminate and be distributed outright to the minors as each reached age 30, but if they both died before reaching that age, the trust would pass to other relatives, the oldest of whom was age 67 at the participant's death. The IRS ruled that the 67-year-old's life expectancy was the ADP because he was the "oldest trust beneficiary." PLRs 2006-10026 and 2008-43042 (see ¶ 6.3.08((B)) are similar.

What the IRS Should do

The IRS's position produces absurd results, as can be seen in these letter rulings. The IRS could easily eliminate this absurdity, and solve the headache of providing for minor beneficiaries, by adopting a simple convention as an add-on to the O/R-2-NLP concept. The IRS could make a rule that an individual will be considered an "unlimited" trust beneficiary (so successors to his interest can be disregarded as "mere potential successors") if his interest in the benefits is to pass to him outright either (1) immediately upon the death of the donor or of another beneficiary [as the rule already provides] *or* (2) upon the beneficiary's attainment of a certain age that is not older than age 45 (or age 35, or age 30, or whatever age the IRS prefers). By adopting that rule, the IRS would immediately make legal the most standard and normal trust provision for minor beneficiaries, which is that they will come into outright possession upon attaining a certain age—an age that (under the vast majority of trust instruments) they have an overwhelming likelihood of attaining, according to the IRS's own actuarial tables.

Here are some possible approaches for dealing with this problem. With each, a separate trust just for the retirement benefits may be required, since the remainder beneficiary provisions may be different for the benefits than for the other assets.

✓ One approach is for the donor to plug in the name of a younger individual as the wipeout beneficiary, perhaps a young niece, nephew, or other relative. The drawback of this approach, obviously, is that the donor ends up potentially leaving the retirement benefits to someone he is not really interested in benefitting.

✓ Another approach, used successfully in PLR 2002-35038, is to give the trustee the power to distribute the remainder to any individual beneficiary who was born in the same year as the donor's oldest child or in a later year (or give the minor children the power to appoint to any younger beneficiaries). Unfortunately, the IRS's rulings approving this approach are seriously defective, in that the rulings *fail to mention what would happen to the benefits if the power of appointment were not exercised.* Realistically, the trust instrument would still have to name a younger individual wipeout beneficiary to address this possibility.

✓ A third approach is to name, as the wipeout beneficiary, heirs at law who are younger than the oldest "real" beneficiary; see ¶ 6.4.08.

D. **Dump the stretch; buy life insurance.** Young parents of young children might consider drafting the trust to say exactly what they want it to say, ignoring the see-through trust requirements, and purchasing life insurance to assure adequate funds for payment of any extra income taxes caused by loss of see-through status. This may make more sense than accepting the drawbacks of approaches A–C.

E. **Staged distributions at various ages.** Trusts for minors often provide for a staged distribution of principal, *e.g.*, half at age 25, balance at age 30. Such staged distributions create several headaches when the trust is beneficiary of a retirement plan. One is whether a retirement benefit is an asset of the trust that is capable of being valued and divided; while many practitioners assume the answer is "yes" with respect to an IRA (which is normally a mere custodial account holding easily-valued securities), the answer is less obvious for a nonassignable benefit under a traditional pension plan.

Another issue is whether the built-in income tax "debt" should be deducted in valuing the retirement benefits for purposes of determining the amount distributable to the beneficiary. A third is the hassle of dividing and transferring an inherited retirement plan; see ¶ 6.1.05. In view of these complications, consider not using such staged distribution for a trust that will hold retirement benefits.

F. **Whether to have a separate trust for each minor.** If the benefits are left to a typical "family pot" trust for the benefit of all of the donor's children collectively, then (assuming the trust qualifies as a see-through) the ADP will be the life expectancy of the oldest child. The donor could leave the benefits to separate trusts, one for the benefit of each child, to enable each child's trust to use that child's life expectancy as the ADP.

The drawbacks of this approach are: the money is divided into rigid predetermined shares, without the ability of the trustee to distribute more money on behalf of a child who needs it more; and, unless the trusts are conduit trusts, you still have the problem of finding a younger remainder beneficiary if the child dies before reaching the age for outright distribution. If the remainder beneficiaries of each individual child's separate trust are the other siblings, you are right back with the oldest child's life expectancy being the ADP for all the trusts.

G.   **Custodianship under UTMA.** Another choice (ideal where there are not enough assets to justify a trustee's fee) is to leave the benefits to a custodian for the child under the Uniform Transfers to Minors Act ("UTMA"). § 3(a) of UTMA permits a "person having the right to designate the recipient of property transferable upon the occurrence of a future event" to nominate ("in a writing designating a beneficiary of contractual rights") a custodian to hold such property under the Act on behalf of a minor beneficiary.

The main drawbacks of leaving benefits to a custodian under UTMA are that the beneficiary becomes entitled to the money outright at a certain age (typically 18 or 21, depending on state law), and that age may be younger than the age the parents would ideally like. Also, the benefits must be left to specific individuals (such as, typically, equal shares to the surviving children). You lose the flexibility of leaving benefits to a "family pot" trust where the trustee has discretion to spend more for one child than another depending on their needs.
The IRS has never ruled on the question of who is considered the Designated Beneficiary when benefits are paid to a custodian under UTMA. Presumably the IRS would recognize that the minor is the "beneficiary."

6.4.06 *Planning choices: Trust for spouse*

Here are options to consider for a trust intended to provide life income to the participant's surviving spouse, including a credit shelter or QTIP trust, when qualifying for see-through trust status is an important goal (¶ 6.2.01). If the client is naming any type of trust for the spouse as beneficiary, be sure the client understands the income tax drawbacks of leaving benefits to a trust for the spouse as opposed to outright to the spouse; see ¶ 3.3.02(B). If qualifying for the marital deduction is important, see ¶ 3.3. See also ¶ 7.5.06(C) regarding use of a charitable remainder trust for the spouse's life benefit.

A.   **Conduit trust as credit shelter or QTIP substitute.** If a retirement plan or IRA is left to a conduit trust of which the participant's surviving spouse is the sole life beneficiary, the surviving spouse will be considered the "sole beneficiary" of the plan or IRA for purposes of the minimum distribution rules but not for purposes of the spousal rollover. ¶ 1.6.06(A).

The primary *drawback* of a conduit-credit shelter trust is that, if the spouse lives long enough, MRDs will eventually cause most of the benefits to be distributed outright to her. Benefits distributed outright to the spouse will not "bypass" her estate and thus to that extent the trust will *not* save estate taxes. Similarly, if the purpose of leaving benefits to a QTIP trust is to preserve the asset for the younger generation, a conduit trust will defeat that purpose, since most of the benefits will be distributed outright to the surviving spouse if she lives long enough. But a conduit trust for the spouse's life may be fine if the participant just wants to make sure the spouse does not spend the entire fund at once.

Here is another problem with using a conduit trust for the benefit of the surviving spouse: If the participant and the surviving spouse *both* die before the end of the year in which participant would have reached age 70½, the IRS will claim there is no "Designated Beneficiary" when the benefits pass to the remainder beneficiaries of the trust, even if the remainder beneficiaries are all individuals, causing the benefits to become subject to the 5-year rule on the death of the spouse. See ¶ 1.6.05 for the special "(B)(iv)(II) rule" that applies on the death of the surviving spouse-beneficiary when both spouses die young, and PLR 2006-44022, discussed at ¶ 1.6.05(C). This drawback is not a factor if the participant has already passed his RBD, but since Roth IRAs have no RBD (¶ 5.2.02(A)) it is a lifelong problem with respect to leaving a Roth IRA to a conduit trust for the participant's surviving spouse.

Contrary to a popular belief, leaving benefits to a conduit trust for the spouse does *not* allow the Applicable Distribution Period to "flip" to the life expectancy of the children or other remainder beneficiaries at the spouse's death; see ¶ 6.3.05(G).

B.   **Accumulation O/R-2-NLP trust.** The typical QTIP or credit shelter trust is an accumulation trust (¶ 6.3.07), meaning that the remainder beneficiaries "count" for purposes of the all-beneficiaries-must-be-individuals rule and the oldest-beneficiary's-life-expectancy-is-the-ADP rule. See, *e.g.*, PLR 9322005 (marital trust to a spouse for life, remainder to children; spouse *and children* regarded as beneficiaries).

If the trust is to terminate and pass outright to the participant's issue on the spouse's death, the trust will "pass" the rules as an O/R-2-NLP trust *provided* that at least one issue of the participant survives the participant; if those conditions are met, the trust can provide whatever the participant wants it to provide regarding disposition of the trust assets if all the issue later predecease the spouse. ¶ 6.3.08. See Form 4.10, Appendix B. If using this format, it is advisable to name the issue *directly* as contingent beneficiaries of the retirement plan if the spouse does not survive the participant; see Form 3.4, Appendix B.

C.   **Accumulation trust: Shares for issue held until certain ages.** If the trust does not pass outright to the participant's issue upon the surviving spouse's death, but rather is to be held in trust for some or all of the issue until they reach certain ages, the trust will not qualify as an O/R-2-NLP trust unless further steps are taken to assure that the benefits must pass outright to younger beneficiaries if all the issue die before reaching the specified ages. Having the trust "convert" at the spouse's death to conduit trusts for the issue will NOT work; see ¶ 6.3.12(B).

Instead, consider providing that the trust terminates early and passes outright to the spouse if the spouse is the only survivor (¶ 6.3.09), and passes outright to the last surviving issue if, at any time after the spouse's death, there is only one issue living ("last man standing"; ¶ 6.4.05(B)). Alternatively, name a younger individual as the outright "wipeout" beneficiary; see ¶ 6.3.08(B), ¶ 6.4.08.

6.4.07 *Generation-skipping and "perpetual" trusts*

The MRD trust rules pose challenges for an estate planner who is trying to either avoid the generation-skipping transfer (GST) tax or take advantage of the GST exemption. For details on the GST tax, see § 2601–§ 2664 and sources in the Bibliography. A client may have the erroneous idea that a trust named as IRA beneficiary can somehow "stretch out" the IRA distributions perpetually over the ever-longer life expectancies of succeeding generations. Actually it is not possible to do that. See ¶ 6.3.05(G).

A.   **Perpetual trusts; GST-exempt shares.** Leaving retirement benefits to a generation-skipping trust is usually not considered advisable because part of the GST exemption will be "wasted" paying income taxes. However, it can be appropriate for a Roth plan (distributions from which are not subject to income tax; see ¶ 5.2.03), or for a traditional plan if the client has no other assets suitable for a generation-skipping gift.

Leaving the benefits directly to grandchildren outright, or to conduit trusts for the benefit of "skip persons," poses no particular problems. If benefits are left to an "accumulation trust" (¶ 6.3.07) for the benefit of the participant's descendants, the problem from the point of view of "passing" the MRD trust rules is to name an individual beneficiary who will receive the trust assets immediately, outright, on the death of all prior beneficiaries. One way to accomplish this is to use the "last man standing" approach so that, if at some time in the future there is only one issue of the participant living, the trust terminates and is distributed to that one individual at that time; see ¶ 6.3.09.

B.   **Leaving benefits to a "GST-nonexempt" share.** A common estate planning technique for larger estates is for a parent to leave the amount of his GST exemption to a generation-skipping trust, and the rest of his estate to "GST-nonexempt" trusts for his children. Since leaving taxable retirement benefits to the GST-exempt trust wastes GST exemption (see "A"), it is usually considered preferable to leave the benefits to the GST-nonexempt shares.

If the benefits are left outright to the children, or to GST-nonexempt trusts that are conduit trusts for the children (¶ 6.3.05), there is no problem—the children are recognized as the Designated Beneficiaries. If the benefits are left to an accumulation trust there can be a problem: The GST-nonexempt trust is by definition not sheltered by the parent's GST exemption. Therefore to avoid having a GST tax imposed on the trust at the child's death (when the trust passes to the child's issue, who are grandchildren of the original donor) it is common practice to give the child a general power of appointment by will over the GST-nonexempt share. This causes the child to be treated as the "transferor" of the GST-nonexempt share for GST tax purposes, so there is no generation-skipping transfer when the share passes to the child's issue at the child's death.

However, a general power of appointment at death requires that the child have the ability to appoint the trust to the child's estate, which is a nonindividual. § 2041(b)(1); see ¶ 1.7.04. Thus, *if the child has a general power of appointment at death the nonexempt share trust will flunk the MRD trust rules, unless it is a conduit trust.*

Another solution is to give the child the right to withdraw all of the trust principal during his life with the consent of a trustee who does not have a substantial interest adverse to the child's exercise of such power, *instead of* giving the child a general power of appointment at death. This causes the trust to be included in the child's estate under § 2041(a)(2), (b)(1)(C), making the child the transferor for GST tax purposes, without causing the trust to have a nonindividual beneficiary. However, this type of withdrawal power would NOT make the trust a grantor trust under § 678, so the remainder provisions of the trust would still have to comply with the MRD trust rules, just as was true for the GST-exempt share (see "A").

6.4.08 *"Younger heirs at law" as "wipeout" beneficiary*

Some practitioners use, as the ultimate or "wipeout" beneficiary of a trust, the "heirs at law" of the participant (or of a particular beneficiary) who are living at the applicable time, with a proviso that any "heir at law" who is older than the oldest trust beneficiary (determined without regard to the wipeout provision) shall be deemed to have died prior to the applicable date.

There is no PLR to date specifically "blessing" this approach. It appears, based on such PLRs as 2006-10026 and -10027 and 2008-43042 (discussed at ¶ 6.3.08), that the IRS would "test" such a provision by determining who would take under the provision if all the *other* trust beneficiaries died immediately after the participant, thus activating the provision; and that the provision would "work" *if* there is some identifiable living individual who would take under the provision at the time of the participant's death.

6.5 Trust Income Taxes: DNI Meets IRD

This ¶ 6.5 deals with the income tax treatment of retirement benefits that are paid to a trust and includible in the trust's gross income. Income taxation of retirement benefits paid to an *estate* is generally the same as the treatment described here for *trusts*. § 641.

Fiduciary income taxation is an extremely complex topic; for complete treatment of the subject see sources in the Bibliography. The purpose of this discussion is solely to explain how the trust income tax rules apply uniquely to retirement plan distributions.

The discussion here does not apply to a nontaxable distribution from a retirement plan; see ¶ 2.1.06 for a catalogue of no-tax and low-tax retirement plan distributions. For income tax considerations in connection with a trust's distributions to <u>charity</u>, see Chapter 7.

This section deals extensively with **income in respect of a decedent (IRD)**. For definition and basic rules of IRD, see ¶ 4.6.

6.5.01 *Income tax on retirement benefits paid to a trust*

When retirement benefits are distributed after the participant's death to a trust that is named as beneficiary of the plan, the distribution is includible in the trust's gross income just as it would have been included in the gross income of an individual beneficiary; see Chapter 2.

Qualifying as a "see-through trust" under the minimum distribution rules (¶ 6.2.03) makes no difference to the trust's income tax treatment. See-through trust status matters only for purposes of determining when the trust must take distribution of the benefits; it has no effect on the tax treatment of those distributions once they arrive in the trust's bank account.

There are several differences between trust (fiduciary) income taxes and individual income taxes. On the bright side, the trust may be able to reduce its tax by passing the income out to the individual trust beneficiaries (¶ 6.5.02); and a trust is not subject to the reduction of itemized deductions under § 68 (¶ 6.5.04).

On the negative side, trusts are generally in a higher income tax bracket than human beneficiaries. A trust (unless its existence as a separate entity is ignored under the "grantor trust rules"; ¶ 6.3.10) or estate is a separate taxpayer and pays tax on its taxable income at the rate prescribed for trusts and estates. A trust or estate goes into the highest tax bracket (35%) for taxable income in excess of $11,200 (2010 rates). For an individual, the top income tax bracket applies only to taxable income above $373,650. Regarding scheduled future income tax rate increases, see ¶ 2.1.02.

Thus, in all but the wealthiest families, income paid to a trust will be taxed at a higher rate than would apply to the individual family members, unless the high trust tax rates can be avoided or mitigated by one of the following means:

✓   **Pass income out to individual beneficiaries.** A trust is entitled to an income tax deduction for distributions it makes from the trust's "distributable net income" (DNI) to *individual* trust beneficiaries, if various requirements are met. See ¶ 6.5.02.

✓   **Charitable deduction.** A trust is entitled to an income tax charitable deduction for certain distributions it makes to *charity.* § 642(c). See ¶ 7.4.03.

✓   **Transfer the retirement plan to a beneficiary.** A trust can transfer the retirement benefits, intact, to the trust beneficiary. ¶ 6.1.05. Following such a transfer, distributions will be made directly to the former trust beneficiary and (in most cases) taxed directly to such former trust beneficiary. See ¶ 6.5.07–¶ 6.5.08.

✓   **Grantor trust rules.** If the individual trust beneficiary is a U.S. citizen or resident, and has the unlimited right to take the retirement benefits out of the trust, the trust is considered a "grantor trust" as to that beneficiary, and distributions from the retirement plan to the trust would be gross income of the beneficiary rather than of the trust. ¶ 6.3.10.

✓   **Use the IRD deduction.** If the participant's estate was liable for federal estate taxes, the trust gets an income tax deduction for the estate taxes paid on the retirement benefits. See ¶ 6.5.04.

6.5.02 *Trust passes out taxable income as part of "DNI"*

A trust gets a unique deduction on its way from "gross income" to "taxable income": The trust can deduct certain distributions it makes to the trust's individual beneficiaries. § 651, § 661. These distributions are then includible in the beneficiaries' gross income. § 652, § 662. The trust's income tax deduction is limited to the amount of the trust's **distributable net income** or **DNI**, so this is usually called the "**DNI deduction**." § 651, § 661.

If the trust's income resulting from retirement plan distributions can be passed out to the individual beneficiaries of the trust as part of DNI, the income tax burden is shifted to the individual beneficiaries, and overall income taxes will be lowered if those beneficiaries are in a lower tax bracket than the trust. Unfortunately, the DNI deduction is not as simple as some practitioners might wish.

First the good news: Retirement plan distributions received by a trust, like other items of IRD, become part of the trust's DNI. See definition of DNI at § 643(a); Reg. § 1.663(c)-5, Examples 6 and 9; and CCA 2006-44016. Accordingly, distributions of such IRD are eligible for the DNI deduction when passed out to the trust beneficiary, and are includible in the beneficiary's income. § 661(a); § 662(a)(2); Reg. § 1.662(a)-3.

Even though IRD, like capital gain, is a form of gross income that is usually allocated to "principal" for trust accounting purposes (¶ 6.1.02), IRD is *not* subject to the special rules that limit a trustee's ability to pass out capital gain as part of DNI. IRD goes straight into DNI just as interest and other "ordinary income" items do. CCA 2006-44016. In contrast, capital gains are not included in DNI (and accordingly cannot be passed through to the trust beneficiary) unless various tests are met. Reg. § 1.643(a)-3(a), (b).

Now the bad news: The mere fact that a trustee receives a retirement plan distribution and later makes a distribution to a trust beneficiary does *not* automatically mean that the distribution to the beneficiary carries with it the gross income arising from the retirement plan distribution. The trust might still be liable for the income tax on the retirement plan distribution it received. The question is (in trust administration lingo) whether such distribution "carries out DNI."

Here are the six hurdles the trustee must clear in order for the trust's distribution of IRD to carry out the income tax burden to the trust beneficiary as part of DNI:

A.   **Trust must authorize the distribution.** The DNI deduction will not be available unless the beneficiary is entitled to receive the money; thus, obtaining this deduction requires attention at the trust drafting stage. See ¶ 6.5.03.

B.   **Income must be required to be, or must actually be, distributed, in year received.** The DNI deduction is available only for gross income that either is required to be distributed, or is actually distributed, to the individual beneficiary *in the same taxable year it is received by the trust* (or within 65 days after the end of such taxable year, if the trustee elects under § 663(b) to have such distribution treated as made during such taxable year). § 651(a), § 661(a). Thus, in the case of *discretionary* distributions, the trustee must take action prior to the deadline; if no one considers the problem until it is time to prepare the trust's tax return, it will be too late.

C.   **Allocation of DNI when separate share rule applies.** If there are two or more beneficiaries, and they have "substantially separate and independent shares," a distribution to one beneficiary will not carry out DNI that is allocated under the "separate share" rule to a different beneficiary. See ¶ 6.5.05–¶ 6.5.06 for how this rule applies to retirement benefits.

D.   **Transfer of the plan does not carry out DNI.** Though a distribution *from* a retirement plan *to* a trust is IRD, and becomes part of DNI, the retirement *plan* itself, which is a "right to receive IRD," is outside the normal DNI rules. Accordingly, transferring the *plan itself* to the beneficiary generally does not "carry out DNI." See ¶ 6.5.07–¶ 6.5.08.

E.   **No DNI deduction for distribution to charity.** The trust generally does not get a DNI deduction for distributions to charity. See ¶ 7.4.02.

F.   **No DNI deduction for certain pecuniary bequests.** Finally, the DNI deduction is not available for distributions in fulfillment of a bequest of a specific sum of money ("straight" pecuniary bequest) unless the governing instrument requires that such distribution is to be paid in more than three instalments (which would be unusual). § 663(a)(1), Reg. § 1.663(a)-1. Thus a trustee's distribution in fulfilment of a typical pecuniary bequest such as "pay $10,000 to my grandchild" will not "carry out DNI" to the grandchild.

A "formula" pecuniary bequest is *not* considered a bequest of a specific sum of money for this purpose, so a formula pecuniary bequest *can* "carry out DNI." Reg. § 1.663(a)-1(b)(1). A "formula pecuniary bequest" does not mean any pecuniary amount determined by a formula; it means a bequest of a sum of money determined by a formula where the amount of the bequest cannot be determined as of the date of death. Many marital deduction bequests are of this type. See PLR 2002-10002 for an example of a formula pecuniary bequest to a credit shelter trust.

Roddy Example: Roddy dies leaving his $10 million IRA to the Roddy Living Trust. The trust provides that, upon Roddy's death, the trustee shall distribute $3.5 million to the Credit Shelter Trust; this is a flat dollar amount (pecuniary) gift, not derived from any formula. The trustee is to distribute the balance of the trust property to Roddy's surviving spouse. The combined federal and state income tax rate applicable to the trust is 45 percent. The trustee withdraws $6,363,636 from the IRA, thus creating $6,363,636 of gross income to the trust. The trustee distributes $3.5 million to the credit shelter trust. This distribution does not "carry out DNI" because it is in fulfilment of a pecuniary bequest that is not payable in three or more instalments, so the trust gets no DNI deduction. The trustee then pays $2,863,636 of income taxes on the IRA distribution. The credit shelter trust is now funded with $3.5 million of after-tax money. The balance of the IRA ($3,636,364) is transferred to Roddy's widow (¶ 6.1.05) in fulfilment of her residuary marital share.

6.5.03 *Trust must authorize the distribution*

The trustee can distribute to the beneficiary only what the trust authorizes the trustee to distribute. This is not an income tax rule; it is part of the law of trusts.

If the trust instrument requires the trustee to distribute to the individual trust beneficiary all retirement plan distributions received by the trust (whether such plan distributions are considered income or corpus for trust accounting purposes), the DNI resulting from the plan distributions would be carried out and taxable to the beneficiary. § 643(a), § 661(a), § 662(a)(2); Reg. § 1.662(a)-3.

The problem is that some trusts are drafted without thought of the income tax consequences of the retirement plan distributions. Trustees can find themselves in the unhappy situation of not being able to pass out retirement plan distributions to the beneficiary because the trust instrument does not authorize it:

Paul Example: Paul leaves his IRA to a credit shelter trust that requires the trustee to pay all income of the trust to Paul's wife for life, and hold the principal in trust for distribution to Paul's issue upon his wife's death. The trustee receives a minimum required distribution (MRD) from the IRA. Under the state law applicable to Paul's trust, 10 percent of the MRD is allocated to trust income and the balance to principal; see ¶ 6.1.02(C). The trustee has no authority to distribute more than 10 percent of the MRD to Paul's wife; the other 90 percent must be retained in the trust, and will be taxed at trust income tax rates. Even if the trust says the trustee can distribute principal to Paul's wife "if her income is not sufficient for her support," the trustee cannot give her more than the 10-percent "income" amount unless she actually needs more for her support.

Accordingly, when drafting a trust that may receive retirement benefits, if you want the trust to take advantage of the DNI deduction to reduce income taxes on distributions from the retirement plan, the trust instrument must give the trustee discretion to distribute principal (or at least the part of principal that consists of distributions from retirement plans) to the individual beneficiaries. If you want the trust to be *forced* to take advantage of this deduction, see "conduit trusts" at ¶ 6.3.05.

6.5.04 *Trusts and the IRD deduction*

If a retirement plan distribution to the trust is IRD when received, the trust is entitled to the applicable § 691(c) deduction, if any (see ¶ 4.6.04), unless the IRD is passed out to the trust beneficiary(ies) in the same year it is received, as part of DNI, in which case the deduction also passes to the beneficiaries. Reg. § 1.691(c)-2. A different rule applies to charitable remainder trusts; see ¶ 7.5.05(C). If the IRD is not passed out to the trust beneficiaries in DNI, then the IRD and the IRD deduction stay in the trust.

The deduction for federal estate taxes paid on IRD (¶ 4.6.04–¶ 4.6.08) is an itemized deduction, subject to reduction (in certain years) under § 68; see ¶ 4.6.08. § 68 does not apply to trusts or estates, however, only individuals. This creates an incentive for a participant whose estate will be subject to federal estate taxes to name a trust or estate as beneficiary of income-taxable benefits.

6.5.05 IRD and the separate share rule

So far we have spoken of the trustee's receiving a retirement plan distribution, including it in the trust's gross income, then paying it out to the trust beneficiary and taking a DNI deduction. This simple pattern becomes more complex if the "separate share rule" of § 663(c) applies. Under this rule, "in the case of a single trust having more than one beneficiary, substantially separate and independent shares of different beneficiaries in the trust shall be treated as separate trusts."

When the separate share rule applies, if a fiduciary distributes money to a beneficiary, that distribution will carry out DNI only to the extent there is DNI that is properly allocable to that particular beneficiary's "separate share."

Separate Accounts vs. Separate Shares

The separate *share* rule of § 663(c) governs the allocation of DNI among multiple beneficiaries of a trust or estate. Do not confuse this rule with the separate *accounts* rule that dictates when multiple beneficiaries of a retirement plan are treated separately for purposes of the minimum distribution rules. See ¶ 6.3.02, ¶ 1.8.01. These are completely different and unrelated rules!

The separate share regulations have the following special rule regarding the allocation of IRD that is "corpus" (principal) for trust accounting purposes: "(3) Income in respect of a decedent. This paragraph (b)(3) governs the allocation of the portion of gross income includible in distributable net income that is income in respect of a decedent within the meaning of section 691(a) and is not...[trust accounting income]. Such gross income is allocated *among the separate shares that could potentially be funded with these amounts....* based on the relative value of each share that could potentially be funded with such amounts." Reg. § 1.663(c)-2(b)(3). Emphasis added.

Here's how the separate share rule would apply to a retirement plan distribution that is corpus for trust accounting purposes:

Jody Example: Jody dies in Year 1, leaving his $1 million 401(k) plan, $1 million of real estate, and $1 million of marketable securities to a trust. At Jody's death, the trust is to be divided into two equal shares, one for each of Jody's children Brad and Angelina, so each child is to receive a total of $1.5 million. Each child's share is to be distributed outright to the child upon attaining age 35. Angelina is already age 36; Brad is 33. In Year 1, the 401(k) plan sends the trustee a check for the entire plan balance of $1 million, creating $1 million of gross income to the trust. The trustee immediately distributes the $1 million it received from the 401(k) plan to Angelina in partial fulfillment of her 50 percent share. The trust has no other income, and makes no other distributions, in Year 1. What is the trust's DNI deduction for the distribution to Angelina?

Step 1: Does the separate share rule apply? The separate share rule applies here because distributions to Jody's children are made "in substantially the same manner as if separate trusts had been created" for them. Reg. § 1.663(c)-3(a). If this had been a "spray" trust, with the trustee having discretion to pay income and/or principal of the entire fund to either child at any time (instead of having to give each child an equal amount) the separate share rule would not apply.

Step 2: Is the plan distribution corpus? The regulation next requires that we determine whether the 401(k) plan is "corpus" for trust accounting purposes. Assume that it is; see ¶ 6.1.02.

Step 3: Does the trust instrument or state law dictate to which share(s) this plan distribution shall be allocated? If either the trust instrument or state law mandates that the plan distribution be allocated to a particular share, that allocation will be followed for purposes of allocating the resulting DNI among the separate shares. To carry out Step 3, therefore, we must look at the terms of Jody's particular trust and/or state law:

Scenario 1: If Jody's trust *required* the trustee to allocate the 401(k) plan proceeds to Angelina's share, then all the income arising from that plan distribution is allocated to Angelina's "separate share" and the $1 million cash distribution from the trust carries out $1 million of DNI to Angelina. Reg. § 1.663(c)-5, Example 9.

Allocation Respected Despite No Economic Effect

Under the regulation, a trust instrument's allocation of an IRD-corpus item to a particular beneficiary's share is given effect for income tax purposes even if such allocation has no independent economic effect (i.e., it does not change the *amount* each beneficiary receives, it affects only the *taxability* of what each beneficiary receives). In other contexts, the regulations give effect to the allocation of a particular class of income to one beneficiary or another "only to the extent that it has an economic effect independent of the income tax consequences of the allocation." See Reg. § 1.652(b)-2(b) and Prop. Reg. § 1.643(a)-5(b), discussed at ¶ 7.4.03(E).

Scenario 2: Alternatively, if Jody's trust requires that each beneficiary receive an equal share of each asset; or if the trust is silent on that topic but applicable state law requires such pro rata funding of the beneficiaries' shares; the separate share rule will require that the DNI resulting from the retirement plan distribution be allocated equally to Brad's and Angelina's shares.

Thus, under Scenario 2, even though the trust distributed $1 million to Angelina, the trust's income tax deduction is only $500,000, and Angelina includes only that much in her gross income for Year 1. The trust will have taxable income of $500,000 for Year 1. This is the fair result the separate share rule was designed to bring about: Under a trust where the beneficiaries "own" fractional shares, no one beneficiary bears a disproportionate share of income tax just because he happened to receive more distributions in a particular year.

6.5.06 IRD, separate shares, and discretionary funding

Scenario 3: Continuing the Jody Example from ¶ 6.5.05, suppose Jody's trust provides that "The Trustee shall not be obligated to allocate each asset equally to the two shares, but rather may allocate different assets to each child's share, provided that the total amount allocated to each child's share is equal." The trust thus authorizes discretionary pick-and-choose (non-pro rata) funding.

The trustee has exercised its authority to choose which assets to use to fund each beneficiary's share: The trustee, in proper exercise of its discretion, allocated the entire $1 million 401(k) plan distribution to Angelina's share. Does this enable the trustee to deduct the entire distribution as DNI?

Probably not. Though other interpretations are possible, the usual interpretation of the regulation is that, since the trustee *could* have elected to fund either beneficiary's share of the trust with the IRD, the trustee *must* (in computing its taxable income and DNI) allocate the IRD equally to the two shares. Under this interpretation, discretionary pick-and-choose funding generally produces the same result as mandatory pro rata funding (see exceptions below).

If the trustee of a trust that (1) is subject to the separate share rule and (2) permits discretionary pick-and-choose funding wants the gross income arising from a retirement plan to be allocated disproportionately, there are two ways to avoid the separate share rule and its apparently-mandatory pro rata allocation of IRD-corpus, assuming these techniques can be used consistent with the fiduciary's obligations to all trust beneficiaries:

✓ **Transfer the plan itself, rather than a distribution.** In the Jody Example, the trustee could transfer the 401(k) plan itself to Angelina, rather than withdrawing money from the plan and distributing the money to Angelina. See ¶ 6.1.05. Such a transfer generates no gross income at the trust level and accordingly the separate share rule for allocation of DNI never comes into play. The problem of Reg. § 1.663(c)-2(b)(3) is avoided. See ¶ 6.5.07.

✓ **Fund other shares first.** If the trustee wants to allocate a particular IRD-corpus item to one beneficiary's share, the trustee can distribute all the *other* assets first, fully funding all the other beneficiaries' shares before the year in which he withdraws funds from the plan. Then he is left with only one asset, the retirement plan, which he cashes out in the later year. This cash can only be used to fund one beneficiary's share (because all other beneficiaries have received their shares in full in previous years), so the distribution carries out all the DNI.

6.5.07 *Income tax effect of transferring plan*

See ¶ 6.1.05 regarding the ability of a trust or estate to transfer an inherited IRA or plan to the beneficiaries of the trust or estate. This ¶ 6.5.07 discusses the *income tax effects* of such a transfer to a specific or residuary legatee. For transfer in fulfilment of a pecuniary bequest, see ¶ 6.5.08.

The general rule is that the transfer of an inherited retirement plan "by the estate of the decedent or a person who received such right by reason of the death of the decedent or by bequest, devise, or inheritance from the decedent" triggers immediate realization of the income represented by the retirement plan, because it is the transfer of a right to receive IRD. § 691(a)(2), first sentence; see ¶ 4.6.03.

However, this general rule does not apply to a "transfer to a person pursuant to the right of such person to receive such amount by reason of the death of the decedent or by bequest, devise, or inheritance from the decedent." § 691(a)(2) (second sentence). Thus, when a retirement benefit is transferred out of an estate or trust to a beneficiary of the estate or trust, the transferring entity is not taxed on the transfer (for exception see ¶ 6.5.08). Instead, the transferee is taxable on the IRD as and when it is paid to such transferee. § 691(a)(1)(C); Reg. § 1.691(a)-4(b).

Clothier Example: Clothier's IRA is payable to his estate. Clothier's will leaves his personal effects, automobile, and IRA to his sister Wanda, and leaves the residue of the estate to his brother. Clothier's executor transfers the personal effects, automobile, and IRA to Wanda. The transfer to Wanda is not a taxable event. Wanda withdraws money from the IRA. The withdrawal is taxable to Wanda as IRD. Reg. § 1.691(a)-4(b)(2).

The "person" to whom the right-to-receive-IRD is transferred could be a charity (see PLRs discussed at "B"), or a trust (see PLR 2008-26028), as long as the transferee is the beneficiary entitled to receive that asset under the decedent's trust or from the decedent's estate.

A.   **Transfer from trust to trust beneficiary.** If the right-to-receive IRD is distributed as a specific bequest from a trust, or upon termination of the trust to a residuary legatee, the beneficiary who is entitled to the item, and not the trust, bears the income tax. Reg. § 1.691(a)-2(a)(3), (b), Example 1; § 1.691(a)-4(b)(2), (3). See PLRs 9537005 (Ruling 7), and 9537011.

What if the right-to-receive is transferred to a trust beneficiary under a discretionary power to distribute principal, but the trust is ongoing? Although the regulation refers to a "terminating" trust, the exception applies to any properly authorized transfer from the trust to its residuary beneficiaries, which is in effect a termination of the trust with respect to such asset. See PLRs 2005-26010, 2006-52028, 2008-03002, 2008-26028, and 2010-13033.

B.   **Transfer from estate to estate beneficiary.** Similarly, the transfer of a retirement plan by an <u>estate</u> to the estate's residuary beneficiaries is a nontaxable event. See PLR 2005-20004, in which the participant died leaving his IRAs and a 401(k) plan to his estate. The executor (who was authorized by the will to make distributions in kind) transferred the IRAs and plan to the estate's residuary beneficiary, a charity, in partial satisfaction of the charity's residuary bequest. This was ruled not to be an income-triggering assignment under § 691(a)(2); accordingly, only the charity realized gross income from the IRAs and plans (when later distributions were received by it). See also the similar PLRs 2002-34019, 2006-17020, and 2006-33009; 2006-18023 (nonqualified annuity transferred to residuary beneficiaries); 2008-50004; and 2008-50058.

Some rulings approving the transfer of an IRA from an estate to the estate beneficiaries as a nontaxable event do not mention § 691(a)(2): See PLRs 2004-52004, 2006-46025, 2006-46027, 2006-46028, 2006-47029, and 2006-47030.

6.5.08 *Funding pecuniary bequest with right-to-receive IRD*

¶ 6.5.07 dealt with the transfer of a retirement plan, intact, to a trust or estate beneficiary in fulfilment of a *specific or residuary* bequest. In Chief Counsel Advice (CCA) 2006-44020, the IRS addressed the tax consequences of a trustee's transferring an IRA to a beneficiary to fulfill a *pecuniary* legacy. The Chief Counsel advised that the trustee's assignment of an interest in an IRA to a trust beneficiary in satisfaction of a pecuniary gift triggered realization of income at the trust level under § 691(a)(2). Citing *Kenan v. Comm'r*, 114 F. 2d 217 (2d Cir. 1940), the IRS said the trust "has received an immediate economic benefit by satisfying its pecuniary obligation to the Charities with property on which neither Trust nor Decedent have previously paid income tax which is a disposition for § 691(a)(2) purposes."

Is the Chief Counsel correct? The *Kenan* case involved a fiduciary's transfer of appreciated property (*not* IRD) in fulfilment of a pecuniary bequest, and dealt with § 663 (*not* § 691). In the author's opinion, the second sentence of § 691(a)(2) should govern (and make the transfer nontaxable) when the right to receive IRD is transferred in fulfilment of a pecuniary bequest in (at least) the following two circumstances: Either the governing instrument requires that such bequest be fulfilled with that asset; or (even if the instrument does not explicitly require use of that asset) the fiduciary has no choice because no other asset is available:

Ron Example: Ron dies, leaving his $1 million IRA payable to his trust as beneficiary. The trust contains a pecuniary formula marital bequest, under which the marital trust is entitled to $400,000. The trust holds no other assets except the IRA. Ron's trustee divides the IRA into two separate inherited IRAs, one with a value of $400,000. The trustee transfers this $400,000 IRA to the marital trust and keeps the other IRA for the residuary credit shelter trust. In this example, in the author's opinion, the IRA is transferred to the marital trust "by bequest from the decedent." The funding trust is not "selling" or "exchanging" the IRA; it is transferring the IRA to the person entitled to it under the terms of the decedent's trust. The trustee has no choice regarding which asset to use to fund the marital trust—the IRA is the only asset available. Thus (in the author's opinion) the transfer is not taxable under § 691(a)(2).

This conclusion is consistent with several PLRs in which the IRS allowed surviving spouses to roll over benefits that were paid to them through pecuniary bequests. See PLRs 9524020, 9608036, 9623056, and 9808043, all of which predate CCA 2006-44020; and 2009-40031 and 2009-43046 (issued *after* CCA 2006-44020). If the transfers of retirement benefits in those rulings had been treated as "sales," the transfers would have triggered immediate realization (deemed distribution) of the underlying income, and there would have been nothing for the spouses to roll over. However, those PLRs did not discuss this issue or mention § 691(a)(2). In PLR 2006-08032, a trustee transferred shares of an IRA to charities in fulfilment of their pecuniary bequests; the IRS ruled that the transfers did not constitute distributions or rollovers under § 408, but did "not address the issue of whether" the trust realized income under § 691 by virtue of these transfers.

For planning purposes, it is wise to assume that the transfer of retirement benefits out of an estate or a trust to a beneficiary in fulfilment of a pecuniary bequest will trigger immediate realization of income under § 691(a)(2) and estate planners should draft their instruments in a way that will avoid the problem; see ¶ 6.1.01, #7.

6.6 See-Through Trust Tester Quiz

Use this quiz to test whether a particular trust qualifies as a see-through trust under the IRS's minimum distribution trust rules (¶ 6.2–¶ 6.3). The quiz is in two parts, PART I (Preliminaries) and PART II (Beneficiaries and substantive terms). PART III provides some answers to the quiz.

In some but not all cases, this quiz will give you "the answer" regarding whether a particular trust qualifies (in the author's opinion) as a see-through. In cases with no definite answer, the quiz will reference the section of this book that explains the issues involved.

PART I: PRELIMINARIES

1.   At the time it receives the retirement benefits, will the trust be valid under state law? See ¶ 6.2.05.
Yes: Go to Question 2.
No: Go to Answer A.

2.   Is the trust irrevocable, or will it become irrevocable upon the participant's death? See ¶ 6.2.06.
Yes: Go to Question 3.
No: Go to Answer A.

3.   Has a copy of the trust instrument (or alternative permitted documentation) been provided to the plan administrator no later than October 31 of the year after the year of the participant's death? See ¶ 6.2.08(A).
Yes: Go to Question 4.
No: Go to Answer B.

4.   Does the trust provide that retirement benefits payable to the trust may not be used to pay debts, expenses, or taxes of the participant's estate, or otherwise be paid to the participant's estate, after September 30 of the year after the year of the participant's death (or at all)? See ¶ 6.2.10.

Yes: Go to PART II of the Quiz.

No: If the participant is living, amend the trust to include such a provision. If the participant is deceased, "fix" the trust using a cleanup strategy as described in ¶ 6.2.10. Then proceed to PART II.

PART II: BENEFICIARIES AND SUBSTANTIVE TERMS

Having dealt with the preliminaries, we now turn to testing the beneficiaries of the trust. In applying this quiz, remember that:

✓   The time to apply these questions is at the moment of the participant's death. If the participant is still alive, pretend that he dies right now; what would happen to the benefits that would flow into this trust if the participant died right now?

✓   Ignore any beneficiary who dies before the participant, even if he/she is named in the trust. See Example 3, below.

✓   The quiz may not work properly in case of "double deaths," i.e., where a trust beneficiary survived the participant, but then died prior to complete distribution of his/her trust share. In such cases, see ¶ 4.4.12.

✓   If the retirement benefits are payable directly to a particular separate trust, share, or subtrust created under the trust instrument as named beneficiary under the participant's beneficiary designation form, apply these questions ONLY to that particular separate trust, share or subtrust. See ¶ 6.3.01(B). Otherwise, see the rest of ¶ 6.3.01 regarding whether to apply these questions to the entire trust.

Example 1: Janice's IRA is payable to "the trust created for the benefit of my son Timmy under Article xxi of the Janice Trust." Apply these questions to the separate trust that is to be created for the benefit of Timmy, *ignoring* the other trusts (if any) created under the Janice Trust. (Of course, if upon Timmy's later death or some other event the assets in his separate trust will flow out to other shares created under Janice's trust, you may end up having to test all the shares anyway.)

Example 2: Godfrey's IRA is payable to the Godfrey Trust. On Godfrey's death, the trust divides into a marital trust and a credit shelter trust. You need to test BOTH subtrusts, since the IRA is payable to the single "funding" trust. If (under the terms of the Godfrey Trust, or applicable state law, or as a result of applying a formula or the trustee's discretion), the IRA ends up being allocated to only one or the other of the two subtrusts, see ¶ 6.3.01 regarding whether you can "ignore" beneficiaries of the other subtrust or share.

Example 3: Doris leaves her IRA to a trust that says "Pay income to my husband Corey for life, and on the death of the survivor of my husband and myself distribute the principal outright to my then-living children." Corey predeceased Doris. Corey is NOT counted as a beneficiary of Doris's trust. You start your trust testing with ONLY those trust beneficiaries (and potential trust beneficiaries) who are actually living at the participant's death or may be born later.

5.   Test for "conduit trust" status. See ¶ 6.3.05–¶ 6.3.06. Is there one individual beneficiary, or is there a group of individual beneficiaries, who is or are entitled to receive from the trust, directly, upon receipt of such amount by the trust, all amounts (net of applicable fees; see ¶ 6.3.05(D)) distributed from the retirement plan during that individual's life (or so long as any member of the group is alive)?

Yes, there is one single individual beneficiary so entitled: Go to Answer C.

Yes, there is a group of individual beneficiaries so entitled: Go to Question 6.

No. Go to Question 7.

When you answer Question 5:
If there is (or may be) another beneficiary who is (or may be) entitled to receive part or all of such distributions, *but* such other beneficiary will have no further interest in the trust or in the benefits as of September 30 of the year after the year of the participant's death, ignore such other beneficiary; see ¶ 6.3.03(A)–(C). If such other beneficiary died, see ¶ 1.8.03(C).

If the answer to Question 5 would be "yes" but for the fact that plan distributions may be paid "for the benefit of" (rather than "to") the conduit beneficiary, see ¶ 6.3.05(C). If the answer to Question 5 would be "yes" but for the fact that the beneficiary merely has the right to demand payment of such plan distributions to himself, rather than such payment's being automatically distributed, see ¶ 6.3.12(A).

Florence Example: Florence's trust says "Following my death, the trustee shall withdraw the annual minimum required distribution (MRD) from my IRA each year, and promptly transmit such MRD to my son Beakie, and shall also pay to Beakie such additional amounts from the IRA or other trust assets as the trustee deems advisable." This trust does not qualify as a conduit trust because the trustee is required to transmit to Beakie only MRDs, not ALL distribution the trustee receives from Florence's IRA. Answer NO to Question 5.

Rhett Example: Rhett's trust says "Following my death, the trustee shall pay $10,000 to Charity X, no later than September 30 of the year after the year of my death; and the trustee shall withdraw the annual minimum required distribution (MRD) from my IRA each year, and such additional amounts as the trustee deems advisable, and shall promptly transmit such MRDs and additional amounts (if any) to my son Bip." Ignore Charity X and Answer YES to Question 5.

6.   We have established that there is a "conduit trust" for the benefit of more than one individual. Of the group of individual "conduit" beneficiaries, is it possible to identify, at the time of the participant's death, which member of the group has the shortest life expectancy? See ¶ 6.2.07.

Yes: Go to Answer D.
No: Go to Answer A.

7.   We have established that the trust is not a "conduit" trust with respect to an individual beneficiary (or group of individuals), so the trust is an "accumulation" trust. We next test whether the trust qualifies as a see-through under one of the qualification methods available to accumulation trusts. Does one individual trust beneficiary have the absolute right to withdraw all assets from the trust at any time?

Yes: The trust qualifies as a grantor trust with respect to the individual beneficiary. See ¶ 6.3.10 regarding whether it qualifies as a see-through trust.

No: Go to Question 8.

8.   Must the trust terminate immediately, and be distributed outright to one of the individual trust beneficiaries, if all *other* individuals who are beneficiaries of the trust die while there is still money in the trust?

Yes: This trust qualifies as a see-through trust because it is a "circle" or "last man standing" trust. See ¶ 6.3.09, ¶ 6.4.05(B).

No: Go to Question 9.

9.   We have determined that the trust does not qualify as a see-through trust either as a conduit, 100 percent grantor, or circle (last man standing) trust. The final step is to test the trust beneficiaries to see whether the trust qualifies as an "O/R-2-NLP" trust, and if so who the oldest (countable) beneficiary is. See ¶ 6.3.08.

To answer Question 9, make a list of *all* beneficiaries of the trust who are or may be entitled to the benefits, in the order in which they are entitled. Go all the way down the chain of beneficiaries and potential future beneficiaries and contingent and even wipeout beneficiaries as far as you can go, UNTIL you come to a beneficiary who (or which) is entitled to *immediate outright* distribution of the benefits upon the death of a prior beneficiary. That "unlimited" beneficiary (to use the IRS's term) is the last beneficiary you have to "count."

If every beneficiary on your list is an individual, the trust qualifies as see-through trust, and the ADP is the life expectancy of the oldest individual on your list. If the list includes a nonindividual, go to Answer A.

PART III: ANSWERS

The "answers" to the quiz are found in different places. In some cases, when you answer a particular question in a particular way, the answer is given to you right then and there. In other cases, you are referred to another section of this book (because the answer is not necessarily clear). Finally, in some cases you are told to "Go to Answer A" (or B, C, or D). Here are Answers A, B, C, and D:

Answer A: This trust does not qualify as a see-through trust under the IRS's minimum distribution trust regulations. For the effect of "flunking," see ¶ 6.2.01. If the participant is still alive and qualification would be desirable, consider having the participant amend his trust so it qualifies. If the participant is deceased, consider disclaimers, reformation, and other "cleanup strategies" at ¶ 4.4–¶ 4.5.

Answer B: This trust has not complied with the documentation requirement (¶ 6.2.08). If the participant is still alive, or he is dead but the filing deadline has not yet passed, comply with the requirement then answer Question 3 "yes" and proceed with the rest of the quiz. If the participant is dead and the filing deadline has passed, go to Answer A.

Answer C: This trust qualifies as a see-through trust for a single individual beneficiary (the "conduit beneficiary") within the meaning of Reg. § 1.401(a)(9)-5, A-7(c)(3), Example 2.

Answer D: This trust should qualify as a conduit trust for the benefit of the multiple individual conduit beneficiaries, subject to caveats in ¶ 6.3.06.

7

——

Charitable Giving

Charitable giving is a tax-efficient way for the charitably-inclined client to dispose of retirement plan benefits, but is not always easy to implement.

This Chapter provides an overview of charitable giving with retirement benefits. For a longer discussion, with more examples and background information, see the *Special Report: Charitable Giving with Retirement Benefits* (Appendix C).

7.1 Three "Whys": Reasons to Leave Benefits to Charity

This Chapter explains the pros, cons, and mechanics of donating retirement benefits to charity. This Chapter discusses charitable gifts of retirement benefits under traditional IRAs, qualified retirement plans, and 403(b) plans. This discussion does not apply to Roth retirement plans. This Chapter assumes the reader is generally familiar with the tax rules of charitable giving. For sources of information about charitable giving, see the Bibliography.

There are three reasons a client should consider leaving his retirement benefits to charity:

A.   **To benefit charity.** The main reason to leave retirement benefits (or any other asset) to charity is to help the charitable organization achieve its goals. There is no advantage to giving retirement benefits to charity if the donor does not want to benefit that charity! Beware of "planning ideas" that purport to give the client the benefit of charitable income tax deductions, and/or to make use of a charity's income tax exemption to shelter the client's income, while providing only a token or speculative benefit to the charity; such schemes are NOT discussed here. The ideas in this Chapter are *only* for use with clients seeking to benefit charity.

B. **Most tax-efficient use of retirement plan dollars.** If a client wishes to leave some of his estate to charity and some to noncharitable beneficiaries, the most tax-efficient allocation of his assets generally is to fund the charitable gifts with retirement benefits and leave other assets to the noncharitable beneficiaries. Because the charity is income tax-exempt, it receives the benefits free of income tax. Thus the benefits may be worth more to the charity than to the client's other beneficiaries. For how a Roth conversion may be even more beneficial than this traditional strategy, see the Trytten article cited in the Bibliography under Chapter 5.

C. **Accomplish other estate planning goals.** Judicious use of charitable giving with retirement benefits can help the client accomplish other estate planning goals at the same time as he fulfills his charitable intentions. See ¶ 7.5.06.

7.2 Seven Ways to Leave Benefits to Charity

Here are the seven ways retirement benefits can pass, upon the participant's death, to a charitable beneficiary.

7.2.01 *Name charity as sole plan beneficiary*

The method of leaving retirement plan benefits to charity that involves the fewest difficulties is simply to name the charity directly as the beneficiary of 100 percent of the death benefit payable under the particular retirement plan. Because the benefits are paid directly to the charity under the beneficiary designation form, § 691(a) (¶ 4.6.01) causes the benefits to be included in the income of the charitable recipient as named beneficiary, and the charity's income tax exemption (§ 501(c)) makes the distribution nontaxable. The estate tax charitable deduction (§ 2055(a)) is available for the value of the charity's interest.

7.2.02 *Leave benefits to charity, others, in fractional shares*

A charity can be named as one of several beneficiaries receiving fractional shares of the retirement plan, with other fractional shares passing to noncharitable beneficiaries, as in "I name as beneficiary of my IRA XYZ Charity and my son Junior in equal shares."

A.   **The problem: The IRS's multi-beneficiary rule.** The problem with this approach is that it risks losing the option of a "life expectancy payout" for the noncharitable beneficiary(ies). A Designated Beneficiary can withdraw inherited retirement benefits in annual instalments over his life expectancy, thus achieving significant income tax deferral. ¶ 1.5.05. However, this favorable life expectancy or "stretch" payout option is available only to *individual beneficiaries* (and qualifying "see-through trusts"); a charity, as a nonindividual, cannot be a Designated Beneficiary. ¶ 1.7.03.

If there are multiple beneficiaries, the general rule is that all of them must be individuals or none of them can use the life expectancy payout method. Reg. § 1.401(a)(9)-4, A-3. There are two exceptions to this rule:

B.   **First exception: separate accounts.** If there are multiple beneficiaries, but the respective beneficiaries' interests in the retirement plan constitute "separate accounts," each such account can be treated as a separate retirement plan for purposes of establishing the Applicable Distribution Period (ADP; ¶ 1.2.03) for the benefits. The drawback of relying on this exception is that the beneficiaries may not meet the deadline for establishing separate accounts; see ¶ 1.8.01(B).

C.   **Second exception: distribution or disclaimer.** The other exception is that a beneficiary is "disregarded" (doesn't count as a beneficiary for purposes of determining the ADP) if such beneficiary ceases to have any interest in the benefits by September 30 of the year after the year of the participant's death (the "Beneficiary Finalization Date"; see ¶ 1.8.03). Thus, the charity's share can be paid out after the participant's death at any time up to the Beneficiary Finalization Date, and the remaining beneficiaries (assuming they are all individuals) will be entitled to use the life expectancy payout method.

Frank Example: Frank dies in Year 1. The beneficiary designation for his $1 million IRA provides that "$10,000 shall be paid to Charity X and the balance shall be paid to my son." Charity X takes full distribution of its $10,000 share of the account shortly after Frank's death. As of the Beneficiary Finalization Date (September 30, Year 2), the son is the sole remaining beneficiary of the IRA, because the charity's interest has been terminated by distribution. As an individual, the son is a Designated Beneficiary, and minimum required distributions (MRDs) will be determined based on the son's life expectancy as the ADP.

D.   **When to rely (or not rely) on the exceptions.** If use of the life-expectancy-of-the-beneficiary payout method would be highly advantageous for the individual beneficiaries, it may not be wise, in the estate planning phase, to rely on the above exceptions, both of which required the beneficiaries to take action after the participant dies. Instead, consider establishing separate IRAs during the participant's life, one payable to the charitable beneficiary(ies) and one payable to the individual beneficiary(ies), rather than putting both types of beneficiaries on the same account and risking loss of the life-expectancy-of-the-beneficiary payout method through the beneficiaries' failure to meet the deadlines for establishing separate accounts (or paying out the charities' share). On the other hand, if establishing separate IRAs prior to death would be disproportionately burdensome compared to the benefits gained thereby, it makes sense to rely on the exceptions.

7.2.03 *Leave pecuniary gift to charity, residue to individuals*

Another way to leave part of the benefits to charity is to name the charity as beneficiary of a pecuniary (fixed-dollar amount) portion of the account, with the balance (residue) going to individual beneficiaries.

Under one approach to funding a pecuniary gift, the IRA provider would create two shares as of the date of death, one funded with the dollar amount of the pecuniary gift and the other containing the rest of the account's assets. Then both shares would share pro rata in gains and losses occurring after the date of death. This treatment could be required by the beneficiary designation form, or (if the beneficiary designation form does not address this question) this treatment might be required as part of the IRA provider's standard procedures. Alternatively, the beneficiary designation form, or the IRA provider's documents, might indicate that the charity is to receive a flat dollar amount, regardless of what appreciation or depreciation occurs in the IRA after the date of death. The planner needs to determine what the client's wishes are and spell out the desired result in the beneficiary designation form.

7.2.04 *Formula bequest in beneficiary designation*

Often, the amount a client wants to leave to charity is neither a fixed dollar amount nor a fractional share of the retirement plan, but rather is derived from a formula based on the size of the client's estate and/or adjustments for other amounts passing to the charity.

Corey Example: Corey wants to leave 10 percent of his estate to his church and the balance to his issue. His assets are a $2 million IRA, a home worth $1 million, and other investments worth $3 million. Thus, based on present values, he would expect the church to receive about $600,000. One way to accomplish that goal is to leave the charity 10 percent of the IRA and 10 percent of the rest of the estate. That approach exactly carries out Corey's intent of leaving 10 percent of all his assets to the church. However, that is not the most tax-efficient way to fund the church's share. Corey could leave more to his children, without reducing the amount the church receives, by funding the church's share entirely from the IRA. His lawyer drafts a beneficiary designation formula leaving the church a fractional share of the IRA equal to 10 percent of Corey's total estate, and leaving the balance of the IRA (if any) to Corey's issue.

For problems with formula beneficiary designations, and ways to avoid the problem, see Question 4(C) in the "Checklist: Drafting the Beneficiary Designation," and Form 3.8, both in Appendix B.

7.2.05 *Leave benefits to charity through a trust*

In many cases it is not feasible to name the intended charitable recipient directly as beneficiary of the retirement benefits. The most common reason for this is that some additional actions must be taken, after the client's death, to carry out the charitable gift. The plan administrator may not be willing to accept a beneficiary designation under which the administrator would not be able to tell, at the participant's death, who is entitled to the benefits.

If the only problem is that the actual charitable recipients are to be selected after the participant's death, consider leaving the retirement benefits to a "donor-advised fund" (¶ 7.5.03). The participant should create the fund prior to death, name it as beneficiary, designate who will be responsible for allocating the fund's assets to charities after his death, and provide the allocators with the guidelines they are to follow. Because the donor-advised fund is itself tax-exempt, the problems discussed in the rest of this section do not arise—and the plan administrator is happy because it knows to whom it must make the check payable.

In some situations, however, the benefits may have to be made payable to the participant's estate (or trust) as beneficiary of the retirement plan, with the will (or trust instrument) specifying that the benefits are to be paid to the not-yet-created (or not-yet-selected) charitable beneficiaries. The executor or trustee is then responsible for carrying out the post-death actions (such as forming the charitable foundation, calculating the formula distributions, or selecting the charities), and the plan administrator can then follow the instructions of the executor (or trustee) in distributing or transferring the benefits.

Unfortunately, this approach involves substantial additional complexity with respect to minimum required distributions (see ¶ 7.3) and fiduciary income taxes (see ¶ 7.4).

7.2.06 *Leave benefits to charity through an estate*

When it is not feasible to name a charity directly as beneficiary, there is an advantage to leaving the benefits to the charity through the participant's estate rather than through a trust. An estate is entitled to an income tax deduction for amounts either paid to or set aside for charity, whereas generally a trust is entitled to an income tax deduction only for amounts "paid" to charity. See ¶ 7.4.04(B), (C). Thus, an estate may have a slight edge; but otherwise the income tax complications of passing retirement benefits through an estate on their way to the charity are the same as for a trust, and require expert knowledge, both at the drafting and administration stages. See ¶ 7.4.

7.2.07 *Disclaimer-activated gift*

This approach may appeal to a client who would like to encourage his individual beneficiary to be philanthropic. The participant names an individual (such as a son or daughter) as primary beneficiary of the plan, and names a charity as contingent beneficiary, specifying that the charity is to receive any benefits disclaimed by the primary beneficiary. See PLR 2001-49015 for an example of this type of planning. See ¶ 4.4 regarding disclaimers.

The contingent beneficiary that will receive the benefits upon the primary beneficiary's disclaimer can be any type of charity that is suitable to receive retirement benefits (see ¶ 7.5.01–¶ 7.5.08), EXCEPT that it CANNOT be:

1.   A private foundation (¶ 7.5.02) of which the disclaimant is a trustee or manager having power to choose recipients of the foundation's funds, unless the foundation is legally required to hold the disclaimed assets in a separate fund over which the disclaimant does not have such powers. This is because of the requirement that disclaimed assets must pass "without any direction on the part of" the disclaimant. See ¶ 4.4.08(B).

According to PLR 2005-18012, a disclaimer in favor of a donor-advised fund (DAF; ¶ 7.5.03) does not violate this requirement, even if the disclaimant is an "advisor" to the DAF, because the advisor merely advises; he cannot "direct" distribution of the DAF's funds.

2.   A charitable remainder trust (¶ 7.5.04) or gift annuity (¶ 7.5.08) of which the disclaimant is an income beneficiary (unless the disclaimant is the participant's surviving spouse), because of the requirement that disclaimed property must pass, as a result of the disclaimer, either to the participant's surviving spouse or to someone other than the disclaimant. See ¶ 4.4.08(A). See *Christiansen*, 130 T.C. 1 (2008), *aff'd* 586 F.3d 1061 (8th Cir. 2009), in which a disclaimer was held not to be qualified for this reason (the disclaimed asset passed to a charitable lead trust (¶ 7.5.09) of which the disclaimant was a remainder beneficiary).

7.3 MRDs and Charitable Gifts Under Trusts

This ¶ 7.3 explains how the minimum distribution rules work with respect to a trust that is named as beneficiary of a retirement plan, when one or more charities are beneficiaries of the trust. For full details regarding the minimum distribution rules as they apply to trusts, also called the "MRD trust rules," see ¶ 6.2–¶ 6.3.

7.3.01 *Trust with charitable and human beneficiaries*

Suppose a client wants to name a trust as beneficiary of his retirement plan. His children are intended to be the primary beneficiaries of the trust, but the trust also has one or more charitable beneficiaries. He wants the plan benefits that pass to this trust to be paid out in installments over the life expectancy of his oldest child. To achieve the desired result, the "MRD trust rules" must be complied with, so that the trust qualifies as a "see-through trust" for minimum distribution purposes (¶ 6.2.03).

One of these rules is that all trust beneficiaries must be individuals. See ¶ 6.2.09. This rule creates two problems in common estate planning situations involving charities:

- First, *any* charitable gift to be paid from the trust at the participant's death, no matter how small, would cause the trust to flunk this requirement. The only *possible* exception to this rule would be if the trustee is forbidden to use the benefits to fund the charitable bequest; see ¶ 6.3.01(D). However, the problem of such payable-at-death charitable gifts can be cured by distributing the charitable bequests prior to the Beneficiary Finalization Date. See ¶ 7.3.02.

- The second problem is that, generally, remainder beneficiaries of the trust are considered "beneficiaries" for this purpose. See ¶ 6.3. Thus, if a trust is the beneficiary of the retirement plan, and any part of the remainder interest in the trust passes to charity (or could be appointed to charity under a power of appointment), the trust will flunk (unless the charitable remainder beneficiary can be disregarded under the IRS's MRD trust rules; see ¶ 6.3). This is not a problem with a true "charitable remainder trust" (¶ 7.5.04), because such trusts are income tax-exempt. The problem is with a trust that is primarily a family trust but which definitely or even possibly has charitable gifts that will be made after the family members' deaths; see ¶ 7.3.03.

Thus, when drafting a trust that is to make charitable gifts, or that may be used to fund charitable bequests under the will, it is important to determine whether any retirement benefits may be payable to that trust, and, if so, to either:

A.   In the beneficiary designation form and in the trust, make the benefits payable directly to the trust shares that benefit only individuals (see ¶ 6.3.01(B) for discussion of this technique), if qualifying for the life expectancy payout is an important goal (see ¶ 6.2.01 for discussion of when this may not be an important goal); or

B.   Match the retirement benefits to the charitable gifts, if the goal is to have the benefits pass to the charity free of income taxes (see ¶ 7.4). Under this approach you are giving up on using the life expectancy payout method for the benefits.

7.3.02 *If charitable gift occurs at the participant's death*

Russ Example: Russ leaves his $3 million IRA to a trust. The trust provides that, upon Russ's death, the trustee is to pay $10,000 to Russ's favorite charity, and hold the rest of the funds in trust for the life of Russ's wife with remainder to Russ's issue.

The trustee can "eliminate" the charitable beneficiary by paying to the charity its $10,000 bequest before the Beneficiary Finalization Date; see ¶ 7.2.02(C). If the charity is paid in full prior to the Beneficiary Finalization Date, then it is no longer a "beneficiary" of the trust as of the Beneficiary Finalization Date, and (assuming the $10,000 bequest to charity was the only defect of the trust under the minimum distribution trust rules) the trust has only individual beneficiaries and qualifies as a "see-through trust." See PLR 2006-08032.

It would make no difference, under the minimum distribution rules, which trust assets were used to fulfill the charity's share, as long as the charity has no further interest in the benefits after the Beneficiary Finalization Date. See ¶ 7.4 regarding income tax treatment of the trust's distribution to the charity.

7.3.03 *If charitable gift occurs later*

If the charitable gift(s) will not occur until after the death(s) of one or more individual beneficiary(ies), the problem of "fixing" the trust so that the retirement benefits can be paid out over the life expectancy of the oldest individual trust beneficiary becomes much more complex.

Heather Example: Heather's trust provides that, upon Heather's death, the trust is divided into equal shares for her four children. Each child receives income for life from his share, plus principal in the trustee's discretion. At death, each child can appoint the principal of such child's share among Heather's issue and any charity. If the child fails to exercise this power of appointment, such child's share is paid to such child's issue if any, otherwise to the other children. The assets coming to this trust at Heather's death are Heather's $1 million IRA and $1 million of other assets. The existence of potential charitable remainder beneficiaries (as appointees under the children's powers of appointment) would mean that, under the multiple beneficiaries rule (¶ 7.2.02(A)), this trust would flunk the IRS's minimum distribution trust rules. The trust would not be able to use the life expectancy of the oldest child to measure MRDs from the IRA to the trust after Heather's death. It would be stuck with the applicable "no-DB rule" (¶ 1.5.06, ¶ 1.5.08).

Including, in the trust instrument, a blanket provision stating that retirement benefits may not be distributed to nonindividual beneficiaries (¶ 6.4.01) is *not* the best way to solve the problem in Heather's trust. For one thing, it is not certain that such prohibitions "work" under the MRD trust rules; see ¶ 6.3.01(D) .

For another, because the potential charitable gifts do not occur until each child dies, the trustee, in order to carry out a blanket prohibition against using retirement benefits to fund any charitable gift, would have to segregate the IRA (and all distributions from the IRA; ¶ 6.2.02(B)) from the other assets of the trust immediately upon Heather's death and keep them segregated for the duration of the trust. So instead of administering four trusts (one for each child) the trustee would end up administering eight trusts (one trust for each child's share of the IRA and IRA distributions, which could not be appointed to charity on the child's death, plus a separate trust for each child's share of the non-IRA assets, which *could* be appointed to charity on the child's death). That is the only way the trustee will be able to tell, when each child dies many years from now, which assets can be appointed to charity and which assets cannot. If the trust instrument or local law does not clearly give the trustee authority to establish two separate trusts for each beneficiary, the trustee may have to go to court to get such authority.

Suppose the trustee sets up the eight separate trust shares. Now Child A needs a discretionary distribution of principal. Does it come out of the retirement assets trust or the nonretirement assets trust for

Child A? Again, this is a question that must be covered in the trust instrument (or, if not covered there, the trustee might have to go to court for authority to pay the distribution out of one share or the other).

If there may be charitable remainder interests in a trust that is being created primarily for individual beneficiaries, and the trust may receive retirement benefits, here are options to consider *instead of* a catchall clause prohibiting payment of retirement benefits to nonindividuals. These are planning options; if the participant has already died, see "cleanup options" at ¶ 4.4–¶ 4.5 instead.

A.   **Jettison the less important goal.** Determine which is a more important goal to the client, the charitable remainders or the life expectancy payout for the retirement benefits, then give up whichever one is less important. For example, if the charitable gifts are high priority, consider giving up the life expectancy payout.

B.   **Create separate trusts.** Consider creating separate trusts to receive the retirement benefits and the nonretirement assets. If Heather places high priority on *both* the deferred payout of her $1 million IRA over the life expectancy of her children, *and* on allowing the children to appoint their shares of the other $1 million of assets to charity, she could direct the trustee to establish two separate trusts for each child, one for the child's share of the IRA and one for the child's share of the other assets. The power to appoint to charity would apply only to the trusts that held no retirement benefits. The drawback of this approach is the administrative inconvenience and cost of extra trust bookkeeping.

C.   **Use a Charitable Remainder Trust.** Consider whether an income tax-exempt Charitable Remainder Trust (CRT; ¶ 7.5.04–¶ 7.5.07) would be a better choice of beneficiary than the client's "regular" trust.

D.   **Use a Conduit Trust.** Under a Conduit Trust, each time the trust receives a distribution from the retirement plan, the trustee must immediately pass that distribution out to the life beneficiary. See ¶ 6.3.05. For MRD purposes, the remainder beneficiary of a Conduit Trust does not count as a beneficiary; thus, having a charity as remainder beneficiary of a Conduit

Trust does not violate the "all trust beneficiaries must be individuals" rule.

7.4 Income Tax Treatment of Charitable Gifts From a Trust or Estate

This ¶ 7.4 discusses the fiduciary income tax treatment of retirement benefits that are paid to charity "through" a trust or estate.

¶ 7.4.01–¶ 7.4.05 assume that the fiduciary receives a distribution from the retirement plan and, in the same year, funds a gift to a "public" charity (¶ 7.5.01) or private foundation (¶ 7.5.02). If the charitable gift is not funded in the same year the distribution is received from the retirement plan, see ¶ 7.4.04. If, instead of taking a distribution from the plan and passing the distributed property out to the charity, the fiduciary transfers the retirement plan itself to the charity, see ¶ 7.4.05.

For ease of reading, this ¶ 7.4 will sometimes refer only to trusts; the same rules apply to estates unless otherwise specified.

7.4.01 *Background: trust income tax rules*

See ¶ 6.5 for discussion of the fiduciary income tax system and how retirement benefits are taxed under that system.

This book does not purport to provide an explanation of fiduciary income taxes. Instead, this book covers (in ¶ 6.5 and this ¶ 7.4) *only* the question of how retirement benefits are taxed within the overall system of fiduciary income taxation. With respect to the underlying rules of fiduciary income taxation, the author relied on secondary sources, namely, the four treatises recommended in the Bibliography, cited in this Chapter as "*Abbin,*" "*Blattmachr,*" "*Ferguson/Freeman/Ascher,*" and "*Zaritsky,*" respectively.

7.4.02 *DNI deduction, retirement benefits, and charity*

See ¶ 6.5.02 regarding the concept of "DNI" (distributable net income) and the DNI deduction.

There is no DNI deduction allowed for a distribution from an estate or trust *to a charity*. § 651(a)(2), § 663(a)(2). Although the Code could be interpreted to mean that a trust can take a DNI deduction for distributions to charity that do not qualify for the charitable deduction, the IRS has not interpreted it that way. See Rev. Rul. 68-667, 1968-2 C.B. 289. The courts have supported the IRS; see *Blattmachr*, § 3:2.1[J], Note 174; *Ferguson/Freeman/Ascher* § 6.10, in which the authors argue that the IRS regulation may be invalid, as the potential abuse it sought to prevent has been obviated by the statutory change that made the separate share rule (see ¶ 7.4.05) applicable to estates as well as to trusts; and *Zaritsky*, ¶ 2.04[6]. Accordingly, if the distribution to charity does not qualify for the charitable deduction under § 642(c) (see ¶ 7.4.03) *it will not be deductible at all.*

A distribution to a *charitable remainder trust* (¶ 7.5.04) is eligible for the DNI deduction, to the extent it meets the other requirements of that deduction. Reg. § 1.664-1(a)(5)(iii).

7.4.03 *Charitable deduction under § 642(c)*

Since a distribution to a charity is not eligible for the DNI deduction (¶ 7.4.02), a distribution to a charity from an estate or trust is deductible, if at all, only as a charitable deduction under § 642(c). § 642(c) allows an estate or trust "a deduction in computing its taxable income...[for] any amount of the gross income, without limitation, which pursuant to the terms of the governing instrument is, during the taxable year, paid for a" charitable purpose (as defined in § 170(c)).

A distribution from an estate or trust to a Charitable Remainder Trust is *not* eligible for the income tax charitable deduction; it is deductible, if at all, only as DNI (¶ 7.4.02). Reg. § 1.642(c)-2(d); § 1.664-1(a)(5)(iii).

A.   **§ 642(c): the fiduciary charitable deduction.** Like an individual taxpayer, a trust is entitled to an income tax deduction for certain payments to charity. There are many differences between the *individual* income tax charitable deduction under § 170 and the *fiduciary* income tax deduction under § 642(c); for example, the fiduciary income tax charitable deduction is unlimited in amount. For discussion of all the differences between the individual and the fiduciary income tax charitable deductions, see *Ferguson/Freeman/Ascher* § 6.01 or *Zaritsky* ¶ 2.04[1].

Suppose a trustee receives a $10,000 distribution from an IRA that is payable to the trust, and then distributes $10,000 from the trust to a charity. To determine whether the trust can take a charitable deduction for the $10,000 payment to the charity, the trustee must answer the following five questions:

First, the trustee must determine whether the "separate share" rule applies, and if so what its effect is. If the separate share rule applies, the trustee may not be entitled to allocate the gross income resulting from the retirement plan distribution to the charity—even if he paid the entire plan distribution to that charity. See ¶ 6.5.05–¶ 6.5.06.

Second, there is the matter of timing. In what taxable year was the plan distribution received by the trust, and in what taxable year did the trust make a distribution out to the charity? There is some limited flexibility regarding the year in which the deduction can be taken relative to these two events; see ¶ 7.4.04.

Third, was the payment to the charity made "pursuant to the governing instrument?" See "B" below. If it was not, there is no deduction. If the answer is yes, then:

Fourth, was the payment paid out of "income?" See "C" and "D." If not, there is no deduction. If the answer is yes, then:

Finally, out of what *class* of income was the payment made? The deduction will be allowable to the extent the payment was made out of gross income that is neither tax-exempt income nor "UBTI" (¶ 8.2). See "E."

As this list shows, taking a charitable deduction for a retirement plan distribution that is paid to a charity through a trust or estate is not a simple matter. A trustee can *sometimes* avoid having to meet all these technical requirements by transferring the retirement plan account, itself, intact, to the charity, rather than taking a distribution from the plan and then paying funds to the charity; see ¶ 7.4.05.

B.   **"Pursuant to the governing instrument."** A trust is entitled to an income tax deduction only for amounts that are paid to charity out of its gross income "pursuant to the governing instrument." § 642(c). This rule is applied in a hyper-technical manner; the IRS regards it as the ultimate weapon for disallowing charitable deductions. If the IRS can find a flaw in the paperwork, the parties' intent and the benefit to charity are irrelevant—the deduction is disallowed. *If there is any question whatsoever regarding whether this requirement is met, consult an expert and/or refer to the treatises cited in the Bibliography.*

For example, in CCA 2008-48020, an IRA was payable to (and was the only asset of) a testamentary trust. The trust called for ongoing annual payments to charities and individuals. The parties caused the trust to be "reformed" after the participant's death (see ¶ 4.5.06) to accelerate the charitable gifts. The purpose of the reformation was to "remove" the charities as beneficiaries of the ongoing trust so it would have only individual beneficiaries (and qualify as a "see-through trust"; see ¶ 7.3.01). The IRS ruled that, *because of the post-death modification* of the trust, the payments to charity were not made "pursuant to the governing instrument" and accordingly the trust could not deduct payments made to the charities.

C.   **Out of gross income, Part I: Tracing.** The Code requires that the payment to charity must come from the trust's *gross income* in order to be deductible. This requires tracing the origin of the item that is distributed to the charity. Rev. Rul. 2003-123, 2003-50 I.R.B. 1200. Note that this is in contrast to the "DNI" system for deducting distributions to noncharitable beneficiaries (¶ 7.4.01), which was explicitly designed to eliminate the need for tracing, according to *Ferguson/Freeman/Ascher*, § 6.09, Note 1.1.

"Income in respect of a decedent" (IRD; ¶ 4.6) that is includible in the gross income of a trust is "gross income" for purposes of the charitable deduction. Reg. § 1.642(c)-3(a). Retirement plan death benefits are IRD to the extent they are includible in the recipient's gross income. Rev. Rul. 92-47, 1992-1 C.B. 198; Reg. § 1.663(c)-5, Example 9. Retirement plan death benefits generally are wholly includible in gross income when received by the beneficiary, but there are exceptions (see ¶ 2.1.06).

D.   **Out of gross income, Part II: Authorization.** Suppose the trust instrument directs the trustee to pay $x to charity (so the payment is "pursuant to the governing instrument"; see "B" above), and the trustee actually makes the payment out of the trust's gross income (so the "tracing requirement" is met; see "C"), but nothing in the governing instrument specifically indicates that the payment to the charity is to come *out of the trust's gross income*. In order for the trust to take the deduction, either the governing instrument or applicable state law must indicate that the gross income *can be* (or must be) the source of such payment. See, *e.g.*, Rev. Rul. 71-285, 1971-2 CB 248.

If the governing instrument (or applicable state law, in the absence of a governing instrument provision) specifies that the payment to charity shall be made first from income, that provision will be honored for purposes of § 642(c), regardless of whether it has any economic effect independent of its income tax consequences. Rev. Rul. 71-285, *op. cit.*

Nongrantor charitable lead trusts, for example, are allowed an income tax charitable deduction for charitable annuity payments paid out of gross income, even though there is no "economic effect" of designating income as the first source for such payments—the charity is entitled to the same annuity amount regardless of whether the trust even has any income. Rev. Proc. 2007-45, 2007-28 I.R.B. 87, Section 5.01(3); see PLRs 2003-39018, 2005-16005, 2005-36013.

This conclusion is consistent with the rules for the allocation of DNI, where a governing instrument provision that a particular beneficiary's "separate share" is to be funded "first" with retirement benefit proceeds that constitute IRD will be respected for purposes of allocation of DNI among beneficiaries' shares even though the provision has no economic effect independent of income taxes. Reg. § 1.663(c)-5, Example 9.

E.   **Out of WHICH gross income?** The charitable deduction under § 642(c) is limited to amounts paid out of gross income *other than tax-exempt income and unrelated business taxable income* (UBTI; see ¶ 8.2). § 681(a); Reg. § 1.642(c)-3(b)(1), (d).

If a trustee has received both ordinary taxable income and tax-exempt income in a particular year, and then makes a distribution to charity out of the trust's income account (pursuant to the governing instrument of course), how does the trustee know whether what he paid the charity was taxable income (deductible) or tax-exempt income (nondeductible)?

That should be easy to answer—look at the governing instrument! After all, Reg. § 1.642(c)-(3)(b)(2) provides that "if the governing instrument specifically provides as to the source out of which amounts are to be paid…" for a charitable purpose, "the specific provision controls." Reg. § 1.643(a)-5(b) says the same thing.

Despite these regulations, the IRS has long maintained that such a specific provision in the governing instrument does *not* control, and a payment to charity from gross income will be deemed to come proportionately from all classes of the trust's income, unless the "specific provision" has *economic effect independent of income tax consequences*. See *Ferguson/Freeman/Ascher* § 6.09, Note 16. The Treasury has now codified this "hidden rule" in Prop. Reg. § 1.643(a)-5(b) and § 1.642(c)-3(b), but the Preamble to the proposed regulations claims the economic effect requirement is not new—it was there all along if you read a chain of regulations cited in the Preamble. Vol. 73 F.R. 118, p. 34670 (6/18/08).

For the meaning of "economic effect independent of income tax consequences," the proposed regulation cross-references Reg. § 1.652(b)-2(b), which deals with the allocation of classes of DNI among beneficiaries.

7.4.04 *Timing of charitable deduction for trust or estate*

¶ 7.4.03 dealt with retirement plan distributions that are paid to a trust and distributed by the trustee to the trust beneficiaries, where the plan-to-trust distribution and the trust-to-beneficiary distribution both occur *in the same taxable year of the trust*. The exact same rules apply when a retirement plan distribution is paid to an estate, and is then in turn distributed by the executor to the estate beneficiaries, where the plan-to-estate distribution and the estate-to-beneficiary distribution occur *in the same taxable year of the estate*.

If the plan distribution is received in one year, but not distributed to the charity until a later year, then different rules apply (and the results may differ depending on whether the plan distribution was received by a trust or by an estate). The following subparagraphs A–C assume that the distribution to the charity meets the other applicable requirements of the income tax charitable deduction (see ¶ 7.4.03).

A. **Distribution to charity in the next year.** If the amount is distributed to the charity in the year (Year 2) *following* the year the income was received (Year 1), the fiduciary can elect to treat the payment to the charity as if it had been made in Year 1 (and so can deduct it in Year 1). § 642(c)(1). This rule applies to both estates and trusts.

B.   **Estate gets a set-aside deduction.** If the distribution to the charity does not occur until even later than that, things get tougher. An *estate* can take a charitable deduction for amounts "permanently set aside for" charity as well as for amounts "paid to" charity. § 642(c)(2). Note: There is no set-aside deduction, even for an estate, for amounts set aside for future distribution to a Charitable Remainder Trust. Reg. § 1.642(c)-2(d).

C.   **Trust may or may not get set-aside deduction.** Trusts, unlike estates, generally *cannot* take a deduction for amounts that are merely "set aside for" charity; a trust generally gets a deduction only for amounts *paid* to charity. There are two exceptions to this general rule: A trust may take a set-aside deduction if the trust is treated as part of the estate pursuant to a § 645 election (see Reg. § 1.645-1(e)(2)(i)), or if the trust is eligible for a grandfather exception for certain pre-10/9/69 instruments (see § 642(c)(2)). PLR 2004-18040.

7.4.05 *Transferring benefits to charity avoids some rules*

This ¶ 7.4.05 discusses transferring a retirement plan benefit (for example, an IRA), intact, from an estate or trust to one or more charitable beneficiaries of the estate or trust. This is discussed primarily in the context of avoiding negative results under the "separate share rule," but the technique can also help the fiduciary sidestep some technical requirements of § 642(c). For example, in PLR 2006-52028, a beneficiary designation form was reformed, after the participant's death, to name a trust rather than the participant's estate, as beneficiary of an IRA; all or part of the trust's residue passed to charities, and the IRS ruled favorably on the transfer of the IRA to the charities as a nontaxable event. Compare CCA 2008-48020 (¶ 7.4.03(B)).

For how to do these transfers, see ¶ 6.1.05. For the income tax treatment of such transfers, see ¶ 6.5.07–¶ 6.5.08.

There is no particular date by which the transfer must occur in order to "work" for the income tax purposes discussed here.

When the separate share rule of § 663(c) applies, if a fiduciary distributes money to a beneficiary, that distribution will carry out DNI only to the extent there is DNI that is properly allocable to that particular beneficiary's "separate share"; see ¶ 6.5.05–¶ 6.5.06. Although § 663(c) states that it applies for the *sole* purpose of determining the amount of DNI "in the application of sections 661 and

662," it appears that the separate share rules *also* apply to determine allocation of DNI to the share of a *charitable* beneficiary, even though, after all the allocating is done, there will be no DNI deduction for distributions to charity (¶ 7.4.02). See Reg. § 1.663(c)-5, Example 11, and *Ferguson/Freeman/Ascher,* § 6.10, where the authors assume this result.

If the participant has already died, leaving retirement benefits to a trust that has "separate shares" within the meaning of § 663; and the beneficiary(ies) of one or more shares is (are) charities, while one or more other shares have noncharitable beneficiaries; and the trust does not include a provision mandating allocation of the retirement benefits to the share(s) of the charitable beneficiary(ies); the deemed allocation to noncharitable beneficiaries' shares of gross income arising from retirement plan distributions can still be avoided, in the trust administration phase, if:

1.   The trust instrument (or applicable state law) gives the trustee authority to distribute assets in kind to beneficiaries in satisfaction of their shares; and

2.   The trust instrument (or applicable state law) gives the trustee authority to pick and choose which asset will be used to fund the charity's share; and

3.   The trustee, instead of taking distribution of the retirement benefits, assigns (transfers) the retirement plan itself to the charity.

Following the assignment, the charity can take distributions directly from the retirement plan. The distributions do not have to be included in the gross income *of the trust* because the benefits are never paid to the trust. The problem of Reg. § 1.663(c)-2(b)(3) is avoided. This approach also sidesteps a requirement of getting a charitable deduction that applies if the trustee takes a plan distribution, namely, that the instrument must specify that the payment to charity must come out of gross income (¶ 7.4.03(C), (D)).

7.4.06 *How to name a charity as beneficiary through a trust*

Here are guidelines to follow if retirement benefits are to be paid to a trust at the client's death, and the trust is to make distributions to charities, and you want the gross income resulting from the retirement plan distributions not to be taxable to the trust, and you also want the maximum estate tax benefit for making the charitable gifts.

These guidelines assume that all or most of the retirement benefits will pass to charity, so that there is no need to be concerned about preserving a "life expectancy of the oldest trust beneficiary" payout for the trust. Preserving a life expectancy payout for noncharitable beneficiaries under a trust when part of the retirement benefits are to be paid to charity is addressed at ¶ 7.3.

✓   **Specify that no estate taxes are to be charged against or paid out of the charity's share.** This is required IF you do not want the estate tax charitable deduction to be reduced by the amount of the estate taxes paid out of the charity's share. Since reducing the charitable deduction would further increase the estate taxes, paying estate taxes out of the charity's share requires a circular calculation to determine the deduction.

✓   **Specify that the retirement plan benefits must be used first to fund the charitable bequests**, and that nonretirement assets are to be used for this purpose only if there are no other assets available. This assures that the trustee will not be required (by state law equitable apportionment principles, the "separate share rule" of § 663, or otherwise) to assign proportionate shares of the retirement benefits and other assets to all beneficiaries; see ¶ 7.4.05.

✓   **Specify that the trustee has authority to distribute assets in kind.** This will assure that the trustee can transfer the retirement plans directly to the charities to fulfill their shares, rather than being compelled to withdraw funds from the retirement plans and then distribute funds to the charities. See ¶ 6.1.05.

✓   **Use fractional rather th7y7uiuikan pecuniary formulas to define the charitable gifts**, if possible. This allows the fiduciary to fulfill the gift by transferring the retirement benefits intact to the charity, as described in ¶ 7.4.05. See ¶ 6.5.07–¶ 6.5.08.

7.5 Seven "Whiches":
Types of Charitable Entities

The Tax Code recognizes various types of charities and "split-interest" partially-charitable entities, not all of which are income tax-exempt. This ¶ 7.5 explains which charitable entities are and are not suitable to be named as beneficiaries of traditional (taxable) retirement plan death benefits.

7.5.01 *Suitable: Public charity*

A public charity is exempt from income tax (except for the tax on "unrelated business income" or "UBTI"; ¶ 8.2). § 501(a), (b).

Lifetime gifts to such charities are deductible for <u>gift tax</u> purposes (§ 2522(a)). Lifetime gifts to *domestic* charities qualify for the <u>income tax</u> charitable deduction. § 170(a). Gifts to some charities qualify for a larger deduction (as a percentage of the donor's gross income) than others, but this distinction is irrelevant to at-death gifts.

Making a bequest of retirement plan death benefits directly to a public charity presents the fewest problems. The planner needs to verify that the organization is an exempt organization under § 501(c)(3) and for a major gift the planner should review each of the Code sections under which a deduction will be claimed, to make sure that the organization in question meets the requirements. This is not generally a problem in the case of gift by a U.S. citizen to typical charities.

7.5.02 *Suitable: Private foundation*

In general, a private foundation is a "501(c)(3) organization" (¶ 7.5.01) that is primarily supported by contributions of one donor or family. However, the definition of a private foundation is notoriously convoluted (see § 509), especially since there are several different types and not all are subject to the same restrictions. Untangling the various definitions and subsets of private foundations is beyond the scope of this book.

Certain private foundations, although exempt from "regular" income taxes (except the tax on UBTI), are subject to a two percent excise tax on net investment income. § 4940. The § 4940 tax "is a limited excise tax that applies only to the specific types of income listed in that section. Amounts from retirement accounts are deferred compensation income," not part of "the gross investment income" of a foundation, and therefore are *not* subject to the tax, according to PLRs 9838028 and 2000-03055.

7.5.03 *Suitable: Donor-advised fund*

A donor-advised fund (DAF) is a "public" (501(c)(3)) charity (¶ 7.5.01) that receives contributions from many individual donors, invests those contributions as separate accounts (one per donor), and distributes the account funds at a later time to "real" charities such as schools, museums, and aid organizations. The donor of the gift (or other individual appointed by the donor) "advises" the DAF which charities to distribute the funds to. The DAF is not obligated to follow the advisor's suggestions but normally does so.

Individuals leaving retirement plan death benefits to a DAF may have to take precautions to make sure the chosen DAF meets any applicable requirements. Gifts may have to be made conditional on the DAF's meeting such requirements, in order to assure the desired tax-free and deductible nature of the contribution, with a contingent gift over to a more typical "public" charity if the chosen DAF does not meet the applicable requirements.

7.5.04 *Suitable: Charitable remainder trust*

A Charitable Remainder Trust (CRT), as that term is used here, means a charitable remainder trust that meets the requirements of § 664 and accordingly is income tax-exempt. § 664(c)(1). The general idea of a CRT is that the trust pays out an annual income to one or more noncharitable beneficiaries (such as the donor's spouse or children) either for life or for a term of not more than 20 years. At the end of the life (or term) interest, the remaining trust assets are paid to charity.

A CRT must meet rigid requirements set forth in § 664 and its related regulations: The annual payout to the noncharitable beneficiary is specified in the trust instrument and must be either a fixed dollar amount, in which case the trust is a "charitable remainder annuity trust" or CRAT, or a fixed percentage of the annually-determined value of the trust, in which case the trust is a "charitable remainder unitrust" or CRUT. The annual payout rate of a CRUT must be at least five percent (but not more than 50%). A CRUT is more flexible than a CRAT because it can provide that the annual payout to the noncharitable beneficiary is the unitrust percentage or the net income of the trust if less, and can even provide for "makeup" distributions to the noncharitable beneficiary if in later years the trust's income exceeds the unitrust percentage. However, neither type of CRT can permit the noncharitable beneficiary to receive anything other than the unitrust or annuity payout amount.

The attraction of leaving retirement plan death benefits to a CRT is that the benefits are paid to the CRT with no income tax. Thus, the client's human beneficiaries can receive a life income from reinvestment of the *entire amount* of the retirement benefit. In contrast, if the individuals inherited the benefits as named beneficiaries under the plan, they would have to pay income taxes on the benefits as those were distributed to them, meaning that (once distribution of the benefits is complete) the amount left over for the beneficiaries to invest is substantially reduced. Thus they could expect a larger annual income from the CRT than they would receive by investing the after-tax value of any retirement benefits distributed to them directly.

Another attraction is that the decedent's estate is entitled to an estate tax charitable deduction for the value of the charitable remainder gift. This value is determined using IRS-prescribed actuarial tables and interest rates, and must be at least 10 percent of the date-of-death value of the trust. § 664(d)(1)(D); § 7520.

This is not to suggest that the client's human beneficiaries will receive more money as life beneficiaries of a CRT than they would receive if they were named directly as beneficiaries of the plan. Normally the opposite is true, because an individual named directly as beneficiary of a retirement plan receives the *entire* benefit, not just the income from the benefit.

7.5.05 *Income tax rules for CRTs; IRD deduction*

A CRT generally pays no income tax itself (see ¶ 7.5.04), but:

A.   **Retirement benefits and UBTI.** In post-2007 years, there is a 100 percent tax on the UBTI of a CRT (but its other income for the year is tax-exempt). § 664(c)(2). PLRs 9237020 and 9253038 involved CRTs that were to be named as beneficiaries of retirement benefits. The IRS ruled that the trusts in question qualified as CRTs (and thus, under rules then applicable, were tax-exempt as long as they did not have UBTI), and that retirement plan death benefits payable to the trusts would be IRD (¶ 4.6.01) and have the same character as the income would have had if it had been paid to the deceased participant. These rulings thus imply that retirement plan distributions are *not* UBTI.

B.   **The multi-tier CRT accounting system.** A CRT has a unique internal accounting system, under which every dollar that the CRT receives is allocated to one of several "tiers" based on its federal income tax character (such as ordinary income, capital gain, tax-exempt income, or principal). § 664(b).

In effect, the CRT "remembers" what types of income it has received. Then, when the CRT makes a distribution to the human beneficiary, the distribution is deemed to come out of one of these tiers, and the federal income tax character of the amount is revived. If the distribution to the noncharitable beneficiary is deemed to come out of the ordinary income tier, the beneficiary will have to include that distribution in his gross income as ordinary income.

Distributions to the noncharitable beneficiary are assigned to tiers on a "worst-first" basis: for example, the noncharitable beneficiary cannot receive any capital gain income from the CRT until the CRT has distributed everything it held in its ordinary income tier. So, although the CRT pays no income tax when it receives a distribution from a retirement plan, the beneficiary of the CRT will have to pay income tax on the distributions *from* the CRT, to the extent those are deemed to represent the CRT's regurgitation of the retirement plan benefit (or other taxable income) under the tier system.

C.   **CRTs and the IRD deduction.** Generally, when the beneficiary of a retirement plan receives a distribution from the plan, he must include it in his gross income as income in respect of a decedent (IRD; ¶ 4.6.01), but he is entitled to an income tax deduction for the federal estate taxes that were paid on those benefits. § 691(c); see ¶ 4.6.04. If retirement benefits are paid to a Charitable Remainder Trust, that deduction for practical purposes disappears—nobody gets to use it. There is no mechanism by which a CRT can pass out the IRD deduction to the CRT's human beneficiaries.

The § 691(c) deduction reduces the taxable income of the CRT (i.e., income assigned to the trust's "first tier") in the year the distribution is received from the plan. Reg. § 1.664-1(d)(2).

Distributions to the individual beneficiary would be deemed to come out of the "net taxable income" of the CRT (first tier) until it had all been used up. The income of the CRT that was sheltered by the 691(c) deduction would become "principal" that could eventually be distributed to the individual beneficiary tax-free as part of the last tier. However, the tax-free principal of the CRT is not deemed distributed until after all net *taxable* income has been distributed. *This point would never be reached in most CRTs funded with retirement benefits.* The § 691(c) deduction is essentially "wasted" when retirement benefits are left to a CRT. PLR 1999-01023. Some practitioners disagree with this result and argue that the unitrust distributions to the noncharitable beneficiary from the CRT should retain their character as IRD and therefore carry out the IRD deduction to the noncharitable beneficiary along with the taxable income, citing Reg. § 1.691(c)-1(d).

7.5.06 *Solving planning problems with a CRT*

For a client with any charitable inclination, naming a charitable remainder trust as beneficiary of retirement benefits can help solve estate planning problems in addition to satisfying the charitable intent.

A.   **To benefit an older individual.** Naming an older nonspouse individual outright as beneficiary of retirement benefits has the effect of dumping the benefits out of the plan and into the beneficiary's gross income rapidly (over the beneficiary's short life expectancy), so the income taxes get paid up front and the elderly person will have less money available in his later years. In contrast, if the benefits are left to a CRT for the life benefit of that person, he will enjoy a more-or-less steady income from the CRT that will last for his entire life (not run out at the end of some artificial life expectancy from an IRS table).

In addition, the participant's estate will get an estate tax charitable deduction which may free up some other funds that can be given to the same or other individual beneficiaries. A charitable gift annuity could also be used in this situation; ¶ 7.5.08. The downside is that the individual beneficiary cannot take out more than the pre-set income stream from the CRT (or gift annuity) regardless of need.

B.   **Provide life income for multiple adults.** Naming a noncharitable trust for multiple adult beneficiaries of varying ages produces a nightmare from the point of view of minimum required distributions (MRDs): Either the trust must use the oldest beneficiary's life expectancy to measure MRDs, or the participant must name multiple separate trusts, one for each beneficiary, which could have the effect of chopping up the assets into too many too-small pots. See ¶ 6.3.02.

By naming as beneficiary, instead, one CRT that pays a unitrust payout for life to several adult beneficiaries, the participant avoids all MRD problems (because the tax-exempt CRT can cash out the plan benefits immediately upon the participant's death, with no income taxes). The trust produces a more-or-less steady income which can be split among the human beneficiaries. As each individual beneficiary dies, his income share passes to the surviving members of the group, thus providing a crude form of inflation protection. Because the value of the charity's remainder interest (determined actuarially using IRS tables) must exceed 10 percent of the total trust value as of the date of the participant's death, this approach will only work with a small group of adult beneficiaries (*e.g.*, a group of 50-something siblings and 80-something parents); see ¶ 7.5.07(B). § 664(d(1)(D).

C.   **For spouse, as a QTIP alternative.** For a charitably inclined participant, leaving retirement benefits to a CRT for the life benefit of his surviving spouse can sidestep the drawbacks and risks involved in leaving such benefits outright to the spouse or to a noncharitable trust for her benefit (but see ¶ 7.5.07(C) regarding spousal consent).

Leaving benefits outright to the spouse has major tax advantages (primarily the spousal rollover; ¶ 3.2), but only if the spouse rolls the benefits over to her own retirement plan after the participant's death, and there is no guarantee she will actually do that. Also, the spouse might blow money left to her outright on expenditures the participant wouldn't approve of, and/or leave what's left of it at her death to a beneficiary the participant wouldn't approve of. If the participant leaves the benefit to a QTIP trust to head off these outcomes, there are major income tax drawbacks; see ¶ 3.3.02(B).

In contrast, if benefits are left to a CRT for the spouse's life benefit, the spouse will get an income stream for life, without the drawbacks of leaving benefits to a QTIP trust. There will be no need for the spouse to roll benefits over on the participant's death. The participant can choose the ultimate beneficiary (which has to be a charity of course). If the spouse is the only noncharitable beneficiary (strongly recommended), there will be no estate tax on the benefits either at the participant's death or at the spouse's death (due to the combination of the charitable and marital deductions). § 2056(b)(8).

D.   Disabled beneficiary. See ¶ 6.4.04(D).

7.5.07 *Reasons NOT to leave benefits to a CRT*

Though it is a great planning tool, there are limitations on leaving retirement benefits to a CRT. For one thing, spousal consent may be required; see ¶ 3.4. Also:

A.   Do not overfund CRT with nonspouse beneficiary. When retirement benefits are left to a CRT, the entire value of the benefit is included in the decedent's gross estate for estate tax purposes. The estate tax charitable deduction for a bequest to a CRT will not shelter the entire value from estate taxes. Rather, only the actuarial value of the charitable remainder is allowed as a charitable deduction. For deaths in 2010, see ¶ 4.3.08.

Accordingly, unless the surviving spouse is the sole noncharitable beneficiary of the CRT (in which case her interest is nontaxable because it qualifies for the marital deduction; § 2056(b)(8)), the noncharitable beneficiary's interest in the CRT will in effect be subject to estate tax. The question of who is going to pay that tax and with what funds needs to be settled as part of the estate plan. Leaving too much money to a CRT could cause a tax meltdown.

B.   CRT for life does not work if beneficiaries are too young. In order to be a qualifying charitable remainder trust, the value of the charitable remainder (as of the date of the gift to the trust, or, in the case of a CRT funded at death, as of the date of death) must be at least 10 percent of the total value of the trust. § 664(d)(1)(D), (2)(D). If the CRT beneficiaries are "too young," and have a life interest, the trust will not meet the 10 percent requirement and it will not qualify as a CRT. A term interest (up to 20 years) can work.

7.5.08 *Suitable: Charitable gift annuity*

Under a charitable gift annuity, a sum is left to a charity and the charity agrees to pay a fixed income to a human beneficiary for life. Leaving a retirement plan to a charity subject to the obligation to pay an annuity to the participant's chosen human beneficiary could be a good way to provide an income for an older beneficiary. The participant's estate gets an estate tax deduction for the value of the retirement benefits left to the charity minus the value of the annuity (determined using IRS tables). The benefits are paid to the charity free of income tax. See PLR 2002-30018.

7.5.09 *Usually unsuitable: Charitable lead trust*

A charitable lead trust (CLT) is the mirror image of a charitable remainder trust: A "unitrust" or "annuity" income stream is paid to a charity for a term of years, then the underlying property passes to the donor's individual beneficiaries at the end of the term. § 170(f)(2)(B).

Unlike a CRT, however, the CLT is not exempt from income taxes. Thus a CLT named as beneficiary must pay income tax on the benefits as they are distributed from the retirement plan. Because of this, leaving traditional retirement benefits to a CLT appears generally to be a disadvantageous way to fund such a trust.

7.5.10 *Unsuitable: Pooled income fund*

The pooled income fund (§ 642(c)(5)) provides approximately the same benefits as a CRT. Unlike CRTs, however, pooled income funds are not exempt from income tax. Reg. § 1.642(c)-5(a)(2); compare § 664(c). Accordingly a pooled income fund is not an attractive choice as beneficiary of traditional retirement benefits.

7.6 Lifetime Gifts of Retirement Benefits

This ¶ 7.6 discusses lifetime charitable giving options for individuals who have money in IRAs and other retirement plans. Most of the considerations discussed here apply to both living participants and beneficiaries (with respect to inherited benefits they hold).

7.6.01 *Lifetime gifts from distributions*

A client who has more money in his retirement plan than he expects to need may wish to give some of it to charity. Generally, the only way he can do this under present law is to first withdraw funds from the plan and then give the funds to the charity. For a temporary exception to this general rule, see "Qualified Charitable Distributions" (¶ 7.6.07).

Withdrawing funds or other assets from a retirement plan generally causes the value of the withdrawn property to be included in the recipient's income. (For exceptions, see ¶ 2.1.06.) If the recipient then donates the withdrawn amounts to charity in the same year that he took the distribution, the income tax charitable deduction *theoretically* should eliminate the tax on the distribution. Unfortunately the following obstacles often prevent the income tax charitable deduction from wiping out the tax cost of the distribution:

A.   **Percent-of-income limit.** The income tax deduction for charitable contributions is limited to a certain percentage (30% or 50%, depending on the type of property given and the type of recipient charity) of the individual's gross income. § 170(b). If the individual's donations exceed the deduction limit, the excess can be carried forward for a limited number of years.

B.   **Deduction-reduction for high-income taxpayers.** Charitable deductions are an itemized deduction, subject to the "reduction of itemized deductions" that applies to high-income taxpayers (before and after 2010) under § 68. The *amount* of the reduction is a percentage of the donor's AGI—so the potential reduction is increased by the plan distribution, which increases AGI.

C.   **Deduction decreases taxable income but not AGI.** Because the distribution is included in the individual's gross income, it may increase his taxes in indirect ways that are not offset by the charitable deduction, because the distribution increases his adjusted gross income (AGI) and the charitable deduction (as an itemized deduction) does not decrease AGI.

D.   **Split-interest gifts are only partially deductible.** If the gift is made to a charitable remainder or lead trust, to a pooled income fund, or in the form of a charitable gift annuity, the amount of the deduction is only part of the total gift (since a portion of the gift is benefitting individuals), even though all of the plan distribution was includible in income.

E.   **Penalty for pre-age 59½ distributions.** If the participant is under age 59½ at the time of the distribution, there is a 10 percent penalty on the distribution unless an exception applies. See Chapter 9. The charitable deduction has no effect on this penalty. The penalty does not apply to beneficiaries; ¶ 9.4.01.

F.   **State income taxes.** In a state that allows no charitable deduction in computing its income tax, the participant would pay state tax on the distribution but get no offsetting deduction.

G.   **Nonitemizers.** An individual who uses the "standard deduction" rather than itemizing his deductions would see no income tax benefit from the charitable contribution.

7.6.02 *Give your MRD to charity*

A retirement plan participant generally must start taking minimum required distributions (MRDs) annually (except in 2009) from his traditional IRAs and other plans after age 70½ (or after retirement in some cases). See Chapter 1. If the participant does not need his MRDs for other purposes, this would be an appropriate source of charitable gifts. The drawbacks listed at ¶ 7.6.01 still apply, but since he has to take the unneeded MRD anyway, he might as well give it to charity; and in most cases he will receive *some* income tax benefit from the charitable gift.

A beneficiary who has inherited a retirement plan is also generally required to take annual MRDs from the plan. If a beneficiary does not need the distributions from an inherited retirement plan, he might consider giving them to charity. If the participant's estate was subject to federal estate taxes, the beneficiary is entitled to an income tax deduction (the "IRD deduction") as he takes distributions from the inherited plan, for the estate taxes attributable to that plan. See ¶ 4.6.04. By giving the distribution to charity, he gets both deductions.

7.6.03 Gifts from a pre-age 59½ "SOSEPP"

A 10 percent additional tax generally applies to retirement plan distributions taken before reaching age 59½. § 72(t); see Chapter 9. A young individual who wanted to give some of his retirement benefits to charity would be discouraged from doing so by this penalty. This penalty does not apply to death benefits (¶ 9.4.01), so it affects only participants, not beneficiaries. One of the more than a dozen exceptions to this penalty is well suited for fulfilling a pledge of annual gifts to a charity. It is called the "series of substantially equal periodic payments" (SOSEPP). See ¶ 9.2–¶ 9.3.

7.6.04 Gift of NUA stock

The Code gives special favorable treatment to distributions, from a qualified plan, of employer stock that contains "net unrealized appreciation" (NUA). Under certain circumstances, NUA is not taxed at the time of the distribution; rather, taxation is postponed until the stock is later sold. See ¶ 2.5. An employee who holds NUA stock apparently has the same options other individuals owning appreciated stock have when they wish to diversify their investments and/or increase the income from their portfolios: Either sell the stock, pay the capital gain tax, and reinvest the net proceeds; or, contribute the stock to a Charitable Remainder Trust (¶ 7.5.04) reserving a life income, thus avoiding capital gain tax *and* generating an income tax deduction. It is advisable to obtain an IRS ruling if using this technique; see PLRs 1999-19039, 2000-38050, and 2002-15032 for examples.

7.6.05 Gift of other low-tax lump sum distribution

"NUA" is not the only special tax deal available for qualifying lump sum distributions (LSDs). An LSD to a participant who was born before January 2, 1936 (or to the beneficiaries of such a participant) qualifies for a special tax treatment under which the distribution is excluded from the recipient's gross income and taxed under a separate rate schedule. See ¶ 2.4.06. The special tax treatment for LSDs has a mixed effect on charitable giving. The effect may be favorable: Since the LSD is excluded from the recipient's gross income, the recipient may be able to pay the low LSD rate on the distribution, give the distribution to charity, and deduct the gift from his other income, thus saving taxes at his regular income tax rate. Or the effect may be unfavorable: If the distribution is large enough, excluding it from gross income may cause a large charitable gift to exceed the percentage-of-AGI limits on charitable deductions (¶ 7.6.01(A)).

7.6.06 *Give ESOP qualified replacement property to CRT*

The Code allows a business owner, if various requirements are met, to sell stock of his company to an "employee stock ownership plan" (ESOP), then reinvest the proceeds in marketable securities ("qualified replacement property"), without paying income tax on the sale. § 1042. The untaxed gain carries over to the qualified replacement property and the capital gain tax thus deferred will be paid when the taxpayer "disposes of" the qualified replacement property. A *gift* of the qualified replacement property does not trigger the recapture provision, but since the Code doesn't define "gift," it's not clear whether transferring qualified replacement property to a Charitable Remainder Trust (which is not totally a gift if the donor retains an income interest) is considered a gift for this purpose. See PLR 9732023.

7.6.07 *Qualified Charitable Distributions*

In a year when "qualified charitable distributions" are permitted, an IRA owner or beneficiary who is age 70½ or older can transfer up to $100,000 directly from his IRA (or inherited IRA, as the case may be) to a public 501(c)(3) charity (¶ 7.5.01), *other than* a DAF (¶ 7.5.03) or support fund, without having the distribution be reportable as a distribution to himself—and the distribution will count towards the MRD for the year. Since this giving method expired at the end of 2009, it is not further reported here. See instead the *Special Report: Ancient History* (Appendix C).

8

Investment Issues; Plan Types

Investment issues with IRAs and Roth IRAs; types of retirement plans.

This Chapter discusses tax issues connected with how an IRA is invested (¶ 8.1–¶ 8.2), and describes the types of retirement plans covered by this book (¶ 8.3).

8.1 IRAs: Issues for Investors

For what an IRA may legally invest in, and how to hold IRA investments, see ¶ 8.1.05. For the tax effects of losses in IRA investments, see ¶ 8.1.02.

8.1.01 *Various investment issues for IRAs*

This ¶ 8.1.01 explains some ordinary and not so ordinary issues that can arise with IRA investments.

A. **IRA contributions, distributions, rollovers: Cash vs. property.** You cannot contribute stock, real estate, your business, or any other noncash asset to an IRA; an IRA may accept only cash contributions. § 408(a)(1). The IRA owner's payment of IRA investment management expenses from "outside" assets does not violate this rule; see ¶ 8.1.04.

The only exception to the cash-contributions-only rule is for rollovers: Property that is distributed from one plan or IRA may be "rolled" into an IRA if the distribution otherwise meets the requirements for a rollover; see ¶ 2.6.02. In fact, if property is distributed from the distributing plan or IRA, you *must* "roll" the *exact same* property to the IRA; see ¶ 2.6.04.

IRA (including Roth IRA) distributions can be in either cash or property. Property distributed is generally included in income at its fair market value; see ¶ 2.1.01. The amount so included then becomes the individual's basis for determining gain or loss on the distributed property on its subsequent disposition. Rev. Rul. 80-196, 1980-2 C.B. 32 (holding #2); Reg. § 1.408A-6, A-16. For minimum distribution effects of a distribution of property, see ¶ 1.2.02(E).

Because the recipient's basis in the distributed property is the value of the property on the date of distribution (i.e., it is not a "carryover" of the IRA's cost basis in the property), the holding period for the distributed property, for purposes of determining whether gain or loss on a subsequent disposition is long- or short-term, would begin the day after the date of distribution, as if the distributee had purchased the securities on the date of distribution—not on the date the IRA acquired the security. See § 1223(2) ("Holding Period of Property"), Reg. § 1.402(a)-1(b)(1).

B.   **Prohibited transaction from standard brokerage account form.** An IRA can be disqualified (i.e., lose its status as an IRA) for such "prohibited transactions" as borrowing from or against the account by the IRA owner. See ¶ 8.1.06(B). In DOL Advisory Opinion 2009-03A, an individual proposed to open an IRA at a brokerage firm. The firm would require the individual to give the firm a security interest (to secure any indebtedness incurred in the IRA) in the individual's nonIRA accounts held at that firm. The DOL ruled that granting a security interest in nonIRA assets to secure an indebtedness of the IRA was a prohibited transaction, namely, an extension of credit between the IRA and a disqualified person (the IRA owner). The DOL noted that a prohibited transaction would similarly arise if an individual granted a security interest in the IRA to secure indebtedness incurred in his nonIRA accounts.

C.   **IRA and nonIRA transactions matched for wash sale purposes.** Under the "wash sale" rule, you cannot deduct a loss on the sale of securities if you repurchase substantially identical securities within 30 days before or after the loss-generating sale. § 1091(a). Rev. Rul. 2008-5, 2008-3 IRB 1, holds that a purchase of securities inside an IRA or Roth IRA *will* be matched with an outside sale of securities within the applicable 30-day period for purposes of applying § 1091. Furthermore, the taxpayer does *not* get to increase his basis in the IRA by the amount of the disallowed loss, despite the fact that § 1091(d) allows such a basis adjustment when the wash sale rule is applied to deny a loss.

This ruling creates a compliance nightmare for tax preparers, who will now apparently have to inspect all of their clients' IRA and Roth IRA brokerage statements to determine whether the wash sale rule applies to outside-the-plan loss sales.

The ruling cites, as its only authority for this position, *Security First National Bank of Los Angeles*, 28 BTA 289 (1933), in which the wash sale rule was applied to a taxpayer's sale of securities when he repurchased identical securities inside a trust that he controlled. However, this case has been "statutorily overruled": Since enactment of the 1954 Code, the grantor trust rules of Subchapter J (§ 671–§ 679) have been the *exclusive* means by which the IRS is permitted to treat trust-owned assets as if they were owned directly by an individual. § 671. But the IRS cannot use the grantor trust rules to achieve its result because the grantor trust rules don't apply to an IRA (see ¶ 8.1.05(C)), thus the reliance on an obsolete case. In the author's opinion, Rev. Rul. 2008-5 is wrong.

8.1.02 *Investment losses and IRAs*

This ¶ 8.1.02 discusses an IRA owner's options for dealing with investment losses inside an IRA. For a loss that occurs upon the conversion of a traditional IRA into a Roth IRA, see ¶ 5.4.03(C).

Generally, losses on investments inside an IRA are not deductible:

Gail Example: Gail made a tax-deductible contribution of $5,000 to her IRA. She used the $5,000 to purchase 100 shares of Omega stock inside the IRA. After a year, the Omega stock value had climbed to $50,000. A market crash caused the Omega stock value to plunge back to $1,000. Although Gail has "lost" $4,000 of her original investment, and $49,000 of its peak value, none of this loss can be deducted because it occurred inside an IRA.

For an IRA "loss" to be deductible, two things have to be true. First, the individual has to have cashed out all of his "aggregated" IRA or Roth IRA accounts; see "A" below. Second, the amount he received as a result of this cashout must be less than his "income tax "basis" in his IRAs or Roth IRAs; see "B." For what type of deduction this loss generates, see "C." For other approaches to dealing with an IRA loss, see "D."

A.   **How to realize an IRA loss.** The individual must close out the Roth account, or the traditional IRA account as the case may be, because there must be a "closed and completed transaction" in order to recognize a loss. Reg. § 1.165-1(b); Notice 87-16, 1987-1 C.B. 446, Part III, D5.

It is the IRS position that the individual actually must close out *all* his Roth IRAs (or all his traditional IRAs), in order to claim a loss on the Roth IRAs (or traditional IRAs), because (according to the IRS) all Roth IRAs are treated as a single account for income tax purposes (and all traditional IRAs are treated as a single account for income tax purposes). Notice 89-25, A-7, 1989-1 C.B. 662.

Here's how the IRS gets there: The applicable Code sections (§ 408(d)(2)(A); § 408A(a); § 408A(d)(4)(A)) require aggregation *for purposes of applying § 72*, the section that governs income taxation of IRA distributions (¶ 2.1.01). Only by applying § 72 can you determine the individual's basis (investment in the contract) with respect to his IRAs or Roth IRAs. Therefore without applying § 72 you cannot determine the amount of the loss that will be deductible. Therefore the aggregation rule applies in obtaining a deductible loss—even though the ultimate deduction is under § 165 (see "C" below) not under § 72.

For which IRAs must (and may not) be aggregated for purposes of calculating and realizing a loss, see: ¶ 5.2.03(B) for Roth IRAs, ¶ 2.2.08(F) for traditional IRAs, and ¶ 2.2.07 for inherited IRAs.

B.   **Loss equals basis minus proceeds.** The amount of the loss is limited to the participant's basis in the Roth IRAs (or traditional IRAs as the case may be). Reg. § 1.165-1(c)(1).

A participant may or may not have basis in a traditional IRA; see ¶ 2.2.06–¶ 2.2.07 regarding how to determine basis in a traditional IRA. Though unusual, it is possible for a participant's account value to be worth less than this basis.

A built-in loss is less unusual with a *Roth* IRA. The participant typically has a relatively high basis in his Roth IRA, especially shortly after creating it, because he has paid income tax on all his contributions to the account. If the Roth IRA subsequently declines in value, the participant now has a built-in loss in his account. See ¶ 5.2.06 and ¶ 5.7.08(D) regarding how to determine basis in a Roth IRA.

C.   **How to deduct the loss.** Everyone agrees that IRA losses are deductible in some fashion, under some Code section. However, the authority for exactly *how* such losses are to be deducted is scant to nonexistent. The problem is that IRA distributions are generally taxed under § 72; see ¶ 2.1.01. But § 72 has no provision for a *loss*. See Rev. Rul. 2009-13, 2009-21 IRB 1029, and PLR 2009-45032.

One possible source for the deductibility of IRA losses is § 165: An individual is allowed an income tax deduction for a loss "incurred in any transaction entered into for profit." § 165(a), (c)(2). Another is § 212, expenses incurred for production of income (see ¶ 8.1.04(B)).
IRS Publication 529 ("Miscellaneous Deductions"; 2009 ed., p. 9) lists IRA losses among the long list of "items" that are deductible as expenses paid either "To produce or collect income that must be included in your gross income" or "To manage, conserve, or maintain property held for producing such income." Those would be § 212 deductions. IRS Publication 590 ("IRAs"; 2009 ed., p. 40) says only that the loss is deductible as a miscellaneous itemized deduction, subject to § 67 (miscellaneous itemized deductions are deductible only to the extent the total of such deductions exceeds 2% of adjusted gross income), and to the reduction of itemized deductions that is applicable, through 2009 and after 2010, to high-income individuals under § 68.

D.   **Ways to deal with a loss (other than deducting it).** If the losses were caused by someone else's malfeasance, see ¶ 8.1.03 regarding the possibility of suing the wrongdoer and depositing the lawsuit winnings in the IRA as a "restorative payment."

If the loss occurred after and with respect to a recent Roth conversion, see ¶ 5.6 regarding the possibility of "recharacterizing" the Roth conversion as a contribution to a traditional IRA.
Another approach to losses is to keep the account alive and hope it recovers its value.

8.1.03 *Restoring lawsuit winnings to IRA*

When an IRA owner has a claim against an investment advisor or firm for losses in connection with products or services provided to the IRA, perhaps the lawsuit should be brought by the IRA custodian as plaintiff rather than by the IRA owner. However, apparently, the IRA owner often or always is the named plaintiff. When the IRA owner recovers, he seeks to have the money restored to the IRA. How can this be done without constituting an excess IRA contribution (¶ 2.1.08)?

The IRS (typically via the "late rollover" procedure; see ¶ 2.6.07) allows the IRA owner to contribute this type of recovery to his IRA as a "restorative payment." The concept is that the recovered amount is replacing losses due to fraud or other breach of fiduciary duty. Rev. Rul. 2002-45, 2002-29 IRB 116; PLR 2006-04039.

See, for example, 11 apparently related PLRs, in which the IRS ruled that the IRA owners' net proceeds from such a lawsuit (which they received in their individual names) could be deposited in their respective IRAs, and these deposits would be treated as tax-free rollovers. Apparently the date the defendant coughed up the money was considered the date of the "distribution" from the IRAs, because the IRS said the owners had 60 days from that date to complete the rollover. PLRs 2004-52043–2004-52046, 2004-52048–2004-52054. PLRs 2001-21034 and 2005-34026 are similar.

The ability to contribute (or "roll over") a "restorative payment" to an IRA applies only to the compensatory payment for the actual investment loss; it does not extend to any portion of the award or recovery that represents attorneys' fees or court costs (see PLR 2007-24040), or interest on the damages award (PLR 2009-21039). It can apply to a payment received from the defendant in a good faith settlement and/or arbitration (see PLRs 2007-24040, 2009-21039) as well as a litigation recovery.

However, this principle does NOT allow the IRA owner to deposit his own funds in the IRA to make up for investment losses, or even for losses caused by the malfeasance of others (PLR 2001-51051).

8.1.04 *Paying, deducting, IRA investment expenses*

This section discusses payment of IRA management expenses using outside funds.

A.   **Payment of IRA expenses.** If the IRA owner pays, from his taxable account, ordinary and necessary expenses that are incurred for the <u>management</u> of the IRA's investments, and that are billed separately to the IRA owner, such payment is *not* considered a contribution to the IRA for purposes of applying the limits on IRA contributions (¶ 5.3.03). Rev. Rul. 84-146, 1984-2 C.B. 61. However, brokerage commissions and similar <u>transaction costs</u> are not considered management expenses. If the IRA owner pays the IRA's brokerage commissions from his taxable account, such payment is considered a contribution to the IRA. Rev. Rul. 86-142, 1986-2 C.B. 60.

With a so-called "wrap" investment account, offered by some brokerage firms, the customer does not pay any separate brokerage commissions. The commissions for trades are included in the "wrap" fee, which is a percentage of the assets in the account. In PLR 2005-07021, the IRS ruled that the wrap fees charged to the applicant-firm's IRA clients could be paid by the IRA owners using outside assets, without causing a deemed contribution, because the wrap fee was "calculated as a percentage of the...assets," included an unlimited number of transactions, and did not "vary with the frequency of the transactions performed."

If the IRA itself has already paid the investment manager's fee, the IRA owner cannot *reimburse* the IRA for that expense. There is no longer a debt to the provider of the investment management services. As a voluntary payment to the IRA, the "reimbursement" would be treated simply as an IRA contribution.

Though an individual can pay his IRA's (or Roth IRA's) separately billed investment management expenses from a taxable account, it would not be proper to cause the investment expenses of his *Roth IRA* to be paid by his *traditional IRA*. The IRS could attack this as a taxable distribution from the traditional IRA.

The IRA's payment of its own expenses (such as an investment management fee) is not a distribution, and accordingly does not count towards fulfilling the minimum required distribution (¶ 1.2.02(G)).

B.   **Deductibility of IRA/Roth IRA management expenses.** § 212 allows individuals an income tax deduction for "all the ordinary and necessary expenses paid or incurred during the taxable year...for the management, conservation, or maintenance of property held for the production or collection of income...."

This is a miscellaneous itemized deduction, subject to the "two percent floor" of § 67, and to the reduction of itemized deductions applicable (through 2009 and after 2010) to high-income individuals under § 68.

The IRS acknowledges in Publication 590, "IRAs" (2009, p. 12), that "Trustees' administrative fees that are billed separately and paid in connection with your traditional IRA...may be deductible as a miscellaneous itemized deduction on Schedule A (Form 1040)."

However, § 265 denies a deduction for otherwise-deductible expenses "allocable" to income that is tax-exempt, or, as the regulations put it, "Wholly excluded from gross income under any provision of Subtitle A" or any other law. Reg. § 1.265-1(b)(1)(i). Though there is as yet no IRS pronouncement on the subject, it would appear that investment management fees allocable to a *Roth IRA* would be nondeductible under this provision once the account owner has fulfilled the Five-Year Period and triggering event requirements (¶ 5.2.04), since after that point all distributions from the Roth IRA would generally be tax-exempt qualified distributions.

8.1.05 *IRAs owning "nontraditional" investments*

The list of assets that an IRA is forbidden to hold is brief: life insurance (§ 408(a)(3)), loans to the owner and other self-dealing investments (¶ 8.1.06), and most "collectibles" (§ 408(m)). So it is perfectly "legal" for an IRA to own real estate, a business, a private investment fund, or other "nontraditional" investment.

Investing an IRA in unconventional choices has come to be misnamed **self-directed IRA** investing. The real meaning of self-directed is that the participant himself (rather than the IRA trustee) chooses the investments. Thus, almost all IRAs are "self-directed," even those invested in publically-traded stocks, bonds, and mutual funds. An IRA that is NOT "self-directed," i.e., whose investment choices are made by someone other than the participant (such as an IRA trustee), is unusual.

Even though it is legal, investing IRA funds in assets other than bank deposits and publically-traded stocks, bonds, and mutual funds creates issues and risks that typically do not arise with more "vanilla" investments. The first problem is to find an IRA custodian or trustee willing to hold title to nontraditional investments. Some IRA providers specialize in this; most IRA providers won't do it at all.

Another problem is the necessity of valuing assets that are not publically-traded. This problem arises annually when the IRA provider must file Form 5498 (reporting the account value to the IRS) and becomes acute when the participant or beneficiary must take annual minimum required distributions (MRDs) computed based on the value of the IRA (¶ 1.2.05).

Even once the valuation is accomplished, fulfilling the MRD can be difficult if the IRA's only assets are illiquid investments. Either the IRA must have cash on hand to fulfill the MRD, or the IRA must distribute interests in the illiquid investment (which creates the need for another valuation). Distributing partial interests in an illiquid asset (such as a parcel of real estate) results in shared ownership of the asset, following the distribution, between the IRA and the participant, which creates potential for a prohibited transaction (¶ 8.1.06). Roth conversion of the illiquid asset prior to attaining age 70½ would require only one valuation of the asset, and eliminate the need for MRDs and their associated problems, as long as the participant is living (¶ 5.2.02(A)).

Other common problems with unconventional investments include titling (see "B" below), and the increased risk of having UBTI (see ¶ 8.2).

A.   **Partnerships.** If an IRA owns a partnership interest, the IRA custodian should NOT provide the IRA owner's Social Security number to the partnership for purposes of reporting the IRA's share of partnership income and losses. Instead, the IRA custodian is supposed to give the partnership the *custodian's* employer identification number. See instructions to IRS Form 1065 (U.S. Return of Partnership Income), 2009, p. 25, under "How to Complete Schedule K-1, Part II, Information About the Partner, Items E and F," first paragraph.

Unlike a "C corporation," a partnership is a "pass-through entity," meaning that the income is taxed directly to the partners. Some businesses (such as oil and gas exploration companies) are typically operated as partnerships rather than in corporate form, and may issue publically-traded shares ("units") in the partnership. An investor (including an IRA) in such a "master limited partnership" is actually a partner in the business, and receives a "K-1" each year reporting the investor's share of the partnership's income. This will indicate the amount of reportable UBTI (see ¶ 8.2.03(C)) attributable to the IRA-owned units, and also may create an obligation to file income tax returns in any state where the partnership operates.

B. **Hedge funds and other "private" investments.** IRA investment in hedge funds and similar private investments sometimes creates logistical difficulties. See, *e.g.*, PLR 2010-13067, in which the participant, to meet a deadline for investing in a particular partnership, deposited cash in the partnership, intending to later (when rollover funds were received from another IRA) "restructure" the partnership investment as an IRA investment, a procedure that obviously does not work. The IRS granted him a late rollover waiver (¶ 2.6.07) because he relied on incorrect financial institution advice.

A more common problem with these investments is titling mistakes. Title to IRA assets must be held by a bank (or other institution that has gone through the IRS process for approval to hold IRA assets). § 408(a)(2). An individual can NOT hold direct title to assets that are supposedly in his IRA. Thus, the title of a partnership unit held by an IRA should be "[Name of bank], as custodian [or trustee] of [name of participant] IRA."

This requirement can be easily overlooked when the IRA owner wants to invest in a hedge fund, LLC, or other private investment vehicle. The hedge fund accepts money that is supposed to be a rollover from an actual IRA or plan, deposits the money in its fund, and opens an account entitled "John Doe IRA." Because there is no bank holding title to the account, however, this investment is not "in" an IRA; it is owned by John Doe directly. The result is a taxable distribution from the original plan or IRA that the money came out of.

If the funds came from an IRA or plan distribution that the participant thought he was simply rolling over or transferring (still inside an IRA) to another investment vehicle, the participant may be able to get a hardship waiver of the 60-day rollover deadline (¶ 2.6.07) that will allow him to get the money back into an IRA. The IRS granted such waivers in PLRs 2007-37047, 2007-37048, 2009-19066 (real estate limited partnership), 2009-21038 (limited partnership), 2009-31063 (investment pool), and 2010-05058. In each of these PLRs, it appears the participant relied on information from the company that was to receive the investment and/or other financial advisors in assuming that the new investment was indeed properly held in a rollover IRA.

However, in PLR 2010-15039, the IRS *denied* a waiver to an IRA owner who withdrew from her IRA and used the money to buy a share of "Company C" based on a seminar she attended and (she claimed) assurances from the lawyer for Company C that this would constitute a valid rollover and IRA investment. The difference between this and the "winning" waiver requests is not entirely clear, except that in this one no advisor or company admitted any error. In the successful deadline-waiver requests based on failure to have a bank hold the "IRA" investment, the financial institutions and/or advisors apparently did admit they had incorrectly advised the participant.

C.   **S corporation stock.** Owning "S corporation" stock inside an IRA or Roth IRA does not disqualify the IRA. However it does cause the corporation to lose its qualification as an S corporation, with the disastrous result that the corporation will be taxed as a regular "C" corporation. Rev. Rul. 92-73, 1992-2 CB 224; Reg. § 1.1361-1(h)(1)(vii).

Though the Code section that creates S corporations does not specifically prohibit S corp. stock ownership by an IRA, the IRS has consistently ruled that IRAs (and Roth IRAs) are considered "trusts" for purposes of the Tax Code. No trust may own S corp. stock other than a "grantor trust" or an "electing small business trust," and an IRA is neither of those. § 1361(b)(1), (c)(2)(A)(I). The Tax Court accepted the IRS view in *Taproot Administrative Services, Inc. v. Comm'r*, 133 T.C. No. 9 (9/29/09).

The Code has a corrective procedure allowing S corp. status to be restored when it is lost inadvertently. § 1362(f). For how an IRA owner can use this procedure to correct inadvertent loss of S corp. status through transfer of S corp. stock into an IRA or Roth IRA, see PLRs 2008-07022, 2009-06015, 2009-15020, 2009-17008, 2009-31039, and 2009-40013.

D.   **Real estate.** Real estate can trigger the same titling problems as hedge funds (see "B"). Direct ownership of real estate by an IRA also has pitfalls of its own. One is the need to buy the property inside the IRA; the participant cannot buy the property outside the IRA and then later contribute the property to the IRA (noncash contribution; ¶ 8.1.01(A)) or sell it to the IRA (prohibited transaction; ¶ 8.1.06(B)). Another problem is personal use of the IRA-owned real estate (IRA owner and his family vacation in the IRA-owned ski chalet, for example), an obvious "prohibited transaction" (¶ 8.1.06(B)).

Another pitfall is commingling of funds. If the IRA owner uses his personal funds to pay expenses associated with the IRA-owned property, that would presumably be considered a contribution to the IRA, which may create an excess contribution problem (see ¶ 5.3.05). If the IRA owner tries to treat such payments as advances, and repays himself out of IRA funds, he either has a taxable distribution or an IRA-disqualifying prohibited transaction (loan; ¶ 8.1.06(B)).

Any shared ownership or expense-sharing between the IRA and the IRA owner in his personal capacity creates prohibited transaction potential.

If the IRA owner works on the IRA-owned real estate (for example painting the place on the weekend), thus contributing "sweat equity," he becomes vulnerable to several possible lines of IRS attack: Disqualifying the IRA for accepting noncash contributions (§ 408(a)(1)); reallocation of the IRA's "income" from sale or rental of the property to the IRA owner's personal return (with resulting penalties for failure to report such income) (see § 482), followed by deemed contribution of the re-allocated income to the IRA (excess IRA contribution penalty), etc.

E.   **Active business.** Theoretically an IRA can operate a business. Of course the business's income would be taxable as UBTI; see ¶ 8.2.02. And the operating business could legally get into the IRA only by being purchased (or started) with cash that had been legally contributed to the IRA (or proceeds of investments arising from legal cash contributions); see ¶ 8.1.01(A). Also, to avoid prohibited transaction problems (¶ 8.1.06), it would appear that neither the IRA owner or any member of his family could work for the business; the only possible limited exception to that would be that it might be permissible for the IRA owner to perform "management" services without compensation. (Note: Despite occasional statements in IRS Publications that a prohibited transaction will arise if the IRA owner is paid "unreasonable" compensation from his IRA, it is actually the case that the payment of *any* compensation to the IRA owner from the IRA would be a prohibited transaction.) And obviously there would be prohibited transaction concerns regarding any transaction between the IRA-owned business and the IRA owner or any of his relatives or entities owned by any of them. With so many risks and limitations, it seems not advisable to operate a business inside an IRA.

8.1.06 *IRAs and prohibited transactions*

Do not engage in a prohibited transaction (PT) involving your IRA. To avoid PT problems, make sure that the IRA never enters into *any* transaction with the IRA owner (other than accepting legal contributions and making permitted distributions), or any person or entity related to the IRA owner, or any person or entity with whom or with which the IRA owner has any type of business or personal relationship outside of the IRA; and that the IRA owner never engages in any transaction *outside* the IRA that involves a payment in connection with assets *inside* the IRA.

A. **The penalty for an IRA PT.** The penalty on an IRA owner (or beneficiary) for "engaging" in a PT involving the IRA is that the IRA is disqualified. The account ceases to be an IRA and is deemed to have been entirely distributed to him on January 1 of the year in which the transaction occurs. § 408(e)(2); Reg. § 1.408-4(d)(1). The result is that the individual must pay income tax on the account value just as if it had been distributed to him. The same penalty applies to a Roth IRA. § 408A(a); Reg. § 1.408A-1, A-1(b). In the case of a Roth IRA, disqualification is an even more drastic punishment because it presumably causes loss of the tax-exempt status otherwise applicable to Roth IRA distributions (¶ 5.2.04).

B. **Transactions that are prohibited.** PTS include just about any direct business transaction (such as sale, leasing of property, payments for goods or services, lending of money or property, etc.) between the IRA and a disqualified person (DQP; see "C" below). § 4975(c)(1)(A)–(D). These transactions are PTS *even if the plan is not harmed.* For example, a participant's bargain sale of property to an IRA would be a PT even though the IRA is getting a good deal.

There are other ways to have a PT besides these catalogued transactions between the IRA and a related party. An IRA transaction with a party who is *not* a DQP can be a PT if it *indirectly benefits* a

DQP. This rule has been used to find PTS when IRAs engaged in transactions with entities that were *less than 50 percent owned* by DQPs; even though the entity was therefore not a DQP (see "C"), the transaction was found to *indirectly benefit* DQPs who were minority owners of (or otherwise related to) the entity. *Rollins*, T.C. Memo 2004-260 (2004); PLR 9119002; DOL Advisory Opinion 93-33A.

A transaction in which the IRA is *not even involved* could be a PT; for example, if the IRA owner receives a payment, outside the IRA, for a transaction involving the IRA's assets. § 4975(c)(1)(F). The IRS and DOL have even been known to claim that any transaction involving a conflict of interest between the IRA and the owner as "fiduciary" is, itself, a PT, without (apparently) the necessity of proving that any DQP benefitted from the transaction, though this IRS/DOL position has not been tested in court. See Reg. § 54.4975-6(a)(5)(i), DOL Advisory Opinion 2000-10A, PLR 2001-28011.

Finally, if the IRA owns or controls an entity, a DQP's transaction with or involving the IRA-controlled entity may be a PT under a set of look-through rules called the "plan asset rules." See 29 CFR § 2510.3-101(a)(1), (f)(2)(ii); DOL Advisory Opinion 2000-10A.

C.   **Who are disqualified persons?** DQPs include the IRA owner (who is considered a "fiduciary" of his own IRA) and certain related parties, namely, the IRA owner/fiduciary's spouse, ancestors, descendants, and spouses of descendants. An entity that is controlled or more than 50 percent owned by DQPs (after application of attribution rules) is also a DQP. § 4975(e)(2). Under the "plan assets rule" (see "B" above), managers of a plan-owned entity are also considered fiduciaries and thus are DQPs.

D.   **Exemptions.** Certain transactions necessary for an IRA to function are either explicitly exempted or assumed to be exempt, such as making legally permitted contributions to the IRA, taking distributions from the IRA (§ 4975(d)(9); see DOL AO-2009-02A), naming or changing the designated beneficiary, and dividing the IRA in the case of divorce (see PLR 2002-15061). The Department of Labor has granted certain "class" exemptions to permit some standard transactions, such as the purchase of life insurance from a QRP and using an IRA balance as part of a collection of accounts to meet a minimum balance requirement (PTE 93-2, PTE 93-33). The DOL can also grant an individual exemption for a proposed transaction, and can issue an "Advisory Opinion" about whether a proposed transaction is a PT. See: http://www.dol.gov/ebsa/compliance_assistance.html.

E. **Enforcement of the PT rules.** The best hope for clients and advisors who come too close for comfort to the PT rules is the chaotic state of the PT law and its enforcement. The statute contains mistakes (has contained them since 1974!) that make the law nonsensical in some respects. The meaning of certain terms such as "beneficiary" and "engages" have never been clarified. Enforcement of the rules with respect to IRAs was originally granted to both the IRS and the DOL, then was supposedly divided between them, and is now claimed sporadically by both of them, so no one seems to know who is really in charge if anyone. The DOL and Courts have issued rulings that appear incorrect. The IRS has issued contradictory rulings on PTS, and is generally so uncomfortable with this area that it tends to use anything other than PTS to attack transactions, such as gift taxes, § 482, improper IRA contributions, and listed transactions.

F. **Recommendations for estate planners and advisors.** Promoters and planners look for flaws in the PT rules that they can exploit to allow the IRA owner to engage in various transactions generally designed to maximize the advantage of investing inside a tax-deferred IRA or tax-free Roth IRA. Hopes have been pinned on such notions as that the PT rules do not apply on formation of an entity; that the IRA owner is not a DQP if he can be positioned so that he is not a "fiduciary" of the IRA; and that any transaction with an in-law, sibling, or nonspouse significant other is not a PT because those persons are not DQPs.

It is not recommended that a client rely on such approaches. It is recommended that the estate planner not "dabble" in PTS. If involved with a transaction that may raise PT questions, the estate planner should either hire or become an expert. To get started, see Chapter 24 of *The Pension Answer Book* (Appendix C). No estate planner should advise regarding a transaction between an IRA and any related party unless (1) there is a class exemption that clearly applies, or (2) the planner devotes the time to study the applicable rules, or (3) an ERISA expert gives an opinion that the PT rules are not violated. Another approach is to follow the Department of Labor and IRS procedures for getting an Advisory Opinion (DOL), PT "exemption" (DOL or IRS), or private letter ruling (IRS).

Since the potential penalty for a PT is disqualification of the IRA, use one IRA for the proposed transaction and a different IRA to hold the owner's other, less controversial, investments. If the separation of the two accounts occurs prior to the year in which the questionable transaction occurs, a PT in one account presumably would not put the other IRA at risk.

8.2 IRAs and the Tax on UBTI

Normally, IRAs are tax-exempt entities; however, like other tax-exempt entities, IRAs are subject to tax under § 511 on "unrelated business taxable income" (UBTI). § 408(e)(1). This ¶ 8.2 provides , for the estate planner, CPA, or financial planner who is advising an individual participant or beneficiary, an *overview* of the tax, emphasizing rules that personal advisers may not be aware of. An IRA owner and his adviser must seek UBTI-expert help (or become UBTI experts) if the IRA invests in nontraditional investments. For more on UBTI, see IRS Publication 598, *Tax on Unrelated Business Income of Exempt Organizations*.

8.2.01 UBTI: Rationale, exemptions, returns, double tax, etc.

The idea of the UBTI tax is that a tax-exempt organization (such as a charity or retirement plan) is granted its tax exemption to foster its exempt purposes, not to enable the entity to compete with tax-paying businesses. Reg. § 1.513-1(b). If the tax-exempt entity has UBTI, it must pay income tax on that income. § 511. However, despite this rationale, an IRA does not have to actually operate a business to become subject to this tax; see ¶ 8.2.03.

The UBTI tax can require not only the complications of figuring out the tax, and filing returns (Form 990-T, 990-W) but also paying estimated taxes (if "adjusted" UBTI exceeds $500), with associated penalties if any of these filings or payments are late. If the UBTI for the year is under $1,000 there is no tax, because there is a $1,000 deduction. § 512(b)(12). Form 990-T must be filed if gross unrelated business income is $1,000 or more. The IRA custodian or trustee is supposed to file the return. Strangely, it is not clear whether an individual's IRAs are aggregated for purposes of applying the $1,000 deduction.

Nothing in the Code gives the IRA owner any "basis step-up" or tax credit to reflect the fact that some of the IRA's income has already been taxed as UBTI. An IRA or Roth IRA distribution will be taxable (or not) under the usual rules for taxation of such distributions (see ¶ 2.2, ¶ 5.2) without regard to how much if any UBTI tax has been paid on the IRA's internal income.

The UBTI tax is not a concern if the IRA invests only in publically-traded corporate stocks and bonds and bank deposits, and never borrows money. However, UBTI can be generated by certain publically-traded securities; see ¶ 8.1.05(A).

8.2.02 *Income from an IRA-operated trade or business*

UBTI includes gross income (minus permitted deductions) from the conduct of an "unrelated trade or business" that is "regularly carried on" by the exempt organization. § 512(a)(1).

§ 513(b) provides that, for a QRP, "unrelated trade or business" means "*any* trade or business regularly carried on by such [plan]…or by a partnership of which it is a member." Emphasis added. Though there is no comparable specific rule for IRAs, which are tax-exempt under § 408(e)(1) not § 401, it appears prudent to assume that *any* "trade or business" conducted by an IRA (or by a partnership or LLC of which it is a member) is unrelated to its exempt purpose.

Under § 513(a)(1), unrelated trade or business "does not include any trade or business—(1) in which substantially all the work in carrying on such trade or business is performed for the organization without compensation…." This might make it appear that, if the IRA owner is the only worker in the business conducted by his IRA, and he does not take a salary or withdraw any profits, he could say he is working without compensation, and the IRA should therefore escape UBTI tax on the resulting income. It seems unlikely that this argument would succeed. Presumably a court would not entertain the notion that the IRA owner is serving "without compensation" where 100 percent of the profits of the business flow to him through his ownership of the IRA, even though his compensation is not currently paid out to him.

8.2.03 *When investment income becomes UBTI*

Most types of investment income are specifically excluded from the definition of "trade or business" income. Thus, the owner of an IRA that receives interest, dividends, and capital gains *generally* has no UBTI worries. § 512(b)(1), (5). However, there are exceptions that can make even these types of "passive" investment income subject to the UBTI tax. One such exception involves income from debt-financed property; see ¶ 8.2.04. The other three are:

A.   **Rent can be UBTI.** Rental income from real estate is generally treated as investment income, rather than as income from a trade or business. However, <u>real estate</u> rental income is treated as UBTI if the amount of rent is determined as a percentage of the tenant's profits. Even stricter rules apply to rental income from <u>personal property</u>. § 512(b)(3).

B.   **Investment income from a controlled entity.** Passive investment income can become UBTI when it is paid to the IRA by a controlled entity. Specifically, if rent, interest, or royalties are received from an entity that is more than 50 percent controlled by the IRA, and such payments have the effect of reducing the business income of the controlled entity, such payments are UBTI to the IRA. § 512(b)(13).

C.   **Business operated by pass-through entity.** If an IRA owns an interest in a business that is a "pass-through" entity for income tax purposes (such as a partnership or an LLC taxed as a partnership), the IRA's share of the partnership's (or LLC's) income from the trade or business is UBTI. This is true regardless of whether the IRA *controls* the pass-through entity. § 512(c)(1). See ¶ 8.1.05(A).

8.2.04 *Income from debt-financed property*

Income from "debt-financed property" is UBTI regardless of whether there is a trade or business. § 512(b)(4), § 514. "Debt-financed property" is property acquired with borrowed funds and held to produce income. § 514(b). Here are some guidelines:

A.   **Margin accounts create UBTI.** An investor may have a loan from his brokerage firm, secured by his securities account, that is used to increase the securities investment activity. This is called a margin account, and if the margin account is held in an IRA, a portion of the plan's investment income will be taxed as UBTI. *Bartels Trust* (see "D").

B.   **Short sales do not create UBTI.** Selling securities short involves two investors at the "selling" end: one (the lender-seller) lends its securities (through the brokerage firm) to the second investor, and the other (the borrower-seller) sells the borrowed securities to the buyer. The lender-seller receives various payments in connection with this transaction, but generally is treated as if he still owns the securities. The lender-seller is exempted from the UBTI tax by § 514(c)(8)(A) and § 512(a)(5), if various requirements are met. Short selling also does not create debt-financed income (or loss) for the borrower-seller; even though it does involve borrowing the securities to be sold, this borrowing creates an "obligation" but it does not create "indebtedness." Rev. Rul. 95-8, 1995-1 CB 107.

C.   **Real estate mortgages create UBTI for IRAs.** A qualified retirement plan (QRP) gets the benefit of an exception for certain mortgages used to finance the plan's purchase of investment real estate. § 514(c)(9). This exception does not apply to IRAs. § 514(c)(9)(C). Thus, owning mortgaged real estate will cause rental income from the property and/or gain upon sale of the property to be UBTI.

D.   **Exception for property used for exempt purpose.** There is an exception to the debt-financed property rule for property that is more than 85 percent used for the exempt entity's exempt purpose (other than its need for funds). § 514(b)(1)(A)(i), Reg. § 1.514(b)-1(b)(1)(ii).

"In furtherance" of the exempt purpose means inherent in or essential to the fulfilment of the exempt purpose. Borrowing for investment purposes, though it may be *useful* for the accumulation of funds in a retirement plan, does not meet this "essential" test. *Elliot Knitwear Profit-Sharing Plan*, 614 F. 2d 347 (3d Cir. 1980), which was followed in *Henry E. & Nancy Horton Bartels Trust*, 209 F. 3d 147 (2d Cir. 2000); Cert. Denied 531 U.S. 978 (2000).

8.3 Types of Retirement Plans

An in-depth discussion of the characteristics of retirement plans is beyond the scope of this book. The purpose of this ¶ 8.3 is to explain the differences among the various types of plans only to the extent such differences are likely to have an impact on individual planning choices.

In this book, a **"retirement plan"** means a corporate or self-employed ("Keogh") pension, profit-sharing, or stock bonus plan that is "qualified" under § 401(a), a tax-sheltered annuity (or mutual fund) arrangement established under § 403(b), or an individual retirement account (IRA) created under § 408 or § 408A. The narrower term **qualified plan** or **qualified retirement plan (QRP)** includes only 401(a) plans. Sometimes the term "plan or IRA" is used to emphasize that a statement applies to both "employer-type" plans (such as QRPs) and "individual account plans" (IRAs and Roth IRAs). Generally the term "IRA" includes both traditional and Roth IRAs, but sometimes the term "IRA or Roth IRA" is used to emphasize that the statement applies to both types.

8.3.01 *Overview of types of plans*

What's most confusing about the various types of retirement plans is that there is not one set of mutually exclusive categories; instead, there are different overlapping classifications for different purposes. For example, Qualified Retirement Plans (QRPs) are divided into two types (Defined Benefit and Defined Contribution) for purposes of the limits (under § 415) on what may be contributed or accrued for a participant, but into three types (pension, profit-sharing, and stock bonus) for purposes of plan aggregation under § 402 (definition of lump sum distribution; ¶ 2.4.04(B)). Profit-sharing and stock bonus plans must be Defined Contribution plans, but a pension plan may be either a Defined Contribution or a Defined Benefit plan. A Keogh plan can be any type of QRP other than a stock bonus plan or ESOP.

8.3.02 *401(k) plan; elective deferral; CODA*

A 401(k) plan is an **elective deferral** plan (also called a **cash-or-deferred arrangement** or **CODA**), meaning that the plan is at least partly funded by voluntary salary reduction (or bonus reduction) contributions. Under a CODA, the participant agrees, in advance, to have part of his compensation contributed to a retirement plan account for his benefit instead of being paid to him in cash. The portion of the account that is funded with the employee's elective deferral contributions is subject to additional rules (over and above the rules that apply to all retirement plan benefits), such as a restriction on distributions prior to age 59½. 401(k) and 403(b) plans, SEP-IRAs, and SIMPLEs are other examples of plans that are often funded by means of elective deferrals. See ¶ 5.7.01 regarding FICA tax treatment of elective deferrals.

The employer that sponsors the 401(k) plan may make additional "matching" or other contributions to the participant's account. A 401(k) plan is a type of QRP and may be a Keogh plan.

8.3.03 *403(b) plan*

403(b) plans (also called "**403(b) arrangements**" or "**TSAs**," which stands for tax-sheltered annuities) are available only to tax-exempt employers. Some 403(b) arrangements are funded exclusively by means of elective deferrals (¶ 8.3.02). Others are funded partly or solely by employer contributions; these latter plans must meet the same requirements as QRPs (¶ 8.3.12).

403(b) plan assets are held in the name of the employee (like an IRA), not in the name of the plan itself (the way QRP assets are held). 403(b) plans may invest *only* in annuity contracts purchased by the employer and issued in the name of the employee and/or in mutual funds held by a bank (or other approved institution) as custodian for the employee. § 403(b)(1)(A), (7).

A 403(b) plan distribution is never eligible for treatment as a lump sum distribution under § 402 (¶ 2.4.02). Also, the minimum distribution rules apply slightly differently; see ¶ 1.4.05.

Regarding rollovers of 403(b) benefits, see ¶ 2.6 (participant), ¶ 3.2.02 (surviving spouse), or ¶ 4.2.04 (other beneficiaries).

Deemed IRA, deemed Roth IRA. See ¶ 5.2.01.

8.3.04 *Defined Benefit plan*

A defined benefit plan is a type of QRP. Under a defined benefit plan, also called a "defined benefit pension plan," the employer promises to pay the employee a specific pension, starting at retirement, and continuing for the employee's life. Defined benefit plans have their own separate set of minimum distribution rules; see ¶ 1.1.05.

A. **"Classic" defined benefit plan.** Under the classic type of defined benefit plan, the amount of the pension is based on a formula, such as "a monthly pension for life, beginning at age 65, equal to 1/12th of 1 percent of final average compensation times years of service, reduced by 10 percent for each year of service less than 10 if the employee has less than 10 years of service, and up to an annual maximum of 40 percent of career average compensation."

The formula may award a lower percentage for compensation below the Social Security tax wage base than for compensation in excess of such base. This is called the "permitted disparity." The formula will contain adjustments for early or late retirement.

The employer hires an actuary to tell it, each year, the minimum amount it *must* contribute to the plan (and how much extra it *may* contribute) (both limits being set by the Code) in order to amortize the employer's future obligations to retiring employees under the plan.

Classic defined benefit plans generally are of greater value to older employees than to younger employees, because of the time value of money. Even if their eventual projected pensions are the same amount, say $36,000 per year starting at age 65, the value is greater to the employee who will be receiving that sooner. $36,000 a year starting in 10 years (how the pension looks to the 55 year-old employee) is a more significant asset than $36,000 a year starting in 30 years (how the pension looks to a 35 year-old employee). The older employee's pension looks more valuable to the employer too, who has to contribute more for the older employee than for the younger.

Classic defined benefit plans were once the normal form of retirement plan for American businesses. Their popularity has declined due to the increasingly complex tax and administrative rules applicable to these plans and due to the lower cost of defined contribution (DC) plans. However, the classic defined benefit plan remains attractive to the one-person business as a way of maximizing tax-deductible retirement contributions. If the business owner/sole employee is over age 50, approximately, a classic defined benefit plan will give him a much larger annual tax-deductible contribution than is permissible under a DC plan.

B.   **Cash balance plans.** There is another type of defined benefit plan, called a **cash balance plan**, that uses a different type of formula. "A cash balance plan is a defined benefit plan that defines benefits for each employee by reference to the employee's hypothetical account. An employee's hypothetical account is determined by reference to hypothetical allocations and interest adjustments that are analogous to actual allocations of contributions and earnings to an employee's account under a defined contribution plan." Reg. § 1.401(a)(4)-8(c)(3)(i). Under a cash balance plan, contributions are more uniform across age groups, making cash plans more attractive than classic defined benefit plans for younger employees (and less generous for older employees).

C.   **Estate planning features.** From an *estate planning perspective*, the defined benefit plan has the following distinctive features.

First, the participant does not have an "account" the way he does in a DC plan. Even under a cash balance plan, though the plan's funding formula is determined by reference to a hypothetical "account" for each employee, the participant does not have an actual account in the plan.

The benefit statement for a classic defined benefit plan will typically say the employee's "accrued benefit" under the plan is (*e.g.*) "$1,450 a month," of which (say) "80 percent is vested." What this means is that the employer has already obligated itself to provide for this employee (if the employee *keeps on working* until retirement age) a pension of $1,450 per month for life starting at the employee's "normal retirement age" under the plan; and if the employee *quits right now*, he's vested in 80 percent of that, meaning that at normal retirement age he would receive 80 percent of $1,450 per month.

The benefit statement may or may not contain more details such as: how much of a pension the employee would receive if he retired early; and (of great significance in estate planning), whether the employee will be permitted upon retirement to withdraw the lump sum equivalent of the accrued pension, or what death benefit, if any, would be available for the employee's beneficiaries. This brings us to the second significant factor in planning for defined benefit pension benefits: Many defined benefit plans do not offer the option of taking a lump sum equivalent in cash (or the client may have already chosen an annuity option and foreclosed his ability to take a lump sum equivalent). Thus under some defined benefit plans there is no ability to "roll over" the benefits to an IRA.

Also, a defined benefit plan may provide *no benefits at all* after the death of the employee other than the required annuity for the surviving spouse (¶ 3.4). If the participant dies prematurely, the money that was set aside to fund his pension goes back into the general fund to finance the benefits of other employees, rather than passing to the deceased employee's heirs.

D.   **Investment and longevity risks.** Under a DC plan, the participant owns identifiable assets held in an account with his name on it. The value of the account fluctuates depending on investment results, but no party to the proceedings has any money staked on the question of how long the participant will live. With a DC plan, the risk that the participant will outlive his money falls on the participant. With a defined benefit plan, the plan (or the insurance company issuing the annuity contract used to fund the benefits) takes the excess-longevity risk.

Theoretically, under a defined benefit plan, the plan also takes all the investment risk. If the plan's investments go down in value, the employee's promised benefit remains the same; the employer must contribute more money to the plan to fund that benefit. However, the employee has the risk that the employer will default on its obligation to fund the plan. If the plan becomes insolvent and/or the employer goes bankrupt, the employee may find his benefits limited to the amount insured by the government's pension insurer, the Pension Benefit Guarantee Corporation (PBGC). The employee will not receive the full benefits promised by the plan.

8.3.05 *Defined Contribution plan*

A Defined Contribution (DC) plan is, along with the defined benefit plan, one of the two broad categories of QRP. DC plans are also called "**individual account plans.**" § 414(i). IRS regulations use the terms individual account plan and defined contribution plan interchangeably; thus even individual account plans that are NOT QRPs (such as IRAs and 403(b) plans) may be called DC plans.

Under a DC plan, the employer may commit to making a certain level of contribution to the plan (such as "10% of annual compensation," an example of a "money purchase plan" formula), or (under a profit-sharing plan) may make such contributions periodically on a discretionary basis or based on profit levels. 401(k) plans and ESOPs are other examples of DC plans.

Once the employer has contributed to the DC plan, the contributions are allocated among accounts for the individual participants who are members of the plan. What the participant will eventually receive from the plan is determined by (1) how much is allocated to his account under the contribution formula and (2) the investment performance of that account. The employer does not guarantee any level of retirement benefits. If the plan's investments do well, the profits will increase the participant's account value. If the plan's investments do poorly, the participant will receive less at retirement.

If the plan is **self-directed**, each participant makes the investment decisions for his own account in the plan, from a menu of alternatives permitted by the plan. The menu may be broad or may be limited to a few mutual funds. If the plan is not self-directed, the investments are determined at the plan level by the trustee of the plan.

Designated Roth account (DRAC). See ¶ 5.7.

8.3.06 *ESOP (Employee Stock Ownership Plan)*

An ESOP is a QRP primarily designed to invest in stock of the sponsoring employer. § 4975(e)(7). ESOPs have various liberalized rules compared with other retirement plans, most of which are of interest only to the employer-sponsor and not to estate planners. Distributions of company stock to the participant or beneficiary from an ESOP or any other retirement plan may be eligible for certain favorable tax treatments if various requirements are met; see ¶ 2.5.

Dividends paid to the employee on employer stock held in the ESOP are entitled to certain special rules: They do not count as distributions for purposes of determining whether an employee has received a "lump sum distribution"; see ¶ 2.4.05. They are not subject to mandatory income tax withholding; see ¶ 2.3.03. They do not count towards fulfilling the minimum distribution requirement; see ¶ 1.2.02(C).

8.3.07 **Individual account plan.** Defined Contribution plan. ¶ 8.3.05.

8.3.08 **Individual Retirement Account (IRA); stretch IRA**

An IRA is a private, one-person retirement account that is created under, and given special tax benefits by, § 408. An IRA can be structured either as a custodial account (most common) or as a trust (in which case it may be called an **Individual Retirement Trust** or **Trusteed IRA**; see ¶ 6.1.07). § 408(a), (h). If the IRA is funded by direct contributions from the participant's employer it is a SEP or SIMPLE; see ¶ 8.3.13. For other ways to fund an IRA see ¶ 5.3.02 (regular contributions) and ¶ 2.6 (rollovers); see also ¶ 5.3.01. IRAs created under § 408 are called **traditional IRAs** when necessary to distinguish them from Roth IRAs (created under § 408A). There is no separate type of retirement plan called a "**stretch IRA**"; that's just a term sometimes used to refer to any IRA that is being paid out gradually over the life expectancy of a beneficiary (see ¶ 1.5.05).

8.3.09 **Keogh plan**

A Keogh plan (also called an **H.R. 10 plan**) is a QRP that covers one or more self-employed individuals. Thus, a Keogh plan is a QRP established by an unincorporated employer (partnership or sole proprietor) for the benefit of the partners and employees of the partnership, or for the benefit of the sole proprietor (and his employees, if any). Any type of QRP other than an ESOP or stock bonus plan may be a Keogh plan.

While the term "Keogh plan" (which never appears in the Code) is still used by self-employed persons to describe their retirement plans, *most* of the once-numerous distinctions between plans adopted by corporations and plans adopted by the self-employed were eliminated by the Tax Reform Acts of 1984 and 1986, and the Unemployment Compensation Amendments of 1992. To read about what the differences *used to be*, see Reg. § 1.401(e). For those that remain, see "B" below; note that some of the differences are applicable to all "self-employed persons" while others apply only to the "owner-employee."

A.   **Definitions.** A **self-employed** person is an individual who has self-employment income. § 401(c)(1). In contrast, a "common law employee" (or, as the Code calls it, "an individual who is an employee without regard to § 401(c)(1)") is an employee of someone else (not himself).

An **owner-employee** is the sole proprietor of an unincorporated business, or a partner "who owns more than 10 percent of either the capital interest or the profits interest" in the partnership. § 401(c)(3). The author has found no rule as to *when* the 10 percent test for determining owner-employee status is applied; do we test only at the end of the plan year? Or must we determine whether the individual owned more than 10 percent of the capital *at any time during* the year? And is the test applied yearly? Or is the individual considered *forever* an owner-employee if he was *ever* an owner-employee?

B.   **How they differ from other QRPs.** Here are the differences that still remain between Keogh plans and other QRPs that may matter from the self-employed individual's personal planning perspective.

Contributions subject to self-employment tax: The self-employed individual's contributions to his Keogh plan are not deductible for purposes of computing his self-employment tax; this is in contrast to employer contributions to a corporate QRP (other than elective deferral contributions; see ¶ 5.7.01), which are excluded from the definition of "wages" for FICA tax purposes.

Lump sum distributions: A lump sum distribution (LSD) may qualify for special tax treatment. ¶ 2.4.06. The definition of LSD is slightly different for self-employed persons vs. common law employees. § 402(d)(4)(A). See ¶ 2.4.03.

Premature distributions: A distribution from a QRP made to an employee "after separation from service after attainment of age 55" is exempt from the 10 percent "premature distributions" penalty. ¶ 9.4.04. Although § 72(t) does not exclude the self-employed from using this exception, it is not clear what would constitute "separation from service" for a sole proprietor. Also see ¶ 9.4.07 regarding the penalty exception for IRA distributions to pay health insurance premiums during unemployment.

Life insurance: If a QRP maintains a life insurance policy on the life of a plan participant, the participant must include the cost of the current insurance protection in his income each year. See ¶ 2.1.04(H). Unlike other participants, an owner-employee does not get to treat the accumulated cost that he has paid tax on as an "investment in the contract" for income tax purposes. Reg. § 1.72-16(b)(4).

Money purchase plan. See ¶ 8.3.10.

8.3.10 *Pension plan*

A **pension plan** is a type of QRP under which the employer is *obligated* to make annual contributions, or, as the Code puts it, it is a plan "subject to the funding standards of section 412." The required annual contribution may be determined by an actuarial formula based on the promised benefits (**defined benefit** pension plan or defined benefit plan; ¶ 8.3.04), or may be simply a percentage of employees' compensation each year (**money purchase** pension plan or money purchase plan). A pension plan is contrasted with a profit-sharing plan, under which the employer's contributions are discretionary or linked to profits. Pension plans have the following features of interest to estate planners:

✓   Pension plans are generally not permitted to make "in-service distributions," i.e., distributions prior to age 62 except upon the employee's termination from employment. See § 401(a)(36)).

✓   Pension plans are subject to the strictest federal spousal-rights rules. See ¶ 3.4.02.

✓   All pension plans are considered "one plan" for purposes of determining whether there has been a distribution, within one calendar year of the recipient, of the employee's entire balance in "the" plan under § 402(d) (lump sum distributions; ¶ 2.4.04(B)), even if they are not the same type of pension plan.

8.3.11 *Profit-sharing plan*

A profit-sharing plan is a QRP (¶ 8.3.12). It is a Defined Contribution plan (¶ 8.3.05) under which the employer's contributions are either entirely discretionary or are a fixed percentage of profits. Most 401(k) plans are profit-sharing plans. Profit-sharing plans qualify for a limited exemption from federal spousal-rights rules; see ¶ 3.4.03.

8.3.12 *Qualified Retirement Plan*

In this book, a Qualified Retirement Plan (QRP) means a retirement plan that meets the requirements of § 401(a), i.e., it is "qualified" under § 401(a). (For a different definition sometimes used in the Code, see ¶ 9.1.02.) Types of QRPS include the 401(k) plan, defined benefit plan, ESOP, Keogh plan, money purchase plan, and profit-sharing plan.

Since § 401(a) has more than 30 separate requirements, some of which cross reference other lengthy Code sections, it is no mean feat to be qualified under § 401(a). Most of the requirements are of little concern to the estate planner who is advising the individual participant or beneficiary. However, it is helpful to be aware of certain § 401(a) concepts that create the landscape in which all QRPs must function. For example:

✓   A QRP is established and maintained by the "**sponsor**" of the plan. Normally, the sponsor of the plan is the employer of the employees who are covered by the plan, but it could also be a labor union or an association of employers. The employer could be a sole proprietor or partnership, in which case the plan is also a Keogh plan (¶ 8.3.09).

✓   The assets of the QRP generally must be kept in a separate trust for the "exclusive benefit" of the employees and their beneficiaries (the "**exclusive benefit rule**"). § 401(a)(2).

✓   § **415 limits** how much may be contributed to the plan (or accrued on behalf of a participant) each year. § 404 limits the employer's tax deduction for contributions.

✓   The plan must prohibit the assignment or alienation of benefits (the "**anti-alienation rule**"). § 401(a)(13)(A). See ¶ 4.4.09(A), ¶ 6.1.05(A).

✓   The plan must contain provisions required by REA. See ¶ 3.4.

Roth IRA. See ¶ 5.2.01.

8.3.13 *SEP-IRA, SIMPLE*

Simplified Employee Pensions (SEP-IRAs, or SEPs) and Simple Retirement Accounts (SIMPLEs) are employer-funded IRAs (¶ 8.3.08). SEPs are created under § 408(k). SIMPLEs are created under § 408(p). These plans were designed by Congress to be retirement plans that a small business could adopt without having to hire a lawyer.

From the point of view of the estate planner advising an individual SEP-IRA or SIMPLE participant or beneficiary, the rules are generally the same as the rules for "regular" (traditional) IRAs, with the following exceptions:

The premature distributions penalty for a distribution from a SIMPLE is increased to 25 percent in case of distributions within the first two years of participation in a salary reduction (elective deferral; ¶ 8.3.02) arrangement; see § 72(t)(6), and ¶ 9.1.02. Employer contributions (including the employee's contributions via elective deferral) to a SEP-IRA or SIMPLE have no effect on the participant's personal IRA contribution limits. ¶ 5.3.03.

As employer-funded plans, SEPs and SIMPLEs may be subject to ERISA requirements that otherwise do not apply to IRAs. ERISA aspects of these and all other plans are beyond the scope of this book.

See also ¶ 2.4.02 (regarding lump sum distributions), ¶ 3.4.04 (regarding spousal rights), and ¶ 5.4.01(A) (regarding Roth conversions).

Traditional IRA. See ¶ 8.3.08.

Trusteed IRA. See ¶ 8.3.08, ¶ 6.1.07.

9

Distributions Before Age 59½

Which "early distributions" the 10
percent penalty under § 72(t) applies to,
and how to avoid it.

This Chapter provides an overview of the 10 percent "early distributions" penalty. For more extensive discussion, see the *Special Report: 10% Penalty on Early Distributions* (Appendix C).

9.1 10% Penalty on Early Distributions

§ 72(t) imposes a 10 percent penalty on retirement plan distributions made to a participant who is younger than age 59½. This ¶ 9.1 describes the penalty. ¶ 9.2 and ¶ 9.3 discuss one useful exception to the penalty, the "series of substantially equal periodic payments" (SOSEPP). ¶ 9.4 explains the other 13 exceptions.

For application of the penalty in connection with Roth retirement plans, see ¶ 5.5. See ¶ 3.2.08 for how the penalty applies to an under-age-59½ surviving spouse-beneficiary.

9.1.01 *What practitioners must know*

Be aware that distributions (even inadvertent distributions) to a participant under age 59½ generally trigger a 10 percent penalty in addition to income taxes. Note carefully the requirements of any possibly applicable exception (*e.g.*, make sure it is available for the type of plan involved). Do not expect the exceptions to operate in a logical, fair, or consistent manner.

The penalty does not apply to post-death distributions (see ¶ 9.4.01), but a surviving spouse who rolls over death benefits to her own retirement plan loses the exemption for death benefits. See ¶ 3.2.08.

9.1.02 *The § 72(t) penalty on early distributions*

§ 72(t) imposes a 10 percent additional tax on retirement plan distributions. The penalty does not apply to distributions made "on or after the date on which the employee attains age 59½." § 72(t)(2)(A)(i); PLR 2004-10023. The tax is *25 percent* rather than 10 percent on certain early distributions from "SIMPLE" (¶ 8.3.13) retirement plans; § 72(t)(6). This additional tax is usually referred to as the 10 percent penalty on "early distributions" or "premature distributions."

§ 72(t)(1) says that the penalty applies to any distribution from a "qualified retirement plan (as defined in § 4974(c))." § 4974(c)'s definition of "qualified retirement plan" includes 401(a) plans (true "qualified" retirement plans) as well as 403(b) arrangements and IRAs (both of which are not normally included in the term "qualified retirement plan"). It also includes other types of plans not dealt with in this book. *Although § 72(t) includes all of these plans in the term "qualified retirement plan," in this book the term "qualified retirement plan" (QRP) refers only to plans qualified under § 401(a), as distinguished from 403(b) arrangements and IRAs*; see ¶ 8.3.12.

There are no regulations. The IRS's position is revealed in IRS publications, Notices, cases, and private letter rulings. Several aspects of the penalty (and its ever-growing list of exceptions) are not clear.

9.1.03 *How the penalty applies to particular distributions*

The penalty is not necessarily 10 percent of the total distribution. Rather, the 10 percent is calculated only with respect to "the portion of [the distribution] which is includible in gross income." § 72(t)(1); Notice 87-16, 1987-1 C.B. 446, Question D9. To the extent the distribution is income tax-free because (for example) it represents the return of the participant's own after-tax contributions (¶ 2.2.01), or because it is rolled over to another plan (¶ 2.6.01), it is also penalty-free. Here is how the 10 percent penalty applies to various types of distributions (and deemed distributions) to a participant who is under age 59½ if no exception (¶ 9.2–¶ 9.4) applies:

A.   **Employer stock and NUA.** An employee who receives employer stock in a lump sum distribution from a QRP is entitled to certain favorable tax treatment regarding the "net unrealized appreciation" in the stock; see ¶ 2.5. The penalty will apply to the portion of the distribution that is includible in the employee's gross income. It will not apply to the NUA (because the NUA is excluded from income for purposes of § 72; § 402(e)(4)(A), (B)) or to the income resulting from later sale of the stock (¶ 2.5.01) (because that event is not a retirement plan distribution subject to § 72).

B. **IRA contributions withdrawn before return due date**. If an IRA contribution for which no deduction has been taken is withdrawn from the account (together with the net earnings on that contribution) before the extended due date of the participant's tax return for the year for which the contribution was made, the withdrawal of the *contribution* is not a taxable distribution (¶ 2.1.08(D)) and accordingly is *also* not subject to the penalty. However, any *earnings on the contribution* that are included in the corrective distribution will be subject to the penalty. Notice 87-16, 1987-1 C.B. 446, Question C2; *Hall*, T.C. Memo 1998-336. According to the Instructions for IRS Form 5329 (2009) (line 23, p. 4), the penalty is reportable for the year the contribution was made (i.e., the same year in which the income is reportable).

C. **Deemed distribution due to plan-owned life insurance.** When a QRP purchases life insurance on the life of a plan participant, § 72(m)(3) generally requires that the cost of the insurance protection be included currently in the participant's gross income. See ¶ 2.1.04(H). This deemed income is not treated as a distribution for purposes of the 10 percent penalty. Notice 89-25, 1989-1 C.B. 662, A-11.

D. **Deemed distribution from failed plan loan.** If an employee borrows, from a QRP, a loan that fails to meet the requirements of § 72(p), the loan is treated as a taxable distribution rather than a loan; see ¶ 2.1.07. The resulting gross income is subject to the penalty. Notice 87-13, 1987-1 C.B. 432, A-20; *Plotkin*, T.C. Memo 2001-71.

E. **Deemed distribution resulting from prohibited transaction.** The penalty apparently applies to the deemed distribution resulting from a prohibited transaction (¶ 8.1.06); see Instructions for IRS Form 5329 (2009), line 1.

9.1.04 *Enforcement of early distributions penalty*

If an under-age 59½ participant takes money from a retirement plan, and does not qualify for any of the very precise and limited exceptions (see ¶ 9.2–¶ 9.4), the penalty is imposed, regardless of the taxpayer's ignorance of the rules, good intentions, or other excuse. Surprisingly many taxpayers litigate their liability for this penalty when they do not have even a colorable argument that they qualify for an exception. The IRS and the courts will (almost) never waive the penalty unless the requirements for an exception are met.

There is no "hardship exception" to this penalty; *Reese*, T.C. Summ. Op. 2006-23; *Gallagher*, T.C. Memo 2001-34; *Deal*, T.C. Memo 1999-352. See, *e.g.*, *Baas*, T.C. Memo 2002-130, and *Czepiel*, T.C. Memo 1999-289, aff'd. by order (1st Cir., Dec. 5, 2000); and *Robertson*, T.C. Memo 2000-100.

9.2 Exception: "Series of Equal Payments"

One exception stands out as a useful planning tool: the "series of substantially equal periodic payments."

9.2.01 *Series of substantially equal periodic payments (SOSEPP)*

The penalty does not apply to a distribution that is "part of a series of substantially equal periodic payments (not less frequently than annually) made for the life (or life expectancy) of the employee or the joint lives (or joint life expectancies) of such employee and his designated beneficiary." § 72(t)(2)(A)(iv). While at first this exception sounds rather rigid, in fact it is highly flexible because:

1. Rollovers and/or IRA-to-IRA transfers can be used to create an IRA of exactly the right size to support the desired payment amount. See ¶ 9.2.04.

2. The payments do not in fact have to continue for the entire life or life expectancy period. The distributions must continue only until the participant reaches age 59½, or until five years have elapsed, whichever occurs later. See ¶ 9.3.02.

3.   The IRS allows several methods for determining the size of the "equal payments" (which do not in fact have to be equal). See ¶ 9.2.05.

This is the most significant exception for planning purposes. All the other exceptions are tied to a specific use of the money (home purchase, college tuition), or to some type of hardship situation (death, disability), or are otherwise narrowly limited; see ¶ 9.4. In contrast, everyone who has an IRA (or who can get one via a rollover from some other type of plan) can use the SOSEPP exception.

There is one significant limitation on the SOSEPP exception: Drastic consequences generally ensue if the series is "modified" before the end of the five year/age 59½ minimum duration; see ¶ 9.3.01.

9.2.02 *How this exception works*

The SOSEPP exception starts from the premise that there is a fund of money (the retirement plan account) that will be gradually exhausted by a series of regular distributions over the applicable period of time (¶ 9.2.01). Thus, the SOSEPP must be designed so that, *if* it continued for that period of time (which it won't; see ¶ 9.3.02), it would exactly exhaust the fund. The participant cannot take annual distributions that are too small to exhaust the account, even if they are equal, regular, payments designed to continue over the applicable time period. See Notice 87-16, 1987-1 C.B. 446, A-12, and PLR 9805023. For how to get around this limitation; see ¶ 9.2.12.

9.2.03 *Notice 89-25 (A-12) and its successor, Rev. Rul. 2002-62*

Notice 89-25, 1989-1 C.B. 662, A-12, laid out three methods a participant could use to compute the payments in his SOSEPP. Revenue Ruling 2002-62, 2002-42 I.R.B. 710, which supercedes Notice 89-25, A-12, continues the same three methods but changes the rules regarding which life expectancy tables, interest rate, and account balance may be used in designing a SOSEPP; see ¶ 9.2.05. Rev. Rul. 2002-62 applies to any SOSEPP commencing after 2002. The IRS posted a document called "FAQs regarding Revenue Ruling 2002-62" at its web site, which is "for general information only and should not be cited as any type of legal authority"; see http://www.irs.gov/retirement/article/0,,id=103045,00.html.

9.2.04 *Steps required to initiate a SOSEPP*

The first step in initiating a SOSEPP is to decide what size payments the participant wants to take. Ideally, the payments desired will not require the participant to use his entire plan balance. With the help of an actuary, the participant determines what size of IRA would be required to support a SOSEPP of the amount he wants, and that amount is transferred into a separate IRA from which the SOSEPP payments are made. This leaves the balance of his funds in a plan or IRA that is not involved in the SOSEPP and which is therefore available for the participant's later needs to, *e.g.*, take an extra payment (on which he would pay the 10 percent penalty) without being deemed to have impermissibly "modified" the SOSEPP (¶ 9.3.01) or even to start another SOSEPP (¶ 9.2.13).

The participant must make several choices about the design of the series: Choose one of the three permitted methods. ¶ 9.2.05. Choose a life expectancy table. ¶ 9.2.07–¶ 9.2.09. If using the amortization or annuitization method, choose an interest rate (¶ 9.2.10) and decide whether or not to use "annual recalculation" (¶ 9.2.06). Choose an initial account balance valuation date. ¶ 9.2.11. Decide whether payments will be monthly, quarterly, or annually. The "periodic payments" must be paid at regular intervals at least annually. Rev. Rul. 2002-62, § 1.02(b). Though Rev. Rul. 2002-62 and its follow-up "FAQs" (¶ 9.2.03) use only annual payments in their examples, monthly payments are apparently also popular (see, *e.g.*, PLRs 2002-14029, 2002-14034, 2002-03072).

9.2.05 *The three methods: RMD, amortization, annuitization*

The participant has a choice of three IRS-approved methods for the design of his SOSEPP:

A.   **RMD method.** Under the "RMD method," the "series" payments are calculated in the same manner as lifetime minimum required distributions under § 401(a)(9) (called "MRDs" elsewhere in this book, "RMDs" by the IRS): The account balance (revalued annually) is divided by a life expectancy factor each year to produce the required payment. See ¶ 1.3.01. Since the youngest age covered under the "real" RMD table (see Table 1, Appendix A) is 70, the IRS created a special under-age-60 "RMD table" for users of this method. See ¶ 9.2.07(A).

"Under this method, the account balance, the number from the chosen life expectancy table and the resulting annual payments are redetermined for each year." Rev. Rul. 2002-62, § 2.01(a). Because this method requires annual revaluation of the account, payments fluctuate (both up and down) with investment performance. The advantage of annual revaluation is that the account will never be wiped out by the SOSEPP payments, as can occur with the fixed payments usually used under the other two methods. The drawback of the RMD method (or any method that employs annual recalculation) is the unpredictability of the payments.

B. **Amortization method:** Under this method, the participant chooses a reasonable interest rate (¶ 9.2.10), and a life expectancy table (¶ 9.2.07–¶ 9.2.09.), then takes regular payments as if the account were a self-amortizing level payment mortgage (except that he is receiving, rather than making, the payments). Once the amount of the first payment is determined, the payments never vary, regardless of the investment performance of the account (unless annual recalculation is used; see ¶ 9.2.06). If using the amortization method, the participant has the option, in any year after the first year, to switch to the RMD method. See ¶ 9.3.04.

C. **Annuitization method:** Under this method, the participant chooses a reasonable interest rate (¶ 9.2.10), and single or joint life expectancy (¶ 9.2.07), then divides the account balance by an annuity factor, as if the account were being annuitized over the applicable life expectancy. "The annuity factor is derived using the mortality table in Appendix B [of Rev. Rul. 2002-62] and using the chosen interest rate." Once the amount of the first payment is determined, the payments never vary, regardless of the investment performance of the account (unless annual recalculation is used; see ¶ 9.2.06). If using the amortization method, the participant has the option, in any year after the first year, to switch to the RMD method. See ¶ 9.3.04.

9.2.06 *Variations on the three methods*

The three methods are not the only possible ways to design a SOSEPP; however, if varying from these pre-approved models it is necessary to obtain advance approval from the IRS via a private letter ruling. See IRS FAQs (¶ 9.2.03), last question.

The IRS has issued several letter rulings blessing SOSEPP designs that incorporated annual adjustments (to reflect changes in the account balance and/or interest rate), within the amortization or annuitization method. See PLRs 2004-32021, 2004-32023, 2004-32024, 2005-51032, 2005-51033, 2005-44023, and 2009-43044. The key to the IRS's approval in these rulings is that approval is sought IN ADVANCE, before the participant starts taking any distributions, and even though the payments will vary in amount, the payment is determined the same way each year. Someone who has already started a fixed-payment SOSEPP using the amortization or annuitization method cannot later change to a recalculation method; see ¶ 9.3.07(D).

9.2.07 *Choose single or joint life expectancy*

The participant must choose a single or joint life expectancy period for the hypothetical duration of his SOSEPP. The choice is among three life expectancy tables if the participant is using the RMD or amortization method ("A"), or among two (three?) "factors" if using the annuitization method ("B"). The choice of payout period is irrevocable if the SOSEPP commenced after 2002. Rev. Rul. 2002-62, § 2.02(a), last two sentences. See ¶ 9.2.08–¶ 9.2.09 for more on these tables.

A.   **Three tables for RMD or amortization method.** Rev. Rul. 2002-62 provides that a taxpayer using the RMD or amortization method must select one of three life expectancy tables for calculating his SOSEPP: the Single Life Table, the Joint and Survivor Life Table, or the Uniform Lifetime Table. Rev. Rul. 2002-62, § 2.01(a), (b), § 2.02(a).

The Single and Joint and Survivor Life Tables are contained in Reg. § 1.401(a)(9)-9, A-1, A-3. The Uniform Lifetime Table (showing the joint and survivor life expectancy of the participant and a hypothetical beneficiary who is 10 years younger than the participant) is contained in Appendix A of Rev. Rul. 2002-62 and of this book

(Table 2). It is an expanded version of the Uniform Lifetime Table contained in Reg. § 1.401(a)(9)-9, A-2, extended down to age 10!

B.   Only two choices for annuitization? For an annuitization-method SOSEPP, the annuity period is "the life of the taxpayer (or the joint lives of the individual and beneficiary)." Notice 89-25 permitted use of any "reasonable mortality table" under the annuitization method. Rev. Rul. 2002-62 took away that option, and supplies its own table of mortality factors that must be used in determining payments under the annuitization method. Rev. Rul. 2002-62, § 2.02(a).

9.2.08 *Notes on Joint and Survivor Life Table*

If the participant elects the Joint and Survivor Life Table, then the factor used to determine the first payment in the series is based on the joint life expectancy of the participant and his ACTUAL beneficiary. Rev. Rul. 2002-62, § 2.02(b). If the participant is using the RMD method (¶ 9.2.05(A)), then the beneficiary (for purposes of determining the factor under the Table) is redetermined every year, as of January 1 of the distribution year, using the same rules as apply for determining the beneficiary for minimum distribution purposes (see ¶ 1.3.03(B)).

Under the annuitization or amortization method, subsequent changes of beneficiary will have no effect on the payments so long as the participant continues using that method—but if he switches in midstream to the RMD method (¶ 9.3.04), and is required (or chooses) to continue using the Joint and Survivor Life Table, then his subsequent payments would be determined using the joint life expectancy of himself and his actual beneficiary.

9.2.09 *Notes on Single, Uniform Lifetime Tables*

The only difference between the Single Life Table and the Uniform Lifetime Table is the size of the annual payment relative to the size of the account. A participant who wants larger payments would choose the Single Life Table. A participant who wants smaller payments would use the Uniform Lifetime Table. When using the "separate IRA" SOSEPP recommended at ¶ 9.2.04, the Single Life Table should always be used, to generate the largest possible payments relative to the account size.

With both these tables, you find the appropriate factor for the first year's payment based on the participant's age on his birthday in that year. Rev. Rul. 2002-62, § 2.02(a). If using the RMD method, you then go back to the originally-chosen table every year to get that year's factor, based on the participant's new age. If using the amortization or annuitization method, you don't go back to the table every year because the payments are fixed in amount (unless your series design is based on annual recalculation; see ¶ 9.2.06).

9.2.10 What interest rate assumption is used

For the amortization and annuitization methods, it is necessary to choose an interest rate (representing the hypothetical projected investment return on the account during the period of the SOSEPP). The participant may use "any interest rate that is not more than 120 percent of the federal mid-term rate (determined in accordance with section 1274(d) for either of the two months immediately preceding the month in which the distribution begins)." Rev. Rul. 2002-62, § 2.02(c). You can find the monthly federal mid-term rates at the IRS web site www.irs.gov/tax_regs/fedrates.html, or at www.tigertables.com or www.leimbergservices.com.

9.2.11 What account balance is used

Whichever method the participant is using, he must apply a certain factor to an account balance. The account balance "must be determined in a reasonable manner based on the facts and circumstances." Rev. Rul. 2002-62, § 2.02(d).

Under all three methods, the participant must select a valuation date for the first year's payment. The IRS provides an example the gist of which is that any date from the last prior year end to the day before the distribution would be fine. There is no specific prohibition against using a date earlier than the last prior year-end, but it would seem that the prior year-end (or any subsequent valuation date, up to the date of the first distribution) would be a safe harbor.

Under the *amortization* and *annuitization* methods, the account balance is determined only once, at the beginning of the series. Since the payments do not fluctuate, there is no need to look at the account balance again after the first year (unless annual recalculation is part of the series design; see ¶ 9.2.06). Under the *RMD method* the account balance is always redetermined annually.

9.2.12 *Applying the SOSEPP exception to multiple IRAs*

Generally, all of an individual's IRAs are aggregated (treated as one account) for purposes of determining how much of any distribution is *included in gross income.* See ¶ 2.2.08(F). However, no provision requires IRAs to be aggregated for purposes of the *penalty* under § 72(t), or the SOSEPP exception.

For purposes of structuring a SOSEPP, the participant has several choices: The series can be based on all of his IRAs, aggregated; or on some of the IRAs aggregated, with others excluded; or on one IRA to the exclusion of others. As the IRS said in PLR 9747039, "If a taxpayer owns more than one IRA, any combination of his or her IRAs may be taken into account in determining the distributions by aggregating the account balances of those IRAs. *The specific IRAs taken into account are part of the method of determining the substantially equal periodic payments....*" Emphasis added.

All IRAs aggregated: In each of PLRs 9830042, 9824047, and 9545018, all of the participant's IRAs were aggregated for purposes of computing the series payments.

Some IRAs aggregated, others excluded: In PLRs 9816028, 9801050, and 2000-31059, the participant had several IRAs, some of which were aggregated to form the basis of his proposed SOSEPP and the rest of which were not to be counted. The IRS ruled favorably in all cases, requiring only that the series payments be made from the aggregated IRAs and not from the other accounts.

Take series from one IRA, not aggregated with others: In PLR 9818055 the participant was taking a SOSEPP from one of her two IRAs. In PLR 9812038 the participant was taking a SOSEPP from one of his three IRAs and wanted to start a second SOSEPP from a new, fourth, IRA, to be created by transfer of funds from one of the other IRAs (not the IRA that was already supporting the first SOSEPP). The IRS permitted this; the ruling stated more than once that the taxpayer's IRAs were not aggregated. In PLRs 9747045, 2001-22048, and 2009-43044, the participant's IRS-approved SOSEPP was taken from one of the participant's multiple IRAs; the accounts were not aggregated.

The account or accounts included in the initial design of the SOSEPP must be the sole source of payments in the series. Once the SOSEPP begins, funds must not be transferred *out of* the IRAs that are being used to support the series (except to make the SOSEPP payments), or *into* any IRA that is part of the support for the series. See

¶ 9.3.09 regarding tax-free rollovers involving IRAs supporting a SOSEPP.

9.2.13 *Starting a second series to run concurrently*

A participant receiving a SOSEPP from one or more IRAs may initiate a *second* series of equal payments from a different IRA or set of IRAs. See, *e.g.*, PLR 9812038, discussed at ¶ 9.2.12. PLR 9747039 also permitted starting a second SOSEPP from a different IRA. See PLR 2003-09028 for a good model of exactly how to do this.

However, the participant may not start a second SOSEPP from *the same IRA* (or plan) that is already supporting the first SOSEPP; such a second series would constitute an impermissible "modification" of the first series. ¶ 9.3.01.

9.2.14 *Procedural and reporting requirements*

There is no specific format for electing one of the three methods. There is no requirement that any of the elections or choices be in writing, or that notice of any choices be delivered to anyone in particular. The usual procedure is for the participant and his advisor to prepare a memorandum or worksheets showing the design of the series and how the distributions are calculated. This normal approach is recommended as the best safeguard for ensuring that the series qualifies for the SOSEPP exception and that such qualification can later be proved to the IRS should that become necessary.

9.3 Modifying the SOSEPP

9.3.01 *Effects of a forbidden modification of series*

If the participant "modifies" his SOSEPP before a certain period of time has elapsed, he is severely punished. His qualification for the SOSEPP exception (¶ 9.2) is retroactively revoked, and he owes the penalty for all series payments he took prior to age 59½, with interest. Once the participant has modified his series, he cannot start a new SOSEPP from the same plan until the following calendar year, according to PLR 2000-33048.

9.3.02 *When the no-modification period begins and ends*

The beginning date of the no-modification period is the date of the first payment in the series. The ending date is the fifth anniversary of the date of the first payment in the series, or, *if later*, the date on which the participant attains age 59½. § 72(t)(4)(A). Once this ending date is passed, payments may be freely taken from the plan without penalty (or the series may be suspended—*i.e.*, the participant can STOP taking payments).

Note that the ending date of the five years is not simply the date of the fifth year's payment. The five years ends on the *fifth anniversary of the first payment. Arnold*, 111 T.C. No. 250 (1998).

9.3.03 *Exceptions for death or disability*

If the series is modified "by reason of death or disability" there is no penalty. § 72(t)(4)(A). Presumably death *automatically* ends the requirement of continuing the series, since death benefits are exempt from the penalty; ¶ 9.4.01. Presumably the same is true of a total disability that justifies penalty-free distributions; see ¶ 9.4.02. Whether a modification that was "caused by" any lesser disability would escape the penalty remains to be seen.

9.3.04 *Changing to RMD method after the SOSEPP commences*

One type of change in the series is specifically permitted: Changing to the "RMD method" of computing the payments (¶ 9.2.05(A)) will not be considered a modification. Rev. Rul. 2002-62 allows a participant using the annuitization or amortization method to change (permanently) to the RMD method; see § 2.03(b) of the Rev. Rul. for details on making this switch.

Because the RMD method requires annual revaluation of the account balance, a downturn in the account value will translate, under the RMD method, into a reduction in the subsequent year's payment. Thus, the series payments will shrink along with the account value and the account will never run dry. Similarly, if the investments perform substantially better than the growth assumption used in designing the SOSEPP (¶ 9.2.10), switching to the RMD method allows the participant to increase his payments to capture some of that investment growth.

9.3.05 *When taking an extra payment is not a modification*

Generally, taking an "extra" payment out of your IRA over and above the prescribed SOSEPP payments would be considered a modification of the series (see ¶ 9.3.07(B)), but not necessarily always.

A.   **Qualified hurricane distributions.** Taking a qualified hurricane distribution (¶ 9.4.13) over and above the participant's SOSEPP payments is not a modification of the SOSEPP. Notice 2005-92, I.R.B. 2005-51, Section 4(H).

B.   **Other payments that qualify for another exception.** If the extra distribution qualifies for some *other* penalty exception, the extra payment is not a modification of the SOSEPP, according to *G.T. Benz*, Dec. 7,810, 132 TC 15 (5/11/09).

C.   **Administrative error.** The IRS generally will rule that there is no modification when a change in the SOSEPP is caused by an administrative action or error of the SOSEPP-paying financial institution; see ¶ 9.3.06(A), (E). However, there is no Revenue Ruling, regulation, or other authority supporting this as a general exception, leaving participants with the unpleasant choice of either applying for their own ruling (expensive) or relying on other peoples' PLRs (with attendant uncertainty).

9.3.06 *What other changes do NOT constitute a modification?*

Converting a SOSEPP-supporting account to a Roth IRA does not constitute a modification; see ¶ 5.5.03 for details. The following other types of changes in a SOSEPP have either been ruled not to be modifications, or have occurred without negative comment in cases or rulings involving other issues:

A.   **Computer system change.** When the paying agent, as part of a change in its computer systems, changed the date of monthly payments in a series to the first day of the month (instead of the last day of the preceding month), the change was ruled to be "ministerial," and not a "modification," even though the change meant that the recipient's income would include one less payment for the year the switch was made. PLR 9514026.

B. **Plan termination.** The participant in PLR 9221052 was receiving monthly payments from a pension plan. When that plan terminated in the middle of his SOSEPP, he sought to roll over the termination distribution to an IRA and continue taking the same monthly payments from the IRA. The IRS ruled that this change would not constitute a modification.

C. **Payments not on anniversary date.** In the case of annual payments, it does not appear to be required that each year's payment occur on the anniversary of the first payment. See Rev. Rul. 2002-62, § 2.02(d). See PLR 9747039, in which the IRS ruled that the participant would qualify for the exception "if [he] received at least five annual payments of $510,000 from IRA Y (at least one during each of the years 1997, 1998, 1999, 2000 and 2001) and does not otherwise modify his IRA distribution scheme."

D. **Plan exhausted.** If investment performance is poor, fixed payments under the amortization or annuitization method might exhaust the account. Running out of money due to taking the payments called for by the SOSEPP will not be considered a modification of the series. Rev. Rul. 2002-62, § 2.03(a).

E. **IRA provider error.** In several cases, the IRS has ruled that a change in a SOSEPP did not constitute a SOSEPP-disqualifying modification where the change was the result of a financial institution error. See PLRs 2005-03036, 2006-31025, 2009-29021 (¶ 9.3.09), and 2009-30053. However: In PLR 2010-03033, the participant was receiving a monthly-payment SOSEPP. Because of financial institution error, an extra payment was sent, so that she received 13 payments instead of 12 in one year. The IRS granted her request for a late rollover of the extra payment (see ¶ 2.6.07), but expressed "no opinion" as to whether the extra payment constituted a modification of the SOSEPP.

F. **Participant error.** In PLR 2006-01044, the participant started an amortization method SOSEPP from four IRAs, but due to a math error his first payment was too small by less than 2/10ths of one percent. The IRS ruled that the underpayment (and subsequent "catch up distribution" to correct the error) did not constitute modifications of the series.

9.3.07 *What changes DO constitute a modification?*

Here are some examples of prohibited modifications of a SOSEPP; see also ¶ 9.3.09 regarding transfers into or out of the SOSEPP-supporting IRA.

A.   **Stopping the payments.** See PLR 9818055, in which the participant terminated the series because she went back to work; she had to pay the penalty.

B.   **Taking extra payment.** Taking a payment that is over and above the payments required as part of the series is a modification. See *Arnold*, ¶ 9.3.02. See ¶ 9.3.05 for exceptions.

C.   **Changing the "period" of periodic payments.** Changing from annual payments to quarterly or monthly payments (or vice versa), even if the total payments for the year add up to the right amount, *could* be considered a modification; there is no authority for the proposition that the size of individual payments in the series does not matter so long as the total is the same each year.

D.   **Changing how the payments in the series are determined.** See PLRs 9821056 and 1999-43050.

9.3.08 *Effect of divorce on the SOSEPP*

If the participant gets divorced in the middle of his SOSEPP, the divorce court may award a share of the retirement plan that is supporting the SOSEPP to the participant's ex-spouse. Usually the spouse's share is transferred tax-free to the spouse's account under a QDRO (§ 414(p)) or the IRA equivalent (§ 408(d)(6)). The participant needs to apply for an IRS ruling allowing the SOSEPP payments to be reduced proportionately to reflect the transfer of part of the participant's SOSEPP-paying retirement plan to the participant's ex-spouse. See PLRs 9739044, 2000-27060, 2000-50046, 2001-16056, 2002-02074, 2002-02075, 2002-02076, 2002-14034, and 2002-25040.

9.3.09 *Transfers to, from, or among IRAs supporting a SOSEPP*

As explained at ¶ 9.2.12, two or more IRAs can be aggregated for purposes of calculating and paying a SOSEPP. Once the SOSEPP commences, it is essential that no assets be transferred into (or out of) those IRAs from (or to) any other IRA (or plan), because of the following rule: "Under all three methods, substantially equal periodic payments are calculated with respect to an account balance as of the first valuation date selected.... Thus, a modification to the series of payments will occur if, after such date, there is (i) any addition to the account balance other than gains or losses, [or] (ii) any nontaxable transfer of a portion of the account balance to another retirement plan...." Rev. Rul. 2002-62, § 2.02(e)(ii).

Note that this rule appears to have two parts, a "no additions" rule and a "no nontaxable transfers" rule. Whether there is any relation or distinction between these two sections of the rule is unclear. See PLR 2009-25044, discussed at "C."

Despite this rule, the IRS ruled in PLR 2009-29021 that there was no modification when, due entirely to a financial institution error, distributions from the participant's workplace retirement plan were rolled into the IRA from which the participant was receiving SOSEPP payment; the participant had asked for these funds to be rolled to a different IRA. See ¶ 9.3.06(E).

A.   **Transfers among IRAs supporting the SOSEPP.** This rule does not preclude moving assets *among the multiple IRAs that are included in the SOSEPP account balance* (¶ 9.2.12). PLR 2000-31059.

B.   **Transfer into a new IRA might or might not constitute a modification.** The principle stated at "A" *should* also protect the individual who is taking a SOSEPP from an IRA and wishes to transfer all or part of the IRA to a different custodian, just for investment reasons, without altering the amount or timing of his SOSEPP payments. (Needless to say, the IRA into which the SOSEPP-supporting IRA is being transferred cannot have in it any other funds.) In this case, the "IRAs supporting the SOSEPP" would be the old IRA and the new IRA, with no commingling of funds from any *other* IRA or plan.

Unfortunately, the IRS has never clearly stated this corollary principle, and there are letter rulings supporting both the principle and its opposite.

There are now four PLRs supporting the conclusion that a SOSEPP-paying IRA may be transferred tax-free to a new, otherwise-empty, IRA account with a different custodian, without causing a modification of the SOSEPP:

PLR 2006-16046 dealt primarily with an inadvertent commingling of the SOSEPP IRA with other IRA funds (due to a financial institution error). In providing the factual background for its ruling regarding the institutional error, the IRS noted *without comment* that, during the SOSEPP (and prior to and unrelated to the occurrence of this financial institution error), the taxpayer had rolled the entire SOSEPP-paying IRA ("IRA M") into a different IRA ("IRA P"), from which he continued taking the SOSEPP payments. The fact that the IRS ruled that he still had a valid SOSEPP after this rollover supports the conclusion that merely transferring the SOSEPP IRA to a different custodian does not violate the no-transfers rule.

There are three other similar PLRs where the IRS was ruling that a financial institution error did not constitute a modification of the series, and in which it is stated as part of the factual background that the IRAs in question had been transferred (prior to and unrelated to the financial institution error incidents) from one custodian to another for investment reasons. If such prior transfers were "modifications," then the subsequent financial institution errors would have been irrelevant because the series would already have been ended via "modification." Since in each of these case the IRS ruled the series had not been modified, this must mean that the prior tax-free transfers were NOT modifications. See PLRs 2006-31025, 2009-29021, and 2009-30053.

And yet...in two other PLRs, the IRS has indicated that the transfer of a SOSEPP-paying IRA to a different account for investment reasons DOES (or might) constitute a modification!

The IRS ruled in PLR 2009-25044 that a participant's trustee-to-trustee transfer of her SOSEPP-supporting IRAs from one financial institution to another, solely for the purpose of changing the investments in the account, was a modification of the series. In this ruling, the SOSEPP-supporting IRA (IRA X) was commingled with funds from another IRA (IRA Y), not involved in the SOSEPP, when both were transferred into a new combined IRA, IRA Z, at the new financial institution. The ruling stated that the problem could not be corrected by unmingling the IRA Y funds and sending them back to

IRA Y. Unfortunately, the ruling does not state that it was *only the commingling* that caused the IRS to rule this a modification; rather, they base the ruling on the provision in Rev. Rul. 2002-62 prohibiting *any* nontaxable transfers in or out of the SOSEPP-supporting IRA.

In PLR 2010-03033, discussed at ¶ 9.3.06(E), the participant's SOSEPP-supporting IRA was moved to a different financial institution when her advisor changed firms, but the IRS did not rule on whether the SOSEPP qualified as a SOSEPP or was modified.

9.4 Other Exceptions to the Penalty

We now turn to the other exceptions to the § 72(t) penalty. Although these lack the broadly applicable planning possibilities of the SOSEPP, each can be useful in particular situations.

9.4.01 *Death benefits*

A distribution "made to a beneficiary (or to the estate of the employee) on or after the death of the employee" is exempt from the penalty. § 72(t)(2)(A)(ii). This exception applies to distributions from all types of plans. Thus death benefits may be distributed penalty-free from any type of plan or IRA, regardless of whether the *beneficiary* is under age 59½ and regardless of whether the *participant* had attained age 59½ at the time of his death.

Despite the unique clarity of this exception, it generates confusion for the following reason: If a surviving spouse rolls over benefits inherited from the deceased spouse to the surviving spouse's *own* IRA, the rolled-over funds cease to be death benefits; they become part of the surviving spouse's own retirement account. Thus, distributions from the rollover IRA will once again be subject to the § 72(t) penalty rules if the surviving spouse is under age 59½—even if the deceased spouse was over age 59½. See ¶ 3.2.08 for planning implications.

9.4.02 *Distributions attributable to total disability*

A distribution (from any type of plan) that is "attributable to the employee's being disabled" is not subject to the penalty. § 72(t)(2)(A)(iii).

Disabled is defined in § 72(m)(7): It means "unable to engage in any substantial gainful activity by reason of any medically determinable physical or mental impairment which can be expected to result in death or to be of long-continued and indefinite duration." See Reg. § 1.72-17A(f)(1), (2). Generally the IRS requires that the individual be eligible to receive Social Security disability benefits to qualify for this exception.

§ 72(m)(7) also states that "An individual shall not be considered to be disabled unless he furnishes proof of the existence thereof [sic] in such form and manner as the Secretary may require." IRS Publication 590 (2009), p. 52, states that "A physician must determine that your condition can be expected to result in death or to be of long, continued, and indefinite duration." This requirement is not waived for those whose religious beliefs prohibit them from consulting physicians. *Fohrmeister*, 73 T.C. Memo 2483, 2486 (1997).

Depression and similar psychiatric problems typically will not constitute "disability" for this purpose, even if they lead to termination of employment or allow the individual to collect disability payments, because these problems are usually temporary.

It is not clear to what extent the plan distribution must be shown to be "attributable" to the disability. In PLR 2001-26037 the IRS said any distributions made after the participant was disabled would be exempt from the penalty

9.4.03 *Distributions for deductible medical expenses*

Distributions from any type of plan are penalty-free to the extent they "do not exceed the amount allowable as a deduction under § 213 to the employee for amounts paid during the taxable year for medical care (determined without regard to whether the employee itemizes deductions for such taxable year)." § 72(t)(2)(B). "During the taxable year" means "during the taxable year in which the distribution is received." *Evers*, T.C. Summ. Op. 2008-140.

9.4.04 *QRPs, 403(b) plans: Early retirement*

A distribution made to an employee "after separation from service after attainment of age 55" is exempt from the penalty. This exception is available for qualified (¶ 8.3.12) and 403(b) (¶ 8.3.03) plans, but *not* for IRAs. § 72(t)(2)(A)(v), (3)(A). For government plan distributions to firemen, policemen, and emergency medical personnel, the age is 50 not 55. § 72(t)(10).

Although § 72(t) limits the exception to distributions made after a separation from service occurring after the employee's 55th birthday, Notice 87-13, 1987-1 C.B. 432, A-20, provides that the separation from service can occur on or after *January 1* of the year the employee reaches age 55. See PLR 2002-15032.

An employee who separates from the company's service *before* the year he reaches age 55 is not entitled to use this exception; he cannot simply wait until age 55 and then take a penalty-free distribution. The exception is available only for distributions "after your separation from service in or after the year you reached age 55." IRS Publication 575, "Pension and Annuity Income" (2009), p. 31; *Humberson*, 70 TCM 886 (1995).

9.4.05 *QRPs, 403(b) plans: QDRO distributions*

Distributions from a *qualified retirement plan or 403(b) arrangement* made to an "alternate payee" under a qualified domestic relations order (QDRO; see § 414(p)(1)) are exempt from the early distributions penalty. § 72(t)(2)(C). This allows a divorcing spouse who is under age 59½ to receive penalty-free distributions from the share of her ex-spouse's QRP or 403(b) plan that is awarded to her in the divorce proceedings (if the QDRO procedures are followed).

However, even though, in § 408(d)(6), Congress provided a means for the tax-free division of *IRAs* between divorcing spouses, analogous to the QDRO procedures for qualified plans, Congress did NOT extend the penalty exception of § 72(t)(2)(C) to IRAs. Thus, a divorced spouse who receives part of her ex's IRA under § 408(d)(6) cannot withdraw from the account prior to reaching age 59½ unless she pays the 10 percent penalty or qualifies for some other exception.

9.4.06 *ESOPs only: Dividends on employer stock*

Under § 404(k), a company can take a tax deduction for dividends paid on stock that is held by an employee stock ownership plan (ESOP), and the ESOP can pass these dividends out to the plan participants, if various requirements are met. Such dividend payments are not subject to the 10 percent penalty. § 72(t)(2)(A)(vi).

9.4.07 *IRAs only: Unemployed's health insurance*

An unemployed individual can take penalty-free distributions from his IRA (but NOT from a qualified plan or 403(b) arrangement) to pay health insurance premiums. See § 72(t)(2)(D) for details.

9.4.08 *IRAs only: Expenses of higher education*

The 10 percent penalty will not apply to *IRA distributions* that do not exceed the participant's "qualified higher education expenses" paid in the taxable year of the distribution. § 72(t)(2)(E).

The distribution does not actually have to be used to pay the education expenses; the exemption applies to the extent the distribution does not exceed the education expenses incurred in the same year the distribution occurs. IRS Publication 590 (2009), p. 52. Using the distribution to repay a loan does *not* qualify for the exception, even if the loan proceeds were used to pay education expenses, if the education expenses were not paid in the same year as the distribution. *Lodder-Beckert*, T.C. Memo. 2005-162.

The distribution must be to pay for education furnished to the participant or his spouse, or to any child or grandchild of either of them. This exception borrows definitions from the Code section allowing various tax breaks to "qualified state tuition programs" (§ 529(e)(3)) for the type of expenses covered ("tuition, fees, books, supplies, and equipment required for the enrollment or attendance of a designated beneficiary at an eligible educational institution") and eligible institutions. The costs of providing the student's computer, housewares, appliances, furniture, and bedding are not qualified expenses. *Gorski*, T.C. Summ. Op. 2005-112.

"Eligible Institutions" include "virtually all accredited public, non-profit, and proprietary post-secondary institutions," according to Notice 97-60, 1997-46 I.R.B. 1, § 4, A-2, which provides details regarding this exception, including the fact that room and board are among the covered expenses if the student is enrolled at least half-time.

To the extent the education expenses in question are paid for by a scholarship, federal education grant, tax-free distribution from an Education IRA (§ 530), tax-free employer-provided educational assistance, or other payment that is excludible from gross income (other than gifts, inheritances, loans, or savings), they cannot also be used to support a penalty-free IRA distribution. § 72(t)(7)(B), § 25A(g)(2); Notice 97-60, § 4, A-1.

9.4.09 *IRAs only: First-time home purchase*

"Qualified first-time homebuyer distributions" from an IRA are not subject to the penalty. § 72(t)(2)(F). An individual can withdraw from his IRA (but *not* from a qualified plan or 403(b) arrangement!) up to $10,000, without penalty, if the distribution is used "before the close of the 120th day after the day on which such payment or distribution is received to pay qualified acquisition costs with respect to a principal residence of a first-time homebuyer who is such individual, the spouse of such individual, or any child, grandchild, or ancestor of such individual or the individual's spouse." § 72(t)(8)(A).

The "date of acquisition" is the date "a binding contract to acquire" the home is entered into, or "on which construction or reconstruction of such a principal residence is commenced"—but, if there is a "delay or cancellation of the purchase or construction" and, solely for that reason, the distribution fails to meet the 120-day test, the distribution can be rolled back into the IRA; this will be a qualified tax-free rollover, even if it occurs more than 60 days after the distribution, so long as it occurs within 120 days of the distribution. See ¶ 2.6.06(A). The rollover back into the IRA will not count for purposes of the one-rollover-per-year limit (¶ 2.6.05(D)). § 72(t)(8)(E).

The $10,000 is a lifetime limit. It applies to the person making the withdrawal (the IRA owner), not the person buying the home. If you withdraw $10,000 in one year to help your son buy a first home, you cannot later withdraw another $10,000 to buy your own first home.

"Principal residence" has the same meaning as in § 121 (exclusion of gain on sale of principal residence), according to § 72(t)(8)(D)(ii). § 121 itself does not contain a definition of "principal residence"; Reg. § 1.121-1(b) says the determination depends on all the "facts and circumstances."

"Qualified acquisition costs" are the costs of "acquiring, constructing, or reconstructing a residence," including "usual or reasonable settlement, financing, or other closing costs." § 72(t)(8)(C). A "first-time homebuyer" is a person who has had no "present ownership interest in a principal residence during the 2-year period ending on the date of acquisition of the" residence being financed by the distribution. If the homebuyer is married, both spouses must meet this test. § 72(t)(8)(D).

Finally, to the extent the distribution in question qualifies for one of the *other* exceptions (*e.g.*, a distribution to pay higher education expenses), it will not count as a "first-time homebuyer" distribution (so it will not count towards the participant's $10,000 limit) even if it is used to pay expenses that would qualify it for the first-time homebuyer exception. § 72(t)(2)(F).

9.4.10 *IRS levy on the account*

Forced distributions after 1999 resulting from an IRS levy under § 6331 will not be subject to the penalty. § 72(t)(2)(A)(vii).

9.4.11 *Return of certain contributions*

Certain excess contributions to "CODA" plans (see ¶ 8.3.02) may be distributed penalty-free if various requirements are met. See § 401(k)(8)(D) and § 402(g)(2)(C). Regarding return of an IRA or Roth IRA contribution prior to the due date of the tax return for the year for which such contribution was made, see ¶ 9.1.03(B).

9.4.12 *Qualified reservist distributions*

The penalty does not apply to "qualified reservist distributions" (QRDs). A QRD is a distribution from an IRA or from the elective-deferral portion of a QRP (¶ 8.3.02), that is made after September 11, 2001, to an individual reservist who is called to active duty. The active duty call or order must be for more than 179 days or for an indefinite period, and occur after September 11, 2001. The distribution must occur on or after the date the participant is called up and before the end of the active duty period. § 72(t)(2)(G)(iii). See ¶ 2.6.06(C) regarding the ability to "roll over" QRDs without regard to normal rollover deadlines and contribution limits.

9.4.13 *Exceptions for tax-favored disasters*

Congress likes to enact special exceptions for individuals affected by natural disasters, provided the disaster is on the national news for at least a week. Someone who lives in a county affected by Hurricane Katrina may thereby qualify for a penalty exception, while someone who suffered worse losses in a local disaster that affected only a few people will not qualify. For penalty exceptions applicable to certain hurricane victims, see § 1400Q, Notice 2005-92, 2005-51 I.R.B.1165, IRS Publication 4492, and IRS Form 8915.

Appendix A: Tables

1.   <u>Uniform Lifetime Table</u>

Table for Determining Applicable Distribution Period (Divisor)			
Age	Distribution period	Age	Distribution period
70	27.4	93	9.6
71	26.5	94	9.1
72	25.6	95	8.6
73	24.7	96	8.1
74	23.8	97	7.6
75	22.9	98	7.1
76	22.0	99	6.7
77	21.2	100	6.3
78	20.3	101	5.9
79	19.5	102	5.5
80	18.7	103	5.2
81	17.9	104	4.9
82	17.1	105	4.5
83	16.3	106	4.2
84	15.5	107	3.9
85	14.8	108	3.7
86	14.1	109	3.4
87	13.4	110	3.1
88	12.7	111	2.9
89	12.0	112	2.6
90	11.4	113	2.4
91	10.8	114	2.1
92	10.2	115 and up	1.9

This table must be used by all taxpayers to compute lifetime required distributions for 2003 and later years, unless the sole beneficiary is the participant's more-than-10-years-younger spouse. See ¶ 1.3.01. This table may not be used: by beneficiaries of a deceased participant (except in the year of the participant's death); or for years prior to 2002 (optional for 2002).

For each Distribution Year, determine: (A) the account balance as of the prior calendar year end (see ¶ 1.2.05–¶ 1.2.08); (B) the participant's age at the end of the Distribution Year (¶ 1.2.04); and (C) the Applicable Distribution Period (divisor) for that age from the above table. "A" divided by "C" equals the minimum required distribution for the Distribution Year.

2.   Uniform Lifetime Table, Younger Ages

For "SOSEPPs" using "RMD Method"; see ¶ 9.2.05(A).

Taxpayer's Age:	Life Expectancy:	Taxpayer's Age:	Life Expectancy:
21	75.3	43	53.4
22	74.3	44	52.4
23	73.3	45	51.5
24	72.3	46	50.5
25	71.3	47	49.5
26	70.3	48	48.5
27	69.3	49	47.5
28	68.3	50	46.5
29	67.3	51	45.5
30	66.3	52	44.6
31	65.3	53	43.6
32	64.3	54	42.6
33	63.3	55	41.6
34	62.3	56	40.7
35	61.4	57	39.7
36	60.4	58	38.7
37	59.4	59	37.8
38	58.4	60	36.8
39	57.4	61	35.8
40	56.4	62	34.9
41	55.4	63	33.9
42	54.4	64	33.0

3.   Single Life Expectancy Table.

For computing MRDs after the participant's death; see ¶ 1.5.02.

Ages 0 to 57

Age	Life Expectancy	Age	Life Expectancy
0	82.4	29	54.3
1	81.6	30	53.3
2	80.6	31	52.4
3	79.7	32	51.4
4	78.7	33	50.4
5	77.7	34	49.4
6	76.7	35	48.5
7	75.8	36	47.5
8	74.8	37	46.5
9	73.8	38	45.6
10	72.8	39	44.6
11	71.8	40	43.6
12	70.8	41	42.7
13	69.9	42	41.7
14	68.9	43	40.7
15	67.9	44	39.8
16	66.9	45	38.8
17	66.0	46	37.9
18	65.0	47	37.0
19	64.0	48	36.0
20	63.0	49	35.1
21	62.1	50	34.2
22	61.1	51	33.3
23	60.1	52	32.3
24	59.1	53	31.4
25	58.2	54	30.5
26	57.2	55	29.6
27	56.2	56	28.7
28	55.3	57	27.9

Single Life Table, cont.

Ages 58 to 111+

Age	Life Expectancy	Age	Life Expectancy
58	27.0	87	6.7
59	26.1	88	6.3
60	25.2	89	5.9
61	24.4	90	5.5
62	23.5	91	5.2
63	22.7	92	4.9
64	21.8	93	4.6
65	21.0	94	4.3
66	20.2	95	4.1
67	19.4	96	3.8
68	18.6	97	3.6
69	17.8	98	3.4
70	17.0	99	3.1
71	16.3	100	2.9
72	15.5	101	2.7
73	14.8	102	2.5
74	14.1	103	2.3
75	13.4	104	2.1
76	12.7	105	1.9
77	12.1	106	1.7
78	11.4	107	1.5
79	10.8	108	1.4
80	10.2	109	1.2
81	9.7	110	1.1
82	9.1	111+	1.0
83	8.6		
84	8.1		
85	7.6		
86	7.1		

Appendix B: Forms

Table of Contents

Checklist: Drafting the Beneficiary Designation 574
1. **SIMPLE BENEFICIARY DESIGNATION FORM**
   1.1   Simple Designation: Spouse, Then Issue 578
2. **MASTER BENEFICIARY DESIGNATION FORMS** 580
   2.1   Master Designation: Traditional or Roth IRA 581
   2.2   Master Designation Form: Qualified Plan 583
   2.3   Additional Clauses for Master Forms 585
3. **SAMPLE INSERTS FOR MASTER FORMS**
   3.1   To Spouse, "Disclaimable" to Trust; Different Contingent Beneficiary (Death vs. Disclaimer) . . 586
   3.2   Spouse Primary Beneficiary; Children Contingent 587
   3.3   Designating Children (Or Their Issue) 588
   3.4   Trust Is Beneficiary, but Only If Spouse Survives 588
   3.5   To Issue; Hold in Trust If below Certain Age 588
   3.6   Spouse as Primary, Issue as Contingent Beneficiary; Hold in Trust If below Certain Age 589
   3.7   Different Benefs. for Roth, Traditional, Accounts 589
   3.8   Formula Gift with Reference to Outside Fiduciary 590
4. **TRUST PROVISIONS DEALING WITH BENEFITS**
   4.1   Administration During Donor's Life; Irrevocability 591
   4.2   Forbidding Payment of Benefits to Nonindividuals 592
   4.3   Excluding Older Adopted Issue 593
   4.4   Limitation on Powers of Appointment in Trust . . 593
   4.5   Marital Deduction Savings Language 594
   4.6   Establishing a Conduit Trust for One Beneficiary 594
   4.7   Conduit Trust for Spouse (Marital Deduction) . . . 595
   4.8   Conduit Provision Included in "Family Pot" Trust 595
   4.9   Last Man Standing Trust for Children 596
   4.10   "O/R-2-NLP" Trust (Spouse then Issue) 597
   4.11   Definitions Used in Certain Trust Forms 597
5. **OTHER FORMS**
   5.1   Power of Attorney for Retirement Benefits 599
   5.2   Will Provision: Formula in Designation Form . . . 600
   5.3   Will Provision: Roth IRA Conversions 601
   5.4   Fiduciary Letter Transferring Plan to Beneficiary 602
   5.5   To Administrator Who Won't Provide Information 603

This Appendix contains sample forms which can be used by practitioners as a starting point for drafting their own forms for various clients and situations.

Checklist: Drafting the Beneficiary Designation

Here is a checklist of "DO'S and DON'T'S" to consider when drafting a beneficiary designation form for a client's retirement plan benefits.

1.   DO impress on the client that the Beneficiary Designation Form is just as important a legal document as a will or trust. Often, more of the client's assets are controlled by this form than by his will. An improperly drafted (or missing) beneficiary designation form could cost the client's family dearly in taxes and increased settlement costs.

2.   DO read the applicable sections of the account or plan documents, to make sure the beneficiary designation and payout method the client desires are permitted. In the case of a qualified retirement plan (QRP) benefit, read the Summary Plan Description or the description of available benefit payout options in the employer-provided beneficiary designation form, then check your conclusions with the plan administrator. In case of doubt read the actual plan documents. Consider, when you quote a fee for a "standard" estate plan, including in the quote the cost of beneficiary designations (including reading plan documents) for up to two retirement plan accounts per client. If the client chooses to have (or for some reason is stuck with) multiple accounts, advise the client of your fee to review the documents and prepare a beneficiary designation form for each additional plan.

If tempted to skip this step, ask yourself with respect to each plan, how bad would it be if this plan does NOT go to the right beneficiary in the right way? You will quickly realize that plans worth hundreds of thousands (or millions) of dollars must be thoroughly taken care of, even if that means reviewing plan documents and multiple communications with the plan administrator, while the client will probably agree that it is not cost effective to have you apply the full court press to a $1,000 IRA.

Bombs Hidden in Plan Documents

The author has seen a bank's IRA beneficiary designation form that contains the statement "I understand that if I become married in the future, this form ceases to apply and I must file a new beneficiary designation." The client may not be aware that marriage has that effect. Some IRA providers require spousal consent to the beneficiary designation even if the spouse has no rights under applicable state law.

Also, many lawyers build an estate plan around the expectation that the primary beneficiary (e.g. the surviving spouse) may disclaim the benefits and allow them to pass to the contingent beneficiary (e.g. a credit shelter trust). But some qualified retirement plans do not recognize disclaimers—the plan will pay the benefits to a named beneficiary who survives the participant regardless of whether the named beneficiary disclaims the benefits. See ¶ 4.4.09.

---

3.   Can the IRA beneficiary transfer the benefits to another inherited IRA? Most IRA providers routinely allow this, but if your client's IRA provider does not it would be nice to know about that policy up front. See ¶ 4.2.02 and Section 3.01 of the IRA/RothIRA Master Beneficiary Designation Form (Form 2.1). (This is not a concern with respect to qualified plans. QRPs are required to allow a direct rollover to an IRA for any *"Designated* Beneficiary," and forbidden to allow it for any *other* beneficiary. See ¶ 4.2.04.)

4.   Problems arise when practitioners submit beneficiary designation forms that place unsuitable duties on the plan administrator or IRA provider ("administrator"). Most IRAs are custodial accounts, under which the IRA provider's duties are limited to custodial and tax reporting services, and the provider's fees are nominal. Most administrators cannot be expected to do much more than send out benefit checks requested by beneficiaries whose names and addresses are listed in the beneficiary designation form. Here are some "do's and don't's" to avert problems with the administrator:

A.   DON'T require the administrator to make legal judgments. A form that says "I leave the benefits to X unless he disclaims the benefits by means of a qualified disclaimer within the meaning of § 2518 of the tax code," appears to require the plan administrator to determine whether the disclaimer is qualified under § 2518 before it can decide who to pay the benefits to. Compare Form 2.2, Section 3.01.

B.   DON'T require the administrator to carry out functions of an executor or trustee. For example, if you say "I designate my son as beneficiary, to receive only the minimum required distribution each year," you are requiring the administrator to control the beneficiary's withdrawals. Most IRAs and plans have no mechanism for restricting the beneficiary's withdrawals. If you want to restrict the beneficiary's withdrawals or make them conditional in any way you generally must either (1) leave the benefits to a trust (so your chosen trustee can enforce the conditions); or (2) use a "Trusteed IRA" (IRT) rather than a "custodial" IRA (¶ 6.1.07).

C.   DON'T require the administrator to determine amounts dependent on external facts. If it is necessary to include, in your beneficiary designation form, a formula that is dependent on external facts (for example, "I leave to the marital trust the minimum amount necessary to eliminate federal estate taxes"), do this in a way that does not make the administrator responsible to apply the formula. Provide that the participant's executor or a trustee will certify the facts to the administrator, who can rely absolutely on such certification, then be sure the will or trust appointing such fiduciary requires him to carry out this duty. See Forms 3.8 and 5.2.

D.   DO avoid redundant or contradictory lists of definitions and payout options. The definitions in Forms 2.1 and 2.2 are intended to be used with IRAs and retirement plans which have either no, or incomprehensible, defined terms. If the plan document already has suitable and clear definitions of "primary beneficiary," "death benefit," "the account," and other terms, using a different set of definitions may just create confusion.

5.   Consider whether to alter applicable presumptions in case of simultaneous or close-in-time deaths. See ¶ 1.7.07.

6.   If the participant is married, and is designating someone other than his spouse as beneficiary, obtain spousal consent if required. See ¶ 3.4.

7.   Consider the extent to which you need to define any terms such as "issue *per stirpes*," "spouse," or "income"; and/or specify which state's law will be used to interpret terms you use in the form. It is highly likely that the QRP or IRA agreement specifies that the law of

the sponsor's state of incorporation will be used. Since that may well not be the state in which your client lives (or dies), there is a potential for problems if the client's chosen disposition depends on a definition that varies from state to state. Although you cannot change the governing law of the "plan," a statement that the *beneficiary designation* will be interpreted according to the laws of a particular state should be accepted in the sense that it will lead to the correct determination of the client's intent. See Section 3.03, Forms 2.1, 2.2.

8.   DO name a contingent as well as a primary beneficiary. DO consider whether different contingent beneficiaries should be named depending on whether the primary beneficiary actually dies before the participant, or merely disclaims the benefits. See Form 3.1. When choosing among competing considerations in naming a primary beneficiary (such as "financial security of spouse" versus "saving estate taxes for children"), name the primary beneficiary based on the relative priorities the client assigns to the choices. For maximum flexibility after the client's death, name the second choice as contingent beneficiary; see ¶ 4.4.13.

9.   Whenever a trust is named as beneficiary, see the Trust Drafting Checklist at ¶ 6.1.01. Some beneficiary designation forms in this book in which benefits are left to a trust describe the trust as "the [TRUST NAME] Trust [optional:, a copy of which is attached hereto]." The phrase "a copy of which is attached hereto" is optional, and would be used solely to identify the trust that is named as beneficiary. You could choose to identify the trust by other means (*e.g.,* "under agreement dated 9/2/10") instead of attaching a copy of the trust to the beneficiary designation form. No matter how you choose to identify the trust, you ALSO must comply with the documentation requirement; see ¶ 6.2.08.

10.   DO include contact information (address and phone) for the beneficiaries, or they and the administrator may never find each other; for reasons of space, not every Form in this Appendix recites the inclusion of contact information. Confirm the administrator's policy regarding whether it will notify the beneficiary; if the administrator declines any responsibility to notify the beneficiary, arrange an alternative mechanism to notify them (or they may never know they have inherited the benefits).

11.   DO require the administrator to provide information to the participant's executor. See ¶ 4.3.01; Section 3.02 of Forms 2.1 and 2.2.

12.   DON'T focus on taxes and minimum distributions to the exclusion of basic drafting issues. For example, if a beneficiary predeceases the participant, does his share pass instead to the surviving beneficiaries, or to his own issue, or to someone else?

13.   Finally, DO get a receipt or other written acknowledgment from the administrator confirming that they have received and accepted the beneficiary designation form. Confirm that the administrator has the beneficiary designation form each time you update the client's estate plan (even if the beneficiary designation is not to change; administrators have a way of losing these documents, especially when there is a corporate acquisition). Admonish the client to see you regarding a new beneficiary designation form, even in between estate plan-update visits, whenever the benefits are moved to a different plan or account (for example, when an IRA is converted to a Roth IRA).

Introduction to the Forms

The rest of this Appendix consists of sample estate planning forms dealing with retirement benefits. [Brackets] indicate instructions to the drafter. [ALL CAPS] in brackets indicate something that needs to be inserted or completed by the drafter. All forms are meant to be modified by the estate planner as needed for a particular client.

Sample beneficiary designation forms are followed by sample trust clauses and miscellaneous other forms.

1.   SIMPLE BENEFICIARY DESIGNATION FORM

1.1   Simple Designation: Spouse, Then Issue

This form may be suitable for a client who wants to leave benefits outright to his spouse if living, otherwise to his children equally (and issue of deceased children). This form is included primarily for use with (1) retirement plans that are of relatively small value and (2) retirement plans that already contain, in the plan documents, the estate plan-friendly additional provisions included in the longer Master Beneficiary Designation forms (2.1, 2.2, 2.3). If the benefit is of substantial value, and the plan documents do not have provisions dealing with the important estate planning issues covered in the longer forms, it would be advisable to use the longer forms.

DESIGNATION OF BENEFICIARY

TO: [Name of IRA or Roth IRA Provider or Plan Administrator]
FROM: [Name of Participant]
RE: [IRA or Roth IRA No._____] or [or Name of Plan]

1.   I hereby designate as my beneficiary, my spouse, [SPOUSE NAME], to receive all benefits payable under the above [account] [plan] in the event of my death. My spouse's address and phone number are [INSERT CONTACT INFORMATION].

2.   If my spouse does not survive me, I designate as my beneficiaries, in equal shares, such of my children as shall survive me; provided, that if any of my children does not survive me, but leaves issue surviving me, such issue shall take the share such deceased child would have taken if living, by right of representation. My children are [INSERT NAMES AND CONTACT INFORMATION].

[Alt. 1: pay minor's benefits to a custodian]
3.   Any benefits becoming distributable to a person under the age of twenty-one (21) years shall be distributed to such person's surviving parent, if any, otherwise to [NAME or DESCRIPTION of proposed custodian, such as "my oldest then living child"], as custodian for such person under the Uniform Transfers to Minors Act. Such custodian shall be entitled to act for the minor in all respects with regard to the benefits.

[Alt. 2: pay minor's benefits to a trust; the drafter must make sure the trust instrument has suitable provision to receive this payment and hold it for the particular minor beneficiary who is entitled to it]
3.   Any benefits becoming distributable to a person under the age of twenty-one (21) years shall be distributed to the Trustee then serving as such under the [NAME OF TRUST] created by [Agreement/Declaration/Instrument/my Will] dated [date of trust instrument] [optional:, a copy of which is attached hereto], to be held

and administered for the benefit of such person as provided therein. The name and address of the current Trustee are: [INSERT].

4.   Regardless of who is named as beneficiary above, you shall provide to the executor, administrator, or other duly appointed representative of my estate such information regarding me, my account, and/or my beneficiary(ies) as such representative may reasonably request in connection with the performance of his, her, or its duties as such representative.

Signed this_____ day of _____, 20 ___.

_____
Signature of Participant

2.   MASTER BENEFICIARY DESIGNATION FORMS

These Master Beneficiary Designation Forms are meant to provide a starting "boilerplate" form, which will be modified by the estate planner when used for a particular client. The modifications will consist of: (1) inserting the names of the beneficiary(ies) in Article II (see sample inserts in Part 3 of this Appendix B); (2) deleting superfluous provisions and/or adding clauses from Form 2.3 if needed; and (3) such other modifications as are necessary or desirable to reflect applicable state law, the client's intent, and the requirements of the plan. See also the "Checklist: Drafting the Beneficiary Designation," at page 574.

Form 2.1 is meant to be used with IRAs (traditional and Roth). Form 2.2 is for QRPs. Form 2.3 contains add-on clauses for both forms.

A particular IRA provider or QRP administrator may not be willing to accept some or all of these provisions, or any modifications to its printed beneficiary designation form. In such cases, the client will have to decide whether to move the benefits to another plan (if that is possible) or compromise his estate planning goals.

2.1   Master Beneficiary Designation: Traditional or Roth IRA

DESIGNATION OF BENEFICIARY

TO: _____

Name of Custodian or Trustee of the Account

FROM: _____

Name of Participant

RE: Account No. _____

I.   Definitions

The following words, when used in this form and capitalized, shall have the meaning indicated in this Section.

"Account" means the "Individual Retirement Account," "Individual Retirement Trust," "Roth Individual Retirement Account," or "Roth Individual Retirement Trust" referred to above, which is established and maintained under § 408 or § 408A of the Code.

"Administrator" means the IRA custodian or trustee named above, and its successors in that office.

"Agreement" means the account agreement between the Administrator and the undersigned establishing the Account.

"Beneficiary" means any person entitled to ownership of all or part of the Account as a result of my death (or as a result of the death of another Beneficiary).

"Contingent Beneficiary" means the person(s) I have designated in this form to receive the Death Benefit if my Primary Beneficiary does not survive me (or disclaims the benefits).

"Death Benefit" means all amounts payable under the Account on account of my death.

The "Personal Representative" of any person means the duly appointed guardian or conservator of such person, or executor or administrator of such person's estate, who is serving as such at the applicable time.

"Primary Beneficiary" means the person(s) designated in this form to receive the Death Benefit in the event of my death.

II.   Designation of Beneficiary

[Here insert the name(s) of the primary and contingent beneficiary(ies). This section must be drafted by the estate planning attorney; see sample inserts in Part 3 of this Appendix B.]

III.   Other Provisions [dispense with any of these that are not appropriate in view of the choice of beneficiary or that are not necessary because already covered in the IRA provider's documents governing the Account; add clauses from Form 2.3 as needed]

    3.01   Transferring Account. The Beneficiary shall have the right to have the Account (or, if the Account has been divided into separate accounts, such Beneficiary's separate Account) transferred to a different individual retirement account or trust, of the same type ("traditional" or "Roth") as the Account, still in my name and payable to such Beneficiary, with the same or a different custodian or trustee.

    3.02   Information to be provided to Personal Representative. The Administrator shall provide to my Personal Representative any information such representative shall request in connection with the performance of such representative's duties (including the preparation of any tax return) regarding the benefits, the terms of the account, and the Beneficiary(ies), including information as to matters prior to such representative's appointment, to the same extent and on the same terms that such information would have been provided to me had I requested it. Any Beneficiary, by accepting benefits hereunder, shall be deemed to have consented to the release of information to my Personal Representative as provided in the preceding sentence.

    3.03   Governing Law. The law of the State of _____ shall apply solely for the purpose of interpreting my intent as expressed in this Designation of Beneficiary form. This provision is not intended to amend or supercede any governing law provision in the Agreement with respect to the interpretation and administration of the Agreement.

    Signed this _____ day of _____, 20 ___.

          _____

          Signature of Participant

    Receipt of the above beneficiary designation form is hereby acknowledged this ___ day of _____, 20 ___.

          _____

_____Name of Custodian or Trustee

    By:_____[Title]

2.2   Master Beneficiary Designation Form: Qualified Plan

DESIGNATION OF BENEFICIARY

TO: _____

       Name of Trustee or Plan Administrator

FROM: _____

       Name of Participant

RE: _____

       Name of Retirement Plan

I.   Definitions

The following words, when used in this form and capitalized, shall have the meaning indicated in this Section.

"Administrator" means the Plan Administrator or Trustee named above, and its successors in such office.

"Beneficiary" means any person entitled to receive benefits under the Plan as a result of my death (or as a result of the death of another Beneficiary).

"Contingent Beneficiary" means the person(s) I have designated in this form to receive the Death Benefit if my Primary Beneficiary does not survive me (or disclaims the benefits).

"Death Benefit" means all benefits payable under the Plan on account of my death.

The "Personal Representative" of any person means the duly appointed guardian or conservator of such person, or executor or administrator of such person's estate, who is serving as such at the applicable time.

"Plan" means the qualified retirement plan or other retirement arrangement described at the beginning of this form.

"Primary Beneficiary" means the person(s) designated in this form to receive benefits under the Plan on account of my death.

II.   Designation of Beneficiary

[Here insert the name(s) of the primary and contingent beneficiary(ies). This section must be drafted by the estate planning attorney; see sample inserts in Part 3 of this Appendix B. If the participant is married, spousal consent is normally required if anyone other than the spouse is named as beneficiary. See ¶ 3.4.]

III.   Other Provisions   [dispense with any of these that are not appropriate in view of the choice of beneficiary or that are not necessary because already covered in the plan documents governing the benefits]

     3.01   Honoring Disclaimers. If a Beneficiary disclaims all or any portion of any interest in the Death Benefit to which such Beneficiary would otherwise be entitled under the foregoing provisions hereof, by means of a written disclaimer delivered to the Administrator within nine months after my death, then that Beneficiary shall be deemed (as to the interest so disclaimed) to have predeceased me, the interest so disclaimed shall pass as if such Beneficiary had predeceased me, and the Beneficiary who takes the interest so disclaimed shall be deemed to be my beneficiary under the Plan for all purposes. This provision shall not be construed to prevent an interest disclaimed by my spouse from passing to my spouse by other means.

     3.02   Information to be provided to Personal Representative. The Administrator shall provide to my Personal Representative any information such representative shall request in connection with the performance of such representative's duties (including the preparation of any tax return) regarding the benefits, the Plan, and the Beneficiary(ies), including information as to matters prior to such representative's appointment, and including copies of Plan documents and returns, to the same extent and on the same terms that such information would have been provided to me had I requested it. Any Beneficiary, by accepting benefits hereunder, shall be deemed to have consented to the release of information to my Personal Representative as provided in the preceding sentence.

     3.03   Governing Law. The law of the State of _____ shall apply solely for the purpose of interpreting my intent as expressed in this Designation of Beneficiary form. This provision is not intended to amend or supercede any governing law provision in the Plan with respect to the interpretation and administration of the Plan.

     Signed this _____ day of _____, 20 ___.

_____
Signature of Participant

> Receipt of the above beneficiary designation form is hereby acknowledged this ___ day of _____, 20 ___.
>
> _____
> _____Name of Plan Administrator or Trustee
> By:_____
> Title:

2.3   Additional Clauses for Master Beneficiary Designations

These clauses can be added to the Master Beneficiary Designations (Forms 2.1 and 2.2) if needed. Use 3.04 if there is any possibility that a minor may become a beneficiary of the plan or account. Use 3.05 if there is any possibility that there could be multiple beneficiaries of the plan or account. If the entire plan benefit or account is payable to a single trust as named beneficiary, for example, there would be no need to use either of these clauses.

Use 3.06 if it may be necessary or appropriate for the beneficiary designated under Article II of the Beneficiary Designation Form to delegate investment authority to an investment manager.

> 3.04   Payments to Minors. If any Beneficiary becomes entitled to any portion of the Death Benefit while under the age of twenty-one (21) years, such Beneficiary's portion of the Death Benefit shall be instead payable to such Beneficiary's surviving parent, if any, otherwise to [NAME or DESCRIPTION of proposed custodian, such as "my oldest then living child"], otherwise to some other person selected by my Personal Representative, as custodian for such Beneficiary under the Uniform Transfers to Minors Act, and such custodian shall have the power to act for such Beneficiary in all respects with regard to the benefits to which such Beneficiary is entitled.
>
> 3.05   Multiple Beneficiaries. If there are multiple Beneficiaries entitled to ownership of the Death Benefit simultaneously, the Beneficiaries shall be entitled, by written instructions to the Administrator, to have the Death Benefit partitioned into multiple accounts, corresponding to each Beneficiary's separate interest in the Death Benefit, as of or at any time after my death, to the maximum extent such division is permitted by law to occur without causing a deemed distribution of the Death Benefit. Following such partition the

newly created separate accounts shall be maintained as if each were an account in my name payable solely to the applicable Beneficiary; no Beneficiary shall have any further interest in or claim to any portion of the Death Benefit other than the separate account representing such Beneficiary's interest.

3.06   Allowing Beneficiary to Appoint Investment Manager. The Beneficiary may designate an Investment Manager for its interest in the Death Benefit. Upon receipt of written authorization from the Beneficiary, and until receiving notice that such authorization is revoked, the Administrator shall comply with investment instructions of the Investment Manager in accordance with the Beneficiary's authorization.

3.   SAMPLE INSERTS FOR MASTER FORMS

The forms in this section are the actual designation of the primary and/or contingent beneficiary. These are designed to be inserted into "Article II" of the Master Beneficiary Designations (Forms 2.1 and 2.2).

These forms are not stand-alone documents. Rather, this is a collection of substantive beneficiary designations, from which you can select the one you want, adapt it to your client's needs, and insert it into another form, for example, one of the Master Beneficiary Designation Forms in Part 2 of this Appendix B.

3.1   Benefits Payable to Spouse, "Disclaimable" to Credit Shelter Trust; Different Contingent Beneficiary Depending on Whether Spouse Predeceases or Disclaims

This form might be used by a client who does not have sufficient non-retirement plan assets to fully fund a credit shelter trust, but nevertheless wants to leave the benefits to his spouse and allow the spouse to make the ultimate decision whether to (1) keep the benefits and roll them over to an IRA or (2) disclaim some or all of the benefits and allow them to flow to the credit shelter trust. See ¶ 4.4.13. If using this form with a nonIRA plan, make sure the plan honors disclaimers; see "Bombs Hidden in Plan Documents," p. 575.

II.   Designation of Beneficiary

A.   Primary Beneficiary

I hereby designate as my Primary Beneficiary my spouse, [SPOUSE NAME], if my spouse survives me.

B.   Contingent Beneficiary in Case of Disclaimer

If my spouse survives me, but disclaims the Death Benefit (or part of it), I hereby designate as my Contingent Beneficiary, to receive the part (or all) of the Death Benefit so disclaimed, [TRUSTEE NAME], as Trustee of the [TRUST NAME] Trust, under agreement dated [TRUST DATE] [optional:, a copy of which is attached hereto].

C.   Contingent Beneficiary in Case of Death

If my spouse does not survive me, I hereby designate as my Contingent Beneficiary my children surviving me, in equal shares; provided, that if any child of mine does not survive me, but leaves issue surviving me, such issue shall take the share such deceased child would have taken if living, by right of representation. My children are: [INSERT NAMES AND CONTACT INFORMATION].

3.2   Spouse is Primary Beneficiary; Children are Contingent

II.   Designation of Beneficiary

A.   Primary Beneficiary

I hereby designate as my Primary Beneficiary, to receive 100% of the Death Benefit, my spouse, [SPOUSE NAME], if my spouse survives me.

B.   Contingent Beneficiary

If my spouse does not survive me, I hereby designate as my Contingent Beneficiary, to receive 100% of the Death Benefit, my children surviving me, in equal shares; provided, that if any child of mine does not survive me, but leaves issue surviving me, such issue shall take the share such deceased child would have taken if living, by right of representation. My children are [INSERT NAMES AND CONTACT INFORMATION].

3.3   Designating Children (Or Their Issue) as Beneficiaries

II.   Designation of Beneficiary

I hereby designate as my Primary Beneficiary, to receive 100% of the Death Benefit, my children surviving me, in equal shares; provided, that if any child of mine does not survive me, but leaves issue surviving me, such issue shall take the share such deceased child would have taken if living, by right of representation. My children are [INSERT NAMES AND CONTACT INFORMATION].

3.4   Trust Is Beneficiary, but Only If Spouse Survives

See ¶ 6.1.01, #6.

II.   Designation of Beneficiary

A.   Primary Beneficiary

I hereby designate as my Primary Beneficiary, to receive 100% of the Death Benefit, if my spouse survives me, [TRUSTEE NAME], as Trustee of the [TRUST NAME] Trust, under agreement dated [TRUST DATE] [optional:, a copy of which is attached hereto].

B.   Contingent Beneficiary

If my spouse does not survive me, I hereby designate as my Contingent Beneficiary, to receive 100% of the Death Benefit, my issue surviving me, by right of representation.

3.5   To Issue; Hold in Trust If below Certain Age

II.   Designation of Beneficiary

I hereby designate as my Primary Beneficiary, to receive 100% of the Death Benefit, my issue surviving me, by right of representation; provided, however, that if any such Beneficiary is under the age of [AGE, such as "thirty"] years at the time of my death such Beneficiary's share shall not be paid to such Beneficiary outright, but shall instead be paid to the trustee then serving as such under the separate trust to be established for such Beneficiary's benefit under Article [NUMBER] of the [TRUST NAME] Trust, dated [TRUST

DATE], a copy of which is attached hereto, to be held, administered, and distributed for the benefit of such Beneficiary as provided therein.

3.6   Spouse as Primary, Issue as Contingent Beneficiary; Hold in Trust If below Certain Age

II.   Designation of Beneficiary

A.   Primary Beneficiary

I hereby designate as my Primary Beneficiary, to receive 100% of the Death Benefit, my spouse, [SPOUSE NAME], if my spouse survives me.

B.   Contingent Beneficiary

If my spouse does not survive me, I hereby designate as my Contingent Beneficiary, to receive 100% of the Death Benefit, my issue surviving me, by right of representation; provided, however, that if any Contingent Beneficiary is under the age of [AGE, such as "thirty"] years at the time of my death such Beneficiary's share shall not be paid to such Beneficiary outright, but shall instead be paid to the trustee then serving as such under the separate trust established for such Beneficiary's benefit under Article [NUMBER] of the [TRUST NAME] Trust, dated [TRUST DATE], a copy of which is attached hereto, to be held, administered, and distributed for the benefit of such Beneficiary as provided therein.

3.7   Different Beneficiaries for Roth, Traditional, Accounts

See ¶ 5.8.06(A) for why a client may want to name different beneficiaries (or different contingent beneficiaries, as in this Form 3.7) for his "traditional" and "designated Roth" (DRAC; see ¶ 5.7) accounts in a single 401(k), 403(b), or 457 plan at his place of employment. This form provides an example of such a bifurcated beneficiary designation. Be aware, however, that the plan may not be willing to accept this type of split beneficiary designation, since it increases the burden on the plan administrator.

This form is not suitable for an IRA. With an IRA, the *entire account* is either a traditional or a Roth IRA. You need a separate beneficiary designation form for *each IRA*, but you could not have different beneficiary designations for different portions of a single IRA.

II.   Designation of Beneficiary

     I hereby designate my Primary and Contingent Beneficiaries for my "Roth" and "traditional" accounts in the Plan:

     A.   I hereby designate, as my Primary Beneficiary with respect to my "designated Roth account" in the plan, to receive 100% of the Death Benefit with respect to said account, my spouse [SPOUSE NAME], if my said spouse survives me, and as my Contingent Beneficiary (to take said account if my said spouse does not survive me, or to the extent my said spouse disclaims the benefits), my issue surviving me, by right of representation.

     B.   I hereby designate, as my Primary Beneficiary with respect to any and all other accounts I have in the plan, to receive 100% of the Death Benefit with respect to said accounts, my spouse [SPOUSE NAME], if my said spouse survives me, and as my Contingent Beneficiary (to take said account(s) if my said spouse does not survive me, or to the extent my said spouse disclaims the benefits), [NAME OF CHARITY], for its general charitable purposes.

3.8   Formula Gift with Reference to Outside Fiduciary

     See the "Checklist: Drafting the Beneficiary Designation," Question 4(C), p. 576. Pair this with Form 5.2.

II.   Designation of Beneficiary

     I hereby designate as my Primary Beneficiaries, to receive 100% of the Death Benefit, the following persons in the following proportions:

     To the trustee then serving of the [NAME OF TRUST], under Agreement of Trust dated _____, a copy of which is attached hereto (hereinafter, the "Trust"), I leave a fractional portion of my Death Benefit. The fractional portion shall be determined by multiplying the value of the Death Benefit as of the date of my death by a fraction, the numerator of which is the amount of "GST exemption" to which my estate is entitled under § 2631 of the Code, after taking into account all other generation-skipping transfers made by me during my life, or at my death under instruments other than this beneficiary designation form ("my GST exemption"), and the denominator of which is the entire value of the Death Benefit as of the date of my death. If the total value of the Death Benefit is less than my GST exemption, I leave the entire Death Benefit to the Trust. If applying said fraction results in less than all of the Death Benefit passing to the Trust, I leave the balance of the Death Benefit to my children surviving me, in equal shares, with the issue of any deceased child of mine taking the share such deceased child would have been entitled to had he or she been living at the time of my death.

In carrying out the terms of this Beneficiary Designation, the Plan Administrator shall be entitled to rely absolutely on any written representation made to it by my Personal Representative with respect to the identities of the beneficiaries hereunder and the amount of the Death Benefit that is payable to each. The Plan Administrator shall have no responsibility or liability to any person for any action or inaction taken by it in reliance upon any representation made to it by, or in carrying out any instructions given to it by, my Personal Representative. The remedy of any person claiming to be aggrieved by any such action or inaction shall be solely against my Personal Representative.

4.   TRUST PROVISIONS DEALING WITH BENEFITS

See ¶ 6.4.01 regarding the "boilerplate" provisions (Forms 4.1–4.4) and why including these provisions in your trust agreement does NOT guarantee the trust's qualification as a "see-through trust."

Note: Some of the following Forms use defined terms (indicated by capitalized initial letters); if using those Forms, you would also need to use the applicable definitions from Form 4.11.

4.1   Administration During Donor's Life; Irrevocability

See ¶ 6.2.06. This form is not suitable for a testamentary trust.

___. Administration During my Life

      .01   The trustee shall distribute to me such amounts of the principal or income of the trust (including all thereof) as I may request from time to time, or (if I am legally incapacitated) as my guardian, conservator, or other legal representative may request on my behalf.

      .02   I reserve the right to amend or revoke this trust by one or more written and acknowledged instruments delivered to the trustee during my lifetime. This trust shall become irrevocable at my death.

4.2   Forbidding Payment of Benefits to Nonindividuals

See ¶ 6.2.10 for why to forbid use of benefits to pay debts, expenses, and taxes of participant's estate. See ¶ 6.3.01(D), ¶ 7.3.03, regarding why this form may not "work" with regard to other possible payments to nonindividual beneficiaries.

Version A:

       Notwithstanding any other provision hereof, the trustee may not distribute to or for the benefit of my estate, any charity, or any other nonindividual beneficiary any Deferrable Retirement Benefit payable to this trust. It is my intent that all such Deferrable Retirement Benefits be distributed to or held for only individual beneficiaries, within the meaning of the Minimum Distribution Rules. Accordingly I direct that such benefits may not be used or applied for payment of my debts, taxes, expenses of administration, or other claims against my estate; nor for payment of estate, inheritance or similar transfer taxes due on account of my death. This paragraph shall not apply to any bequest or expense which is specifically directed to be funded with Deferrable Retirement Benefits by other provisions of this instrument.

Version B:

       Notwithstanding any other provision hereof, the trustee may not, after September 30 of the calendar year following the calendar year in which my death occurs, or such earlier date as may be established under the Minimum Distribution Rules as the final date for determining whether this trust meets the requirements for treatment of the trust's beneficiaries as if they had been named directly as beneficiary of any retirement plan payable to this trust ("Such Date") for purposes of such Rules, distribute to or for the benefit of my estate, any charity, or any other nonindividual beneficiary any Deferrable Retirement Benefits payable to this trust. It is my intent that all such Deferrable Retirement Benefits held by or payable to this trust as of Such Date be distributed to or held for only individual beneficiaries, within the meaning of the Minimum Distribution Rules. Accordingly I direct that such benefits may not be used or applied after Such Date for payment of my debts, taxes, expenses of administration, or other claims against my estate; nor for payment of estate, inheritance or similar transfer taxes due on account of my death. This paragraph shall not apply to any bequest or expense which is specifically directed to be funded with Deferrable Retirement Benefits by other provisions of this instrument.

4.3   Excluding Older Adopted Issue

See ¶ 6.2.07(A).

A person's "issue" shall not include an individual who is such person's issue by virtue of adoption if such individual was so adopted after my death and is older than the oldest individual who was a beneficiary of this trust at my death.

4.4   Limitation on Powers of Appointment in Trust

See ¶ 6.3.11(E) for why this clause may be needed.

Notwithstanding any other provision hereof, no Deferrable Retirement Benefit may be appointed, distributed, or transferred to any other trust unless (1) under the Minimum Distribution Rules, beneficiaries of such other trust are treated as having been designated directly as beneficiaries of such Deferrable Retirement Benefit for purposes of such Rules, and (2) the oldest beneficiary of such other trust was not born in a year earlier than the year of birth of the oldest beneficiary of this trust.

4.5   Marital Deduction Savings Language

See ¶ 3.3.03(B).

If this trust is or becomes the beneficiary of any Retirement Benefit, the trustee must withdraw from the trust's share of such Retirement Benefit, each year:

A.   So long as my spouse is living, the net income of the trust's share of such Retirement Benefit for such year; and

B.   Regardless of whether my spouse is then living, such amount or such additional amount (if any) as is required to be distributed from such share under the Minimum Distribution Rules (if applicable).

This paragraph shall not be deemed to limit the trustee's power and right to withdraw from the marital trust's share of the Retirement Benefit in any year more than the amount(s) stated above.

4.6   Establishing a Conduit Trust for One Beneficiary

See ¶ 6.3.05.

From and after my death, this trust shall be held for the benefit of [NAME OF INDIVIDUAL TRUST BENEFICIARY] (hereinafter referred to as the "Beneficiary"). Each year, beginning with the year of my death, my trustees shall withdraw from any Deferrable Retirement Benefit the Minimum Required Distribution for such Deferrable Retirement Benefit for such year, plus such additional amount or amounts as the trustee deems advisable in its discretion. All amounts so withdrawn (net of expenses properly charged thereto) shall be distributed to the Beneficiary, if the Beneficiary is then living. Upon the death of the Beneficiary (or upon my death if the Beneficiary does not survive me) all remaining property of this trust [here insert the provisions that will apply after the conduit beneficiary's death; since the see-through trust rules "do not care" what these provisions say, they can be anything you want. Examples: "shall be paid to [NAME OF REMAINDER BENEFICIARY]," or "shall be held in further trust pursuant to the provisions of Article [NUMBER] of this trust instrument."].

4.7   Conduit Trust for Spouse (Marital Deduction)

See ¶ 3.3.08.

> From and after my death, this trust shall be held for the benefit of my spouse [NAME OF SPOUSE] (hereinafter referred to as "my spouse"), if my spouse survives me. Each year, beginning with the year of my death, and so long as my spouse is living, the trustee shall withdraw from any Retirement Benefit the income of such Benefit, or (in the case of any Deferrable Retirement Benefit) the Minimum Required Distribution for such Deferrable Retirement Benefit for such year if greater than the income of such Deferrable Retirement Benefit, plus such additional amount or amounts as the trustee deems advisable in its discretion. All amounts so withdrawn (net of expenses properly charged thereto) shall be paid directly to my spouse upon receipt by the trustee. Upon my spouse's death (or upon my death if my spouse does not survive me) all remaining property of this trust [here insert the provisions that will apply after the conduit beneficiary's death; since the see-through trust rules "do not care" what these provisions say, they can be anything you want. Examples: "shall be paid to [NAME OF REMAINDER BENEFICIARY]," or "shall be held in further trust pursuant to the provisions of Article [NUMBER] of this trust instrument."].

4.8   Conduit Provision Included in "Family Pot" Trust

See ¶ 6.4.03. As a reminder, this approach works only for benefits that pass directly to this "Family Trust" upon the participant's death under the participant's beneficiary designation form. It will not work for a trust that is not established until the death of a prior beneficiary; see ¶ 6.3.12(B).

> Administration of Family Trust
>
> From and after my death, the trustee shall hold and administer all amounts then held by the trust, or that become payable to this trust as a result of my death, for the benefit of my children surviving me, upon the following terms.

A.	While there is any child of mine living who is under the age of [AGE, such as "thirty"] years, the trustee shall hold, administer, and distribute Deferrable Retirement Benefits as provided in Paragraph B and shall hold, administer, and distribute all other property of the trust as provided in Paragraph C.

B.	Each year, beginning with the year of my death, the trustee shall withdraw from any Deferrable Retirement Benefit the Minimum Required Distribution for such Deferrable Retirement Benefit for such year, plus such additional amount or amounts (if any) as the trustee deems advisable in its discretion. The trustee shall forthwith pay all amounts so withdrawn (net of expenses properly charged thereto) to such one or more of my children as are then living, and in such proportions among them, as the trustee deems advisable in its discretion.

C.	The trustee shall pay such amounts of the income and/or principal of property subject to this paragraph to (or apply it for the benefit of) such one or more of my children as are then living, and in such proportions among them as the trustee deems advisable in its discretion.

D.	At such time as there is no child of mine living who is under the age of [AGE, such as "thirty"] years, the trust shall terminate and be distributed outright and free of trust to my issue then living by right of representation, or, if there are no such issue then living, shall be distributed to [NAME OF DEFAULT REMAINDER BENEFICIARY].

## 4.9	Last Man Standing Trust for Children

See ¶ 6.3.09 and ¶ 6.4.05(B).

___. Administration of Family Trust

From and after my death, the trustee shall hold and administer all amounts then held by the trust, or that become payable to this trust as a result of my death, for the benefit of my children surviving me, upon the following terms. While there is any child of mine living who is under the age of [AGE, such as "thirty"] years, the trustee shall pay such amounts of the income and/or principal of the trust to (or apply it for the benefit of) such one or more individuals as the trustee shall select from the class consisting of all my issue then living, and in such proportions among them as the trustee deems advisable in its discretion for their care, support, education, comfort, and welfare. The trust shall terminate at the earlier of the following times:

A.   Such time as there is no child of mine living who is under the age specified above.

B.   Such time as there is only one child of mine living (regardless of such child's age).

Upon termination, the trust property shall be distributed, outright and free of trusts, to my issue then living, by right of representation.

4.10 "O/R-2-NLP" Trust (Spouse then Issue)

See ¶ 6.3.08. Note that the distribution to issue on the spouse's death must NOT be contingent upon their having reached any particular age. This trust is not intended to qualify for the marital deduction.

Following my death, the trustee shall pay to or apply for the benefit of my spouse, as long as my spouse is living, all income of the trust and such amounts of the principal as the trustee deems advisable in its discretion for my spouse's health and support in the standard of living to which my spouse had become accustomed during my life. Upon my spouse's death (or upon my death, if my spouse does not survive me), the trust shall terminate, and all property of the trust shall be distributed, outright and free of trust, to my issue then living by right of representation.

4.11 Definitions Used in Certain Trust Forms

This Form contains definitions that are used in Forms 4.2 and 4.4–4.8. Delete any definitions not used in the particular Form you are using.

__. Certain Definitions

The following definitions shall apply in administering this Trust:

1.   The **Code** means the Internal Revenue Code of 1986, as amended.

2. A **Retirement Benefit** means the trust's interest in one of the following types of assets if payable to this trust as beneficiary or owned by this trust: a qualified or nonqualified annuity; a benefit under a qualified or nonqualified plan of deferred compensation; any account in or benefit payable under any pension, profit-sharing, stock bonus, or other qualified retirement plan; any individual retirement account or trust; and any and all benefits under any plan or arrangement that is established under § 408, § 408A, § 457, § 403, § 401, or similar provisions of the Code. **Retirement Benefits** means all of such interests collectively.

3. A **Deferrable Retirement Benefit** means any Retirement Benefit that meets the following two requirements: First, it is subject to the Minimum Distribution Rules. Second, a designated beneficiary of such Benefit has the option (either under the terms of the plan or arrangement that governs such Benefit, or by causing the Benefit to be transferred to an inherited IRA) to take distribution of such Benefit in annual instalments over the life expectancy of the (or of the oldest) designated beneficiary. **Deferrable Retirement Benefits** means all of such interests collectively. Benefits payable under a plan or arrangement that is not subject to the Minimum Distribution Rules (such as, under current law, a "nonqualified deferred compensation plan") are not Deferrable Retirement Benefits.

4. The **Minimum Distribution Rules** mean the rules of § 401(a)(9) of the Code, including Regulations thereunder.

5. The **Minimum Required Distribution** for any year means, with respect to any Retirement Benefit: (1) the value of the Retirement Benefit determined as of the preceding year-end, divided by (2) the Applicable Distribution Period; or such greater or lesser amount as the trustee shall be required to withdraw under the laws then applicable to this Trust to avoid penalty. Notwithstanding the foregoing, the Minimum Required Distribution for the year of my death shall mean (1) the amount that was required to be distributed to me with respect to such Benefit during such year under the Minimum Distribution Rules, minus (2) amounts actually distributed to me with respect to such Benefit during such year. The terms "life expectancy," "designated beneficiary," and "Applicable Distribution Period" shall have the same meaning as under the Minimum Distribution Rules.

5.   OTHER FORMS

5.1   Power of Attorney for Retirement Benefits

This clause could be added to the client's power of attorney or set up as a separate power of attorney just dealing with benefits. The form and formalities of execution need to be appropriate for the applicable jurisdiction and the client's circumstances. For any significant retirement plan benefit, determine in advance whether the plan will honor this form; some IRAs, for example, require customers to use a particular form prepared by the IRA provider.

My Agent shall have the power to establish one or more "individual retirement accounts" or other retirement plans or arrangements in my name.

In connection with any pension, profit sharing or stock bonus plan, individual retirement arrangement, Roth IRA, § 403(b) annuity or account, § 457 plan, or any other retirement plan, arrangement or annuity in which I am (or my spouse is) a participant or of which I am a beneficiary (whether established by my Agent or otherwise) (each of which is hereinafter referred to as "such Plan"), my Agent shall have the following powers, in addition to all other applicable powers granted by this instrument:

1.   To make contributions (including "rollover" and/or "conversion" contributions) or cause contributions to be made to such Plan with my funds or otherwise on my behalf.

2.   To receive and endorse checks or other distributions to me from such Plan, or to arrange for the direct deposit of the same in any account in my name or in the name of [NAME OF CLIENT'S LIVING TRUST].

3.   To elect a form of payment of benefits from such Plan, to withdraw benefits from such Plan, and to make, exercise, waive or consent to any and all elections and/or options that I or my spouse may have regarding contributions to, investments or administration of, distributions from, or form of benefits under, such Plan.

4.   With respect to any contribution to an IRA or Roth IRA, to "recharacterize" all or part of said contribution with the effect of having said contribution (or part thereof) deemed to have been made to the other type of IRA.

[Alt. 1: Agent can choose beneficiary]

5.   To designate one or more beneficiaries or contingent beneficiaries for any benefits payable under such Plan on account of my death, and to change any such prior designation of beneficiary made by me or by my Agent; provided, however, that my Agent shall have no power to designate my Agent directly or indirectly as a beneficiary or contingent beneficiary to receive a greater share or proportion of any such benefits than my Agent would have otherwise received unless such change is consented to by all other beneficiaries who would have received the benefits but for the proposed change.

[Alt. 2: Agent is to name a particular beneficiary]

5.   To designate my spouse, [SPOUSE NAME], if living, otherwise my issue surviving me by right of representation, as beneficiary of any benefits payable under such Plan on account of my death.

5.2 Will Provision Regarding Formula in Beneficiary Designation Form

See "Checklist: Drafting the Beneficiary Designation," Question 4(C), p. 576. Something like this clause should be included in the client's will (or trust) if the executor (or trustee) is to be responsible for certifying the amounts payable to respective beneficiaries under the client's beneficiary designation form, as in Form 3.8.

ARTICLE ____. I own (or at my death may own) retirement plan accounts and benefits that become payable, upon my death, to beneficiaries I have (or will have) designated by forms filed with the respective sponsors, administrators, and/or trustees of said retirement plans. The firm or entity that administers any such retirement plan or account is herein referred to as the "plan administrator." My Executor shall certify to the plan administrator of any such retirement plan any and all facts that my Executor can ascertain with reasonable effort, and that are needed by such plan administrator to enable the plan administrator to identify and locate the beneficiaries entitled to ownership of my benefits in the plan and the amount payable to each, including: The identities, taxpayer identification numbers, addresses, and other information concerning the beneficiaries; and the amount payable to each under any formula in the beneficiary designation form.

My Executor's reasonable fees and expenses in carrying out this instruction shall be paid by my estate. My Executor shall have no responsibility to any person for any error or omission in carrying out the terms of this paragraph that is caused by or is the result of my Executor's inability to obtain the required information despite reasonable efforts; or that is the result of fraud or misrepresentations of another person; or that arises from changes in valuations or tax treatments as a result of a tax audit.

5.3   Will Provision: Roth IRA Conversions

If an individual dies after converting a traditional retirement plan to a Roth IRA (¶ 5.4) but before the deadline for "recharacterizing" the conversion (see ¶ 5.6), the recharacterization election may be made by his executor. See ¶ 4.1.02. The individual may want to give his executor instructions regarding the Roth IRA conversion. What those instructions are will differ from one individual to another. Here's one approach; another would be to leave a compensating cash bequest to the beneficiary of the Roth IRA if the executor elects to recharacterize.

ARTICLE ____ : If I have (within the meaning of § 408A of the Code) "converted" any traditional IRA or retirement plan owned by me to a "Roth IRA," and during the time that my Executor is serving as such my Executor would be permitted under the IRA documents and applicable regulations to "recharacterize" the transfer as a contribution to a "traditional" IRA, I direct my Executor to exercise its powers with respect to the Roth IRA as follows: My Executor shall bear in mind that my purpose in converting was to provide tax-free income to myself and/or the beneficiary(ies) of the Roth IRA. Accordingly, I direct my Executor not to "recharacterize" any Roth conversion made by me merely because such conversion caused depletion of my estate and/or merely because recharacterization would augment my estate by the amount of the income tax liability on the conversion. Rather, I direct my Executor to exercise my Executor's discretion to recharacterize any Roth conversion made by me only if one or more of the following conditions exist (any such recharacterization still to be within the discretion of my Executor even if such conditions do exist): Either, (1) my Executor is requested to do so by the beneficiary of the Roth IRA or (2) the value of the Roth IRA has declined by more than five (5%) percent between the date of the conversion and the date of the recharacterization or (3) the loss of the funds required to pay the income taxes on the conversion causes a hardship (in my Executor's sole judgment) to my estate or the beneficiaries of my estate.

5.4   Fiduciary Letter Transferring Plan Account to Beneficiary

See ¶ 6.1.05.

To the Plan Administrator of the [NAME OF RETIREMENT PLAN] (hereinafter "the Plan"):
Re: Benefits of [NAME OF DECEASED PARTICIPANT], deceased (hereinafter "Participant")

[Alt. 1: From executor, if benefits were payable to participant's estate]:
I am the [TITLE, SUCH AS EXECUTOR, ADMINISTRATOR, OR PERSONAL REPRESENTATIVE] of the estate of the Participant, who was a participant in the Plan. I enclose a certificate evidencing my appointment. In that capacity, I am transferring the Participant's interest in the Plan to the beneficiary/ies of Participant's estate who is/are entitled to receive it under [THE TERMS OF PARTICIPANT'S WILL/APPLICABLE INTESTACY LAW].

[Alt. 2: From trustee of trust named as beneficiary]:
I am the Trustee of the [NAME OF TRUST] (the "Trust") which was the named beneficiary of the Participant under the Plan. In my capacity as such Trustee, I am transferring the Participant's interest in the Plan to the beneficiary/ies who is/are entitled to receive it under the terms of the Trust.

[Alt. 1: transfer to one beneficiary]
Accordingly, I hereby instruct and direct you to change the titling of this plan benefit to "[NAME OF BENEFICIARY TO WHOM THE BENEFIT IS BEING TRANSFERRED] as successor beneficiary of [NAME OF DECEASED PARTICIPANT]."

[Alt. 2: transfer to several beneficiaries, in separate accounts]
Accordingly, I hereby instruct and direct you to divide the benefit into [NUMBER OF SEPARATE ACCOUNTS TO BE

ESTABLISHED] separate accounts, and to change the titling of each such account to the name of one of the beneficiaries to whom the benefit is being transferred "as successor beneficiary of [NAME OF DECEASED PARTICIPANT]." The names, addresses, and Social Security numbers of the individual beneficiaries of the separated accounts are: [INSERT].

In accordance with the instructions for IRS Form 1099-R, this transfer is a plan-to-plan transfer and is not to be treated or reported as a distribution from the Plan. Please advise what if any further information or documentation you require to complete this transfer.

Yours truly, [SIGNATURE OF EXECUTOR OR TRUSTEE]

5.5   Letter to Administrator Who Won't Provide Information

See ¶ 4.3.01.

To the Plan Administrator of the [NAME OF RETIREMENT PLAN] (hereinafter "the Plan"):

Re: Benefits of [NAME OF DECEASED PARTICIPANT], deceased (hereinafter "the Participant")

I am the executor of the estate of the Participant, who was a participant in the Plan. I enclose a certificate evidencing my appointment. I have requested from you certain information in order that I may fulfill my responsibility to prepare and file a federal estate tax return for the Participant's estate. You have informed me that you will provide no information regarding the Participant's benefits under the Plan to anyone other than the Participant's designated beneficiary. You will not tell me the name of the Participant's designated beneficiary. As required by § 6018(b) of the Internal Revenue Code, I will include with the estate tax return I will file for the Participant's estate a statement that I am unable to make a complete return regarding the Participant's interest in the Plan, and I will submit your name and address as the person holding legal title to this property. The Internal Revenue Service will then require you to prepare and file an estate tax return regarding this asset on behalf of the Participant's estate.

Very truly yours,

[SIGNATURE OF EXECUTOR]

Appendix C
Resources

This Appendix lists resources available to help professionals in planning for their clients' retirement plan benefits. See also the Bibliography for more books and articles. Prices, ordering information and features change constantly, so check with the vendor before placing an order.

The Pension Answer Book

For "ERISA" law or other matters related to retirement plans that are primarily of importance to the plan administrator, plan trustee, and employer, and any other retirement plan question not covered by this book, I turn to the easy-to-navigate well-written *Pension Answer Book,* by Stephen J. Krass, Esq.; I strongly recommend it as the best resource for us non-ERISA specialists regarding retirement plan legal and tax issues. It covers "employer" issues such as the design, funding and qualification of retirement plans, as well as other pension topics not covered in this book, such as QDROs, prohibited transactions, life insurance in plans, etc.. Www.aspenpublishers.com. $309; discount may be available if purchased at a trade show.

Ataxplan Website

Updates to this book, when available, may be downloaded free from the publisher's website, www.ataxplan.com.

Software

Most providers offer a downloadable demo at their web sites.

Brentmark Retirement Plan Analyzer. $570. Includes 6 months' free maintenance; $179 annual update fee. Powerful feature-filled software to help planners analyze proposed plan distribution strategies from QRPs, IRAs and Roth IRAs (comparing multiple scenarios simultaneously), including income tax, estate tax and spousal rollover aspects. It also analyzes whether it is worthwhile to convert a traditional plan to a Roth IRA and computes pre-59½ SOSEPP distributions. The ideal user is an experienced planner with some training to understand the impact that changing assumptions has on outcome. For just running MRD and SOSEPP calculations (including MRDs for multiple beneficiaries), use Brentmark's Retirement Distributions Planner ($224). Brentmark Software, Inc., 3505 Lake Lynda Drive # 119, Orlando FL 32817-8333; 1-800-879-6665 or 407-306-6160; www.brentmark.com. The Brentmark web site has lots of free information and useful links; a top web site for professionals on retirement distributions planning.

NumberCruncher by Stephen Leimberg runs projections for pre-age-59½ "SOSEPPs" (see ¶ 9.2) as well as "almost 100" estate planning calculations (CRTs, CLTs, GRATs, etc.). It is an indispensable tool for estate planners; extremely easy to use and intuitive for non-techie types. Leimberg & LeClair Inc., PO Box 1332, Bryn Mawr, PA 19010, (610) 924-0515. Order at www.leimberg.com.

Many financial institutions offer free **Roth conversion analysis** programs for their customers and/or the general public, including Fidelity Investments ("Roth Conversion Evaluator," https://calcsuite.fidelity.com/rothconveval/app/launchPage.htm), and Charles Schwab ("Roth IRA Conversion Calculator"; http://www.schwab.com/).

Another commercially available Roth-conversion analyzer is **The Roth IRA Conversion Expert™** from CCH, developed in connection with Robert S. Keebler and Stephen J. Bigge of Baker Tilly Virchow Krause, LLP, http://tax.cchgroup.com/roth-ira-conversion-expert.

Newsletters

Ed Slott's IRA Advisor. Ed Slott, CPA, is one of America's most knowledgeable retirement benefits experts, plus he writes beautifully and is a great speaker. Each issue has in-depth discussion of practical retirement tax info by top practitioners. $125 for twelve 8-page issues per year (includes all back issues). Sent by mail (800-663-1340), or download (and find lots of other useful info) at www.irahelp.com.

Choate's Notes, by Natalie B. Choate. Published irregularly, free for now, sent by regular USPS mail to customers of Ataxplan Publications and to professionals who request it by handing in business card at a

Natalie Choate seminar (or sign up at www.ataxplan.com). Each issue contains a short article on some aspect of planning for retirement benefits, plus other info of interest to estate planning professionals.

Steve Leimberg's Employee Benefits and Retirement Planning Newsletter. E-mail-only. Expert analysis of breaking news "as it happens, such as rulings, cases, and legislation. Written by Bob Keebler, Barry Picker, me, and others, edited by the incomparable Steve Leimberg, Esq. Includes 24-hr access to extensive database. $28 per month (includes all four of Steve's newsletters). Indispensable. Visit one-time free or subscribe at www.leimbergservices.com. Access is provided free through membership in some Estate Planning Councils and possibly other professional associations, so check with yours. In addition to being a nationally recognized expert on estate planning, retirement benefits, and life insurance, and a major supplier of helpful tools for our industry, Steve also has ready-to-go seminars for estate planners at www.Leimberg.com.

Quick Reference Guides

I highly recommend Denise Appleby's "IRA Quick Reference Guides." These are laminated charts neatly summarizing such subjects as what plan can be legally rolled over into what other plan (see "IRA Portability Quick Reference Guide"), the current limits on contributions to every type of plan (see "Rollover Chart and 2010 Limit Table"), and the distribution options/requirements for inherited plans and IRAs (see "IRA Beneficiary Options"). You will find yourself using these "cheat sheets" more than you expect. Purchase at http://www.applebyconsultinginc.com/. Denise also offers consulting services and a free newsletter.

Choate Special Reports

The following other publications by Natalie B. Choate are available for download at www.ataxplan.com:

Special Report: Ancient History. This report contains text from prior editions of *Life and Death Planning for Retirement Benefits* and/or from past seminar materials covering rarely-applicable grandfather rules as well as tax rules that are no longer effective (but that you may need to know because when you are trying to clean up tax questions from a back year). Subjects covered include: The minimum distribution rules for pre-2003 years under the proposed minimum distribution regulations; TEFRA 242(b) elections; pre-1987 403(b) plan balances; special averaging for participants born before 1936; federal estate tax exclusion for retirement benefits; pre-2010 limits applicable to Roth conversions; the 15 percent tax on excess retirement plan contributions and distributions; special tax treatment of 1998 Roth conversions; the limits applicable to Roth "reconversions" in 1998 and 1999; the suspension of MRDs for 2009; and qualified charitable distributions (2006–2009).

For more information about how to qualify retirement benefits for the **estate tax marital deduction** (for both citizen and noncitizen spouses) see the *Special Report: Retirement Benefits and the Marital Deduction (Including Planning for the Noncitizen Spouse)*.

Almost all of the material in the following three *Special Reports* was also contained in the 2006 edition of *Life and Death Planning for Retirement Benefits* but had to be cut for space reasons from this edition:

Special Report: When Insurance Products Meet Retirement Plans. This report provides full detail on the minimum distribution rules applicable to defined benefit plans and annuity payouts from defined contribution plans (¶ 1.1.05); the income, gift, and estate tax treatment of life insurance held in or distributed from a qualified plan; and various special rules dealing with annuities in plans.

Special Report: Charitable Giving with Retirement Benefits. This is an expanded version of Chapter 7 (a little more than twice as long), providing more detail, discussion, background, and examples in connection with charitable giving with retirement benefits.

Special Report: 10% Penalty on Early Distributions. This is an expanded version of Chapter 9 (about twice as long), providing more detail, discussion, background, and examples in connection with the early distributions penalty of § 72(t).

Bibliography

Trusts & Estates magazine is published by Penton Media, New York, NY. Subscribe or purchase back issues ($35) at www.trustsandestates.com.

"T.M." refers to the Tax Management Portfolio series published by the Bureau of National Affairs, Inc., 1801 S. Bell St., Arlington, VA 22202. Each Portfolio has its own publication number. A publication date is not provided for books in this series because they are kept up to date by annual supplements.

"CCH" is a division of Wolters Kluwer. Www.cch.com.

ACTEC Journal is published by the American College of Trust and Estate Counsel, 901 15th St. NW, #525, Washington, DC 20005, (202) 684-8460; www.actec.org.

IRS Publications can be downloaded free from the IRS website, http://www.irs.gov/formspubs/lists/0,,id=97819,00.html.

A star (★) indicates an article that is particularly useful.

Introduction

The best book for lawyers on tax-oriented estate planning is *Estate Planning Law and Taxation* (4th ed., 2001, with Supp. Aug. 2010) by Professor David Westfall and George P. Mair, Esq., published by Thomson Reuters/WG&L. Obtain the paperback "Financial Professionals' Edition."

Estate and Gift Tax Issues for Employee Benefit Plans (TMP 378) and *An Estate Planner's Guide to Qualified Retirement Plan Benefits* (American Bar Assoc., Section of Real Property, Probate and Trust Law, 1992), both by Louis A. Mezzullo, Esq. are excellent overviews of the subject. The former also covers subjects not covered in this book, including non-qualified deferred compensation plans, QDROs, and gift and estate tax issues.

Estate Planning for Retirement by Marcia Chadwick Holt, Esq. (Bradford Publishing Co., Denver CO, 2007) is another excellent book on the same general subject as this one. It covers several subjects not covered in *Life and Death Planning for Retirement Benefits*, including creditors' rights, QDROs, and the tax treatment of nonqualified deferred compensation and Social Security benefits, and includes a CD with the entire text in pdf format.

Chapter 1: Minimum Distribution Rules

Economics of retirement: Blyskal, Jeff, "Questionable Assumptions," *Worth*, July/August 1993, p. 70.

Choate, N., "The 'Estate' As Beneficiary Of Retirement Benefits," *Trusts & Estates*, Vol. 138, No. 10 (Sept. 1999), p. 41.

Chapter 2: Income Tax Issues

For more discussion of lump sum distributions, see *Qualified Plans: Taxation of Distributions*, by Janine H. Bosley *et al.*, TMP 370-3d; and *Taxation of Distributions from Qualified Plans*, by Diane Bennett *et al.*, Thomson Reuters/WG&L (2010).

Chapter 3: Marital Matters

For more on spousal waivers under REA, see Lynn Wintriss, Esq. "Practice Tips: Waiver of Rights Under the Retirement Equity Act and Premarital Agreements," 19 *ACTEC Journal*, no. 2, Fall 1993.

"The 'Probate Law' of ERISA," by Mary Moers Wenig, Esq., in *Estate Planning Studies*, April 1996 issue (page 5), newsletter published for members of the bar by State Street Bank and Trust Company, 225 Franklin St., Boston MA 02101 (thoughtful and well written review of the background of REA and how it has been interpreted by the courts).

For more on community property issues regarding retirement benefits, see "Practicalities of Post-Mortem Distribution Planning for Community Property Retirement Benefits and IRAs—Trusts as Beneficiaries, Separate Shares and Aggregate Theory Agreements," by Edward V. Brennan, Esq., *California Trusts and Estates Quarterly*, Vol. 5, No. 4 (Winter 1999).

Chapter 4: Inherited Benefits: Advising Executors, Beneficiaries

Disclaimers:

Choate, Natalie B., "Disclaimers vs. ERISA," *Trusts & Estates* (Oct. 2009), p. 24.

Income in respect of a decedent (IRD):
Book: Acker, Alan S., Esq.: *Estate Planner's Guide to Income in Respect of a Decedent*, CCH (2007).

Articles:
     Hoyt, Christopher R. Esq., "Inherited IRAs: When Deferring Distributions Doesn't Make Sense," *Trusts & Estates*, Vol. 137, No. 7 (June 1998), p. 52, and "Sometimes It's Better to Avoid Stretch IRAs," *Trusts & Estates*, Vol. 142, No. 3 (March 2003), p. 38.
     For more on transfers of the right to receive IRD, see Choate, N., "Mysteries of IRD," *Tax Management Memorandum*, Vol. 38, No. 20, p. 235 (Tax Management Inc., Washington, D.C., 9/29/97).

Chapter 5:   Roth Retirement Plans

     For financial analysis of Roth IRAs, see Keebler, Robert S. CPA, MST, *A CPA's Guide to Making the Most of the New IRAs* (AICPA); *The Rebirth of Roth: A CPA's Ultimate Guide for Client Care* (available through www.cpa2biz.com or by calling 888-777-7077); and *100+ Roth Examples and Flowcharts* (edited by Barry Picker, CPA) (800-809-0015). Also visit www.RothIRA.com.

Books: Bledsoe, John D., *Roth to Riches* (Legacy Press, 2009). http://www.johnbledsoe.com/John's%20Books.htm
     Keebler, Robert S., *The Rebirth of Roth: A CPA's Guide for Client Care* (AICPA, 2009).

Articles:
     ★Trytten, Steven E., "Are IRAs and Charities the Perfect Match?", *Trusts & Estates* (Sept. 2010).
     ★Keebler, Robert S., CPA, *et al.*, "To Convert or Not To Convert—That Is The Question!", *Journal of Retirement Planning* (CCH, May–June 2007 issue).
     Choate, N., "Retirement Benefits: Unexpected Drama," 143 *Trusts & Estates* 1 (Jan. 2004), p. 40.
     ★DeFrancesco, Roccy, "Even Ed Slott is Wrong about Roth IRA Conversions" (7/1/09). www.producersweb.com. Arguing that the Roth conversion is not profitable for most Americans.
     Holt, Marcia Chadwick, "Traditional vs. Roth IRAs," *Trusts & Estates* (Sept 2009), p. 18.

Hoyt, Christopher, "Want to Convert to a Roth IRA?" *Trusts & Estates* (Sept 2009), p. 26.

Jones, Michael J., "Roth IRA Gifts May Terminate Income Tax Benefits," *Tax Notes*, 6/1/98, p. 1156.

Jones, Mike, "Do Roth IRA Conversions Offer a Brand-NUA Opportunity?," *Steve Leimberg's Employee Benefits and Retirement Planning Email Newsletter* (www.leimbergservices.com), Archive Message #390, 11/1/2006.

★Keebler, Robert S., "Roth Segregation Conversion Strategy," *Taxes* (CCH), June 2003, page 3. Detail regarding the strategy discussed at ¶ 5.6.04, second paragraph.

Keebler, Robert S., *et al.*, "3.8% Surtax Requires Another Look At Roth Conversions," *Steve Leimberg's Employee Benefits and Retirement Planning Email Newsletter*, Archive message #523, (April 6, 2010).

Trytten, Steven E., "Show Me the Money," *Trusts & Estates* (Sept 2009), p. 34.

Chapter 6:   Leaving Retirement Benefits in Trust

★Keene, David, "Trusts Holding IRAs: Income and Estate Tax Issues and Planning Options," *Journal of Retirement Planning* (CCH), May–June 2009, p. 37. Excellent overview of all the issues.

Trust accounting for retirement benefits:

Doyle, Jeremiah W., Esq., "IRA Distributions to a Trust After the Death of the IRA Owner—Income or Principal?", *Trusts & Estates*, Vol. 139, No. 9, p. 38 (Sept. 2000).

★Golden, A.J., "Total Return Unitrusts: Is This a Solution in Search of a Problem?," 28 *ACTEC Journal* Vol. 2, p. 121 (Fall 2002).

Trusteed IRA (IRTs):

Two articles in the Sept. 2009 issue of *Trusts & Estates* offer differing perspectives on the trusteed IRA: Morrow, Edwin P., III, "Trusteed IRAs: An Elegant Estate-planning Option," p. 53, and Steiner, Bruce D., "Before Setting up a Trusteed IRA," p. 48.

For an article comparing the trusteed IRA with a trust named as beneficiary of a custodial IRA, see Kavesh, Philip J., and Morrow, Edwin P., III, "Ensuring the Stretchout," *Journal of Retirement Planning* (CCH, July–August 2007), p. 31.

Trusts and the minimum distribution rules:

★Blattmachr, J., et al., "A Beneficiary as Trust Owner: Decoding Section 678," 35 *ACTEC Journal* No. 2 (Fall 2009), p. 106. Excellent article on how to make a trust a 100 percent grantor trust as to the *beneficiary* (the tests are different from the standards applied to the actual trust *grantor*).

★Tryttten, Steven E., "Got Stretch-Out?," *Trusts & Estates* (July 2009), p. 41. Excellent article recommending, and providing drafting tips for, conduit trusts.

Other articles:

Blase, James G., et al., "Consider the MAT," *Trusts & Estates* (Feb. 2010), p. 38.

★Choate, Natalie B., "Tax opinion: Transferring an IRA out of trust," *Estate Planning Studies* (Merrill Anderson Publishing, July 2008), http://www.ataxplan.com/bulletinBoard/ira_providers.cfm.

Choate, Natalie B., "Trustees' Dilemma with Section 643," *Trusts & Estates*, Vol. 143, No. 7, July 2004, p. 26,

Jones, Michael J., "Transferring IRAs," 145 *Trusts & Estates* No. 4 (April 2006), p. 38.

Kavesh, Philip J., and Morrow, Edwin P., III, "Ensuring the Stretchout," *Journal of Retirement Planning* (CCH, July–August 2007), p. 31.

Fiduciary income tax matters:

The following four treatises are recommended for an understanding of the income tax treatment of trusts and estates:

Abbin, Byrle M., *Income Taxation of Fiduciaries and Beneficiaries* (CCH, 2007, 2 vols.).

Boyle, F.L., and Blattmachr, J.G., *Blattmachr on Income Taxation of Estates and Trusts*, 15th Ed. (2007), Practicing Law Institute, 810 Seventh Ave., New York, NY 10019, www.pli.edu (cited in this book as "*Blattmachr*").

★Ferguson, M. Carr, Freeland, James L., and Ascher, Mark L., *Federal Income Taxation of Estates, Trusts, & Beneficiaries*, CCH/Wolters Kluwer (3rd Ed. 1999–2010).

Zaritsky, H. and Lane, N., *Federal Income Taxation of Estates and Trusts*, ("Checkpoint" On-line Edition, updated through May 2010; Warren, Gorham & Lamont) (cited as "*Zaritsky*").

Chapter 7:   Charitable Giving with Retirement Benefits

Books:

The Harvard Manual on Tax Aspects of Charitable Giving, by the late David M. Donaldson, Esq., Carolyn M. Osteen, Esq., et al.(8th edition, 1999) is a magnificent summary of charitable giving techniques, with citations, written from the point of view of counsel for the charitable donee. The Harvard University Office of Planned Giving, Cambridge, MA 02138, 800-446-1277 (donation of $105).

Conrad Teitell, Esq., is one of the country's top experts in the tax law of charitable giving, and fortunately for the rest of us he is also a prolific author and superb public speaker. For access to his books, newsletters, and seminars, visit http://www.taxwisegiving.com/.

Articles and seminar outlines:

Babitz, M.S., et al., "The IRA Double Tax Trap: The Private Foundation Solution," 29 *Estate Planning* 8 (Aug. 2002), p. 411.

Blattmachr, J.G., "Income in Respect of a Decedent," 12 *Probate Notes* 47 (1986). This excellent article discusses numerous strategies for reducing taxes on retirement benefits and other IRD, including charitable dispositions.

Burke, F.M., "Why Not Allow Lifetime Charitable Assignments of Qualified Plans and IRAs?" *Tax Notes* 7/7/97.

★Finestone, William, "Charitable Gift Annuities," 29 *ACTEC Journal* 37 (Vol. 29, No. 1), Summer 2003. Excellent explanation of charitable gift annuities, including what is known about funding them with retirement benefits.

Hoyt, C.R., "Solution for Estates Overloaded with Retirement Plan Accounts: the Credit Shelter CRUT," 141 *Trusts & Estates* 5 (May 2002), p. 21.

Hoyt, C.R., "Stretch This: Using a CRT to help heirs of employees of companies that liquidate retirement accounts at death," 145 *Trusts & Estates* (Feb. 2006), p. 50.

Mulcahy, T.W., "Is a Bequest of a Retirement Account to a Private Foundation Subject to Excise Tax?," *Journal of Taxation*, August 1996.

Newlin, Charles F., "Coping With the Complexity of Separate Shares Under the Final Regs.," *Estate Planning*, July 2000 (Vol. 27, No. 6, p. 243).

Shumaker, R.L., and Riley, M.G., "Strategies for Transferring Retirement Plan Death Benefits to Charity," 19 ACTEC Journal, no. 3,

p. 162 (1993), and follow-up comments published in 20 ACTEC Journal, p. 22 (1994). Compares the economic effects of various ways of funding a $1 million charitable gift from a $4 million estate, including the use of retirement benefits.

Shumaker, R.L. (with Riley, M.G.), "Charitable Deduction Planning with Retirement Benefits and IRAs: What Can Be Done and How Do We Do It?," American Bar Association Section of Real Property, Probate and Trust Law meeting outline, August 1995.

Chapter 8: Investment Issues; Plan Types

Taxation of IRA transactions and investments:

Regarding the effects of the IRS application of the wash sale rule to IRA sales (Rev. Rul. 2008-5): Jones, Michael J., CPA, "Tossing IRAs into the Wash" (*Trusts & Estates*, Feb. 2008).

Prohibited transactions:

For thoughtful discussion of many of the issues, see materials by Noel C. Ice, Esq., at his web site www.trustsandestates.net.

The Department of Labor web site, www.dol.gov/ebsa/, has posted copies of the DOL's advisory opinions (back through 1992 only), PT exemptions (1996 to date) and interpretive bulletins, and the "Presidential Reorganization Plan #4 of 1978." Generally this excellent government web site is easy to use. An oddity of the web site is that it clumps several exemptions together into one document; for example, if you click on the exemption for Dr. Smith's IRA, you will find yourself reading about the DeutscheBank Pension Plan...just keep scrolling down until you come to Dr. Smith. Older PT exemption requests and advisory opinions are not posted at the DOL web site.

Nontraditional IRA investments:

Michael J. Jones, CPA, "Roth IRA Conversions, Nontraditionally," *Trusts & Estates* (March 2010, p. 36), and "Roth IRA Conversions: Dealing with Nontraditional Assets in Traditional IRAs," *Ed Slott's IRA Advisor*, April 2010, p. 6.

Chapter 9: Distributions before Age 59½

Toolson, Richard B., "Structuring Substantially Equal Payments to Avoid the Premature Withdrawal Penalty," *Journal of Taxation*, Nov 1990, page 276.

Index

Page number in **bold** indicates the page where the term is defined and/or that contains complete cross-referencing to other sections relevant to the term being defined. If a term is used on multiple consecutive pages, this index generally cites only the first of such pages.

$5,000 death benefit
exclusion 307
§ 72 . . . . 122, 131, 139,
140, 144, 545
403(b) plan 535
Grandfather rule 53
Lump sum distribution . 165
MRDs 29, 49
RBD 53
Spousal consent 238
Spousal rollover 211
415 limits 543
457(b) plan 181, 365
691(c) deduction 311
5-year rule (MRDs) 34, 39, 58,
74-76, 82, 97
Rollover 187
Spousal rollover . . . 77, 216
Switch to life exp. 83
10-year averaging 171
10% Penalty (§ 72(t)) . 177, 545
Death benefits 563
Divorce 565
Education expenses 566
ESOP 565
Life insurance 547
NUA stock 546
Rollover 218
Roth IRA 348
Roth IRA conversion . . 349
Self-employed person . . 541
SOSEPP 352
60 day deadline
Direct rollover 125
Exceptions 191
Hardship waiver 192
IRA-to-IRA transfer . . . 198

60 day rollover 149, **182**
Property distributed . . . 187
Account balance
2d distribution year 55
Decline in value 35
How to determine 40
IRAs (income tax) 154
Outstanding rollover . . . 155
Pre-1987 . . . . 53, 144
Recharacterization . 43, 154
Rollover 42
Separate accounts 110
SOSEPP 554, 561
Spousal election 91
Valuation 44
Accumulation trust 439
Adjusted gross income
Roth IRA 334
ADP: see "Applicable
Distribution Period"
After-tax money (see also
"Basis") 138
10% penalty 546
DRAC 372
Inherited IRA 151
IRA 150
MRD 36
Rollover 184
Age
MRD purposes 39
Age 70½ 51
Distribution year 50
IRA contribution 366
MRD 33
NUA stock 177
RBD 52
Rollover 42, 186
Roth IRA 333

Roth IRA conversion . . 320
Aggregation of accounts . . 170
    Accounts within a QRP . . 50
    Husband and wife 156
    Income taxes 143
    Inherited 80, 151
    IRAs (income tax) 152
    Lump sum distribution . 170
    MRD purposes 49
    Roth IRAs 322
    Series of payments 555
Alimony
    As compensation 332
Alternate valuation method   268
Alternative minimum tax . . 314
Annuity
    Contract 36, 82, 129
    Disclaimer 284
    Inside DC plan **32**
    Minimum distributions . . 32
    QTIP election 234
    Withholding 161
Applicable Distribution Period
    (ADP) 34, **38**
    Spousal rollover 208
At least as rapidly rule . . 56, 67
(B)(iv)(II) rule 94
Basis (see also "After-tax
    money")
    Deaths in 2010 275
    NUA stock 172-175
    Qualified plan 140
    Recovery of 327
    Road Map 139
    Roth IRA 327, 328
Beneficiary; see also contingent,
    successor, etc. **24**
    Age 39
    Basis 151
    Changing, post mortem . 113
    Death of 60, 85, 107
    Designated 101
    Estate 66, 69, 104

Handicapped (disabled) . . . 453
    How to determine 100
    Life expectancy 71
    MRD 34, 60
    Multiple 62, 66, 104
    Multiple beneficiaries   66, 70
    NUA stock 174
    Spouse 47, 64, 68, 87
    Trust 65
Beneficiary designation form (see
    also "Checklists")
    Contested 301
    Invalid 299
    Marital deduction 227
    Reformation 301
Beneficiary Finalization
    Date 86, 89,
        111, **113**, 422, 432
    Death before 116
    Disclaimer 292
    Trust as beneficiary   417, 449
Beneficiary IRA 254
Bush tax cuts 123
Capital gain 171
    NUA stock 172
Cash balance plan 537
Charity
    As beneficiary 112
    Lifetime gifts 511
    Roth IRA 391
    Trust as beneficiary . . . 446,
        452, 456, 467
Checklists
    Drafting   beneficiary
        designation 574
    Trust drafting 394
Cleanup Strategies 299
CODA **364**, 535
Collectible 127
Community property 128,
        236, 416
Compensation 331, 332
Conduit IRAs 183

Conduit trust **433**
   Combined with other . . 447
   Disabled beneficiary . . . 452
   For spouse 98
   GST tax 463
   Marital deduction 233
   Minors 454
Constructive receipt 126
Contingent beneficiary **85,**
                292, 298, 396
Contribution
   Income attributable to . . 354
Contribution(s)
   By executor 247
   By spouse 213
   Deadline 359
   Employee, other . . 170, 173
   Property 515
Corrective distributions . . . **133**
   10% penalty 547
   MRD 37
   Rollover 183
   Roth IRA 324
Cream-in-the-coffee rule 140, 147
   Examples 156
   Exceptions . . . 143, 158, 159
   Formula (IRAs) 152
Credit shelter trust 225
   Conduit trust 460
   For spouse 99
Deadline
   60-day rollover . . . 125, 191
   Beneficiary election 77
   Beneficiary Finalization 113
   Conversion to Roth IRA 359
   Corrective distribution . 134
   Disclaimer 284
   IRA contribution 331
   MRDS . . . 34, 50, 55, 59, 77
   Recharacterizing . . 358, 360
   Rollover 191
   Roth IRA conversion . . 358
   Spousal election . . . 93, 214

Spousal rollover 216
Suspension 2009 31
Trust documentation . . . 419
Deemed distributions 126
   MRD 37
   Rollover 183
Deemed Roth IRA 319
Default beneficiary . . . 101, **299**
Defined benefit plan 536
   Disclaimer 284
   Minimum distributions . . 32
   Planning considerations 537
   Spouse's rights 237
   Trust accounting 401
Defined contribution plan . 538
Department of Labor 528
Designated beneficiary 62,
                 100,102
   By executor 249
Designated Roth account; see
   "DRAC"
Direct rollover **181**
   Partial 142
   Post-death 262
Disability **166, 563**
   DRAC 368
   Lump sum distribution . 166
   Roth IRA 323
   Series of payments 557
Disaster exceptions 362
   60 day deadline 191
Disclaimer
   Deadline 284
   Definition **276**
   Fiduciary 280, 294
   Income taxes 279
   Non-qualified 279
   Partial 277
   Pitfalls 296
Distributable net income: see
   "DNI"
Distribution Year **50**
   Age 70 1/2 55

Distribution(s)
    Annuity 129
    Deemed 126
    From multiple plans 48
    How to take 202
    Income taxes 122
    Maximum required 35
    Non-taxable 128
    Partial rollover 142
    Plan loan offset 132
    Property 37, 122
    Tax treatment 121
    When does it occur 124
Divisor 34
Divorce 127, 130
    10% penalty 565
    MRD 48
    SOSEPP 560
    Spouse's rights 240
DNI 464, 466
Documentation requirement 418
Double deaths 207, 294
DRAC 364, 365
    Contributions 365
    In-plan conversion 379
    Income taxes 371
    MRD 368
    Nonqualified
        distribution(s) . 370, 371
    Qualified distribution .. 368
    Rollover 372
Due date of return
    Definition 358
Early distributions 545
Education expenses 566
    10% penalty 566
    Roth IRA 323
EGTRRA 123, 183
Elective deferral 535
Eligible rollover distributions 183
    Withholding 161
Employee **24**, 28
Employee contribution acct   144

Employer stock
    10% penalty 546
    Distributions, tax
        treatment 172
ERISA
    Disclaimer 288
    IRA 238
    Spouse's rights 236
ESOP
    10% penalty 565
    Definition 539
    Lump sum distribution . 171
    Minimum distributions .. 37
    Spousal consent
        requirements 237
Estate
    As beneficiary 104, 475
    Minimum distributions .. 66
    Spousal rollover 220
    Transferring plan out of 402
Estate taxes 267
    "Repeal" in 2010 275
    Alternate valuation date 268
    Disclaimer 297
    Exclusion for retirement
        plan 274
    IRD deduction 310
    Marital deduction 223
Excess IRA contributions . 133,
                            335
Excise tax: see "Penalty"
Executor
    Naming beneficiary 103
    QTIP election 227, 234
    Recharacterizing .. 244, 601
    Special spouse rules ... 215
    Spousal rollover 215
Extended due date 360
Exxon Valdez 330
Failed Roth conversion ... 345
FICA tax
    DRAC contributions ... 364

Financial inst. error
  60 day deadline . . . 192, 194
First-time homebuyer 191
Five-Year Period (for Roth
      qualified distributions)
  Beneficiary 325
  DRAC 369
  Roth IRA 325
Five-year rule; see "5-year rule"
Fixed-term method 39
Form 706 . . . . 227, 267
Form 1040 174
Form 1065 523
Form 1099-R 142, 198
  NUA stock 173
Form 4972 169
Form 5498 198
Form 8606 . . . . . 151, 154, 156
Forms in this book, list of . 573
Frozen deposits 192
Gift tax
  Spousal consent
      requirements 242
Grandfather rules
  10-year averaging 171
  403(b) plan 53
  Rollover of inherited IRA 257
  TEFRA 242(b) 57
Grantor trust 309, 443
  Disabled beneficiary . . . 453
  For spouse 98
  Income taxes 464
Hardship distribution
  Rollover 184
Hardship waiver 360
  60 day deadline 192
Health insurance
  10% penalty 566
Health Savings Account . . . 130
Hedge funds 524
Home purchase
  10% penalty 567
In-plan conversions 379

Incidental death benefit 54
Income in respect of a decedent
  (IRD) 306, **307**
  Deduction 174, 310
  Right-to-receive 308
  Separate share rule 470
Income taxes
  Deduction 311
  Disclaimer 279
  Distributions 122
  Special averaging 171
  Withholding 160
Indirect rollover 182
Individual account plan . . . 540
Individual retirement plans: see
  "IRAs"
Individual retirement trusts (IRT)
  Conversion to Roth IRA   337
Inherited benefits
  10% penalty 563
  Aggregation of plans 80
  Basis 151
  Beneficiary dies 84
  Combining 259
  Disclaimer 276
  How to title 254
  Rollover 183
  Roth IRA conversion . . 336
  Spousal rollover 208
  Surviving spouse 205
  Titling 254
  Transfer 257, 403
Inherited IRA 254, **255**
  Beneficiary rollover . . . 262
  Roth conversion 265
Insurance; see type (life, health)
Investment expenses 520
Investment in the contract (see
      also "Basis") . . 122, 139
IRAs 540
  Assignment 126
  Income tax 156
  Investment(s) 127, 522

Lump sum distribution . 165
Minimum distributions . . 28
Spousal consent
    requirements 238
Spousal election 211
Traditional 24
Transferring 126
UBTI 530
IRA-to-IRA rollover
One per 12 months rule . 188
IRA-to-IRA transfer 197
Post-death 256
IRD deduction 310
Joint and Last Survivor
Table 38, 47
Keogh plan 540
Lump sum distribution . 165
Kiddy tax 307
Lawsuit winnings 520
Life expectancy
Participant 78
Life expectancy payout 30, **60**, 70
Economic effect(s) 73
Life insurance
10% penalty 547
Income taxes 127, 129
Self-employed person . . 541
Spouse's rights 238
Loan(s) 126, 127, **131**
10% penalty 547
MRD 37
Rollover 184
Spousal consent 131
Losses 517
Lump sum distribution 164
Plan's only option 82
Self-employed person . . 541
Special averaging method 171
Margin account 533
Marital deduction **223**
Annuity 234
Entitled to all income . . 228

Medical expenses
10% penalty 564
Medicare surtax 123
Military death gratuities . . . 330
Minimum distribution rules . 27
Enforcement 116
Post-death 59
Regulations 28
Roth IRA 319
Minimum required distribution
Account balance 40
Basic rules 33
Executor responsibility . 251
Income vs. 229
Lifetime 44
Missed 252
Reporting 117
Rollover 184
Spousal rollover 209
Suspension 2009 . . . . **30**
Vs. maximum 34, 35
What counts 36
Year of death 62, 252
Multiple beneficiaries
Inherited IRA 259
IRD deduction 313
Multiple beneficiary
    rule 103, 104
Net unrealized appreciation
    (NUA) 172
10% penalty 546
Charitable gift 176, 513
Partial rollover . . . 176, 177
Post-death 174
No-DB rules 74, 100
Non-citizen spouse 224
Roth IRA 391
Non-deductible contributions 141
IRAs 152
Reporting 150
Non-qualified plan 141
Nonqualified distribution
Roth IRA 327

Nonspouse beneficiary
  Rollover 254, **260**
Notice 2009-68 .. 142, 143, 148
O/R-2-NLP trust 441
One per 12 months rule ... 188
  IRA-to-IRA transfer ... 198
Owner-employee 541
Participant 24
Partnership 523
Past service credits 144
Patient Protection etc. Act . 122
Pecuniary bequest 111, 225, 468
Penalty
  10% penalty 545
  Excess IRA contribution 135,
                          335, 346
  Executor responsibility . 253
  MRD 117
Pension plan
  Definition 542
Pension Protection Act 123
Periodic payments
  Withholding 160
Plan administrator 418
  Disclaimer 288
  Obligations 263
  Planning considerations 575
Plan document
  Payout options 82
Plan loan offset 132
Plan loans; see "Loan(s)"
  Defaulted 141
Power of appointment 445
  Disclaimer ... 282, 288, 432
  Trust rules ... 444, 445, 463
Pre-nuptial agreement
  Spousal consent 240
  Spousal rollover 213
Premature distributions
  10% penalty 545
Pretax money 139
Private letter ruling 450
Profit-sharing plan 542

Spousal consent 237
Prohibited transaction(s)
  Brokerage agreement .. 516
  IRAs 527
  Roth IRA 324
QHSAFDs 130, 159
QTIP trust 99
  As beneficiary 225
  MRD effects 226
Qualified airline employees 330
Qualified Charitable
  Distribution 159, 514
Qualified distribution (from Roth
  plan) 370
  DRAC 368
  Roth IRA 323
Qualified domestic relations order
  (QDRO) 130
  10% penalty 565
  MRD 34
  SOSEPP 560
Qualified joint survivor annuity
  (QJSA) 236
Qualified plans 40, 116
  Definition 543
  Lump sum distribution .. 82
  RBD 52
  Spousal rollover 210
Qualified pre-retirement survivor
  annuity (QPSA) 236
Qualified reservist
  distribution 150, 568
  Rollover 191
RBD (Required Beginning
  Date) 51
  5-percent owner 51
  Death before 74
  Distributions before 35
  Qualified plan 52
  Roth IRA 51
  Surviving spouse 93
  Suspension 2009 58
  Traditional IRA 51

REA 236
Real estate 525
Recalculation method 39
Recharacterization . . . 154, 353
    By executor 244
    Effect on MRD 43
    Minimum distributions . 320
    Partial 358
    Which contributions . . . 353
Reconversions 363, 607
Reduce by one method 40
Reformation
    Beneficiary designation 301
    Trust or will 303
Regular contribution to IRA 331
Required Commencement
    Date 59
    Surviving spouse 93
Restorative payment 520
Retirement **54**
    RBD 52
Retirement Equity Act of
    1984 236
Retirement plan 534
Returned contribution
    IRAs 154
Rev. Rul. 2000-2 228
Rev. Rul. 2005-36 282
Rev. Rul. 2006-26 227
Rev. Rul. 89-89 232
Road Map
    Advising a beneficiary . 314
    Advising married client 203
    After-tax money 139
    Executor's 243
    Leaving benefits to spouse224
    Leaving to marital trust . 224
    Lifetime distributions . . 198
    Lifetime MRDs 45
    MRDs to spouse 89
    Post-death MRDs 60
    Rollover decisions 199
    Special spouse rules 87

Surviving spouse 204
When 5-year rule applies . . . 75
Rollover 179, **181**
    After-tax money . . 139, 150
    Age 70 1/2 42
    By executor 247
    Conversion to Roth IRA 346
    Deadline 360
    Definition 180
    Distributions eligible . . . 183
    Effect on MRD 41
    Employer stock 176
    Inherited IRA 254
    IRA to nonIRA plan . . . 158
    MRDs 41, 184
    NUA stock 176
    One per 12 months rule . 188
    Outstanding 41
    Partial 145
    RBD 42
    Surviving spouse 208
    Vs. plan-to-plan transfer 180
    Withheld income tax . . . 183
Rollover contribution 181
Roth conversion
    After-tax money 139
    Failed conversion 345
    How to do it 346, 347
    In 2010 344
    MRD effects 320
    Nonspouse beneficiary . 264
    Partial 158
    Planning 381
    Surviving spouse 215
    Tax treatment 340, 342
    Type of plan 337
    Who is eligible 339
Roth IRA
    1998 or 2010 conversion 344
    Contribution limit 332
    Conversion: 340, 352
    Deemed 319
    Distributions 321

Eligibility 333
Five-Year Period 325
Gift during life 393
How to fund 329
Minimum distributions . 319
Ordering Rules 328
Planning   381, 389, 391, 393
Qualified distribution . . 321
RBD 51
Spousal consent 238
Spousal rollover 211
Who may contribute . . . 333
Roth plans
10% penalty 348
Abuses 317
Estate planning 391
S corporation stock 525
See-through trust 413
Minimum distributions 65, 69
Self-directed IRA 522
Self-employed 540
SEP-IRA 333, **544**
Separate accounts
Income taxes 143
Separate accounts rule 109
During life 50
Separate share rule 470
Separation from service . . . 166
10% penalty 564
Series of equal payments . . 548
Charitable gift 513
Modification 556
Rollover 183
Roth IRA conversion . . 352
Short sales 533
SIMPLE IRA **544**, 546
Minimum distributions . . 28
Simultaneous deaths 207
Single Life Table 39, 571
Software 604
Special averaging method . 171
Spousal consent requirements 236
Exceptions 239

Transfer tax aspects . . . 242
Spousal election against will 300
Spousal IRA election **205**
Alternate valuation date 272
How to make 213
Minimum distributions . . 90
Spousal rollover **205**
5-year rule 77
Advantages 208
By executor 215
Compared to QTIP 225
Deadline 216
Disclaimer 293
Minimum distributions . . 90
Pros and cons 208
Under age 59 1/2 218
Spousal rollover
Through estate or trust . 220
Spousal Roth conversion . . 206
State law 121, 160, 446
Trust as beneficiary 415
Stretch IRA 60, 70, 540
Successor beneficiary 84
Minimum distributions . . 92
Summary plan description . 170
Surtax investment income . 123
Surviving spouse **87**
10 years younger 47
Early death 94
Multiple beneficiaries . . 206
Sole beneficiary 48, 88
Special rules for 87
Table(s), IRS 38
Tax-sheltered annuity 535
Taxable account **24**
TEFRA 242(b) elections . . . 57
Traditional account 24
Traditional IRA **540**
Contribution limit 332
Recharacterizing 353
Roth IRA conversion . . 336
Trustee-to-trustee transfer . 182
Minimum distributions 37, 41

Vs. rollover 180
Trusteed IRA 407
Trusts as beneficiary
    Accounting 397
    Checklist 394
    Disclaimer 288
    Distributing plan out of
        trust 402, 475
    Income taxes 464
    Marital deduction 226
    MRD trust rules 410
    Spousal consent
        requirements 241
    Spousal rollover 220
    Testamentary 415
Uniform Lifetime Table . . . 38,
                                46, 569
Uniform Principal and Income
    Act 398

Marital deduction 228
Uniform Principal and Income
    Act 228
Uniform Table 569
Unrelated business income
    (UBTI) 530
User fee, Hardship waiver . 193
Wages for FICA purposes . 364
Wash sale rule 516
Withholding 160
    Eligible rollover
        distribution 183
    Mandatory 162
    Roth conversion 162
WRERA 30
Year of death
    MRDs 62, 64, 67, 252

What's New in this Edition

This 7th edition 2011 is up to date for the *Small Business Jobs Act* enacted September 27, 2010, and contains NEW Road Maps to make finding everything you need faster and easier. See list of Road Maps in the Index and on the back cover. A brand new "See-Through Trust Tester Quiz" is included by popular demand; see page 477. Also: greatly expanded coverage of distributions and Roth conversions of after-tax money; see Chapter 2. New material in Chapter 4 covers what executors need to know about retirement benefits, and how to advise beneficiaries. To make room for all this, life insurance was removed to a *Special Report*, charitable giving and pre-age 59 ½ distributions were abbreviated; save your old edition if you want that material!

Where to Buy this Book

At the web site www.ataxplan.com you can buy this book, get FREE updates for the book as they are posted, learn about the author Natalie B. Choate, find out where Natalie is speaking, and see her *Special Reports* on topics relating to personal planning for retirement benefits.